Power From On HIGH

Power From On HIGH

Jack Cottrell

COLLEGE PRESS PUBLISHING COMPANY · JOPLIN, MISSOURI

College Press Publishing Co
Since 1959, publishers of resources for preachers, teachers, and Bible students
Order toll-free 800-289-3300
On the web at www.collegepress.com
Publishers also of HeartSpring Books

International Standard Book Number: 978-0-89900-517-1

Abbreviations Used in this Book and Others in the Series

AD.....................*Anno Domini*
ASV ....American Standard Version
BC ....Before Christ
CRD ....Campbell-Rice Debate
CSB ....Holman Christian Standard Bible
CEV...................Contemporary English Version
ESV....................English Standard Version
KJV ....King James Version
LB......................Living Bible
LXX ....*Septuagint*
MT ....Masoretic Text
NAB ....New American Bible
NASB ....New American Standard Bible
NEB...................New English Bible
NIV ....New International Version
NKJV.................New King James Version
NLT ....New Living Translation
NRSV ....New Revised Standard Version
NT.....................New Testament
OT.....................Old Testament
RSV ....Revised Standard Version
TEV ....Today's English Version
TNIV ....Today's New International Version

ABOUT THE SERIES

"What does the Bible say about that?" This is a question that should concern every Bible-believing Christian, whatever the particular subject being discussed. Granted, we know there are situations and activities that are not directly addressed by the Bible, because of changes in society, culture, and technology. However, if we truly believe that the Bible is to be our guide for living and especially for developing our relationship with God, then we need to look to it for information that will impact our everyday decisions. Even what may seem like abstract doctrinal matters will affect our religious practices, and if the Bible is indeterminate on a particular issue, then we need to know that too, so that we don't waste time on the kinds of controversies Paul warns about in 1 Timothy 1:4.

College Press Publishing Company is fully committed to equipping our customers as Bible students. In addition to commentary series and small study books on individual books of the Bible, this is not the first time we have done a series of books specifically dedicated to this question: "What DOES the Bible say?" Part of this stems from the background of CPPC as a publishing house of what has generally been known as the "Restoration Movement,"[1] a movement that gave rise to Churches of Christ and Christian Churches. The "restoration" of the movement's name refers to the desire to restore biblical teaching and emphases to our religious beliefs and activities.

It is important to understand what this series can and cannot do.

[1] In order to be more specific and recognize that these churches are not necessarily unique in the plea to restore the church of the apostles, it is also known as the "Stone-Campbell Movement," after the names of some of the 19th-century leaders of the movement.

Every author in the series will be filtering the exact words of the biblical text through a filter of his or her own best understanding of the implications of those words. Nor will the Bible be the only source to be quoted. Various human authors will inevitably be referenced either in support of the conclusions reached or to contradict their teachings. Keeping this in mind, you should use them as tools to direct your own study of the Bible, and use the "Berean principle" of studying carefully every part of the Bible to see "whether these things [are] so" (Acts 17:11, ASV). We would not be true to our own purpose if we encouraged you to take any book that we publish as the "last word" on any subject. Our plea, our desire, is to make "every Christian a Bible Student."

A Word about Format

In order to emphasize the theme of "What the Bible Says," we have chosen to place Scripture quotations and Scripture references in distinct typestyles to make them stand out. Use of these typestyles within quotations of other works should not be taken as an indication that the original author similarly emphasized the highlighted text.

IN THIS BOOK

This volume is dedicated, with appreciation and affection, to all my students in the CHOSEN ONES class at the Miamitown (OH) Church of Christ. I will always fondly remember all the years we studied the Word of God together, and I pray that your love for His Word will never cease!

— Your teacher, friend, and brother in Christ, Jack Cottrell

INTRODUCTION

From the outset I affirm my reasoned conviction that the Bible is the inspired and inerrant Word of God. Thus the Bible alone and the Bible in its entirety is our only norm for all doctrine, including the doctrine of the Holy Spirit. Everything that can be known in this life about the Holy Spirit must be learned from this Book.

Since the whole Bible is God's inerrant Word, it possesses the quality of *epistemic unity*. That means that everything it teaches from Genesis to Revelation is a single body of consistent truth. This is true of all its doctrines combined, and also of any one specific doctrine such as the doctrine of the Holy Spirit. Thus to have a complete understanding of the Spirit (or as nearly so as our finite minds will allow), we must study everything the Bible says about Him and His work, and then set forth our conclusions as a unified whole.

As a justification for this task, I will also affirm from the outset my strong belief that human beings are made in the image of God and are thus endowed with the rational ability to understand, analyze, and organize truth learned from any source, including the Bible. As a result my method of presenting the doctrine of the Holy Spirit is called *systematic theology*, which is simply a subject-by-subject study of what the Bible teaches. Here we are seeking to learn what it teaches about the subject of the Holy Spirit.

In this introduction I will set the stage for this study by examining the various relevant biblical terms about the Holy Spirit, the concept and characteristics of spiritual beings as such, and the various biblical expressions and phrases used to describe the Holy Spirit.

RELEVANT TERMS

The word "spirit" in English versions of the Bible is almost always a translation of one Hebrew word, *ruach*, and one Greek word, *pneuma*.[1] These words are equivalent in meaning; each has three main connotations or usages in biblical literature.

OLD TESTAMENT: *RUACH*

The Hebrew word *ruach* is used over 380 times in the OT. Heron (**3-4**) says its root meaning "probably had to do with the movement of air," or air in motion. This is seen in the fact that two of its main meanings are "wind" and "breath."

Wood says that "wind" seems to be *ruach*'s most basic meaning; it is used in this sense about 100 times (**16-17**). Wind is often used as an instrument of God's providence, a force by which He accomplishes His purposes in the world (e.g., ***Gen 8:1***; ***Ex 15:10***; ***Num 11:31***; ***Ps 148:8***; ***Jonah 1:4***; ***4:8***). Based on this usage *ruach* thus becomes associated with the concept of *power*. As Morris says, "It is plain that the throbbing note of power characterizes *ruach*" (***Spirit***, **17**).

In over 25 of its occurrences, *ruach* has the connotation of "breath," most often human breath. When used poetically to represent the breath of God, the main point again seems to be *power*. In other words, the breath of God, whether emanating from His nostrils or His mouth, becomes a mighty wind that accomplishes His purposes, both benevolent and punitive. *"'At the blast [ruach] of Your nostrils the waters were piled up'"* (***Ex 15:8***), thus allowing Israel to escape the Egyptian army. *"By the breath of His mouth"* God created the heavens (***Ps 33:6***). *"His breath is like an overflowing torrent"* of wrath by which He punishes the nations (***Isa 30:28***). See also ***2Sa 22:16***; ***Job 4:9***; ***Ps 18:15***; ***Isa 11:4***; ***33:11***; ***40:7***.

Since breath in human beings is associated with life, some connect *ruach* with life-giving power and see God's *ruach* as the source of

[1]Exceptions are ***Job 26:4*** and ***Prov 20:27***, where "spirit" translates the Hebrew word *neshamah*.

life. This is the main connection between *ruach* and another Hebrew word, *neshamah*. In most of its approximately 25 uses, *neshamah* refers to ordinary human breath as the indicator of life. ***Genesis 2:7*** describes God as breathing into the inert Adam's nostrils the "*neshamah* of life." When used of God, the "*neshamah* of God" is equivalent to the "*ruach* of God" in the sense of God's creative and destroying breath. See ***2Sa 22:16***; ***Job 4:9***; ***32:8***; ***33:4***; ***37:10***; ***Ps 18:15***; ***Isa 30:33***.

The third main connotation of *ruach* is most relevant for our purposes. Over 230 times this Hebrew word is translated "spirit," mostly in the sense of spiritual entities or nonmaterial personal beings. Why would the same Hebrew word sometimes refer to wind and breath, and sometimes to spiritual entities? The most obvious thing they have in common is invisibility. Wind and breath are real in their effects, but they cannot ordinarily be seen; likewise spiritual beings are real but are invisible to our normal sight.[2]

The spiritual beings to which *ruach* is applied include angelic beings, especially fallen angels or evil spirits (e.g., ***Jdg 9:23***; ***1Sa 16:14-16***), and also the human spirit (e.g., ***Num 16:22***; ***Ps 31:5***; ***142:3***; ***Isa 26:9***; ***Eze 36:26***). Most significantly, *ruach* is the word that designates the Holy Spirit in the OT, approximately 80 times. When the OT thus refers to the *Ruach* of God, hovering in the background are the thoughts of wind and breath with their implications of power.

NEW TESTAMENT: *PNEUMA*

The relevant Greek word, *pneuma*, appears in the NT about 380 times (just as *ruach* is found over 380 times in the OT). We need not spend a lot of time discussing it, since it is practically equivalent in meaning to *ruach*: on a few occasions it means "wind" (***Jn 3:8***; see ***Heb 1:7***) and "breath" (***2Th 2:8***; ***Rev 11:11***; ***13:15***), but in an overwhelming majority of cases it is translated "spirit."

When translated "spirit," *pneuma* on a few occasions means an attitude or state of mind (e.g., ***Rom 8:15***; ***11:8***; ***Eph 4:23***; ***1Pet 3:4***); most of the time it refers to personal spiritual beings including angels (***Heb 1:14***), demons (e.g., ***Mt 8:16***; ***10:1***; ***Mk 5:2***; ***Acts 5:16***), the human spirit (e.g., ***Mt 26:41***; ***27:50***; ***Lk 1:47***; ***8:55***; ***Rom 8:10***), and the Holy Spirit. This

[2] "The relation of 'wind' to 'spirit' is not so easily seen, but probably is based on the idea that both are invisible" (Wood, 17).

last usage is by far the most common, with *pneuma* referring to the Holy Spirit about 260 times.

English Words: *Spirit* and *Ghost*

The English word "spirit," which translates both *ruach* and *pneuma,* is taken directly from the Latin word *spiritus*. This word, like *ruach* and *pneuma,* means "breath" and "wind." The translators of the Latin Vulgate Bible decided to use *spiritus* to translate *ruach* and *pneuma* also when these words refer to invisible entities—angels, demons, the human spirit, and the Holy Spirit. Thus the *ruach* or *pneuma* of God became the *spiritus* of God, and most present-day English versions simply use the English derivative, "spirit." Thus today we speak of "the Holy Spirit."

This is by no means unanimous, though, because of the influence of the KJV, which with few exceptions speaks of "the Holy Ghost." This is carried over into the last line of the common "Doxology": "Praise Father, Son, and Holy Ghost." In Middle English "ghost" was "gost," and in the earlier Old English it was "gast." This word did not mean "guest," as is sometimes suggested. Rather, it meant "soul, spirit, life, breath."[3] Thus it was originally a worthy English translation of *ruach* and *pneuma*.

Prior to the appearance of the KJV in 1611, Christian writing in Old and Middle English used both "Holy Ghost" and "Holy Spirit" for the Spirit of God. On the one hand, as early as AD 900 a document known as the *Durham Ritual* referred to the "halig gast"; in 1340 Hampole's *Psalter* spoke of the "haly gast"; in 1535 G. Joyce's *Apology of Tyndale* used the term "holigost." On the other hand, around 1300 a poem called *Cursor Mundi* spoke of the "hali spirite," and the 1549 *Book of Common Prayer* said, "Laude and praise be . . . to the holy spirite."[4]

Either English term might have sufficed if the word "gost" or "ghost," near the end of the 14th century, had not taken on the meaning of "disembodied spirit of a dead person."[5] Since this is the prevailing connota-

[3] "Online Etymology Dictionary," www.etymonline.com/index.php?l=g&p=4, accessed 6/29/05.

[4] "Spotlight on . . . the Holy Spirit," *Take Our Word for It*, issue 82 (4/17/00), www.takeourword.com/Issue082.html, accessed 6/29/05.

[5] "Online Etymology Dictionary," etymonline.com. See the Greek word *phantasma*, ***Mt 14:26***; ***Mk 6:49***.

tion of the word "ghost" today, it is now misleading and confusing to use this word to translate *ruach* and *pneuma*. Thus it is appropriate to speak of the "Holy Spirit" rather than the "Holy Ghost."

THE CONCEPT OF SPIRIT

We have seen that the relevant biblical terms, *ruach* and *pneuma*, have several key meanings. How do we know when these words mean "breath" or "wind," and when they mean "spirit"? Only the context in which the words appear can determine this, and in most cases the intended connotation is quite straightforward.

When a translator has determined that in a specific text the relevant word means "spirit," he must still decide whether this means "spirit" in the sense of a mental state or attitude (e.g., ***Num 5:14***; ***Rom 8:15***), or in the sense of an existing metaphysical entity, a spiritual *being*. Again the decision is usually not difficult. Our concern here is only with the latter.

In the Bible there are two basic kinds of stuff or substance: material (or physical) and spiritual (see ***Isa 31:3***; ***Mt 26:41***). Spiritual substance is real substance, but it is metaphysically different from physical matter. In the Bible three kinds of beings are called "spirit," i.e., are composed of spiritual "stuff." One is the human soul or spirit, which is distinct from the physical body but is designed to be "at home" in it (***2Cor 5:6***). Another is the world of angelic beings (***Heb 1:14***), called the invisible creation (***Col 1:16***). Since demons are fallen angels (***2Pet 2:4***), they too are composed of spiritual substance and thus are called evil *spirits* (***Acts 19:11-16***). The third kind of spiritual being is God Himself: *"God is spirit"* (***Jn 4:24***). This is true of all divine beings and applies to God the Father, God the Son, and God the Spirit.

While all substantive beings can be divided into the two categories of material and spiritual, it is important to see that they must all be divided into two other categories as well, namely, created and uncreated (***Rom 1:25***). Human beings (both body and spirit) and angelic beings are in every sense created and therefore finite entities; only divine spirit is uncreated and therefore infinite. The difference is crucial.

Why, then, are the same biblical words (*ruach* and *pneuma*) used to denote both created and uncreated spirit? Because all spiritual beings share certain basic characteristics in contrast with material substance as such. (This is part of what it means to say that human

Why are the same biblical words used to denote both created and uncreated spirit?

beings are made *"in the image of God," Gen 1:26-27*.) The following attributes thus apply to all spiritual beings, though to divine spirit they apply innately and infinitely.[6]

Spirit Is Nonmaterial

That spiritual essence is nonmaterial is the most obvious thing we can say about it. Spiritual beings are not "made out of" material stuff; they are not formed of atoms and molecules and the elements of this world (see ***Lk** 24:36-43*). Physical stuff has certain innate limitations that do not apply to spiritual substance (***Isa** 31:3*); this is infinitely true of *uncreated* spiritual being. This is one of the main points of the second commandment (***Ex** 20:4*): do not try to capture the essence of uncreated, divine spirit in any material form or substance.

Divine spirit, including the essence of the Holy Spirit, thus exists on a metaphysical level that is different from both this material universe and the invisible world of angels. God the Spirit is not limited as created beings are. This is important in understanding the *power* of the Holy Spirit.

Spirit Is Invisible

Some material stuff is invisible to unaided human vision, e.g., most gases and all molecules and atoms, but is "visible" through such instruments as microscopes. Spiritual stuff, on the other hand, is invisible to all material sensing devices, including divinely created eyes and humanly created machines and instruments. This invisibility is a major similarity between breath and wind on the one hand, and spirit on the other (see ***Jn** 3:8*). Human eyes cannot see created spiritual reality except by divine permission (e.g., ***2Kgs** 6:17*), and created beings cannot see the pure spiritual essence of God at all. He is "the invisible God" (***Col** 1:15*). No man *has* seen God (***Jn** 1:18*; *5:37*; ***1Jn** 4:12*); no man *can* see God (***Ex** 33:20*; ***1Tm** 6:16*). Even when God chooses to make Himself visible to men and to angels (in theophanies), we are not viewing His uncreated, transcendent essence.

This is important for our understanding of the way in which the

[6] For more detail on these points see Cottrell, *Creator*, 222-239.

Spirit works in the world, and of the way we experience His working. We may see the *results* of the Spirit's presence (His "footprints," so to speak), but we will never see the Spirit Himself. From this we may infer that we will never actually sense or feel the presence of the Spirit in our lives and bodies, in the way we may detect or be conscious of the presence or movement of any created essence within us.

We may see the results of the Spirit's presence, but we will never see the Spirit Himself.

Spirit Is Living

A third characteristic of spiritual beings is that they are *living*, or *alive*. They have the quality of life. Of course, there is a certain kind of life that is present within material stuff in the world of plants and animals. The life of spiritual beings seems to be life on a different level, however. Earlier we pointed out the relation between the concepts of breath (as an indicator of life) and spirit. In human beings, *"the body without the spirit is dead,"* says ***James 2:26***.

Created spiritual beings are living beings, but their life is not innate; it is a gift of God and can be withdrawn by Him. This is not the case with uncreated, divine spirit, namely, God, who has "life in Himself" (***Jn 5:26***). In contrast with false gods and idols, He is "the Living God" (***Isa 37:4***; ***Heb 3:12***).

This helps us to understand the role of the Holy Spirit as the giver of life, especially the new spiritual life bestowed as part of the gift of salvation: *"It is the Spirit who gives life; the flesh profits nothing"* (***Jn 6:63***; see ***2Cor 3:6***). He is the "Spirit of life" (***Rom 8:2***), bestowing life not only upon our sin-deadened spirits in this life but also upon our death-defeated bodies in the day of resurrection (***Rom 8:9-11***).

Spirit Is Personal

There is no such thing as impersonal or nonpersonal spirit-stuff; the very idea is foreign to Scripture. "Impersonal spirit" is a contradiction of terms. All spiritual beings are *personal* beings. Animals are *not* persons because they do not have a true spiritual essence. Human beings are persons because we are

"Impersonal spirit" is a contradiction of terms.

not just bodies but are also spirits. Angels as pure spirit are fully personal.

This is of course true of God as divine spirit; God is personal. In fact, the trinitarian God revealed in the Bible (especially in the NT) is *three* persons. God is inherently personal; He is the original model for all created personhood. This is true of God the Holy Spirit; He is one of three divine persons. (The biblical data for this will be examined in the next chapter.)

Here we may summarize the four main elements of personhood. First, a person has *rational consciousness,* or thought processes. A personal being is a thinking being, having knowledge, wisdom, and understanding. Second, a person has *self-consciousness,* an awareness of the self as a thinking individual. Third, a person has the power of *self-determination,* the ability to plan and to choose and to decide. This is the concept of volition or free will. Fourth, a person has the capacity for *interpersonal relationships*. This is the awareness of the existence of other persons as persons, and the ability to relate to them on a personal level, e.g., the ability to give and to receive love.

All of these things are true of God in an eminent way. Each person of the Trinity, including the Holy Spirit, has rational consciousness, self-consciousness, self-determination, and relationships with other persons. The Holy Spirit says "I think," "I am," "I will," and "thou art." The implications of the Spirit's personhood will be discussed in the next chapter.

Spirit Is Powerful

Every spiritual being has a certain amount of power, a power that derives from existing as a *personal* being who knows how to make plans and how to carry them out. Compared with human beings, angels are supernatural and have a finite measure of supernatural power. Even human persons, as free-will beings, have the power to create events, sometimes with far-reaching consequences (e.g., ***Gen 3:1-7***).

The power inherent in uncreated, divine Spirit far surpasses the power of any created spirit. It is indeed infinite or unlimited; it is omnipotence. As noted above, the term *ruach* in itself, in its connotations of both wind and breath, expresses the very notion of power. "Symbolically, the expression 'the *breath* of Yahweh's nostrils' (probably referring to the wind), is used to describe the force of Yahweh's power" (**Van Pelt, 1074**). Look at, for example, ***Exodus 15:8***, *"At the blast [ruach] of your nostrils the waters were piled up,"* and ***Isaiah 11:4***, *"With the breath [ruach] of His lips He will slay the wicked."*

Morris concludes, "Passages like these prepare us for the thought that when *ruach* is used of God it points to Him as completely irresistible, and strong in might. . . . The Spirit of the Lord acts with the power of a mighty wind. Man cannot resist Him" (***Spirit***, **18, 19**). It is no surprise, then, that when the Spirit was poured out on the Day of Pentecost, *"suddenly there came from heaven a noise like a violent rushing wind"* (***Acts 2:2***).

Based upon the nature of spiritual being as such, and in view of the fact that the Spirit of God is uncreated, infinite spirit, we may think of the Holy Spirit as a nonmaterial, invisible, living-and-life-giving, omnipotent divine person.

NAMES AND DESCRIPTIONS OF THE SPIRIT

How is the Holy Spirit described or referred to in the pages of Scripture? Regarding the OT especially, there is some disagreement as to which *ruach* texts are referring to the Holy Spirit and which are referring simply to the active power of God, e.g., ***Genesis 1:2***. This issue would be more difficult if we were considering the OT in isolation from the NT writings. However, given the unity of all Scripture, and viewing the OT references to God's *ruach* in the light of the more clear NT teaching about the Spirit, we conclude that most OT texts about the *ruach* of God do indeed refer to the Holy Spirit. There are approximately 80 such references, using the following names and descriptions:

1. The Spirit. ***Numbers 11:17,25,26; 27:18; Isaiah 32:15; Ezekiel 2:2; 3:12,14,24; 8:3; 11:1,24; 43:5; Malachi 2:15.***
2. The Spirit of God. ***Genesis 1:2; Exodus 31:3; 35:31; Numbers 24:2; 1 Samuel 10:10; 11:6; 19:20,23; 2 Chronicles 15:1; 24:20; Job 33:4; Ezekiel 11:24.***
3. The Spirit of the LORD (literally, the Spirit of Yahweh). ***Judges 3:10; 6:34; 11:29; 13:25; 14:6,19; 15:14; 1 Samuel 10:6; 16:13,14; 2 Samuel 23:2; 1 Kings 18:12; 22:24; 2 Kings 2:16; 2 Chronicles 18:23; 20:14; Isaiah 11:2; 40:13; 63:14; Ezekiel 11:5; 37:1; Micah 2:7; 3:8.***
4. The Spirit of the Lord GOD [Adonai Yahweh]. ***Isaiah 61:1.***

5. My Spirit. ***Genesis 6:3; Isaiah 30:1; 42:1; 44:3; 59:21; Ezekiel 36:27; 37:14; 39:29; Joel 2:28,29; Haggai 2:5; Zechariah 4:6.***
6. His Spirit. ***Numbers 11:29; Isaiah 34:16; 48:16; Zechariah 7:12.***
7. His Holy Spirit. ***Isaiah 63:10,11.***
8. Your Spirit. ***Nehemiah 9:30; Psalms 104:30; 139:7.***
9. Your Holy Spirit. ***Psalm 51:11.***
10. Your good Spirit. ***Nehemiah 9:20; Psalm 143:10.***
11. The Spirit of wisdom. ***Exodus 28:3; Deuteronomy 34:9; Isaiah 11:2.***
12. The Spirit of grace and supplications. ***Zechariah 12:10.***

The NT references to the Holy Spirit are more varied and more descriptive. They are as follows:

1. Spirit (*pneuma* without the definite article; a maximum of 41 times, depending on the interpretation of some texts, e.g., ***Revelation 1:10; 4:2***).[7] ***Matthew 22:43; John 3:5; 7:39; Acts 6:3; Romans 2:29; 7:6; 8:4,5,9,13; 15:19; 1 Corinthians 2:4,13; 12:13; 2 Corinthians 3:6,18; Galatians 3:3; 4:29; 5:5,16,18,25; Ephesians 2:18,22; 3:5; 4:4; 5:18; 6:18; Philippians 2:1; Colossians 1:8; 2 Thessalonians 2:13; 1 Timothy 3:16; 1 Peter 1:2; 3:18; Jude 19; Revelation 1:10; 4:2; 17:3; 21:10.***
2. The Spirit (*to pneuma,* using the definite article; a total of 70 times). ***Matthew 4:1; 12:31; Mark 1:10,12; Luke 2:27; 4:1,14; John 1:32,33; 3:6,8,34; 6:63; 7:39; Acts 2:4; 6:10; 8:18,29; 10:19; 11:12,28; 20:22; 21:4; Romans 8:5,6,11,16,23,26,27; 15:30; 1 Corinthians 2:10; 12:4,7,8,9,11; 2 Corinthians 1:22; 3:6,8,17; 5:5; Galatians 3:2,5,14; 5:17,22; 6:8; Ephesians 4:3; 6:17; 1 Thessalonians 5:19; 1 Timothy 4:1; 1 John 3:24; 5:7,8; Revelation 2:7,11,17,29; 3:6,13,22; 14:13; 22:17.***
3. My Spirit (with the definite article). ***Matthew 12:18; Acts 2:17,18.***
4. His Spirit (with the definite article). ***Romans 8:11; Ephesians 3:16; 1 John 4:13.***
5. Holy Spirit (*pneuma hagion,* no definite article, the words being reversed in the Greek fashion; a total of 48 times). ***Matthew 1:18,20; 3:11; Mark 1:8; Luke 1:15,35,41,67; 2:25; 3:16; 11:13; John 1:33; 20:22; Acts 1:2,5,8; 2:4; 4:8,25; 6:5; 7:55; 8:15,17,19; 9:17; 10:38; 11:16,24; 13:9,52; 19:2; Romans 5:5; 9:1;***

[7] It should be noted that the given phrase may occur more than once in some verses in this and other lists.

14:17; 15:13,16; 1 Corinthians 12:3; 2 Corinthians 6:6; 1 Thessalonians 1:5,6; 2 Timothy 1:14; Titus 3:5; Hebrews 2:4; 6:4; 1 Peter 1:12; 2 Peter 1:21; Jude 20.

6. The Holy Spirit (*to pneuma to hagion*, with the definite article before both the noun and the adjective, in the Greek fashion; 27 times). ***Matthew 12:32; Mark 3:29; 12:36; 13:11; Luke 2:26; 3:22; 10:21; John 14:26; Acts 1:16; 2:33; 5:3,32; 7:51; 10:44,47; 11:15; 13:2; 15:8,28; 19:6; 20:23,28; 21:11; 28:25; Hebrews 3:7; 9:8; 10:15.***
7. His Holy Spirit (*to pneuma to hagion*, with "His"). ***1 Thessalonians 4:8.***
8. The Holy Spirit of promise (*to pneuma to hagion*, with "of promise"). ***Ephesians 1:13.***
9. The Holy Spirit (*to hagion pneuma*, using one definite article; 11 times). ***Matthew 28:19; Luke 12:10,12; Acts 2:38; 4:31; 9:31; 10:45; 13:4; 16:6; 1 Corinthians 6:19; 2 Corinthians 13:14.***
10. The Spirit of holiness. ***Romans 1:4.***
11. Spirit of the Living God. ***2 Corinthians 3:3.***
12. Spirit of God (no article). ***Matthew 3:16; 12:28; Romans 8:9,14; 1 Corinthians 7:40; 12:3.***
13. The Spirit of God (with article). ***1 Corinthians 2:12,14; 3:16; 6:11; Philippians 3:3; 1 John 4:2.***
14. The Holy Spirit of God. ***Ephesians 4:30.***
15. The Spirit of your Father. ***Matthew 10:20.***
16. Spirit of the Lord (no article). ***Luke 4:18; Acts 8:39.***
17. The Spirit of the Lord (with article). ***Acts 5:9; 2 Corinthians 3:17.***
18. The Spirit of Jesus Christ. ***Philippians 1:19.***
19. The Spirit of Jesus. ***Acts 16:7.***
20. The Spirit of His Son. ***Galatians 4:6.***
21. Spirit of Christ. ***Romans 8:9; 1 Peter 1:11.***
22. The Spirit of truth. ***John 14:17; 15:26; 16:13; 1 John 4:6.***
23. The Spirit of life. ***Romans 8:2.***
24. Spirit of adoption. ***Romans 8:15.***
25. The Spirit of grace. ***Hebrews 10:29.***
26. The Spirit of glory and of God. ***1 Peter 4:14.***
27. Eternal Spirit. ***Hebrews 9:14.***

Is there any significance to this wide variety of expressions, especially in the use or nonuse of the definite article (*to*, "the") in the NT texts? Some have suggested as much. In his book, *The Spirit and the Word* (**15**), Z.T. Sweeney says that in many of the 264 references to the Spirit in the

NT, "there is no allusion to the Holy Spirit. In many places the expressions 'the Spirit' and 'the Holy Spirit,' should be rendered by 'Spirit' and 'holy Spirit,' or frequently 'a holy Spirit,'" depending on the presence or absence of the definite article. What Sweeney seeks to make of this distinction is not clear. He does dismiss ***Luke 11:13*** as referring to the Holy Spirit, since there is no definite article there. It refers, he says (**86**), to God's gift of a holy spirit or disposition.

A more serious use of the presence or absence of the article is made by Victor Paul Wierwille, founder of the cult known as The Way International, in his book *Receiving the Holy Spirit Today*. He says (**14**) that "*the* Holy Spirit" (with the article) refers to God, while "holy spirit" (*pneuma hagion* without the article) refers simply to the power from on high, the GIFT given by the Holy Spirit (the GIVER) on the Day of Pentecost. "The gift of (from) The Holy Spirit, **the Giver**, is *pneuma hagion*, holy spirit, power from on high, spiritual abilities, enablements." Wierwille uses this distinction to construct a faulty view of God and a faulty view of tongue-speaking.

My own conclusion is that the presence or absence of the Greek definite article in texts referring to the Spirit is irrelevant. When we compare the various descriptions of the Spirit as they appear in parallel passages or in the same context, we see that they are used interchangeably and synonymously for the Holy Spirit. If there is a question as to whether the Holy Spirit is the intended referent in a particular text, only the context can decide. The following comparisons show that this is the case.

1. ***John 3:5***, *pneuma* (Spirit); ***John 3:6***, *to pneuma* (the Spirit)
2. ***Matthew 22:43***, *pneuma* (Spirit); ***Mark 12:36***, *to pneuma to hagion* (the Holy Spirit)
3. ***Luke 2:25***, *pneuma hagion* (Holy Spirit); ***Luke 2:26***, *to pneuma to hagion* (the Holy Spirit); ***Luke 2:27***, *to pneuma* (the Spirit)
4. ***John 7:39***, *to pneuma* (the Spirit) and *pneuma* (Spirit)
5. ***Matthew 3:16***, *to pneuma tou theou* (the Spirit of God); ***Mark 1:10***, *to pneuma* (the Spirit); ***Luke 3:22***, *to pneuma to hagion* (the Holy Spirit)
6. ***Matthew 12:18***, *to pneuma mou* (my Spirit); ***Matthew 12:28***, *pneuma theou* (Spirit of God)
7. ***Acts 2:4***, *pneuma hagion* (Holy Spirit) and *to pneuma* (the Spirit); ***Acts 10:45***, *to hagion pneuma* (the Holy Spirit); ***Acts***

11:15, *to pneuma to hagion* (the Holy Spirit); ***Acts 11:16***, *pneuma hagion* (Holy Spirit)

8. ***Acts 8:15,17***, *pneuma hagion* (Holy Spirit); ***Acts 18:18***, *to pneuma* (the Spirit)
9. ***Acts 19:2***, *pneuma* (Spirit); ***Acts 19:6***, *to pneuma to hagion* (the Holy Spirit)
10. ***2 Corinthians 3:6***, *pneuma* (Spirit) and *to pneuma* (the Spirit)
11. ***Galatians 3:2***, *to pneuma* (the Spirit); ***Galatians 3:3***, *pneuma* (Spirit)
12. ***Galatians 5:16-25***, *pneuma* (Spirit), 4 times; *to pneuma* (the Spirit), 3 times

THE NAME "HOLY SPIRIT"

Why is the name "Holy Spirit" or "the Holy Spirit" used for the third person of the Trinity? We can only speculate about this, but several points may be suggested. First, we must remember that the essence of all three persons of the Trinity is spirit: "God is spirit" (***Jn 4:24***). The fact that one person is called "the Spirit" helps us to remember this. That the Holy Spirit is specifically called "the Spirit" does not make the Father or the Son any less spirit. The same thing is true of the principal names applied to the Father and the Son by the Apostle Paul, namely, "God" and "Lord" (see ***1Cor 12:4-6***; ***Eph 4:4-6***). That Paul refers to the Father as "God" (*theos*) does not make the Son and the Spirit any less God. That he calls the Son "Lord" (*kurios*) does not make the Father and the Spirit any less Lord. It is simply convenient to have a readily identifiable name for each person of the Trinity, even if the attribute designated by that name is shared by all.

But why is the Spirit so often called the *Holy* Spirit? What is the significance of the word "Holy"? "Holy Spirit" was not a common name for the Spirit in the OT, being used only in ***Psalm 51:11*** and ***Isaiah 63:10-11***. In the NT, though, it is applied to the Spirit around 90 times. Why is this name significant?

Why is the Spirit called the Holy Spirit? To be holy means to be separated from the ordinary.

The biblical terms for holiness seem to have the root meaning of separation; to be holy means to be *separated* from the ordinary, to be *set apart* from something (**Cottrell, *Creator*, 212-216**). Holiness is thus a basic attribute of God as such: *"Holy, Holy, Holy, is the LORD of hosts"* (***Isa 6:3***). This means that God as the infinite Creator is in a separate category of being; everything else is a part of creation. As explained earlier, even though God is spirit and some created things are spirits, divine spirit is still in a category of its own compared with created spirits. Divine spirit is thus holy, separate, distinct, set apart, transcendent. This is called God's *ontological* holiness.

Another sense in which God is holy is that He is totally separate from *sin* and from *sinners*. He is completely righteous and pure and upright in character; He is the very opposite of evil. This is called God's *ethical* holiness.

Thus it is appropriate when referring to "the Spirit" to speak of Him as "the *Holy* Spirit," the Spirit who is different from all created spirits and separate from all sin.

Another reason for the appropriateness of the name "*Holy* Spirit" has to do with the Spirit's work in the NT era. Even though the three persons of the Trinity share the same basic nature of uncreated, divine spirit, and even though they are often involved in the same works in relation to this world, nevertheless each person has certain roles and tasks that are unique, especially in relation to the redemption of sinners. As we shall see, one of the unique works of the Holy Spirit, perhaps His main work, is the sanctification of Christians. The Spirit indwells us for the specific purpose of sanctifying us, i.e., to *make us holy* (in the ethical sense) as He is holy (***1Pet 1:15-16***). Since holiness is His distinctive work, it is fitting that He be called the *Holy* Spirit, indeed, the "Spirit of holiness" (***Rom 1:4***).

CHAPTER ONE

THE PERSON OF THE HOLY SPIRIT

In the study of Christology (what the Bible says about Jesus Christ), the biblical material is usually divided into two main categories: (1) the *person* of Christ, or who He is; and (2) the *work* of Christ, or what He has done and is doing for our salvation. The same division is made in presenting the biblical material about the Holy Spirit. We first ask about the person of the Spirit; then we ask about His work. This chapter deals with the former; the rest of the book deals with the latter.

As we approach the subject of the person of the Spirit, we find that there are three main issues. First, is the Holy Spirit a *person*? Second, is He a *divine* person? Third, as a divine person is He distinct from the Father and the Son? Before addressing these issues, we will set forth a brief survey of the history of the doctrine of the Spirit.

THE HOLY SPIRIT IN CHRISTIAN HISTORY

For over two hundred years after the NT writings were completed, relatively little attention was given to the doctrine of the Holy Spirit. Christian writers directed their efforts mainly toward explaining the Christian faith in general and defending it against attacks from both Judaism and paganism (especially Gnosticism). In this period the most controversial doctrine was the person of Christ, specifically His deity in relation to the one God as revealed in the OT. This controversy reached an initial resolution with the Creed of Nicea (AD 325), which asserted the essential deity of Jesus, declaring Him to be of the same essence as the Father.

Up until this time, during the second and third centuries, brief trinitarian references were presented with little theological reflection. For example, Clement of Rome (early second century) asked, "Have we not one God and one Christ and one Spirit of grace that was shed upon us?" (¶46; **Holmes, 54**). He introduces another comment with these words: "For as God lives, and as the Lord Jesus Christ lives, and the Holy Spirit, who are the faith and hope of the elect . . ." (¶58; **Holmes, 61**). Likewise Ignatius of Antioch (early second century) uses the formula, "in the Son and the Father and in the Spirit" ("To the Magnesians," ¶13; **Holmes, 96**). Another second-century document, "The Martyrdom of Polycarp," refers to "the Lord Jesus Christ . . . , to whom be the glory with the Father and the Holy Spirit forever and ever" (22:3; **Holmes, 144**).

In the late second century Irenaeus wrote that the church believes "in one God, the Father Almighty, Maker of heaven, and earth, and the sea, and all things that are in them; and in one Christ Jesus, the Son of God, who became incarnate for our salvation; and in one Holy Spirit, who proclaimed through the prophets the dispensations of God" and the coming advents of Christ ("Against Heresies," I.x.1). In the third century some attention was given to the subject by Tertullian and Origen (**Heron, 67-73**), but the Creed of Nicea itself (AD 325) reflects the relative neglect of the doctrine of the Spirit up to that time. The first paragraph of this creed is one sentence about the Father: "We believe in one God, the Father All Governing, creator of all things visible and invisible." The next paragraph is about six times longer than this and is all about Jesus. Then comes one brief sentence about the Spirit: "And [we believe] in the Holy Spirit." To this is added several more lines about Jesus (**Leith, 30-31**).

After Nicea, however, the issue of the deity of the Holy Spirit was specifically raised. The Arians, having lost the battle over the deity of Christ, now began to question the divine nature of the Spirit and to speak of Him as a created being. But in the decades following Nicea there were many who strongly defended the full personhood and deity of the Spirit. These included Cyril of Jerusalem, Athanasius, and the Cappadocian Fathers (Basil, Gregory of Nazianzus, and Gregory of Nyssa). For example, Athanasius wrote, "It is sufficient for you to believe that the Spirit is not a creature, but is Spirit of God; and that in God there is a Triad, Father, Son, and Holy Spirit" (*Ad Serapionem*, IV.7; cited in **Heron, 77-78**).

The matter was resolved at the Council of Constantinople in AD 381, where the Arians were denounced and the Nicene Creed of AD 325 was revised to include a stronger statement of faith in the Holy Spirit. In this creed faith was affirmed "in the Holy Spirit, the Lord and life-giver, Who proceeds from the Father, Who is worshiped and glorified together with the Father and Son, Who spoke through the prophets" (**Leith, 33**). Bethune-Baker (**224-225**) makes this comment on the pronouncement of Constantinople:

> And so the faith in the triune personality of God was proclaimed against the last attempt of Arianism, and the Catholic interpretation established—one God existing permanently and eternally in three spheres of consciousness and activity, three modes, three forms, three persons: in the inner relations of the divine life as well as in the outer relations of the Godhead to the world and to men.
>
> From this time forward it was only in connexion with the procession of the Spirit that any fresh development of the doctrine is to be noted. . . .

The issue of the procession of the Spirit will be discussed later in this chapter.

The conclusions of Nicea and Constantinople remained the accepted orthodoxy for over a thousand years. Then in the late sixteenth century unitarianism was reintroduced by Socinus, who "denied that the One God could properly be spoken of as three Persons" (**Kent, 590**). He taught that "the Holy Spirit is nothing but God's power and influence" (**Heick, 2:140**). This view took firm root in England and America, not just in unitarianism as such but also in most forms of classical Liberalism. Liberal theology challenged the idea that the Holy Spirit is a distinct person within a "trinity." An example is Hopper (**172**), who says that "in terms of Trinitarian speculation it [the Holy Spirit] clearly risks distortion the moment it is hypostatized or affirmed as a 'Person.'" The Liberal theologian William

Newton Clarke explains that Father, Son, and Spirit are "three modes of being" rooted in "divine self-consciousness. . . . They are not personalities, in the modern sense of the term, but are separate aspects of one personality" (175).

This anti-trinitarianism continues in modern Neo-liberalism, in which "Holy Spirit" is simply the name applied to God as He works in the world today or as we anticipate His working in the future. An example is Blaikie, for whom "the Holy Spirit" is "God who acts in the world" (28). More specifically, God who acts at all times and places we call God the Father; God made known to us in the past as Jesus Christ we call God the Son. "And *God here and now*, God acting in the continuing present of our world-time, God in His fulness as we meet Him today, we call God the *Holy Spirit*" (211).

The orthodox (Nicene) concept of the Holy Spirit is also denied by many modern cults. For example, Jehovah's Witnesses equate the "holy spirit" (never capitalized) with God's impersonal active force or power. "So the holy spirit is the invisible active force of Almighty God which moves His servants to do His will" (***Let God Be True*, 108**). "It is the impersonal, invisible active force that finds its source and reservoir in Jehovah God and that he uses to accomplish His will even at great distances, over light-years of space" (***Let Your Name Be Sanctified*, 269**). Thus on Pentecost, the disciples "'became filled with holy spirit.' Were they 'filled' with a person? No, but they were filled with God's active force" (***The Truth That Leads to Eternal Life*, 24**). "Satan is the originator of the trinity doctrine" (***Let God Be True*, 101**).

Herbert W. Armstrong's original Worldwide Church of God embraced this same view of the Spirit. An early edition of Armstrong's "Correspondence Course" (8:8) said, "God's Spirit is not a 'third person' in the God Family. It is His divine POWER that emanates from Him and permeates the universe!" One WCG publication offered "proof positive that the Holy Spirit is not a person but the power God the Father uses—much as a man uses electricity" (**"Is the Holy Spirit a Person?" 32**).

As noted in the Introduction, Victor Paul Wierwille, founder of "The Way International" cult, taught that "*the* Holy Spirit" (with the article in the Greek, and capitalized) is just another name for God, and that "holy spirit" (no article, small case) is God's impersonal power (**Wierwille, 14, 59, 252**). There is no divine person called the Holy Spirit who is distinct from the Father. Since he also denied that Jesus Christ is God, Wierwille was basically a unitarian. "Trinitarianism, then, according to Wierwille, is baptized paganism" (**J.L. Williams, 72**).

Mormons distinguish between the Holy *Spirit* (the Spirit of God, the Spirit of Christ) and the Holy *Ghost.* As an eminent Mormon writer explains, the former is the impersonal power, energy, or enlightenment that works within all human beings. The latter is a personal divine being, the third person of the Godhead (**Richards, 111-132**). But Mormons are polytheists; there are many other personal gods besides the Father, the Son, and the Holy Ghost. Also, Mormon deities are finite, bearing no resemblance to the transcendent, infinite God of the Bible. Thus we are not surprised to hear that, for Mormons, the Holy Ghost is "a male personage" who has a "spirit body" (instead of a material body like the Father and other gods). He is "a personage of spirit in the form of a man" and is "confined in His personage to a limited space" (**Richards, 118-120**). In summary, the Holy Ghost "is one of many gods in the universe. These Mormon gods continually produce spirit children which are given bodies on different planets. The Holy Ghost is unique among these gods in that it has no body and cannot reproduce like other gods" (**Spiritual Counterfeits Project letter, 7/26/85**).

There is considerable confusion and false teaching about the person of the Holy Spirit today.

It is clear that there is considerable confusion and false teaching about the person of the Holy Spirit today, and therefore there is a great need to carefully examine what the Bible says about the subject. That is what the rest of this chapter seeks to do.

THE HOLY SPIRIT IS A PERSON

Many have concluded, for one reason or another, that the Holy Spirit is not a person. Some have been unable to reconcile the idea with the oneness of God, thus favoring unitarianism. Others have felt that references to "the spirit of God" (especially in the OT) more naturally refer to God's power or influence. A few, especially in the Restoration Movement, have been so wary of Calvinism and subjectivism that they have adopted the radical view that the Holy Spirit is actually the Bible itself. Carl Ketcherside (7) tells of attending a Bible class in a Missouri church where the teacher held His Bible aloft and declared, "This Book is the Holy Spirit, and all the Holy Spirit there is. When I have it in my overcoat pocket, the Holy Spirit is in my pocket. The Holy Spirit is the Word of God, and that's what this Book is, the Word of God, and the Holy Spirit."

Against such views it is very important to see that the Holy Spirit is a *person*. This is true not just for the sake of maintaining the doctrine of the Trinity, but also for making sense of the many activities or works attributed to the Spirit in the Bible, especially as related to revelation and salvation. The things the Holy Spirit is said to do simply cannot be done by an impersonal, lifeless force. The Bible mocks inert idols because of their inactivity and helplessness: *"Like a scarecrow in a cucumber field are they, and they cannot speak; they must be carried, because they cannot walk! Do not fear them, for they can do no harm, nor can they do any good"* (**Jer 10:5**). *"What profit is the idol when its maker has carved it . . . ? For its maker trusts in His own handiwork when he fashions speechless idols. Woe to him who says to a piece of wood, 'Awake!' To a mute stone, 'Arise!' And that is your teacher? . . . There is no breath at all inside it"* (**Hab 2:18-19**).

Only a Spirit who is *personal* can speak and teach and act—things that Scripture says the Holy Spirit does.

It is not immediately self-evident, however, that the Holy Spirit is a person. Morris points out that the very designation "Father" implies personhood, and that the incarnation of the Logos as the living human being Jesus of Nazareth makes it easy to remember that He is a person. "But it is different with the Spirit. 'Spirit' is not such an aggressively personal word as 'Father'. The Spirit has not become incarnate like the Son. We find it hard to picture Him" (***Spirit*, 34**).

Only a Spirit who is personal can speak and teach and act.

Thus it is necessary to concisely set forth the biblical evidence for the Spirit's personhood.

All Spiritual Beings Are Persons

First of all, we must remind ourselves of a point made in the Introduction namely, that in the Bible all spiritual entities are personal. A being of spirit is by nature a personal being. This is true of human souls, of angels, and of God Himself (***Jn 4:24***). There is no such thing as an "impersonal spirit." This in itself supports the personhood of the Holy Spirit.

The Spirit Is "Another Helper"

A second evidence of the Spirit's personal nature is Jesus' description of Him as "another Helper" in ***John 14:16***. Here, on the eve of His crucifixion, from which point Jesus would be physically separated from His disciples for the rest of their earthly lives, He comforts them with this promise: *"I will ask the Father, and He will give you another Helper, that He may be with you forever."* This "other Helper" is identified in ***verse 17*** as *"the Spirit of truth."*

The Greek phrase for "another Helper" is *allos parakletos*; each of these two words supports the fact that the Spirit is a person. The word *parakletos* has been translated several ways, including "Helper" as in the NASB (also NKJV, TEV, ESV), "Comforter" (KJV, ASV, LB), "Counselor" (RSV, NIV, NLT, CSB), "Advocate" (NEB, Weymouth, NRSV, TNIV), and "Paraclete" (NAB). The literal meaning of *parakletos* is "called alongside," or someone called upon for assistance. Phillips translates *allos parakletos* as "someone else to stand by you"; Knox has it as "another to befriend you." The main point is that the word itself was used to refer to *persons*.

In the Greek world the word was commonly used of someone called upon for help with a legal matter, such as a "counsel for the defense," or an advocate (as it seems to mean in ***1Jn 2:1*** as applied to Jesus). Thus it would be equivalent to "attorney" or "lawyer"—clearly a personal concept. Morris thinks this meaning might be too narrow in ***John 14:16***, though (***Spirit*, 35**). Barclay agrees, and suggests "Encourager" instead—"one who puts courage into the fainthearted, one who nerves the feeble arm for fight, one who makes a very ordinary man cope gallantly with a perilous and a dangerous situation" (***Words*, 221**). Either way, the word simply would not be used of anything but a person.

Jesus said the Holy Spirit would be "another" Helper or Advocate or Encourager. The word for "another" is *allos*, one of two Greek words with this general meaning. The other word is *heteros*. The fact that Jesus uses *allos* instead of *heteros* is significant; as used here this word also establishes the personhood of the Spirit. How is this the case?

Because *heteros* basically means "another of a *different* kind," while *allos* means "another of the same kind," i.e., a Helper of the same kind as Christ Himself. "The most natural interpretation of all this is that the Spirit is to be thought of as another like Jesus. As Jesus is a Person, the inference is that the Spirit is a Person. . . . The most natural way of understanding 'another' [*allos*] is "another of like kind'" (**Morris, *Spirit*, 36**). Trench rightly says, "Thus Christ promises to His disciples that He will send, not *heteron*, but *allon, Parakleton* (***John xiv.16)***, 'another' Comforter therefore, similar to Himself" (***Synonyms*, 357**).

Thus both words, "another" and "Helper," in themselves affirm the Spirit's personhood. Their use in this context only reinforces this. Would anything less have been of consolation to the disciples, in view of Christ's impending departure? As Torrey says, "Is it possible that Jesus Christ could have used such language if the other Comforter who was coming to take His place was only an impersonal influence or power? . . . No, one Divine Person was going, another Person just as Divine was coming to take His place" (**20-21**).

The Holy Spirit Is Listed with Other Persons

In two NT texts the Holy Spirit is listed or juxtaposed with other persons in such a way that it makes sense only if the Spirit is also a person. One is the familiar baptismal formula, *"baptizing them in the name of the Father and the Son and the Holy Spirit"* (***Matt 28:19***). Linking the Spirit with the Father and the Son (who are indisputably persons), in equal connection with a single "name," points to the Spirit's personhood.

The same is true of ***Acts 15:28***, which is part of the letter from the Jerusalem church to Antioch: *"For it seemed good to the Holy Spirit and to us to lay upon you no greater burden than these essentials."* The "us" here includes "the apostles and the elders, and the whole church" in Jerusalem, as named in ***verse 22***. Thus once again the Spirit is listed alongside other persons, this time as sharing the responsibility for the contents of this letter.

Neuter Noun, Masculine Pronouns

An interesting but not decisive consideration is the fact that sometimes the Greek noun for "spirit" (*pneuma*), which is neuter in gender, is followed by masculine pronouns when referring to the Holy Spirit. This is significant because, simply as a matter of Greek grammar, pronouns and adjectives are expected to agree with the gender of the noun to which they refer.

The fact that the word *pneuma* is neuter in gender is totally irrelevant to the issue of the personhood of the Spirit, contrary to the following contention of Tommy Baker (**23**): "In the original language of the New Testament, which is Greek, the Holy Spirit is consistently 'neuter' as well as the pronouns, articles, and participles which refer to 'It.' In the English translations where a masculine pronoun or noun appears the original neuter gender has so been changed by a translator." Thus the translators have proceeded to "tamper with the gender of the Godhead," perhaps because of "some ancient bias for the masculine."

Baker is wrong in two ways. First, he implies that since the word used for the Holy Spirit (*pneuma*) is grammatically neuter, this gender somehow should carry over into the Spirit "Itself." This is an implicit questioning of the personhood of the Spirit. But this whole contention is wrong, because in fact the gender of a Greek noun, i.e., the word used to represent some aspect of reality, is not necessarily related to the gender of the reality for which it stands. Nonpersonal things (neuter in reality) can be represented by words that are either masculine or feminine grammatically. For example, *ho artos* (masc.) means "bread," and *he aspis* (fem.) means "shield." At the same time, words representing persons, male or female, may well be grammatically neuter: *to andrapodon* (neut.) means "slave, captive in war"; *to paidion* (neut.) means "infant, child." Thus the fact that *pneuma* is neuter is completely irrelevant to the issue of the Spirit's personhood.

Baker's second problem is a straightforward factual error. He says that since *pneuma* is neuter, the related Greek pronouns, articles, and participles used for the Spirit are "consistently 'neuter.'" This is simply wrong, and significantly so. Grammatically, they *should* be neuter. But in a few key texts they are masculine, in deliberate defiance of the grammatical rule and seemingly as a deliberate affirmation of the Spirit's personhood. One such text is ***John 14:26***, *"But the Helper, the Holy Spirit* [*pneuma*, neut.], *whom the Father will send in My name, He* [*ekeinos*, masc.] *will teach you all things."* Here we would expect the pronoun *ekeinos* ("that one") to be neuter since the noun to which it seems to refer (*pneuma*) is neuter, but it is masculine. The same is true in ***John 15:26***. See also ***John 16:13-14***, where *ekeinos* (masc.) is used at the beginning of each verse. Another such verse is ***Ephesians 1:14***, where the masculine relative pronoun *hos* refers back to the Holy Spirit (*pneuma*, neut.) in ***verse 13***.

Under these circumstances the fact that *pneuma* is neuter actually supports the case for the Spirit's personhood rather than weakening it.

The Holy Spirit Does What Persons Do

Another reason for accepting the personhood of the Spirit is that the Bible constantly depicts Him as doing the sorts of things that persons do. First, He engages in rational or *intellectual* activity. ***John 16:8*** says the Spirit will "convict the world." Carter says, "*Convict* is a forensic term which implies a rational and just exercise of the mind" (**24**). ***Romans 8:26-27*** specifically refers to "the mind of the Spirit," which He exercises in reading our own unarticulated thoughts. Most significantly, ***1 Corinthians 2:10-11*** says that *"the Spirit searches all things, even the depths of God,"* and thus knows the very thoughts of God. Such activity is eminently personal.

Second, the Holy Spirit performs *volitional* acts, exercising His judgment, using His will to make decisions, and even authoritatively imposing them upon human beings. In ***Acts 13:1-4*** the Spirit chooses Barnabas and Saul, calls them to missionary work, and sends them out. In ***Acts 15:28*** He decides what burden to bind upon the Gentile brethren. In ***Acts 16:6-7*** the Spirit forbade Paul and Silas to preach in certain places. ***First Corinthians 12:11*** says that the Holy Spirit decides which gifts to bestow upon Christians, distributing *"to each one individually just as He wills"* (see ***Heb 2:4***).

"The Spirit searches all things, even the depths of God."

Third, the Holy Spirit is described over and over as *speaking,* both to and through the apostles and prophets. In ***Acts 8:29***, "the Spirit said to Philip, 'Go up and join this chariot.'" Paul tells us that "the Spirit explicitly says that in later times some will fall away" (***1Tm 4:1***). See also ***Matthew 10:20***; ***John 15:26***; ***16:13***; ***Acts 13:2***; ***21:11***; ***Hebrews 3:7***; ***10:15***; ***Revelation 2:7***.

The fourth personal activity attributed to the Holy Spirit is *teaching*. *"You gave Your good Spirit to instruct them"* says **Nehemiah 9:20.** Jesus promised His apostles that the Spirit "will teach you all things" (***Jn 14:26***; see ***Jn 16:13-15***). As an inspired Apostle, Paul spoke words "taught by the Spirit" (***1Cor 2:12-13***).

Finally, the Holy Spirit is described in Scripture as one who feels the kinds of *emotions* that persons feel, such as grief: *"But they rebelled, and grieved His Holy Spirit,"* ***Isaiah 63:10*** says of Israel. Christians are exhorted, *"Do not grieve the Holy Spirit of God"* (***Eph 4:30***). The word used here (*lupeo*) is used often in the NT for ordinary sorrow and sadness. Also, Paul may be attributing the feeling of love to the Spirit when he exhorts the brethren *"by our Lord Jesus Christ and by the love of the Spirit"* (***Rom 15:30***). This could mean either the Spirit's love for us or our love for the Spirit. Either way, both the giving and the receiving of love are something experienced by persons.

The Holy Spirit Is Treated as a Person

The last line of evidence in support of the Spirit's personhood is that He is described as being treated as a person would be treated. In the episode with Ananias and Sapphira in ***Acts 5:1-11***, Peter declared that they both *lied to* the Holy Spirit (*v. 3*) and *tempted* the Spirit of the Lord (*v. 9—peirazo*, the common word for "tempt"). These acts are meaningful only when directed toward a person. Also, **Hebrews 10:29** says it is possible to *insult* (provoke, arrogantly despise) the Spirit of grace. Some would include here the blasphemy of the Spirit (***Mt 12:31***).

The Nature of the Evidence

The biblical evidence that the Holy Spirit is a person is overwhelming, but some are concerned that most of it comes from the NT. It is a fact that the portrait of the Spirit in the OT is not as clear and distinct as it is in the NT. This does not mean, however, that the OT *denies* the personhood of the Spirit. In a way that is perfectly consistent with the historical, progressive unfolding of God's plan of salvation, the explicit picture of the Spirit as a person distinct from the Father is simply not revealed until the New Covenant dispensation.

This is true of the doctrine of the Trinity as such, including our knowledge of God the Son. The trinitarian nature of God comes to light historically only in relation to the work of redemption, beginning with the incarnation and continuing with the Pentecostal outpouring of the Spirit. Thus we would actually expect the NT revelation of the nature of the Holy Spirit to be more detailed than that of the OT (see **Cottrell, *Redeemer*, 117-120**).

THE HOLY SPIRIT IS A DIVINE PERSON

The Christian faith affirms not only that the Holy Spirit is a person, but also that He is a *divine* person. He is God the Holy Spirit, the third person of the Trinity, being of the same divine spiritual essence as the Father and the Son. Several lines of biblical evidence confirm this.

Trinitarian Statements

Several NT texts refer to the Father, the Son, and the Spirit in ways that support Their unity and equality and thus the deity of the Holy Spirit. The best known and most commonly used text is ***Matthew 28:19***, *"Go therefore and make disciples of all the nations, baptizing them in the name of the Father and the Son and the Holy Spirit."* The one name unites the three persons. The phrase "into [*eis*] the name of" can mean generally "into a relationship with," which in this context would be a saving relationship in which all three persons of the Trinity participate. In the Greek world the phrase was used specifically as an accounting term for the entry of an item into the list of one's owned assets. Thus the phrase means that in accepting God's salvation a person becomes the "property" equally of the Father, the Son, and the Spirit and surrenders to Their shared lordship. This is difficult to understand if the Spirit is not divine in the same way as are the Father and the Son.

Another trinitarian text is the blessing of ***2 Corinthians 13:14***, *"The grace of the Lord Jesus Christ, and the love of God, and the fellowship of the Holy Spirit, be with you."* This expresses our continuing dependence on all three persons.

Another text that parallels the three is ***1 Corinthians 12:4-6***, *"Now there are varieties of gifts, but the same Spirit. And there are varieties of* *ministries, and the same Lord. There are varieties of effects, but the same God who works all things in all persons."* Here all three persons of the Trinity are equally involved in the bestowing of what we call "spiritual gifts."

These three texts together show that there is no one proper order for listing the Father, the Son, and the Spirit. We usually use this order because of the influence of the baptismal text, and as a result we usually speak of the Holy Spirit as "the third person of the Trinity." In view of these last two texts, however, we can see that this order is more traditional than normative. It also shows the fallacy of Boles's statement that "the Holy Spirit is always put third when spoken of in the Bible; as God is placed first in the Trinity, so the Holy Spirit is put third" (**21**). But as we can see, in ***1 Corinthians 12:4-6*** the Spirit is actually mentioned first; and in the three texts God (the Father) is placed in all three positions.

Other trinitarian texts include ***Ephesians 4:4-6***, where "one Spirit," "one Lord," and "one God and Father" are each included in the seven basic doctrines that unite believers. Also relevant are ***2 Corinthians 1:21-22***, *"Now He who establishes us with you in Christ and anointed us is God, who also sealed us and gave us the Spirit in our hearts as a pledge,"* and ***1 Peter 1:2***, which says we are chosen *"according to the foreknowledge of God the Father, by the sanctifying work of the Spirit, to obey Jesus Christ and be sprinkled with His blood."* These latter two texts again involve all three persons of the Trinity in the work of salvation.

One text that should not be cited to support the Trinity and therefore the deity of the Spirit is ***1 John 5:7*** in the KJV, *"For there are three that bear record in heaven, the Father, the Word, and the Holy Ghost: and these three are one"* (see also the NKJV). Most modern translations omit this verse because it is a clear case of a very late addition to the text of the Bible; it is present in no early or even moderately early Greek manuscripts of the NT (see **Metzger, 101-102**).

THE HOLY SPIRIT HAS DIVINE ATTRIBUTES

Another biblical basis for affirming the Spirit's deity is the fact that He is said to possess divine attributes. ***Hebrews 9:14*** speaks of Him as "the eternal Spirit." According to ***1 Timothy 6:16***, only God "possesses immortality," i.e., is inherently eternal (see ***Ps 90:2***).

Also, ***1 Corinthians 2:10-11*** presents the Holy Spirit as omniscient or all-knowing, since the content of His mind is the same as the content of the Father's mind:

> *For the Spirit searches all things, even the depths of God. For who among men knows the thoughts of a man except the spirit of the man which is in him? Even so the thoughts of God no one knows except the Spirit of God.*

Isaiah 40:13-14 suggests that "the Spirit of the LORD" by nature knows all there is to know:

> *Who has directed the Spirit of the LORD, or as His counselor has informed Him? With whom did He consult and who gave Him understanding? And who taught Him in the path of justice and taught Him knowledge and informed Him of the way of understanding?*

Psalm 139:7-10 clearly involves the Spirit of God in divine omnipresence:

> *Where can I go from Your Spirit? Or where can I flee from Your presence? If I ascend to heaven, You are there; if I make my bed in Sheol, behold, You are there. If I take the wings of the dawn, if I dwell in the remotest part of the sea, even there Your hand will lead me, and Your right hand will lay hold of me.*

Also, the fact that the Holy Spirit simultaneously indwells all immersed believers worldwide shows that His essence is not limited by space, which is the very presupposition of omnipresence. (His indwelling is more than His omnipresence, however.)

Though the Bible does not explicitly attribute omnipotence to the Spirit, it does say that He performs works of such great power that we normally think of them as things that only God can do. A main example is creation (***Gen 1:2***; ***Ps 104:30***); another is raising the dead (***Rom 8:11***). Creation and resurrection are the two masterworks in God's repertoire of omnipotence (***Rom 4:17***), and the Spirit does both. He is the Spirit of power (***Mic 3:8***; ***Zec 4:6***; ***Acts 1:8***; ***Rom 15:13,19***).

The Spirit performs works of umistakably divine power.

BLASPHEMY AGAINST THE SPIRIT

Jesus teaches that the worst sin anyone can commit is blasphemy against the Holy Spirit, since it is the only sin that "never has forgiveness" (***Mk 3:29***). His full statement is thus:

> *Therefore I say to you, any sin and blasphemy shall be forgiven people, but blasphemy against the Spirit shall not be forgiven. Whoever speaks a word against the Son of Man, it shall be forgiven him; but whoever speaks against the Holy Spirit, it shall not be forgiven him, either in this age or in the age to come.* (***Mt 12:31-32***; see ***Lk 12:10***)

This is incomprehensible if the Holy Spirit is not divine, since blasphemy against the Son of Man—Jesus, God the Son—can be forgiven. Surely blasphemy against the Spirit can be worse than this only if the Spirit is also divine.

THE HOLY SPIRIT IS CALLED GOD

We believe the Holy Spirit is divine because the Bible specifically speaks of Him as God. When the Apostle Peter addresses Ananias's deceit in ***Acts 5:1-4***, he asks him, *"Why has Satan filled your heart to lie to the Holy Spirit . . . ?"* He then characterizes this lie thus: *"You have not lied to men but to God."* Thus Peter specifically equates the Holy Spirit with God; lying to the Spirit is the same as lying to God.

Another such text is ***1 Corinthians 3:16***, *"Do you not know that you are a temple of God and that the Spirit of God dwells in you?"* Using the analogy or type of the OT temple as the literal locale of the Shekinah glory, the visible manifestation of God to the Jews (***Ex 40:34-38***), Paul says the church is God's temple, God's dwelling-place today; and we are indwelt specifically by "the Spirit of God." See also ***Ephesians 2:22***, *"You also are being built together into a dwelling of God in the Spirit."* The same applies to the body of the individual believer (***1Cor 6:19***).

> **The church is God's temple, indwelt specifically by "the Spirit of God."**

The Bible identifies the Holy Spirit as God in a very dramatic way when OT events and sayings of which Yahweh (the LORD) is the subject are in the NT attributed to the Holy Spirit. Some put ***Hebrews 3:7-11*** into this category (**Torrey, 30**), since it is introduced with *"just as the Holy Spirit says,"* and since the events described were directed toward Yahweh in ***Exodus 16:7***; ***17:1-7***. However, it is possible that "just as the Holy Spirit says" is simply acknowledging the Spirit's authorship of ***Psalm 95:7-11***, which is being quoted in ***Hebrews 3:7-11***.

Another such NT text is ***Acts 28:25-27***, where Paul directly cites ***Isaiah 6:8-10***. Whereas Paul says, *"the Holy Spirit rightly spoke through*

Isaiah the prophet," the OT text clearly places the quoted words in the mouth of Yahweh (the LORD). The same is true of ***Hebrews 10:15-17*** and ***Jeremiah 31:31-34***. Hebrews says that in these words *"the Holy Spirit also testifies to us,"* while Jeremiah clearly shows that they are the declaration of Yahweh (the LORD). Based on these texts, Pache says, "The Spirit is therefore undeniably God Himself" (**16-17**). Walvoord agrees: "The title of Jehovah, reserved in Scripture for the true God, is therefore used of the Holy Spirit" (**12**).

THE ISSUE OF THE PROCESSION OF THE HOLY SPIRIT

When the early Christians (in the second through the fourth centuries) tried to understand how Jesus could be of the same nature as God the Father, they decided that in some mysterious way that can be neither understood nor explained, the Father generates the Son in an eternal act of begetting. Therefore the Son has no beginning and is of the same essence as the Father. This is the concept of the eternal Sonship of the Logos; it is set forth in the Nicene Creed of AD 325.

Seeking to ground the full deity of the Holy Spirit in some similar association with the Father, the church fathers in the fourth century focused on the language of ***John 15:26***, *"the Spirit of truth who proceeds from the Father."* This language was incorporated into the revised creed of AD 381, and the concept of the eternal procession of the Holy Spirit from the essence of the Father was made official. Later the Eastern and Western branches of the church split over whether to say that the Spirit "proceeds" only from the Father (in the East) or also from the Son (*filioque*—in the West).

The imagery of procession is different from that of generation. In the latter, the second person of the Trinity is derived from the divine essence like a Son is derived from His Father's essence. In the procession of the Spirit, however, building on another meaning of *ruach* and *pneuma*, the third person of the Trinity is derived from the divine essence like breath comes forth from the mouth (see **Heron, 83**; **Palmer, 15-16**). "The Spirit is of the Father, not created or made in time, but eternally proceeding, or breathed out, as it were, from the Father" (**Candlish, 32**). Like the Son's eternal generation, this is of course an eternal relationship of "proceeding" or an eternal act of spiration (breathing).

There is no need to ask what this means, however, since it simply cannot be explained. As Palmer says, "It is difficult to describe what is meant by the procession of the Spirit of God; we can do little more than repeat the words of Scripture" (15). In any case the imagery serves to affirm that the Spirit is of the same essence as the Father and is therefore fully divine.

The Spirit is of the same essence as the Father and is therefore fully divine.

Those who accept these concepts of the eternal generation of the Son from the Father and the eternal procession of the Spirit from the Father (and Son) infer from them an eternal relationship of subordination within the Trinity. Though all three persons are coeternal and are equally divine in essence, the Son is eternally subordinate to the Father, and the Spirit is eternally subordinate to the Father (and Son). (See **Palmer, 16-17**.) As Torrey says, "From the fact that the Holy Spirit is a Divine Person, it does not follow that the Holy Spirit is in every sense equal to the Father. . . . Though the Holy Spirit is a Divine Person, He is subordinate to the Father and to the Son" (**36**). According to Ware, within the eternal, immanent, ontological Trinity, there is a relationship of both subordination and obedience (**"Trinity," 270**). "This hierarchical structure of authority exists in the eternal Godhead," as the Son submits to the Father and "the Spirit submits to both the Father and the Son" (**Ware, *Father*, 21**).

In my judgment, both the concept of the eternal generation of the Son (and therefore the concept of eternal sonship as such), and the concept of the eternal procession of the Holy Spirit, are based more on human speculation than on solid biblical data. They are useless ideas in the sense that no one claims to know in the least what is meant by "eternal generation" and "eternal procession." They are also unnecessary ideas because both the full deity of Christ and the full deity of the Spirit are well documented in Scripture without them.

The biblical language of subordination, as it is used both of the Son and of the Spirit, applies to Their adopted and assumed roles in the working out of the plan of redemption. The eternal Logos took on the role of a servant and voluntarily submitted to the will of the Father (***Php 2:5-11***) in His work as Redeemer. Likewise the Holy Spirit took on a parallel role, allowing Himself to be "sent" or "poured out" upon the church especially on Pentecost, and voluntarily assuming the task of glorifying the Son (***Jn 16:13-15***).

The language of ***John 15:26b***, *"who proceeds from the Father,"* does not refer to some mysterious eternal relationship but to the imminent *sending* of the Spirit, which is a main point of this whole discourse (***14:16,26***; ***15:26a***; ***16:7***). This redemptive Pentecostal "sending" is not just the work of the Father but of the Son also—*filioque!*—as Jesus says in ***John 16:7***, *"I will send Him to you"* (see ***Jn 15:26a***; ***Acts 2:33***). This is the only "procession" of the Spirit—His "procession into this world of fallen human beings," to use Ware's own words (**"Trinity," 262**).

THE HOLY SPIRIT IS A DISTINCT DIVINE PERSON

The Holy Spirit is not only a divine person equal with the Father; He is also distinct from the Father in that He is a separate, distinct person, i.e., a separate center of consciousness with His own distinct thoughts, emotions, and actions. This point seems more than obvious to most Christians; but occasionally, in a misguided effort to explain the Trinity, some have embraced a seriously false view called modalism. From its earliest known forms in the late second century, modalism seems to have been a serious—though heretical—attempt to account for God's threeness while emphasizing His oneness.

Modalism is a misguided and false attempt to explain the Trinity.

Modalism is basically the view that in His inner nature there are no distinctions within God, threefold or otherwise. However, in His external relationships with His creatures, God assumes different modes in which to make Himself known and accomplish His purposes among men. In its original form the contention was that in the Old Testament era God revealed Himself as Father; then He became incarnate as the Son; finally, after Jesus' ascension, God relates to His creatures as the Holy Spirit. Thus these modes of relationship are successive, not simultaneous. Viewing the Trinity this way allows one to say that the Holy Spirit is fully divine. The problem is that the Father, Son, and Spirit are not really distinguished from one another. In Their true being They are one and the same person, a person who assumes different modes in His outward relationships to His creatures. God the Father *is* God the Son, who also *is* God the Holy Spirit.

The best known early modalist was Sabellius in the early third century; thus the view is sometimes called Sabellianism. In more recent times varying versions of this view are found mainly in modernistic religion, but also in certain conservative circles such as Oneness Pentecostalism (see **Cottrell, *Redeemer*, 141-142**). Modalism also appears from time to time within the Restoration Movement (**ibid., 143**).

All forms of modalism must be rejected as seriously false doctrine. This view simply cannot do hermeneutical justice to the many, many passages of Scripture which speak of Father, Son, and Spirit together, not only alongside each other but interacting with one another. The relationship or interaction is real and not just a charade. ***Luke 1:35*** is an example:

> *The angel answered and said to her, "The Holy Spirit will come upon you, and the power of the Most High will overshadow you; and for that reason the holy Child shall be called the Son of God."*

The most natural explanation is that both the Father (Most High) and the Spirit were involved in the incarnation of the Son. Another example is the baptism of Christ, where Father, Son, and Spirit are described as simultaneously being involved in different ways: *"And the Holy Spirit descended upon Him in bodily form like a dove, and a voice came out of heaven, 'You are My beloved Son, in You I am well-pleased'"* (***Lk 3:22***). Here the Father speaks to the Son in direct address, with the Spirit manifesting Himself separately. Also, Jesus' teaching concerning the coming of the Holy Spirit in ***John 14–16*** is a welter of double-talk if Father, Son, and Spirit are not distinct. For example, Jesus said, *"I will ask the Father, and He will give you another Helper"* (***Jn 14:16***; see also ***Jn 14:26***; ***15:26***). The same applies to the record of the fulfillment of this promise in ***Acts 2***; see especially ***2:33***.

Many other passages are robbed of their natural meaning by modalistic presuppositions. The following examples will suffice: ***Romans 8:11*** speaks of *"the Spirit of Him [the Father] who raised Jesus from the dead."* ***Romans 8:26*** says the Spirit *"intercedes for us."* If the Spirit is not distinct from the Father, the concept of intercession is meaningless. In ***1 Corinthians 6:11*** Paul says we are washed, sanctified, and justified *"in the name of the Lord Jesus Christ and in the Spirit of our God."*

If the Spirit is not distinct from the Father, the concept of intercession is meaningless.

Galatians 4:6 says *"God has sent forth the Spirit of His Son into our hearts, crying, 'Abba! Father!'"* **Ephesians 2:18** says that *"through Him [the Son] we both have our access in one Spirit to the Father."* **Titus 3:4-6** says *"God our Savior"* saved us *"by the washing of regeneration and renewing by the Holy Spirit, whom He poured out upon us richly through Jesus Christ our Savior."* **First Peter 1:2** says we are chosen *"according to the foreknowledge of God the Father, by the sanctifying work of the Spirit, to obey Jesus Christ and be sprinkled with His blood."* **Jude 20-21** exhorts us thus: *"Praying in the Holy Spirit, keep yourselves in the love of God, waiting anxiously for the mercy of our Lord Jesus Christ."*

Many other passages could be cited, but these are enough to show that Father, Son, and Spirit are distinct persons who exist simultaneously and interact with one another. The Holy Spirit is thus a distinct divine person.

IMPLICATIONS

When we understand that the Holy Spirit is a divine person, the third person of the Trinity who is fully God in every sense of the word, several implications suggest themselves. First of all, we must always speak of the Holy Spirit in personal terms. We should never speak of the Spirit as "it" or "itself." The Holy Spirit is not a thing; He is not an *IT*. Following biblical precedent, we should use masculine pronouns when referring to Him. The point is not to suggest that He is male; it is simply a way of affirming His personhood.

A second implication is the likelihood that Yahweh (the LORD) in the OT *is* the Trinity, i.e., that Yahweh is not just God the Father but is also God the Son and God the Holy Spirit. That Jesus is Yahweh can be shown by comparing certain NT texts about Jesus with OT texts about Yahweh (see **Cottrell, *Redeemer*, 127-128**), and we have seen above that certain NT texts about the Spirit may identify Him with Yahweh in the OT as well. This is not to say that every reference to Yahweh in the OT must refer to all three persons of the Trinity. It simply means that any given mention of Yahweh may be a reference to any one of the Trinity or to all three.

A third implication is that we should worship the Holy Spirit. If the Holy Spirit is God, in every way equal to the deity of the Father and the Son, how can we *not* worship Him? The AD 381 revised Nicene creed says that the Holy Spirit is to be "worshiped and glorified together with the Father and Son" (**Leith, 33**). Some say this should not be done, though, since there is no clear biblical precedent for it. Boatman, for example, says that "nowhere in the book of Revelation, nor elsewhere in the Scripture, is the Holy Spirit said to be worshipped by anyone at any time" (**16**). He says there is "neither Scripture precedent nor command for the Holy (Ghost) Spirit to be 'worshipped and glorified.' No patriarch, prophet, priest, apostle, evangelist, nor any angel, seraphim, or other heavenly being of record (that is, of the Biblical record) is reported as doing so, nor is it intimated that it is God's intent that any one ever should, or shall" (**ibid., 73**).

I grant that there is no biblical precedent for direct worship of the Spirit, especially for addressing the Spirit specifically in an act of adoration. We must remember, though, that silence does not imply prohibition, especially if a practice is the result of a necessary inference. In my judgment, worship of the Holy Spirit is a necessary inference from the biblical teaching of His full deity. I confess that the absence of express biblical precedent makes me personally wince at songs such as "Spirit, we love You, we worship and adore You; glorify Thy name in all the earth." But I cannot say that this is wrong.

I offer two biblical considerations for putting such overt worship of the Spirit into perspective, however. One, it is the Spirit's stated purpose to glorify Jesus Christ (***Jn 16:14***). Any worship practice, public or private, that elevates the Spirit above Jesus Christ is therefore wrong. Second, the consistent biblical teaching about prayer indicates that we should pray *to* the Father (***Mt 6:9***; ***Lk 11:2***), *through* the intercession of the Son (***Jn 16:23-24***; ***1Tm 2:5***; ***Heb 4:14-16***), with the assistance of the Holy Spirit (***Rom 8:26,27***; ***Eph 6:18***). Even prayers about the Spirit's power and working in our lives are addressed to the Father (***Eph 3:14-16***). ***Ephesians 2:18*** sums up the roles of the Trinity in our prayers: *"For through Him [Jesus] we both have our access in one Spirit to the Father."*

It is the Spirit's stated purpose to glorify Jesus Christ.

Thus while acts of worship to God cannot exclude worship of the Holy Spirit nor worship of Jesus Christ, I believe we must use caution and self-restraint in prayers of direct address to the Spirit. This does not demean the Spirit, but simply acknowledges that in the working out of the plan of redemption, the three persons of the Trinity have adopted different roles. We must seek to honor Their "division of labor," as it were.

A final implication of realizing that the Holy Spirit is a divine person, rather than just an impersonal power available for our use, is well stated in these words of R.A. Torrey (**7-9**):

> It is . . . of the highest importance from the practical standpoint that we decide whether the Holy Spirit is merely some mysterious and wonderful power that we in our weakness and ignorance are somehow to get hold of and use, or whether the Holy Spirit is a real Person, infinitely holy, infinitely wise, infinitely mighty and infinitely tender who is to get hold of and use us. The former conception is utterly heathenish, not essentially different from the thought of the African fetish worshipper who has His god whom he uses. The latter conception is sublime and Christian. If we think of the Holy Spirit as so many do as merely a power or influence, our constant thought will be, "How can I get more of the Holy Spirit," but if we think of Him in the Biblical way as a Divine Person, our thought will rather be, "How can the Holy Spirit have more of me?" The conception of the Holy Spirit as a Divine Influence or power that we are somehow to get hold of and use, leads to self-exaltation and self-sufficiency. One who so thinks of the Holy Spirit and who at the same time imagines that he has received the Holy Spirit will almost inevitably be full of spiritual pride and strut about as if he belonged to some superior order of Christians. . . . But if we once grasp the thought that the Holy Spirit is a Divine Person of infinite majesty, glory and holiness and power, who in marvellous condescension has come into our hearts to make His abode there and take possession of our lives and make use of them, it will put us in the dust and keep us in the dust. I can think of no thought more humbling or more overwhelming than the thought that a person of Divine majesty and glory dwells in my heart and is ready to use even me.

We should think not of "How can I get more of the Holy Spirit," but rather, "How can the Holy Spirit have more of me?"

CHAPTER TWO

THE HOLY SPIRIT AND THE BIBLE

We have explained the *person* of the Holy Spirit; we now begin our discussion of His *work*. The work of the Spirit may be divided according to the two main kinds of gifts He gives to mankind, namely, *knowledge* and *power*. It is crucial that we keep these aspects of His work distinct. In this chapter we are discussing the main way the Holy Spirit gives us knowledge, which is through the *Bible*.

When God gives us knowledge, we usually call this *revelation*. God can reveal and has revealed knowledge to human beings in many different ways. Some of these are called "general revelation," since they convey knowledge to all people in general. There are two basic kinds. First, God reveals His own glory as the Creator to all people through the marvels of His creation (***Ps 19:1-2***; ***Rom 1:19-20***). Second, He reveals His general will for all mankind by engraving His moral law upon the hearts of the human race by virtue of their being made in His own image (***Rom 2:14-15***).

Other kinds of revelation are called "special revelation" because they have

C. Will God Help Us Understand the Bible?
1. Providential Intervention in Answer to Prayer
2. Prayer for Wisdom
3. Taking Advantage of the Spiritual Gifts of Others
4. The Process of Sanctification
III. The Holy Spirit and the Truth of the Bible

come to certain human beings at specific points in history and in specific locations. Such special revelation has taken numerous forms. God has spoken directly and audibly to many individuals of Bible history, e.g., Adam and Eve (***Gen 3:8-19***), Abraham (***Gen 12:1,7; 17:1-22***), Moses (***Ex 3:4-14***), and Peter (***Acts 10:19-20***). He has spoken directly and audibly to large groups (e.g., ***Ex 20:1-22***). He has spoken directly to individuals in dreams and visions (e.g., ***Num 12:6; 1Sa 3:1-18***). He has spoken to individuals and groups through prophets and apostles (e.g., ***2Sa 12:1-15; Acts 2:14-39***). He has spoken to individuals through angels (e.g., ***Mt 1:20; Lk 1:26-38***). He has given messages to men through direct writing (***Ex 31:18; Dan 5:5,24-28***). He has communicated His will through the guiding of lots (***Jonah 1:7; Acts 1:24-26***). He has spoken directly to many in the words of Jesus of Nazareth. In these and other ways, God has given knowledge to mankind.

As dramatic as some of these forms of special revelation were during the era of Bible history, and as important as all of them were for their purposes, no form of special revelation from God is more important than the written words of Scripture, the Bible. This may be intuitively recognized by simply observing the fact that our very knowledge of all of these other revelatory events comes to us through one and the same source: the Bible. Of course, the Bible gives us knowledge of these things and *much more*. The point is that the Bible is God's one comprehensive means of communicating knowledge from Himself to the whole human race today. Scripture can serve this purpose because it is by definition God's *written* message (*scriptura* is Latin for "something written"). As such it preserves the knowledge that God desires for all mankind in an objective, permanent form and thus transmits this knowledge to all cultures in all ages, including our own.

The Bible is God's one comprehensive means of communicating to the whole human race.

The importance of this phenomenon we call "the Bible" cannot be overstated. Since (as we shall see) the Holy Spirit is mainly responsible for its origin, we may think of the Bible as the Spirit's most important gift to mankind. In years past I sometimes gave a lesson on the Holy Spirit which I called, "Who Is the Holy Spirit, and What Is the Most Important Thing He Ever Did for Us?" The answer to the latter question is: He gave us the Bible. I agree with Abraham Kuyper: "Among the divine works of art produced by the Holy Spirit, the Sacred Scripture stands first. It may seem incredible that the printed pages of a book should excel His spiritual work in human hearts, yet we assign to the Sacred Scripture the most conspicuous place without hesitation." He adds, "That the Bible is the product of the Chief Artist, the Holy Spirit; that He gave it to the Church and that in the Church He uses it as His instrument, can not be over-emphasized" (**56, 60**).[1]

In this chapter we will discuss the Holy Spirit's role in relation to the *origin* of the Bible, the interpretation or *understanding* of the Bible, and the *truth* of the Bible.

THE HOLY SPIRIT AND THE ORIGIN OF THE BIBLE

What is involved in the origin of the Bible is the process of communication. Communication is the transfer of data, thoughts, ideas, and concepts from one mind to another mind. This may be accomplished through means such as gestures, looks, pictures, or hand signs. The most efficient and precise means of communication, though, is *words*. Now, God desires to communicate with those whom He has created in His own image, i.e., He desires to transfer certain data and concepts from His mind to our minds. As noted above, He can do and has done this in different ways; but again, the most effective way of doing this is by words, and this is the main means God has employed.

Communication is the transfer of data, thoughts, ideas, and concepts from one mind to another.

This is where the Bible enters the picture. It is designed to be an instrument of communication; its principal and immediate purpose is to transfer ideas from God's mind to ours. By accomplishing this

[1] When we speak of "the Bible," we are referring primarily not to a physical object as such (e.g., a book), but to its verbal content, its inscripturated message.

purpose it is then able to achieve further ends, of course, such as generating faith (***Jn 20:30-31***; ***Rom 10:17***) and equipping for righteousness (***2Tm 3:16-17***). But its primary intention is to communicate. How does God ensure that the Bible will succeed in transferring what is in His mind to our minds? He does this with two major related works commonly known as *revelation* and *inspiration*. These are the works of the Holy Spirit by which He gives us the wonderful gift of knowledge.

Revelation and Inspiration

Revelation and inspiration are the two main steps by which the Bible has been produced. To understand the nature of the Bible it is important to understand these two works and to understand how they are related to one another. That is the focus of this section.

Revelation

The main NT noun for "revelation" is *apokalupsis*, which means "an unveiling, an uncovering, a disclosure." The verb (*apokalupto*) means "to unveil, to uncover, to lay bare, to make known." Communication, as the transfer of data and concepts from one mind to another, is basically an act of revelation. One person is revealing or disclosing what is in his mind to another person. This is what God is doing in every act of revelation, including those reported in the Bible and those involved in the very origin of the Bible itself. In most cases God uses the phenomenon of human language—words, phrases, sentences—as His means of communication. This is certainly the case with the origin of the Bible. That God is able to communicate with us through our own words is possible because our being created in His image involves a language capacity designed for this very purpose.

Revelation would be all that is needed for God-to-man communication if God chose to reveal directly to each individual everything He wants everyone to know. God could certainly do this; He could transfer all the knowledge He wants us to know directly from His mind to every individual's mind through universal private revelation.

God has chosen to reveal some things directly to some individuals; for example, God spoke directly with Adam and Eve and with Abraham. It is no doubt a fact that God said a lot more to Adam and Eve than is recorded in Genesis, and that Jesus said a lot more to His disciples than is recorded in the Gospels. Every word Jesus spoke was a revelation from God to all who heard Him, whether it was written down or not.

What is significant for our purposes, though, is that God has chosen to communicate *some* of His revealed words to people other than their immediate, original recipients. This is where inspiration enters the picture.

Inspiration

Sometimes God wants to communicate the contents of His mind to others without speaking to them directly. Sometimes He reveals what is in His mind to one recipient or group of recipients, and then uses a mediator, a go-between, an intermediary, a spokesman, to pass that revelation along to others. This is technically what a *prophet* is: one who speaks for another, a spokesman. A prophet of God is someone who speaks God's revealed word to others. Often God simply speaks the message directly to the prophet's mind, who then respeaks it to another audience, as in every case of a *"thus says the LORD God of hosts"* (e.g., **Isa 10:24**).

A prophet can perform this "respeaking" function either orally or in written form. Either way, when God chooses to use a prophet or spokesman to transmit His revelation, there is one potential problem with which He must deal. That problem is human fallibility, which is complicated further by the sinfulness of every human being. How can God use fallible, sinful people to transmit His precious revelation, and trust them to do so without messing it up in some way? How can He guarantee that the message will be passed along exactly as He wants it to be? He does this through the work of inspiration.

Inspiration is the name given to God's own active participation in the human act of transmitting or mediating a message (oral or written) from Himself to others. It is a divine influence exerted upon the prophet, an influence that includes whatever it takes to make sure the message is communicated correctly. Revelation may occur without inspiration. When God spoke to Adam and Eve, this was revelation; but He never intended for them to pass this along to us, so they were not inspired. But when God revealed His Word to Moses, Samuel, Elijah, Isaiah, Paul, John, and others, He commissioned them also to pass His word along to the rest of us. When they did so, it was necessary for them to be *inspired.* Often revelation and inspiration occurred at the same time, as when a revealed message was proclaimed or written down at the very moment it was received.

This next statement is of crucial importance for understanding the origin and nature of the Bible: some parts of the Bible are revealed, and some are not; but *all* parts of the Bible are *inspired.* Certainly we must regard material such as the creation account (***Genesis 1 and 2***) and predictive prophecies (e.g., ***Isa 9:6-7; Mal 3:1-4; 4:5-6***) as revelation. But not everything in the Bible was revealed directly from God to the writers. Much of its content was known to the writers from human sources, such as existing documents (***Josh 10:13***), personal investigation (***Lk 1:3***), personal experiences (***Acts 20:6-7,13-15***), and even personal subjective feelings (***Pss 51:3; 119:97***).

Some parts of the Bible are revealed, some are not, but all parts are inspired.

What does this mean? It means that sometimes God used prophets and apostles to pass along to us not only revealed material but some nonrevealed material also. In the latter case the work of inspiration is all-important. Its overall purpose is the same as the inspiration of revealed material, namely, to guarantee the accurate transmission of the data God wants to communicate to us. But in this case some extra elements may be required, e.g., memory assistance, judicious selection of data, and omission of erroneous material. Boles gives an example: "Some of the prophets had an accurate knowledge of the condition of affairs in Israel; they did not need the Holy Spirit to *inform* them of these things, but they did need the Holy Spirit to guide them in selecting just such things as were best to be included in the divine record" (**86**). The point again is that in the work of inspiration God exerts upon the speaker or writer whatever influence is necessary to guarantee that the message is true and trustworthy.

Inspiration therefore is the term applied to God's involvement in the prophetic transmission of His message, in order to ensure its accuracy. Whether it was applied to revealed or nonrevealed material, the result was the same. As explained by Kuyper, "But whether He dictates directly, as in the Revelation of St. John, or governs the writing indirectly, as with historians and evangelists, the result is the same: the product is such in form and content as the Holy Spirit designed, an infallible document for the Church of God" (**77**).

The following chart helps to show the relation between revelation, nonrevealed material, and inspiration:

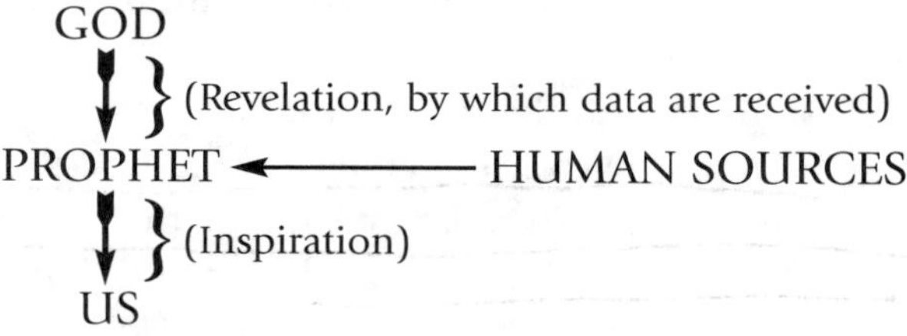

In reference to the Bible, then, we can see that inspiration is not the source of the data included therein; the data comes either from revelation or from various human sources. Inspiration is, however, the immediate source of the written product itself, namely, the Bible. In the final analysis the authority of the Bible is based upon the fact of its inspiration rather than on revelation as such.

Revelation, Inspiration, and the Holy Spirit

Our purpose in this section is to show that the Bible teaches in much detail that the Holy Spirit is active in both the work of revelation and the work of inspiration. Since these works are often combined in a single event, we may speak of them together as signifying the *divine origin* of the Bible.

Setting the stage for the biblical testimony about the Spirit's work of producing the Bible is testimony about the Spirit as the source of oral or spoken prophecy. Examples from the OT include the seventy elders chosen to assist Moses: *"When the Spirit rested upon them, they prophesied"* (***Num 11:25***). Also included is the pagan prophet, Balaam. Contrary to Balaam's intention, *"the Spirit of God came upon him,"* and He spoke an inspired blessing upon Israel (***Num 24:2***). Another example is King Saul (***1Sa 10:10***; ***19:20-24***); see also ***1 Chronicles 12:18***; ***2 Chronicles 15:1***; ***20:14***; ***Nehemiah 9:30***; ***Zechariah 7:12***.

New Testament references to the Holy Spirit as the source of oral prophecy include Jesus' promise to His apostles in ***Mark 13:11***, *"When they arrest you and hand you over, do not worry beforehand about what you are to say, but say whatever is given you in that hour; for it is not you who speak, but it is the Holy Spirit."* Also included here are the apostles' initial testimonies in unlearned languages on the Day of

Pentecost (***Acts 2:4***) and other episodes of tongue-speaking (***Acts 10:44-46***; ***19:6***; see ***1Cor 12:8-11***). The words of Peter (***Acts 4:8***) and Agabus (***Acts 21:10-11***) were delivered through the power of the Spirit (see ***1Pet 1:12***).

Turning now to the origin of the biblical writings themselves, we find numerous references to the Holy Spirit's active involvement both in the receiving of revelation and in the writing of all that God decreed should be inscripturated. In the OT, the inspiration of the prophets is indicated in **Nehemiah 9:30**, *"However, You bore with them for many years, and admonished them by Your Spirit through the prophets."* The Spirit puts words into their mouths, which words they speak: *"My Spirit which is upon you, and My words which I have put in your mouth shall not depart from your mouth"* (***Isa 59:21***). David uses a similar image of spoken words to represent all the Psalms he wrote under the Spirit's inspiration: *"The Spirit of the Lord spoke by me, and His word was on my tongue"* (***2Sa 23:2***).

The NT likewise testifies to the Holy Spirit's authorship of the OT Scriptures. Echoing the Psalmist's own claim, Jesus declares that David's words in ***Psalm 110:1*** were written *"in the Holy Spirit"* (***Mt 22:43***; ***Mk 12:36***). Likewise referring to David's Psalms (***69:25***; ***109:8***), Peter says that *"the Scripture had to be fulfilled, which the Holy Spirit foretold by the mouth of David concerning Judas"* (***Acts 1:16***; see ***4:25***). Paul says that *"the Holy Spirit rightly spoke through Isaiah the prophet"* the words of ***Isaiah 6:9-10*** (***Acts 28:25-27***). In ***Hebrews 3:7*** a quote from ***Psalm 95:7-11*** is introduced with the words, *"Just as the Holy Spirit says"* (see ***Heb 9:8***; ***10:15***). OT prophets made predictions concerning the Christ through *"the Spirit of Christ within them"* (***1Pet 1:10-11***). Most significantly, ***2 Peter 1:20-21*** says that we must understand

> *that no prophecy of Scripture came about by the prophet's own interpretation of things. For prophecy never had its origin in the human will, but prophets, though human, spoke from God as they were carried along by the Holy Spirit.* (TNIV)

Speaking their "prophetic message" (***2Pet 1:19***) while being "carried along by the Holy Spirit" is an extremely strong affirmation of the Spirit's work of inspiration.

There are also many clear NT references to the Spirit's role in the divine origin of the NT itself. Many of these texts may be referring to the oral preaching and teaching of NT apostles and prophets, but we cannot deny an application to their writings as well. This is certainly true of Jesus' promises concerning the coming "Spirit of truth" in ***John 14–16***. In ***John 14:26*** Jesus says that the future teaching ministry of His apostles would be informed by revelation from the Holy Spirit: *"He will teach you all things"*; and by the Spirit's inspiration: He will *"bring to your remembrance all that I said to you"* (see ***Jn 15:26***). Jesus' promise in ***John 16:12-13*** focuses on the revealing work of the Spirit:

> *I have many more things to say to you, but you cannot bear them now. But when He, the Spirit of truth, comes, He will guide you into all the truth; for He will not speak on His own initiative, but whatever He hears, He will speak; and He will disclose to you what is to come.*

In ***1 Corinthians 2:9-13*** Paul clearly attributes both revelation and inspiration to the Holy Spirit. *"For to us,"* he says, that is, to us *apostles, "God revealed"* the hidden things mentioned in ***verse 9*** (see ***Eph 3:5***). How did He reveal them? *"Through the Spirit; for the Spirit searches all things, even the depths of God . . . . The thoughts of God no one knows except the Spirit of God."* Now, says Paul, *"we [apostles] have received"* this *"Spirit who is from God, so that we may know the things freely given to us by God."* Up to here (***vv. 9-12***) Paul has declared the Spirit's work of revelation (see ***1Tm 4:1***); then in ***verse 13*** he moves on to His work of inspiration: *"which things also we speak, not in words taught by human wisdom, but in those taught by the Spirit, combining spiritual thoughts with spiritual words."* Referring to the authority of his own teaching, Paul says in this same epistle, *"I think that I also have the Spirit of God"* (***1Cor 7:40***; see **Kuyper, 147**).

In ***1 Peter 1:10-12*** Peter says that the Holy Spirit was not only responsible for the OT prophecies about Christ, His suffering, and His glories; He was also at work in the apostolic proclamation of the fulfillment of these prophecies in Jesus—the things, he says, *"which now have been announced to you through those who preached the gospel to you by the Holy Spirit sent from heaven"* (***v. 12***).

The Spirit not only inspired the prophecies about Christ, but also proclamation of their fulfillment.

When John received his Patmos visions and recorded them for us in the book of Revelation, he declares that he was "in the Spirit" (***Rev***

1:10; ***4:2***), and that his message was the message of the Spirit to the churches: *"He who has an ear, let him hear what the Spirit says to the churches"* (***Rev 2:7,11,17,29***; ***3:6,13,22***).

The most well-known passage about the divine origin of Scripture is ***2 Timothy 3:16***, where Paul says, *"All Scripture is breathed out by God and profitable for teaching, for reproof, for correction, and for training in righteousness"* (ESV). The key word here is *theopneustos,* translated *"given by inspiration of God"* in the KJV and the NKJV, and *"inspired by God"* in some recent versions (NASB, NRSV, CSB). The word "inspired" comes from the Latin *inspiro,* "to blow on or in, to breathe into, to inspire." The Latin Vulgate used a form of this word in both ***2 Timothy 3:16*** (*divinitus inspirata*) and ***2 Peter 1:21*** (*inspiriti*). This may have influenced the KJV translators to use the English word "inspire" to translate *theopneustos* in ***2 Timothy 3:16***. This is an unfortunate choice, since neither the Latin nor the English meaning of "inspire" is an adequate translation of this Greek word.

Theopneustos does have to do with breathing. *Theo-* is from *theos,* which means "God"; and *-pneustos* is from *pneo,* which means "to blow, to breathe out." The word "inspire," though, connotes more of a "breathing in," and implies that God is somehow breathing His power into the writers of Scripture. This is an accurate concept, but it is not the point of ***2 Timothy 3:16***, where the subject of "is *theopneustos*" is not the writers but the writing itself: *"all Scripture* is *theopneustos."* The point is not that God breathes something into Scripture, but that He "breathes Scripture out." Thus the ESV translates it, *"All Scripture is breathed out by God,"* and the NIV has *"All Scripture is God-breathed."* This is very strong testimony to the divine origin of the "sacred writings" (***v. 15***), and it embraces both the OT and the NT.[2]

The point is not that God breathes something into Scripture, but that He "breathes Scripture out."

The idea of Scripture being "breathed out" is a powerful figure, and it is general enough to include both revelation and inspiration. In other words, some Scripture is breathed out by God in the sense that the

[2]The "sacred writings" in ***v. 15*** are the OT; and "*all* Scripture" in ***v. 16*** adds to that the NT writings. See ***2Pet 3:16***, where Peter refers to Paul's letters and "the rest of the Scriptures," thus including Paul's letters in the general category of Scripture.

words are revealed directly from Him to the writers; other Scripture is breathed out by God in the sense that He works inside the minds of the writers to monitor, adjust, supplement, and protect from error the material authored by the writers themselves. Either way, Scripture goes forth from the writers' pens with the full approval of God.

The Holy Spirit is not specifically mentioned in **2 Timothy 3:16**, but the fact that the word for "spirit" (*pneuma*) can also mean "breath" leads some to suggest that the word *theopneustos* is an implicit reference to God the Spirit. This may be the case, but it is little more than speculation. We may rightly infer that the *theos* ("God") in *theopneustos* is indeed God the Holy Spirit; but this inference is based on the many references to the Spirit as the origin of Scripture in the passages noted above, rather than on the word itself.

We must briefly address the issue of the manner of the Holy Spirit's works of revelation and inspiration. In particular, we must inquire concerning the extent to which the Spirit is responsible for the very *words* of Scripture. There can be no doubt that the Bible itself regards its own words as being the words of God (**Rom 3:2**, NIV). Several of the texts surveyed above speak of the Spirit as being responsible for the spoken or written words of those who were inspired. For example, when Jesus told His apostles not to worry about what they should *say* when arrested, because the Holy Spirit would speak through them (**Mk 13:11**), this assurance certainly refers to their *words*. David said the Spirit's *word* was on his tongue (**2Sa 23:2**). In **1 Corinthians 2:13** Paul specifically says that the *words* he speaks are "taught by the Spirit." **Second Timothy 3:16** must be referring to God-breathed *words*, since what is God-breathed is *Scripture*, i.e., what is *written* (see **v. 15**, "sacred *writings*"). By its very nature any writing, sacred or not, consists of words.

Calling attention to the inspiration of the very words of Scripture (a concept usually called "verbal inspiration") has led to the charge that some Bible believers are teaching that the Holy Spirit actually *dictated* every word of Scripture (in the original texts), thus minimizing the participation of the human writers to the role of a machine. This is labeled "mechanical dictation." For example, Boatman speaks pejoratively of "verbal inspiration" as meaning that "the very *words* of the original manuscripts were chosen by the Holy Spirit," indeed, that "the Holy Spirit Himself *supplied* the words—all of them" (**273**).

Several times Boatman quotes a statement by Rene Pache as an example of this, namely, that "the superintendency of the Holy Spirit extended even to the choice of words used by the original writer" (**Boatman, 277, 281, 282**). Such a concept of verbal inspiration, says Boatman, has been called "the robot, mechanical dictation theory of inspiration" (**277**). Such is "the doctrine of word for word dictation, alias verbal inspiration" (**284**).

Boatman asks, "Are we misreading the fundamentalists and hard-line plenary verbal inspirationists?" (**281**). The answer to that question is a resounding YES! Equating Pache's statement with "word for word dictation" is a complete misreading of his statement and of the concept of verbal inspiration as such. Pache's key word is "superintendency," which is a deliberate alternative to dictation. The point is that the Holy Spirit *superintends* (monitors, supervises) what the human authors of Scripture write, and that He monitors even the words *chosen by these authors*. The human authors (except for matters of direct revelation) *do* choose the words they use, but in His work of inspiration the Spirit looks over their shoulders, so to speak, to make sure that every necessary word and no false word is chosen. To accomplish this purpose the Spirit may supply or substitute an occasional word (below the level of the writer's consciousness), while allowing the main flow of words to be the writer's own. This is Pache's point, and the point of "verbal inspiration." The Scriptures cited above not only allow us such a view of the Spirit's inspiration, but actually require it.

We may agree with Boles here. Though he rightly rejects a mechanical view of verbal inspiration (**77**), he declares, "The Holy Spirit seems to have exercised a special providential and miraculous influence over both the words and the thoughts of the writer" (**80**). He adds with emphasis, "Every theory which does not recognize the Holy Spirit in *every word* as well as in *every thought* is to be rejected" (**83**). As Pache himself explains, surely the Spirit *guided* the biblical writers in their choice of words. "Since every idea is expressed in words, it would be difficult to imagine an inspiration that did not in some way bear upon the form in which the truth should be expressed" (**48-49**). The key words here are "in some way." If the Spirit's work of inspiration does not *in some way* affect the words of Scripture, then it is a futile effort with no meaningful results.

This explanation of inspiration should lay to rest all accusations that a concept of verbal inspiration makes the writers nothing more than dictating machines. On the contrary, their full individual personalities, backgrounds, and vocabularies are expressed and utilized in what they wrote. The Holy Spirit's work simply ensures that each writer's individuality is kept within the boundaries of truth.

Sola Scriptura

The result of the Holy Spirit's work of revelation and inspiration is a unique book of infallible truth, a book that serves as the basis for all true knowledge of all that truly matters. As Kuyper says, "The men employed in this work were consciously or unconsciously so controlled and directed by the Spirit, in all their thinking, selecting, sifting, choice of words, and writing, that their final product, delivered to posterity, possessed a perfect warrant of divine and absolute authority" (**78**). This is indeed the Holy Spirit's most wonderful gift to us, His gift of *"the knowledge of the truth"* (***1Tm 2:4***).

The Holy Spirit's most wonderful gift to us is "the knowledge of the truth."

But here the question arises, is the Bible our *only* source of Spirit-given knowledge? Or does the Spirit give us knowledge in some other way? One of the major emphases of the Protestant Reformation was the principle of *sola scriptura*, "Scripture alone." The reformers espoused this in deliberate opposition to the Catholic church, which accepts church tradition as having authority equal to that of the Bible; and also in opposition to many of the radical reformers, who believed in continuing revelation from the Holy Spirit. Contrary to such ideas, the mainstream Protestants taught the sufficiency and finality of the Bible and its sole authority in all matters of faith and morality. This principle is also associated with the Restoration Movement, usually worded thus: "The Bible alone is our only rule of faith and practice."

In my judgment this is a true and important principle. What it says in effect is that the only way the Holy Spirit gives anyone knowledge today is through the Bible. We should not expect to receive revelations from God or to hear some "still, small voice" of the Spirit speaking within us. We must reject all claims from others who say they are receiving prophecies or inspired messages from God in any sense. The written Word gives us all the knowledge that is needed to produce faith in the hearts of unbelievers (***Jn 20:30-31***; ***Rom 10:17***) and to produce holiness in Christians (***2Tm 3:17***).

Unfortunately there are many who do not accept the *sola scriptura* principle, and who believe that the Spirit still gives knowledge to Christians today as the result of His indwelling presence. On the one hand, many believe the revelatory spiritual gifts (prophecy, knowledge, tongues plus interpretation) are still being bestowed on Christians by the Spirit; we will examine this issue toward the end of this book. On the other hand, there are many who reject miraculous gifts but believe that the indwelling Spirit still gives inward, subjective guidance to Christians.

Examples of this latter view are numerous. I was teaching an adult Bible class at a local church some years ago when the subject of the need and use of the Bible was raised. A man in the class—a deacon and the church treasurer—literally declared that Christians no longer need the Bible because we have the Holy Spirit. Many who are not this radical still believe that the Spirit speaks to us or teaches us apart from the Bible. In a letter to *Christian Standard* a writer said that "the same Holy Spirit that told holy men of old what to write in the Bible also indwells Christians today and continues to prompt, lead, and speak to us." Texts cited as confirming this claim included ***1 Corinthians 2:12-13***; ***John 16:13***; and ***Galatians 5:18***. The writer said that such leading and speaking "does not mean we are receiving new revelation" (**Criminger, 23**).

In another example from *Christian Standard,* Gary Zustiak says that ***Hebrews 1:1-2*** does not eliminate the possibility of continuing "individual guidance and direction" from God "in matters of personal decision-making." Over time, one can "learn to recognize God's voice." When He speaks, "not only will God's voice be clear, but it will be specific." Of course, "whatever God speaks to us, it will never contradict what has already been written in the Bible" (**4-6**). The only NT text cited to support this view is ***John 10:4***.

Citing ***John 14:26***, ***John 16:12-14***, and ***Nehemiah 9:20***, R.A. Torrey declares that "in all these passages it is perfectly clear that the Holy Spirit is . . . a Person who comes to us to teach us day by day the truth of God. It is the privilege of the humblest believer . . . to have a

Divine Teacher to daily teach him the truth he needs to know" (**18-19**). "We shall never truly know the truth until we are thus taught directly by the Holy Spirit" (**ibid., 144**). Leon Morris similarly applies ***John 16:13*** to all Christians: "Here the Christian has a wonderful promise from the Master Himself. . . . This gives a general charter which we may claim in all sorts of situations" (***Spirit*, 78-79**).

I acknowledge the sincerity and the piety with which such claims to inner teaching and guidance are made, but I sincerely believe they are unfounded. The main biblical texts on which they are based fall into two categories. One set of Scriptures is composed of promises Jesus made to the *apostles* and to them alone; they refer to the revealing and inspiring work of the Spirit in the lives of the apostles. This is especially true of ***John 14:26*** and ***16:12-14***, and also of ***1 Corinthians 2:9-13***. Torrey does say that the primary application of these texts is to the apostles, but he says that "we cannot limit this work of the Spirit to them" (**143, 147**). In my judgment this is a serious error. I agree with Bales (**51**):

> Because the word needed to be preached by men who knew the mind of God, the Spirit came to teach and to guide certain men into all truth (***John 14:26***; ***16:12-13***). The promise of ***John 16:12-13***, that they would be guided into all truth was made to the twelve (***Matt. 26:20-25***; ***John 13:1-30***; ***17:6-12***). Although others were given certain gifts (***I Cor. 12***), yet the promise in ***John 16:12-13*** was to the apostles. Thus it followed that by the time the last apostle died the "all truth" had been delivered and confirmed (***Heb. 2:3-4***), or the promise of Jesus, that they would be guided into all truth, failed. . . . The faith has once for all been delivered to the saints (***Jude 3***). . . . The "all truth" is in the Bible.

The "all truth" is in the Bible.

The other group of texts used as a basis for this extrabiblical teaching of the Spirit today includes those that speak of our being "led by the Spirit," especially ***Romans 8:14*** and ***Galatians 5:18***. Some may acknowledge that the Bible itself is the Spirit's "chief means of affording us guidance" (**Morris, *Spirit*, 80**), but they then add to the Bible inward feelings and impressions. Despite denials, the latter would have to be regarded as forms of revelation, new revelation from the Spirit and thus a denial of *sola scriptura*. In my judgment this is a seriously wrong approach to these texts. We *are* led by the Spirit, but His leading affects our *wills*, not our *intellects*. This will be discussed later in the chapter on sanctification.

Two other problems with this approach may be noted. First, the Bible does teach its own sufficiency as a guide for holy living: *"All Scripture is inspired by God and profitable for teaching, for reproof, for correction, for training in righteousness; so that the man of God may be adequate, equipped for every good work"* (***2Tm 3:16-17***). We should pray for wisdom in understanding the Bible (see the next section) and in applying the Bible (***Jas 1:5***), but we should not expect new information to "pop into our minds."

Second, any dependence upon inward, subjective feelings for "guidance," or upon personal experiences of any kind as an assurance of the Spirit's presence and will, is very risky and leaves one open to Satanic deceit. Bob Russell (**14**) tells of a man who brought him occasional messages from God, e.g., "God spoke to me last night and told me I should share this Scripture with you." Russell expressed to the man his doubts about such claims to verbal revelation today. The man was undaunted. He told Russell that God had spoken to him and revealed that his estranged wife would return to him within two weeks. The man reappeared six months later and declared, "God spoke to me several months ago and told me I needed to go to another church." Unfortunately his wife had not returned to him, but he was still listening to these "messages from God."

Jesus' teaching in ***Matthew 7:21-23*** must be solemnly heeded:

> *Not everyone who says to Me, "Lord, Lord," will enter the kingdom of heaven, but he who does the will of My Father who is in heaven will enter. Many will say to Me on that day, "Lord, Lord, did we not prophesy in Your name, and in Your name cast out demons, and in Your name perform many miracles?" And then I will declare to them, "I never knew you; depart from Me, you who practice lawlessness."*

Jacoby rightly says, "If anything is certain, it is the fact that it is dangerous to follow our feelings. Feelings have little to do with being led by the Spirit" (**65; see 65-75**).

"Feelings have little to do with being led by the Spirit."

See again some sound advice by Bales (**54**):

> Since there are no inspired men living today—and those who claim to be such contradict the word of God in some of their teaching—the only witness which we have of the Spirit to us is found in His written Word. This witness is borne not

> through a still, small voice; not through our emotions; but through the written Word of God. It is the only witness of the Spirit concerning God's will because the Bible is the only Word of the Spirit which we have.

See **Palmer, 126-128**. *Sola scriptura* is still one of the solid principles upon which the church is built.

THE HOLY SPIRIT AND THE UNDERSTANDING OF THE BIBLE

The second topic to be discussed in this chapter is the work of the Holy Spirit in relation to our *understanding* of the Bible. It is commonly believed that the Holy Spirit is not only the ultimate author of the Bible, but also its only infallible interpreter. In other words, just as the Spirit worked in the minds of the writers to produce the Bible, so does He work in the minds of the readers to help them to understand it. This latter work of the Spirit is usually called *illumination.*

Belief in the Spirit's guidance in understanding the Bible is a frequent aspect of sincere piety. An old hymn entreats, "Open my eyes, illumine me, Spirit divine." Another says, "O send Thy Spirit, Lord, now unto me, that He may touch my eyes and make me see! Show me the truth concealed within Thy Word, and in Thy book revealed I see the Lord." A Christian worker tells of spending two months in confinement waiting for a broken leg to heal, and of using that time just reading the Bible, "with no commentary of man but rather looking to the Holy Spirit to open my eyes to spiritual understanding." A Bible college professor writes that "the Holy Spirit's purpose here is to teach us Jesus and to reveal the meaning of Scripture." A member of a task force attempting to come to an understanding of the Bible's teaching on gender roles asked, "Why can't I just trust the Holy Spirit to lead me into the truth on this subject without my having to read what others have written on it?" A Christian lady who "felt led to write" me a letter said that ***2 Peter 1:20-21*** "notes the Holy Spirit as *author* and *interpreter* of Scriptures." A "workers ready for service" request in the *Christian Standard* reads, "Inexperienced minister looking for small church. . . . Has . . . never been to college but is guided by the Holy Spirit."

Does the Holy Spirit indeed enable us to understand the Bible?

What should we think about such claims and expectations? Does the Holy Spirit indeed enable us to understand the Bible? If so, how?

The Protestant Doctrine of Illumination

Within the conservative Protestant world it is almost universally agreed that the Holy Spirit does enable the Christian to come to the correct understanding of the Bible. An explanation of this doctrine of illumination can be found in most books and treatises on the general doctrine of the Holy Spirit. Some examples are as follows.

The Doctrine of Illumination Stated

In his book, *The Person and Work of the Holy Spirit*, R.A. Torrey devotes a chapter to "The Holy Spirit as a Teacher." Torrey acknowledges that ***John 16:12-14*** was first given to the apostles, but declares that "the Apostles themselves applied it to all believers" in ***1 John 2:20,27***. Thus "it is the privilege of each believer in Jesus Christ, even the humblest, to be 'taught of God.' Each humblest believer is independent of human teachers" (**143**). Thus, "while we may learn much from men, we are not dependent upon them. We have a Divine Teacher, the Holy Spirit" (**144**). "Not even a diligent study of the Word either in the English or in the original languages will give us a real understanding of the truth. We must be taught directly by the Holy Spirit and we may be thus taught, each one of us. . . . The Spirit will guide the one whom He thus teaches 'into all the truth'" (**144-145**). Torrey cites also ***1 Corinthians 2:9-13***, again declaring that this text cannot be limited to the apostles (**146-147**). Thus "it is always our privilege to have the author of the Bible right at hand when we study it. . . . He stands ready to interpret its meaning to every believer every time he opens the Book. . . . It is not enough that we have the revelation of God before us in the written Word to study, we must also have the inward illumination of the Holy Spirit to enable us to apprehend it as we study" (**147-148**). "We must daily be taught by the Spirit to understand the Word" (**150**).

Pache's view is the same. "The Spirit who guided the authors of the sacred book is also He who directs the sincere reader of the Scriptures. He teaches him all things and also leads him into all truth, meaning that He explains the word which is the truth (***John 14:26***; ***16:13***; ***17:17***)" (**49**). "Having inspired the Scriptures He enables us to understand them and expound to us the things that pertain to God," according to ***1 Corinthians 2:9-10*** and ***1 John 2:20,27*** (**149**). Men need "the Spirit's teaching in addition to the written word of the Bible," because of "the darkness of their understanding." Thus "without the Holy Spirit's illumination, we should understand nothing" (**149**). "The Spirit renders the Bible intelligible" (**150**).

Kuyper explains, "'Illumination' is the clearing up of the spiritual consciousness which in His own time the Holy Spirit gives more or less to every child of God" (**76**). "He, the Inspirer, alone can give the right interpretation" (**193**).

Griffith Thomas agrees: "We do indeed need a teacher, an interpreter, and we have it in the Author of the Book, who also is its Expounder. This is the work of the Holy Spirit as the Spirit of Truth." Why is this necessary? Because of "the intellectual and moral darkness caused by sin" (**160**). "The unction from the Holy One will enable a Christian to perceive the true and reject the false (***I John ii.20,21***)" (**ibid.**). "It is simply impossible to understand a Book which emanates from the Holy Spirit without the Spirit Himself as the Illuminator of our spirit" (**163**).

As Palmer says, "The sum of the matter is, then, that when the Holy Spirit comes into people's lives he enlightens them, gives them understanding, teaches them, opens their eyes, removes the veil from their hearts, and softens their hearts so that they can know the things of the Spirit of God." Palmer observes "that the Holy Spirit does not enlighten man by giving to him a secret revelation—new knowledge. . . . No, the Holy Spirit enlightens man . . . by mysteriously operating on his heart so that he can see the revelation already given" (**58-59**).

The 1978 "Chicago Statement on Biblical Inerrancy" included the following affirmation: "The Holy Spirit, Scripture's divine Author, both authenticates it to us by His inward witness and opens our minds to understand its meaning" (**Geisler, *Inerrancy*, 494**).

The Alleged Biblical Basis for the Doctrine

Those who accept the idea of illumination appeal to a wide array of Scripture texts as the basis for the doctrine. Frequently cited are the

Johannine promises in ***John 14:26, 15:26***, and ***16:12-15***. Even when acknowledged as referring primarily to the apostles, these texts are said to apply also to every "sincere reader of the Scriptures" (**Pache, 49**). "Note how often Scripture states that the Spirit will lead us into *all* truth and will teach us *all* things" (**ibid., 150**). Torrey likewise cites these same passages (**141-145**). "The Spirit will guide the one whom He thus teaches 'into all the truth.' The whole sphere of God's truth is for each one of us" (**ibid., 144-145**).

Included also are John's references to the "anointing" in ***1 John 2:20,27***:

> *But you have an anointing from the Holy One, and you all know. . . . As for you, the anointing which you received from Him abides in you, and you have no need for anyone to teach you; but as His anointing teaches you about all things, and is true and is not a lie, and just as it has taught you, you abide in Him.*

This shows that "we have a Divine Teacher, the Holy Spirit," says Torrey (**144**). Palmer likewise appeals to this text to prove the Spirit's illumination (**58**), as do others.

One of the most cited texts is another passage about revelation and inspiration, i.e., ***1 Corinthians 2:9-13***. Usually ***verses 14 and 15*** are added:

> *But a natural man does not accept the things of the Spirit of God, for they are foolishness to him; and he cannot understand them, because they are spiritually appraised. But he who is spiritual appraises all things, yet he himself is appraised by no one.*

Torrey says this text "refers primarily to the Apostles but we cannot limit this work of the Spirit to them. The Spirit reveals to the individual believer the deep things of God" (**147**). Palmer says this passage shows that "the Holy Spirit is necessary for the enlightenment of one's mind" (**58**). Many others agree.

These are the main proof-texts, but others are also cited. Some use ***Hebrews 8:10-11***, which quotes from ***Jeremiah 31:31-34***. Under the New Covenant, prophesies Jeremiah (as quoted in Hebrews), *"I will put My laws into their minds, and I will write them on their hearts. . . . And they shall not teach everyone his fellow citizen, and everyone his brother, saying, 'Know the Lord,' for all will know Me, from the least to the greatest of them."* "The Lord has achieved this through the Spirit," says Pache (**150**).

Palmer refers to Paul's description of his own preaching as *"not in persuasive words of wisdom, but in demonstration of the Spirit and of power"* (***1Cor 2:4***; see also ***1Th 1:5***). Such texts show, says Palmer, that the Holy Spirit "comes into hearts in an indescribable, mysterious way" and "irresistibly convinces a person of the truth of the gospel, and . . . thereby causes him to believe" (**57-58**). Without this Spirit-caused new birth, no one can "see," i.e., understand, the Kingdom of God (***John 3:3***), says Griffith Thomas (**160**).

Also cited are David's prayer in ***Psalm 119:18***, *"Open my eyes, that I may behold wonderful things from Your law"*; and Paul's prayer for all saints in ***Ephesians 1:17-18***, that God *"may give to you a spirit of wisdom and of revelation in the knowledge of Him,"* and that *"the eyes of your heart may be enlightened."* The former shows, says Palmer, that "the opening of one's spiritual eyes is an act of God and not of man"; and the latter is "unequivocal as to the fact that it is the Holy Spirit who enlightens the mind" (**57-58**).

For most of its defenders, the real basis of the doctrine of illumination is not just certain specific passages understood as above, but is primarily the acceptance of the Augustinian doctrine of total depravity. The major reformers of the sixteenth century taught that every human being, as the result of Adam's sin, is born totally depraved. This means that inborn sin has affected every aspect of human nature, including both the will and the intellect. Regarding the latter, the depraved mind is so warped by sin that it cannot possibly understand and accept the teachings of Scripture unless the Holy Spirit deliberately opens the mind and enables it to do so. Most defenders of illumination approach the issue with the presumption of total depravity (or at least, serious depravity), which in fact necessitates some form of spiritual illumination.

This connection between total depravity and illumination is seen, for example, in Griffith Thomas's explanation of "the Spirit of truth": "Scripture is full of the thought of the intellectual and moral darkness caused by sin, the necessity of spiritual illumination, and the light and leading bestowed by the Spirit on the repentant and trustful soul. Our Lord speaks of the new birth to enable us to *see* the Kingdom of God (***John iii.3***)," and Paul shows us in ***1 Corinthians 2:14-16*** that the Spirit must reveal and teach "that which man cannot see for himself" (**160**). Pache says, "Man left to himself cannot see the kingdom of God; he lies in spiritual death and the god of this age (world) has blinded his intelligence." Evil has perverted "his thoughts and his reason," and he cannot receive the things of the Spirit (***1Cor 2:14***). Because of "the darkness of their understanding," Scripture "remains closed to all those whose hearts are not set at rights." Thus the Holy Spirit must "correct the conceptions of our spirit, warped by sin" (**148-149**).

Palmer especially stresses depravity as the reason why illumination is necessary. "Because of the spiritual blindness that has been caused by our own sin," he says, "man cannot know a single thing of either general or special revelation without the Holy Spirit" (**43**). "The New Testament intimates that natural man is blind, blind as a mole, so that he cannot see the great and clear truths even when they are presented to him by an apostle" (**ibid., 54**). Appealing especially to ***1 Corinthians 2:14-15***, Ramm declares that "the testimony of God is not known to the natural man because he is ignorant in his sin." Also, "lacking the Holy Spirit and possessing a rebellious mind, the unregenerate simply has no grounds for comprehending God's revelation" (**53-54**). We are asking "nothing short of impossible" when we expect "those whose hearts are desperately evil, deceitful, and corrupted by sin to understand holy things," says Donald Williams, likewise citing ***1 Corinthians 2*** (**39-40**). "What makes it impossible is a perverse, rebellious, and sinful indisposition to the truth built into our natures since the fall" (**ibid., 41**). Ware says that "people who do not truly know Christ are simply unable to understand some of Scripture's spiritual truths," as shown by ***1 Corinthians 2:14***. "Natural" persons—the unsaved—simply "lack the Spirit who is necessary to make these truths correctly understood." "Until the Spirit changes their hearts, they will not be able to accept these Scripture truths" (**"Sense," 35-36**).

As understood from this Augustinian perspective, the Holy Spirit's primary act of illumination is an aspect of the sinner's initial experience of irresistible grace; it is a part of the monergistic work of regeneration that bestows the gift of faith upon the totally depraved sinner. Donald Williams states this very clearly: "The work of the Holy Spirit in illumination begins with regeneration, and before that with conviction and calling. He changes the sinner's heart, softening it and enabling it to repent, to change its mind and believe. . . . At regeneration, sinners are brought from death to life and given for the first time the possibility of understanding aright the Word of God" (**43-**

44). This is the point of Palmer's statement, that "the sum of the matter is, then, that when the Holy Spirit comes into people's lives he enlightens them, gives them understanding," and "opens their eyes . . . so that they can know the things of the Spirit of God" (**58**).

The Spirit's ministry of illumination does of course continue throughout the Christian's life, but its starting point is the act of regeneration included in the initial irresistible bestowing of saving grace.

Critique of the Doctrine of Illumination

Despite the fact that the doctrine of illumination is a staple in Protestant theology, I cannot personally accept it. In my judgment it is a false doctrine with no solid biblical basis. My reasons for rejecting it are as follows.

Illumination and *Sola Scriptura*

My first problem with this doctrine is that it seems to contradict the essence of the *sola scriptura* principle (see pages 59-63 above). Those who hold to this doctrine usually distinguish it from revelation: "It should be carefully observed that the Holy Spirit does not enlighten man by giving to him a secret revelation—new knowledge" (**Palmer, 59**). But such a protestation fails for two reasons.

In the first place, it is difficult to understand just *how* illumination is different from revelation. If a person makes a statement and is then asked to explain or interpret what he has said, is not the explanation a separate act of communication with additional information? As an illustration, I said above that "illumination is a staple in Protestant theology." If someone (confused by the word "staple") asks me to explain that, I will say, "It means that this doctrine is a basic or principal element in Protestant pneumatology, like flour and sugar are staples in the average kitchen." If someone (not understanding "pneumatology") says, "I'm still confused; explain further, please"; I will say, "Most Protestant theologians endorse the concept of illumination as part of their doctrine of the Holy Spirit." In each explanation, though I am not saying anything that is basically new, I am revealing more of what is in my mind in more detail. In the same way, in whatever way it is understood, if the Holy Spirit in a separate and direct work upon the reader's mind interprets a biblical text to that mind, this sounds very much like an act of revelation.

In the second place, knowledge or information does not have to be *revealed* to have divine authority; even the parts of the Bible that are not revealed are *inspired* by the Holy Spirit and are thus the Word of God. As described by its adherents, illumination is at least equivalent to inspiration, even if somehow distinguished from revelation. As noted above, some of the main biblical texts used as proof for illumination are the main passages that teach both revelation and inspiration, e.g., ***John 14:26***; ***John 16:12-15***; ***1 Corinthians 2:9-13***. How can "interpretation" so produced be that different in authority, then, from revelation or at least from inspiration? The line between illumination on the one hand and at least inspiration on the other hand is thus erased, and *sola scriptura* is severely compromised.

Illumination and God's Ability to Communicate with Man

My second problem with the doctrine of illumination is that it seems to deny God's ability to communicate with man. Most conservative Protestants believe that God is omniscient or all-knowing, and that He is omnipotent or all-powerful. They also believe that this omniscient and omnipotent God has created human beings in His own image, which includes an inherent rationality and an inherent capacity for language, the very purpose of which is to enable communication between God and man. If these things are true, how can we deny God's ability to communicate with His creatures in language understandable by those designed for this very purpose?

Donald Williams cites the qualitative difference between God and man as part of the rationale for illumination: "That we should need supernatural aid in understanding the Bible should not be all that strange a notion to us. After all, when we proclaim the Word of God to people, we are asking quite a lot of them. We are asking people whose only experience is of earth to understand heavenly things; we are asking those whose lives are like a wisp of smoke blown away by the wind to understand eternal things" (**39**). He says further that some divine concepts "will stretch our minds to the limits of their capabilities and beyond. . . . The exalted nature of the ideas makes some, though not all, of the teaching difficult" (**41**). But in this very context Williams undermines this alleged rationale for illumination by citing God's words to Moses in **Exodus 4:11**, *"Who has made man's mouth? Or who makes him mute or deaf, or seeing or blind? Is it not I, the LORD?"* Williams then comments, "God, who made the organs of human speech and implanted in the first man the ability to generate language (indeed an irresistible impulse to do so), is certainly capable of using it to achieve His purposes" (**40**).

But this is just the point! God is *capable* of using human language, as He does in Scripture, to achieve His purposes of communication, without an added layer of subjective, mystical illumination. As Donald Williams says, "The Bible is written in normal human language, with all the grammatical and lexical cues used in a normal way" (**40**) Thus Bodey is so wrong when he compares reading the Bible with listening to an Italian or German opera without knowing the language, and being completely unable to understand it. "The same thing is true when we approach the Word of God," he says. "It is written in the language of heaven, but we speak the language of earth" (**18**).

This is simply false. The language of heaven—the language God uses to communicate with us—*is* the language of earth. To say that communication with us in such language is impossible, thus requiring illumination, is to say that God has failed in His creation purposes.

The more commonly cited rationale for illumination, though, is not human finitude but human *sinfulness*.[3] The idea is that the noetic effects of sin—sin's corruption of the mind and of the reasoning processes—make it impossible for sinners to understand the Bible without the Spirit's illumination. This is Donald Williams' main point. When we proclaim the Word of God to people, he says, "we are asking those whose hearts are desperately evil, deceitful, and corrupted by sin to understand holy things. . . . Without the aid of the Holy Spirit, what we are asking is nothing short of impossible" (**39-49**). "What makes it impossible" to understand biblical teaching "is a perverse, rebellious, and sinful indisposition to the truth built into our natures since the fall" (**ibid., 41**).

It is actually because of our *sinful* nature, says Bodey, that we cannot understand the Word of God. "The Bible reads to us like a book

[3] This will be discussed further in the point about total depravity, pp. 76-78.

in an unknown foreign tongue." It is "as unintelligible and unmeaningful to us as an encyclopedia to a newborn infant. We not only reject it, we cannot even begin to make sense out of it" (**18**).

In my judgment this is another version of the same problem, namely, it is in effect just another way of denying that the omniscient God is able to communicate with man. The difference in this case is to say that God cannot communicate with *sinful* man. In response to this we must remember that every prophetic word ever delivered to mankind, and every word of Scripture in our possession, were given to and directed to men *as sinners*. God's very purpose in giving us inspired Scripture is to communicate with man *as he is*, in his fallen state.

This is especially true of the message of the gospel, which is *"the power of God for salvation"* (***Rom 1:16***). Faith itself *"comes from hearing, and hearing by the word of Christ"* (***Rom 10:17***). The apostle John assumes that the unbelieving sinner will be able to read his Gospel, understand it, be convicted by it, and come to saving faith on the basis of it:

> *Therefore many other signs Jesus also performed in the presence of the disciples, which are not written in this book; but these have been written so that you may believe that Jesus is the Christ, the Son of God; and that believing you may have life in His name.* (***John 20:30-31***)

*"**These have been written so that you may believe**"*! John says that the very purpose of his written word is to produce faith. If sinful man is unable to understand the written word well enough to place saving faith in Jesus, then God has failed in His purposes of revelation and inspiration.

If man cannot understand the written word, then God's revelation and inspiration have failed.

Illumination Bypasses the Normal Learning Processes

Many of those who defend the doctrine of illumination find it necessary to stress that the Holy Spirit's subjective enlightenment does not preclude the usual objective learning processes, such as diligent personal study and guidance by learned teachers. Fearing that some may use illumination as an excuse for dismissing the latter, Klein *et al.* declare that "this illuminating work of the Spirit does not circumvent nor allow us to dispense with the principles of hermeneutics and the techniques of exegesis" (**84**). Donald Williams is quite clear about this, declaring that the Spirit "does not illumine the minds of the readers by striking them with the right interpretation, but by working through the normal processes of reason, study, and understanding. . . . No one is ever justified in claiming the Spirit's authority for any interpretation which cannot be successfully defended on lexical, grammatical, and contextual grounds." He also says, "The Holy Spirit's work of illumination then is no substitute for an alert mind, an honest heart, a sensitive ear, common sense, and a good concordance. These will not work without the Holy Spirit; neither does the Spirit normally work apart from them, but rather through them" (**46**).

These statements are quite correct, but in my judgment such assertions are inconsistent with the usual concept of illumination. The consistent view is well expressed by Torrey, who says that we can learn much from human teachers but we are not dependent on them. He says (**144**),

> We shall never truly know the truth until we are thus taught directly by the Holy Spirit. No amount of mere human teaching, no matter who our teachers may be, will ever give us a correct and exact and full apprehension of the truth. Not even a diligent study of the Word whether in the English or in the original languages will give us a real understanding of the truth. We must be taught directly by the Holy Spirit and we may be thus taught, each one of us. The one who is thus taught will understand the truth of God better even if he does not know one word of Greek or Hebrew, than the one who knows Greek and Hebrew thoroughly and all the cognate languages as well, but who is not taught of the Spirit.

When we compare Torrey's comments with the ones in the previous paragraph, it would appear that there is a spectrum of opinions among defenders of illumination as to the value and necessity of the usual learning processes. Torrey's view practically excludes their necessity, while Williams seems to be saying that the normal use of "reason, study, and understanding" is the main means by which the Spirit enlightens our minds. In my judgment the closer one comes to the latter position, the more insignificant the doctrine of illumination becomes.

We know from Scripture that God intends for us to learn the meaning of Scripture through the normal learning processes. When Paul and Silas preached the gospel at Berea, their audience *"received the word with great eagerness, examining the [OT] Scriptures daily to see whether these things were so."* Their diligent study was directly responsible for their coming to faith in Christ: *"Therefore many of them believed"* (***Acts 17:11-12***).

A principal spiritual gift, named in ***1 Corinthians 12:28*** and ***Ephesians 4:11***, is the gift of teaching. God sent Philip, a human teacher, to explain Scripture to the Ethiopian eunuch (***Acts 8:26-35***). When Philip asked him if he understood the passage he was reading from the prophet Isaiah, the eunuch replied, *"Well, how could I, unless someone guides me?"* (***vv. 30-31***). Philip then explained the passage to him. One qualification for a church elder is that he must be *"able to teach"* (***1Tm 3:2***), i.e., *"able both to exhort in sound doctrine and to refute those who contradict"* (***Tts 1:9***).

As we shall see in the third main section of this chapter (pp. 87-92), God does actively help us in our efforts to understand the Bible. The primary means by which our minds are thus enlightened, however, are the normal objective teaching and study processes.

God does actively help us in our efforts to understand the Bible through normal processes.

Illumination and Contradictory Beliefs

Another reason for rejecting the common Protestant concept of illumination is the fact that those who believe and teach this doctrine, and thus claim to be illumined by the Spirit, often have different and even opposite or contradictory understandings of the same biblical passages. If the Spirit truly leads all believers into "all truth," then how may we explain Christendom's radically different views of the millennium and the end times? Why are great numbers committed to infant baptism and others equally committed to believers' baptism? Why are some believers egalitarian and others complementarian, with each group reaching opposite conclusions from the same texts of Scripture? Why are there such strong differences on matters relating to the Holy Spirit Himself, e.g., do miraculous gifts continue or have they ceased? Why don't we all see ***1 Corinthians 13:8-13*** alike?

How may we explain Christendom's radically different views on controversial subjects?

In their explanation of illumination, Klein *et al.* express their regret that "some deeply spiritual people have purported some obviously incorrect interpretations of the Bible" (**85**). Of course, all believers with strong convictions about any side of any contested issue within Christendom would say the same thing—about those who disagree with them. Does this mean that each defender of illumination actually believes that the Spirit is enlightening only himself and those who agree with him, and is not enlightening those who disagree? Klein *et al.* add this statement to the one cited above: "Being indwelt by the Spirit does not guarantee accurate interpretation" (**ibid.**). How may one be sure that this does not apply to himself? Of what value, then, is belief in illumination?

The same problem arises with regard to the beliefs of each individual who, in the course of his Christian life, changes his mind about the interpretation of a particular passage or doctrine. Such change is to be expected, according to Palmer, who says that even as Christians "we still have considerable dimness in our eyes (some more than others); we still are not free from blindness; we still cannot see as well as we should. So we should pray constantly as Christians that the Spirit of wisdom and revelation will come and illuminate our minds so that we may see more of the great truths of revelation" (**61**).

Where, then, does the doctrine of illumination apply? How can it be a valid idea, if even those who believe in it recognize that individual Christians grow in their understanding and sometimes change their interpretations of Scripture? If yesterday I was premillennial but today I decide that amillennialism is a better approach to prophetic Scriptures, was I illumined yesterday or am I illumined today? If I renounce complementarianism and embrace egalitarianism, am I to assume that only the latter interpretation is from the Holy Spirit? Is every change an improvement? But if such changes in belief can be made on the assumption that my *latest* view is the truly illumined one, implying that my former view was incorrect, how can I be sure that my *present* view is my final, "correct" one, and that I will not be given a still different view tomorrow? After all, while I was holding to my former view, did I not assume that *it* was the illumined one?

In view of such ambiguities I conclude that in the final analysis the concept of illumination is a useless idea.

Illumination and Total Depravity

Another problem with the idea of illumination is its dependence on the doctrine of total depravity, which itself is not a biblical teaching. It does not surprise us that the concept of an inner testimony of the Holy Spirit arose within the context of the Protestant Reformation, given the fact that the major reformers were committed to the Augustinian doctrine of total depravity. The main point of total depravity is that all aspects of every person's being are corrupted as the result of the sin of Adam. This includes all of one's intellectual or reasoning abilities. Each individual is thus born with an inherent inability to properly understand spiritual matters, including Scripture. Only the divine intervention of the Holy Spirit can restore one's depraved mind and enable him to understand God's revelation.

Speaking of the general concept of the inner witness of the Spirit, Ramm says that John Calvin based his doctrine of this inward testimony on several presuppositions, including the following:

> *The human mind is corrupted. Sin has made it blind and perverse. It has lost its inward spiritual vision and cannot read the plainest revelation of God. Its original knowledge of God is replaced by every sort of religious fancy. It is a labyrinth, and man wanders around in the labyrinth of his mind without ever finding the truth of God. Only a divine act can bring light into this darkness.* (**16**)

Ramm says that the doctrine of the inner testimony of the Spirit presupposes that one's ability to understand the truth of God "is now crippled and perverse so that the ear is dull, the eye dim, and the heart fat with insensitivity." The point of the inner working of the Spirit is to restore this power of understanding (**38**). It is no wonder, then, as Ramm notes, that this doctrine "has received its best interpretation by the nineteenth- and twentieth-century Reformed theologians" (**26**).

An example is the Reformed writer Edwin Palmer. In explaining the need for illumination Palmer emphasizes man's blindness: "The New Testament intimates that natural man is blind, blind as a mole, so that he cannot see the great and clear truths even when they are presented to him by an apostle" (54). But "when the Holy Spirit comes into people's lives he enlightens them, gives them understanding, teaches them, opens their eyes . . . so that they can know the things of the Spirit of God. Without him, man is blind to see the truths of revelation; but when there is a demonstration of the Spirit and of power, man knows all things" (58-59).

This implies that the initial act of illumination is a part of the Calvinist concept of irresistible grace, the unilateral act of the Spirit by means of which the unconditionally chosen, totally depraved sinner becomes an eternally secure believer. This is the Reformed concept of regeneration. This is why, in their explanation of the work of the Holy Spirit, many Reformed writers "confine their remarks to illumination under the general topic of regeneration" (**Ramm, 26**).

This raises a serious question, namely, if the doctrine of total depravity had not been adopted by men such as Luther and Calvin, would we even be talking about the doctrine of illumination today? In my judgment the answer is no. The doctrine of illumination as it is known and taught today is so dependent on the idea of total depravity that without the latter it would never have developed as it has. Thus if the doctrine of total depravity is false, then the whole concept of illumination must be completely rethought.

> **If total depravity is false, then illumination must be rethought.**

My strong conviction is that total depravity is *not* taught in Scripture. In its usual form total depravity is an aspect of the Augustinian doctrine of original sin, which itself is a false doctrine. The biblical passage that is used as the main proof-text for original sin is ***Romans 5:12-19***. In my commentary on Romans I have shown that this passage actually teaches the opposite of original sin. Rather than teaching that all human beings are conceived and born under the curse of Adam's sin, this text affirms that the cross of Christ has counteracted the Adamic curse, and that all children come into existence under the original *grace* of Jesus Christ rather than under the curse of original sin. For details, see my treatment of this in ***Romans,* I:330-364**, and in ***Faith,* 179-190**.

Concerning the question of total depravity as such, the Bible does teach that all human beings have personally sinned (***Rom 3:23***) and as a result have developed (not inherited) a depraved or sinful nature (**Cottrell, *Faith*, 195-197**). The main effect of sin upon our natures, however, is upon our wills rather than our intellects. Sinners do not deny the truth because they *don't* understand it, but because they *do* understand it and deliberately refuse to accept it and to live by it. They *"suppress the truth in unrighteousness"* (***Rom 1:18***), which is an act of the will. *"They exchanged the truth of God for a lie"* (***Rom 1:25***), again as an act of the will. They are *"darkened in their understanding, excluded from the life of God because of the ignorance that is in them, because of the hardness of their heart"* (***Eph 4:18***). In other words, the problem with the *understanding* is due to "the hardness of their heart," which is a matter of the *will*.

Defenders of illumination do not adequately distinguish between the mind and the will. Illumination is essentially an *epistemological* concept, relating to knowledge and understanding. But this is not where the sinner's main problem lies. A resistant will is the roadblock to understanding. The Holy Spirit does act upon the sinner's will through the power of the gospel, and He continues to rehabilitate the Christian's will through His work of sanctification. This is not, however, the same as the concept of illumination.

A resistant will is the roadblock to understanding.

Thus in my judgment there is no biblical basis for thinking that human depravity is "total" in the Augustinian sense, thus requiring an act of irresistible grace to restore a sinner's ability to understand the Bible. In particular, the Bible does not teach that a regenerating (illuminating) act of the Holy Spirit must precede a sinner's decision to believe and repent. Again, see my discussion of this in ***Faith*, 197-200**.

Without the concept of total depravity as its starting point, the Protestant doctrine of illumination is deprived of its foundation and thus collapses.

Illumination and Biblical Exegesis

But what about the alleged biblical teaching concerning the doctrine of illumination? What about the many passages that supposedly affirm that the Spirit enlightens us and teaches us and gives us an inward knowledge of the truth? In my judgment these texts, rightly understood, do *not* teach such a doctrine. Ironically, the very passages used to support the idea that the Holy Spirit enables us to rightly interpret Scripture are themselves misinterpreted by the defenders of illumination.

John 14:26; 16:12-15. This is true preeminently of the texts that are most often used to support illumination, including ***John 14:26*** and ***16:12-15***. These passages are cited over and over as teaching illumination, as summed up in ***16:13***, *"The Spirit of truth . . . will guide you into all the truth."* The fact is, however, that neither of these texts has anything at all to do with the idea of illumination. Rather, they refer to the Spirit's work of revelation and inspiration, and they apply only to the apostles.

One of the most basic principles of hermeneutics is to discern *to whom* a particular biblical statement is made. In reference to this section of the Gospel of John, it is quite clear that the above passages are a part of Jesus' private discourse with His apostles on the night before His death. These are promises that were meant for them alone. By taking them out of context and applying them to all Christians, the defenders of illumination are thus breaking a primary rule of hermeneutics and (according to the doctrine of illumination itself) are implicating the Holy Spirit in the same error.

We need to know to whom a particular biblical statement is made.

Though he defends illumination on other grounds, Kuyper acknowledges that the Johannine passages are intended for the twelve alone. ***John 16:13***, he says, is "a rare promise . . . that may not be applied to others, but to the apostles exclusively." Also, ***John 14:26*** "was not intended for all, but for the apostles only, securing them a gift evidently distinct from illumination" (153-154). Kuyper is absolutely correct. These are not general promises to all Christians. To apply them thus is a serious and glaring hermeneutical error, a fact that weakens the doctrine of illumination in more ways than one. It not only strips this view of some of its most basic proof-texts; it also casts doubt upon the very reality supposedly established by these texts. In other words, if the Holy Spirit guides Christians into all truth, why have these texts been so badly misunderstood?

1 Corinthians 2:10-16. What is true of these Johannine texts is true also of another favorite text used to support illumination, namely, ***1 Corinthians 2:10-13***. As opposed to this doctrine, it seems that Paul is speaking here not of any concept of illumination, but of the Holy Spirit's work of revelation and inspiration with reference to his own ministry as an apostle. This seems to be the point of his use of first person plural (*"For to* ***us*** *. . .* ***we*** *have received . . . so that* ***we*** *may know . . .* ***we*** *also speak"*), in contrast with his addressing the Corinthians in second person plural. He uses the first person plural to include himself and other apostles (***4:9***), and in this context he also seems to be including Apollos as one who received revelation and spoke inspired messages from the Spirit (see ***1:12***; ***3:4-6,22***). This places Apollos in the category of NT prophets, who were recipients of revelation and inspiration alongside the apostles (***Eph 2:20***; ***3:5***).

This distinction between *we/I* and *you* persists throughout ***chapters 1–4***, where Paul is discussing the subject of unity and division, especially division based on excessive loyalty to a particular church leader (***1:12***). See especially ***1:23***, *"****We*** *preach Christ"*; ***3:9***, *"****We*** *[Paul and Apollos] are God's fellow workers;* ***you*** *are God's field"*; ***4:1***, *"Let a man regard* ***us****"* (Paul, Apollos, and Cephas, ***3:22***); and ***4:8-13***. Thus it is natural to take the first-person-plural references in ***2:10-13*** as applying specifically to apostles and prophets. In addition to this, it is obvious from the content of the verses that Paul is speaking of revelation and inspiration.

But what about ***1 Corinthians 2:14-16***? These verses are almost always cited as teaching illumination, and as affirming the need for it based on the total depravity of the unsaved. These verses read thus:

> *But a natural man does not accept the things of the Spirit of God, for they are foolishness to him; and he cannot understand them, because they are spiritually appraised. But he who is spiritual appraises all things, yet he himself is appraised by no one. For who has known the mind of the Lord, that he will instruct Him? But we have the mind of Christ.*

The key point is the contrast between the "natural man," who "cannot understand" the things of the Spirit, and the "spiritual" man, who *can* understand them. The usual interpretation is that the "natural man" is the totally depraved, unregenerate person, and the "spiritual" man is the one who has been regenerated and enlightened by the Holy Spirit.

I see this as a serious misunderstanding of these verses that is based on a complete ignoring of the context in which they appear. As noted above, the divisions in the Corinthian church were related in part to excessive loyalty to specific individuals, including Paul himself (***1:12***). In addressing this problem Paul attempts to put his own place in Christ's kingdom into proper perspective. In so doing he finds it necessary to defend his apostolic authority against his critics (***4:3-5***; ***9:1ff.***), while at the same time humbly admitting that he possessed no great earthly talent or charisma or claim to fame (***2:1-5***). His apostolic authority rested not on human wisdom and great oratorical ability, but solely on the fact that the message he spoke was received from God.

Paul declares that his message is the hidden wisdom of God that has been shrouded in mystery (***2:7***), a wisdom that cannot be discovered and known by natural means (***2:8-9***). But Paul and God's other inspired spokesmen knew this wisdom because God revealed it to them through the Holy Spirit (***2:10a***), who alone knows the things (Greek, *ta*) that are in the mind of God (***2:10b-11***). This is the very same Spirit of God that we have received, says Paul, so that *we* (apostles) may know these things (*ta*) that are hidden (***2:12***). These are the things we have spoken to you, in words taught to us by the Spirit Himself (***2:13***).

The three verses that follow (***2:14-16***) are a continuation of Paul's defense of his apostolic authority. He is not a *natural* man, but a *spiritual* man, he says. The designation "natural man" has nothing to do with *moral* qualities; it is not a synonym for sinful, depraved, or unregenerate. It refers rather to one who is limited to merely natural or human abilities and resources, as contrasted with one who is endowed with the Holy Spirit and His supernatural gifts of revelation and inspiration. A natural man does not have access to "the things" (*ta*) of the Spirit of God (***2:14a***). "The thoughts of God" in ***2:11*** (NASB, NIV) are literally "the things [*ta*] of God"; these are *"the things [ta] freely given to us [apostles] by God"* (***2:12***).

A natural man—one without revelation from the Spirit—"cannot understand" these things (**2:14b**). The word translated "understand" is *ginosko*, i.e., the natural man cannot *know* the kinds of things I am revealing to you. The issue is not whether he can understand them, but whether he is even aware of them. Paul says he cannot know them, i.e., he is not aware of them. Why not? Because only the Holy Spirit *knows* (*ginosko*) the things (*ta*) of God (***2:11***). These secret things can be discerned only by the Holy Spirit, and by those to whom the Spirit has revealed them, i.e., the "spiritual" man in ***2:15a***. Paul is such a "spiritual" man, endowed by the Spirit with revealed knowledge and with the words by which to speak it. Thus you cannot sit in judgment on me, says Paul (***2:15b***; "appraise" in the NASB). Why not? Because I am speaking words which ultimately come from the mind of Christ Himself! Only if you, too, have such access to the mind of Christ can you sit in judgment on me (***2:16***; see ***4:3-5***).

These verses (***2:14-16***) thus follow directly upon the flow of thought in ***2:1-13***. The content of ***verses 10-13*** interprets the content of ***verses 14-16***. There is nothing here about the Spirit's regeneration of sinners, and nothing about His illumination of Christians. Paul applies it all to himself in the concluding words of ***2:16***: *"But we have the mind of Christ."* (See **Sweeney, 110-112.**)

1 John 2:20,27. The next passage to be discussed is ***1 John 2:20,27***. Here John says,

> *But you have an anointing from the Holy One, and you all know. . . . As for you, the anointing which you received from Him abides in you, and you have no need for anyone to teach you; but as His anointing teaches you about all things, and is true and is not a lie, and just as it has taught you, you abide in Him.*

The advocates of illumination usually say that "the Holy One" is Jesus, and that the "anointing" that He gives us is the Holy Spirit, who then teaches us all things. As Kistemaker says concerning ***verse 27***, "The believers have no need of deceivers who try to teach false doctrine. They have the gift of the Holy Spirit who leads them in all truth (***John 16:13***)." That the *"anointing teaches you about all things"* means that "the Spirit of Christ will teach the believer everything (***John 14:26***) and will guide him in distinguishing truth from error" (**287**).

These verses from 1 John are not in the same category as the previous ones because their application is not limited only to the apostles (contrary to Kistemaker's use of passages referring only to the latter). They do refer to Christians in general. But even a cursory reading indicates that their subject is not illumination but (as in the previous texts) revelation itself. When John says that as a result of the anointing *"you all know"* (***2:20***), there is no indication that he is referring to a Spirit-bestowed understanding of some previously received revelation (such as the Bible). It is not an inward enlightenment as to the meaning of the revealed/inspired messages from God in the Bible. In these verses the anointing *is* the revealed knowledge, or at least the direct and immediate source of the revealed knowledge. Contrary to the whole concept of illumination, the knowledge comes directly from the anointing without being related to an intermediate factor.

But if this is a reference to direct revelation apart from the Bible, it would seem to make the Bible superfluous. Some avoid this conclusion by supposing that John is referring to the miraculous gifts of prophecy and supernatural knowledge that were present in the apostolic era prior to the completion of the NT canon. Such gifts did involve direct revelation. This is a possible understanding of the anointing, but in my judgment it is too limited in its scope.

To my mind the best understanding of the anointing is that it refers to the revealed/inspired Word of God itself in all its forms, including apostolic preaching, prophetic messages, and the written Scriptures. If the anointing is the Word of God, then the "Holy One" (***2:20***) is the Holy Spirit, who gives us the anointing by His work of revelation and inspiration upon prophets and apostles.

This interpretation seems to be most consistent with the context and teaching of the passage as a whole. This is seen in several ways. For one thing, John speaks of the anointing as if it were in the category of *knowledge*, something known. In ***2:27*** he says the anointing *"is true and is not a lie."* In this connection we should remember that one of John's major concerns in this letter is to warn the Christians in late-first-century Ephesus of the dangers of various anti-Christian heresies, including what appears to be an incipient Gnosticism. A major theme of Gnosticism was the claim to a special kind of saving knowledge available only to its followers. Over against such claims, John tells the Christians that they already *have* an anointing of true knowledge that has already taught them the truth. They do not need someone else to come along and teach them alien ideas contrary to what they already know. The anointing they already have *"is true and is not a lie"*; it is true knowledge from God. It makes more sense to think of the Word of God in these terms than to think of the Holy Spirit Himself as "true" and "not a lie."

A second indication that the anointing is the revealed/inspired Word of God is that the "knowing" in ***2:20*** seems to be the result of the revealed message the Christians had heard from the beginning. They *know* because they heard the Word from the beginning. The whole of this second chapter of 1 John refers to the message already heard. ***Verse 7*** speaks of *"an old commandment which you have had from the beginning. The old commandment is the word which you have heard."* In most versions ***verses 13-14*** are translated as referring to *"**Him** who has been from the beginning."* This is possible, but in view of ***2:7*** I believe these verses are actually speaking of "the (Word) which you have known from the beginning." In both verses (***13 and 14***) the clause reads *"hoti egnokate ton ap' arches."* What is known is represented simply by the article, *ton*. I take this article to refer not to Jesus the person but to "the word [*ho logos*]" in ***2:7***. The phrase *ap' arches* ("from the beginning") ties these verses together, and they form the background for ***2:20***—"You all know" not because of some present inner revelation from the Spirit but because of the Word which you have heard from the beginning.

John's point is this: the original truth, which you heard from the beginning (***2:7,13,14***) is still true; it is the standard of truth. Go back to it and you will see that these false teachers are lying.

Another indication from the context that the anointing is the Word of God is the statement in ***2:27*** that the "anointing which you received from Him [the Holy One] *abides in you*." It is certainly true that the Holy Spirit Himself abides in us, but in this context it is specifically stated in ***2:14b*** that "the word of God" abides in us, and in ***2:24*** that the message heard from the beginning abides in us:

> *I have written to you, young men, because you are strong, and the word of God abides in you. . . . As for you, let that abide in you which you heard from the beginning. If what you heard from the beginning abides in you, you also will abide in the Son and in the Father.*

This is perfectly consistent with the point just made, that the anointing is the Word of God which had been heard from the beginning.

This means that it would be possible to translate the last clause in ***2:27*** as "you abide in *it* [the Word of God]," rather than "you abide in Him." Jesus uses this very language in ***John 8:31***, *"If you abide in My word."* See also ***2 Timothy 3:14***.

The main point is that the best understanding of ***1 John 2:20,27*** is that the anointing is the revealed/inspired Word of God which every Christian has heard from the beginning of his Christian life. Making sure that the Word abides in us helps to protect us against false and heretical ideas.

Making sure the Word abides in us helps protect us against false and heretical ideas.

Hebrews 8:10-11. Another text to which defenders of illumination sometimes appeal is ***Hebrews 8:10-11*** (cited from ***Jer 31:33-34***),

> *For this is the covenant that I will make with the house of Israel after those days, says the Lord; I will put My laws into their minds, and I will write them on their hearts. And I will be their God, and they shall be My people. And they shall not teach everyone his fellow citizen, and everyone his brother, saying, "Know the Lord," for all will know Me, from the least to the greatest of them.*

We note immediately that here there is no reference at all to the Holy Spirit, nor to divine aid in understanding Scripture. Finding the notion of illumination here is a rather forced inference.

In my judgment this passage has nothing to do with illumination or with any kind of inward work of the Spirit. These verses are part of God's promise through Jeremiah of a new covenant. One of the main points of the promise is that the new covenant would be very different from the old covenant. A major difference is that membership in old-covenant Israel was a matter of physical birth only. A child was already a member of the covenant people before he was taught to know the Lord and His laws. A person could be born a member of the covenant people and remain a member all his life without ever surrendering from his heart to God's claims upon him. Thus Paul's statement in ***Romans 9:6***, *"They are not all Israel who are descended from Israel."*

The new covenant is very different from this. One becomes a member of new-covenant Israel (the church) and enters into this covenant relation with God not by physical birth but by the new birth only. The terms of the new covenant are not written simply on external instruments such as stone or parchment; rather, they are written upon the heart and accepted in the heart (see ***Rom 6:17***). How God writes them on the heart is not stated and is not the point.

This is why, under the new covenant, it will not be necessary to teach a covenant brother to know the Lord (***v. 11***). Since old-covenant membership was by physical birth, every person who belonged to the covenant people was taught about Yahweh and His Word *after* becoming a member. But one does not enter the new covenant until he has already been taught, and has come to "know the Lord" and has believed in Him. Every member of the new-covenant people of God, from the newest Christian to the most senior saint, already knows the Lord as a condition for membership. *How* we come to "know the Lord" is not addressed here but is learned from other biblical teaching (e.g., ***Rom 10:17***).

This passage is simply not relevant to the issue of illumination.

John 3:3 is sometimes cited in support of illumination: *"Jesus answered and said to him [Nicodemus], 'Truly, truly, I say to you, unless one is born again he cannot see the kingdom of God.'"* This is interpreted to mean that the unbeliever's mind is so corrupted by sin that he cannot "see"—in the sense of "understand"—the kingdom of God (representing all spiritual things) until he has been born again or regenerated by the Holy Spirit (***3:5***). The crucial point is taking the word "see" (*horao*) in the sense of "understand."

This interpretation of *horao* in this context is completely unwarranted. This is the ordinary word for "to see," and usually it means to see with one's physical eyes. It is sometimes used in other senses; and a few times it does mean "to perceive, to understand," as at the end of ***Matthew 13:14*** (also ***Mk 4:12***). The sense of *horao* that fits the ***John 3:3*** context much better, however, is "to experience." An example of this meaning is ***Matthew 16:28***, *"Truly I say to you, there are some of those who are standing here who will not taste death until they* ***see*** *the Son of Man coming in His kingdom"* (also ***Lk 9:27***). See also ***Acts 2:27***, *"Nor will you let your Holy One* ***see*** *decay"* (NIV); and ***Hebrews 11:5***, *"By faith Enoch was taken up so that he would not* ***see*** *death."* In the third chapter of John itself (***v. 36***) *horao* is used thus: *"He who does not obey the Son will not* ***see*** *life."*

That this is the intended meaning in ***John 3:3*** is clear enough from Jesus' own explanation of it in ***John 3:5***, *"Unless one is born of water and the Spirit he cannot* ***enter into*** *the kingdom of God."* "Enter into" explains "see" in ***3:3***. This text thus has no relevance to the doctrine of illumination.

1 Corinthians 2:4; 1 Thessalonians 1:5. Also irrelevant to the issue are ***1 Corinthians 2:4*** and ***1 Thessalonians 1:5***, where Paul says he preached the gospel *"in demonstration of the Spirit and of power,"* and *"in power and in the Holy Spirit."* These texts are irrelevant because they describe how Paul *delivered* his message, not how it was *received* by his audience.

2 Peter 1:20-21. Finally, a word should be said about ***2 Peter 1:20***, which says that *"no prophecy of Scripture is a matter of one's own interpretation."* **Verse 21** adds, *"Men moved by the Holy Spirit spoke from God."* Ambiguous translation and careless reading have led many to conclude that these verses are speaking of the *interpretation* of Scripture, which comes only from the Spirit. On the contrary, this text has nothing to do with the interpretation of the Bible (illumination), but is all about its origin (revelation and inspiration). The word "interpretation" is used not in reference to the reader's interpretation of Scripture, but in reference to the writer's interpretation of reality. The TNIV is more clear: *"No prophecy of Scripture came about by the prophet's own interpretation of things."*

The bottom line is that, with a right interpretation of Scripture, the alleged biblical basis for the doctrine of illumination disappears. The irony of this could not be more striking.

Will God Help Us Understand the Bible?

If the doctrine of illumination must be rejected as false, does this mean that we receive no help from God in our efforts to study and understand His Word? Does it do any good to pray for God to help us when we are struggling to understand a specific passage, or when we are trying to build a sermon or Bible lesson around a specific text? In her monthly newsletter a missionary told how she was trying to witness to the woman who was her language teacher. She made this request: "I need your prayers that the Holy Spirit will help her understand what I am saying and it will bear good fruit in her." Would such a prayer be futile, or would it be "fruitful"? What can we expect God to do in answer to such prayers?

I believe that such prayers are valid, and that God can and will help us in our efforts to understand His Word. Here I will present four ways in which God aids our understanding. The first two are not unique works of the Holy Spirit, but may be performed by any of the three persons of the Trinity. The last two are the result of the Spirit's specific works in the church and in the lives of individual Christians. It should be stressed that these works of God are not substitutes for our own diligent and informed study of Scripture, but are accomplished through and along with our own study.

Providential Intervention in Answer to Prayer

Through His general providence the sovereign Creator rules over His creation by permitting the two relatively independent created forces—natural law and free will—to "go their own way." However, He has the ability and reserves the right to intervene within these processes if He so chooses. He can intervene in dramatic supernatural ways, e.g., by performing miracles, which violate or suspend natural law (and even free will if necessary). But He can also intervene in a way called special providence, whereby His divine power alters the course of nature without violating natural laws, and works within the human mind and upon the human will for the purpose of influencing that will toward a certain decision.[4]

This latter mode of divine activity, special providence, is usually the way God works when He answers our prayers (**Cottrell, *Ruler*, ch. 10**). When we pray for healing, we expect God to touch our bodies or the bodies of friends and family in hidden yet powerful ways, arresting infection or pain and beginning a healing process. When we pray for a family member to forgive us for some wrong we have done, we expect God to touch that person's heart or mind in some way, perhaps by bringing certain memories into their consciousness or by causing them to forget certain things.

When we pray for God to help us to understand Scripture, we can expect Him to providentially intervene in our lives in similar ways. This does not mean that He will reveal new ideas to us, but He may work within our minds to help us remember something we encountered long ago but have forgotten. He may sharpen our mental processes, giving us insights and helping us to see connections between ideas previously overlooked. He may help to clear our preoccupied minds so that we can concentrate. He may arrange for us to have an uninterrupted period of time for diligent study. He may lead

[4] See Cottrell, *Ruler*, especially chapters 4 and 5, on special providence. See also Thomas, chapter 5.

us to cross paths with another person who can help us (remember Philip and the eunuch, ***Acts 8:26-40***).

Several things should be noted about such providential answers to our prayers for understanding. One, the Holy Spirit may be the one who answers such prayers, but it may be the work of the Father or the Son. This is not an exclusive work of the Spirit. Two, we need not limit such prayers to our understanding of the Bible or spiritual matters as such. We can pray for such help in understanding college textbooks or instruction manuals. Three, such providential intervention is not limited to the lives of Christians. Thus it is proper for us to pray, as in the missionary's request above, that God will give such help to sinners to whom we are witnessing.

Prayer for Wisdom

This may not be much different from the point just discussed, but the Bible does make a special point of singling out prayers for wisdom. ***James 1:5*** says, *"But if any of you lacks wisdom, let him ask of God, who gives to all generously and without reproach, and it will be given to him."*[5]

In general, the difference between knowledge and wisdom is something like this: knowledge is an awareness and understanding of the facts; wisdom is knowing what to do with these facts, or the ability to put one's knowledge to practical use. In reference to Bible study, knowledge refers more to what the Bible *means*; wisdom refers to what it means *for me*, or to the proper application of the text to one's daily living. A thorough understanding of the Bible will include both, just as an effective sermon or Bible lesson will include both facts ("What's so?") and application ("So what?").

> **Knowledge refers more to what the Bible means; wisdom refers to what it means for me.**

In ***James 1:5*** God invites us to pray specifically for wisdom in general, which would include praying for wisdom in knowing how to apply the Word of God to our lives. Perhaps this was the main thrust of David's prayerful meditation upon God's law: *"O how I love Your*

[5]This is not the same as the spiritual gift called the "word of wisdom" in ***1Cor 12:8***, which was probably miraculous.

law! It is my meditation all the day. . . . I have not turned aside from Your ordinances, for You Yourself have taught me" (***Ps* 119:97,102**).

Again, God's answers to prayers for wisdom in applying His Word are not the exclusive work of the Holy Spirit.

Taking Advantage of the Spiritual Gifts of Others

Another way God helps us understand the Bible—this time as an exclusive work of the Spirit—is by bestowing upon some members of the body of Christ spiritual gifts that are for the specific purpose of helping others to learn. In our day this includes especially the gift of teaching (***1Cor* 12:28-29**) or the role of pastor-teacher (***Eph* 4:11**). The distinctive ability of such a Spirit-gifted teacher is to explain the content of the messages received from God through inspired apostles and prophets. (It is likely that other gifts sometimes identified as teaching gifts, e.g., "the word of wisdom," ***1 Corinthians* 12:8**; and "the distinguishing of spirits," ***1 Corinthians* 12:10**, were limited to the first century.)

Such a gift of teaching is especially associated with those who serve as elders in the church (***1Tm* 3:2; 5:17; *Tts* 1:9**), but need not be limited thereto. To have the gift of teaching does not necessarily involve having a charismatic personality and dramatic teaching skills, but rather involves the desire to learn what Scripture teaches, the time to pursue such knowledge, the insight to grasp it, and the passion to share it. The Holy Spirit gives the gift of teaching by strengthening an individual in all these areas.

> **The gift of teaching involves desire, time, insight, and passion.**

What does this mean for Christians in general who want to understand the Bible, and who pray for God to help them understand it? It means that they should seek out such teachers and learn from them! Here is more advice from Ware: "So, what shall we do when we come across passages that are hard to understand? *Remember,* God provides us with His Spirit and Spirit-gifted teachers to lead us into clearer and deeper understandings of His Word. Pray for the teachers and preachers of our churches, Bible schools, and seminaries; that they would be diligent, hard-working, careful, and faithful to what God has revealed in His Word" (**"Sense," 38**).

In view of this specific way in which the Spirit helps us understand the Word, what shall we say about someone who prays that the Holy Spirit will help him to have more knowledge of the Bible, and yet never participates in Sunday school classes and Bible study classes provided by the church? If the Spirit indeed helps us understand the Bible by providing "Spirit-gifted teachers," and we do not take advantage of their teaching, would not such prayers be hypocritical?

Is it not hypocritical to ask for the Spirit's help and yet neglect the classes of Spirit-gifted teachers?

The Process of Sanctification

A final way that God may help us to understand the Bible is through the main work of the Spirit in the life of a Christian, namely, sanctification. As we will see later, the indwelling Spirit sanctifies us by giving us the moral power to become more and more holy in our character and conduct, which we do by becoming more and more obedient to the Word of God. In His sanctifying work the Spirit operates mainly upon our wills, increasing our desire and ability to obey God's will.

Since sanctification means becoming more and more conformed to the will and nature of God as revealed in His Word, it requires that we have a clear understanding of what the Bible teaches about His will for us. We have seen above some of the ways God helps us in coming to such a clearer understanding. Sometimes, though, the greatest barrier to a proper interpretation and understanding of a particular biblical teaching is not an intellectual gap but a roadblock created by our wills. That is to say, the reason we do not understand a particular commandment or teaching aright is because we do not *want* to. If we accepted its real meaning, we would have to give up some cherished false idea or some desired sinful pleasure. Thus we *"suppress the truth in unrighteousness"* (***Rom 1:18***). As Ware says, "Sometimes what is hard to understand may simply be scriptural truths that run contrary to the sinful perspectives we carry into our lives as Christians" (**"Sense," 38**).

Here is where the Holy Spirit can help us understand Scripture aright, namely, by softening our resisting wills and helping us to rearrange our

By reshaping our wills, the Spirit reshapes our understanding of the Word.

inward desires toward specific things, so that we are willing to accept openly the meaning of a specific biblical teaching (e.g., about drinking, gender roles, divorce, or fornication) that we knew in our hearts was the correct one all along. This is part of what sanctification is all about. By reshaping our wills, the Spirit reshapes our understanding of the Word.

In conclusion, when we pray for God to give us a better understanding of His Word, He may help us in any or all of the above ways. In these ways the following biblical prayers may be answered. In ***Psalm 119:18*** David prays, *"Open my eyes, that I may behold wonderful things from Your law."* Paul's prayer for the Ephesians is one that we can also utter for ourselves and for others,

> *that the God of our Lord Jesus Christ, the Father of glory, may give to you a spirit of wisdom and of revelation in the knowledge of Him. I pray that the eyes of your heart may be enlightened, so that you will know what is the hope of His calling, what are the riches of the glory of His inheritance of the saints, and what is the surpassing greatness of His power toward us who believe.* (***Eph 1:17-19***)

This Pauline prayer from ***Philippians 1:9-11*** fits well into the sanctification process discussed above:

> *And this I pray, that your love may abound still more and more in real knowledge and all discernment, so that you may approve the things that are excellent, in order to be sincere and blameless until the day of Christ; having been filled with the fruit of righteousness which comes through Jesus Christ, to the glory and praise of God.*

All of God's means of giving us understanding seem to be in view in this final prayer:

> *For this reason also, since the day we heard of it, we have not ceased to pray for you and to ask that you may be filled with the knowledge of His will in all spiritual wisdom and understanding, so that you will walk in a manner worthy of the Lord, to please Him in all respects, bearing fruit in every good work and increasing in the knowledge of God.* (***Col 1:9-10***)

THE HOLY SPIRIT AND THE TRUTH OF THE BIBLE

We have discussed the Holy Spirit and the *origin* of the Bible, and the Holy Spirit and the *understanding* of the Bible. One other issue under the heading of "The Holy Spirit and the Bible" is his relation to the *truth* of the Bible. The question here is this: how is it possible to know that the Bible is true? On what basis can we accept the Bible as true?

How is it possible to know that the Bible is true?

This issue is parallel in many ways to the previous one. Many believe that only through an internal working of the Spirit can we come to a true understanding of the Bible, and likewise many also believe that only through the internal testimony of the Spirit can one acknowledge that the Bible is true. One does not need to be convinced by external evidences; the Spirit testifies directly to our hearts and internally convinces us of the Bible's truth and authority. This is usually called "the internal witness of the Holy Spirit," or just the *testimonium* (**Ramm, 7**).

An affirmation of the *testimonium* was a part of "The Chicago Statement on Biblical Inerrancy" cited earlier: "The Holy Spirit, Scripture's divine Author, both authenticates it to us by His inward witness and opens our minds to understand its meaning" (**Geisler, *Inerrancy*, 494**). Another part of the Chicago Statement declares, "We affirm that the Holy Spirit bears witness to the Scriptures, assuring believers of the truthfulness of God's written Word" (**ibid., 497**).

R.C. Sproul devotes an entire chapter in the *Inerrancy* volume to this subject.[6] The main point of the *testimonium,* he says, "is found in its focus on the question of *certainty*. The Spirit in His internal testimony works to confirm the reliability of Scripture, giving us certainty that the Bible is the Word of God" (**338**). This does not happen contrary to or apart from objective evidence; rather, "the Spirit causes us to submit or yield to the evidence" (**342-343**). Why is this work of the Spirit necessary? Because of the effects of sin upon the heart. "Thus the *testimonium* is directed primarily at the heart of man, with the effect on the mind being a consequence of the change of the disposition of the heart" (**348-349**).

Sproul acknowledges that "the New Testament does not provide us with a thoroughgoing exposition of the 'internal testimony' as such." He insists, though, that "the New Testament is replete with

[6] See also Ramm's *The Witness of the Spirit.*

allusions to the work of the Spirit in securing our confidence in the Word." Sproul simply mentions **2 Corinthians 4:3-6**; **1 John 1:10**; **2:14**; **5:20**; **Colossians 2:2**; **1 Thessalonians 1:5**; **Galatians 4:6**; and **Romans 8:15-16**. A "classic text" for the *testimonium*, he says, is **1 Corinthians 2** (353-354).

In this book I will not give a detailed examination of this doctrine. In most ways its origin, its alleged biblical basis, and its exegetical lapses are parallel to what we have seen regarding the doctrine of illumination. I will stress just two points.

First, this concept of the internal testimony of the Spirit arises out of the teaching of John Calvin and is integrally related to the doctrines of total depravity and irresistible grace. Sproul notes, "John Calvin is usually credited with developing and giving the clearest expression to the Reformation principle of the *testimonium*" (338). Ramm says that this was in part a response to the Catholic church's claim to be the only authenticator of the Bible. "Calvin replaced the voice of the Church, which supposedly tells us with great assurance that the Scriptures are the Word of God, with the *internal witness of the Holy Spirit*" (12).

Why did Calvin not simply appeal to objective evidence as the basis for such assurance? Because, as in the case of man's *understanding* of Scripture, the innate and universal state of total depravity has rendered the mind and heart incapable of honestly examining such evidence. Thus for Calvin it is "the sinful condition of fallen man that makes the *testimonium* necessary" (Sproul, 348). One reason Calvin "opposed rationalistic Christian apologetics," says Ramm, is that "the darkness of the human mind prevents it from being a fit instrument to prove the divinity of the Christian faith" (13). "Therefore we need a special persuasion that we may see the Scriptures as the Word of God" (18). Bodey well explains the dependence of the *testimonium* upon total depravity (17-18):

> Paul explains it by saying that the natural man, the unregenerate man, the man who does not have the indwelling Spirit of God, does not receive the things of God. Indeed, he cannot. His mind and heart and will are so perverse and steeped in rebellion against God that no amount of objective testimony will ever convince him of divine truth. He must be born again, or he cannot see the kingdom of God, much less believe the book of the Kingdom. Only by the inner witness of the Holy Spirit in our hearts can any of us accept the

> Scriptures as the Word of God. Without this internal confirmation we can only continue in blind rejection and unbelief.

In the section on illumination I have already addressed the fallacy of attempting to ground any other doctrine on the concept of total depravity. The main point was that no such doctrine as total depravity is taught in the Bible. That discussion applies here as well. Thus the concept of the *testimonium* has no true theological basis.

The other point I will briefly mention is the weakness of the alleged *exegetical* basis for the *testimonium*. Many of the same passages used to support illumination are appealed to here as well, with similar misinterpretation and misapplication. I judge it to be unnecessary to examine them in detail. When I survey the kind of passages brought into this discussion by the defenders of the *testimonium*, I cannot help but conclude that no one would ever have "discovered" this doctrine in these texts if it were not for the notion that the doctrine of total depravity makes it a cognitive necessity.

CHAPTER THREE

THE HOLY SPIRIT'S WORK IN THE OLD TESTAMENT

This chapter will present a summary of the work of the Holy Spirit in OT times, from creation to the first coming of Christ. Our information for this subject comes mainly from the OT itself, but not from the OT *by* itself because we are looking back at the OT through the lens of the NT. If we had only the OT to go by, we would have a very tentative and limited pneumatology, since the fuller revelation of the Spirit is found in the new-covenant Scriptures. But the Bible is in reality one book, held together in a transcendent unity that is grounded in its one underlying redemptive theme and in its common divine authorship. This unity of the Bible is the presupposition of a proper understanding of the OT's teaching about the Holy Spirit. It helps us in several ways.

On the one hand, the NT helps us to understand OT texts about "the Spirit of the Lord" as truly referring to the Holy Spirit, one of the three persons of the Trinity. Without the NT perspective, crucial texts such as ***Genesis 1:2***; ***2 Samuel 23:2***; ***Psalm 139:7***; and ***Zechariah 4:6*** might be taken as referring simply to God's power, presence, or influence. Garth Black goes so far as to say, "There is no clear indication in the Old Testament of a belief that the Spirit of God is a personality distinct from God" (**10**). This conclusion may be too extreme, but we must admit the presence of some ambiguity in this area.

When we see the OT in the light of the NT, however, this ambiguity melts away. The NT writers clearly present the Holy Spirit as a divine person distinct from the Father and the Son, and they often identify the Holy Spirit thus understood with the "Spirit of God" in the OT. This is especially true of the Spirit who spoke through the OT writers. Compare ***2 Samuel 23:2*** with ***Matthew 22:43***; ***Mark 12:36***; ***Acts 1:16***; and ***Hebrews 3:7***. Also, compare ***Isaiah 59:21*** with ***Acts 28:25***; ***1 Peter 1:11***. (See **Wood, 32.**)

The NT helps us to understand OT texts about "the Spirit of the Lord"; the OT helps us to better understand certain NT teachings about His work.

On the other hand, what the OT says about the Holy Spirit helps us to better understand certain NT teachings about His work. This is true especially regarding the equipping work of the Spirit, which is found in both the old-covenant and new-covenant ages. The principle is basically the same in each age, namely, the Spirit bestows specific ministries and skills upon selected individuals to enable them to perform certain tasks vital to the people of God as a whole. Two particular OT examples give us helpful insight into NT teaching about such gifts. One example is the equipping of certain Israelites with the skills necessary for constructing the tabernacle. There are some parallels between this incident and NT gifts in general. Another example is the calling and equipping of the 70 elders to assist Moses in his administrative work (***Num 11:16-30***). This episode provides a key to understanding the purpose of tongues on the Day of Pentecost.

This chapter focuses on three main subjects. First, we will examine what the OT says about the Spirit's role in creation. Second, we will survey its teaching about the equipping work of the Spirit in the old-covenant age. Finally, we will address the question of what the OT says about the Holy Spirit's saving work.

THE HOLY SPIRIT'S WORK OF CREATION

Several OT texts link God's *ruach* to the work of creation. We must remember, though, that the word *ruach* can mean "spirit," "breath," or "wind." Deciding which of these is the intended meaning is not always obvious. Another complication is that some of the relevant texts regarding the creation of man use another Hebrew word that usually means "breath," namely, *n^eshamah*. The issue is whether this word should be understood as "spirit" in certain texts.

In any case it is clear enough that the Spirit did have a role in the original work of creation. Boles's claim (**35**) that "the work of the Holy Spirit in the material world is as great as in the spiritual realm" is probably too extreme, but there is no doubt that His participation was significant. We shall see that this is the case first in reference to the creation of the material universe as a whole, then in reference to the creation of man in particular.

It is clear that the Spirit did have a role in the original work of creation.

THE CREATION OF THE UNIVERSE

Theologians sometimes speak of the *economic* Trinity, which refers to the fact that each person of the Trinity performs unique works not necessarily shared by the other two. This is especially true in reference to redemption; e.g., only God the Son became incarnate as Jesus of Nazareth. This may also be true of creation. Though the Father, the Son, and the Spirit were all involved in the work of creation, they were not all necessarily doing the same specific things.

Exactly how this applies to creation is somewhat a matter of speculation. Kuyper, for example, says that in every work shared by the Trinity, "the power *to bring forth* proceeds from the Father; the power *to arrange* from the Son; the power *to perfect* from the Holy Spirit" (**19**). "The Father brings forth, the Son disposes and arranges, the Holy Spirit perfects" (**ibid., 27**). As applied to creation, the Holy Spirit did not create the stuff from which the universe is made, but began His work only after matter had been brought into existence by the Father through the Son (**ibid., 29-30**). Wood outlines a similar division of labor: "In general, the work of the Father is that of serving as supreme planner, author, and designer; that of the Son as worker, carrying out the directives of the Father . . . ; and that of the Holy Spirit as completer or consummator, bringing to final form that which has been brought into existence by the Son at the Father's command" (**16**). Also, "The Spirit . . . quite clearly worked with what the Son had already created, fashioning it into the design planned by the Father" (**33**).

Such distinctions as these are probably too tidy and overly simplified. Nevertheless some specialization of the Spirit's work in creation can be seen in ***Genesis 1:1-2***, *"In the beginning God created the heavens and the earth. The earth was formless and void, and darkness was over the surface of the deep, and the Spirit of God was moving over the surface of the waters."* Since the Holy Spirit is not specifically mentioned until ***1:2***, ***1:1*** is often understood as saying that the *ex nihilo* creation of the material of the universe was *not* His work. This is not necessarily the case, however. The subject in ***1:1*** is *Elohim*: *"In the beginning* Elohim *created the heavens and the earth."* We cannot assume that *Elohim* refers only to God the Father. This Hebrew word, usually translated "God" when referring to Yahweh, may be used for any member of the Trinity or for all three at the same time (as is the case with the divine name, *Yahweh*, itself). ***Genesis 1:1*** certainly does refer to the act of *ex nihilo* creation, but it also serves as a summary statement for the entire initial creation process. I do not think the Holy Spirit can be excluded from ***1:1***.

Some specialization of the Spirit's work can be seen in Genesis 1:1-2.

It is certainly true, though, that after the general reference to creation in ***1:1***, the first creative act of God specifically mentioned is a work of the Holy Spirit: *"The Spirit of God was moving over the surface of the waters"* (***1:2b***). Exactly what this means can be no more than inference at best, and mostly speculation. Much is drawn from the fact that the little-used[1] verb translated "moving" is also used in ***Deuteronomy 32:11*** to describe an eagle "that hovers over its young." Thus the Holy Spirit "moving over the surface of the waters" is compared with a mother hen sitting on her nest, hovering or brooding, perhaps incubating her eggs or providing protection for her young in their infancy. Morris (***Spirit***, **19**) cites Milton's interpretation in *Paradise Lost*: "His brooding wings the Spirit of God outspread, and vital virtue infused, and vital warmth throughout the fluid mass."

In ***Genesis 1:2*** the Spirit is pictured as giving life to and bringing order out of the just-created, barren and chaotic earth: *"The earth was*

[1] The verb, *rachaph*, is used only three times: here, ***Deu 32:11***, and ***Jer 23:9***.

formless and void, and darkness was over the surface of the deep, and the Spirit of God was moving over the surface of the waters." Boatman says the image "suggests a vital force exerted upon the primordial sea" (**44**). Kuyper describes this work of the Spirit as *"impregnating* inanimate matter" (**24**), as "the kindling and fanning of the spark of life" (**ibid., 33**). Carter says, "The Spirit's brooding over the natural chaos brought out of those primal elements a living, Spirit-sustained organism that we call the cosmos, or universe" (**52**). From this image it is sometimes concluded that the Spirit's role in the physical creation is parallel to His spiritual work of regeneration and sanctification in the new-covenant era.

From this verse it is also concluded that the Spirit's work is to organize, perfect, or bring to completion what has been planned by the Father and initiated by the Son. In Torrey's words, "The development of the earlier, chaotic, undeveloped states of the material universe into higher orders of being is effected through the agency of the Holy Spirit" (**79**). Boles declares that "the completion of the work of creation was done by the Holy Spirit. The ministry of the Holy Spirit in creation was to organize the matter, and set in motion all of the functioning of the parts of the universe" (**38**).

This understanding has led some to conclude that the entire work of the six days of creation (after ***Gen 1:1***) was the work of the Holy Spirit. Wood says that the Spirit serves "as completer or consummator, bringing to final form that which has been brought into existence by the Son at the Father's command." To accomplish this the Spirit "moved" on the face of the chaotic waters, "and in six days brought them to a complete state of order" (**16**). Wood states further, "The idea of the word in ***Genesis 1:2***, then, is that the Holy Spirit 'fluttered over,' 'took care of,' 'moved upon' the chaotic state of the world in the interest of bringing order and design. Since the indication comes immediately before the description of the six-day creative activity, the implication is that the work of the six days was performed by the Spirit" (**30**).

While this seems quite speculative, some confirmation may be found in ***Psalm 33:6***; ***Job 26:13***; and ***Isaiah 40:12-14***. In the Isaiah text ***verse 12*** seems to be a poetic reference to creation events in the first chapter of Genesis: *"Who has measured the waters in the hollow of His hand, and marked off the heavens by the span, and calculated the dust of the earth* *by the measure, and weighed the mountains in a balance and the hills in a pair of scales?"* ***Verse 13*** then seems to link the Holy Spirit to these works: *"Who has directed the Spirit of the LORD, or as His counselor has informed Him?"* The Spirit's "intimate connection with the plan and management of the universe is apparent," says Walvoord (**38**).

A more specific statement is ***Psalm 33:6***, which is usually taken to mean that the Holy Spirit was directly involved in the creation and organization of the heavens above, i.e., our solar system and all other stars and galaxies. It says, *"By the word of the LORD the heavens were made, and by the breath of His mouth all their host."* Here the word "breath" is *ruach*, which many take to be a specific reference to the Holy Spirit.[2] "This passage reveals that all the host of heaven were made by the Holy Spirit," says Walvoord (**37**). Wood takes the reference to "the word" in ***33:6a*** to signify Jesus, and the reference to "breath" in ***33:6b*** to mean the Holy Spirit. "So taken, the verse means that all the heavenly bodies were made by a combined effort of the Son and the Spirit" (**31**). Since "the heavens more than any other portion of God's creation reveal His order," this confirms the Spirit's role in creation as bringing order out of chaos, says Walvoord (**40**).

In creation, the Spirit brings order out of chaos.

Job's uninspired comment (recorded by inspiration) in ***Job 26:13*** is taken as reflecting this idea: *"By His breath [ruach] the heavens are cleared."* The word translated "cleared" literally means "made beautiful" ("garnished," KJV; "adorned," NKJV; "gained their beauty," CSB). "The word . . . carries the thought of beautifying or bringing to a state of order and design," says Wood (**31**). Whether *ruach* here means "wind" (NRSV), "breath" (most versions), or "Spirit" is a matter of debate. If the last, this verse along with ***Psalm 33:6*** implies "that the Holy Spirit put on the finishing touches in the heavens, drawing out the glory and beauty that were possible in the hosts of heaven" (**Palmer, 23**).

Another verse usually brought into the discussion at this point is ***Psalm 104:30***, *"You send forth Your Spirit, they are created; and You renew the face of the ground."* The main thought here is God's creation and

[2] ***John 20:22*** shows that "the breath of His mouth must signify the Holy Spirit," says Kuyper (29).

care for *animals*. For some the central idea is that of maintaining and renewing the lives of living creatures (**Torrey, 78**), or the Spirit's "continuing, providential control over creation" (**Wood, 31**). The entire Psalm seems to be thematically linked to Genesis one, however; and the strong word for creation, *bara'* (used in ***Gen 1:1***) is used in ***Psalm 104:30***. This latter fact, says Walvoord, "points to the original creation" as the subject in ***verse 30*** (**37**; see **Kuyper, 30**). Probably both the original creation of days 5 and 6 (***Gen 1:20-25***) and the continuing care for this living universe are indicated. As Palmer puts it, "Thus the psalmist indicates that the Holy Spirit is the one who gives life to all living creatures: to the storks in the fir trees, the wild goats in the mountains, and the leviathans in the great seas—to bird, beast, and fish" (**24**).

THE CREATION OF MAN

That the Holy Spirit was specifically involved in the creation of man (mankind, the human race, Adam and Eve) can be affirmed in view of ***Genesis 1:26***, *"Then God said, 'Let Us make man in Our image.'"* The plural pronouns here are usually seen as reflecting God's trinitarian nature; for our purposes they indicate that the making of man was a trinitarian project.

The Holy Spirit was specifically involved in the creation of man.

Genesis 2:7 is usually seen as a more specific indicator of the Spirit's work in the creation of man: *"Then the LORD God formed man of dust from the ground, and breathed into his nostrils the breath of life; and man became a living being."* The Spirit's presence in this verse is inferred from the references to the act of *breathing* and to "the *breath* of life." In view of this, let us be very clear about one point: the usual word for "Spirit," *ruach*, is not used in this verse at all, though some writers assume or imply that it is. For example, Pache quotes ***Genesis 2:7*** thus: "'The Lord God formed man . . . He breathed into his nostrils the breath [Spirit] of life" (**29**; brackets in the original). Palmer says that ***Genesis 2:7*** uses "the words *breathed* and *breath*, the latter being the name of the Holy Spirit" (**25**). Staton says that ***Genesis 2:7*** shows that "man had God's own breath . . . which is the same as the word for 'Spirit'" (***Holy Spirit*, 9**).

I contend that anyone reading such comments would assume that in ***Genesis 2:7*** "the breath of life" is actually "the *ruach* of life." But since this is not the case, such statements are very misleading. The actual word for "breath" in ***2:7*** is *n^e^shamah*, the basic meaning of which is "breath," not "spirit." It is used only about 25 times in the OT. Once it means animal breath (***Gen 7:22***); about 17 times it refers to human breath, with several of these paralleling human breath and human spirit. Seven times the word refers, metaphorically, to the breath of God. In five of these the clear meaning is the powerful breath expelled from God's nostrils, figuratively speaking: ***2 Samuel 22:16***; ***Job 4:9***; ***Psalm 18:15***; ***Job 37:10***; ***Isaiah 30:33***. In the first three *ruach* is also used; and it clearly means "breath," as it absorbs the meaning of the dominant word *n^e^shamah*.

In only two places (other than ***Gen 2:7***) is it possible for *n^e^shamah* to mean "spirit": ***Job 32:8***, *"But it is a spirit* [*ruach*] *in man, and the breath* [*n^e^shamah*] *of the Almighty gives them understanding"*; and ***Job 33:4***, *"The Spirit* [*ruach*] *of God has made me, and the breath* [*n^e^shamah*] *of the Almighty gives me life."* It is possible that in these two verses *n^e^shamah* is intended to take on the meaning of *ruach* in the sense of "spirit." If that is so, then these two verses may well reflect the event described in ***Genesis 2:7***.

My conclusions are as follows. I believe ***Job 32:8*** and ***33:4*** do echo ***Genesis 2:7***, but I deny that *n^e^shamah* in these or any other verses is ever used as a synonym for God's Spirit, in the sense of the Holy Spirit. In every case the *n^e^shamah* of Yahweh/God/the Almighty refers figuratively to an *act* of God, not to the *essence* of God in any sense. This is true, I believe, even in ***Job 33:4***, where "the *n^e^shamah* of the Almighty" may refer indirectly to the creative act by which God breathed life into the inanimate clay form of Adam.[3] In other words, the powerful, divine breath—the *n^e^shamah* of God—is the *means* by which Adam was endowed with his human, biological breath, the "*n^e^shamah* of life." There is no specific reference either in ***Genesis 2:7*** or in ***Job 33:4*** to the Holy Spirit.

The "breath" of God refers to an act of God, not His essence.

It is very important to understand this. Anyone who tries to identify the *n^e^shamah* in ***Genesis 2:7*** with the Holy Spirit is confusing the

[3] Elihu here says that *"the breath of the Almighty gives* ***me*** [Elihu] *life."* But he does seem to be echoing ***Gen 2:7***.

divine "breath" with ordinary *human* breath. This not only blurs the difference between cause and effect; it also violates the very nature of creation by identifying the creature with the Creator. This is true because the *n^e^shamah* in **Genesis 2:7**, as the result of the divine creative act, becomes a part of Adam's own existence. The "*n^e^shamah* of life" is breathed *into* Adam; it is then a part of Adam's life. Thus if the *n^e^shamah* in **Genesis 2:7** is the Holy Spirit, then Adam received the essence of God as a part of his own essence.

Some have succumbed, perhaps inadvertently, to this conclusion. It is in fact the very premise of Staton's book, *Don't Divorce the Holy Spirit* (see **pp. 9-10**). Boles comes very close to saying this: "Man is the product of the Holy Spirit; the nature of the human soul comes from the nature of the Godhead" (**41**). Walvoord quotes, approvingly, from John Owen's *Discourse Concerning the Holy Spirit*: "'Into this formed dust, "God breathed the breath of life"; . . . a vital immortal spirit; something of himself; somewhat immediately of his own; not of any pre-created matter'" (**41**). The effect of such statements is to partially deify man.

Is there any basis, then, apart from **Genesis 1:26**, for discerning a role for the Holy Spirit in the creation of man? Is there anything about **Genesis 2:7** which points us in this direction? If so, it is not the word *n^e^shamah*, or the phrase "breath of life." The only other possibility is the reference in this verse to the *act* of breathing as the cause of the clay's coming to life: *"God . . . breathed into his nostrils."* This is the Hebrew verb *naphach*, which is not directly related to *ruach*. There is nothing special about it. It is used only about a dozen times in the OT, only two of which have the connotation of "breathe." The only reason for identifying "the LORD God" in **Genesis 2:7** specifically with the Holy Spirit is the fact that the act of creation is thus pictured as an act of *breathing*, and the word for "Spirit" also happens to mean "breath." This is a very slender thread of an argument.

Some infer that the Holy Spirit must be the agent of creation in **Genesis 2:7** simply because the Spirit is pictured elsewhere in the Bible as the giver of life, and **Genesis 2:7** speaks of the moment when life began in the first human being. Walvoord says, "The Holy Spirit is related to life as the Giver of life," as in regeneration. "The Holy Spirit probably imparts life to all creation, particularly to man" (**41**). Morris says of **Genesis 2:7**, "The term 'Spirit' (*ruach*) does not occur here, but it is surely implied. Life in man comes only from God's Spirit" (***Spirit*, 20**).

I have no objection to anyone's affirming that the Holy Spirit was the specific agent in the creation of man, especially in ***Genesis 2:7***, as long as this is recognized as an inference. The strongest basis for the inference is Genesis ***1:26***; the next strongest is the fact that the Spirit is indeed the giver of life (***Jn 6:63***); trailing at a distance is the imagery of breathing in ***Genesis 2:7***. Inferences based on the identification of "the *n^eshamah* of life" with "the Spirit of God" must be rejected; they lead only to the deification of man.

THE SPIRIT'S EQUIPPING WORK IN THE OLD TESTAMENT

From the NT perspective we can clearly distinguish between the Spirit's *equipping* work and His *saving* work, with the emphasis falling on the latter. But what of the OT era? Whether and to what extent the Spirit was performing any saving activity in this time are matters of dispute. No one questions, though, that He was very much involved in the life of the people of God, bestowing upon them special ministries and skills that enabled them to perform needed services for Israel as a whole. This section focuses on this equipping work.

The Spirit gave people special ministries and skills that enabled them to serve Israel as a whole.

Wood refers to this as "empowerment by the Spirit," and he distinguishes four categories of servants so empowered: judges, craftsmen, prophets, and civil administrators (**53-63**). In discussing these I will absorb the judges into the category of administrators.

PROPHETS

A prophet is literally a spokesman, someone who speaks on behalf of someone else. In this sense Aaron was Moses' prophet (***Ex 7:1***). A prophet of God is thus someone who delivers inspired messages from God, whether orally or in writing. Since such inspiration is the work of the Holy Spirit, all true prophets are thus empowered by the Spirit, whether the Spirit's role is specifically mentioned or not.

The presence of such prophets among the people of Israel is mentioned in a general way in a prayer of confession and praise in

Nehemiah 9:30, where God is praised for bearing with His rebellious people during the wilderness wanderings and the era of judges and kings: *"However, You bore with them for many years, and admonished them by Your Spirit through Your prophets"* (see ***v. 20***; see ***Num 12:6***). Even in pre-Israelite times, specific individuals are identified as prophets or described as speaking messages from God. ***Jude 14*** says that *"Enoch, in the seventh generation from Adam, prophesied."* God identifies Abraham as a prophet (***Gen 20:7***). Joseph was empowered by God to interpret dreams (***Gen 41:16,38***). Aaron was a prophet once removed, so to speak (***Ex 7:1***); and Miriam is called a prophetess (***Ex 15:20***). Since true prophesying was due to empowerment by the Spirit, even a pagan could be used as a prophet. Such was the case with Balaam, when *"the Spirit of God came upon him"* (***Num 24:2***) and caused him to speak a blessing upon Israel.

Since prophesying was due to empowerment by the Spirit, even a pagan could be used as a prophet.

In the era of the judges and kings other specific individuals are named as prophetesses or prophets, e.g., Deborah (***Jdg 4:4***), Nathan (***2Sa 7:2***), Gad (***2Sa 24:11***), and Huldah (***2Kgs 22:14***). The equipping role of the Holy Spirit is specifically mentioned in the case of the prophet Azariah: *"Now the Spirit of God came on Azariah the son of Oded,"* and he delivered a prophetic message to King Asa (***2Chr 15:1-8***). Similar statements are made about Jahaziel (***2Chr 20:14***) and Zechariah the son of Jehoiada (***2Chr 24:20***). Since most of these men and women are not given prominent roles in the history of God's people, it is likely that they prophesied only occasionally, as the need arose. They were perhaps similar to many who had the gift of prophecy in the early church. Wood believes they were filled with the Spirit only intermittently or temporarily (**43-44**); Walvoord concludes that their prophetic utterances dealt largely with contemporary problems (**48**). This is why they wrote no books of the Bible for use by future generations, i.e., they were "nonliterary" prophets.

A few other nonliterary prophets seem to have had more prominent roles within Israel, serving as God's spokesmen on a more ongoing basis. An example is Samuel, who "was confirmed as a prophet of the LORD" (***1Sa 3:20***). Also in this category are Elijah and Elisha. The account of the prophetic succession (from Elijah to Elisha) in ***2 Kings 2:9-16*** is sometimes taken as confirmation that the Holy Spirit was upon each (see ***vv. 9,15-16***).

Other prophets of Israel were empowered by the Spirit in a somewhat different manner. Wood says their filling with the Spirit was continuous rather than temporary (**44-47**). Whether this is the case or not, their distinction was that they were enabled not only to speak prophetic words but also to put their inspired messages into written form to be used by future generations. These are called the "literary" prophets. That they were Spirit-empowered is true of all writers of the books of the OT, though not all are specifically said to be under the influence of the Spirit. Those who are so named are Moses (***Num 11:17***; see ***Num 12:7-8***), Joshua (***Deu 34:9***), David (***2Sa 23:2***; see ***1Sa 16:13***; ***Ps 51:11***), Isaiah (***Isa 59:21***), Micah (***Mic 3:8***), Ezekiel (***Eze 2:2***; ***37:1***; ***43:5***), and Daniel (***Dan 2:19***; ***4:8***; ***5:11-14***; ***6:3***).

While the main point of prophecy was the content of the message delivered thereby, in certain OT contexts the gift of prophecy involved some very unusual physical activity. In such cases it seems that the *form* of the prophesying was more important than its content. Such activity occurred in relation to certain groups of prophets (see ***1Kgs 18:4***; ***2Kgs 2:3,5,15***), sometimes called "schools" for prophets. In ***1 Samuel 10:5-6*** the prophet Samuel directed the newly anointed Saul to find such a group and prophesy with them:

> *Afterward you will come to the hill of God,* [and] *you will meet a group of prophets coming down from the high place with harp, tambourine, flute, and a lyre before them, and they will be prophesying. Then the Spirit of the* L*ORD* *will come upon you mightily, and you shall prophesy with them and be changed into another man.*

It happened exactly as Samuel had foretold:

> *Then it happened when he turned his back to leave Samuel, God changed his heart; and all those signs came about on that day. When they came to the hill there, behold, a group of prophets met him; and the Spirit of God came upon him mightily, so that he prophesied among them.* (***1Sa 10:9-10***)

Because of this one event, it was rumored that Saul was now a prophet:

> *It came about, when all who knew him previously saw that he prophesied now with the prophets, that the people said to one*

> *another, "What has happened to the son of Kish? Is Saul also among the prophets?"* (**1Sa 10:11**)

Toward the end of his reign Saul, pursuing David, heard that the latter was staying with Samuel; and he sent his men to capture David. But when these men

> *saw the company of the prophets prophesying, with Samuel standing and presiding over them, the Spirit of God came upon the messengers of Saul; and they also prophesied. When it was told Saul, he sent other messengers, and they also prophesied. So Saul sent messengers again the third time, and they also prophesied.* (**1Sa 19:20-21**)

Saul then decided to do the job himself. But when he reached the area,

> *the Spirit of God came upon him also, so that he went along prophesying continually until he came to Naioth in Ramah. He also stripped off his clothes, and he too prophesied before Samuel and lay down naked all that day and all that night. Therefore they say, "Is Saul also among the prophets?"* (**1Sa 19:23-24**)

How can we explain this type of prophesying, and Saul's participation in it? There is no doubt that what he did was very unusual for him, but apparently it was not unusual for prophets to do it. What exactly were they doing? Whatever it was, it was the result of the Spirit of God coming upon them (**1Sa 10:6,10**; **19:20,23**). Some say the resulting display was in the category of "supernatural manifestations" (**Walvoord, 47**). These are usually described with the term "ecstasy," a word that literally means "standing outside of oneself," i.e., having one's spirit or mind displaced by another power with the result that one's body is under the control of that alien power. As Moody describes Saul's experience, "the ecstatic *ruach* of the Lord . . . displaced the normal ego" (**16**). "It was a state of wild, ecstatic possession," says Heron (**13**). Morris describes it as a "prophetic frenzy" (***Spirit*, 24**).

Whatever the prophets were doing, it was the result of the Spirit of God coming upon them.

In his book on *The Holy Spirit in the Old Testament,* Leon Wood goes to great lengths to deny this interpretation of this kind of prophesying (**90-125**). In his mind such "ecstaticism" is too much like pagan practices to be attributed to the Spirit of God. The only "prophesying" these schools of prophets were doing was singing praises to God, accompanied by their instruments (**111**). When Saul prophesied with them, "the thought would be that he simply joined in singing with them" (**112**). In ***1 Samuel 19***, when Saul followed his three groups of messengers in search of David, he found them all singing along with the prophets, "enjoying the songfest," forming "quite a choir" (**ibid.**). This was significant in Saul's case because it was "behavior that was so different from what was customary for him" (**94**). Saul's "stupor" in ***1 Samuel 19:24*** is explained as a case of "extreme melancholy and despair" (**116**).

In my judgment Wood's explanation of this particular kind of prophetic phenomenon is highly implausible, if not absurd. Whatever these prophets, and Saul, were doing must have been supernatural to say the least. Even if it were something of an ecstatic nature, which it probably was, this is no sign of a pagan origin or association. The Holy Spirit caused similar activity in the apostolic era by causing some to speak in tongues. Such activity served as an unmistakable sign of the Spirit's presence, which in Saul's case was the main point (***1Sa 10:7,9***). Because of their supernatural (indeed, miraculous) nature, these phenomena functioned as signs. We will address this point again when we discuss the anointing of the 70 elders in ***Numbers 11***, an event that is quite parallel to the Pentecostal event of ***Acts 2***.

CRAFTSMEN

A second category of the Holy Spirit's equipping work in OT times is His bestowing of physical skills of craftsmanship and artisanship upon those who built the tabernacle, Israel's first center of worship. Part of the law God revealed to Moses was composed of detailed instructions as to how the tabernacle and all its furnishings should be built. (See ***Ex 31:7-11*** for a summary of the items that had to be constructed.) Because the tabernacle was the focus of Israel's religious life and because it was in a real sense God's own dwelling place among His people (***Ex 40:34-38***), it was important that it be built with the highest measure of quality. As Morris says, "The tabernacle was to be a place made to the divine plan. It was to be worthy of worship of so great a God" (***Spirit***, **23**).

In order for it to be built according to God's specifications, "the construction of the tabernacle required capable workmen, skilful carpenters, goldsmiths, and silversmiths, and masters in the arts of weaving and embroidering. Who will furnish Moses with them? The Holy Spirit" (**Kuyper, 38**). The Spirit bestowed upon certain Israelites skills in the "mechanical arts" (**ibid., 39**) or the ability to work with their hands. This included the abilities necessary to make the garments to be worn by the priests as they carried out their tabernacle duties (***Ex 28:3***).

The Spirit gave certain Israelites skills in the mechanical arts.

God gave to Moses the names of the two men whom He Himself had selected to be the foreman and assistant foreman for the project, namely, Bezalel and Oholiab. Since they were in charge of every phase of the work, the Spirit gave to them the knowledge and skills that would make them experts in all of the necessary forms of craftsmanship. In addition to these men, God said that He was giving specific skills to others for the accomplishment of this task. Here is how God announced His plan to Moses in ***Exodus 31:1-6***:

> *Now the LORD spoke to Moses, saying, "See, I have called by name Bezalel, the Son of Uri, the son of Hur, of the tribe of Judah. I have filled him with the Spirit of God in wisdom, in understanding, in knowledge, and in all kinds of craftsmanship, to make artistic designs for work in gold, in silver, and in bronze, and in the cutting of stones for settings, and in the carving of wood, that he may work in all kinds of craftsmanship. And behold, I Myself have appointed with him Oholiab, the son of Ahisamach, of the tribe of Dan; and in the hearts of all who are skillful I have put skill, that they may make all that I have commanded you."*

Three things may be noted about this plan. First, the role of the Holy Spirit is specifically mentioned regarding Bezalel: *"I have filled him with the Spirit of God"* (***v. 3***). By implication we may assume that the Spirit's equipping presence was with the other workers also. Second, the skills with which these people were equipped were not supernatural in themselves. The *source* of their skills was in one sense supernatural, but the various types of artisanship were quite ordinary. Third, it seems from ***verse 6*** that in many cases God was using those who had providential skills already present, and was supernaturally enhancing those skills for application to His work. As God said, *"In the hearts of all who are skillful I have put skill."* See ***Exodus 36:1,3***.

Here is how Moses reported God's plan to the people in ***Exodus 35:30–36:2***:

> *Then Moses said to the sons of Israel, "See, the LORD has called by name Bezalel the son of Uri, the son of Hur, of the tribe of Judah. And He has filled him with the Spirit of God, in wisdom, in understanding and in knowledge and in all craftsmanship; to make designs for working in gold and in silver and in bronze, and in the cutting of stones for settings and in the carving of wood, so as to perform in every inventive work. He also has put in his heart to teach, both he and Oholiab, the son of Ahisamach, of the tribe of Dan. He has filled them with skill to perform every work of an engraver and of a designer and of an embroiderer, in blue and in purple and in scarlet material, and in fine linen, and of a weaver, as performers of every work and makers of designs. Now Bezalel and Oholiab, and every skillful person in whom the LORD has put skill and understanding to know how to perform all the work in the construction of the sanctuary, shall perform in accordance with all that the LORD has commanded."*

One important point is added here in ***35:34***, namely, that the Spirit was equipping Bezalel and Oholiab not only with expertise and dexterity to actually work with gold and cloth and wood, but also with the ability to *teach* others how to do the same.

Following the NIV translation of ***1 Chronicles 28:11-12***, many think that the Holy Spirit gave King David similar knowledge and skills for the planning of the tabernacle's successor, namely, the temple. This passage (in the NIV) reads thus:

> *Then David gave his son Solomon the plans for the portico of the temple, its buildings, its storerooms, its upper parts, its inner rooms and the place of atonement. He gave him the plans of all that the Spirit had put in his mind for the courts of the temple of the LORD and all the surrounding rooms, for the treasuries of the temple of God and for the treasuries for the dedicated things.*

We can certainly see how the Spirit would have been involved in the building of the temple.

Given the Spirit's extensive involvement in equipping the workers who built the tabernacle, we can certainly see how He would have at least this much participation in the building of the temple.[4]

[4]The suggestion that the Holy Spirit endowed the pagan Hiram with skills for building the temple, based on ***1 Kgs 7:13-14*** (Wood, 42, 56) is an unlikely inference. His skills were probably providential in origin.

When we later come to examine the NT teaching on spiritual gifts, we will need to remember the Spirit's empowerment of these craftsmen to build the tabernacle. This is especially true in view of the nature of OT typology, where physical objects and events stand in prophetic anticipation of their spiritual counterparts under the New Covenant. According to this principle the tabernacle and the temple are forerunners of the NT church, which is *"a spiritual house for a holy priesthood"* (***1Pet 2:5***) and *"a dwelling of God in the Spirit"* (***Eph 2:22***). The spiritual gifts God gives to Christians today serve the same purpose of the gifts of craftsmanship in the OT, namely, to build up the house of God.

Spiritual gifts given to Christians today serve the same purpose as gifts of craftsmanship in the OT.

Also, the stated manner of the bestowing of these OT gifts may help us resolve a question often asked about spiritual gifts in this age, namely, are they entirely new abilities, or are they an enhancement of already-present talents? As we saw, Bezalel and Oholiab may have received new abilities, but those who actually worked on the tabernacle were skillful people whose skills the Spirit enhanced, sharpened, and intensified.

Administrators

The third category of those equipped by the Spirit in the OT may be grouped under the heading of administrators, or civil administrators as Wood calls them (**49, 59**). As Kuyper puts it, the Holy Spirit qualified various men for "official functions" by bestowing upon them "military genius, legal acumen, statesmanship, and power to inspire the masses with enthusiasm" (**38-39**). Moses may be mentioned as the first of these. In addition to being a prophet, he was endowed by the Spirit with wisdom and power for his forty-year role of leadership for the Israelites. ***Numbers 11:25*** speaks of *"the Spirit who was upon him"* for this purpose (see ***11:17***). ***Isaiah 63:10-12*** speaks of the way the Holy Spirit used Moses in leading the people.

Moses' successor, Joshua, was likewise *"filled with the spirit of wisdom, for Moses had laid his hands on him"* (***Deu 34:9***). "Spirit" should probably be capitalized here, especially in view of ***Numbers 27:18***, which speaks of *"Joshua the son of Nun, a man in whom is the Spirit."*

Those who later served as judges of the people were also empowered by the Spirit. Concerning Othniel, ***Judges 3:10*** says that *"the Spirit of the LORD came upon him, and he judged Israel."* The same is said of Gideon (***Jdg 6:34***) and Jephthah (***Jdg 11:29***). The role of the Holy Spirit is noted several times in connection with Samson's illustrious career as a judge. Even in his youth *"the Spirit of the LORD began to stir him"* (***Jdg 13:25***). He was especially endowed by the Spirit with great physical strength (***Jdg 14:6,19***; ***15:14***).

Morris says this of the Spirit's role in the liberating work of the judges:

> The whole narrative makes it clear that the judges did not accomplish their great deeds of deliverance because of any natural strength, leadership, or wisdom that they possessed. Each is God's chosen man for the particular hour. God has given him the gifts he needs to carry out the work of deliverance. In other words he is a judge only because God has put His Spirit within him. (**Spirit, 23-24**)

As Wood notes, in each case the Spirit empowered these men for physical and military action. "None of them had to do with salvation from sin in any sense" (**41, 53-55**).

Of all the kings of Israel and Judah, the Holy Spirit's administrative empowerment is specifically mentioned only for the first two, Saul and David—the latter, like Moses, being also gifted as a prophet. Saul's temporary Spirit-induced experiences as a prophet have already been noted (***1Sa 10:6,10***; ***19:23***). Before he was confirmed as king, *"the Spirit of God came upon Saul mightily"* (***1Sa 11:6***) as He had earlier come upon the judges. When God rejected him as king, *"the Spirit of the LORD departed from Saul"* (***1Sa 16:14***). When Samuel anointed the shepherd David to be Saul's successor, *"the Spirit of the LORD came mightily upon David from that day forward"* (***1Sa 16:13***). After his sin with Bathsheba, knowing what had happened to Saul, he prayed to God sincerely, *"Do not take Your Holy Spirit from me"* (***Ps 51:11***). As Wood sums up the Spirit's presence upon them, "Both Saul and David . . . needed special empowerment. Neither was sufficient in himself for his God-given task. Accordingly, God sent His Spirit on both" (**62**).

An episode that requires special attention is the occasion when 70 elders from the people of Israel were chosen to assist Moses in his overwhelming responsibility of ministering to the needs of the wandering nation. When Moses complained to God that he needed some administrative help (***Num 11:10-15***), God answered his prayer thus (***11:16-17***):

> *The* Lord *therefore said to Moses, "Gather for Me seventy men from the elders of Israel, whom you know to be the elders of the people and their officers and bring them to the tent of meeting, and let them take their stand there with you. Then I will come down and speak with you there, and I will take of the Spirit who is upon you, and will put Him upon them; and they shall bear the burden of the people with you, so that you will not bear it all alone."*

After further instruction,

> *Moses went out and told the people the words of the* Lord. *Also, he gathered seventy men of the elders of the people, and stationed them around the tent. Then the Lord came down in the cloud and spoke to him; and He took of the Spirit who was upon him and placed Him upon the seventy elders. And when the Spirit rested upon them, they prophesied. But they did not do it again.* (***11:24-25***)

Actually only 68 men showed up for the induction ceremony; two men, Eldad and Medad, were late and were still in the camp among the people when the Spirit came upon them. *"And the Spirit rested upon them (now they were among those who had been registered, but had not gone out to the tent), and they prophesied in the camp. So a young man ran and told Moses and said, 'Eldad and Medad are prophesying in the camp'"* (***11:26-27***). When Joshua advised Moses to restrain them, Moses replied, *"Are you jealous for my sake? Would that all the* Lord's *people were prophets, that the* Lord *would put His Spirit upon them!"* (***11:28-29***).

We must carefully note that two distinct works of the Spirit were performed on these 70 men at this time. One was a permanent empowerment for leadership comparable to the gift of leadership given to Moses. This is the point of God's words, *"I will take of the Spirit who is upon you [Moses], and will put Him upon them; and they shall bear the burden of the people with you"* (***11:17***). This was not a miraculous empowerment, but more of a gift of wisdom.

The other work of the Spirit upon these 70 men was the one-time gift of prophesying, which occurred at the moment the Spirit was placed upon them for the former purpose. That is, in addition to giving them the permanent gift of leadership, the Spirit gave them the temporary gift of prophesying (***11:25***).

It is important to see that the latter *was* a temporary gift. ***Verse 25*** specifically says, *"But they did not do it again."* The problem here is that the KJV says the very opposite: *"They prophesied, and did not cease."* How is this to be explained? It is generally agreed today that the KJV at this point was following a faulty manuscript reading, one that is mostly rejected today. Even the NKJV says, *"They never did so again."*

We must ask two questions about this one-time gift of prophesying: what was its nature, and what was its purpose? Regarding the former question, the issue is whether the prophesying was miraculous or not. Seeking to avoid any semblance to pagan ecstatic experiences, Wood insists that it was completely nonmiraculous. The prophesying of these 70 men, he says, was the same as that of Saul in ***1 Samuel 10 and 19***, which Wood concludes was no more than singing praises to God. Likewise, these men were just praising God with great emotion. "This praising activity likely was in the form of singing one or more songs of praise." That Eldad and Medad "continued on in the activity is not strange. They probably enjoyed singing and were perhaps given to more exuberance in their joy than the others. They apparently wanted all the camp to know of their joy and so moved through the camp letting the fact be known" (**109, 111**).

Just as in the case of Saul's experiences with the school of prophets, I find Wood's explanation here to be completely unacceptable to the point of superficiality. Though we are not told what the exact nature of this prophesying was, it is clear that it was much more than enthusiastic praise. I conclude that it was indeed a form of miraculous, ecstatic speaking based on the following reasons. First, *"they did not do it again,"* meaning, what they did was so special that it was a *unique* occurrence. This surely would not apply to ordinary praise to God.

Second, ***verses 25-26*** and ***verse 29*** show that the prophesying was an involuntary act directly caused by the Holy Spirit, something the men were *enabled* to do by the Spirit. They did not simply make a *decision* to do what they did because they now knew that the Spirit had been given to them. That is to say, it was not just their voluntary response of thanksgiving. The experience of Eldad and Medad makes this clear. Wood's explanation implies that these two men were present at the tabernacle with the other 68 when the Spirit came upon them, and that they were so happy about it that they continued to praise God longer than the others, even when they returned to the campground. This misses the point entirely. Eldad and Medad, delayed for some reason, never made it to the tabernacle; the Spirit rested on them and they prophesied before they ever got to the meeting place (*v. 26*). In this case, if the prophesying were mere praise—a song of thanksgiving for the Spirit's being given to them—how would they have known when to begin their singing? Under such circumstances it could not have been just voluntary, natural praise; it must have been directly *caused* by the Spirit's presence.

Third, that this prophesying activity caused by the Spirit was a supernatural manifestation is seen from the young man's response to it (*v. 27*). His response hardly makes sense if Eldad's and Medad's prophesying was just ordinary praise, however emotional it may have been. To this lad it was so unusual and abnormal that he considered it necessary to report it to Moses.

Prophesying activity was a supernatural manifestation.

The fourth reason for understanding this prophesying as miraculous leads us into the other question about it, namely, what was its *purpose*? Since the Holy Spirit Himself did cause the 70 to prophesy, there must have been a reason for it. This reason is easily discernable if the prophesying was indeed miraculous, namely, it served the purpose of any miracle: it was a sign confirming to the people that the Spirit had bestowed a leadership role upon these 70 men, and that the people must now accept them in this role. It was providential and not accidental, I believe, that Eldad and Medad were still in the camp when this sign was manifested, so that it could be witnessed by the people.

Keil and Delitzsch have it exactly right, I believe, when they say that the transfer of the Spirit from Moses to the 70 elders "must have been effected in such a way, that Moses and the elders received a convincing proof of the reality of the affair. When the Spirit descended upon the elders, *'they prophesied, and did not add;' i.e.* they did not repeat the prophesyings any further." These authors opine that the prophesying here refers to

> . . . speaking in an ecstatic and elevated state of mind, under the impulse and inspiration of the Spirit of God, just like the "speaking with tongues," which frequently followed the gift of the Holy Ghost in the days of the apostles. But we are not to infer from the fact, that the prophesying was not repeated,

> that the Spirit therefore departed from them after this one extraordinary manifestation. This miraculous manifestation of the Spirit was intended simply to give to the whole nation the visible proof that God had endowed them with His Spirit, as helpers of Moses, and had given them the authority required for the exercise of their calling. (**70-71**)

As Keil and Delitzsch suggest, what happened here in ***Numbers 11*** is almost exactly parallel to the Pentecost event of ***Acts 2***. There, as here, two separate and distinct workings of the Holy Spirit took place, one temporary and one permanent. The temporary one—the miraculous tongue-speaking—was temporary because its purpose was to function as a one-time *sign* that from this moment on the permanent gift of the Spirit's indwelling presence was now available to the church. This will be discussed in more detail in chapter 5.

DID THE SPIRIT WORK REDEMPTIVELY IN THE OLD TESTAMENT?

We have accepted the common distinction between the equipping and the saving works of the Holy Spirit, and we have seen that the former was definitely present throughout the history of Israel in the OT era. But what about the Spirit's saving work? Was the Holy Spirit active in the salvation of individuals in pre-Christian times? What does the Bible say?

First, here are some points that cannot be disputed (both of which will be discussed in detail later). One, the Holy Spirit's saving work consists of regeneration and sanctification. As we shall see later, salvation as such has two main aspects: (a) justification or forgiveness, which is an objective or legal pronouncement by God based upon the atoning blood of Jesus Christ; and (b) regeneration and sanctification, which are subjective or inward changes in the sinner's nature accomplished by the Holy Spirit. If the Holy Spirit was directly involved in the salvation of sinners in the OT era, this is what He was doing. Two, the OT prophesies and John the Baptist and Jesus both promise, that the Holy Spirit would begin to perform a new kind of work in the New Covenant era, with ***John 7:37-***

The Holy Spirit's saving work consists of regeneration and sanctification.

39 specifying that it would not happen until after Christ's ascension. In the light of ***Acts 1 and 2***, it seems apparent that this new work began on the day of Pentecost.

Second, these two facts present us with a seeming dilemma. If we affirm that the Holy Spirit was performing His saving work in OT times, then what is the nature of His *new* work from Pentecost onward? But if we deny that the Holy Spirit was performing His saving work before this, then we are declaring that it must be possible for sinners to be saved without being regenerated and sanctified. But how can this be? Did not Jesus say, *"You must be born again"* (***Jn 3:7***)? Did He not say, *"Unless one is born of water and the Spirit he cannot enter into the kingdom of God"* (***Jn 3:5***)? And how can one be born again without the Spirit?

Affirming the Spirit's Old Testament Saving Work

This latter aspect of the dilemma has led many to affirm without hesitation that the Holy Spirit was performing His regenerating and sanctifying work on (some) sinners in the OT. Some believe that the OT specifically teaches this in a few places. Under the heading of the Holy Spirit as "the agent for man's restoration and redemption," Boatman says that ***Genesis 6:3*** "informs us that God's Spirit serves as an agent for men's restoration" (**46**). In this text God simply says, *"My Spirit shall not strive with man forever."* Carter says this is "a clear indication of the Spirit's efforts to bring alienated and wayward humanity back to the living relationship with God enjoyed before the Fall" (**45**).

Others see an act of salvation in ***1 Samuel 10:6***, where Samuel promises Saul that when the Spirit comes upon him he will *"be changed into another man."* Then when Saul left Samuel's presence, *"God changed his heart"* (***v. 9***). Carter cites this passage likewise as an occasion of "the Spirit's re-creative function exemplified in man" (**45**).

The OT text most commonly cited as proof of the Spirit's saving work in that era is ***Psalm 51***, David's prayer of repentance after the Bathsheba incident. He prays that God will change him within and will not take the Holy Spirit from him: *"Create in me a clean heart, O God, and renew a steadfast spirit within me. Do not cast me away from Your presence and do not take Your Holy Spirit from me"* (***vv. 10-11***). This Psalm, especially in these verses, "focuses on the redemptive aspect of

God's holy Spirit," says Boatman (**46**). Carter says, "David is well aware that his only hope of restoration is through the operation of the Holy Spirit. . . . Without the Spirit this could never be accomplished. This is the re-creative work of the Spirit" (**45**). "Should He be withdrawn, all hope of salvation would disappear" (**ibid., 72**). Lehman says of ***Psalm 51***, "Here, for the first time in Scripture, the Holy Spirit was viewed as the agent of spiritual cleansing" (**23**).

Even if these texts do teach that the Spirit's saving work was present in OT times, one might be concerned that there are so few references to such an important subject. The fact is, however, that even these texts most likely are *not* talking about saving activity. The most that can be said of the Spirit's work in ***Genesis 6:3*** is that He was possibly working indirectly to evoke repentance through the preaching of Noah. This is not the same as the direct saving works of regeneration and sanctification. Most likely, though, it means simply that the Spirit was acting to restrain sin (see ***2Th 2:6-7***), which is quite different from saving activity as such.

There is no basis for saying that ***1 Samuel 10:6,9*** refers to a moral change in Saul's internal character. This same kind of language is used elsewhere in the OT for external empowering (see ***1Kgs 3:9,12; 10:24***). At times God exercised a limited control over men's hearts, even those of unbelievers (see ***Ex 4:21; Deu 2:30; Ezra 6:22; Prov 21:1***).

But what about ***Psalm 51:11***? Surely, if any OT text refers to the saving work of the Spirit, this one does. But does it? The fact is that it does not! In his roles as psalmist and king, David knew that he had received the *empowering* presence of the Spirit (***2Sa 23:2; 1Sa 16:13***). He knew that shortly after the Spirit had come upon him when he was anointed for kingship, *"The Spirit of the LORD departed from Saul"* (***1Sa 16:14***). Knowing this, in ***Psalm 51:11*** he prays that God would not do the same thing to him, i.e., he prays that God would not withdraw the empowering Spirit from him, thus effectively ending his service to God. His prayer for God not to withdraw His Spirit is distinct from his prayer for God to renew his heart.

Kuyper recognizes that this is David's point; his prayer "must . . . refer to gifts qualifying him for the kingly office" (**39**). Wood agrees that those who see personal salvation in ***Psalm 51:11*** are wrong: "David was not thinking of this; he simply did not want to lose the special Spirit-empowerment that had been his from the day of his anointing by Samuel. He had seen Saul lose his empowerment when the Holy Spirit had been taken from him—his manner of rule had rapidly deteriorated after that—and he did not want the same to happen to him" (**51**).

It is very interesting, though, to see that many of those who find no actual references to the Spirit's saving work in the OT nevertheless still affirm that the Spirit was regenerating (some) sinners in pre-Christian times anyway. Wood, for example, says that every alleged reference to such work involves "empowerment for a task"; none is "found to involve spiritual renewal" (**53**). Why does Wood conclude that the main texts usually cited as involving saving activity—***1 Samuel 10:6,9*** and ***Psalm 51:11***—cannot refer to salvation? Because both passages teach that the Spirit may *depart* from someone after coming upon him. This is specifically stated of Saul (***1Sa 16:14***) and is implied by David's prayer (***Ps 51:11***). Now, if salvation were the purpose of the Spirit's presence in these cases, "this . . . might imply . . . that the Old Testament person could be saved and then lost, depending on whether the Holy Spirit was on him or not." But such a conclusion, says Wood, "would not square with the biblical truth of the security of the believer. Surely Old Testament believers enjoyed eternal security, as well as believers in the New Testament time" (**12**).

Eternal security, of course, is the same as "once saved, always saved." Since Woods is committed to the "once saved, always saved" doctrine, he realizes that he cannot consistently use these crucial texts to support a saving activity of the Spirit in OT times. Thus he comes to the right conclusion—that the OT does *not* specifically affirm that the Spirit was working redemptively in that era, but for the wrong reason. Even if one denies eternal security (as I do), he should still acknowledge that the relevant texts are about empowerment, not salvation.

But here is the main point: Wood and others committed to an Augustinian doctrine of original sin affirm nevertheless that the Holy Spirit *was* working redemptively in the OT, even though it is not specifically so mentioned. Spiritual renewal, or regeneration, was being experienced, even if "not declared in writing" (**64-65, 68**). How do we know this? Because many people in the OT era were saved. And since everyone is born a sinner, no one can live as a saved person unless the Holy Spirit regenerates him. Thus the affirmation of the

Spirit's saving activity in the OT is required by the doctrine of original sin (**65-66, 70, 146**).

Kuyper says the same thing, even more strongly: "In the ages before Christ God's elect shared the blessings of the work of re-creation," i.e., the "regenerating and sanctifying" of the Holy Spirit" (**51-52**). How do we know this? Because "believing Israelites were saved. Hence they must have received saving grace. And since saving grace is out of the question without an inward working of the Holy Spirit, it follows that He was the Worker of faith in Abraham as well as in ourselves" (**119**). Anyone who believes in total depravity would have to agree.

So what is *new* about the working of the Spirit in the NT age? Only the baptism of the Holy Spirit, which is not the same as regeneration and is not necessary for individual salvation. Rather, it is a means of unifying all Christians into one body. Its purpose and result are church unity (**Wood, 74-76**). This unifying effect of Holy Spirit baptism from Pentecost onward was earlier taught by Kuyper (**123-126**).

If one asks why there is so much OT teaching on the Spirit's empowerment for service and none at all about this alleged OT saving work of the Spirit, Wood's puzzling reply is this: "God evidently saw more important that man recognize the secret of successful service than the secret of a right spiritual relationship to Himself" (**81**).

Denying a Saving Work of the Spirit in the Old Testament

I have shown above that the only OT texts that allegedly teach a saving work of the Spirit in OT times do not actually support the idea. Thus if one affirms it, he must *infer* it from some other doctrine. This is exactly what Wood and others are doing, i.e., they are inferring a saving work of the Spirit in the OT from their understanding of the nature of salvation. They state that salvation is impossible without the regenerating and sanctifying work of the Spirit, and since many in the OT were undoubtedly saved, the Holy Spirit must have regenerated and sanctified them.

I find this argument to be challenging, but not convincing. As an argument it is simply not strong enough to negate the force of the Bible's teaching about the newness of the Spirit's working in the NT age. All the evidence supports the conclusion that regeneration and sanctification *are* this new work of the Spirit. And since His new work did not begin until Pentecost, we must conclude that the Holy Spirit was not regenerating and sanctifying sinners before then. This is certainly consistent with the absence of any teaching about such a work of the Spirit in the OT. Certainly if it were happening, what could have been more important (*contra* Wood) than explaining this to God's people?

Regeneration and sanctification are the new work of the Spirit.

Pache argues that the Spirit's regenerating work in man's heart could not be accomplished until Christ's atoning work was done. "Christ having not yet died and been raised for sinners, the Spirit could not raise them up with Him." If the Spirit "now lives within us, it is because of the blood of the Lamb which cleanses us from all our sins. But the atonement was not yet accomplished for believers under the Old Covenant" (31). This is faulty reasoning, though, because God was already applying the blood of Christ to people's lives in OT times as the basis for their forgiveness. OT saints were truly forgiven. Thus this cannot be the reason why the Spirit was not working redemptively in the OT.

The bottom line seems to be simply that God was saving this blessing of the Spirit for the messianic age, as part of the larger package of blessings to be bestowed upon those who know Jesus personally. This will be discussed in more detail in chapter five. Candlish (17) sums up the main point thus, that from the OT perspective,

> . . . the general bestowal of the spirit as the source of holiness is spoken of as a thing of the future, one of the blessings of the promised reign of God over His people. In the theocracy in Israel, the spirit of God had been given to certain chosen men as leaders and rulers of the nation, and doubtless wherever there was genuine godliness, that was due to the working of the spirit; but there is no indication that the mass of the nation, though the professed people of God, was filled with the spirit, in the sense in which the Christian Church after the Pentecostal gift was so.

This raises the question, though, as to *how* a person can be saved without the regenerating and sanctifying work of the Holy Spirit. The following are some thoughts on this issue. First, it seems to me that such working of the Holy Spirit would be absolutely necessary only if the doctrine of total depravity were true, which (as discussed earlier) is not the case. The original grace of Jesus Christ intercepts and nullifies any possible inheritance or imputation of original sin, including the total depravity usually associated therewith. Also, no Bible text rightly interpreted supports the idea of an *acquired* total depravity. Thus every person who is confronted by God's offer of salvation has a functioning free will which has the ability to choose to enter upon that path.

Second, the only thing absolutely necessary to be saved (i.e., to have the hope of going to heaven) is to be justified or forgiven. This is something that God does for us on the basis of Christ's atoning sacrifice, and He was doing this even in OT times in assured anticipation of the cross. For example, Abraham is the "poster child" for justification (see ***Rom 4:1-22***). So in this sense, yes, one can be saved without regeneration.

Third, the only absolute conditions for justification are faith and repentance. In NT times confession and baptism have been added as conditions (**Cottrell, *Faith*, chs. 19, 20**), but these are too intimately related to the person and work of Christ to have been meaningful in OT times. But OT sinners *could* believe and repent. There was no total depravity to preclude these decisions; and there *was* a power that could impel and stimulate them, namely, the power of God's Word. Of course, there is a unique power in the gospel of Christ to induce saving faith (***Rom 1:16***; ***10:17***), but the Word of God in any form *"is living and active and sharper than any two-edged sword"* (***Heb 4:12***). Surely the powerful messages of the OT prophets were intended and were able to lead one to faith and repentance and thus to a state of forgiveness. In this sense one can say that in OT times the Holy Spirit worked *indirectly* to bring sinners to salvation, even if He did not work a work of salvation directly upon their hearts. Also, He worked indirectly through the Word to provide motivation and instruction for holy living (see ***Psalm 119*** *passim*, especially ***vv. 97-105***). In this sense Candlish is right to say that "doubtless wherever there was genuine godliness, that was due to the working of the spirit" (**17**), even if that working was only indirect.

The only absolute conditions for justification before Christ are faith and repentance.

Fourth, we must grant that without the redemptive indwelling of the Spirit, living a holy life would be a great challenge even for someone like Moses or Jeremiah. This, I believe, is the main reason why God was so insistent that the nation of Israel should exist in its own land, in geographical and cultural isolation from the rest of the world. They did not have the heart-changing, indwelling Holy Spirit as a source of inward spiritual power. This may be why Moses' law had to take account of the Jews' "hardness of heart" (***Mt 19:8***). Christians, however, *do* have the sanctifying presence of the Spirit within, and thus can "go into all the world." We can say that in OT times God's plan was holiness through separation; in NT times it is separation through holiness.

Fifth, NT teaching makes it very clear that since Pentecost, regeneration and sanctification through the Holy Spirit *are* a part of the total salvation package. This is one of the new blessings of the messianic age, the kingdom age. In this era, at the same moment God forgives sins, the Holy Spirit also regenerates and begins His indwelling for the purpose of sanctification. Sinners cannot receive the one without the other. If one is justified, he is regenerated; if one is regenerated, he is justified. Regeneration is the same as the new birth. Thus Jesus can say to Nicodemus, in anticipation of the kingdom age that would begin on the day of Pentecost, that one must be born again; and unless one is born of water and the Spirit, he will not enter the kingdom of God (***Jn 3:3-7***). It is not proper to apply this condition for entering the kingdom to the OT, *pre-kingdom* era, though.

CONCLUSION

We may summarize the above discussion in a few succinct statements about the work of the Spirit in the OT age. One, the Holy Spirit was very active in the work of creation (***Gen 1:2***). Two, the Spirit was not working directly upon the hearts of any sinners in a saving way. Three, the main work of the Spirit in the lives of individuals was to equip or empower them for service. Four, even in terms of empowerment, the Spirit was not given to all Israelites, and not even to all saved Israelites. Five, the Spirit was given to various individuals not for their personal benefit but for the good of the whole body of Israel. Six, in some cases this empowerment was temporary and lasted only as long as the need for that person's service remained (cf. ***1Sa***

10:10 and ***16:14***; cf. ***1Sa 16:13*** and ***Ps 51:11***). Seven, at times, miraculous signs accompanied nonmiraculous gifts; but these were temporary (***Num 11:25***). Eight, a person did not have to be a believer to receive this empowering from the Spirit (***Num 24:2***; ***1Sa 19:20-24***). Nine, sometimes the Spirit came upon a person through human agency (***Deu 34:9*** [see ***Num 27:18-23***]; ***1Sa 16:13***) and sometimes without a human agent (***Num 11:25-26***).

CHAPTER FOUR

THE HOLY SPIRIT AND JESUS CHRIST

The subject of this chapter is the Holy Spirit and Jesus Christ. This does not include what Jesus *taught* about the Spirit; we are concentrating rather on the working of the Spirit in connection with His life and ministry. Our data come mostly from the Gospels; thus our focus moves from the OT to the NT Scriptures. This does not mean, however, that we are moving from the old-covenant to the new-covenant era. The covenantal transition does not happen technically until Christ's death on the cross, and does not happen functionally or practically until Pentecost. Thus the role of the Spirit in the life of Jesus still follows the pattern of His working as detailed in the previous chapter. As yet there is nothing qualitatively new.

Under this subject the most difficult issues have to do with Christology more than with the Holy Spirit. Here we are assuming the traditional understanding of Christ as having both a fully divine and a fully human nature. The eternal, divine Logos became incarnate as the human person Jesus of Nazareth. The Gospels are filled with inspired testimony to supernatural events surrounding the life of Jesus and supernatural acts performed by Jesus. It is easy to assume that the immediate cause of all these supernatural events was the divine nature of Jesus. Since He was truly God in the flesh, He certainly could heal the sick, raise the dead, walk on water, and order demons around.

When we read the Gospels carefully, however, we will see that the supernatural powers exercised by Jesus were derived largely, if not exclusively, from empowerment by the Holy Spirit. This in no way detracts from the glory and power of Jesus Christ or from the reality of His divine nature. It does, however, emphasize how important Jesus' *human* nature was to the accomplishment of His mission, and also how important the Holy Spirit's role was in the same. Specifically, what we shall see is that the Holy Spirit equipped and strengthened Jesus Christ in His *human* nature throughout His earthly ministry.

The Holy Spirit equipped and strengthened Jesus Christ in His human nature.

THE HOLY SPIRIT AND PREPARATION FOR THE MESSIAH

In a general sense the entire history of Israel was a preparation for the first coming of Jesus the Messiah. Thus all of the Spirit's works in relation to God's chosen people were helping to lead up to this event. Here we are looking at those works of the Spirit which *specifically* laid the groundwork for Christ's coming and ministry.

OLD TESTAMENT PROPHECY

The first way the Holy Spirit specifically prepared the way for Christ's coming was to reveal certain prophecies about His own role in the life of Jesus. Of course, the Holy Spirit is the divine author of *all* prophecies about Christ (***1Pet 1:10-12***; ***2Pet 1:19-21***). Here we are thinking only of those that specifically mention the Spirit's empowerment of Jesus. All are from the prophet Isaiah.

The first of these is ***Isaiah 11:1-2***:

> *Then a shoot will spring from the stem of Jesse, and a branch from his roots will bear fruit. The Spirit of the LORD will rest on Him, the*

spirit of wisdom and understanding, the spirit of counsel and strength, the spirit of knowledge and the fear of the LORD.

This text is not specifically quoted in the NT, but all agree that it points ahead to the Messiah. That *"the Spirit of the* LORD *will rest on Him"* is similar to John the Baptist's testimony that when the Spirit came upon Jesus at His baptism, *"He remained upon Him"* (***Jn 1:32-33***).

The next passage is ***Isaiah 42:1-4***,

> *Behold, My Servant, whom I uphold; My chosen one in whom My soul delights. I have put My Spirit upon Him; He will bring forth justice to the nations. He will not cry out or raise His voice, nor make His voice heard in the street. A bruised reed He will not break and a dimly burning wick He will not extinguish; He will faithfully bring forth justice. He will not be disheartened or crushed until He has established justice in the earth; and the coastlands will wait expectantly for His law.*

We know that this refers to Jesus because the apostle Matthew cites most of it and says that it was fulfilled in Jesus (***Mt 12:17-21***). Thus again it is prophesied that the Holy Spirit will be upon Him.

Another such prophecy is ***Isaiah 61:1-2***:

> *The Spirit of the Lord* GOD *is upon me, because the Lord has anointed me to bring good news to the afflicted; He has sent me to bind up the brokenhearted, to proclaim liberty to captives and freedom to prisoners; to proclaim the favorable year of the Lord and the day of vengeance of our God.*

Most of this prophecy is likewise cited in the NT and is said to be fulfilled in Jesus. Actually, it was Jesus Himself who declared that He is the one of whom Isaiah was speaking, when He read the passage aloud in a synagogue meeting and then said, *"Today this Scripture has been fulfilled in your hearing"* (***Lk 4:17-21***).[1]

The content of these texts will be looked at more closely below. The point here is simply that they have helped to prepare the way for the coming of a Spirit-filled Messiah.

PROPHETS ANNOUNCING THE INFANT REDEEMER'S PRESENCE

Very early in the life of Jesus God sent two nonliterary prophets to

[1] Some add ***Isa 48:16*** to this list (e.g., Lehman, 35), but it more likely refers to Isaiah himself.

announce that the Savior of Israel and of all the world had at last been sent to the earth. Their prophecies are given on the occasion of Jesus' presentation in the temple in Jerusalem, as recorded in ***Luke 2:22-38***. Every Israelite mother was designated unclean for 40 days following the birth of a son, after which an offering was to be brought to a priest at the temple (***Lev 12:1-8***). Also, every firstborn male Israelite had to be presented for redemption from Yahweh through the payment of a redemption price (***Ex 13:2,12; Num 18:15-16***). Mary and Joseph, with the infant Jesus in their arms, were fulfilling these requirements of the law when they were met by two prophets (***Lk 2:25-38***).

The first was Simeon, who is specifically said to be under the influence of the Spirit (***2:25-28***):

> *And there was a man in Jerusalem whose name was Simeon; and this man was righteous and devout, looking for the consolation of Israel; and the Holy Spirit was upon him. And it had been revealed to him by the Holy Spirit that he would not see death before he had seen the Lord's Christ. And he came in the Spirit into the temple; and when the parents brought in the child Jesus, to carry out for Him the custom of the Law, then he took Him into his arms, and blessed God.*

He proceeded then to give two brief Spirit-inspired prophecies about Jesus, which Luke records in ***verses 29-35***.

The second was a prophetess, Anna (***2:36-37***). She is not specifically said to be under the Spirit's influence, but we can infer that she was from the fact that she is called a prophetess and from the fact that she immediately knew the identity of this infant and declared Him to be the redeemer: *"At that very moment she came up and began giving thanks to God, and continued to speak of Him to all those who were looking for the redemption of Jerusalem"* (***2:38***).

John the Baptist

Whether the Spirit used Simeon and Anna beyond this one occasion we do not know. There was another prophet raised up by the Spirit, however, whose whole life was devoted to preparing for the coming of the Messiah. His name was John, known to us as John the Baptist. That the Spirit should have a large role in the life and ministry of John the Baptist is not surprising in view of just how special his mission was. Carter says, "It fell to him to prepare the way for Christ, to baptize Him, and introduce Him as the Savior of the world.

Furthermore, it was his mission to call Israel, in particular, to repentance and return to faith in God's promise of the coming Messiah, that Christ might be recognized and received by them at His advent" (**94**).

Luke tells us that John was fulfilling Isaiah's prophecy (***Isa 40:3-5***), that he was *"the voice of one crying in the wilderness, 'Make ready the way of the LORD, make His paths straight'"* (***Lk 3:4***). John was fully aware of his own mission, and cites the same prophecy to those who questioned him (***Jn 1:23***). Jesus confirms John's divinely determined purpose by declaring that he is the fulfillment of the prophecy in ***Malachi 3:1***: *"This is the one about whom it is written, 'Behold, I send My messenger ahead of You, who will prepare Your way before You'"* (***Mt 11:10***).

To empower him for such a crucial role, the Holy Spirit was active in John's life from beginning to end. Even before he was born, his parents were filled with the Spirit and were given the temporary gift of prophecy. His mother Elizabeth actually foreshadowed John's role of preparing for Jesus when she encountered the newly pregnant Mary and *"was filled with the Holy Spirit."* Through the Spirit's inspiration she knew that Mary was supernaturally pregnant, and she declared that the baby in Mary's womb was *her Lord*. Through the Spirit she uttered a prophetic blessing upon Mary (***Lk 1:41-45***).

After John was born his father Zacharias likewise *"was filled with the Holy Spirit, and prophesied"* (***Lk 1:67***). His prophecy praised the coming Messiah (***Lk 1:68-75***), and gave honor to his own son for his role of preparation: *"And you, child, will be called the prophet of the Most High; for you will go on before the LORD to prepare His ways; to give to His people the knowledge of salvation by the forgiveness of their sins"* (***Lk 1:76-77***).

Of John the Baptist himself, the angel of the Lord who foretold his birth to Zacharias declared, *"He will be filled with the Holy Spirit while yet in his mother's womb"* (***Lk 1:15***). The Spirit's presence within him is evidenced by the baby John's leaping in the womb for joy when Mary greeted Elizabeth (***Lk 1:41,44***). After his birth, *"the child continued to grow and to become strong in spirit"* (***Lk 1:80***). In my judgment "in spirit" should here be translated "in the Spirit." In any case his filling with the Spirit was continuous. The purpose for this filling was not John's moral and spiritual cleansing (*contra* **Carter, 95**), but his empowerment for his unique service of preparing the way for the Christ. This was similar to the Spirit's empowerment of OT prophets.

That John the Baptist was himself a prophet is specifically stated. The Spirit-filled Zacharias declared that his son would *"be called the prophet of the Most High"* (***Lk 1:76***). Speaking to the crowds about John, Jesus asked, *"But what did you go out to see? A prophet? Yes, I tell you, and one who is more than a prophet"* (***Mt 11:9***). He was the equivalent of the greatest OT nonliterary prophet, Elijah (***Mal 4:5-6; Mt 11:14***). Swete calls him "the last of the prophets of Israel" (**22**). In view of Jesus' testimony in ***Matthew 11:11***, He could have said John was "the last *and greatest* of the prophets of Israel."

As a prophet who was filled with the Spirit, John the Baptist's preaching was fully inspired. Things were revealed to him that he could not have known through his own resources (see, e.g., ***Jn 1:19-34***). As Swete says, "In the Baptist the prophetic Spirit uttered its last testimony to Him that was to come, completing the witness of the Old Testament at the moment when the Christ was ready to enter upon His work" (**ibid.**).

THE HOLY SPIRIT AND THE BIRTH OF JESUS

The incarnation—enfleshment—of the eternal, divine Logos as the man Jesus of Nazareth is one of the greatest and most mysterious of all of God's works. *How* the infinite being of God could enter into or become united with the finite human person of Jesus is simply beyond our understanding, and the Bible does not attempt to explain it. We are simply told, *"The Word [Logos] became flesh"* (***Jn 1:14***). The eternally preexisting Logos in a unique way entered into this spatial, material universe by becoming united with the newly conceived male infant miraculously formed in Mary's womb.

How the infinite God could become united with a finite human person is beyond our understanding.

Most agree that all three persons of the Trinity participated in some way in this wondrous event (e.g., **Kuyper, 80**). While this is no doubt true (see ***Heb 10:5***), the role of the Holy Spirit is what receives special emphasis in the Gospels. When Gabriel announced Jesus' birth to Mary, she asked, *"'How can this be, since I am a virgin?' And the angel answered and said to her, 'The Holy Spirit will come upon you,* *and the power of the Most High will overshadow you; and for that reason the holy Child shall be called the Son of God'"* (***Lk 1:34-35***). Thus it was that *"when His mother Mary had been betrothed to Joseph, before they came together she was found to be with child by the Holy Spirit"* (***Mt 1:18***). An angel explained to Joseph what was happening, saying, *"Joseph, son of David, do not be afraid to take Mary as your wife; for the Child who has been conceived in her is of the Holy Spirit"* (***Mt 1:20***).

Thus as Palmer says, "although the incarnation was an act of all three Persons of the Godhead, yet it was especially the work of the Holy Spirit. He, and not the Father nor the Son, was the efficient cause by which Mary was found with child" (**65**).

The Holy Spirit Was the Agent of Jesus' Conception

Though we usually speak of the "virgin birth" of Jesus, it was more precisely a virgin *conception*.[2] The miraculous[3] or supernatural aspect of Jesus' origin was not His birth as such, or His coming forth from Mary's womb. The miracle was in His conception, or the moment when the ovum in Mary's womb was transformed into a person. The human nature of Jesus actually began as an ovum naturally produced by Mary; Jesus was thus literally Mary's offspring or "seed" (***Gen 3:15***). At a time chosen by God, two supernatural events occurred that turned this natural ovum into the God-man, Jesus Christ.

First, Mary's ovum was supernaturally altered so that it became a complete human being, body and spirit, without the addition of the chromosomes usually provided by a male sperm. This was the specific work of the Holy Spirit, which He performed in the moment when He *came upon* Mary and *overshadowed* her (***Lk 1:35***). We should note that this work of the Spirit was performed not on Mary's body as such but upon the tiny ovum produced by her body. From the moment when the Spirit's power touched this ovum and miraculously caused this transformation to occur, the human nature of Jesus began to develop in a natural way.

[2] In this context I will continue to use the term "virgin birth," but with the understanding that the conception of Jesus is what was special, as explained here.

[3] Since the virgin conception of Jesus was not a public event and thus lacks sign or evidential value, it was technically not a miracle. With this caveat, I will continue to apply this term to it.

The second supernatural event, which occurred simultaneously with the first, was the joining of the eternal, personal, divine Logos with this newly formed human being, Jesus. In this moment the divine nature of our Savior entered into some unexplainable union with His human nature. This coming together of the two natures was not the Spirit's work, but the work of the Logos. In this moment *"the Word became flesh"* (**Jn 1:14**).

The Purpose of the Supernatural Conception of Jesus

Why was the virgin birth necessary? *Was* it really necessary? A common answer is that it was necessary as the means of preserving Jesus' human nature from the effects of original sin, which was necessary to ensure His personal sinlessness, which was a prerequisite for His viability as a sacrifice for sin. As Palmer puts it, "This conceiving act of the Holy Spirit was essential in order to secure Christ's sinlessness, which, in turn, was necessary in order for Him to become our Savior. It preserved Christ from that original sin which is the lot of every person born into this world." Original sin includes two elements: inherited guilt and an inherited corrupt nature. But "because of his conception by the Holy Spirit, Christ was preserved from this twofold aspect of original sin." His "spotless and morally beautiful" human nature "was due to the operation of the Holy Spirit whereby Jesus was immaculately and miraculously conceived without Joseph's taking part" (**66-67**). As Lehman sums it up, "Conceived by the Holy Spirit the child was holy and sinless" (**37**).

Why was the virgin birth necessary?

I completely reject this rationale for the virgin birth. There is no biblical basis for such an idea. As noted several times already, the concept of original sin is itself not taught in the Bible. The original grace of Jesus Christ resulting from the cross preserves the entire human race from all the spiritual consequences of Adam's sin. But if this is true, does this not imply that without Christ's atoning work there *would* have been such a thing as original sin? Yes, it does. But does this not in turn raise the question of Christ's own preservation from original sin? Yes, it does. But we cannot say that His own exemption from such original sin was the result of His own atoning work, since the former must be a prerequisite for the latter.

My contention is that the human nature of Jesus was preserved from all consequences of original sin simply by divine fiat or miracle. There is nothing about the virgin conception as such that would prevent the impartation or imputation of original sin. The idea that the "corrupt nature passes from the father to the child" (**Kuyper, 90**) cannot be established; thus excluding male parenthood as such would not explain Christ's exemption from any possible original sin. But "the power of the Most High" could simply will it to be so. Surely if the Spirit of God can cause Mary's ovum to become a fully-human person without a male sperm, He can also (as a distinct and separate act) prevent any taint of Adam's sin from entering into that person. The one does not have to be the cause of the other. In fact, it is possible that the Spirit could have prevented all aspects of original sin from being applied to Jesus even if He had had two human parents.

> **The Spirit could have kept original sin from being applied to Jesus even with two human parents.**

The fact is, of course, that Jesus had only one human parent, and was supernaturally conceived by the power of the Holy Spirit. Why did it happen this way? Was it inherently necessary for the God-man to be conceived thus? If the entrance of the Logos into this human being was an act separate from the miraculous conception as such, could the former have happened without the latter? Perhaps, but the former would not have been *fitting* or *appropriate* without the latter. The divine nature of the child formed in Mary's womb calls for a unique, supernatural conception. In other words, the virgin conception was fitting in view of Christ's *deity*. The key to understanding this is Gabriel's statement to Mary, *"The Holy Spirit will come upon you, and the power of the Most High will overshadow you; and* ***for that reason*** *the holy Child shall be called the* ***Son of God"*** (***Lk 1:35***, emphasis added).

The Greek word for "shall be called" is *kaleo*, "to call, call by name, provide with a name." According to Arndt and Gingrich, when this word is used, "very often" the emphasis is less on the fact that one's name is such and such, "than on the fact that the bearer of the name actually is what the name says about him. . . . *Be named* thus approaches closely the mng. *to be*" (**400**). If that applies here, Gabriel is thus saying, *because* Jesus is conceived by the power of the Spirit, He *is* the Son of God—"Son of God" being an unmistakable title of deity. The absence of a *human* father makes it clear that Jesus is the Son of *God*. Swete warns against pressing this point too far; "'shall have a right to the title' is perhaps the nearest rendering," he says (**28, fn 3**). See ***1 John 3:1*** for a comparable usage of the term.

The bottom line is that the virgin birth of Jesus is inseparably connected with His divine nature. It is the means by which the divine Savior was born, and it is the guarantee to us of His deity.

WAS JESUS "FILLED WITH THE SPIRIT" FROM BIRTH?

Scripture says that Jesus was *"full of the Holy Spirit"* (***Lk 4:1***). Was this true of Jesus from His birth, or did it begin at some later point such as His baptism? A case can be made for the latter; but many say it was so from Jesus' birth, indeed, during "every moment of His existence" (**Kuyper, 94**). Though the Bible does not specifically teach this, it is a "reasonable inference that Christ was filled with the Holy Spirit from the very moment of conception" (**Walvoord, 92**). If it was true of John the forerunner (***Lk 1:15***), surely it must have been true of Christ Himself (**ibid.; DeWelt, *Power*, 3:6, 9**).

Whether at His conception or birth, or at a later time, Christ was indeed filled with the Spirit. To what end? What were the purpose and result of such filling? All agree that its main purpose, after the pattern of the Spirit's OT work, was to empower Jesus for His ministry, or to equip Him with those gifts necessary to fulfill His mission. In this respect the difference between Jesus' filling and the filling of OT leaders thus was not qualitative but *quantitative*. This seems to be confirmed by ***John 3:34***, *"For He whom God has sent speaks the words of God; for He gives the Spirit without measure."* The key statement is the latter part of the verse, *"for God gives the Spirit without limit"* (NIV). The KJV translates it thus: *"for God giveth not the Spirit by measure **unto him**,"* i.e., unto Jesus. The words *"unto him"* are not in the original; but the "preferable" understanding is as the KJV has it, that "the Father gives the Spirit to the Son without measure" (**Morris, *John*, 246-247**).

The Father gives the Spirit to the Son without measure (or limit).

What does this mean? Kuyper says it means that the Holy Spirit endowed Christ's "human nature with the glorious gifts, powers, and faculties of which that nature is susceptible." And in terms of ***John 3:34***, "He lacked nothing, possessed all; not by virtue of His divine nature, which can not receive anything, being the eternal fulness itself, but by virtue of His human nature, which was endowed with such glorious gifts by the Holy Spirit" (**94-95**). Walvoord agrees: being filled with the Spirit, Christ's human nature "possessed every spiritual gift from the moment of conception" (**93**).

Some add to this the idea that Christ's being filled with the Spirit was the source or cause of His ongoing holiness or sinlessness, as distinct from His "official" empowerment. In Kuyper's opinion, human nature as such, even apart from the need to overcome sin, cannot have holiness without the Holy Spirit. This was true even of Adam in his pre-Fall sinlessness, and thus it must be true of Christ, i.e., "His human nature could not dispense with the constant inshining of the Holy Spirit" (**102-103, 110**). Palmer says that Jesus' filling with the Spirit is equivalent to the way the Spirit indwells Christians, and thus the Spirit "was the author of holiness in Jesus' human nature" (**67**). "All the time, . . . even as a baby, he was indwelt by the Spirit." All of his spiritual growth "was due to the operation of the Holy Spirit" in his life (**ibid., 68-69**).

I have serious difficulty with this latter point. There is no biblical evidence that the indwelling of the Spirit is an element of humanness as such[4] or that He was the author of Adam's pre-Fall holiness. The indwelling of the Spirit for the purpose of producing holiness is the essence of the new, post-Pentecostal work of the Spirit. It is God's gift to Christians as they struggle to overcome sin, not the prerequisite of original sinlessness as such. Thus in my judgment the only purpose for Christ's being filled with the Holy Spirit was empowerment for His mission; it was not for the purpose of ensuring His perfect holiness. And if this is true, the idea that this infilling occurred not at His conception but at His baptism becomes more acceptable.

The Spirit's indwelling to produce holiness is the post-Pentecostal work of the Spirit.

[4] *Contra* the thesis of Staton's entire book, *Don't Divorce the Holy Spirit.*

THE HOLY SPIRIT AND JESUS' BAPTISM

The first main event in Jesus' time of public ministry was His baptism at the hands of His forerunner, John. Since John's baptism was *"a baptism of repentance for the forgiveness of sins"* (**Mk 1:4**), Jesus could not have received baptism for the same reason everyone else did. It is likely, though, that He was accepting this baptism vicariously in the sense that He was identifying Himself with sinful mankind as He did on the cross. Thus His baptism as the beginning of His public ministry was a foreshadowing of the cross as the end of His public ministry, so much so that He can even speak of His death on the cross as a figurative baptism (**Mk 10:38-39**). His baptism was the start of His public journey to the cross.

Jesus' baptism was the start of His public journey to the cross.

We can say, then, that Jesus' baptism was the official inauguration ceremony of His unique mission and ministry. He is now beginning to do what He came to do when He said, *"Behold, I have come . . . to do Your will, O God"* (**Heb 10:7**). This is the meaning of Jesus' statement that His baptism was *"to fulfill all righteousness"* (**Mt 3:15**). He is speaking here of His own personal righteousness, i.e., His personal conformity to God's unique will for Him and Him alone. By being baptized He is saying, "I hereby plant my feet on the road that will lead me to the cross." Its connection with His unique mission means that Jesus' baptism had neither the content of John's baptism of repentant Israelites nor the content of the later Christian baptism. All efforts to equate Jesus' baptism with Christian baptism should be vigorously resisted, especially in reference to the Spirit's connection thereto.

THE DESCENT OF THE DOVE

All four Gospel writers place the Holy Spirit at Jesus' baptism in the accompanying descent of the dove coming down from heaven and lighting upon Him. By Matthew's account (**3:16**), *"After being baptized, Jesus came up immediately from the water; and behold, the heavens were opened, and he saw the Spirit of God descending as a dove and lighting on Him."* **Mark 1:10** says, *"Immediately coming up out of the water, He saw the heavens opening, and the Spirit like a dove descending upon Him."* In Luke's words,

Now when all the people were baptized, Jesus was also baptized, and while He was praying, heaven was opened, and the Holy Spirit descended upon Him in bodily form like a dove, and a voice came out of heaven, "You are My beloved Son, in You I am well-pleased." (***3:21-22***)

John's Gospel gives us John the Baptist's perspective:

John testified saying, "I have seen the Spirit descending as a dove out of heaven, and He remained upon Him. I did not recognize Him, but He who sent me to baptize in water said to me, 'He upon whom you see the Spirit descending and remaining upon Him, this is the One who baptizes in the Holy Spirit.'" (***1:32-33***)

Luke 3:21 tells us that after Jesus was baptized (aorist participle) and while He was praying (present participle), heaven was opened, meaning the dimensional barrier between the divine heaven and our universe parted, somewhere in the space above where Jesus and John were standing. This did not happen during the baptism itself, but after Christ had come up out of the water. When He did so, immediately John and probably Jesus saw the Spirit of God coming down toward Jesus. The Spirit descended as a dove, in bodily form. This was not just a vision, nor was the dove just some ethereal, nonmaterial form. It was a literal dove, created *ex nihilo* for the occasion of this theophany—a dove which the Holy Spirit was using to make Himself visible. The dove came down "to" (*eis*) Jesus (Mark), or "upon" (*epi*) Jesus (Matthew, Mark, John). The Matthew translation, *"lighting upon Him,"* gives the correct sense. It seems that the visible form of the dove actually settled upon the head or shoulder or arm of Jesus, while at the same moment the invisible Holy Spirit Himself came upon Jesus.

That the latter is the main point is seen from the fact that none of the Gospel writers says that John "saw a dove" or that "a dove came down." What they say is that the *Holy Spirit* came down *as* a dove, and that Jesus and John saw the *Holy Spirit* coming down *as* a dove. John the Forerunner testifies that the Spirit (in the form of a dove) not only rested upon Jesus, but *remained* upon Him. This was followed by God the Father speaking audibly from heaven, *"You are My beloved Son, in You I am well-pleased"* (***Lk 3:22***).

The question of whether the dove was visible to all and the voice audible to all, or whether these were perceived only by John and probably Jesus, has no conclusive answer. We know from his own testimony that John the Forerunner saw the dove, which implies that he heard the voice (though this is not specifically stated). We know that Jesus heard the voice, since (in Mark's and Luke's accounts) it is addressed directly to Him. Also, in Matthew's and Mark's accounts, "he saw" probably refers to Jesus. Nothing is said about whether anyone else saw or heard these things, though we cannot rule this out.

Some ask why the Spirit chose to make Himself visible in the form of a *dove*. There is no sure answer to this question. Moody suggests that because the dove is a bird, this calls to mind "the brooding of the Spirit over the water chaos" in ***Genesis 1:2***, thus symbolizing the beginning of a new creation (**36**). Sometimes a connection with Noah's dove (***Gen 8:8-12***) is also sought (**ibid.**). Such speculation cannot take us very far. It may be that a dove's form was chosen simply because doves are a nonthreatening creature, and were a common and familiar presence throughout the land. Thus one appearing in the sky at this time would not have been alarming or distracting.

The Significance of the Descent of the Spirit

Speaking of distractions, we should not allow ourselves to be distracted by the question of "why a dove?" The issue is not the significance of the dove as such, but the significance of the *Holy Spirit's* descending and remaining upon Jesus. What is actually happening here?

The issue is not the significance of the dove as such.

The fact is that the descent of the Holy Spirit upon Jesus has all the appearances of an anointing ceremony, as when Samuel anointed David to be king of Israel (***1Sa 16:13***). In the OT, in addition to kings, priests were anointed (***Ex 29:7***; ***Lev 8:10-13,30***), and sometimes prophets (***1Kgs 19:16***). Such an anointing ceremony was like an ordination service; the one being anointed was publicly submitting himself to God's will and committing himself to the designated task or office. Those doing the anointing were consecrating or setting apart the anointed one for a sacred purpose. It was a public declaration of and dedication to the specified service to God.

The exact meaning of the oil used in such a ceremony is not spelled out, but the description of the occasion of David's anointing suggests a connection with the Holy Spirit: *"Then Samuel took the horn of oil and anointed him in the midst of his brothers; and the Spirit of the* LORD *came mightily upon David from that day forward"* (***1Sa 16:13***). The outpouring of the oil seems to symbolize the outpouring of the Holy Spirit upon the anointed one, the outpouring of the latter being an empowerment for service.

This seems to be the significance of the descent of the Spirit upon Jesus at His baptism. The dove takes the place of oil, symbolizing the presence of God's Spirit upon Jesus to empower and equip Him in every way for His imminent mission. This connection between the outpouring of the Spirit upon Jesus and His anointing for His redemptive work is seen in ***Isaiah 61:1***,

> *The Spirit of the Lord* GOD *is upon me, because the* LORD *has anointed me to bring good news to the afflicted; He has sent me to bind up the brokenhearted, to proclaim liberty to captives and freedom to prisoners.*

When the Spirit came upon Jesus, so did the power.

Peter's words in ***Acts 10:38*** show the same thing: *"You know of Jesus of Nazareth, how God anointed Him with the Holy Spirit and with power, and how He went about doing good and healing all who were oppressed by the devil, for God was with Him."* When the Spirit came upon Jesus, so did the power.

This anointing with the Holy Spirit is why we refer to Jesus as "the Christ," which means "the anointed one." As Lehman explains,

> This anointing energized Christ for His threefold mission: (1) Jesus was the Anointed Prophet who proclaimed the good tidings; (2) He was the Anointed High Priest who "made purification for sins"; (3) He was the Anointed King who "[reigns] in righteousness." He who heightened Jesus' powers in this threefold ministry was the Holy Spirit. Nowhere is it said that Jesus performed these extraordinary functions in His own power. (**39**)

Is this *anointing* with the Spirit the source of Christ's being *filled* with the Spirit (***Lk 4:1***)? To be sure, Jesus Christ was chosen before the creation to fill the roles of prophet, priest, and king. In this sense we can agree with Kuyper that "He was anointed from eternity" (**98**). We have seen that some say Jesus was filled with the Spirit from His conception or birth (e.g., **Walvoord, 95**). But even those who say Jesus was filled with the Spirit from conception must admit that the descent of the dove at His baptism began "a new phase of the ministry of the

Holy Spirit" (**ibid.**). "The Messiah was about to enter on His official life, and at . . . this inception of His Messianic work, He must receive a new outpouring of the Spirit." Thus His baptism "invested Jesus with new powers and a new mission. It was the spiritual, invisible, but effectual anointing of the Christ *with Holy Spirit and power* for His unique work" (**Swete, 46-47**).

As I stated earlier, a good case can be made for the view that the descent of the Spirit at Christ's baptism was actually the time when He was filled with the Spirit. The baptismal accounts are the only specific clues we have as to a particular time or occasion for this filling. Assertions of a prebaptismal filling are only inferences; there are no specific statements to that effect. Also, Luke's statement that Jesus was "full of the Holy Spirit" follows directly upon His baptism and seems to be related to His baptism: *"Jesus, full of the Holy Spirit, returned from the Jordan,"* i.e., where He was baptized (***Lk 4:1***).

Either way, the "descent of the dove" at His baptism prepares Jesus for everything that is to follow.

THE HOLY SPIRIT AND JESUS' TEMPTATION

Immediately after His baptism, as a prelude to His public ministry, *"Jesus was led up by the Spirit into the wilderness to be tempted by the devil"* (***Mt 4:1***). As ***Mark 1:12-13*** tells it, *"Immediately the Spirit impelled Him to go out into the wilderness. And He was in the wilderness forty days being tempted by Satan; and He was with the wild beasts, and the angels were ministering to Him."* Mark's word, "impelled" (*ekballo*) is stronger than Matthew's "led up" (*anago*). It sometimes carries a "sense of violence" (**Heron, 41**), as in "to throw out or drive out forcibly"; it is often used of driving out demons. We need not take it to this extreme, though; it can also mean simply "to lead or send out." In any case the Spirit's role is more than a simple presence in Jesus' life at this point. He is not merely passive, but seems to be initiating and encouraging Jesus' departure into the wilderness. He is actively leading the Savior into a decisive encounter with the devil.

In any case the Spirit's role is more than a simple presence in Jesus' life at this point.

Matthew 4:1-11 and ***Luke 4:1-13*** give a few details about this wilderness ordeal. Both writers describe three main temptations directed against Jesus by the devil. We should not assume that these were the only temptations Jesus experienced during the 40 days He was in the wilderness. Luke's account suggests that He was tempted during the entire 40 days: *"Jesus, full of the Holy Spirit, returned from the Jordan and was led around by the Spirit in the wilderness for forty days, being tempted by the devil"* (***Lk 4:1-2***). *"Being tempted by the devil"* (present participle) seems to apply to the whole time Jesus was in the wilderness. Mark specifically says, *"He was in the wilderness forty days being tempted by Satan."* Matthew indicates that it was *"after He had fasted forty days and forty nights"* and had become hungry, that *"the tempter came"* and enticed Him with these three specific temptations (***4:2-3***). We conclude, then, that Jesus faced many temptations in addition to these three during this time.

What was the role of the Holy Spirit during these 40 days? It is reasonable to conclude that the Spirit was with Jesus, strengthening and encouraging Him in the face of the devil's attacks, helping Him to overcome them, during this entire time. ***Luke 4:1*** remarks that Jesus was *"full of the Spirit"* when He entered the wilderness, and ***Luke 4:14*** says that after the 40 days He *"returned to Galilee in the power of the Spirit."* The terminology of ***Luke 4:1-2***, that Jesus *"was led around by the Spirit in the wilderness for forty days,"* suggests that the Spirit not only led Him into the wilderness, but was guiding and strengthening Him during the whole time. This understanding is based on a slight difference in Luke's wording. Matthew and Mark say that the Spirit led or impelled Jesus "into" (*eis*) the wilderness; Luke says the Spirit led Jesus "in" (*en*) the wilderness, i.e., while He was in the wilderness.

What was the nature of the Spirit's "leading" during the temptations? Many assume that His role was the same for Jesus as it is for all human beings who are fighting to resist the devil. As Palmer says, "The whole period of temptation from beginning to end was under the control of the Holy Spirit, and it was by means of the Spirit that Jesus' human nature was given the strength to overcome the severe tempta-

What was the nature of the Spirit's "leading" during the temptations?

tions placed before him." He could not rely on His divine nature for such strength. "Instead, being complete man, he relied upon the indwelling of the Spirit for ability to resist" (**71**). This agrees with Swete, who says that "the strength by which He resisted was not other than that by which we ourselves may conquer," i.e., He did so "in the power of the Holy Spirit and not simply by the force of a sinless human will" (**55**).

Some say this was the case during Jesus' whole life, namely, being filled with the Spirit at conception, He resisted all temptations during His entire life through the power of the indwelling Spirit. Thus the role of "the eternal Spirit" was to make sure Jesus was "without blemish" when He came to the cross (***Heb 9:14***); see **Torrey, 257-258**. Ware cites ***Isaiah 11:1-2*** to support the idea that Jesus' "empowerment for obedience" was "linked to the Spirit being in him and working through him" (***Father*, 88-89**).

I cannot accept this simple explanation of the Spirit's role in reference to Christ's temptations. I have already expressed my doubts about Jesus' being filled with the Spirit at His conception or birth. That human beings must have the indwelling of the Holy Spirit to overcome temptations is inconsistent with the fact that such indwelling was not given to anyone prior to Pentecost. Even without the Holy Spirit, Jesus in His human nature had the resources to resist temptation that every other pre-Pentecost human being had. Being "filled with the Spirit" is not necessarily equivalent to the *indwelling* of the Spirit; it often refers just to empowerment for service. Regarding Jesus, the main (if not only) point of His being filled with the Spirit was *empowerment* for His mission.

Being "filled with the Spirit" is not necessarily equivalent to the indwelling of the Spirit.

This is why I believe we cannot interpret the temptations of Jesus as *mere* temptations, comparable to those faced by all other human beings. Jesus' encounter with Satan in the wilderness was not just a moral struggle, nor just a hurdle to clear in order to maintain His qualifications as a spotless sacrifice (see ***Heb 9:14***). It was rather a central aspect of His messianic purpose, namely, to do battle with *"the god of this world"* (***2Cor 4:4***) and *"to destroy the works of the devil"* (***1Jn 3:8***). Satan did not initiate this confrontation; *God* did, when the

Spirit *impelled* Jesus into the wilderness. He is "calling the devil out," so to speak. As the second Adam[5] He is beginning His work of crushing the serpent's head (***Gen 3:15***) and reversing the Edenic curse. He is beginning His work of binding the devil (***Mt 12:29***)[6] and rendering him powerless (***Heb 2:14***). As the Messianic King He is confronting His enemies (***Pss 2, 45***) and setting up His kingdom (***Mt 12:28***).

Yes, Jesus did all this *as a human being;* no wonder He needed the empowerment of the Holy Spirit! His battle against the devil in the wilderness was on a completely different level from the ordinary temptations faced by ordinary people. *"Greater is He who is in you than he who is in the world"* (***1Jn 4:4***) does apply to us just as it did to Jesus, but we must not equate our own spiritual warfare with what was happening during those 40 days in the wilderness. At His baptism Jesus had been anointed with the Holy Spirit and with power (***Acts 10:38***) for the purpose of encountering and defeating the devil on a cosmic scale. The result was as Carter describes it: "It was the Spirit that '*impelled*' Christ to go into the wilderness to meet Satan's challenge, and it was by *the power of the Spirit* that He came forth from that wilderness ordeal a complete victor over Satan. From that time forth Christ walked in the power and authority of His Spirit-wrought victory over Satan and all the evil forces" (**103**).

THE HOLY SPIRIT AND JESUS' MINISTRY

Whether at His conception or at His baptism, Jesus *was* filled with the Spirit and thus empowered for His public ministry. As Kuyper says, "He was guided, impelled, animated, and supported by the Holy Spirit at every step of His Messianic ministry" (**101**). We remember again ***Luke 4:1***, that Jesus was *"full of the Spirit,"* and ***Luke 4:14***, that He began His ministry in Galilee *"in the power of the Spirit."* We remember ***John 3:34***, that the Father gives the Spirit to the Son without measure. ***Matthew 12:17-21*** tells us that Jesus was the fulfillment of the prophecy in ***Isaiah 42:1-4***. In this prophecy God says, *"Behold, My Servant, whom I have chosen, My Beloved in whom My soul is well-*

[5] "Under the compulsion of the Holy Spirit, Jesus is driven into the desert, the traditional abode of demonic powers, to do battle against Satan against whom the First Adam was helpless" (Moody, 37).

[6] "The issue of the Temptation was the binding of Satan by the Christ" (Swete, 53).

pleased; I will put My Spirit upon Him, and He shall proclaim justice to the Gentiles" (***Mt 12:18***).

Early in His ministry, in a synagogue service in Nazareth, Jesus announced that He was anointed with the Spirit for messianic purposes. He read these words from the scroll of Isaiah (***61:1-2***): *"The Spirit of the Lord is upon Me, because He anointed Me to preach the gospel to the poor. He has sent Me to proclaim release to the captives, and recovery of sight to the blind, to set free those who are oppressed, to proclaim the favorable year of the Lord"* (***Lk 4:18-19***). Then He declared to the people, *"Today this Scripture has been fulfilled in your hearing"* (***Lk 4:21***).

The Spirit empowered Jesus for every aspect of His ministry.

When we examine these and other relevant texts, we see that the Spirit empowered Jesus for every aspect of His ministry.

Jesus' Prophetic Ministry

A prophet of God is someone who speaks inspired messages from God. Such revelation and inspiration are the work of the Holy Spirit. The OT was written by those who had this prophetic gift, and it refers to many others who spoke for God in that age. The prophet Moses spoke of a coming prophet that would be like him in many ways: *"The Lord said to me, '. . . I will raise up a prophet from among their countrymen like you, and I will put My words in his mouth, and he shall speak to them all that I command him'"* (***Deu 18:17-18***). Most understand this as referring to Jesus, who was God's prophet *par excellence* (see ***Acts 3:22***; ***7:37***).

Every word that Jesus spoke was a word from God, not just because He Himself was divine but also because He was filled with the Spirit: *"For He whom God has sent speaks the words of God; for He gives the Spirit [to Him] without measure"* (***Jn 3:34***). In other words, that Jesus speaks the words of God is causally related to His being filled with the Spirit. The prophecy in ***Isaiah 61:1-2***, which Jesus applied to Himself in ***Luke 4:17-19***, specifies that one purpose of the Spirit's anointing is to enable prophetic proclamation: *"The Spirit of the Lord is upon Me, because He anointed Me* ***to preach*** *the gospel . . .* ***to proclaim*** *release . . .* ***to proclaim*** *the favorable year of the Lord"* (emphasis added). The same is found in the prophecy from ***Isaiah 42:1-4***, cited of

Jesus in ***Matthew 12:17-21***. Speaking of His chosen Servant, God says, *"I will put My Spirit upon Him, and He shall* ***proclaim*** *justice."*

Speaking of the ***Luke 4*** passage, Lehman says that Jesus "was saying that His preaching with its accompanying spiritual works was the direct result of His being anointed with the Spirit" (**40**). "The preaching of our Lord was *in the power of the Spirit,"* says Swete (**57**). Walvoord says, "While there was resident in the person of Christ all the attributes of deity, in the limitations of His earthly walk Christ chose to be dependent on the Holy Spirit for the exercise of His prophetic gift" (**96**). As an example, ***Acts 1:2*** says that Jesus *"had by the Holy Spirit given orders to the apostles."*

One purpose of the Spirit's anointing is to enable prophetic proclamation.

In view of this biblical testimony concerning the Spirit's role in His prophetic ministry, it seems that the Son of David Himself could speak the words of the original King David: *"The Spirit of the LORD spoke by me, and His word was on my tongue"* (***2Sa 23:2***). These roles were reversed after Jesus was glorified, though (***Jn 16:12-15***).

JESUS' KINGLY MINISTRY

Jesus' ministry was characterized and energized by *"the power of the Spirit"* (***Lk 4:14***; see ***Acts 10:38***). This relates especially to His role as the Messianic King who came to establish His authority over all things. As noted in the section on Jesus' temptations, it has particular relevance to His purpose of overthrowing the devil's usurped dominion and establishing His own eternal kingdom in its place (***Acts 26:18; Col 1:13***).

The Holy Spirit's role in Christ's kingly mission is clearly stated in reference to Christ's work of casting out demons, something He did throughout His ministry. On one occasion He cast out a demon that was causing a man to be blind and mute (***Mt 12:22***). His enemies accused Him of doing so by the power of Beelzebul, i.e., Satan (***vv. 23-24***). Jesus refutes this charge (***vv. 25-27***) and then declares, *"But if I cast out demons by the Spirit of God, then the kingdom of God has come upon you"* (***v. 28***). This is in effect exactly what He was claiming to be doing; He was binding the strong man (the devil) and was plundering his domain (***v. 29***). In doing so He was fulfilling that part of the

Isaiah 61 prophecy for which the Spirit of the Lord had anointed Him, *"to set free those who are oppressed"* (***Lk 4:18b***).

Jesus says He is doing this *"by the Spirit of God."* In ***Luke 11:20*** He says the same thing, only here He says He is casting out demons *"by the finger of God."* In the OT "the finger of God" is a symbol of His mighty power (***Ex 8:19***; ***31:18***; ***Ps 8:3***); here it is a symbol of *"the power of the Spirit"* (***Lk 4:14***). As Moody says, "The Spirit came to Jesus . . . at his baptism to enable him to invade the demon-infested dominion of Satan and deliver those in bondage" (**36**). Also, "By the power of the Holy Spirit poured out on him after his baptism, Jesus bound the Strong One, Satan, so now his underlings are unable to stand before the Stronger One, Jesus" (**40**). When Jesus shared His Spirit-given power over Satan's kingdom with His disciples, He shared their joy in seeing people delivered from Satan's clutches (***Lk 10:17-21***). *"At that very time He rejoiced greatly in the Holy Spirit,"* Luke says (***v. 21***). See **Swete, 60**.

Can we assume that this same "power of the Spirit" that energized Jesus to cast out demons was the source of His power to perform miracles in general? This is inferred by many. Building upon ***Matthew 12:28***, Torrey says, "Jesus Christ wrought His miracles here on earth in the power of the Holy Spirit" (**260**). Palmer reasons the same way. Beginning with ***Matthew 12:28*** he says, "Here again, we see clearly that at times Jesus performed miracles, not by the Father nor because he as man received supernatural power from the second Person of the Trinity, but because the Holy Spirit had given him the gift to do so" (**71**). "It was the Holy Spirit who was really the author of those miracles, even if they were done through Jesus" (**ibid.**). Walvoord, though, thinks it is going too far to attribute *all* Jesus' miracles to the power of the Spirit. Sometimes this was the case, but only because Jesus *chose* to do it that way. At other times, Walvoord says, the power came from His own divine nature (**97-98**).

Either way, the power that enabled Christ to perform His kingly ministry was divine power, and at least some of it was the result of His being filled with the Spirit.

Jesus' Priestly Ministry

"Jesus' priestly ministry" refers to His offering Himself as the one-and-only efficacious and all-sufficient sacrifice for the sins of the world. The one passage that specifically relates the Holy Spirit to Christ's priestly work is ***Hebrews 9:14***, which declares that Christ *"offered Himself without blemish"* to God *"through the eternal Spirit."* Since Christ's entire life was in a sense a preparation for this one climactic event, some think that this text may be referring to everything "the eternal Spirit" did for Christ up to this point. As noted earlier, those who believe Christ was indwelt by the Spirit for the specific purpose of maintaining His holiness see in this text a reference to the Spirit's work of helping Christ to remain "without blemish."

One verse is not a lot to go on, but I believe there is something more in view here than just a recap of all that the Spirit did in Jesus' life up to this point. I believe it refers to something the Holy Spirit was doing for Jesus in the very circumstances of His crucifixion, probably beginning in Gethsemane. In the few hours that Jesus spent in the garden of grief (***Mt 26:38***), every strand of His messianic purpose came together and was unfolded before His human nature as never before. When He became aware of the magnitude, the enormity, the infinite weight of the burden He was about to bear, His first reaction was to recoil: *"My Father, if it is possible, let this cup pass from Me"* (***Mt 26:39***).

The cosmic scale of the task that lay immediately before Him at this point was comparable to what took place during the 40 days of temptation. Then, of course, He was confronting the devil as an enemy who was using every means at his disposal to prevent the Messiah from accomplishing His purpose. Then, the Holy Spirit gave Him the strength necessary to resist Satan's adversarial power. Here in Gethsemane, there is no indication of a tempter's presence. The dialogue is between Jesus and His heavenly Father, and both are on the same side; both are of the same purpose. Jesus' hesitation comes not from a moral weakness exploited by Satan, but from the simple finitude of His human nature. He is overwhelmed by the seeming impossibility of this next step in His messianic journey.

As He continues to pray, though, His initial recoiling from this next step disappears, and His mind and heart are calmed and made ready for the unspeakable ordeal that awaits Him: *"My Father, if this cannot pass away unless I drink it, Your*

If there is a specific point when the Spirit strengthened Jesus Christ in the shadow of Calvary, this was it.

will be done" (***Mt 26:42***). If there is a specific point when "the eternal Spirit" strengthened the man Jesus Christ in the shadow of Calvary, this was it. Here we can picture the power of the Spirit undergirding the finite humanity of Jesus and infusing Him with the resolve to see His "mission impossible" through to the end. Downer ties this in with ***Hebrews 9:14*** thus: "It was through the eternal Spirit that His sacred will conquered its aversion to death, and for love to His Father and His people made Him a Sacrifice for sin without blemish, as a perfect offering" (**57-58**).

This is of course an inference, but the inference seems sound. If the Spirit's presence empowered Jesus throughout His earthly ministry, which it did, surely there was no point in this ministry where the Spirit's power was more needed than here. This is why Walvoord concludes, "In the difficult hours of Gethsemane and all the decisive moments leading to the cross, the Holy Spirit faithfully ministered to Christ" (**100-101**).

"In the difficult hours of Gethsemane . . . the Holy Spirit faithfully ministered to Christ."

In view of this understanding of ***Hebrews 9:14***, Walvoord offers an interesting possibility for explaining Christ's difficult lament from the cross, *"My God, My God, why have you forsaken Me?"* (***Mt 27:46***). Is it possible that He is referring here to God the Spirit? Is Jesus saying that the Spirit, having strengthened Him at every point during His ministry up to the cross itself, has now withdrawn for those hours when Jesus was actually on the cross? Says Walvoord, "It is possible that there was a cessation of the Spirit's ministry during this period without altering the fact that Christ offered Himself by the Spirit of God. While the Holy Spirit could succor Christ in making His decision and in fulfilling the eternal purpose of God in taking the path which led to the cross, only Christ could bear the load of sin. In this the Holy Spirit could not avail" (**101**).

THE HOLY SPIRIT AND JESUS' RESURRECTION

As it was in the initial creation, so it was in the first act of God's new creation, the resurrection of Jesus: all three persons of the Trinity were involved. In ***Ephesians 1:17-20*** Paul clearly says that *"the God of* *our Lord Jesus Christ, the Father of glory,"* raised Jesus from the dead. In ***John 10:17-18*** Jesus says that He will lay down His own life and that He will take it up again. But there are also several texts that attribute Christ's resurrection to the Holy Spirit.

One such text is ***Romans 8:11***, *"But if the Spirit of Him who raised Jesus from the dead dwells in you, He who raised Christ Jesus from the dead will also give life to your mortal bodies through His Spirit who dwells in you."* Here Paul seems to say that the one who raised Jesus from the dead is actually God the Father, but that He did so through the agency of the Holy Spirit. Paul's point is to give us assurance of our future bodily resurrection. This assurance is based on the indwelling presence of the Spirit: God *"will also give life to your mortal bodies through His Spirit who dwells in you."* For this argument to have any force, Paul must be implying that God raised Jesus from the dead through the same Spirit who dwells in us.

Another text is ***Romans 1:4***, which says that Jesus *"was declared the Son of God with power by the resurrection from the dead, according to the Spirit of holiness."* The best understanding of this is that the "Spirit of holiness" is here pictured as the agent of Christ's resurrection. The preposition *kata*, translated in the NASB as "according to," sometimes has a causal sense, i.e., "through, by means of." This is how the NIV understands it, thus it translates the phrase "through the Spirit of holiness."

Another text probably relating the Spirit to Christ's resurrection is ***1 Peter 3:18***, which says that Christ was *"put to death in the flesh, but made alive in the spirit."* The issue is whether "in the spirit" (*pneumati*) refers to Christ's human spirit or to the Holy Spirit. By not capitalizing it the NASB supports the former option. The NIV and TNIV translate it as referring to the Holy Spirit: *"He was put to death in the body but made alive by the Spirit."* Walvoord shows that the latter is the better option (**102-103**). In light of this, it seems best to understand ***1 Timothy 3:16*** in the same way when it says Christ was *"vindicated by the Spirit"* (NIV), i.e., by the Spirit's raising Him from the dead.

Christ was put to death in the flesh, but made alive in the spirit.

The exact role of the Spirit in raising Jesus' body from the dead is not explained in the Bible. Since He is the *"Spirit of life"* (***Rom 8:2***), and since *"it is the Spirit who gives life"* (***Jn* 6:63**), we should not be surprised that He was the person of the Trinity whose life-giving power brought Jesus' crucified body back to life.

CONCLUSION

Boles declares that "mystery shrouds much of the relationship existing between Christ and the Holy Spirit" (**123**). That is certainly and even inevitably true, since this subject involves two of the most incomprehensible realities: the Trinity and the incarnation.

Whatever were the relationships among the persons of the Trinity prior to creation, prior to the incarnation, and prior to Pentecost, in their works in relation to the world and especially in relation to redemption these divine persons have taken upon themselves relationships that did not necessarily exist in their eternally preexistent state. One type of relationship that the persons of the Trinity assumed in their creative and redemptive purposes was a relationship of authority and submission. Since this kind of relationship was *assumed* (voluntarily entered into) by the Trinitarian persons, it implies no inequality in their essence, authority, and power.

The incarnation itself is a major example of how these assumed relationships of authority and submission take shape in the course of God's working out of the redemptive plan. In the incarnation the eternal, divine Logos became a human person, Jesus of Nazareth. The result was that this unique person has two natures: a fully divine nature and a fully human nature.

In His divine nature, Jesus is fully God, with all the attributes of God in place. In the incarnation He did not lose or surrender any of His divine essence or attributes. But this raises a serious question: if Jesus was fully divine, why did He need to be filled with the Spirit? The answer is, because He was also fully human, and for the purposes of His redemptive mission His human nature had to be fully operative. For this to be the case, in His divine-human personhood as Jesus of Nazareth, God the eternal Logos voluntarily placed Himself in the role of a *servant* to God the Father. As Jesus of Nazareth He submits Himself to the Father's will and authority. (See **Cottrell, *Faith*, 255-257**.)

If Jesus was fully divine, why did He need to be filled with the Spirit?

Also, in order to allow His human nature to be fully operative, in His incarnation Jesus voluntarily surrendered or suspended the *use* of at least some of His divine attributes. (This is the point of ***Php 2:6-7***.) He came to earth as a man; He was born, He grew up, and He lived among men as a man. But what He had to accomplish as the Messiah required more than human nature by its own resources can achieve. However, rather than using His own divine nature for His tasks, He used the supernatural power of the Holy Spirit. Explaining how this was so is what this chapter has been about. We have seen, as Boles says, that Christ assumed a "dependence upon the Holy Spirit" (**128**), not necessarily for His holy living, but for His supernatural works. As Ware says, "Although Jesus was fully God, as a man he chose to rely not on his own divine nature but on the power of the Spirit" (***Father*, 91**).

How was His dependence on the Spirit different from OT prophets, priests, and kings? The difference is not qualitative, but quantitative. This is the point of ***John 3:34***. The uniqueness of Christ's mission required that the Father give Him the Spirit without measure, to empower and equip Him for this mission. If this is indeed the main way the Spirit worked in the life of Jesus, and I believe it is, we must not try to draw too many parallels between the Spirit in Jesus' life and the Spirit in our own lives as Christians.

CHAPTER FIVE

THE HOLY SPIRIT AND THE NEW AGE

World history, indeed time itself, has been variously divided into significant contrasting periods. The NT quite clearly sets "this age" or "this time" over against "that age" or "the age to come" (***Mt 12:32***; ***Mk 10:30***; ***Lk 18:30***; ***20:34-35***; ***Eph 1:2***1).

Sometimes "this age" refers to the entire period between the original creation in Genesis 1 and the second coming of Christ. Often, however, it is not just a quantitative concept, referring to a period of time a certain number of years in length. It is also a qualitative concept, i.e., "this age" refers to the world characterized by the fallen condition that began with the sin of Adam and Eve in ***Genesis 3***. As such it is "this present evil age" (***Gal 1:4***), whose god is the devil himself (***2Cor 4:4***), whose wisdom is foolishness (***1Cor 1:20***; ***2:6,8***; ***3:18***), and to which we must not conform (***Rom 12:2***).

In contrast with "this age" in the above sense, "the age to come" is the eternal age that will be inaugurated by the second coming of Christ, the climactic event that will happen at the end of this age (***Mt 13:39-40,49***; ***24:3***). For believers it

III. Pentecost and the Holy Spirit
- A. Pentecost Is the Beginning of the New Age
- B. The Main Event of Pentecost
  1. The Prophecy of Joel
  2. The Outpouring of the Holy Spirit
  3. The Pentecostal Tongues

will be the age of "resurrection from the dead" (***Lk 20:35***) and "eternal life" (***Mk 10:30; Lk 18:30***), the age in which all the powers of salvation will be experienced in full (***Heb 6:5***) in the everlasting "new heavens and a new earth" (***2Pet 3:13***).

"This age" as the entirety of world history between creation and Christ's second coming is itself divided in different ways. Many dispensationalists distinguish seven stages of history, each marked by a specific way God relates to the world and to His people. Each begins with a major event: the creation, the fall, the flood, the call of Abraham, the giving of the Law of Moses, the first coming of Christ, and the second coming of Christ.

A more universally accepted way of dividing world history, and in the minds of most Christians a more biblical way, is represented by the BC/AD system of dating events. "BC" stands for "before Christ," and AD stands for *anno Domini*, Latin for "in the year of the Lord," i.e., Jesus. This system is surely biblical in that it acknowledges Jesus as the hinge or turning point of history. It is slightly askew, however, in that it identifies the *birth* of Jesus as the crucial event, rather than His death and resurrection.

The main point is that the first coming of Christ introduced a new age in the history of the world. It brought a new era marked by significant differences in the life of God's people on earth as compared with pre-Christian times. A major aspect of this newness has to do with the work of the Holy Spirit. As a result of Christ's first coming, the Holy Spirit is now working in the lives of God's people in a new and glorious way.

As a result of Christ's first coming, the Holy Spirit is now working in the lives of God's people in a new and glorious way.

THE PROMISE OF A NEW AGE

The OT is a precious record of God's dealings with people from the creation to the first coming of Christ. Because it is *"the very words of God"* (***Rom 3:2***, NIV), it contains absolute truth and eternal wisdom that are *"profitable for teaching, for reproof, for correction, for training in righteousness"* (***2Tm 3:16***). Yet the OT is marked by the themes of preparation and promise. In all His dealings with the Jews God is preparing for even greater works; God's prophetic word to Israel is filled with promises of a new age to come.

Promise and Fulfillment

The NT directs our attention to the *promise* elements of the OT. Israel's glory included the fact that the Israelites received God's promises (***Rom 9:4***). The Old Covenant was a covenant of promise (***Eph 2:12***). ***Hebrews 6:13*** reminds us of the time *"when God made the promise to Abraham"* (see ***Gen 12:1-3***; ***15:5-7***; ***17:1-8***; ***22:15-18***). Though he personally did not receive the *fulfillment* of the promises (***Heb 11:13***), Abraham "received the promises" as such, in the sense that he was the one to whom the promises were made (***Heb 11:17***; see ***Heb 7:6***). In his sermon at Antioch of Pisidia Paul preached about *"the promise made to the Fathers,"* i.e., to Abraham, Isaac, and Jacob (***Acts 13:32***; see ***Acts 26:6***; ***Rom 15:8***). In the third chapter of ***Galatians*** Paul contrasts the promise elements of the Old Covenant with the law elements (***3:16-18***). He refers to Jesus—Abraham's seed—both as the one to whom the promise was made (***3:16,19***) and as the content of the promise (***Acts 13:23,33***; ***Gal 3:22***).

The OT saints "did not receive what was promised" (***Heb 11:39***), but NT saints do receive it *"by faith in Jesus Christ"* (***Gal 3:22***; see ***Rom 4:16***). As believers in Jesus we inherit everything promised to Abraham's seed; we are *"heirs according to promise"* (***Gal 3:29***). We *"inherit the promises"* (***Heb 6:12***; see ***v. 17***), i.e., we inherit the content of the promises. In the new age Jews and Gentiles alike are *"partakers of the promise in Christ Jesus through the gospel"* (***Eph 3:6***).

The Coming of the New

In ***Isaiah 42:9*** God states a significant truth: *"Now I declare new things."* Likewise in ***Isaiah 43:19*** He says, *"Behold, I will do something new, now it will spring forth; will you not be aware of it?"* The new age promised by God would certainly be filled with new things. God declared that it would be introduced by a new Elijah (***Mal 4:5-6***), ruled over by a new David (***Eze 37:24***), administered by a new covenant (***Jer 31:31-34***), resulting in a new kind of righteousness and peace. The prophets did indeed "announce a new and saving divine activity in the future" (**Haarbeck, 670**).

Paul sums up this concept of newness quite well in ***2 Corinthians 5:17b***, *"The old things passed away; behold, new things have come."* For our purposes the most relevant aspects of this newness, as affirmed in the NT, are the new creation and the new covenant.

The New Creation

The first kind of newness that characterizes the new age is the concept of the *new creation*, as compared and contrasted with the original creation, which now exists in a state of fallenness. The new creation is already a reality, having been established in the very midst of the old creation through the work of the Messiah at His first coming. Those who accept Jesus Christ as Savior become a part of this new creation: *"Therefore if anyone is in Christ, he is a new creature"* (***2Cor 5:17a***). This new creation will ultimately embrace the entire cosmos in the form of a *"new heavens and a new earth"* (***2Pet 3:13***).

The new creation is already a reality.

The present, ongoing work of the new creation consists of the aspect of personal salvation usually called regeneration (which will be discussed in chapter seven). Every individual who accepts Christ as Savior and Lord by obeying the gospel undergoes a literal *"regeneration and renewing"* in his heart (***Tts 3:5***). This is the fulfillment of the promise of ***Ezekiel 36:26***, *"Moreover, I will give you a new heart and put a new spirit within you; and I will remove the heart of stone from your flesh and give you a heart of flesh."* The result is a *"newness of life"* (***Rom 6:4***) that enables us to walk in obedience to God's commandments (***Eze 36:27***).

This is what Paul means when he says that *"if anyone is in Christ, he is a new creature"* (***2Cor 5:17a***), and when he says, *"For we are His workmanship, created in Christ Jesus for good works"* (***Eph 2:10***). This new creation is not something external; rather, it takes place within the heart. As Paul says, *"For neither is circumcision anything, nor uncircumcision, but a new creation"* (***Gal 6:15***).

The reality of the new creation is one of the most marvelous blessings of the new, messianic age.

The New Covenant

The other main aspect of newness is the *new covenant*, as compared and contrasted with the old covenant as given through Moses. Actually, the first or old covenant was given in two stages: the *promise* stage, given to Abraham; and the *law* stage, given through Moses (***Gal 3:15-19***). The former aspect of the first covenant was not replaced by the new covenant, nor does it continue into the new-covenant era. Since it consisted solely of promises made by God to Abraham and "the fathers," when these promises were fulfilled through the incarnation and work of the Messiah, it simply ceased to exist. When the Bible depicts the old covenant as being *replaced* by a new covenant, it is usually referring to the Mosaic or law aspect of that first covenant. This is clearly seen in the classic new-covenant promise in ***Jeremiah 31:31-34***:

> *"Behold, days are coming," declares the LORD, "when I will make a new covenant with the house of Israel and with the house of Judah, not like the covenant which I made with their fathers in the day I took them by the hand to bring them out of the land of Egypt, My covenant which they broke, although I was a husband to them," declares the LORD. "But this is the covenant which I will make with the house of Israel after those days," declares the LORD, "I will put My law within them and on their heart I will write it; and I will be their God, and they shall be My people. They will not teach again, each man his neighbor and each man his brother, saying, 'Know the LORD,' for they will all know Me, from the least of them to the greatest of them" declares the LORD, "for I will forgive their iniquity, and their sin I will remember no more."*

Here the old covenant is clearly the *law* covenant written upon stone and other such materials at Mount Sinai following the exodus from Egypt, a covenant that was binding upon all Israelites from birth even if they were ignorant of it or were unfaithful to it.

By its very nature this first covenant was incomplete and unable in itself to accomplish God's ultimate purpose of restoring a relationship between Himself and sinful human beings. This is why it was, by God's design, merely a prelude to a *new* and *better* covenant (***Heb 7:22; 8:6,13***). The book of Hebrews, citing the Jeremiah prophecy in ***Hebrews 8:8-12*** and ***10:16-17***, spells out in detail the difference between the covenants and shows that the old or first covenant has now been replaced by the new one. *"When He said, 'A new covenant,'*

He has made the first obsolete" (***Heb 8:13***). *"He takes away the first in order to establish the second"* (***Heb 10:9***).

One of the main differences between the covenants is that the old one was by nature physical and external, while the new one is by nature spiritual and internal. Membership in the old covenant was by physical birth; membership in the new covenant is by spiritual or new birth (see ***Jer 31:34***). Individual Jews were bound by the terms of the old covenant even if their hearts were not committed to it; those under the new covenant have accepted it in their hearts. In other words, the former was written on stone; the latter is written on the heart (see ***Jer 31:33***; ***2Cor 3:6-7***). In the old covenant the sacrifices and worship were physical and finite, and addressed ceremonial uncleanness—cleansing the flesh, as it were. By contrast the new covenant sacrifice of Jesus Christ had a spiritual and eternal dimension that cleanses the heart and the conscience (***Heb 9:1-15***; ***10:19-22***). This contrast between the old covenant as physical and the new covenant as spiritual is summed up in ***Hebrews 12:18-24***:

> *For you have not come to a mountain that can be touched and to a blazing fire, and to darkness and gloom and whirlwind, and to the blast of a trumpet and the sound of words which sound was such that those who heard begged that no further word be spoken to them. For they could not bear the command, "If even a beast touches the mountain, it will be stoned." And so terrible was the sight, that Moses said, "I am full of fear and trembling." But you have come to Mount Zion and to the city of the living God, the heavenly Jerusalem, and to myriads of angels, to the general assembly and church of the firstborn who are enrolled in heaven, and to God, the Judge of all, and to the spirits of the righteous made perfect, and to Jesus, the Mediator of a new covenant, and to the sprinkled blood, which speaks better than the blood of Abel.*

This new, spiritual covenant, along with the new, spiritual creation, embodies the essence of the newness that God promised would be introduced by the Messiah at His first coming.

THE BEGINNING OF THE NEW AGE

Jesus Christ is the transition point from the old to the new.

Exactly when did this new age begin? This is the same as asking when the new covenant and new creation began. All Christians agree that *Jesus*

Christ is the transition point from the old to the new. He is the beginning of the new covenant; He is the beginning of the new creation. It is a mistake, though, to equate this cosmic turning point with the *birth* of Jesus, or the incarnation as such. The new age literally, specifically, and officially began with the death and resurrection of Jesus considered as a single redemptive event.

Jesus' Death and the New Covenant

Jesus' death on the cross has many levels and many dimensions. One result of His death was that it inaugurated and established the new covenant, thereby setting the old one aside and bringing the old-covenant age to an end. As the great High Priest, Jesus is called *"the mediator of a new covenant"* (***Heb 9:15***; ***12:24***), *"the mediator of a better covenant"* (***Heb 8:6***). According to ***Hebrews 9:16-18***, as a matter of principle a covenant, in the sense of a testament or will, becomes effective only when its maker dies:

> *For where a covenant is, there must of necessity be the death of the one who made it. For a covenant is valid only when men are dead, for it is never in force while the one who made it lives. Therefore even the first covenant was not inaugurated without blood.*

"A covenant is valid only when men are dead."

This applies to Jesus and the new covenant. Through His one self-sacrifice on the cross, Jesus established once and for all the new covenant promised in ***Jeremiah 31:31-34*** (***Heb 10:12-16***). The blood that He shed in His death was *"the blood of the covenant"* (***Heb 10:29***), *"the blood of the eternal covenant"* (***Heb 13:20***).

Jesus Himself made this point clear when He instituted the Lord's Supper. When He gave His disciples the cup, He declared, *"This is My blood of the covenant, which is poured out for many for forgiveness of sins"* (***Mt 26:28***; see ***Mk 14:24***). According to ***Luke 22:20*** He also said, *"This cup which is poured out for you is the new covenant in My blood"* (see ***1Cor 11:25***).

God's own visual testimony to the fact that Jesus' death replaced the old covenant with the new was the tearing of the temple veil at the moment Jesus died: *"Jesus cried out again with a loud voice, and yielded up His spirit. And behold, the veil of the temple was torn in two from top to bottom"* (***Mt 27:50-51***; see ***Mk 15:37-38***; ***Lk 23:45***). From that moment on, the old covenant was inoperative, and the new covenant was technically in force. This means that everything that happened during the lifetime of Jesus, as recorded in the Gospels, happened under the administrative authority of the old covenant. Also, as we shall soon see, the new covenant, though established by Christ's death, did not become functional until the day of Pentecost. Between the cross and Pentecost, the motor was running, so to speak, but the car was not yet in gear.

Jesus' Resurrection and the New Creation

Jesus' resurrection likewise had many levels and many dimensions (**see Cottrell, *Faith*, 272-282**), including the fact that it was the literal beginning of the new creation (**ibid., 277-278**). The first or old creation in its entirety has suffered the effects of sin, particularly evidenced by the presence of disease, decay, and death. It will continue in this state until the second coming of Jesus, when it will be destroyed by a cosmic holocaust and replaced by a new universe (***2Pet 3:10-13***). However, in the very midst of this old creation God inaugurated the first phase of the new creation when He raised Jesus from the dead and gave Him a new, glorified human nature as a prototype of the final resurrection (***Php 3:21***; ***1Jn 3:2***).

Thus we declare that the resurrection of Jesus (including its natural extension in His ascension in His glorified body) was the actual beginning of God's new creation. As such Jesus was *"the firstborn from the dead"* (***Col 1:18***), meaning that His resurrection was the first event of its kind, ever. It was something entirely new, unlike any previous miracle or even any previous resurrection. Jesus alone was *"raised from the dead . . . never to die again"* (***Rom 6:9***; see **Acts 13:34**). Through the glorification of His body He was raised into a new kind of existence, a new dimension of physical creation. This was a stupendous event comparable only to the original creation of ***Genesis 1:1***.

Jesus' resurrection actually inaugurated the whole new order of existence associated with the new heavens and new earth. It is the first event of the eschatological age, the most significant feature of which is that the universe will be cleansed of all the effects of sin and death and will never again be touched by their alien power. The glorified body of Jesus was the first instance of this new order from which death is forever excluded. The eschaton has begun; it began with Jesus' resurrection!

In the case of the covenants, when the new one began, the old one ended. The one immediately replaced the other. This is not the case with the new creation. It has begun in the very midst of the old creation and will exist alongside it and continue to progressively displace it until the second coming. Only then will the old creation cease to exist, and the new creation will be all in all.

What interests us here is this continuing growth and expansion of the new creation. Jesus' resurrection unleashed the *"power of an indestructible life"* (***Heb 7:16***), a power that infuses new life into the souls and bodies of sin-damaged human beings and sustains the living church in the midst of a dying world. This is what Paul calls *"the power of His resurrection"* (***Php 3:10***). This life-giving resurrection power is what God poured out upon mankind on the day of Pentecost in the person of the Holy Spirit.

Jesus' resurrection unleashed the "power of an indestructible life."

THE NEW AGE AS THE "LAST DAYS"

What is the relation between the new age and the "last days"? Sometimes the NT uses the expression "last days" or "later days" to refer to the period of time just before the second coming of Jesus. This seems to be the case in ***1 Timothy 4:1*** and ***2 Timothy 3:1***, and in John's reference to the day of resurrection as "the last day" (***Jn 6:39,40,44,54***; ***11:24***; see ***12:48***).

Sometimes, though, the concept of the "last days" seems to be equivalent to the entire new age, beginning generally with Christ's first coming. That is, the messianic era inaugurated by Jesus is the "last days" in contrast with premessianic times, which would then be the "first days." That Jesus set the "last days" in motion with His first coming is clearly indicated in ***Hebrews 1:1-2***, where Jesus is contrasted with the OT prophets as a new mode of revelation: *"God, after He spoke long ago to the fathers in the prophets in many portions and in many ways, in these last days has spoken to us in His Son."* Likewise in

1 Peter 1:20 Jesus' first coming is described as a "last days" event: *"For He was foreknown before the foundation of the world, but has appeared in these last times, for the sake of you."* This may also be the meaning in ***2 Peter 3:3*** and ***Jude 18***, and especially in ***1 John 2:18***, where John refers to his own era as "the last hour."

The reason this is important is that Peter says that Joel's prophecy concerning the outpouring of the Holy Spirit (***Joel 2:28-32***) was being fulfilled on the day of Pentecost (***Acts 2:16-21***), and by the inspiration of the Spirit he says that Joel meant that this prophecy would be fulfilled in "the last days" (***Acts 2:17***). Thus Pentecost must be included in the "last days." When we understand that the expression "last days" is used elsewhere in the NT to refer to the new age begun by Jesus' first coming, Peter's use of ***Joel 2:28-32*** to explain the tongues phenomena on Pentecost presents us with no problem.

THE NEWNESS OF THE SPIRIT[1]

A major element in the newness of the new age has to do with the Holy Spirit. As we have seen, the OT presents us with considerable testimony to the activity of the Spirit in that era. Until now, however, I have deliberately avoided any discussion of one of the most important OT themes regarding the Holy Spirit. I am speaking of several crucial prophecies of a new phase in the Spirit's work, prophecies of a time when the Spirit would be poured out upon God's people in a new and unprecedented way.

As we shall see, this new outpouring of the Spirit corresponds to the beginning of the new age. Indeed, it is one of the main blessings of the new covenant, one of the main gifts of the Messiah to His new people, the church. And as we shall also see, this new gift of the Spirit is indeed *new*. The marvelous work of the Spirit to which the OT prophets, John the Baptist, and Jesus all point is not just a continuation of what the Spirit has already been doing; it is a new kind of work, a work which now constitutes an aspect of salvation itself.

[1]Though this expression occurs in ***Rom 7:6*** (*kainoteti pneumatos*), I take this as a reference to the human spirit, not the Holy Spirit. See Cottrell, *Romans*, I:429.

Old Testament Prophecies of the Spirit

Most OT messianic prophecies refer, naturally, to the coming of the Messiah Himself, Jesus Christ. Prophecies of the new coming of the Holy Spirit are much fewer, but they are very significant. Those OT saints who carefully studied their holy Scriptures would be expecting not just a coming Redeemer, but a significant outpouring of the Holy Spirit as well. As befits a culture with a relatively dry climate where water was so highly prized, most of these prophecies depict the coming of the Spirit in the imagery of the outpouring of life-giving water. This is the point of ***Isaiah 32:15***, *"Until the Spirit is poured out upon us from on high, and the wilderness becomes a fertile field, and the fertile field is considered as a forest."* A similar prophecy is ***Isaiah 44:3-4***, *"For I will pour out water on the thirsty land and streams on the dry ground; I will pour out My Spirit on your offspring and My blessing on your descendants; and they will spring up among the grass like poplars by streams of water."*

Its proximity to ***Isaiah 44:3-4*** and its similar imagery cause us to understand ***Isaiah 43:19-20*** as likewise referring to the Holy Spirit, though He is not specifically mentioned therein. Here Isaiah says,

> *Behold, I will do something new, now it will spring forth; will you not be aware of it? I will even make a roadway in the wilderness, rivers in the desert. The beasts of the field will glorify Me, the jackals and the ostriches, because I have given waters in the wilderness and rivers in the desert, to give drink to My chosen people.*

Here God promises to give rivers of water to His thirsty people, and He specifically says this will be "something new."

Intermingling prophecies of the revival of the collective nation of Israel from its Babylonian stupor and prophecies of the new messianic era, Ezekiel tells us what God will do in this latter time:

> *Then I will sprinkle clean water on you, and you will be clean; I will cleanse you from all your filthiness and from all your idols. Moreover, I will give you a new heart and put a new spirit within you; and I will remove the heart of stone from your flesh and give you a heart of flesh. I will put My Spirit within you and cause you to walk in My statutes, and you will be careful to observe My ordinances.* (***Eze 36:25-27***)

Verses 26 and 27 especially are usually taken as God's promise of a new saving work that He would begin in the new age, with ***verse 26*** referring to the "regeneration and renewing" of which ***Titus 3:5*** speaks, and ***verse 27*** referring to the power that brings it about, namely, the indwelling Holy Spirit. The difference between this promise and those in ***Ezekiel 37:14*** and ***39:29*** is that the latter texts seem to refer to the Spirit's presence within Israel collectively, and ***36:27*** seems to refer to the Spirit's presence within individual believers—a blessing not given until the new age.

Zechariah 12:10 adds this prophecy: *"I will pour out on the house of David and on the inhabitants of Jerusalem, the Spirit of grace and of supplication, so that they will look on Me whom they have pierced."* The imagery of "pouring out" the Spirit like water is poured out of a pitcher is continued here.

The figure of pouring out water is also used in the most significant of the OT prophecies of the coming of the Spirit, ***Joel 2:28-32a***:

> *It will come about after this that I will pour out My Spirit on all mankind; and your sons and daughters will prophesy, your old men will dream dreams, your young men will see visions. Even on the male and female servants I will pour out My Spirit in those days. I will display wonders in the sky and on the earth, blood, fire and columns of smoke. The sun will be turned into darkness and the moon into blood before the great and awesome day of the LORD comes. And it will come about that whoever calls on the name of the LORD will be delivered.*

The reason this text is so important, of course, is that it is the one cited by Peter in ***Acts 2:16-21*** as being fulfilled on the day of Pentecost. The similarity between Joel's language and the language of most of the other prophecies cited above supports the decision to take the latter as referring to the Pentecost event as well.

JOHN'S AND JESUS' PROMISES OF THE SPIRIT

Prophecies of the newness of the Spirit do not end with the OT prophets. In continuity with them, and perhaps of even greater significance, are the promises of John the Baptist and of Jesus Himself. Those that stand out are the references to being *baptized* with the Spirit and to the Holy Spirit as *living water*.

Baptism with the Spirit

John the Baptist distinguished himself from Jesus thus: *"As for me,*

I baptize you with water for repentance, but He who is coming after me is mightier than I, and I am not fit to remove His sandals; He will baptize you with the Holy Spirit and fire" (**Mt 3:11**). Luke reports John's promise in almost the same words: *"I baptize you with water; . . . He will baptize you with the Holy Spirit and fire"* (**Lk 3:16**). Mark's report is more condensed: *"I baptized you with water; but He will baptize you with the Holy Spirit"* (**Mk 1:8**). John the Baptist tells us that he himself did not originate this language. In his testimony about Jesus he says, *"I did not recognize Him, but He who sent me to baptize in water said to me, 'He upon whom you see the Spirit descending and remaining upon Him, this is the One who baptizes in the Holy Spirit'"* (**Jn 1:33**). Jesus reminded His apostles of this promise in His final instruction to them: *"For John baptized with water, but you will be baptized with the Holy Spirit not many days from now"* (**Acts 1:5**).

Except for **Mark 1:8**, which has the simple dative case, *pneumati hagio*, all the other passages cited above have the prepositional phrase with the dative, *en pneumati hagio*. In every case this action of baptizing "with the Spirit" is compared with John's baptizing "with water." In the latter case the form is both the simple dative, *hudati* (**Mk 1:8**; **Lk 3:16**) or the prepositional phrase, *en hudati* (**Mt 3:11**; **Jn 1:33**; **Acts 1:5**). The interchangeable use of the simple dative and the prepositional phrase shows that they have the same meaning. In reference to the Spirit, either form can be translated "baptized *in* the Spirit" or "baptized *with* the Spirit," indicating the element in which one is baptized; or either can be translated "baptized *by* the Spirit," indicating the agent performing the baptism. Only the context can decide which of these is intended. I conclude that either of the first two translations is appropriate, since baptism *en* the Spirit is compared with baptism *en* water and *en* fire. Thus the Holy Spirit is the element *in* or *with* which one is baptized. Also, the promise identifies Jesus as the agent doing the baptizing, so we cannot speak of being baptized *by* the Spirit as if He were the one baptizing us in or with something else.

> **In every case, baptizing "with the Spirit" is compared with John's baptizing "with water."**

The image in this promise is that of being baptized or *immersed* in the Holy Spirit just as John was immersing repentant sinners in water.

Though water is again the element of comparison, the action is different from the OT image of water being *poured out*. The continuity of thought, however, is this: the Holy Spirit will be poured out in such abundance—think of Niagara Falls—that His presence will be like flowing rivers (***Isa 43:20***) and streams (***Isa 44:3***) in which one may be completely immersed in His life-giving power.

The Holy Spirit as Living Water

The other main set of references to the coming of the Spirit are Jesus' promises to give "living water" to those who thirst, that living water being the Holy Spirit. After Jesus requested a drink of water from the Samaritan women at Jacob's well, He said to her, *"If you knew the gift of God, and who it is who says to you, 'Give Me a drink,' you would have asked Him, and He would have given you living water"* (***Jn 4:10***). When the woman inquired as to the meaning of this offer, Jesus replied no less cryptically, *"Everyone who drinks of this water will thirst again; but whoever drinks of the water that I will give him shall never thirst; but the water that I will give him will become in him a well of water springing up to eternal life"* (***Jn 4:13-14***).

How do we know this is a reference to the Holy Spirit, and why is Jesus not more specific about it? The answers to both questions are found in ***John 7:37-39***. Here John describes an incident that happened on the last day of the Feast of Tabernacles:

> *Now on the last day, the great day of the feast, Jesus stood and cried out, saying, "If anyone is thirsty, let him come to Me and drink. He who believes in Me, as the Scripture said, 'From his innermost being will flow rivers of living water.'"* (***vv. 37-38***)

Here again is a promise of living water that can quench spiritual thirst, and again Jesus does not explain what He means. But in his narrative John the Apostle explains it: *"But this He spoke of the Spirit, whom those who believed in Him were to receive; for the Spirit was not yet given, because Jesus was not yet glorified"* (***v. 39***). Here we are told specifically that the living water is the Holy Spirit, and it is suggested that Jesus did not explain this at the time because the promise would not be fulfilled until after He was glorified, i.e., raised from the dead and enthroned in heaven at the right hand of the Father.

These promises of bestowing the Spirit in the sense of giving living water to the thirsty are in complete continuity with the OT prophecies of the coming of the Spirit and with John's promise that Jesus would baptize with the Spirit. These are all referring to the same new-age newness of the work of the Holy Spirit. The Spirit will be poured out like a cataract of water, forming rivers abundant enough to be immersed in and abundant enough to provide a never-ending supply of life-giving, thirst-quenching refreshment.

It is important to see that the images and terminology of "being baptized" in the Spirit and "drinking" the Spirit are incidental to the circumstances in which they originated. By God's inspiration John spoke of baptism in the Spirit because he was comparing it with being baptized in water. Jesus spoke of the Spirit as water that can be drunk because He was comparing this with water from a well and from a specific religious ceremony. *Baptism in the Spirit and drinking the Spirit are not two different things,* which is clear from Paul's juxtaposition of both images in ***1 Corinthians 12:13***, *"For in one Spirit we were all baptized into one body . . . and were all made to drink of one Spirit"* (ESV).

Baptism in the Spirit and drinking the Spirit are not two different things.

Luke 11:13

Another promise of Jesus concerning the Holy Spirit is found in ***Luke 11:13***, *"If you then, being evil, know how to give good gifts to your children, how much more will your heavenly Father give the Holy Spirit to those who ask Him?"* In my judgment this promise should be equated with the ones already discussed, and should be understood in light of ***John 7:39***; that is, it would not be fulfilled until after Jesus' ascension.

Promises to the Apostles Only

One other group of promises concerning the Spirit are those passages from ***John 14–16***, discussed earlier, in which Jesus promises that the special presence and the special power of the Spirit will be with His apostles after Jesus returned to the Father in heaven. Though Jesus Himself would be separated from them, He promises to be with them in the person of His representative, "another Helper," the Holy Spirit (***Jn 14:16-19,25-27***; ***15:26***; ***16:5-15***).

These promises of the Spirit should not be placed in the same category as those discussed above, since they are given to the apostles only and not to God's people in general. Also, they have to do with the equipping work of the Spirit, not His new saving work. They refer especially to the Spirit's work of revelation and inspiration that would enable the apostles to speak with divine authority.

In my judgment these are the texts in the light of which we should understand the difficult passage that describes the risen Christ as breathing on His disciples (probably the apostles) and in some sense giving them the Holy Spirit: *"And when He had said this, He breathed on them and said to them, 'Receive the Holy Spirit'"* (***Jn 20:22***).

Some think that this act had something to do with the apostles' receiving the Holy Spirit's indwelling, saving presence. One possibility is that Jesus was giving them this blessing in advance of Pentecost. If so, this would be unique and would be an exception to ***John 7:39***. Another possibility is that it was just a symbolic foreshadowing of the Pentecostal gift of the indwelling Spirit. It is much more likely, though, that this has nothing to do with the outpouring as promised by the prophets, by John the Baptist, and by Jesus in ***John 4 and 7***. Rather, what is happening here is that Jesus is bestowing upon His apostles (at least symbolically) what He has promised to them alone in ***John 14–16***, i.e., that special comforting and empowering presence of the Spirit that will now enable them to speak with divine inspiration and authority, and will now equip them to fulfill their unique role as the founding leaders of the church. Just as the Spirit who was upon Moses was also given to the 70 elders to equip them for leadership, and the Spirit who was upon Elijah was also given to Elisha to equip him as a prophet to Israel, so here the Spirit who was present "without measure" upon Jesus (***Jn 3:34***) is being given to the apostles in a new and special way.

Conclusion

God made many promises that would be fulfilled to His people under the new covenant, and none is more significant than the promise of a new kind of presence of the Holy Spirit. In ***Galatians 3***, where Paul emphasizes the promises *"spoken to Abraham and to his seed"* (***v. 16***), he focuses on the words of ***Genesis 12:3***, *"All the nations will be blessed in you"* (***v. 8***). This "blessing of Abraham" (***v. 14***), i.e., a blessing to be given to all peoples through Abraham and his seed, was promised to all who will accept the promise through faith. *"So then those who are of faith are blessed with Abraham, the believer"* (***v. 9***).

Exactly what is the content of this promise? As part of the general gift of salvation through Jesus Christ, it specifically includes the new gift of the Holy Spirit: *"in order that in Christ Jesus the blessing of Abraham might come to the Gentiles [nations], so that we would receive the promise of the Spirit through faith"* (***v. 14***). Paul's main point is to remind the Galatians of *how* they received the promised Spirit: *"This is the only thing I want to find out from you: did you receive the Spirit by the works of the law, or by hearing with faith?"* (***v. 2***). My main point is this: should we not be impressed by the fact that the Holy Spirit is singled out as a main element of the promised Messianic blessing?

The Holy Spirit is singled out as a main element of the promised Messianic blessing.

That the Holy Spirit is a central aspect of the promise is also indicated by ***Ephesians 1:13*** (NIV): *"And you also were included in Christ when you heard the word of truth, the gospel of your salvation. Having believed, you were marked in him with a seal, the promised Holy Spirit"* (lit., "the Holy Spirit of the promise").

One of the very last things Jesus said to His Apostles before His ascension was to instruct them *"not to leave Jerusalem but to wait for what the Father had promised"* (***Acts 1:4***), which was, specifically, that *"you will be baptized with the Holy Spirit not many days from now"* (***Acts 1:5***). ***Luke 24:49*** reports that Jesus said to the apostles, *"And behold, I am sending forth the promise of my Father upon you; but you are to stay in the city until you are clothed with power from on high."* Peter later explained the Pentecostal phenomena thus: *"Therefore having been exalted to the right hand of God, and having received from the Father the promise of the Holy Spirit, [Jesus] has poured forth this which you both see and hear"* (***Acts 2:33***). In ***Acts 2:37-39*** Peter announces that this promised and now present Holy Spirit is intended for all: *"For the promise is for you and your children and for all who are far off, as many as the Lord our God will call to Himself"* (***v. 39***).

In all of these texts, that which is promised is the Holy Spirit. One simply cannot think of the Messianic promise without also thinking of the newness of the Spirit.

The Nature of the Newness of the Spirit

That the Messiah's gift of the Holy Spirit would be something *new* has been emphasized. Our question here is, what is the *nature* of this newness? Based on the content of the prophecies and promises noted above, what conclusions can we draw concerning this newness of the Spirit in the new age? Why is it new? How is this new work of the Spirit different from what He was already doing in the OT era?

What Is *Not* New about the Spirit

First, it is very important to understand what is *not* new about the work of the Spirit in the new age. For one thing, the bestowing of *spiritual gifts* is not new. In OT times, as we have seen, the Spirit equipped many individuals with such things as leadership ability and construction skills. As we shall see, the Spirit continues to equip God's people with gifts and abilities of various kinds; but since such things had already been occurring, they cannot be the newness of the Spirit that is the point of the many prophecies and promises.

For another thing—and this is a very critical point—the new thing cannot be *miraculous powers* of any kind, since the Holy Spirit had already bestowed miracle-working abilities on various individuals in OT times, as needed. The main examples are Moses, Elijah, and Elisha. Also, in the waning days of the old-covenant era, Jesus gave to His apostles the power to work miracles (***Mt 10:1***; ***Lk 9:1***).

Understood in the general sense of supernatural abilities, the most prevalent miraculous power given by the Spirit in OT times was the gift of prophecy, i.e., the ability to speak inspired messages from God. The Holy Spirit thus empowered nonwriting prophets such as Elijah, Elisha, and John the Baptist; and also those who wrote the books of the OT, such as Moses, Samuel, David, and Isaiah. Sometimes the Spirit gave the gift of prophecy not for the sake of the content thus transmitted, but as an evidential sign. Notable here are the examples of Saul (***1 Sam 10:1-11***) and Moses' 70 assistants (***Num 11:25***).

The reason this is important is that many have the mistaken idea that the newness of the Spirit, beginning with Pentecost, was a specific miraculous power, i.e., the gift of tongues. One reason this is a mistaken idea is that the new-age outpouring of the Spirit must be seen as something new; and at that point miraculous abilities, including the ability to prophesy, were *not* a new thing. ***Joel 2:28*** foretells that the outpouring of the Spirit would be *accompanied* by prophesying, which Peter equates with the tongue-speaking on Pentecost (see ***Acts 2:17***); but this prophesying or tongue-speaking cannot be the *content* or *purpose* of the outpouring, since it was nothing new. Rather, this form of prophesying must be understood as the miraculous, evidential sign that the outpouring itself was indeed taking place at that time. As such it had the same general function as the prophesying of the 70 elders in ***Numbers 11***. Again, it was not a new kind of gift from the Spirit.

What *Is* New about the Spirit

What, then, *is* the new work of the Spirit in the new age? What do the prophecies and promises themselves suggest about this? Three main points may be identified. First, from the standpoint of the prophets themselves, the new-age gift of the Spirit would be *universal*. That is, it would be available to and offered to anyone desiring to receive it, and it would be given to all who called upon the Messiah for salvation.

The bestowal of the Spirit would be universal in two senses. First He would be given to all *groups* of people, Gentiles and Jews alike. The promise to Abraham, identified by Paul in ***Galatians 3:2,14*** as including the Holy Spirit, embraced *"all the families of the earth"* (***Gen 12:3***). The prophecy in ***Joel 2:28*** says, *"I will pour out My Spirit on all mankind,"* lit., "all flesh." Though he did not seem to understand what the Spirit was saying through Joel or even through himself, at the fulfillment of Joel's prophecy on Pentecost Peter said that this promise, the promise of the Spirit (***Acts 2:33***), *"is for you,"* i.e., for the Jews who were his audience, *"and for all who are far off,"* referring to the Gentiles (***Acts 2:39***).

The second sense in which the new-age outpouring of the Spirit would be universal is that this gift would be given to every member of God's new-covenant people, not just to selected individuals within the covenant as was the case in the OT era. This universality is seen in Joel's prophecy, not so much in his reference to sons and daughters, old men and young men, male and female servants (***2:28-29***), but in the climactic promise in this prophecy: *"And it will come about that whoever calls on the name of the LORD will be delivered"* (***2:32***). The "whoever" makes it universal. It is important that on Pentecost Peter quotes Joel's prophecy up through this universal promise (***Acts 2:21***), thus connecting it with the promise of the Spirit. Peter then offered the promised Spirit to *"each of you"* in the audience (***Acts 2:38***), and he later declared that *"God has given"* the Holy Spirit *"to those who obey Him"* (***Acts 5:32***), i.e., to whoever calls upon the name of the Lord (***Acts 2:21***) in the manner specified in ***Acts 2:38***.

"God now lavishes His Spirit upon everyone near and afar who accepts His Christ as Lord and Savior."

Robert W. Shaw has well summed up this point thus:

> How revolutionary is this generous promise of the gift of God's Spirit! Limited in His entrance into men in previous ages, God now lavishes His Spirit upon everyone near and afar who accepts His Christ as Lord and Savior. It is as though a dam which had allowed only rivulets of water to ease a parched land had opened all its floodgates, that each and every parcel of ground might be so abundantly supplied with life-giving water as to ensure its producing an abundant harvest. (**3-4**)

The second element of newness about the new-age gift of the Spirit is its *inwardness*. Though the language itself cannot be pressed too far, it seems that in the OT era the Spirit came *upon* individuals in an external way, by empowering them from outside their inmost being. For example, God said to Moses concerning the 70 elders, *"I will take of the Spirit who is upon you, and will put Him upon them"* (***Num 11:17***). When this happened, *"the Spirit rested upon them"* (***v. 25***). Later concerning Saul, *"the Spirit of God came upon him mightily"* (***1Sa 10:10***); and concerning David, *"the Spirit of the LORD came mightily upon David"* (***1Sa 16:13***). Such an external presence ("upon") sufficed for bestowing abilities and powers for service.

It is true that the OT prophecies of the new-age coming of the Spirit also speak of the Holy Spirit as being "poured out" (***Isa 32:15***; ***44:3***; ***Joel 2:28***; ***Zec 12:10***), but not so as to remain on the "outside" of the recipient, so to speak. ***Ezekiel 36:27*** specifically says, *"I will put My Spirit within you,"* not merely to equip you with powers for service, but to *"cause you to walk in My statutes, and you will be careful to observe My ordinances."* Such inwardness will characterize the new covenant, says ***Jeremiah 31:33***: *"I will put My law within them and on their heart I* *will write it."* This is part of the new-covenant *"ministry of the Spirit,"* says Paul (***2Cor 3:8***). It is the Spirit Himself who writes upon our hearts; the provisions of the new covenant are *"written not with ink but with the Spirit of the living God, not on tablets of stone but on tablets of human hearts"* (***2Cor 3:3***). In this way God has *"made us adequate as servants of a new covenant, not of the letter but of the Spirit"* (***2Cor 3:6***).

That the new-covenant gift of the Spirit will be an inward blessing is seen most clearly in Jesus' reference to the coming Spirit as "living water" meant to be drunk (***Jn 4:10***; ***7:38***). The imagery of drinking this living water emphasizes the truth that the Spirit will be present within us: *"The water that I will give him will become in him a well of water springing up to eternal life"* (***Jn 4:14***). *"He who believes in Me,"* says Jesus, *"from his innermost being will flow rivers of living water"* (***Jn 7:38***).

What is the point of this new inwardness of the Spirit? The answer leads us to the third aspect of the Spirit's newness in this new age, namely, the Spirit's work will be *soteriological* in nature. This means that the Spirit's new presence will not be for the purpose of equipping us with various and specific powers for service; it will be for the purpose of *salvation*.

The Spirit's new presence will be for the purpose of salvation.

Certainly OT saints were saved, in the sense that their sins were fully forgiven by God's grace and they had the hope of eternal life. But, as we have seen, they did not have the gift of regeneration that is caused by the inner working of the Holy Spirit. They did not have the indwelling of the Spirit as a source of power for holy living. This inward saving work of the Spirit was reserved for new-covenant saints. Ezekiel's prophecy describes this promised work of regeneration: *"I will give you a new heart and put a new spirit within you; and I will remove the heart of stone from your flesh and give you a heart of flesh"* (***Eze 36:26***). The next words identify the promised Spirit as the source of this regenerating, sanctifying power: *"I will put My Spirit within you and cause you to walk in My statutes"* (***Eze 36:27***).

The prophets' use of *water* to represent the promised Spirit emphasizes this saving purpose. The coming Spirit will be like *"rivers in the desert"* (***Isa 43:19-20***), producing new and verdant life (***Isa 44:3-4***). Jesus said that those who receive this "living water" will have within them an ever-flowing *"well of water springing up to eternal life"* (***Jn 4:14***). Such was Joel's point when he connected the outpouring of the Spirit (***2:28-29***) with calling on the Lord's name for deliverance or salvation (***2:32***; ***Acts 2:21***).

We have seen that two of the principal components of the new age are the new covenant and the new creation. Characteristic of both is the reality of the new spiritual life flowing into our hearts from the poured-out Spirit. The old covenant, written on "tablets of stone," was not intended to bring such life; but the new covenant, written on "tablets of human hearts" (lit., "hearts of flesh"), provides such life. How? In that the new covenant is *"not of the letter but of the Spirit; for the letter kills, but the Spirit gives life"* (***2Cor 3:3,6***). Likewise, following its initiation in the bodily resurrection of Jesus, the continuation of the new creation consists of the spiritual resurrections of countless converts who arise from the baptismal grave to *"walk in newness of life"* (***Rom 6:4***; see ***Col 2:12-13***). This experience of spiritual resurrection, of new birth, of "regeneration and renewing" is the continuing work of new creation (***2Cor 5:17***; ***Eph 2:10***); and it is accomplished *"by the Holy Spirit"* (***Tts 3:5***).

The prophecies and promises of the newness of the Spirit—in the OT, from John the Baptist, and by Jesus—all are pointing ahead to the *same thing*: the coming of an age when God would offer to everyone an inward, saving presence of the divine Spirit Himself. As an offer of salvation, this gift of the Spirit thus becomes a part of the very gospel of salvation. Referring especially to John's image of this work of the Spirit, Stott says, "In the light of all this biblical testimony it seems to me clear that the 'baptism' of the Spirit is the same as the promise or gift of the Spirit and is as much an integral part of the gospel of salvation as is the remission of sins" (***Baptism*, 25**).

PENTECOST AND THE HOLY SPIRIT

Thus far in our discussion of the Holy Spirit and the new age, we have made a number of references to the day of Pentecost. This has been unavoidable, because the fact is that everything related to the new age and the newness of the Spirit had its practical beginning on the day of Pentecost. All the prophecies and promises of the beginning of a new phase in God's redemptive plan, especially as this involves the Holy Spirit, are pointing ahead to Pentecost. The events of Pentecost described in ***Acts 2*** are the fulfillment of it all. This is why Broomall says, "The second chapter of Acts is one of the pivotal chapters of Scripture" (**78**).

Pentecost Is the Beginning of the New Age

As we saw earlier, in a precise technical sense the official, literal turning point of history was the death and resurrection of Jesus Christ. Jesus' death began the new covenant, and His resurrection began the new creation. In a practical or functional sense, however, the beginning point for the new age was the day of Pentecost. This in no way diminishes the significance of Christ's death and resurrection. In reality the outpouring of the Spirit on Pentecost was the consummation of a single yet complex redemptive process. I said earlier that the death and resurrection of Jesus may be considered as a single redemptive event. The total event is actually even more comprehensive, including also Christ's ascension, His enthronement at the Father's right hand, and the Pentecostal outpouring of the Holy Spirit. Peter links all of these stages together in his Pentecost sermon (***Acts 2:22-33***). They are bound together in unbroken continuity, the climax of the process being the outpouring of the Spirit. This is when the new-age clock actually begins to run.

Pentecost is when the new-age clock actually begins to run.

Not everyone agrees with this, though the dissenters are few and are found mainly in ultradispensational circles.[2] The greater number, it seems, do accept the pivotal nature of ***Acts 2***. Pettegrew says, "The Day of Pentecost was, as it were, the divine starting gun of a new era; the new covenant was officially functional" (**89**). "The new dispensation is formally introduced at Pentecost," says Broomall (**81**). In ***Acts 2***, says Barclay, "the great days which the prophets promised . . . have come, and the new age has dawned" (***Promise*, 52**). "Pentecost marked the dividing line between the old economy and the new," says Hunley

[2] Some ultradispensationalists say the turning point (i.e., the suspension of God's dealing with Israel and the beginning of the Church) did not happen until ***Acts 13***; others say ***Acts 28***. See Pettegrew, 113-114; G.R. Lewis, 1129-1121.

(**18**). "The Pentecostal outpouring of the Holy Spirit . . . was the beginning of a new era," says Swete (**79**). Lindsell says Pentecost was "the beginning of the latter days" (**77**). Unger declares that "Pentecost initiated a new epoch in the economy of God," and as such "it is as unrepeatable as the creation of the universe" (***Baptism*, 62, 63**).

As the beginning of the new age, Pentecost was the fulfillment of all the old-covenant prophecies and promises of the coming of the Spirit. As Carter says, "The preparations and promises of the ages concerning the future Age of the Spirit came to their culmination and fulfillment on the Day of Pentecost with the mighty effusion of the Holy Spirit. This was what the prophets had foreseen, what John the Baptist had promised . . . , what Jesus Christ and His Father had promised" (**157**).

Most Bible versions translate ***Acts 2:1a*** similarly to the NASB, *"When the day of Pentecost had come"* ("came," NIV; "arrived," ESV). The verb translated "had come" is the present passive infinitive of *sumpleroo*, from the verb *pleroo*, "to fill up, to fulfill" (see ***Acts 2:2***). Thus the connotation in ***Acts 2:1*** is something like "When the day of Pentecost came to fulfillment." The KJV hints at this: *"And when the day of Pentecost was fully come."* Lohse says it should be translated, "When the promised day of Pentecost had come" (**50**).

The Main Event of Pentecost

In truth, everything that happened on the day of Pentecost was in one way or another a part of this fulfillment. Still, the main event or centerpiece of the fulfillment was the outpouring of the Holy Spirit. This is how Peter interprets Pentecost in his explanatory message following the episode of tongues: *"This is what was spoken of through the prophet Joel"* (**Acts 2:16**); and then he quotes Joel's prophecy about the outpouring of the Spirit (***Acts 2:17-21***). *"The promise of the Spirit"* is what was being poured out on this day, he said, i.e., the promised *"gift of the Holy Spirit"* (***Acts 2:33,38-39***).

The Prophecy of Joel

Peter quotes a rather lengthy section from the prophecy in ***Joel 2***, including references to the outpouring of the Spirit, prophesying, cosmic wonders, and calling on the Lord for salvation. Some say that not every aspect of the prophecy was fulfilled on Pentecost. For example, Pettegrew says it "has not been at this time fulfilled literally in its entirety because the heavenly wonders mentioned by Joel did not occur" (**43**). "The sun was not turned into darkness, nor was the moon turned into blood" (**ibid., 105**). Unger agrees: "It is obvious that Peter did not quote Joel's prophecy to claim its fulfillment in the events that had just taken place. The apostle purposely overquoted the passage beyond any possibility of its fulfillment then. He included events still unfulfilled, which would take place in the still-future day of the Lord preceding kingdom establishment (***Acts 2:19-20***)" (***Baptism,*** **75**).

In my judgment, however, Peter would not have quoted the entire prophecy if it were not all being fulfilled on that day. This was the day of the initial outpouring of the Spirit: *"I will pour forth of My Spirit on all mankind"* (***Acts 2:17a***). This was also the day when prophesying occurred as the evidence of the outpouring: *"And your sons and your daughters shall prophesy"* (***Acts 2:17b***). This was the day when men began to call upon the name of the Lord Jesus for salvation: *"And it shall be that everyone who calls on the name of the Lord will be saved"* (***Acts 2:21***; see ***2:36***). And it was also the day when there were *"wonders in the sky above and signs on the earth below, blood, and fire, and vapor of smoke. The sun will be turned into darkness and the moon into blood"* (***Acts 2:19-20***).

How can we say that these last events, these cosmic calamities, occurred on Pentecost? They did not occur literally, of course, and were not intended to do so. As Kik points out, this apocalyptic language was used figuratively by the OT prophets to describe "great national disasters. Familiar symbols are used to articulate the destruction of nations" (**71**). As an example, see ***Isaiah 13:10***, about judgment on Babylon; ***Isaiah 34:4-5***, about Edom; ***Ezekiel 32:7-8***, about Egypt. The similar apocalyptic language in ***Joel 2:30-31***, as cited by Peter in ***Acts 2:19-20***, symbolically expresses God's judgment upon the nation of Israel. The inauguration of the new-covenant age, the age of the Holy Spirit, was at the same time the termination of Israel's exclusive status as God's covenant people. Thus understood, we can see that even this aspect of Joel's prophecy was fulfilled on that day.

The focal point of Joel's prophecy was the outpouring of the Spirit.

The Outpouring of the Holy Spirit

The focal point of Joel's prophecy, the singular event which was the common content of all the old-era prophecies and promises, was the outpouring of the Spirit. This was *"the Holy Spirit sent from heaven"* (***1Pet 1:12***) as a mighty stream of life-giving water, ready to enter into the hearts and bodies of all who would call upon the name of the Lord Jesus for salvation. This was the new thing, the new work of the Spirit—His inward work of regeneration and continuing indwelling for the purpose of saving penitent sinners not from the guilt of sin (which occurred in the OT era) but from the *power* of sin.

All of the various prophetic ways of speaking of this coming of the Spirit are referring to this one new thing: the pouring forth of the Spirit, as in Joel's and other prophecies; putting the Spirit within, as Ezekiel says; being baptized in the Spirit, to use John the Baptist's figure; drinking the living water, as Jesus put it; and *"the gift of the Holy Spirit,"* as Peter described it in ***Acts 2:38***. All are pointing to the gift of the saving presence of the Spirit that the risen and enthroned Messiah would lavish upon His people from Pentecost onward.

Those who believe that the Holy Spirit was already performing an inward, regenerating work in OT times have some difficulty explaining or doing justice to the outpouring of the Spirit on Pentecost. Kuyper is an example. He affirms the inward working of regeneration by the Spirit in OT times (**119**). What difference, then, does Pentecost make? In the days of the OT the Spirit worked only on individual persons. "But when we come to the day of Pentecost, this no longer suffices. For His particular operation, on and after that day, consists in the extending of His operation to a *company of men* organically united" (**ibid., 120**). The result of the Pentecostal outpouring, then, is that all the individuals regenerated by the Spirit are now formed into one body, the Church (**ibid., 120-121**). In my judgment this is an extremely anemic explanation and hardly does justice to the collective content of the prophecies and promises.

Another example is Arthur Lewis, who defends "the new birth under the old covenant" (**35**). How does he explain the coming of the Holy Spirit in ***Acts 2***? He sees it not as a saving gift, but as an equipping gift, specifically, "a prophetic and evangelistic gift" (**37**). He is saying that on Pentecost the Spirit gave the gift of prophecy to the 120 disciples, "which enabled them to become evangelists and witness to the Jewish citizens and pilgrims in Jerusalem" (**42**). Even ***John 7:39*** is interpreted as referring to "the *prophetic* gift, not the new birth" (**43**). "The gift of the Spirit at Pentecost was . . . a prophetic gift, signalling the mission to all nations, and providing the power for that task" (**43-44**).

Green says much the same thing: "The prime purpose of the coming of the Spirit of God upon the disciples was to equip them for mission." "The Holy Spirit is for Mission." That is, "the coming of the Spirit upon the Church is to equip it for evangelism" (**58-60**).

The problem with such views is rather obvious: they cannot account for the implicit *newness* in the various promises of the Spirit. They present us with just further extensions of the Spirit's equipping work, amply performed in various contexts throughout the OT era. These views also fail to distinguish between Jesus' promises regarding the equipping work of the Spirit directed especially to His apostles, and the universal promise of the Spirit's saving work. Both became present on Pentecost, but they must be kept separate. Jesus did promise witnessing power from the Holy Spirit to His apostles (and perhaps by extension to the entire original group of 120 disciples—***Acts 1:15***): *"But you will receive power when the Holy Spirit has come upon you; and you shall be My witnesses both in Jerusalem, and in all Judea and Samaria, and even to the remotest part of the earth"* (***Acts 1:8***). On Pentecost *"they were all filled with the Holy Spirit and began to speak with other tongues, as the Spirit was giving them utterance"* (***Acts 2:4***). This was their first empowerment for witnessing.

But here is the crucial point: This was *not the same* as the outpoured gift of the Spirit, but rather the accompanying evidence of it. The Holy Spirit did equip these original servants, giving first the tongue-speaking (***Acts 2:1-13***), and then the gift of prophetic inspiration for Peter when he preached his great Pentecost sermon (***Acts 2:14-40***). But the Spirit had done this same kind of work in the OT era, so this was nothing new. Also, even equipping work as powerful as described in ***Acts 2*** cannot do justice to the salvation themes that pervade the prophecies and promises of Pentecost.

The Pentecostal Tongues

Perhaps the most widely known phenomenon associated with Pentecost is the tongue-speaking described in ***Acts 2:4***, *"And they were* *all filled with the Holy Spirit and began to speak with other tongues, as the Spirit was giving them utterance."* Whether the "all" includes only the apostles or the entire company of 120 disciples (***Acts 1:15***) is a matter of disagreement. It certainly included all of the apostles, and in view of ***Acts 2:17*** (*"Your sons* ***and your daughters*** *shall prophesy"*) may have included the entire group. That the crowd labeled them all as Galileans (***Acts 2:7***) is not decisive. Even if all the 120 were speaking in tongues, the apostles as the authoritative leaders were no doubt in the forefront and were the most conspicuous of the group. Also, the term "Galilean" was probably intended more as an insult than as a precise term of origin.

The events described in ***Acts 2*** began in a house the disciples were using as their gathering place while they were waiting *"for what the Father had promised"* (***1:4***; see ***1:13***; ***2:1-2***). While they were all gathered here, *"Suddenly there came from heaven a noise like a violent rushing wind, and it filled the whole house where they were sitting"* (***2:2***). Then *"there appeared to them tongues as of fire distributing themselves, and they rested on each one of them"* (***2:3***). After these external manifestations of the Spirit had occurred, they were all filled with the Spirit and spoke in tongues (***2:4***).

We are not told where in Jerusalem this house was, but it must have been in a neighborhood where many other people were gathered, since a large number of people heard the sound coming from the group of disciples (***2:6***). It must also have been a place where many people could assemble as a single audience since Peter later preached his sermon there and about 3,000 responded to it. Most likely it was in the temple area, since the converts—the newly formed church—continued to gather in the temple (***2:46***). Also, the audience who had gathered to hear Peter's sermon were not permanent residents of the area; they were Jewish pilgrims from many surrounding countries visiting Jerusalem for the feast of Pentecost (***2:5,8-11***). The one place they were all likely to be together was the temple area.

In any case, *"When this sound occurred, the crowd came together"* (***2:6***). They may have heard the windlike noise, but more likely the "sound" they heard was that of the tongue-speaking. (The word for "sound" is *phone*, which can refer to any sound but is commonly used of an audible voice.) The circumstances described in ***2:5-13*** make it clear that the disciples who were speaking in tongues did not remain in the house but came outside, making the sound even more audible. As the crowd was gathering, those speaking in tongues probably circulated among them so that all those assembled could hear exactly what they were saying.

The main reaction of the crowd was summed up in their question, *"What does this mean?"* (*2:12*). That is my question here as well: exactly what was going on here? What was the nature of the tongue-speaking, and what was its purpose? How do the Pentecostal tongues fit into this most pivotal event of all history?

How do the Pentecostal tongues fit into this most pivotal event of all history?

The Nature of the Tongues. What was the nature of the "tongues" (*glossai*, sing. *glossa*) spoken on the day of Pentecost? Some say it was a kind of ecstatic speech, i.e., a nonhuman, heavenly language (**C.R. Smith, 34-39**), but this is not consistent with the hearers' testimony that their own languages were being spoken (*2:8,11*). Also, it is not consistent with the fact that the hearers *understood* what was being said: *"We hear them in our own tongues speaking of the mighty deeds of God"* (*2:11*).

Another view is that the tongues were not foreign languages of any kind, but were simply the disciples' ordinary language (probably Aramaic, or possibly Greek) being used in an especially powerful and impassioned way as a result of the Spirit's filling. Moody (**62**) calls this the "fiery eloquence" view. An example is Barclay, who says that Luke's language in ***Acts 2*** "is a vivid and dramatic way of saying that the disciples were empowered by the Spirit to speak the message of the gospel in such a way that it found a road straight to the heart of men and women of every origin and of every background. This, we think, is the true explanation of this passage" (***Promise*, 55**).

Barclay is proceeding on the assumption that the purpose of the speaking in tongues was simply to communicate "the message of the gospel" to all in the audience. If this were indeed the purpose of the *glossai* in ***Acts 2***, then Barclay is correct to say that the use of foreign languages was unnecessary (**ibid., 54**). This is so because Greek was the common language known to all in the civilized world at the time, and Aramaic was probably known by all in the audience since all were Jews. "In a world where Greek and Aramaic would serve all necessary purposes, a miracle whereby the disciples spoke in foreign languages was unnecessary" (**ibid.**).

Barclay is right to say that foreign languages were not necessary to communicate the gospel, as many have recognized. However, this does not support his own view, because (as we shall see) the communication of the gospel was *not* the purpose of the tongues. The purpose of the *glossai* required that the phenomenon had to be a genuine miracle, which "fiery eloquence" is not.

The third and correct view is that the Pentecostal tongues were indeed foreign languages, or as **Acts 2:4** says, "other tongues." As for those in the audience—Jews and proselytes from a dozen or more parts of the world—*"each one of them was hearing them speak in his own language"* (**2:6**; see **2:8**). That these are real languages is shown by the fact that the hearers refer to them not only as *glossai* (**2:11**) but as *dialektoi* (**2:6,8**), or dialects. Also, Moody notes that "the church fathers are almost unanimous on foreign languages" (**62**). The point is that the tongue-speakers were speaking in an understandable way in languages that they had never studied and learned. The phenomenon was indeed a miracle, and its miraculous nature was part of its very essence and purpose.

The Purpose of the Tongues. Exactly what was the purpose of the miracle of tongues on the day of Pentecost? Many continue to defend the unwarranted idea that the purpose of the great variety of languages was to enable all the nationalities represented in the audience—Parthians, Medes, Egyptians, Romans, etc.—to hear and understand the message of the gospel. For example, F.S. Smith says, "Tongues were . . . the means by which the gospel which is 'the power of God unto salvation' was proclaimed immediately and probably simultaneously unto the nations. . . . The miraculous use of foreign languages was the medium God used . . . to disseminate the good news to all the world" (**23**).

As noted above, Barclay denies that the *glossai* were foreign languages, since the common languages of Greek and Aramaic made the use of the former unnecessary for the purpose of communicating the gospel. Barclay's alternative, however—the "fiery eloquence" view, is likewise not acceptable since it is based on the same assumption that he is reading into the foreign-language view, namely, that the purpose of the *glossai*, however interpreted, was to facilitate the communication of the gospel.

Such an idea, however, is simply not the case; it misses the whole point of the Pentecostal tongues. To assume it is so leads both to a misunderstanding of the nature of the tongues (**Barclay**) and to a misunderstanding of the purpose of the tongues (**F.S. Smith**). Pettegrew has it right: "The gift of speaking in tongues was not intended to be an aid in communication" (**91**). ***Acts 2*** gives no indication whatsoever that the *content* of what was spoken in tongues had anything to do with the gospel of Christ. The content is summed up in one phrase: they were *"speaking of the mighty deeds of God"* (***2:11***). Nash, probably assuming the view espoused by F.S. Smith above, declares that the tongue-speakers "were no doubt talking about the works of Jesus as the Christ of salvation just as in Peter's message to follow" (**21**).

The text does not warrant such a conclusion, however. Nothing about the crowd's response to the *glossai* indicates that they had thus far heard anything about Jesus. Swete's conclusion is valid and to the point: "To regard the gift of tongues, as many of the Fathers of the Church did, as having answered the wider purpose of qualifying the Apostles and other early missionaries for their work of evangelizing the world is scarcely possible" (**73**).

In my judgment the *"mighty deeds of God"* extolled by the tongue-speakers were the great works of God among the Israelites recorded in the OT. That is to say, the *content* of the messages given in tongues was familiar and raised no questions. This is because the whole point of the tongues was *not* the content of the message spoken thereby, but their *form*, namely their *miraculous* nature. In a way the content was irrelevant, because the purpose of the tongue-speaking was to provide an obvious *miracle* that would serve as a *sign* or as *evidence* that God was working a great redemptive work, and would also be a confirmation of the accompanying revelation that explained it (i.e., Peter's sermon).

The bottom line is this: the purpose of the Pentecostal tongues was to provide a God-given sign that the great crescendo of prophecies and promises of the new age of the Holy Spirit were finally being fulfilled. God is saying to His people, "This is the day, and here is the proof!"[3] Unger explains this point very well. He says, "The supernatural display of fire, wind, and tongues of Pentecost were the outward

[3] Pettegrew is right to recognize that speaking in tongues was a sign, not an aid to communication (91). I believe he is wrong, though, to suggest that the purpose of the sign of unlearned foreign languages was to demonstrate the international character of the new-age institution of the church (92-93). Despite their different languages, the Pentecostal audience were all, after all, just one nation; all were Jews.

visible signals that the new age was being introduced." Also, "the tongues, wind, and fire were unmistakable signs to the Jews, showing them that God was doing a new thing" (***Baptism*, 73, 74**). Gromacki well says that the speaking in tongues on Pentecost was "a sign of the never-to-be-repeated advent of the Holy Spirit into the world" (**96**).[4]

The fact is that the miraculous sign of speaking in tongues accomplished its purpose on that day. As a result of hearing of *"the mighty deeds of God"* in their own languages, the hearers showed no signs of conviction of sins or faith in Jesus. This is because the gospel of Jesus was not the subject of what they heard. The fact is that they responded not to the content of the message at all, but to the miracle as such—which is what they were supposed to do. What was their response? *"They were bewildered because each one of them was hearing them speak in his own language. They were amazed and astonished"* (***2:6-7a***). *"They all continued in amazement and great perplexity, saying to one another, 'What does this mean?'"* (***2:12***). In other words, they were now sufficiently ready to hear and to believe the gospel that Peter proceeded to preach to them.

We should remember that the main purpose of every miracle is to function as a sign (see **Cottrell, *Ruler*, 231-244**). Indeed, one main NT word for miracle is *semeion*, "sign." The tongue-speaking on Pentecost was the main miraculous sign that the promise of the outpouring of the Spirit was beginning at that very time. As such, Pentecostal tongues had the very same purpose as the prophesying by the 70 elders in ***Numbers 11:25***. Neither was the main event of the day, but rather was a confirmation of the main event.

It is extremely important that we do not confuse the sign of the promise with the promise itself as Pentecostals usually do. In Joel's prophecy, the outpouring of the Spirit is one thing, and the prophesying (i.e., tongues) is another (***Acts 2:17***). The main point of Pentecost is the outpouring of the Spirit for salvation purposes, not the tongues. Roger Thomas put it this way: "Many of us make a tragic mistake when we read

It is important that we do not confuse the sign of the promise with the promise itself.

[4] Kuyper (128-131) is completely off base when he says the miracles of Pentecost were not intended to be signs; they were just inevitable results of God's great work on that day.

the Scriptural account of Pentecost. We mistake the signs for the promise. We behave like the people whom James rebukes for paying more attention to the clothing worn by their fellow worshipers than to the character of those who wear it (*Jas 2:2-4*). This is precisely what many of us have done with the gift of the Spirit. We have missed the real 'person' while absorbed with the trappings in which He came" (**"Promise," 1:15**).

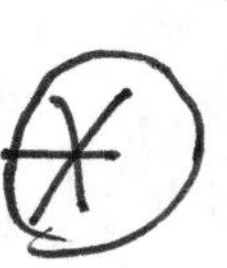

Stated another way, we should not confuse the gift with the wrappings in which it arrived. Those today who still focus on the tongues aspect of Pentecost are like someone who receives a beautifully wrapped birthday gift. After carefully removing the velvet ribbon and the expensive paper, the lovely box is opened to reveal the keys to a fancy new Mercedes automobile! But then this confused celebrant nonchalantly tosses aside these keys with a casual "That's nice." Then he turns back to the wrapping in which they came: "Wow! What wonderful ribbon!" he cries. "What beautiful paper! What a gorgeous box! I love it! I'm going to keep this ribbon and box and paper forever!" The tongues were only the wrapping, to be laid aside so we can enjoy the permanent blessing of Pentecost.

The Source of the Tongues. It is commonly assumed that on the day of Pentecost the apostles (and perhaps others) spoke in tongues *because* they had been baptized in the Holy Spirit. In ***Acts 1:5*** Jesus promised them, *"You will be baptized with the Holy Spirit not many days from now."* Then in ***Acts 1:8*** He said, *"You will receive power when the Holy Spirit has come upon you."* At first it might appear that these are just two ways of saying the same thing. But are they?

In ***Acts 2:1-4*** there is no specific reference to baptism with the Spirit. It is simply assumed by many that this is what the text is referring to, and that Jesus is here keeping the promise stated in ***Acts 1:5***. But what does Luke actually say? *"They were all filled with the Holy Spirit and began to speak with other tongues, as the Spirit was giving them utterance"* (***2:4***). In other words, the ability to speak in tongues was the result of their being *"filled with the Holy Spirit."* Do we have any reason to equate this *filling* with the Spirit with the promised *baptism* with the Spirit (***Acts 1:5***)? I think not. Rather, *being filled* with the Spirit is the same as having the Spirit *come upon* them (***Acts 1:8***).

From the perspective of Pentecost being filled with the Spirit was hardly a new concept or a new reality. This language had already been used a number of times in reference to an *equipping* work of the Spirit upon certain individuals (see ***Ex 28:3***; ***31:3***; ***35:31***; ***Lk 1:15,41,67***; ***4:1***). This terminology would also be used several times after Pentecost for such equipping work (***Acts 4:8,31***; ***6:3***; ***7:55***; ***13:9***). The OT also commonly spoke of the Holy Spirit as "coming upon" individuals, also in reference to their being equipped for service (e.g., ***Num 11:17,25-26***; ***Jdg 3:10***; ***6:34***; ***14:6***; ***1Sa 10:10***; ***16:13***).

I agree with Boles's point, that "a distinction should be made between the 'baptism of the Holy Spirit' and being 'filled with the Holy Spirit'" (147). And I believe that being filled with the Spirit is the same as having the Holy Spirit come upon a person. Also, being baptized with the Spirit is the new thing promised up to and including Jesus' promise in ***Acts 1:5***; being filled with the Spirit—having the Spirit come upon a person—was an old concept. Being baptized with the Spirit is a salvation event; "filling" and "coming upon" refer to equipping with power for service. Tongue-speaking is an example of the latter. Thus ***Acts 2:1-4*** fulfills the promise of ***Acts 1:8***, not ***Acts 1:5***.

Being baptized with the Spirit, unlike "filling" and "coming upon," is a salvation event.

How does this relate to the issue of tongues in ***Acts 2***? In view of the clear statement in ***2:4*** that the tongue-speaking was the result of *being filled with the Spirit*, it shows that the tongue-speaking on Pentecost was *not* the *result* of being baptized with the Holy Spirit. Jesus made two separate promises in ***Acts 1:5*** and ***1:8***. He promised the imminent baptism with the Spirit, which was a universal gift of saving power; and a filling with the Spirit, which equipped the apostles (and perhaps others) with the miraculous power to speak in tongues. The latter was the sign that the former was taking place. The latter is the point of ***Acts 2:1-13***; and the former is the point of ***Acts 2:37-39***.

The events of Pentecost line up this way: (at least) the apostles were *filled* with the Spirit, which gave them the power to speak in tongues, which was the sign or evidence that the baptism or outpouring or gift of the Spirit was now a reality.

CHAPTER SIX

THE WORK OF THE HOLY SPIRIT BEFORE CONVERSION

Thus far we have discussed the work of the Spirit at various stages of history, up to and including Pentecost as the practical beginning of the new age or the New Covenant era. The Pentecostal outpouring made available for the first time "the gift of the Holy Spirit" as a saving presence and power in the lives of all who accept the gift. This is a new aspect of salvation, offered to sinners in addition to the forgiveness of sins, which up until Pentecost had been the main gift of grace. This new component of salvation, based upon the indwelling of the Holy Spirit as its cause, consists of the cleansing of the heart from its sinful condition. This begins with the Spirit's work of regeneration (new birth, new creation, spiritual resurrection) and continues in the ongoing process of sanctification.

In this and the next three chapters we turn our attention to a detailed examination of *how* the Holy Spirit works in the lives of individuals in order to accomplish such salvation. The issue is not *whether* the Spirit operates within individual hearts for this purpose. Most would certainly agree with Boles: "Let it be understood now that since the church was established there has never been a genuine case of conversion that was not begun, carried on, and consummated by the Holy Spirit" (**195**). There is serious disagreement, however, as to *how* the Spirit does this. As many see it, there are two main choices here: either the Spirit works indirectly upon the human heart by means of the Word of God, or He works immediately and directly upon the heart in a way not easily understood. Of course, it is possible that He works both directly and indirectly, and many take this option.

Alexander Campbell on the Meaning of "Conversion"

This question of how the Holy Spirit works is a perennial issue in the Restoration Movement. Many have been influenced by the views of Alexander Campbell, especially as stated in his debate with N.L. Rice in 1843 (henceforward referred to as the Campbell-Rice debate, or CRD). Many of the relevant issues were raised and dealt with in this debate, though not necessarily well. My own judgment is that Campbell was wrong on several crucial points in this discussion, and that he thus sowed some seeds of serious confusion that are still producing faulty fruit.

Specifically, (1) Campbell was seriously mistaken about the nature of conversion, in that he did not adequately distinguish between a sinner's decision to believe and repent, and the subsequent work of the Spirit in regeneration. Also, (2) contributing to the above error and causing even further confusion is Campbell's virtual equation of several crucial terms and the events denominated thereby. He declares concerning the terms "regeneration, conversion, reconciliation, new creation, illumination, remission, adoption, redemption, salvation," that "each one of these" is "a *complete view* of man." He says, "Hence regeneration, conversion, justification, sanctification, &c. &c., are frequently represented as component parts of one process"; but this is wrong, he says, since "any one of these, independent of the others, gives a full representation of the subject. Is a man regenerated? He is converted, justified, and sanctified. Is he sanctified? He is converted, justified, and regenerated" (CRD, 612). Also, "Conversion is a term denoting that whole moral or spiritual change, which is sometimes called sanctification, sometimes regeneration. These are not three changes, but one change indicated by these three terms, regeneration, conversion, sanctification" (ibid., 613). Campbell was also wrong, I believe, (3) in arguing that the *only* way the Spirit can work upon the human heart in conversion or sanctification (or whatever!) is *indirectly*, through the instrumentality of the Word of God alone.

I believe it is crucial to distinguish three stages in the salvation process as it involves the Holy Spirit. A main source of confusion is how to use the term *conversion* itself. Is it a general term referring to the whole process of salvation? Or does it refer to a single specific aspect of that process? In either case, is conversion something done *by* us or *to* us? Is it something accomplished by a human decision or act, or is it something that only God can do? Or are we both actively involved?

I believe it is crucial to distinguish three stages in the salvation process as it involves the Holy Spirit.

In the approach that Alexander Campbell and others have taken, the central element in conversion seems to be *man's* decision to turn to God in faith and repentance. This human act thus constitutes regeneration or the beginning of new life in the sinner's heart. Others see conversion as including (in addition to the above) a working of God upon the life or spirit of the sinner. This work of God, specifically of the Holy Spirit, is not something the sinner can do for himself but something that must be done by God. Others take a third approach, seeing conversion in itself as consisting solely of this working of the Holy Spirit.

How one chooses to use the term *conversion* is perhaps arbitrary, and I am not basing any aspect of my view on the term in and of itself. I am using the term the way I do for the sake of convenience, and I am explaining it now for the sake of clarity. In this discussion, unless otherwise noted, the term *conversion* refers to the single moment in time when the sinner's state or condition changes from unsaved to saved. Before this moment of conversion a person is lost; after it he is saved. Also, I see it in the third sense above, namely, as a work of God the Spirit. Thus we may speak of the Holy Spirit's saving work upon the sinner's heart *before* conversion, *during* conversion, and *after* conversion. The use of the term itself may be arbitrary, but this threefold distinction of the Spirit's work is not. Indeed, it is very important to think of it this way in order to avoid the errors noted above and to do justice to the Bible's teaching.

This chapter deals with the work of the Holy Spirit before conversion. The main issue here is this: what exactly does the Spirit do to help bring the lost sinner to faith and repentance? What role does the Spirit play in leading a sinner to believe and repent? What He does in the moment of regeneration and in the process of sanctification are totally separate questions, and will be discussed in the next three chapters.

How we answer the present question is interrelated with many serious theological and practical issues. For example, those who accept the doctrine of *total depravity* will answer the question one way, and those who reject it will answer it another way. For instance, what we believe about how the Spirit works before conversion will (or should) affect our practice of *praying for the lost*. When we pray for the lost, specifically what do we expect God to do in answer to that prayer? A missionary I know says of a Shinto couple in Japan, "We are praying and hoping that some day this couple will accept Christ." Another Christian leader requests concerning a spiritualist friend, "Please pray that the Holy Spirit will convict him of the truth." This very day I received a newsletter from another missionary with this note: "We continue to be able to preach to the professionals but we need to pray that they would be convicted to make decisions for Christ." Do we believe that God can answer such prayers? If so, what exactly do we believe the Spirit can or will do in the hearts of such sinners?

What we believe about how the Spirit works before conversion affects how we pray for the lost.

THE NATURE OF THE SINNER'S PRECONVERSION CHANGE

Prior to the moment of conversion, i.e., the specific moment when the lost sinner becomes saved, another kind of change must take place in the sinner's heart. This preconversion change is the sinner's own decision to believe and repent. This is a conscious change that occurs within the sinner's mind as the result of the sinner's own decision. What is the nature of it?

A Decision to Believe

This change includes first of all a decision to believe, a transition from unbelief to faith. Scripture always presents this as something the sinner must do to prepare himself for receiving the gift of salvation. *"He who has believed and has been baptized shall be saved; but he who has disbelieved shall be condemned"* (***Mk 16:16***). John says he wrote his Gospel *"so that you may believe that Jesus is the Christ, the Son of God; and that believing you may have life in His name"* (***Jn 20:31***). *"Believe in the Lord Jesus, and you will be saved"* (***Acts 16:31***). *"If you confess with your mouth Jesus as Lord, and believe in your heart that God raised Him from the dead, you will be saved"* (***Rom 10:9***). *"For by grace you have been saved through faith"* (***Eph 2:8***). See ***Romans 3:28; Galatians 2:16; 3:26.***

The faith that saves includes two aspects. One is called *assent*, which is a judgment of the intellect and an act of the will that acknowledge the truth of a statement or truth-claim. It has also been called "belief in testimony" (**CRD, 618**). That is, it is accepting the truth of someone else's testimony or stated truth-claims in the absence of one's own firsthand experience. *"We walk by faith, not by sight"* (***2Cor 5:7***). Faith is *"the conviction of things not seen"* (***Heb 11:1***).

In biblical terminology the assent aspect of faith is represented by the phrase "believe that" (*pisteuo hoti*), i.e., believing with the mind *that* various statements and claims are true. ***Hebrews 11:6*** says that we must "believe that" God exists and that He rewards those who seek Him. Jesus exhorts Philip to "believe that" He is in the Father, and the Father is in Him (***Jn 14:10-11***). John wrote his Gospel so that we may "believe that" Jesus is the Christ, the Son of God (***Jn 20:31***). Those who "believe that" God raised Jesus from the dead will be saved (***Rom 10:9***).

Such assent involves several changes within the mind. For one thing, it involves a purely quantitative change in the content of one's knowledge. To believe something, one must first of all *know about* it, or come to an awareness of it as a possible truth. Also, one must *understand* the truth-claim. Such understanding is not a part of assent, but a prerequisite for it. Next, the intellect must assess the evidence supporting the truth-claim, to see whether it warrants being accepted as true. Finally, assent itself is an act or decision of the will to accept or admit the truth or validity of a specific truth-claim. Even though it is the task of the intellect or reason to evaluate the relevant evidence, in the final analysis it is the will that decides whether to reject a statement's truth (sometimes in spite of sufficient evidence to the contrary) or to admit that it is true. The latter is assent. In this way a sinner comes to *believe that* Jesus is the Christ, the Son of God (***Jn 20:31***), and *believe that* God raised Him from the dead (***Rom 10:9***). Whether this act is "merely a cold assent to truth" or "a cordial, joyful consent to it" (**Campbell, CRD, 618**) is irrelevant to its nature. The latter is still just assent.

The second aspect of faith is called *trust,* which is altogether a decision of the will to act upon the truth assented to. It is a personal surrender to the implications and consequences of this truth. Such trust is most often directed toward persons. To trust a person is to surrender ourselves or something in our power to that person, as when we place our health and life in the hands of a doctor, or our children into the care of a babysitter.

To trust a person is to surrender ourselves or something in our power to that person.

The faith that leads to salvation includes such trust, specifically, a decision of the will to surrender everything about ourselves—our time, our possessions, our abilities, our life itself, and our eternal destiny—into the hands of Jesus Christ. Trust is the decision to rest our hope of eternal life upon the saving power of Christ's cross and resurrection. It is the decision to say, with Paul, *"I know whom I have believed and I am convinced that He is able to guard what I have entrusted to Him until that day"* (***2Tm 1:12***).

The biblical concept of trust is represented by the same Greek words as assent (*pistis, pisteuo*), but by a different phrasing. Assent is believing "that" (*hoti*) the gospel facts are true; trust is believing "in" (*eis*) or believing "on" (*epi*) the person and work of Jesus Christ Himself. *"Whoever believes in Him shall not perish, but have eternal life"* (***Jn 3:16***). *"Everyone who believes in Him receives forgiveness of sins"* (**Acts 10:43**). *"Believe in the Lord Jesus, and you will be saved"* (***Acts 16:31***). We *"believe in Him for eternal life"* (***1Tm 1:16***).

Our question here is, whence comes this faith? How does it arise in the sinner's heart? Whence comes the awareness of the truth claims to which a sinner must assent in order to be saved? What moves the will to accept their truth? What moves the will to act upon these truths, to surrender oneself to Christ and to rest one's eternity upon His promises? In particular, what role does the Holy Spirit play in this?

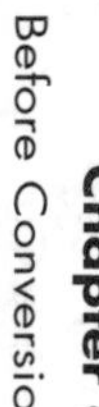

A Decision to Repent

The sinner's preconversion change also includes a decision to repent of one's sins. Such repentance is also a change required for the reception of salvation. Jesus says that *"unless you repent, you will all likewise perish"* (***Lk 13:3,5***). Our only choices are "to perish" or "to come to repentance" (***2Pet 3:9***). Sinners in need of salvation are called to repentance (***Mt 3:2; Lk 5:32; Acts 8:22; 17:30; 26:20***), and repentance is specifically linked to forgiveness of sins (***Mk 1:4; Lk 3:3; 24:47; Acts 2:38; 3:19; 5:31; 8:22***). Repentance leads to life (***Acts 11:8***) and to salvation (***2Cor 7:10***).

What is repentance? The NT noun is *metanoia* and the verb is *metanoeo*, from a combination of the Greek words *meta*, meaning "after," and *noeo*, meaning "to perceive, know, understand, think." Thus the basic meaning is to "know after" in the sense of reconsidering or rethinking a past act or opinion. Such repentance is an *intellectual* change, literally a change of *mind* about *sin*—one's own sin in particular. This involves knowing what sin is as such, knowing what specific attitudes and acts count as sin, and knowing that one is personally a sinner.

Repentance also involves an affective or *emotional* change, or a change in one's *attitude* toward sin. This involves first of all a *hatred* of sin. This is the heart and core of repentance. Instead of loving sin, we hate it. The repentant person has come to despise sin because the holy God Himself despises it, because it is counter to and destructive of true human nature, and because this is what sent the Savior to the cross. Another emotional aspect of repentance is *remorse* (sorrow, grief) for having committed sins against God. When David repented of his sin with Bathsheba, he spoke of his "broken spirit," his broken and contrite heart (***Ps 51:17***). Paul relates repentance to godly sorrow (***2Cor 7:9-10***).

The repentant person has come to despise sin because the holy God Himself despises it.

Finally, repentance is a *volitional* act, i.e., an act of the will. It is a desire, a decision, and a determination to surrender to the Lordship of Christ, and thus to forsake sin and to conform one's life to God's will as found in His Word.

Again our question is, whence comes this repentance? How does it arise in the sinner's heart? What changes the mind about sin, leading to a hatred of it and a desire to be rid of it? What moves the will to surrender to the Lordship of Christ? In particular, what role does the Holy Spirit play?

A Decision to Turn

A biblical concept embracing both faith and repentance is expressed by the Greek word *epistrepho*, usually translated "turn" or "return." It is used seventeen times in the NT to represent turning *away* from sin and idolatry and turning *to* the true God. Basically the "turning away" is repentance, and the "turning to" is faith. Uses of the term include **Matthew 13:15** (citing **Isa 6:10**), *"For the heart of this people has become dull, with their ears they scarcely hear, and they have closed their eyes, otherwise they would see with their eyes, hear with their ears, and understand with their heart and return [epistrepho], and I would heal them"* (see also **Mk 4:12**; **Acts 28:27**; **Jn 12:40**). The word is used in this sense eight times in Acts. In one instance Peter exhorts, *"Therefore repent and return [epistrepho], so that your sins may be wiped away, in order that times of refreshing may come from the presence of the Lord"* (**Acts 3:19**). Luke reports, *"And the hand of the Lord was with them, and a large number who believed turned [epistrepho] to the Lord"* (**Acts 11:21**). Jesus sent Saul (Paul) to the Gentiles, *"to open their eyes so that they may turn [epistrepho] from darkness to light and from the dominion of Satan to God, that they may receive forgiveness of sins and an inheritance among those who have been sanctified by faith in Me"* (**Acts 26:18**). Paul praises the Thessalonian Christians for *"how you turned [epistrepho] to God from idols to serve a living and true God"* (**1Th 1:9**). The noun *epistrephe* is used once, in **Acts 15:3**, to refer to *"the conversion of the Gentiles."* Also, the verb *strepho* is used twice in this sense (**Mt 18:3**; **Jn 12:40**).[1]

As Laubach says concerning these terms, "When men are called in the NT to conversion, it means a fundamentally new turning of the human will to God" (355). Such turning is a decision of the sinner, a change the sinner makes in his own heart. In no case does the NT say that God turns the sinner. Salvation from God is something that *follows* the human turning. In **Matthew 13:15** and **Mark 4:12**, healing and forgiveness are given by God only after the sinner returns to Him. In **Acts 3:19**, returning to God is a condition for forgiveness and refreshing. The same is true in **Acts 26:18**. In **2 Corinthians 3:16**, turning to the

[1] In some translations the word "conversion" or "converted" is used in some of these texts, but this rendering is contrary to the way I am using these words, as explained above in the introduction to this chapter. The "turning" in these texts is the preconversion change willed by the sinner, not the actual change from lost to saved which only God can accomplish.

Lord precedes the removal of the veil that prevents a right understanding of His Word. (All of these texts are contrary to the Calvinist understanding of the Holy Spirit's work in conversion, which assumes the doctrine of total depravity and therefore the need for the divine work to precede the human. This will be discussed in more detail below.)

In this turning, which consists of faith and repentance, all aspects of the mental or spiritual life are involved: the intellect, the emotions, and especially the will. All such willful changes are decisions made by sinners. What moves them to make these decisions? Is the Holy Spirit involved? If so, in what way?

> **In this turning, all aspects of the mental or spiritual life are involved.**

THE POWER OF THE WORD OF GOD

What has the power to move a sinner's heart to accept the truth about sin and salvation, to hate his own personal sins, and to turn to Jesus and trust Him for eternal life? What can make such an impact on the intellect, the emotions, and the will? One thing about which Scripture is absolutely clear, and one thing upon which all agree, is that such power is inherent in the Word of God, especially in the gospel of Jesus Christ. The Word of God is not only *able* to bring sinners to faith and repentance; its role is absolutely *necessary* if this is to be accomplished.

The Bible's Testimony to Its Own Power

"The Word of God" includes any information or message revealed to mankind by God through prophets and apostles, plus any nonrevealed messages that come to us via inspiration from the Holy Spirit. For those of us who live in postapostolic times, the Word of God is the Bible. We can learn something and benefit in some way from every part of this book, but all its parts do not have the same purpose or produce the same benefit. Regarding the power of the Word to bring about faith and repentance, we are thinking specifically of its *law* portions and its *gospel* message. These are strands of teaching that run throughout the OT and the NT. The Bible's own teaching underscores the power of these aspects of the Word of God to move us to faith and repentance.

In the OT the experiences and writings of David emphasize the power of God's law to convict of sin and to generate commitment to obey God's will. David cries out to God, *"My flesh trembles for fear of You, and I am afraid of Your judgments"* (***Ps 119:120***). He is filled with godly sorrow because of his sin when confronted by the law: *"My eyes shed streams of water, because they do not keep Your law"* (***Ps 119:136***). *"I cried with all my heart; answer me, O LORD! I will observe your statutes"* (***Ps 119:145***). From God's law he learns righteousness and is motivated to live thereby: *"From Your precepts I get understanding; therefore I hate every false way"* (***Ps 119:104***). *"Your word I have treasured in my heart, that I may not sin against You"* (***Ps 119:11***). He sums this up in ***Psalm 19:7***, *"The law of the LORD is perfect, restoring the soul."*

The Bible's own teaching underscores the power of the Word of God to move us to faith and repentance.

When David committed adultery with Bathsheba and murdered her husband Uriah, God sent the prophet Nathan to pronounce the law's condemnation against him (***2Sa 12:1-12***). This moved David to repent: *"Then David said to Nathan, 'I have sinned against the LORD'"* (***2Sa 12:13***). He expressed his repentance in ***Psalm 51***, where he acknowledged the impact of God's Word through Nathan: *"Against You, You only, I have sinned and done what is evil in Your sight, so that you are justified when You speak and blameless when You judge"* (***Ps 51:4***). He prayed for restoration: *"Restore to me the joy of Your salvation and sustain me with a willing spirit"* (***Ps 51:12***). If restored, David promised to use God's Word to convert other sinners: *"Then I will teach transgressors Your ways, and sinners will be converted to You"* (***Ps. 51:13***).

Another OT example of the power of the law of God to convict sinners is the rediscovery of the book of the law in the days of Josiah the king. *"Then Hilkiah the high priest said to Shaphan the scribe, 'I have found the book of the law in the house of the LORD.' And Hilkiah gave the book to Shaphan who read it"* (***2Kgs 22:8***). Shaphan took the book to Josiah and *"read it in the presence of the king. When the king heard the words of the book of the law, he tore his clothes"* (***2Kgs 22:10-11***). He declared, *"Great is the wrath of the LORD that burns against us, because our fathers have not listened to the words of the book, to do according to all that is written concerning us"* (***2Kgs 22:13***).

The NT gives even more testimony to the power of the Word of God. We have noted the use of the Greek word *epistrepho* to describe a sinner's act of turning to God in faith and repentance. Several of the relevant texts make it clear that hearing the Word is a major factor in prompting such turning. ***Matthew 13:15*** and its parallels show that hearing and understanding God's Word is a prerequisite for this turning. Luke tells us that Christian evangelists came to Antioch, *"preaching the Lord Jesus. And . . . a large number who believed turned to the Lord"* (***Acts 11:20-21***). Paul and Barnabas told the pagans at Lystra that they were there to *"preach the gospel to you that you should turn from these vain things to the living God"* (***Acts 14:15***). Paul tells King Agrippa that he obeyed his divine commission and preached *"to the Gentiles, that they should repent and turn to God"* (***Acts 26:19-20***).

The NT gives even more testimony to the power of the Word of God.

In these examples from Acts, God uses human agents to proclaim His Word and thereby to elicit faith and repentance from sinners. John the Baptist's mission was likewise to preach and to *"turn [epistrepho] many of the sons of Israel back to the Lord their God"* (***Lk 1:16***). ***James 5:20*** says that *"he who turns [epistrepho] a sinner from the error of his way will save his soul from death."* All those who preach and exhort from the Word are thus secondary instruments for leading sinners to turn to God, but the power of the *Word* is still the primary motivator for such turning.

Campbell recounts twenty-one examples of conversion from the book of Acts, and shows that in every case the converts were acting upon the Word that was proclaimed to them (**CRD, 745-747**). Boatman likewise surveys the conversion episodes of Acts (**248-258**) and remarks that "conversion is uniformly recorded as occurring in direct response to the preaching of the gospel" (**ibid., 248**). ***Acts 2*** is a prime example. When Peter preached the first gospel sermon (**Acts 2:14-36**), the audience was brought under conviction: *"Now when they heard this, they were pierced to the heart"* (***Acts 2:37***). Likewise ***Acts 4:4*** says on another occasion that *"many of those who had heard the message*

believed." The Ethiopian eunuch believed through Philip's explanation of a messianic prophecy from Isaiah (***Acts 8:29-38***). *"And many of the Corinthians when they heard were believing and being baptized"* (***Acts 18:8***).

Many other NT texts declare the power of the Word. In Jesus' parable of the sower (***Lk 8:4-8***) *"the seed is the word of God"* (***8:11***). In His explanation of the parable Jesus shows that the sowing of the seed is the preaching and hearing of the word, and that the word thus planted can produce faith and salvation (***8:12***). Jesus says that the truth, when known, makes one free (***Jn 8:32***). The very purpose for which John wrote his Gospel is *"so that you may believe that Jesus is the Christ, the Son of God; and that believing you may have life in His name"* (***Jn 20:31***). The written word thus has the power to lead to faith. Paul declares that the gospel is *"the power of God for salvation to everyone who believes"* (***Rom 1:16***). What prompts such faith? *"So faith comes from hearing, and hearing by the word of Christ"* (***Rom 10:17***). ***Hebrews 4:12*** says that the Word is powerful enough to pierce the most calloused heart: *"For the word of God is living and active and sharper than any two-edged sword, and piercing as far as the division of soul and spirit, of both joints and marrow, and able to judge the thoughts and intentions of the heart."*

WHAT GIVES THE WORD ITS POWER?

What is there about the Bible—the Word of God—that gives it such power? First of all, it has power because it is *true*. Wherever the Word is proclaimed, the truth is proclaimed; and there is an inherent power in truth. Wells observes, "Biblical conversion is conversion that is brought about by *truth*." The gospel "is a deep and profound gospel because it is a gospel of truth." The apostles' secret in the book of Acts "was this gospel of truth" (**95**). Boles says, "The instrumentality of truth in conversion is a fact abundantly substantiated in the New Testament" (**197**). This was shown in the preceding section.

First of all, the Word has power because it is true.

Lies and falsehood are also quite powerful, but the truth always "rings true" to honest seekers. That God's Word is truth (***Jn 17:17***) is one thing that causes it to pierce through our defenses into the hidden recesses of our hearts and to lay us bare not only before God but also before our own eyes (***Heb 4:12-13***). This was the power of Nathan's message to David (***2Sa 12:1-13***) and of Peter's sermon on Pentecost (***Acts 2:37***).

The second thing that gives the Word its power is the very *content* of the gospel message about Jesus Christ. Its ability to move hearts is due to more than just the fact that it is true. There is also a moving and stirring force in the very story of the gospel as recorded in the Word. The message of how Christ died for our sins and arose from the dead has the power to stir our emotions and prod our wills to make the decisions that are the necessary elements of faith and repentance.

The message of what Christ did has the power to stir our emotions and prod our wills.

The third thing that gives the Word its power is the fact that it is, by virtue of the phenomena of revelation and inspiration, the Word *of God*. There are many appeals that move the heart and motivate us to action, such as accounts of the devastation and need caused by tsunamis and hurricanes. There are many written messages that stir us up and motivate us to action, such as letters from our creditors, from the I.R.S., or from some other agency of authority. But there is only one message that actually comes to us from *God Himself*, and that is the Bible. When we understand its true origin, how can we not be moved by it? Yes, it is true; yes, its message of salvation is inherently moving. But the thing that should stimulate a response to it most of all is the fact that it is "the very words of God" (***Rom 3:2***, NIV), the words of the omnipotent Creator and sovereign Lord of the universe! This leads to our next section.

THE SPIRIT AND THE WORD

"In the very nature of things," says Sweeney, "the work of the Spirit is to make believers out of unbelievers" (**99**). This is certainly not His only work, but it surely is a main one. Our question in this chapter is just this: *how* does the Holy Spirit "make believers out of unbelievers"? What is His role in bringing sinners to faith and repentance? All would agree that whenever someone makes a conscious decision to believe and repent, the Word of God is involved. All would also agree that whenever the Word is working, the Holy Spirit

The Holy Spirit works to bring unbelievers to faith and repentance through the Word of God.

is working through the Word. Thus at the very least we can say that the Holy Spirit works to bring unbelievers to faith and repentance through the Word of God as His instrument. Boles puts it thus: "The Holy Spirit and the word of God are never separate in conversion and sanctification" (**197**). Also, "it is clear that the Holy Spirit always operates upon the heart of the sinner in conversion through the truth, and that truth is the gospel" (**198**).[2]

(Whether the Spirit works in some manner apart from or in addition to the Word will be discussed below, pp. 213-228.)

The Implication of Inspiration

The most basic reason we can say that the Holy Spirit is always working where the Word is working is that He is in fact the divine author of everything in the Bible. This is the result of His work of revelation and inspiration. Whenever an inspired prophet or apostle speaks or writes an inspired message from God, in a true sense that is the Holy Spirit Himself speaking or writing. Anyone who is moved by such a message is thus being moved by the Spirit.

Several texts specifically make this point. ***Nehemiah 9:30*** records this prayer to God concerning Israel: *"However, You bore with them for many years, and admonished them by Your Spirit through Your prophets, yet they would not give ear."* That the people did not respond ("give ear") does not negate the fact that the Spirit was speaking through the prophets with the intent of eliciting a response. That they did not respond simply reflects the reality of human free will.

First Peter 1:12 is another text that links the Spirit and the Word. Here Peter refers to the *"things which now have been announced to you through those who preached the gospel to you by the Holy Spirit sent from heaven."* This is obviously referring to the post-Pentecostal preaching of the gospel by the apostles. They preached this inspired Word, says Peter, "by the Holy Spirit."

Bales discusses the ***Nehemiah*** and ***1 Peter*** texts (***52***), and also refers to Jesus' messages to the seven churches of Asia given to the apostle

[2] It should be remembered that some of the writers I am quoting do not use the word "conversion" in the same sense that I am using it.

John in ***Revelation 2 and 3***. Though Jesus Himself dictated these letters to John (e.g., *"And to the angel of the church in Thyatira write: The Son of God . . . says this"* [***Rev 2:18***]), in each letter these words are included: *"He who has an ear, let him hear what the Spirit says to the churches"* (***2:7,11,17,29; 3:6,13,22***). Even though the letters were dictated by Jesus and written down by John, the Spirit was involved because He was inspiring John's writing to ensure that it was accurate and true (see ***Rev 1:10-11***). Bales makes this comment: "The written word of the Spirit was the voice of the Spirit. He who listens to the written word is listening to what the Spirit saith to the churches" (**53**). This is true of Scripture as a whole.

We should also remember that Christians are exhorted to defend themselves against the devil with *"the sword of the Spirit, which is the word of God"* (***Eph 6:17***). Whether we are using this Word in self-defense or in an attempt to rescue others who are being held captive by the devil, we are at the very least using a sword that has been forged by the Holy Spirit; thus every victory must be credited to Him. It may be that when we thus use the Word, the Spirit Himself is the "sword-wielder" (**J.D. Thomas, 12**).

We are using a sword that has been forged by the Holy Spirit.

Our main point is that the Holy Spirit always works through the Word because of His role in the origin of the Bible. Because of His works of revelation and inspiration, God the Spirit is the ultimate author of everything in the Bible. Therefore whatever is accomplished by the biblical message is ultimately accomplished by the Spirit Himself. The Spirit influences the hearts of sinners by working on them *indirectly* through His own inspired Word.

The Spirit Convicts the World

A key text describing the Spirit's role in bringing sinners to faith and repentance is ***John 16:8-11***, which is part of Jesus' final instructions to His apostles on the eve of His crucifixion. Much of this teaching has to do with the work of the promised Helper (*parakletos*), the Holy Spirit. Jesus says,

> *And He, when He comes, will convict the world concerning sin and righteousness and judgment; concerning sin, because they do not believe in Me; and concerning right-*

eousness, because I go to the Father and you no longer see Me; and concerning judgment, because the ruler of this world has been judged.

The subject here is the Holy Spirit. His work will be to "convict the world." The "world" (*kosmos*) is the unbelieving or unsaved world, "mankind as alienated from God, as opposed to God and in need of the saving grace of God" (**Erdman, 107**). What does Jesus say will be "the Spirit's mission to unconverted men" (**Carter, 138**)? He will "convict" them.

The word Jesus uses here for "convict," i.e., *elengcho*, has received a lot of attention. Some take it in a legal or forensic sense, with the Spirit being portrayed as a prosecuting attorney who demonstrates the guilt of sinners by presenting evidence against them in a court of law. This seems to be the sense of the word in ***James 2:9***, which speaks of certain ones as being *"convicted by the law as transgressors"* (see ***Rom 3:19-20***). ***Jude 15*** pictures the judgment day as the time when the Lord will come *"to execute judgment upon all, and to convict all the ungodly of all their ungodly deeds."*

Donald Williams elaborates on this supposed legal connotation of the term:

> This was a technical term used to describe what a prosecuting attorney does in a courtroom in order to convict the accused of a crime. The attorney presents the incriminating evidence, argues the case, anticipates and refutes objections and rationalizations until there is no reasonable doubt of the prisoner's guilt.

"The Spirit acts as God's prosecuting attorney to convince the sinner of his own guilt and need of Christ as Savior"

Williams then applies this to the Spirit: "That is exactly what the Holy Spirit does in the courtroom of the sinner's mind before the jury of personal conscience: the Spirit acts as God's prosecuting attorney to convince the sinner of his own guilt and consequently his desperate need of Christ as Savior" (**52**).

It may be that we should not press the forensic interpretation of this word too far. Whether we do or not, the word certainly does contain the idea of the presentation of evidence that clearly shows the accused to be guilty. Thus the original NIV translation of ***John 16:8*** said that the Holy Spirit "will prove the world wrong." This seems to be the idea in ***Matthew 18:15***, *"If your brother sins, go and show him his fault [elengcho] in private; if he listens to you, you have won your brother."* Jesus challenged His opponents, *"Which one of you convicts me of sin?"* (***Jn 8:46***). What He is saying is, do you think you can really produce any genuine evidence that I have sinned? See also ***1 Timothy 5:20***; ***James 2:9***; ***Jude 15***.

A major issue in the interpretation of *elengcho* is whether the result of the action is merely an objective demonstration or also a subjective acknowledgment by the accused. In other words, does one merely present sufficient evidence to make his case, or does the evidence actually convince the accused to acknowledge his guilt? Those who hold the latter view are usually not satisfied with the forensic connotation, since a prosecutor and jury may agree that the accused is guilty, while the latter adamantly refuses to acknowledge his wrongdoing. Thus the word "convict" may be misleading if it is limited to a courtroom decision. The proponents of the subjective view thus prefer the translation "convince," in the sense that the accused is personally convicted of his wrong, and is brought to admit it and acknowledge it in his own heart. Trench's opinion is often quoted in support: "But *elengchein* is a much more pregnant word; it is so to rebuke another, with such effectual wielding of the victorious arms of the truth, as to bring him, if not always to a confession, yet at least to a conviction, of his sin" (***Synonyms*, 13**). Barclay agrees: "The basic meaning of this word is so to demonstrate the truth to a man that he sees it as the truth, that he is convinced of, and admits, his error, and that he accepts the new consequences which follow from the new acceptance of the truth. . . . The whole essence of the word is that the truth is so presented to a man that he cannot fail to see it, that he cannot deny it, and that he must accept it" (***Promise*, 43**).

I would like to accept this view, but I do not think the evidence warrants it. Erdman rightly says that "convince" (the subjective view) is more than Jesus was intending to convey here (**108**). Certainly he is right in the sense that the Holy Spirit does not actually persuade the entire world of unbelievers to admit that they are wrong. He certainly *proves* that they are wrong, and at best we can say that he makes such a case that no honest sinner can truly deny it. The sinner's conscience will surely be pierced. When this happens, though, not every-

The sinner's conscience will surely be pierced, but not everyone will admit his wrong.

one will admit his wrong, perhaps not even to himself. In ***Matthew 18:15*** Jesus tells us to show a sinning brother his fault, i.e., to "convict" him; then He says, *"if he listens to you." "If* he listens" shows that it is possible that he will not be *convinced*. Also, when Herod was "reprimanded" (*elengcho*) by John the Baptist (***Lk 4:19***), his response was hardly that of a humble penitent.

The fact is, though, that some who are thus "convicted" *will* be fully convinced and will turn to God. Paul says that an unbeliever may attend a church service and hear Christians prophesying, and thus be *"convicted by all; the secrets of his heart are disclosed; and so he will fall on his face and worship God"* (***1Cor 14:24-25***). In ***Titus 1:9*** Paul says that elders must be able to *"refute* [*elengcho*] *those who contradict sound doctrine."* In ***1:13*** he adds, *"For this reason reprove* [*elengcho*] *them severely so that they may be sound in the faith."* This anticipates a positive response to the convicting work.

Whatever nuance we place upon this word, whether it be objectively proving one wrong via the presentation of evidence, or also convincing one subjectively to acknowledge his guilt, we should not equate the immediate result of this convicting work with repentance as such or faith as such. It is, however, a prerequisite for true faith and repentance. When one submits to the Spirit's convicting work, he is ready to believe and repent. See ***Revelation. 3:19***, *"Those whom I love, I reprove* [*elengcho*] *and discipline; therefore be zealous and repent."*

Of what does the Spirit "convict the world"? Of sin, righteousness, and judgment. We may be ready to give our own ideas about what should be included in these terms, but Jesus points us toward certain specific applications of them. First, the Spirit convicts concerning sin, He says, *"because they do not believe in me."* Thus Jesus is not speaking of a conviction about sins in general (which the Spirit does accomplish through the law portions of God's Word), but of the specific sin of "not believing in Jesus" (**Foster, "Conversion," 8**). As Barclay says, "The work of the Holy Spirit will compel a man to see that not to believe in Jesus Christ is to sin" (***Promise*, 43**). Carter calls such unbelief "the sin of all sins, and it is to convince man of this sin . . . that the Spirit was sent into the world of unconverted men" (**140**). It does not matter if a man is convicted of any other or all other of his sins; until he comes to grips with his unbelief in Jesus, none of his sins can be dealt with. No matter what else one believes about Jesus, until he knows Him as the one who *"came into the world to save sinners"* (***1Tm 1:15***), he is still an unbeliever.

Second, the Spirit convicts the world concerning righteousness, Jesus says, *"because I go to the Father and you no longer see Me."* By referring to His own departure from the world in His death, resurrection, and ascension, Jesus shows that the Spirit will convict sinners concerning *Jesus' own righteousness*. Most take this to mean that Jesus' resurrection and ascension are proof that He was not a sinner and was not the guilty scoundrel His enemies made Him out to be. By exalting Jesus to His own right hand and making Him *"both Lord and Christ"* (***Acts 2:33-36***), the Father affirmed once and for all Christ's eternal righteousness and sinless perfection. As Barclay says, without the resurrection and ascension "it might be possible to see in Jesus a glorious failure; with them we cannot but see the triumphant, victorious, vindicated Lord" (***Promise*, 44**). See **Carter, 141**.

Another possibility is that the Holy Spirit will convict the world of the gift of the righteousness of Jesus Christ which He can share with the world by virtue of His high-priestly sacrifice on the cross and His mediatorial work from His throne in heaven. When convicted of their own sin, and then of this righteousness Christ offers to sinners (***2Cor 5:21***; ***Php 3:9***), sinners can then see that their only hope of heaven is Christ's righteousness and not their own.

Third, the Spirit convicts the world concerning judgment, *"because the ruler of this world has been judged."* The "ruler of this world" is the devil, and he was judged and "cast out" by the very instrument he thought was his triumph over Jesus, namely, the cross. Jesus had said earlier, *"Now judgment is upon this world; now the ruler of this world will be cast out. And I, if I am lifted up from the earth, will draw all men to Myself"* (***Jn 12:31-32***). The world comforts itself by denying a future judgment day, but the cross proves the inevitability of judgment in that it was God's decisive judgment upon the father of all sin-

The world comforts itself by denying a future judgment day, but the cross proves its inevitability.

ners, the devil himself. Through His death Jesus crushed the serpent's head (***Gen 3:15; Rom 16:20***) and rendered the devil powerless (***Heb 2:14***; see ***1Jn 3:8***). Certainly if the devil himself has been judged, no sinner can hope to escape his own judgment.

In all of this we must remember that Jesus' main point is that the *Holy Spirit* will convict the world of sin, righteousness, and judgment. The main question for our purposes is this: *how* does the Spirit convict the world? What means does He use, if indeed He uses means at all? One view is that He convicts the world through the holy living of Christians, whose holiness is the result of their being indwelt by the Spirit. Pettegrew says that this "should come as no surprise to us because we know that believers under the new covenant have the universal indwelling of the Spirit. Thus, we become the Spirit's instruments of conviction as we preach, teach, and live the Word of God" (73).

This is not a bad idea. We can agree that the Holy Spirit does indirectly influence sinners through His indwelt people. However, I doubt if that is specifically what Jesus had in mind here in ***John 16:8-11***. It is more likely that He was referring to the way the Holy Spirit indirectly convicts sinners through the Word of God which is produced by His own work of revelation and inspiration. This is suggested here in the context of ***John 16:8-11*** itself, in the fact that the next few verses include Jesus' most specific promise to His apostles that they would be guided into all truth by the Spirit of truth, especially the truth that glorifies Jesus (***Jn 16:12-15***). This is the very truth, the gospel truth, that convicts the world.

In the abstract, we might think that the best means of convicting the world of sin, righteousness, and judgment would be through the inspired *law* elements of the Word of God. But Jesus narrows all of these subjects down to Himself: the sin of unbelief in Him, the righteousness of the risen and ascended Lord, and God's judgment against Satan through the cross. This means that no one can be convicted of these specific aspects of sin, righteousness, and judgment without knowing the facts of Jesus' sinless life and redeeming work. Thus the only way the Holy Spirit can convict the world of these things is by inspiring the apostles and NT prophets to accurately recount all the relevant historical data about Jesus, and by revealing to them the things about Jesus' death, resurrection, and ascension that could originally be known only by God. This is simply to say, again, that the

Holy Spirit works to bring sinners to faith and repentance indirectly through the inspired truth of the gospel.

The prime example of the Spirit's convicting work, thus understood, is Peter's sermon on the day of Pentecost, which we infer (from Jesus' promise in ***Jn 16:12-15***) was inspired by the Spirit. Here Peter was enabled to preach gospel facts about Jesus that he could have known only by revelation. He emphasized the facts and the implications of Jesus' death, burial, resurrection, and exaltation; and the result was that thousands came under conviction (***Acts 2:37***) and received salvation through faith, repentance, and baptism (***Acts 2:38-42***).

Another example is Stephen's sermon in ***Acts 7***. Stephen was also speaking as a prophet by the Spirit's power (***Acts 6:8-10***; ***7:55***). After preaching a powerful sermon on God's working in the OT, he sensed the growing hostility of the Jewish opponents of the gospel and said, *"'You men who are stiff-necked and uncircumcised in heart and ears are always resisting the Holy Spirit; you are doing just as your fathers did'"* (***Acts 7:51***). The Holy Spirit was convicting them through Stephen's inspired words, but they closed their ears to his message. By rejecting his message, they were resisting the Holy Spirit Himself.

These examples show the meaning of ***John 16:8-11***. When the Word of God is resisted, the Holy Spirit Himself (as the ultimate author of the Word) is also being resisted. But when the Word of God succeeds in producing faith and repentance, it succeeds as an instrument of the Holy Spirit which He prepared for that very purpose (see ***Jn 20:31***).

When the Word of God is resisted, the Holy Spirit Himself is also being resisted.

How the Spirit Uses the Word

An issue of disagreement is the *manner* in which the Spirit uses the Word to convict sinners. One possibility is that the Spirit's divine authorship of the Word (via revelation and inspiration) makes Him ultimately responsible for anything legitimately accomplished by it. This would be parallel to the way any human author's writing affects the thoughts and lives of its readers. If someone pens a letter of endearment to a loved one, that letter will stir the recipient's emotions even if it is read days or weeks after being written and even if the writer is thousands of miles away. The power of the words resides in those words as such, even in the absence of the author. Everyone who writes articles and books trusts that this is so.

If one believes that this is the only way the Spirit works through the biblical message, he would be holding to the "*Word alone* system," as Campbell calls it (**CRD, 614**). A.B. Jones sums it up thus: "Another view is that the Holy Spirit . . . supernaturally inspired the prophets and apostles to write the Bible; and after this revelation of truth was given the Holy Spirit, like Christ, ascended back to heaven; and that this revealed word, in the hands of a living ministry, is the only agency or means for the conversion of men" (**333**). In his debate with Rice, Campbell said that he rejected this view as "the parent of a cold, lifeless rationalism and formality" (**CRD, 614**). The view has often been compared with deism.

The other possibility is that the Holy Spirit is always actually present with and alongside the Word of God, and that He is personally using the Word as His instrument whenever its message is being received by human hearts. Not only did He forge the sword of the Word; He actually wields it as it works its way into *"the thoughts and intentions of the heart"* (***Heb 4:12***). This is the view A.B. Jones defends: "*The Holy Spirit converts sinners*, and not the Word, except in a secondary and subordinate sense, as an instrument in the hands of the Spirit" (**221**). "A thousand Bibles," he says, "thrown out in heathen lands, in the language of the people, would not convert them to Christ. It requires a living ministry—a ministry *in* whom the Holy Spirit operates, and *with* whom he co-operates, in order to carry the truth along the spiritual avenues to the spiritual understanding of man" (**222**).

Not only did He forge the sword of the Word; He actually wields it.

Alexander Campbell Debates N.L. Rice on the Working of the Holy Spirit

Campbell's view in his debate with Rice is in line with that cited by Jones. This view, he said, "never speculatively separates the Word and the Spirit; which, in every case of conversion, contemplates them as co-operating; or, which is the same thing, conceives of the Spirit of God as clothed with the gospel motives and arguments—enlightening, convincing, persuading sinners, and thus enabling them to flee from the wrath to come" (CRD, 614). He declares, "I have, indeed, no faith in conversion by the Word, without the Spirit; nor by the Spirit without the Word. The Spirit is ever present with the Word, in conversion and in sanctification" (ibid., 678). He repeats the same point with emphasis: "I conclude, that the Spirit of Truth . . . whose sword or instrument this book is, is always present in the work of conversion, and through this truth changes the sinner's affection, and draws out his soul to God. . . . Its author not only ever lives, but is ever present in it, and with it, *operating through it, by it,* and *with it,* upon saints and sinners" (ibid., 732). Campbell compares this to a man using an axe to cut down a tree. The axe fells the tree, but only through the power put forth through the axe by the axe-wielder himself (ibid., 719).

Rice attacked Campbell on this point, twice quoting a statement that Campbell had made in his book *Christianity Restored* (350), a statement in which Campbell seems indeed to equate the way the Spirit works through the Word with the way an absent man's writings impact a reader's mind. Here is the passage as quoted (and emphasized) by Rice:

> But to return. *As the spirit of man puts forth all its moral power, in the words which it fills with its ideas; so the Spirit of God puts forth all the converting and sanctifying power, in the words which it fills with its ideas.* Miracles cannot convert. They can only obtain a favorable hearing of the converting arguments. If they fail to obtain a favorable hearing, the arguments which they prove are impotent as an unknown tongue. If the Spirit of God has spoken all its arguments; or, if the New and Old Testament contain all the arguments which can be offered to reconcile man to God, and to purify them who are reconciled; *then all the power of the Holy Spirit which can operate upon the human mind is* SPENT, *and he that is not sanctified and saved by these, cannot be saved by angels or spirits, human or divine.* (CRD, 754; see 627)

Rice then comments, "The gentleman could not have employed language more clear and definite. He puts the Holy Spirit, in regard to conversion and sanctification, on a perfect equality with man, except so far as he may present more powerful motives than man. In the most definite terms, he denies any influence of the Spirit, other than that of his words or arguments" (ibid., 754).

Rice's interpretation of Campbell seems to be supported in Campbell's adamant denial that the Holy Spirit works in any other way in conversion and sanctification except through the instrumentality of the Word. Indeed, this is the very proposition Campbell is defending in the debate: "In Conversion and Sanctification, the Spirit of God operates on Persons only through the Word" (ibid., 611). Also, he is very clear that conversion and sanctification and similar terms indicate "a moral or spiritual change," and that "a moral change is effected only by motives, and motives are arguments; and all the arguments ever used by the Holy Spirit, are found written in the book called the Word of Truth." Therefore such a change as conversion or regeneration or sanctification is "accomplished through the arguments, the light, the love, the grace of God expressed and revealed, as well as approved by the supernatural attestations of the Holy Spirit" (ibid., 613-614). The very nature of the human mind dictates that this is the only way a man can be changed by the Spirit: "He merely receives new ideas, and new impressions, and undergoes a great moral, or spiritual change—so that he becomes alive wherein he was dead, and dead wherein he was formerly alive" (ibid., 617).

In view of this, it is no wonder that Rice sees an inconsistency between the statement made in *Christianity Restored* and Campbell's statements in the course of this debate. And I believe we are warranted in raising this question: even if the Spirit is present in and with the Word, and is personally using the Word as it impacts the sinner, what difference does this make? How is this *practically* different from the first view above? Campbell affirms that the Spirit is definitely working through the Word, as a man must use an axe, but he grants that he has no idea what this means:

> If I see a man take an axe and fell a tree, I call the axe the instrument, and I say, whatever power he puts forth in felling the tree is put forth through the axe. Not one chip is removed without it. This illustrates so much of the subject as pertains to *instrumentality*. I am at a loss to understand his additional power. I see but the man and the axe, and the tree falls. That the Spirit *operates* through the instrumentality of the Word I doubt not; but if asked to explain the *modus operandi*, I confess my inability. (ibid., 719)

Rice challenges Campbell thus: "He tells us, the Spirit of God is always present with his Word. I have asked, and now ask again, what does he mean by this language?" (ibid., 737). Campbell has no answer.

The bottom line is this, that whichever of the two views one holds of *how* the Spirit works through the Word, it is still true *that* He works through the Word and does in this manner lead sinners to faith and repentance. This leads us to a much more important issue, and our next main point, which is the question of whether the Spirit ever works for this purpose in some way *other than* or *in addition to* the Word.

Whichever view one holds of how the Spirit works through the Word, it is still true that He does.

DOES THE SPIRIT WORK IN ADDITION TO THE WORD?

The most controversial issue in relation to our present subject is whether the Spirit works in addition to the Word. When the question is asked in such general terms, everyone will say yes. He works in inspiration, in miracles, in tongue-speaking, in spiritual gifts, and perhaps in providence. But such matters are not the point. As Campbell says, "In how many other ways the Spirit of God may operate in nature, or in society, in the way of dreams, visions and miracles, comes not within the premises contained in our proposition. To what extent He may operate in suggestions, special providences, or in any other way, is neither affirmed nor denied in the proposition before us. It has respect to *conversion* and *sanctification* only" (**CRD, 617**). What the Spirit "may do in the way of suggestions or impressions, by direct communication of original ideas, or in bringing things to remembrance long since forgotten, I presume not to discuss. I believe he has exerted, and can exert, such influences" (**ibid., 722**). But the crucial issue is whether the Spirit works "in conversion and sanctification" (or in our terminology, to produce faith and repentance) in any way other than through the Word.

Many in Christendom respond to this question with an emphatic YES! This is true especially of everyone in the Augustinian camp, the primary examples of which today are Calvinists. In short, Calvinistic theology *demands* a positive answer to the question; it is inherent in the system. It is a necessary implication of the doctrine of total depravity, upon which the whole Calvinistic system of sin and salvation is built. Since all of Adam's natural descendants are born totally depraved, then the Word of God by itself is simply unable to move anyone to faith and repentance. Only a direct work of the Spirit can change the totally depraved heart, thereby unlocking the human potential to believe and repent.

This direct work of the Spirit is called *irresistible grace*. It is performed only upon those sinners whom God has unconditionally elected to salvation, and under normal circumstances it is performed only in connection with the preaching of the gospel.[3] The main aspect of this direct work of the Spirit, this irresistible grace, is the unilateral divine act of regeneration, which lifts the sinner out of his condition of total depravity and restores to him the ability to believe and repent. In the same moment, the Spirit directly bestows upon the being-regenerated sinner the actual gifts of faith and repentance. Thus what Campbell calls a "moral or spiritual change" is wrought directly by the Spirit, by some kind of supernatural operation of the naked Spirit of God upon the naked spirit of man.

Kuyper is an example of this view. He says the Word and the Spirit work together in conversion. The Word presents an external call, and the Spirit presents an internal call. The internal call of the Spirit is regeneration in its initial and most precise sense. It involves the implanting of the new life-principle within the sinner, along with the faith-faculty and even faith itself. "Not only the faith-*faculty*, but faith itself . . . are gifts of grace." (**295-296**). Only when the Spirit has thus regenerated the sinner does the latter have any consciousness of faith. "Hence the first *conscious* and comparatively cooperative act of man is always *preceded* by the original act of God, planting in him the first principle of a new life, under which act man is wholly *passive* and *unconscious*" (**294**).

This "original act of God," this "operation of the Holy Spirit in man's innermost being," may be performed "in the sinner's heart *before, during,* or *after* the preaching of the Word." This initial act of regeneration, "when the Lord plants the new life in the dead heart," is a work performed "*without means.*" Therefore it "is not dependent upon the preaching of the Word; and therefore may *precede* the preaching" (**Kuyper, 317-318**).

Palmer is another example. In chapter seven of his book, which discusses "The Holy Spirit and Regeneration," Palmer begins with total depravity: "By himself man can never turn to God. He is totally depraved. His intellect, will, and emotions are corrupt through and

[3] Exceptions include infants and mentally-handicapped persons who die before or without attaining the rational capacity to believe and repent. All such are usually considered to be among the elect.

through" (77). "Thus it is an absolute impossibility for natural man to turn to God without the Spirit of the living God" (78-79). When the time for regeneration arrives, "the Holy Spirit comes and does something to the soul of man," touching the spirit at its innermost core (81). "Man is entirely passive" in this event. The regeneration of the Spirit causally precedes any conscious act of believing on man's part (83). "And the beauty of it all is that man cannot resist the Spirit's work" (86).

Walvoord, another Calvinist, prefers to call this work of the Spirit "efficacious grace," and says, "it is an act of God dependent solely upon God for its execution." It is never attributed to human choice. "In keeping with their doctrine of total depravity and total inability, Reformed theologians have insisted that efficacious grace is an immediate act of God accomplished without human assistance" (121). It is "always effectual" and is "never resisted"; those who receive it are "instantly saved" (122-123). This doctrine, he says, is required by total depravity. "If one accepts the Biblical revelation of man's state of spiritual death and total inability, he must accept the doctrine of efficacious grace as the solution to the problem" (124-125).

Campbell's Position on Direct and Indirect Working of the Spirit

The early leaders of the Restoration Movement adamantly rejected Calvinism, and also generally opposed the view that the Holy Spirit works directly upon the sinner's heart in conversion. They interpreted any such idea as some version of Calvinism. This seems to be the assumption of Campbell, especially in his debate with Rice. Like others, Campbell distinguished between the ideas of a *direct* work and an *indirect* work of the Spirit. The former was almost always understood and explained in the Calvinist sense.

But even apart from this, Campbell taught that the very nature of man precludes a direct work of the Spirit in conversion. The change of heart called conversion (or regeneration, or sanctification) is a moral or spiritual change, not a physical (or metaphysical), legal, or even purely intellectual change (CRD, 613). It is a change of one's feelings, emotions, and motives; and this sort of change takes place only by the person's own choice under the influence of words or arguments. This is why Campbell said that the Spirit cannot operate on the heart directly, but must operate indirectly through his inspired Word. "Physical force and the power of motives are very different things. Reasons, containing *motives*, constitute the elements and materials of all moral, *converting*, or *sanctifying* power, so far as known to man. . . . God's moral power is infinitely superior to ours. *Yet all that power is in the gospel*" (ibid., 643).

Therefore a direct work of the Holy Spirit, which would be a kind of physical change, is impossible for the purpose of conversion. For those who defend such a view, "the philosophy of mind is converted into a heap of ruins. They have the Spirit of God operating without testimony—without apprehension or comprehension—without sense, susceptibility, or feeling. . . . I, therefore, . . . repudiate their whole theory of mystic influence, and metaphysical regeneration . . ." (ibid., 619). Interestingly, Campbell allows for this possibility after death, as in the case of infants who die (ibid., 654-655). But in this life there can be no direct, naked-Spirit-on-naked-spirit acts of God. "The naked Spirit of God never has operated upon the naked spirit of man, so far as all science, all revelation teach" (ibid., 750).*

*Rice comments, "This is mere assertion. How can the gentleman prove it true?" (CRD, 753-754).

Thus Campbell, and many after him, have declared that in conversion the Spirit operates only through the Word, i.e., this is the only instrument by which He touches the spirit of man.

> The term *only* is, indeed, redundant; because a moral change is effected only by motives, and motives are arguments; and all the arguments ever used by the Holy Spirit, are found written in the book called the Word of Truth. . . . If, then, I prove that conversion, or sanctification, is effected by the Word of Truth at all, I prove that it is a moral change, and consequently, accomplished by the Holy Spirit, through the Word alone" (**CRD, 613**).

He says this is in effect the same as saying the Spirit operates (for conversion) *always* through the Word (**ibid., 613, 663, 673**). It is a mistake to try to interpret Campbell here as saying that he does not really mean "only"; he just means "always." Actually, he means "only and always."[4]

[4]Thus I disagree with Foster, who says that by defining "only" as "always"

Denial of the "Spirit Alone" View by Restoration Movement Writers

What does Campbell mean, then, when he says that he denies the "Spirit alone" view (CRD, 614, 678)? As explained in the previous section, he means that, as he sees it, the Word is *not alone* when it operates on the sinner's heart; the Spirit is there *with* the Word, wielding it like a sword. But in defending the debate's proposition, that in conversion and sanctification "the Spirit operates only through the Word," he argues (1) that the Spirit uses *no other instrument* in addition to the Word, and (2) that the Spirit does not operate *directly* on the heart at all.

Others in the Restoration Movement have perpetuated this view. One example is the nineteenth-century writer G.W. Longan. Regarding the influence of the Spirit in saving men, there are only two possibilities, he said. "One of these is the notion of an influence by direct, or naked impact; the other, that of an influence mediated by truth." Only the second "meets the demands of enlightened reason, and fully accords with every utterance in the word of God." Therefore, "Let us insist that God, in the sphere of redemption, is immanent in truth, in the forces of truth—that he quickens morally dead sinners, sustains and comforts believers, in no case, by naked, mechanical impact, but evermore through influences mediated by truth, and thereby divinely correlated with the voluntary activities of the human soul" (75-77).

B.F. Hall (1837) states succinctly, "I believe that the Holy Spirit exerts *no influence* on the hearts of sinners over and above the word: that his influences are in the facts he has revealed in the gospel, the evidence by which he has confirmed these facts, and in the motives to obedience presented in the Scriptures of Truth" (cited in Leonard Allen and R. Hughes, 85).

A final example is Garth Black, who asserts "that the Holy Spirit operates in conversion only through the instrumentality of the word." As proof he cites the biblical texts showing the power of the Word of God and the role of the Word in converting sinners. He concludes, "From these scriptures it is evident that the Holy Spirit operates upon the heart of the sinner in conversion through the

Campbell "was denying that the Spirit sometimes convicts in conversion without the presence of the Word, but he was not saying that the work of the Spirit was limited to the Word alone" ("Conversion," 8). Actually Campbell was saying both.

truth, and that truth is the gospel message, the word of God. The New Testament does not teach that the Holy Spirit operates in any other way in conversion than through the instrumentality of the word" (27-28).

In my judgment there are serious problems with this view that the Spirit operates in conversion and sanctification only through the Word. Much of the difficulty stems from some confusion in the use of terminology, but this itself in part stems from a failure to make a proper distinction between *two separate stages* in the Spirit's saving work upon the unsaved. That is, no distinction is made between what the Holy Spirit does to bring the sinner to faith and repentance, and what He does to regenerate the sinner. The tendency is to lump both of these stages together and to identify the emergence of faith and repentance in the sinner's heart with regeneration, and then to refer to all of this as "conversion."

Adding to the confusion is the fact that when Campbell and other early Restoration leaders were addressing this issue, their main antagonist was Calvinism, with its doctrine of the necessity of a direct regenerating operation of the Spirit upon the totally depraved sinner's heart as the origin of faith and repentance. It is not surprising, then, that in such a context, when these men thought about the difference between a *direct* and an *indirect* work of the Spirit upon the soul of man, the only kind of direct working they could picture was Calvinism's irresistible grace. Thus the whole concept of a direct working of the Spirit ("naked Spirit on naked spirit") was rejected as a Calvinist doctrine.

Many in Restoration Movement Equate Direct Working of the Spirit with Calvinism

Though he does not name a specific representative, Campbell seems to be thinking of Calvinism (remember: his opponent in the "Campbell-Rice debate" was a Calvinist) when he describes a system

> . . . claiming both the Spirit and the Word—representing the naked Spirit of God operating upon the naked soul of man, without any argument, or motive, interposed in some mysterious and inexplicable way—incubating the soul, quickening, or making it spiritually

alive, by a direct and immediate contact, without the intervention of one moral idea, or impression. But after this creating act, there is the bringing to bear upon it the gospel revelation, called conversion. Hence, in this school, regeneration is the cause; and conversion, at some future time, the result of that abstract operation. (CRD, 614)

Of the same view he says, "Their notion, as far as we can gather it, is, that the Spirit of God comes into a personal contact with the spirit of a man, and either new-moulds or attempers, or changes, or imbues it with something from himself, which is sometimes called the infusion of a holy principle. . . . This divine touch is sometimes compared to that which reanimated the body of Lazarus, or raised to life the dead body of Jesus" (ibid., 685).

In Restoration circles the tendency remains to equate all "direct operations" of the Spirit upon the sinner with Calvinism. Speaking specifically of "*Direct Operation* in the conversion of an alien sinner," J.D. Thomas says (8),

> This modern denominational concept, held by many, basically comes from Augustine (died 430 A.D.) but is also to be credited to John Calvin of the Reformation period who embellished and enhanced it somewhat. It holds that man is hereditarily totally depraved and is powerless to take even a first step in the direction of his own salvation until he is personally singled out and acted upon in a direct and immediate way by the Holy Spirit. This direct operation "saves" the individual but also is that which makes him to be an intellectual believer. . . .
>
> None of this "direct operation" doctrine is taught in the New Testament. Faith is not based upon any power other than the word of the gospel. No divine power of any kind ever "forces faith" in an irresistible way.

Boatman likewise ties the idea of a direct operation of the Spirit to Calvinism:

> Those influenced by Calvinism, consciously or otherwise, have taken the position that the Holy Spirit operates directly (and, if need be, apart from the Scriptures) to turn men to God and Christ, and hence unto salvation. He is said to operate directly upon the mind, the emotions, the conscience and even the will of 'the elect.' Thus sinners do not 'turn' to God. They are said to 'be turned' (be converted) (245-246).

The consequence of this linking of "direct operation" with Calvinism is that most Restoration writers simply rule out all possibility of any kind of direct working of the Spirit upon the sinner's heart. E.g., Boles says, "The New Testament does not teach that the Holy Spirit operates directly upon the heart of the sinner; there is no teaching that the Holy Spirit comes *directly, immediately, independently* into the hearts of sinners and converts them. There is no case on record in the New Testament where anyone was converted who did not first hear the truth, believe in Christ, repent of sin, and was baptized into Christ" (199). The assumption is that if one opts for a direct operation of the Spirit upon the sinner's heart, he has (a la Calvin) made the Holy Spirit the sole author of faith and repentance and has thus compromised the role of the Word of God in conversion.

In my judgment we can reach a more nearly biblical idea of the work of the Spirit in bringing sinners to salvation if we take the following approach. First, we should by all means repudiate Calvinism's view of sin and salvation, beginning with its doctrine of total depravity.[5] This means we should reject all notions inherent in the doctrine of irresistible grace, including the following: regeneration precedes faith; faith and repentance are gifts of God; regenerating grace is given only to those whom God has unconditionally elected; and such grace is irresistible.

We *must* understand that all of these ideas are the necessary consequence of the doctrine of total depravity. Rice acknowledges this in his debate with Campbell: "The necessity of the agency of the Spirit in the hearts of men, I have said, arises simply from their deep depravity" (**CRD, 754**). As Walvoord says, "In keeping with their doctrine of total depravity and total inability, Reformed theologians have insisted that efficacious grace is an immediate act of God accomplished without human assistance" (**121**). What we must realize is this: the idea of total depravity leads not just to the necessity of a "direct operation" of the Spirit upon the sinner, but to a direct operation *of a specific kind*. In other words, the Calvinist, because of total depravity, must believe that the Holy Spirit directly bestows a regenerating grace upon the sinner (1) that is selective (via unconditional election), (2) that is irresistible, and (3) that *precedes* (i.e., is the source of) faith and repentance.

In other words, the problem with Calvinism is not a direct operation of the Spirit as such, but a *specific kind* of direct operation, one that is the spawn of total depravity. We can—and should—reject this *kind* of direct operation of the Spirit, but we can do this without

[5] See my discussion of both original sin and total depravity in *Faith*, 179-190, 187-200.

rejecting the concept of direct operation as such. For some reason Campbell missed this point and completely separated the issue of the influence of the Spirit from the total-depravity doctrine: "This matter is wholly foreign to the subject. The question is not about total depravity" (**CRD, 640-641**). He was wrong.

Why did he miss this point? I believe this goes back to the confusion (mentioned earlier) over the very concept of "conversion," and the failure to distinguish between the change wrought *indirectly upon* the sinner's heart via the Word of God, leading him to faith and repentance; and the change wrought *directly within* the sinner's heart via the act of regeneration (which will be discussed in the next chapter). Though the latter is a direct operation of the Spirit, it *follows* the sinner's decision to believe and repent; it does not cause it, nor is it identical with it.

Campbell, however, seemed to think that the moral change wrought by the Spirit indirectly through the Word *is* regeneration. From the Spirit's working through the Word, a man "merely receives new ideas, and new impressions, and undergoes a great moral, or spiritual change—so that he becomes alive wherein he was dead, and dead wherein he was formerly alive" (**CRD, 617**). This is regeneration terminology. Campbell says specifically that "faith in God is . . . the soul-renewing principle of all religion; as it is the regenerating, justifying, and sanctifying principle" (**ibid., 618**). Such regeneration "is a change of heart. . . . What sort of change?—not of the flesh, but of the spirit—a *change of the affections,* of the feelings *and sympathies of the soul"* (**ibid., 654**). When regeneration is thus identified with the sinner's own self-willed change of heart (under the influence of the Word, to be sure), there is nothing left for the Holy Spirit to do as an act of regeneration. So in Campbell's mind anything other than the indirect operation of the Spirit via the Word must be the *Calvinist* view of direct operation, which he rightly repudiated. His error was to rule out direct operation as such.

When we make the distinction between the faith/repentance change worked *indirectly* by the Spirit in the sinner's heart through the Word of God, and His later *direct* work properly called regeneration, much of this confusion disappears. Faith and repentance *are* the moral or spiritual change Campbell speaks of, and they are the result of the power of the Word operating on the heart. This is the way the Spirit moves *men* to act, and faith and repentance *are* their acts.

Faith and repentance are the moral change Campbell speaks of, the result of the power of the Word on the heart.

Regeneration, though, is not a human act but a divine act; the Holy Spirit does not move men to regenerate themselves but to submit to His own direct work of regeneration.

This approach should not be confused with the Calvinist concept of the direct operation of the Spirit. When the Spirit works via the Word to bring the sinner to faith and repentance, this is *not* a direct operation of the Spirit, and it is *not* selective and irresistible. The direct operation of regeneration is something the Spirit performs only upon those who have already believed and repented. But this is perfectly acceptable and perfectly biblical, as long as this direct operation is neither selective nor irresistible. The whole bugaboo of a "direct operation of the Spirit" is a red herring.

THE SPIRIT AND SPECIAL PROVIDENCE

The previous section began with the question, "Does the Spirit work in addition to the Word?" Specifically, does He work upon the hearts of unsaved sinners in any way besides the Word of God? Calvinists say *yes*, but I reject their approach because it is part of a false view of sin and salvation grounded upon the false doctrine of total depravity. Many in the Restoration Movement say *no*, but we reject this approach because it usually fails to distinguish between two separate stages or events in the heart of an unsaved sinner: the human decision to believe and repent, and the divine act of regeneration. In the latter event the Spirit is definitely working upon the sinner's heart in a way that is in addition to the Word.

In the previous section another question was raised, "Does the Spirit work only *indirectly* upon the sinner's heart, i.e., through the Word, or does He also work *directly* upon the sinner's heart in some way?" We can answer this question correctly only when we make the proper distinction between the two events named in the previous paragraph. When we understand the difference between the faith/repentance event and the regeneration event, we can see that the Spirit works both indirectly *and* directly. He works indirectly, through the Word, to convict the sinner and lead him to faith and repentance; and He works directly in the sinner's heart to regenerate him.

But now I want to focus only upon the *first* event, the human decision to believe and repent; and I want to ask concerning this alone, "Does the Spirit work upon the heart of a sinner *to lead him to faith and repentance* in any way, directly or indirectly, in addition to the Word of God?" The answer to this question is *yes*, the Spirit can and probably does work thus upon a sinner's heart through acts of *special divine providence*.

The Spirit can and probably does work on a sinner's heart, but not in the absence of the Word.

Whatever may be involved in this, one must never think that it happens in the absence of the Word or instead of the Word. As J.D. Thomas says, "A clear distinction as to what the Spirit does through the word and separate from it is this. *Revelation* comes only through the word; *Providential Activity* of God (or of the Spirit) may occur in addition to the influence of the word" (**11**). In other words, in reference to influencing a sinner toward faith and repentance, special providence is always *along with* and *in addition to* the message of the gospel. After all, the whole point of such acts of special providence is to influence the sinner to surrender his mind and will to Jesus Christ, and Jesus can be known only through the Word.

This role for providence seems to be allowed by Campbell when he speaks of "the co-operation of secondary causes; of various subordinate instrumentalities; the ministry of men; the ministry of angels; the doctrine of special providences" (**CRD, 614**). He does not elaborate on this, however.

Though I am presenting this concept of special providence as part of the work of the Holy Spirit, I must qualify it thus: divine providence is not necessarily the exclusive work of any one person of the Trinity. Acts of special divine providence may indeed occur in the life of a sinner to urge him toward faith and repentance, and these may be the work of the Holy Spirit. But such providential intervention is not limited to God the Spirit; it is not one of His unique works. With this qualification in mind, we may certainly affirm that the Holy Spirit does work upon the sinner's heart through providential means.

What do we mean by "special divine providence"?[6] Our understanding of providence begins with the fact that the sovereign God

[6] On the subject of providence, see Cottrell, *Ruler*, chapters 3–5.

has complete knowledge of and is in complete control of everything that happens, both in the natural world and in human history. The great majority of events are simply monitored and permitted by God via what is sometimes called His "general providence." However, if God so chooses, He may intervene in the flow of world events and cause things to happen that would not have happened without such intervention. Some of these things are called "miracles"; these are events that are contrary to the laws of nature. Some are not contrary to the laws of nature but still take place only through God's special intervention; these are what we mean by "special providence."

God has complete knowledge of and is in complete control of everything that happens.

One aspect of special providence is that God may work outside of the human heart, manipulating natural processes in order to fulfill His purposes toward human beings. One of these purposes is to influence sinners to repent of their sins and turn (or return) to Him. For example, God may providentially cause a drought or bring rain; or He may cause sickness or heal a sick person. By the manipulation of events in nature and in people's lives, the Spirit may confront the sinner with circumstances that disturb him, or that cause him to think seriously about his life, or that "put the fear of God into him" as we sometimes say. As ***Job 37:13*** says, the Lord sometimes uses storm systems to administer "correction."

At times such special providence may involve something drastic, such as natural disasters, personal sickness, accidents, or tragedy involving a loved one. I once heard a Christian man say, "Thank God for my heart attack." The attack came when he was an unbeliever. He had to lie in bed quietly for six weeks while recovering. During that time he could not help but think about his close call with death, his wrong relationship with God, and his bleak prospects for eternity. He came under conviction and was converted. We do not know this for sure (since only inspired prophets can give sure interpretations of providence), but it is possible that God may have caused this heart attack for this very purpose.

Another example of how the Spirit may bring conviction through special providential intervention is an account told by a missionary who was active in China when this country was taken over by communists (**"One Man," 9-10**). The missionary was arrested and subjected to severe questioning and mental torture. Throughout the procedure he continually uttered a quotation from the Psalms, *"My times are in Thy hands."* In what he describes as his "final ordeal," he was offered a knife and tempted to take his own life. He responded, *"My times are in Thy hands."* He reports, "The screaming voice of the interrogator demanded to know where the words came from and he threw a Bible before his victim. The sacred volume fell open at ***Psalm xxxi***. . . . Here was a description of the present situation in detail" (see ***vv. 4,11,13-15,18,23-24***). In the midst of the open page was the very statement the missionary had been citing all along: *"My times are in thy hand"* (***v. 15***). "This was too much for the still superstitious inquisitor who fled from the room." The missionary was then released and allowed to go home. The inquisitor did not come to saving faith and repentance, but he clearly was convicted of sin and filled with fear of judgment.

How do we explain the fact that the Bible, flung down on a table by the enemy, happened to open to that very place? The sovereign God has the power to manipulate muscles and wind currents; making sure the book opened to this text was an easy act of special providence.

Not all providential events will be this dramatic. For example, the Spirit could work upon a sinner's heart by causing him to hear a specific meaningful song as he scans stations on his car radio Or the Spirit may providentially lead him to cross paths with an unexpected person who will be able to touch his heart. (Though not strictly an act of providence, the meeting of Philip and the eunuch in ***Acts 8:26-40*** shows how something like this could happen.)

In the above examples of special providence, God is working outside the human heart, working upon it *indirectly* through experienced events. But there is another whole aspect of special providence, wherein God may work *within* a person, i.e., within his thought processes, *directly* impacting his heart and mind in order to influence that person to make a certain decision (e.g., in the hardening of Pharaoh's heart). In the case of unbelieving sinners, the Spirit may so work for the purpose of bringing the unbeliever to conviction, to faith, and to

God may work within a person to influence a certain decision.

repentance. As noted above, though this working is in addition to the Word, it is never done in the absence of the Word.

An example is that the Spirit may work within a person's thought processes by bringing forgotten or suppressed ideas or facts into one's consciousness. He may work by keeping certain thoughts on a sinner's mind. We often speculate that the devil tempts us by bringing evil ideas into our consciousness. If this can happen, then it is even more likely that the Holy Spirit may cause certain good memories to haunt our minds, pressing us to conviction. Examples are the memory of a convicting song, or a convicting statement or look from an acquaintance; or the memory of a loving spouse's example and prayer (see ***1Cor 7:16***; ***1Pet 3:1-2***); or the memory of an appropriate sermon or Bible text. (This is something very different from the revelation of new ideas, of course.)

What can the Spirit accomplish by such special providence (along with the Word)? Certainly such activity may make the sinner more responsive to the Word, thus "opening his heart" to the power of the gospel (see ***Acts 16:14***). Such events may help the sinner to better understand the Word, in the manner described on pages 87-92 above. Or they may simply soften a sinner's resisting will in ways that we do not understand.

This does not mean, however, that the Spirit's providential urgings will infallibly and irresistibly produce faith and repentance; providence is very different from Calvinism's "irresistible grace." The decision to believe and repent is still up to the sinner, whose will is free to say yes or no. Sometimes providential warnings are ignored or go unheeded, as is made clear in ***Amos 4:6-12***. Here the prophet declares that God had been sending drought and pests and plagues of various kinds against Israel, *"'Yet you have not returned to Me,' declares the LORD"* (***vv. 6,8,9,10,11***). Clearly the purpose of this providential activity was to lead the Israelites to repentance, but they closed their minds to it and did not go where it was meant to lead them.

Nevertheless the Spirit does work upon sinner's hearts, both through the Word and through special providence. There are two very practical implications from this. First, if we do not believe the point about special providence, why do we pray for the lost? What do we expect to happen, if the Holy Spirit is not doing something *in addition to* the Word? What do we expect God to do in answer to such a prayer? We must expect Him to do *something*, or we would not so pray. And if we *do* believe that God can answer such prayers, why do we not pray more often and more fervently for the lost?

Unless we believe that there is something the Spirit does in addition to the preaching of the Word, there really is no rationale for prayer for the lost. Rice offered this criticism against Campbell's view: "His doctrine makes it both useless and improper to pray for the conversion of men" (**CRD, 729**). Campbell rightly pointed out that Rice's Calvinism also leaves no place for prayer for the lost (**ibid., 732**), but Rice correctly replied that Campbell still "makes no attempt to prove, that his doctrine is at all consistent with prayer" (**ibid., 737**). He does not respond to Rice's criticism. Thus Rice says, "I repeat the argument. If his doctrine be true, there is absolutely no propriety in praying" (**ibid., 752**). Rice is correct.

Unless we believe in this kind of work, there is no rationale for prayer for the lost.

But there is a second practical implication. In view of how the Spirit works in bringing sinners to faith and repentance, we should be more conscious of *His* role in the evangelistic process. Many Christians are filled with doubts about their ability to win sinners to Christ; many do not even attempt it for fear of failure. But we should remember that the success of our evangelistic efforts is not really in our hands; it does not depend upon how clever and how professional we are as "soul-winners." We must simply sow the seed of the Word (***Mt 13:3-9***); we must simply *"go into all the world and preach the gospel to all creation"* (***Mk 16:15***), remembering that there is a greater power at work in our preaching and witnessing than our own puny reason and oratory.

The other side of this coin is that we should not get puffed up when we do lead someone to the Lord, as if this is accomplished by our great knowledge and expertise. As a young minister I often went calling with revival preachers. I remember one instance when I and the evangelist sat at a kitchen table with a Christian man and his unbelieving wife. As a result of sharing the gospel with this lady, we rejoiced to see her come to faith and repentance, and I baptized her that evening. As we left this couple's house after this evangelistic visit, the revival preacher turned to me and asked, "What do you think I said that caused her to make her decision?" My first thought was, maybe it was not "something you said"; maybe it was simply the power of the gospel. I don't remember if I voiced that sentiment aloud, and maybe I was reading too much into his question. But it did impress upon me the need to rely upon the power of the Spirit in evangelizing.

BLASPHEMY AGAINST THE HOLY SPIRIT

Before we leave this chapter on the Holy Spirit's work prior to conversion, we must try to explain the sin of blasphemy against the Holy Spirit, commonly called the "unpardonable sin" or "unforgivable sin." Three texts in the Gospels speak of this sin in this terminology. One is ***Matthew 12:31-32***,

> *Therefore I say to you, any sin and blasphemy shall be forgiven people, but blasphemy against the Spirit shall not be forgiven. Whoever speaks a word against the Son of Man, it shall be forgiven him; but whoever speaks against the Holy Spirit, it shall not be forgiven him, either in this age or in the age to come.*

A parallel passage is ***Mark 3:28-29***, *"Truly I say to you, all sins shall be forgiven the sons of men, and whatever blasphemies they utter; but whoever blasphemes against the Holy Spirit never has forgiveness, but is guilty of an eternal sin."* See also ***Luke 12:10***, *"And everyone who speaks a word against the Son of Man, it will be forgiven him; but he who blasphemes against the Holy Spirit, it will not be forgiven him."*

Luke says this sin *"will not be forgiven."* **Matthew** also says *"it shall not be forgiven,"* and adds *"either in this age or in the age to come."* **Mark** says this sin *"never has forgiveness"*; it is *"an eternal sin."* None of these texts actually says that this sin *cannot* be forgiven—just that it *will not* be forgiven. However, the fact that it is contrasted with all other sins and blasphemies, which, says Jesus, *will* be forgiven, implies that "*will not* be forgiven" is a final and irrevocable judgment upon this sin. This is supported by its description as an *eternal* sin, i.e., one who commits this sin will suffer its consequences for eternity.

Few teachings of Scripture leave us more frustrated than this one. Of all the sins mentioned in the Bible, this is the one our hearts want most to be sure about, since it does seem to be the one *unpardonable* sin. But at the same time Scripture says so little about it that we can do little more than speculate about its true nature. Among those who have attempted to explain it, there is much disagreement about so many questions related to it. Speaking of the Matthew passage, Winter says that "it remains, after all the centuries, a passage that finds no absolutely satisfactory exposition. Nowhere in sacred writ or in early Christian literature is there to be found one really exact parallel by aid of which it may be determined and defined. To generalize upon it is easy, and to define some particular aspect of it is not difficult; but always there is something to be desired" (**12**).

Yet we shall plunge ahead and seek to explain this doctrine the best that we can. For those who want more detail, I highly recommend W. Carl Ketcherside's treatment of it in his book, *Heaven Help Us*, chapter 7.

There are two main views of this sin. One is that it is a general state or attitude; the other is that it is a specific act. The former says that the unpardonable sin is persistence in the state of unbelief until death, or "resistance against the call of the Spirit until death overtakes the sinner" (**Ketcherside, 105**). Some leave out the "until death" aspect, thus denying the finality of the unforgiveness. Such blasphemy "is not a single event that, once done, is too late to undo," says Thompson. "Rather, it is a sustained stance toward Jesus that denies the power of the Spirit of God at work in Jesus. So long as one persists in attributing Jesus' work to any other power than the power of God, one is guilty of 'blasphemy of the Holy Spirit.' None of the Gospels says that once this stance is taken it can never be altered" (**82**). In any case, according to this view, "Rather than a particular act, it is a disposition of the will" (**Burge, 1017**).

The other main view is that the blasphemy against the Spirit does involve a specific act of speaking against the Spirit. As Berkhof sums it up, "The sin consists in the conscious, malicious, and wilful rejection and slandering, against evidence and conviction, of the testimony of the Holy Spirit respecting the grace of God in Christ, attributing it out of hatred and enmity to the prince of darkness. . . . The sin itself consists, not in doubting the truth, nor in a simple denial of it, but in a contradiction of it. . . . It is nothing less than a decided slandering of the Holy Spirit" (**253**). Ketcherside says, "Without speaking, it is impossible to commit the sin of blasphemy. Blasphemy is a sin of the tongue and not merely of the heart" (**113**). He says, "Blasphemy is a specific sin against the Spirit as contrasted with every other sin" (**103**).

Actually, these two views are not necessarily exclusive, except those who hold to the first view usually make it so. That is, they usually do not equate the blasphemy against the Spirit with a single act and thus do not include a specific act of blasphemy within their view. Those who hold the second view, though, usually do not make it exclusive. In other words, they combine the notion of blasphemy against the Spirit as a single act with the idea that it is committed only by someone who has a specific and persistent attitude of unbelief. As Ketcherside, says, it is a sin of the tongue and not *merely* of the heart. It is both.

I believe that the unpardonable sin is better understood in this second sense. It does involve a specific act of *speaking against* the Spirit. The English word "blasphemy" comes directly from the Greek noun *blasphemia* (verb, *blasphemeo*), which comes from two other Greek words, *blapto*, "to harm"; and *phemi*, "to speak." Thus "to blaspheme" means to speak evil or speak harmfully against someone; to slander, revile, malign, insult, defame, or curse someone. That it refers to an act of evil speaking seems to be clear from the fact that in our three Gospel texts, Jesus uses the word "blaspheme" interchangeably with "speak a word against." That it refers to a specific act seems to be indicated by Jesus' statement in Matthew that such a sin will not be forgiven *"in this age,"* i.e., even while a person is still alive. This would be difficult to explain if the unpardonable sin is by definition simply persisting in a certain *attitude* up until the moment of death.

"To blaspheme" means to speak evil or speak harmfully against someone.

But even if we say that this sin is a specific act, a sin that is so heinous as to be unforgivable must grow out of an exceptionally hard and sinful heart. It is true in general that all sins begin in the heart (***Mt 15:18-19***), and this is no less true of the unpardonable sin. Jesus Himself makes this connection for us in the verses that follow His warning against Spirit-blasphemy: *"You brood of vipers, how can you, being evil, speak what is good? For the mouth speaks out of that which fills* *the heart. The good man brings out of his good treasure what is good; and the evil man brings out of his evil treasure what is evil"* (***Mt 12:34-35***). As Morris puts it, "It is plain that Jesus does not refer to the uttering of a few idle or slanderous words only. Blasphemy may be in act as well as in word. Jesus is referring to a whole attitude of life" (***Spirit*, 48**).

The key to understanding the nature of blasphemy against the Spirit, then, seems to be a proper understanding of the state of mind that gives rise to it. Of crucial importance here is the historical context in which Jesus first taught about the blasphemy against the Spirit, as reported in ***Matthew 12:22-29*** (see ***Mk 3:22-27***). Jesus had just healed a deaf-mute man by casting a demon out of him, inducing the crowds to think of Him as the Messiah (the Son of David). *"But when the Pharisees heard this, they said, 'This man casts out demons only by Beelzebul the ruler of the demons'"* (***Mt 12:24***). ***Mark*** reports that they were saying, *"He is possessed by Beelzebul"* (***3:22***). The warning about blaspheming the Spirit was part of Jesus' response to these unbelieving Jewish leaders.

What we learn from this is that the unpardonable blasphemy of the Holy Spirit is a sin that can be committed only in the context of an attitude of unbelief and open hostility toward Jesus. On this occasion ***Matthew*** tells us that Jesus' teaching is directed specifically to these unbelieving Pharisees (***12:25***; see ***12:34***). ***Mark*** says that Jesus even *"called them to Himself"* to give them this teaching (***3:23***), and that He gave them the warning about Spirit-blasphemy specifically *"because they were saying, 'He has an unclean spirit'"* (***3:30***).

> **The blasphemy of the Holy Spirit can be committed only in the context of open hostility toward Jesus.**

This tells us that blasphemy against the Spirit is a sin that can be committed only by someone who refuses to accept Jesus as the divine Messiah, and who is deliberately trying to prevent others from accepting Jesus by openly attacking and opposing Him and by blaspheming or speaking evil against Him (i.e., Jesus). Those who commit this sin are those who "rebel against Christ openly, brazenly, and without any remorse" (**Palmer, 183**).

Perhaps the most amazing thing Jesus says in His lecture to the Pharisees is this: *"Whoever speaks a word against the Son of Man, it shall be forgiven him"* (***Mt 12:32a***). This suggests to me that nothing the Pharisees had done thus far had crossed the line between forgivable and unforgivable. Even their hostile, open attacks on Jesus could be forgiven. Even attributing His miracles to the power of Satan could be forgiven. As great as these sins are, they can be forgiven! Amazing!

What is the line, then, between the forgivable and the unforgivable? When do open hostility against and attacks upon Jesus become blasphemy against the Holy Spirit? The answer seems to be this: when one *knows in his heart* that Jesus' Messiahship has been fully confirmed and authenticated by the power of the Holy Spirit, but continues to *reject Christ anyway*. I think Boatman is right (**230-231**), that there is no reason to think that at this point the Pharisees had already crossed this line and had committed the unforgivable sin. Yes, they had accused Jesus of being possessed by the devil and of using the devil's power to cast out demons. But there is no evidence that they knew that Jesus' power was from the Holy Spirit, and that by their accusations against Jesus they were actually attacking the Spirit Himself.

But from this point on, they had no excuse for not knowing this. Jesus totally refutes, with logic, the Pharisees' charge that He was using Satan's power to cast out demons (***Mt 12:25-27***). Then He clearly informs them that He is casting out demons *"by the Spirit of God"* (***12:28***). Now they have been warned! They can no longer reject and attack Jesus without also attacking—blaspheming—the Holy Spirit.

This is why it is valid to say that the sin of Spirit-blasphemy is a deliberate rejection of the Holy Spirit's testimony to Jesus *while at the same time knowing that it is true.* Herman Bavinck says that this sin is not simply a matter of "doubting or simply denying the truth." It is rather "a denial which goes against the conviction of the intellect, against the enlightenment of conscience, against the dictates of the heart; in a conscious, wilful and intentional imputation to the influence and working of Satan of that which is clearly recognised as God's work."[7] In other words, what qualifies such an attack on Jesus as blasphemy against the Spirit is

Spirit-blasphemy is rejection of the Holy Spirit's testimony while knowing that it is true.

[7] Bavinck, *Gereformeerde Dogmatiek,* 2nd ed., 3:157, cited in Geldenhuys, 352.

when one understands that the power behind Jesus' miracles is the Holy Spirit, but continues to attack Jesus and attribute His power to Satan anyway.

This helps to explain why this sin is unforgivable: if one has come face to face with the truth about Jesus, *and* with the undeniable power of the Holy Spirit working through Jesus' miracles to confirm that truth, and if he then still refuses to accept Jesus and even openly attacks Him, he has thereby *closed every door* to the Holy Spirit's convicting power through the Word, through miracles, and through special providence. Winter says, "The blasphemy against the Holy Spirit is unforgivable because when a man rails against the promised Paraclete and attributes His works to the power of the devil, he has rejected God's last effort to reach him" (**15**). Candlish says, "The Messiah may be reviled ignorantly, by men who do not see His divine Sonship in the human nature which He wears; and for such sin there is forgiveness by God's grace to those who repent: but if a man reviles that very spirit of holiness whereby God reveals himself, he sets himself against holiness itself, seen and known as such; and how shall such an one be delivered from sin and obtain forgiveness?" (**22**).

When one deliberately, knowingly, and blasphemously rejects the Holy Spirit's clear testimony to the world's only Savior, he has thereby rejected God's final Word, and his own last hope. Jesus was trying to warn the Pharisees not to cross over this line.

When one deliberately rejects the Holy Spirit's testimony to the only Savior, he has rejected his own last hope.

Can this sin be committed today? Some may question this possibility, especially if they believe that the Holy Spirit has not given the power to work miracles since the days of the apostles. Does one have to actually witness a miracle to be convicted by its verifying power? No. The Bible's Spirit-inspired testimony to such miracles is still able to confirm the truth about Jesus and engender faith in Him (***Jn 20:30-31***). The power of the Word of God today in many ways is parallel to the power of the miracles Jesus Himself performed. Both the Word and the miracles are the product of the power of the Holy Spirit. Thus I believe one may commit the unpardonable sin today by deliberately, knowingly, and blasphemously rejecting the Spirit-inspired *Word's* clear testimony to Jesus Christ.

Can this sin be committed by a Christian? On the one hand, many will say *no*, but for the wrong reason. That is, they have accepted the false doctrine of "once saved, always saved." Palmer is an example: "Because some Christians have deprived themselves of great peace out of fear that they have committed this sin, it is necessary to state emphatically that Christians cannot blaspheme against the Holy Spirit. The grand truth of the Bible is: Once saved, always saved" (**180**).

On the other hand, many sincere believers understand that it is possible for a Christian to fall from grace, and they are filled with spiritual agony and doubt about their salvation because of some sinful remark they have made about the Holy Spirit. They believe they have committed the unpardonable sin. For their peace of mind and a restored genuine assurance of heaven, these folks should come to realize that not every *sin* against the Spirit is the unpardonable *blasphemy* against the Spirit. It is generally agreed that blasphemy against the Spirit cannot be committed by a Christian. Given the explanation above, it should be clear that the key element of Spirit-blasphemy is an open and hostile rejection of Jesus Himself—which by definition cannot be true of a Christian. It is also generally agreed that the unpardonable sin can be committed only by someone whose heart is evil (***Mt 12:34-35***) and irrevocably hardened against Jesus, like the Pharisees. Ketcherside says it well: "The kind of heart that would engage in such reprehensible conduct will not repent. It is the heart of stone or flint that would willingly see the world of mankind destroyed to justify its own cruelty and gratify its own inhumanity" (**117**). One may say that this sin arises only from a "hopeless hardness of heart" that "makes repentance and faith impossible" (**Candlish, 65**).

The usual, and correct, pastoral advice in this situation is that if any Christian is worried about whether he has committed this unpardonable sin, that in itself is a comforting sign that he has not. As Ketcherside puts it, "A simplistic, but relatively safe, criterion is that anyone who is worried about having blasphemed the Spirit has not done so, for the kind of person Jesus described would never worry about it" (**119**).

If any Christian is worried whether he has committed the unpardonable sin, that is a sign that he has not.

We should note that while we can have confidence concerning

who has *not* committed the unforgivable sin, namely, sincere Christians, we cannot say that we know anyone who *has* committed it. As Winter says, "Only God can read the hearts of men and tell when they have gone so far in their wicked insults to the Holy Spirit that they have indeed blasphemed the Holy Spirit" (**16**). Pache agrees that we cannot thus judge anyone, but he rightly admonishes us to "warn those who are in sin, praying for them that they may escape such a terrible danger" (**65**).

This raises a final question, one about the relation between the unpardonable sin and ***Hebrews 6:4-8***. Many equate the sin named in this passage with the unpardonable sin, since most translations say that when people commit this sin *"it is impossible to renew them again to repentance"* (***v. 6***). Now, if one believes the "once saved, always saved" doctrine, and also believes that ***Hebrews 6:4-8*** speaks of a sinner's being truly lost, he will say that this text cannot be talking about *Christians* or about something that is possible for a *Christian* to do. It applies only to unbelievers (see, e.g., **Palmer, 180-186**; **Pache, 61**). There are many, however, who believe that it is possible for a true believer to truly fall away, which I think is the only reasonable interpretation of ***Hebrews 6:4-8***. But then they read (in ***v. 6)*** that when this falling away occurs, *"it is impossible to renew them again to repentance."* Thus they conclude that any Christian who falls from grace, under any circumstances, has in effect committed the unpardonable sin. Thus, they say, in this manner it *is* possible for a Christian to commit the unpardonable sin (see, e.g., **Barron, 15, 18**; **Spratt, "Sin," 4**). Christians can commit apostasy, and all apostasy is final.

The bottom line is that this is a false interpretation of ***Hebrews 6:6***, especially of the statement, *"It is impossible to renew them."* In most Bible versions this statement is followed by the word "because" or "since," leaving the impression that Hebrews is saying that renewing an apostate to repentance is impossible, *period*—and here's the reason why. . . . In my judgment this is an incorrect interpretation and a seriously misleading translation. The present participles in the verse should be taken as temporal, not causal, and as referring to continuing action, not a completed sin. Thus the correct interpretation is that it is impossible to renew the apostate to repentance *while* or *as long as* he *continues* to crucify Christ again and *continues* to put Him to an open shame. But there is no reason to conclude that he *must* continue to do so. There is nothing at all in this verse that suggests that the falling away is irrevocable and irreversible; this cannot be equated with the unpardonable sin. (See my fuller discussion of this verse in ***Faith*, 382-383**).

We conclude that the unpardonable sin is a specific *act* of speaking against the Holy Spirit's testimony to Jesus in His miracles and in His Word, and that this always occurs in connection with the specific *attitude* of rejection of and opposition to Jesus Himself.

CHAPTER SEVEN

THE WORK OF THE HOLY SPIRIT IN CONVERSION

In the previous chapter I explained that the term "conversion" is used in different ways. Some see it as a general concept embracing the whole process by which a sinner becomes saved, including hearing and being convicted by the Word; believing and repenting; and being regenerated and forgiven. I am using it in a much more restricted sense, namely, to refer to the exact moment when a sinner is "converted" from an unsaved state and condition to a saved state and condition.

Exactly what happens to a sinner to cause this transition from the unsaved to the saved state? Several things happen simultaneously. In this single transitional moment the sinner enters into a saving *union with Jesus Christ* (***Rom 6:3-4***; ***Gal 3:27***), by virtue of which all the saving benefits of Christ's death and resurrection are received. One of these benefits, received in this moment, is *justification* or forgiveness with respect to the guilt of one's sins (***Rom 5:1***). As a result the sinner is no longer under the condemnation of hell (***Rom 8:1***). Also in this moment the sinner is *reconciled* to God, or enters into a state of peace with God (***Rom 5:1,10***). At the same time the sinner is *sanctified* in the sense of an initial separation from Satan's "domain of darkness" and a transfer of citizenship to the Kingdom of Christ (***1Cor 6:11; Col 1:13***). This is also the moment of *adoption*, when one officially and in reality becomes a member of the redeemed family of God (***Rom 8:15; Gal 3:26; 4:5***). Finally, in this same moment the sinner is *regenerated* or born again, being infused with new spiritual life (***Jn 3:3-5; Tts 3:5***).

Regeneration is the specific work of the Holy Spirit in the moment of conversion.

The last of these events—regeneration—is the specific work of the Holy Spirit in this moment of conversion. This chapter will thus focus on how the Holy Spirit works His work of regeneration.

THE NATURE OF REGENERATION

The biblical term usually translated "regeneration" (*palingenesia*) occurs only twice in the NT, in ***Matthew 19:28*** and ***Titus 3:5***. In the former text it seems to refer to the cosmic eschatological renovation of the universe, resulting in the new heavens and new earth; thus it will not be relevant in this chapter. In ***Titus 3:5*** there is no doubt that the word is referring to a salvation event that happens in the life of individual sinners: *"He saved us, not on the basis of deeds which we have done in righteousness, but according to His mercy, by the washing of regeneration and renewing by the Holy Spirit."*

In spite of the fact that this is the only time this word is used in the NT with this connotation, it has become the standard theological term for this particular work of the Spirit. In this section we shall explore the meaning not just of this term but of the whole concept represented by it and by several other NT expressions.

Regeneration as a Salvation Event

The familiar hymn "Rock of Ages" calls upon the blood of Christ to "be of sin the *double cure*; save me from its guilt and power" (or "save from wrath and make me pure"). I have come to think of salvation as this "double cure," and of the sin-condition from which it saves us as the "double trouble" of guilt and power. The biblical basis for these concepts is abundant and solid.

The most serious consequence of personal sin is the *guilt* that results from breaking the law of God (***1Jn 3:4; Jas 2:10***). Guilt in itself is the state of being in a wrong relationship with God and His law. This is an external, objective state, not to be confused with subjective guilt feelings. It simply means that the sinner has broken God's law and as a result is under God's wrath and is liable to the penalty prescribed by the law, which is eternal condemnation in hell. It is comparable to a state of indebtedness; the sinner owes God the debt of eternal punishment. God the righteous Judge must see that this debt is paid.

How does God save a sinner from this guilt and wrath? He does so through the atoning death of Jesus Christ, in which the Savior takes our guilt and punishment upon Himself and suffers the full force of the wrath of God in our place. This is the sense in which He is our Redeemer and our Propitiation (***Rom 3:24-25***). Because Jesus has thus paid sin's debt, God freely offers to cancel the debt of eternal punishment for anyone who freely accepts the offer through obedience to the gospel. Those who accept the offer are thus *justified* or forgiven, which means that God the Judge declares that the forgiven person no longer owes the debt. Justification is the Judge's official pronouncement: "*No penalty for you!*" This is the first part of the "double cure," accomplished through the spiritual but actual application of the blood of Christ to the individual sinner.

The second consequence of personal sin, the second part of the "double trouble," is that the sinner acquires a *sinful nature*. That is, sin affects not only our objective relationship with God and His law; it also affects us subjectively and personally, in our very being. It brings about a weakness of the soul, making it harder to resist temptation. The sinner's spirit is corrupted, diseased, and depraved. The sinner is spiritually sick and evil in his inner nature; he has a sinful heart.[1]

The biblical teaching to this effect is abundant and clear. The sinner is described as sinful in his very nature or being. Sin is the soul's fatal disease, affecting our spirits in a way analogous to the way physical disease affects our bodies. In ***Isaiah 1:5-6*** the prophet describes the

[1] This should not be confused with the Augustinian concept of *total* depravity. See Cottrell, *Faith*, 197-200.

collective body of Israel thus: "The whole head is sick and the whole heart is faint. From the sole of the foot even to the head there is nothing sound in it, only bruises, welts and raw wounds, not pressed out or bandaged, nor softened with oil." This is simply an analogy for the spiritual condition of the sinful heart or soul: *"The heart is more deceitful than all else and is desperately sick"* (***Jer 17:9***). See ***Ezekiel 36:26***; ***Acts 7:51***; ***Ephesians 4:18*** regarding the sinner's hardened, uncircumcised heart.

Sinners are in a condition of weakness or helplessness (***Rom 5:6***), a state of captivity to the devil (***Col 1:13***; ***2Tm 2:26***), a state of slavery to sin (***Rom 6:6,16-20***). Their condition is so bad that it is described as a kind of *death*: sinners are *"dead in your trespasses and sins, . . . dead in our transgressions"* (***Eph 2:1,5***; see ***Col 2:13***). ***Jude 12*** describes sinners as "doubly dead," i.e., not just facing physical death but even now being in a state of spiritual death. Such spiritual death refers to the soul's separation from God and its loss of all sensitivity to godly things. This is the second part of the "double trouble."

How does God save us from this sinful *condition*? Here is where the second part of the "double cure" comes into the picture. God not only saves us from the guilt of sin; He saves us from its power also. He not only saves us from wrath; He also makes us pure. He does this through the saving works known as *regeneration* and *sanctification*. Regeneration is that instantaneous, one-time event that happens in the moment of conversion, the moment when a sinner passes from his lost state to his saved state. As such it is the beginning point and prerequisite for the ongoing process of becoming more and more holy (***1Pet 1:15-16***), known as sanctification. (This is *progressive* sanctification, not to be confused with the *initial* sanctification mentioned on page 238 above.) These marvelous aspects of our salvation are primarily the works of the Holy Spirit, and are the subjects of this and the next two chapters.

God not only saves us from the guilt of sin but also its power.

Biblical Images of Regeneration

The second part of the double cure is represented in the NT by many images or metaphors, all of which seem to be referring to the same instantaneous event known as regeneration. A survey of all of these images will help us to understand exactly what the Holy Spirit is doing in this saving work.

Death and Resurrection

In my judgment the key metaphor describing this event is the dual concept of *death and resurrection*. **Romans 6:1-14** gives us the most complete explanation of this idea. Here Paul says that in the moment of baptism the sinner's "old self," i.e., the "heart of stone" (**Eze 36:26**) was crucified or put to death with Jesus (**v. 6**); in this moment we "died to sin" (**v. 2**). In **Galatians 2:20** Paul declares that this has happened to him: *"I have been crucified with Christ."* He refers here not to the historical event of Christ's death on Golgotha, but to that moment in his own life when the bestowal of the benefits of Christ's death resulted in his own death to sin.

This death-event is just one side of the coin; it is immediately accompanied by the experience of resurrection and the infusion of new life (**Rom 6:4-5**), by virtue of which the sinner is now *"alive from the dead"* (**v. 13**) and able to *"walk in newness of life"* (**v. 4**). As the result of regeneration one is thus *"dead to sin, but alive to God in Christ Jesus"* (**v. 11**). Thus Christians are described as the "living stones" out of which the church is being built (**1Pet 2:5**).

In **Colossians 2:12-13** Paul describes the regeneration event in almost the same way. He says that we have been *"buried with Him in baptism,"* recalling the union with Christ in His death outlined in **Romans 6:1-6**. Likewise, the death-by-burial is followed by an act of resurrection: *"In which [baptism] you were also raised up with Him through faith in the working of God, who raised Him from the dead"* (**v. 12**). The fact of resurrection from spiritual death is reemphasized in **verse 13**: *"When you were dead in your transgressions and the uncircumcision of your flesh, He made you alive together with Him, having forgiven us all our transgressions."* See also **Colossians 3:1**.

In view of the centrality of Christ's death and resurrection in the scheme of redemption, it is no accident that the saving act of regeneration should itself have the character of death and resurrection. Paul speaks of *"the surpassing greatness of [God's] power toward us who believe,"* which is *"in accordance with the working of the strength of His might which He brought about in Christ, when He raised Him from the dead"* (***Eph 1:18-20***; see ***Php 3:10***). In other words, Christ's resurrection unleashes the power of life that destroys the curse of death in all its forms. This includes the power to give new life to souls that are dead in their trespasses and sins. Thus the language of resurrection—being made alive—is used for the act of regeneration more than any other imagery. Besides ***Romans 6:1-14*** and ***Colossians 2:12-13***, we may cite ***Ephesians 2:5-6***, which says that God *"made us alive together with Christ . . . and raised us up with Him."* John also speaks of the Christian as having *"passed out of death into life"* (***Jn 5:24***; ***1Jn 3:14***).

Hodge sums up the thrust of this biblical teaching very well: "By a consent almost universal the word regeneration is now used to designate . . . the instantaneous change from spiritual death to spiritual life. Regeneration, therefore, is a spiritual resurrection; the beginning of a new life" (**III:5**). As Torrey says, "Regeneration is the impartation of life, spiritual life, to those who are dead, spiritually dead, through their trespasses and sins" (**101**).

"Regeneration is a spiritual resurrection, the beginning of a new life."

Rebirth

The next most significant metaphor for regeneration is *birth* or *rebirth*. The key passage using this image is Jesus' conversation with Nicodemus in ***John 3***. In response to Nicodemus's unspoken inquiry Jesus says, *"Truly, truly, I say to you, unless one is born again he cannot see the kingdom of God"* (***v. 3***). The word rendered "born" is *gennao*, which (in the passive voice) can mean either "begotten" or "born." The context clearly shows that here it means "born." The word translated "again" is *anothen*, which can also mean "from above" (as in ***Jn 3:31***; ***19:11***; ***Jas 1:17***; ***3:15,17***). Nicodemus obviously understands Jesus to mean "again" (***v. 4***; see ***v. 7***; ***Gal 4:9***). Jesus does not contradict this understanding, but by emphasizing *"born of the Spirit"* (***vv. 5,6,8***) He shows that He does not mean simply "again." Both meanings are probably intended: "You must be born again, and this rebirth must be from above, from the power of the Holy Spirit."

Jesus' specific reply to Nicodemus's question in ***verse 4*** is this: *"Truly, truly, I say to you, unless one is born of water and the Spirit [ex hudatos kai pneumatos] he cannot enter into the kingdom of God"* (***v. 5***).

Jesus specifically contrasts this with physical birth in ***verse 6***, *"That which is born of the flesh is flesh, and that which is born of the Spirit* [*ek tou pneumatos*] *is spirit."* He is talking about something that happens not to the body but to the spirit of man. He refers again to *"born of the Spirit"* (*ek tou pneumatos*) in ***verse 8***. Laying the groundwork for Pentecost (cf. the reference to "the kingdom"), Jesus is saying that one cannot participate in salvation in the New Covenant era unless his soul or spirit has been "born again" by the power of the Holy Spirit.

John the Apostle refers several times to the fact that Christians are "born of God" (***1Jn 3:9***; ***4:7***; ***5:1,4,18***; see ***2:29***). Early in his Gospel, speaking of Jesus, John says, *"But as many as received Him, to them He gave the right to become children of God, even to those who believe in His name, who were born, not of blood nor of the will of the flesh nor of the will of man, but of God"* (***Jn 1:12-13***).

The Apostle Peter likewise refers to this event of spiritual rebirth, saying that God *"has caused us to be born again to a living hope through the resurrection of Jesus Christ from the dead"* (***1Pet 1:3***). Also, *"You have been born again not of seed which is perishable but imperishable, that is, through the living and enduring word of God"* (***1Pet 1:23***). In these verses "born again" is a single Greek word, *anagennao*, or *gennao* (which Jesus used in ***John 3***) plus *ana*, which adds the thought of "again" (or "re-"). In ***1:3*** the verb is active, emphasizing the divine act; in ***1:23*** it is passive, emphasizing the human experience. Though the KJV and NKJV translate *anagennao* in ***1:3*** as "begotten," almost all translations give it the connotation of *birth* in ***1:3*** and ***1:23***. Though Peter does not specifically mention the Holy Spirit, it is clear that he is referring to the same divine act of rebirth of which Jesus speaks in ***John 3***.

One other NT reference to the new birth is ***James 1:18***, *"In the exercise of His will He brought us forth by the word of truth, so that we would be a kind of first fruits among His creatures."* James uses the verb *apokueo*, which means "to give birth" (see ***Jas 1:15***).

All of these texts refer to the same event, the regeneration of the sinner by the Holy Spirit. Any attempt to divide this work of the Spirit into two separate events—first, an act of begetting, and later, an act of birth—is pressing the analogy with physical birth too far. The main point of this image of birth is that a *new life* has begun, corresponding exactly with the image of regeneration as a resurrection from the dead. This overlapping of birth and resurrection is seen in the description of the risen Christ as *"the firstborn from the dead"* (***Col 1:18***; ***Rev 1:5***; see ***Acts 13:33***) and in James's description of reborn Christians as *"a kind of first fruits"* (***Jas 1:18***; see ***1Cor 15:10,23***). Peter says we have been *"born again . . . through the resurrection of Jesus Christ from the dead"* (***1Pet 1:3***). Thus these images of resurrection and rebirth are two pictures of the same event: regeneration by the Holy Spirit.

"Regeneration and Renewing"

Another pair of terms describing the regeneration event are used together in ***Titus 3:5***, *"He saved us, not on the basis of deeds which we have done in righteousness, but according to His mercy, by the washing of regeneration and renewing by the Holy Spirit."* The main verb here, *esosen*, "he saved," is aorist tense and thus refers to a completed past action upon us by *"God our Savior"* (***v. 4***). He saved us *"by the washing"* (*dia loutrou*), which is a reference to our Christian baptism. This is described as a washing *"of regeneration and renewing by the Holy Spirit."* In this phrase "regeneration" and "renewing" are parallel terms and are related to "washing" in the same way, i.e., it is a *"washing of regeneration and renewing."* The phrase *"by the Holy Spirit"* modifies both regeneration and renewing in the same way, i.e., this one act, called a regeneration and a renewing, is accomplished *"by the Holy Spirit."* One should never simply divide this whole expression in the middle, as if *"the washing of regeneration"* were one thing, and the *"renewing by the Holy Spirit"* were something altogether different. It is a washing—of regeneration and renewing—by the Holy Spirit.

"Regeneration" and "renewing" are parallel terms, both related to "washing."

As indicated earlier, this is the only NT use of the term "regeneration" in the sense of individual salvation. The word is *palingenesia*, from *palin*, "again," and *genesis*, "beginning, birth." (The word *genesia* means "birthday," as in ***Mt 14:6***; ***Mk 6:21***.) Thus *palingenesia* means "new beginning, new birth, rebirth" (and the day of our conversion is our "rebirthday"). In Greek and Jewish literature it was used to mean "coming back from death to life," or "the restoration to life of individuals." Of ***Titus 3:5*** Büchsel says, "Here *palingenesia* is the result of baptism and parallel to *anakainosis* [renewing]. It does not mean only attainment to a new life with the end of the old life, nor does it mean only moral renewal; it embraces both. The former, however, is the more important" (**686-688**).

In ***Titus 3:5*** the word "renewing" is the noun *anakainosis,* from a verb which means "to make new, to renew." The root word is *kainos,* which means "new," not just in terms of time but also of quality (**Trench, *Synonyms,* 220**). It refers to the new, not just as contrasted with the old, but as "what is new in nature, different from the usual, impressive, better than the old, superior in value or attraction" (**Behm, 447**). "*Kainos* is the epitome of the wholly different and miraculous thing which is brought by the time of salvation" (**ibid., 449**). Thus our word in ***Titus 3:5*** "refers to the unique and basic beginning which the Spirit makes in man at baptism" (**ibid., 453**). This fulfills the prophecy of ***Ezekiel 36:26***, *"Moreover, I will give you a new heart and put a new spirit within you; and I will remove the heart of stone from your flesh and give you a heart of flesh."*

It should be clear that these two words, regeneration and renewing, are parallel not only to one another but also to the concepts of spiritual resurrection and the new birth.

New Creation

Another biblical term for regeneration is "new creation," which according to ***2 Corinthians 5:17*** is one result of our saving union with Christ: *"Therefore if anyone is in Christ, he is a new creature; the old things passed away; behold, new things have come."* See also ***Galatians 6:15***, *"For neither is circumcision anything, nor uncircumcision, but a new creation."* This is the saving act of which ***Ephesians 2:10*** speaks: *"For we are His workmanship, created in Christ Jesus for good works."* The phrase *"created in Christ Jesus"* is not the creation of ***Genesis 1:1***, but the new creation of ***2 Corinthians 5:17***.

This is simply another concept parallel with new life, new birth, and new beginning. Raising the dead and creation from nothing are mentioned together as the greatest masterworks in the repertoire of divine omnipotence (***Rom 4:17***). That both of these metaphors are applied to the conversion event shows what an incomprehensible work of divine power is being performed there. Behm says, "Without any human co-operation there arises in baptism the *kaine ktisis* [new creation] . . . by the miracle of renewal through the Holy Spirit, who created a life that was not there before" (**453**).

"Circumcision Made without Hands"

A final image representing the regeneration event is circumcision. **Colossians 2:11** says that *"in Him,"* i.e., when you entered into that saving union with Jesus Christ, *"you were also circumcised with a circumcision made without hands, in the removal of the body of the flesh by the circumcision of Christ."* This is obviously a spiritual event ("without hands") and a salvation event, foretold in **Deuteronomy 30:6**, *"Moreover the LORD your God will circumcise your heart and the heart of your descendants, to love the LORD your God with all your heart and with all your soul, so that you may live."*

The OT prophets sometimes exhorted the Israelites to circumcise their own hearts (***Deu 10:16***; ***Jer 4:4***), meaning that they should repent and change their ways before the Lord. The spiritual circumcision of ***Colossians 2:11***, though, is not something accomplished by the sinner himself; it is passive voice, referring to something done to him. It seems comparable to the image of dying with Christ in ***Romans 6:1-6***, where Paul says our old self was crucified with Christ, *"in order that our body of sin might be done away with"* (***v. 6***). The "body of sin" in ***Romans 6:6*** is equivalent to the "body of the flesh" in ***Colossians 2:11*** (cf. *"the uncircumcision of your flesh"* in ***Col 2:13***). In other words, the "death" of the old self or old being is like a spiritual circumcision in which the sinful side of our nature is removed and left behind us, buried with Christ in baptism, as it were, paving the way for the resurrection of the new man (***Col 2:12***).

By using this image, says Dunn, Paul "is expounding the radical nature of the spiritual transformation which takes place at conversion." It is an "operation which takes place in the innermost being of man and affects his total personality. . . . It is the work of God, not of man." In contrast with physical circumcision, "it is the spiritual, internal, invisible work of God in the heart of man" (***Baptism*, 153-154**).

This is confirmed in Paul's words addressed especially to Jews who trusted in their physical circumcision as a mark of their salvation, in ***Romans 2:28-29***. He says in ***verse 29***, *"But he is a Jew who is one inwardly; and circumcision is that which is of the heart, by the Spirit, not by the letter; and his praise is not from men, but from God."* Here the "circumcision made without hands" is called the circumcision "of the heart," i.e., of the soul or spirit. Significantly, Paul says this circumcision of the inner man is performed "by the Spirit."

What Kind of Change Is This?

Alexander Campbell on Regeneration

It is obvious that regeneration is a monumental change in the soul or spirit of the sinner. But what kind of change is it? In his debate with Rice, Alexander Campbell distinguishes several kinds of change. There is *physical* change, which "has respect to the essence or form of the subject." Another kind is a *legal* change, which "is a change as respects a legal sentence, or enactment." Next, an *intellectual* change is "a change of views." Finally, a *moral* or *spiritual* change "is a change of the moral state of the feelings, and of the soul." It is "a change of the affections—a change of the heart." Such "a moral change is effected only by motives, and motives are arguments" (CRD, 613).

In this debate and in his book, *The Christian System*, Campbell explains his view that regeneration is a general term that describes the whole process of spiritual or moral change, culminating in the new birth at Christian baptism. This "moral regeneration" is "the renovation of the mind and character," or "the change of heart and of character," or the "change of heart and life" (*System*, 220, 222, 227). This change is summed up as faith, or belief in testimony; repentance, or sorrow for sin; and reformation of life, or abandonment of sin (ibid., 222). It is solely a response to the testimony of the Word pertaining to the gospel facts.

> . . . Fact, testimony, faith, feeling, action, are therefore bound together by a natural and gracious necessity, which no ingenuity can separate. And will not every Christian say, that when a person *feels* and *acts* according to the faith, or the testimony of God, he is a new creature—regenerate—truly converted to God? He that believes the facts testified in the record of God understands them, feels according to their nature and meaning, and acts in correspondence with them—has undergone a change of heart and of life which makes him a new man.
>
> This is that moral change of heart and life which is figuratively called *regeneration*. We are not to suppose that regeneration is something which must be added to the faith, the feeling, and the action or behavior, which are the effects of the testimony of God understood and embraced; or which are the impress of the divine facts attested by Prophets and Apostles. It is only another name for the same process in all its parts. (ibid., 227)

It is in the process of undergoing this moral change that the spiritually dead sinner becomes alive again. "He merely receives new ideas, and new impressions, and undergoes a great moral, or spiritual change—so that he becomes alive wherein he was dead, and dead wherein he was formerly alive" (CRD, 617).

This leads to what Campbell calls "the last act of regeneration," namely, the "bath of regeneration" (Tts 3:5) or Christian baptism, "which completes the whole." Baptism (immersion) is called regeneration because it is the culmination of the whole *process* called regeneration. Here is where the new birth takes place. That is, the new birth of John 3:3-5 is not equivalent to the whole process, but only to its final component (*System*, 230-232).

This consummating act of regeneration—immersion, the new birth—is altogether a change of *state*, which is similar to what Campbell calls a *legal* change in that it is a change of relationships only. All moral change—the change of views, heart, and feelings—precedes this change of state. A change of views leads to a change of heart or feelings, which is followed by a change of state. The change of state is not moral or internal; it is solely a change of relationship with God. And it is this change of state or relationship which marks the transition from unsaved to saved. "A man may change his views of Jesus, and his heart may be changed towards him; but, unless a change of state ensues, he is still unpardoned, unjustified, unsanctified, unreconciled, unadopted, and lost to all Christian life and enjoyment" (ibid., 164-165). As a change of state this final act of regeneration is equivalent to marriage, naturalization as a citizen of a new country, or adoption into a new family (ibid., 166).

What is the role of the Holy Spirit in all of this? Campbell is very clear on this point: "All that is done in us before regeneration"—i.e., before this final, state-changing step of regeneration, this new birth—"God our Father effects by *the word*, or the gospel dictated and confirmed by his Holy Spirit" (ibid., 234). This is the point of the proposition Campbell defended against Rice: in the moral change known as conversion, "the Spirit of God operates on persons only through the Word" (CRD, 611).

I believe Campbell's approach to regeneration does not do justice to the biblical testimony to the change in the sinner's heart known as regeneration. I agree that regeneration must not be confused with justification or forgiveness of sins, which is a *legal* change and does not really involve a change within the sinner himself. Such confusion is seen in the following comment by Root on **Ephesians 2:1**: "*And you hath he quickened* (**Eph 2:1**). To quicken anyone is to make him alive. Since the wages of sin is death (**Romans 6:23**), we who sinned were *dead in trespasses and sins*: that is, we were condemned, doomed, sentenced to die. But God forgave our sins, canceled our condemnation, and thus made us alive" (**"Knots," 11**). This is wrong. "Made us alive" is a change in our spiritually dead nature, not just the legal cancellation of our death penalty.

I also agree that regeneration must not be equated with an *intellectual* change, or the change of views that is involved in the assent aspect of faith. Such a change is necessary, but only as a prerequisite to regeneration and not as a part of regeneration itself.

Contrary to the contention of Campbell, however, I do not believe that regeneration involves what he calls the *moral* change in the sinner's heart that is motivated by the Word of God. Such a moral change does occur, and must occur as a prerequisite to regeneration. This moral change includes both aspects of faith, i.e., assent and trust, as well as repentance. The error of Campbell and many others, though, is to identify this moral change with regeneration as such, or at least with the heart of the regeneration event.

The main reason why this is completely inadequate and unacceptable is this. A moral change, as described by Campbell, is a change which the sinner makes in himself. Whatever the motivation or reason for the change, when a sinner believes and repents, that is a voluntary change of mind and heart that the sinner himself accomplishes through his own will. If we do not see faith and repentance as the sinner's own decisions or acts, then we have compromised the reality of free will. However, the variety of biblical images surveyed in the previous section depict regeneration as an event so unspeakably wondrous and prodigious that it cannot possibly be regarded as something that can be accomplished by mere human effort. Can a man raise himself from the dead? Can a man give birth to himself? Can a man create himself? Such an event cannot possibly be equated with a sinner's personal decision to believe, repent, and reform his own life. It is something only God can do. Here is Morris's apt comment:

> . . . Now, this great variety of forms of expression points impressively to one great central truth, namely, that the Christian life is due to supernatural action. Christianity does not simply mean a moral change within men. It is more than merely "turn-

> ing over a new leaf". It is such a radical change that the man can be said to have been born all over again. He can be said to be created anew (***2 Cor. v. 17***). This is not anything that men may do for themselves. It takes place as a result of the work of the Spirit of God. We cannot begin to understand what Christianity is all about until we have grasped this. (***Spirit*, 73**)

We must understand this: our moral self-change (faith and repentance) occurs prior to regeneration and is a prerequisite for it, but it is not the same as regeneration and cannot of its own power produce regeneration. Regeneration itself is more like the kind of change Campbell absolutely rules out, namely, a *physical* change, or more appropriately a *metaphysical* change (see **Campbell, CRD, 619**). That is, regeneration is a change that takes place in the very essence of the soul.

This does not mean, of course, that the soul's essence is transformed into a different kind of stuff, or that anything is added to its essence. It means simply that the damage sin inflicts upon the soul is repaired; it means that what was dead is now alive; it means that the sin-sickness that infects the soul is healed. Or rather, it means that the long process of healing and repair has begun. By way of analogy, a bodily sickness is healed first of all by an initial treatment, e.g., an injection or an operation, which is then followed by a period of recuperation and recovery. On the spiritual level the initial operation is the act of regeneration, and the period of recovery is sanctification.

In regeneration the damage sin inflicts upon the soul is repaired.

To follow this analogy, in the act of regeneration God assumes the role of the Great Physician, rather than the role of Judge as in justification. ***Ezekiel 36:26*** prophetically describes this work in terms of a heart-transplant operation: *"Moreover, I will give you a new heart and put a new spirit within you; and I will remove the heart of stone from your flesh and give you a heart of flesh."* Here the "heart of stone" is the soul hardened and calcified by sin. It is figuratively removed and replaced by a "heart of flesh," i.e., one that is soft and yielding to the will of God.

It should also be clear that such a change, under the image of the new birth, is not merely a change of *state.* A change of state does take place at that point (initial sanctification, adoption, reconciliation), but this is *not* regeneration. Regeneration as a new birth is an inward change of the heart.

As indicated above, regeneration is a change in the sinner's nature, but it is not a complete change or a complete healing of the soul's sin-sickness. It is rather the reversal of the general direction of one's life. It is the beginning of a process of further change, which is the lifelong healing process known as sanctification (see chapter 9, below). It is similar to an event often depicted in old Western movies where a principal in the story would be wounded and develop an infection and a fever. With no antibiotics the local doctor could only monitor the sick man's condition until either the latter died or "the fever broke," as they would say. The time when "the fever broke" was the turning point, the beginning of the wounded man's recovery. Likewise, regeneration is the time when the sin-fever breaks and the life-giving power of the Holy Spirit sets the sinner on the road to spiritual wholeness.

The result of regeneration, then, is that the saved person can now say, "I can obey God's will; *I am able* to obey the law's commands"—which the unregenerated person was unable to do (***Rom 8:7-8***). We died and rose with Christ, *"so that we would no longer be slaves to sin"* (***Rom 6:6***). A bad tree cannot produce good fruit (***Mt 7:18***); but the regenerated person is no longer a bad tree. He is a good tree who is now able to bear good fruit (***Mt 7:17***). The spiritual heart transplant of which Ezekiel speaks (***36:26-27***) enables one to walk in God's statutes and observe His ordinances. *"For we are His workmanship, created in Christ Jesus for good works"* (***Eph 2:10***). That is, the ability to do good works is the very purpose and result of regeneration.

THE HOLY SPIRIT AS THE CAUSE OF REGENERATION

As just indicated, the very nature of the regenerating event precludes any definition of it that sees it as something the sinner can accomplish for himself. It is not a work of man, but a work of God. As ***John 1:13*** says, God's children are *"born, not of blood nor of the will of the flesh nor of the will of man, but of God."*[2] Our death with Christ and resurrection with Him are "the working of God" (***Col 2:12***); thus in our new natures *"we are His workmanship"* (***Eph 2:10***). As J.C. Smith

[2] The interpretation that this verse refers to Christ's supernatural birth rather than to Christians' new birth is based on extremely poor manuscript evidence. See Morris, *John*, 100.

Our rebirth "is no human process, but a divine accomplishment."

says, "The new birth is God's act in response to man's acceptance of the gospel by the obedience of faith" (**10**). Gresham says that our rebirth "is no human process, but a divine accomplishment"; "it is a spiritual act wrought by God" (**I:3**).

When the Bible gets specific about God's role in regeneration, it assigns this redemptive act to the Holy Spirit. Thus we may speak of the Spirit as the agent or cause of regeneration.

The Spirit's Indirect Work in Regeneration

The Holy Spirit's work in relation to regeneration is both indirect and direct. Regarding the former, He works indirectly upon the sinner's heart through the Word of God, as explained in the previous chapter. Through the power of the Word the Spirit convicts sinners of sin, righteousness, and judgment and moves them to faith and repentance. This in itself is not regeneration, but it is a necessary precondition or preparation for it. The gift of regeneration is bestowed only upon those who believe and repent; faith and repentance are aroused by the Word of God; the Holy Spirit is the divine author of the Word. In this way the Spirit's work is indirectly responsible for regeneration.

This crucial role of the Word in leading us to the moment of the new birth is seen in ***James 1:18***, *"In the exercise of His will He brought us forth by the word of truth."* Peter asserts the same thing: *"For you have been born again not of seed which is perishable but imperishable, that is, through the living and enduring word of God"* (***1Pet 1:23***). Though it is tempting to think of this aspect of the Spirit's work as an act of *begetting* as distinct from a later moment of birth as such, I do not believe this distinction is intended or warranted by these texts. The point is simply this, that when we come to the moment of actual regeneration, we must acknowledge that we have been brought to that point by a work of the Holy Spirit, namely, His indirect working through the Word.

We must think of this work of the Spirit as *necessary* for regeneration. This is the sense in which Morris is correct: "We would not even begin to be Christians without some work of the Spirit within us" (***Spirit,*** **71**). This applies first of all to His working upon our hearts indirectly via His inspired Word. The error of many is to think that this is the *only* way the Spirit works in regeneration.

We may note that the Word has the same indirect role in bringing a sinner to the moment of justification or pardon, in that it leads us to faith and repentance, which are necessary preconditions for receiving this saving gift also. No one would say, though, that the Word actually *accomplishes* the pardon. Pardon or forgiveness is received only through a direct act of God in which He applies the blood of Christ to the believing, repentant sinner. We should view regeneration in the same way. Working indirectly through the Word to incite us to faith and repentance, the Spirit thus leads us to the moment when the distinct act of regeneration can be accomplished. The latter also is a work of the Spirit, but it is His *direct* work upon the soul.

The Spirit's Direct Work of Regeneration

I know that Campbell and many others in the Restoration Movement were and are adamantly opposed to the concept of a direct operation of the Spirit upon human spirits—"the naked Spirit of God operating upon the naked soul of man" (**CRD, 614**), but I believe the biblical teaching about the divine act of regeneration cannot be understood in any other way. The ultimate power for salvation, both for justification and for regeneration/sanctification, flows from the saving work of Jesus Christ. In ***Romans 6:1-14*** even regeneration is attributed to Jesus' sin-slaying, life-giving death and resurrection. Christ died to sin; and when we are united with Him in His death, we too die to sin *by virtue of His death*. Christ also rose from the dead, and when we are united with Him in His resurrection, we too pass from spiritual death to spiritual life *by virtue of His resurrection*. This does not happen through some inner strength of our own.

Why do we say, then, that the *Holy Spirit* is the one who works regeneration in the believing sinner's heart? Because a specific saving work of the Spirit is to *apply* the saving benefits of Christ's death and resurrection to the sinner. He is the person of the Trinity who brings the power of Christ's death and resurrection to bear upon us. As such He is the very embodiment of the death-dealing and life-giving power that changes us in the moment of regeneration.

Not only does the Spirit apply to us *"the power of His [Christ's] res-*

urrection" (***Php 3:10***); He Himself is an inherent source of life. He is *"the Spirit of life"* (***Rom 8:2***), even for the physical world: *"You send forth Your Spirit, they are created; and You renew the face of the ground"* (***Ps 104:30***; see ***Gen 1:2***). God promises that the Holy Spirit will give life to our dead bodies in the day of resurrection (***Rom 8:11***), an assurance for which He is now a pledge or down payment (***2Cor 1:22***; ***5:5***; ***Eph 1:13-14***). Likewise as the Living Water (***Jn 4:10-14***; ***7:37-39***), the Spirit is the one who even now imparts and implants new life into our spiritual natures. *"It is the Spirit who gives life"* (***Jn 6:63***; see ***2Cor 3:6***).

The Spirit of God is specifically named as the agent of regeneration in ***Titus 3:5***, which says that the regeneration and renewing that take place in baptism are *"by the Holy Spirit."* Jesus specifically attributes the new birth to the Holy Spirit; He uses the phrase *"born of the Spirit"* three times in ***John 3:5-8***. Here, says Morris, "Jesus is referring to the miracle which takes place when the divine activity re-makes a man. He is born all over again by the very Spirit of God" (***John***, **218**). Under the figure of spiritual circumcision, Paul likewise attributes regeneration to the Holy Spirit in ***Romans 2:29***. In Peter's second recorded gospel sermon in Acts, he invites sinners to repent and return to God *"in order that times of refreshing may come from the presence of the Lord"* (***Acts 3:19***). The "times of refreshing" are parallel to the promise of *"the gift of the Holy Spirit"* in his first sermon (***Acts 2:38***). When the Spirit comes, the soul is refreshed and renewed.

The Spirit of God is specifically named as the agent of regeneration.

A main reason why many reject the idea of regeneration as a direct work of the Spirit upon the sinner's heart is that they think it is an implicit form of Calvinism, similar to the Calvinist doctrine of irresistible grace. As we will remember, Calvinism's doctrine of total depravity includes the belief that all unsaved people are totally unable to respond to the gospel or to the influence of the Word, and thus are totally unable to make the decision to believe and repent. Therefore, if anyone at all is going to be saved, God Himself must decide who that will be (via unconditional election); and then He must act directly upon the chosen ones' hearts *to enable them to believe*. This direct, efficacious, and irresistible act, performed by the Holy Spirit, is a main element of the total package called irresistible grace, and is the Calvinist version of regeneration. As a consequence of this act, the sinner immediately begins to believe in Jesus Christ. Thus regeneration precedes and bestows faith as an irresistible gift.

Thus it is true that in Calvinism regeneration is a direct work of the Spirit upon the sinner's heart, but this is completely different from the view of regeneration explained here as the biblical view. In the latter view the Spirit does work upon sinners' hearts to influence them to believe and repent, but this work is mainly *indirect* (through the Word), and is always resistible. Some choose to believe and repent, and some choose not to do so. Only after one has chosen to believe and repent does he submit himself to the Great Physician's healing touch, and only then does the Holy Spirit work directly upon his heart to effect regeneration. Such an understanding is quite the opposite of Calvinism.

I cannot describe the way or manner or method of the Spirit's regenerating touch upon the sinner's spirit. Scripture does not explain it, and spiritual being by its very nature is not something we can observe and analyze as we do with material objects. Jesus reminds us of the element of mystery related to this work of the Spirit: *"The wind blows where it wishes and you hear the sound of it, but do not know where it comes from and where it is going; so is everyone who is born of the Spirit"* (***Jn 3:8***). We assert that it happens and believe that it happens simply because the Bible so teaches it.

THE TIME OF REGENERATION

We have discussed the *nature* of regeneration and the *cause* of regeneration; now we must inquire concerning the *time* of the Spirit's direct work of regeneration. How we answer this question is very important for a proper understanding of how God saves us. It is also closely interrelated with one's understanding of the nature of regeneration as well. Two views concerning this question will now be presented.

One View: Regeneration Happens at the Time of Faith and Repentance

Probably the most prevalent view in Christendom today is that the Holy Spirit performs His work of regeneration in direct connection with the sinner's coming to faith and repentance. This idea is not only nearly universal among the denominations; it is also widely held within the Restoration Movement. There are, however, several different approaches to this view that regeneration immediately accompanies faith and repentance.

Protestantism in General

Almost all Protestant denominations agree that the Spirit works regeneration upon the sinner's heart at the same moment the sinner believes and repents. They disagree, however, as to which is the cause and which is the effect, or at least as to the logical order of the two. The division is along Calvinist and non-Calvinist lines.

Because of their commitment to the doctrine of total depravity, most Calvinists believe that the Spirit's work of regeneration must *precede* the convert's faith and repentance. This all happens in the single moment when irresistible grace is bestowed, so there is no temporal gap between the Spirit's regenerating work and the convert's faith and repentance; but there is a logical order. That is to say, regeneration precedes faith and repentance as cause precedes effect. For all practical purposes, though, everything happens simultaneously. As soon as regeneration occurs, the sinner begins to believe and repent.

An example is Palmer, who says, "According to Scripture, faith does not precede and cause regeneration but rather, regeneration precedes and causes faith" (**84**). Pink says, "A man is not regenerated because he has first believed in Christ, but he believes in Christ because he has been regenerated" (**55**). As James White puts it, "Men believe the gospel to be saved. No question about it. I believe it, I preach it, I call men to do it. I just know that no man *will* do it unless and until the miracle of regeneration takes place first" (**305**). As Donald Williams puts it,

> Which is cause and which is effect? Here the biblical answer seems to be that regeneration comes first. If the unsaved do not have it in them to respond to Christ and if repentance itself must be granted by God (***2Tm. 2:23***), then it seems clear that, while both God and the sinner perform a significant act in conversion, it is God's act which comes first. God takes the initiative. (**75**)[3]

[3] Millard Erickson, though basically a Calvinist, acknowledges that the biblical evidence supports the fact that faith and repentance are (logically) prior to

The standard non-Calvinist Protestant approach agrees with Calvinism that faith and repentance occur at the same time as regeneration, but it recognizes that faith and repentance are logically first and that regeneration is the Spirit's gift to the believing heart. Pache asks, "When does regeneration take place?" His answer: "At that very moment when the heart, under the Spirit's double conviction of sin and righteousness, accepts the Saviour, who is presented to him. . . . By means of new birth we receive life eternal; this grace is given us as soon as we believe" (**68-69**). "As soon as I am in Christ through faith, Christ is also in me to give me life by new birth" (**72**).

Restoration Movement

Contrary to what some might expect, the idea that regeneration takes place as soon as a sinner believes and repents occurs frequently in other Christian circles, though never in the Calvinist sense as described above. This view takes two forms.

The more common of these views is basically Alexander Campbell's approach to the whole issue of the work of the Holy Spirit in conversion. As we have seen, Campbell basically limits the role of the Spirit in conversion to what He accomplishes through His inspired Word. Under this indirect influence of the Spirit the sinner is motivated to believe and repent, thus undergoing a self-caused moral change of heart that is part of the essence of regeneration. In other words, the "change of heart and of character"—wrought by the sinner himself as convicted and moved by the Word—"constitutes moral regeneration" (***System*, 222**). Review again Campbell's comments virtually equating faith, repentance, and reformation of life with regeneration as quoted in the box on page 247.

This same approach to the time of regeneration has been taken by other Restoration Movement authors. This is seen especially in their explanation of ***Romans 6:1-6***, where they equate the sinner's dying to sin and rising to new life with his prebaptismal decision to believe and repent. For example, Moses Lard declares that "we die to sin

regeneration. The difference is inconsequential, though, since he uncharacteristically distinguishes between what Calvinists call God's "effectual calling" and regeneration. He then assigns to effectual calling the usual role of irresistible grace, i.e., the bestowing of faith and repentance. This allows him to maintain his Calvinism while being true to the Bible's sequence of faith, then regeneration (944-945).

when we believe in Christ and repent of our sins"; thus "we died to sin before our baptism" (***Romans***, **195-196**). Following Lard, DeWelt says that the sinner's death to sin "was brought about by our belief and repentance preceding our baptism"; that is, "the method of attaining the crucifixion of self and thus being released from the bondage of the flesh is by way of faith and repentance before baptism" (***Romans***, **90-91**). K.C. Moser says the same: "In repentance one dies and is raised to righteousness." In our repentance, which is a human act, "two changes take place. First, like Christ and with him, we die unto sin. Second, like Christ and with him, we are raised to live unto God" (**89-90**).

As we have already seen, this death and resurrection are the same as regeneration; thus according to this approach a sinner regenerates himself when he believes and repents. This observation alone is sufficient to show the fallacy of this notion, in view of the fact that regeneration is clearly a change which can be accomplished only by supernatural power (as seen in the previous section). Also, it seriously violates the clear biblical connection between regeneration and baptism, which will be shown below.

We are discussing the view that the time of the Spirit's regenerating work is directly related to the moment when the sinner believes and repents. Another approach to this view, one that is quite popular in Restoration circles, is the life-before-birth proposal. This approach focuses on the concept of regeneration as a new birth, and proceeds to expand the analogy into a two-step process. The contention is that if regeneration is parallel to physical birth (***Jn 3:3-5***), then it must be preceded by an act of *begetting* in which a seed is planted and immediately initiates new life which continues to grow until the time of birth. In reference to regeneration this act of begetting is identified with the planting of the seed of the Word (***Jas 1:18***; ***1Pet 1:23***). When the Word is believed, the new life begins. Thus the convert is already spiritually alive before he is "born of water" in Christian baptism.

Campbell's "Birth" Analogy

The view that there is a "begetting" stage before the actual birth is implicit in the Campbellian view explained above. Campbell himself lays the groundwork for it in his explanation of regeneration:

"The Spirit of God is the begetter, the gospel is the seed; and, being thus begotten and quickened [made alive], we are born of the water. A child is alive before it is born, and the act of being born only changes its state, not its life. Just so in the metaphorical birth. Persons are begotten by the Spirit of God, impregnated by the Word, and born of the water" (*System* 173). He declares, "Begetting and quickening necessarily precede being born." Also, "Being born imparts no new life; but is simply *a change of state*, and introduces into *a new mode of living*" (ibid., 179). "Birth itself is not for procuring, but for enjoying, the life possessed before birth" (ibid., 233).

Many have followed Campbell's reasoning on this point, often applying it in ways Campbell never intended. A detailed example is Root's article, "How to Be Born Again." He distinguishes these elements in the process of physical birth: 1) sperm; 2) conception; 3) prenatal development; and 4) birth itself. In spiritual rebirth these correspond to 1) the gospel; 2) belief; 3) repentance and commitment; and 4) baptism. At point two—conception—"a new life begins" ("Born Again," 3). Crouch makes a similar distinction between begetting and birth: "The new nature of the redeemed man is begotten by the Spirit of God. Then when the Father has regenerated the life, birth follows at the baptismal waters. Life is begotten by the Father; the birth at baptism brings that new life into a new relationship in the kingdom of Christ" (15). Phillips asserts that "the Spirit is the author of life, and the divine begetting is from Him. . . . One is begotten when one believes. . . . Through the Word faith produces regeneration" (3-5). Van Buren (9) says,

> . . . Physically a person must be alive before birth in order to be alive after birth; otherwise he will be stillborn. So spiritual life in us is originated by faith through hearing the preaching of the good news of Jesus. This is the medium through which the "seed" of the Holy Spirit is planted in us and life is conceived. . . . So a person who is "born again" has spiritual life *conceived* in him when he believes in Jesus as Messiah, Savior, and Lord. He is *born of water* when he is baptized into Christ; that is, the birth process is completed.

A common application of this idea is seen in Bill Putman's identification of unimmersed believers as "brothers yet unborn." He says, "In preparation for the physical birth there must be the implanting of seed that fertilizes the prepared egg cell. From that point on the new life is in process of becoming." Now, "the spiritual process is very much the same. The word of God must be planted in the heart." This leads to faith and repentance, and ultimately to birth itself in

Christian baptism. But since Ananias referred to Saul as "Brother Saul" even before he was baptized (Acts 22:13), we should think of unimmersed believers as "brothers yet unborn" (10).

Putman overlooks the fact that Jews often referred to their fellow Jews as "brethren," even after they became Christians. This occurs often in Acts; see also Rom 9:3. (See Cottrell, *Baptism*, 70, 77 [fn 3]).

This approach to the time of regeneration has serious problems that should cause us to reject it. For one thing, it is an unwarranted extension of the metaphor of birth. In dealing with figures of speech, we must resist the ever-present temptation to go beyond the point being made in the text. The figure of the new birth, as applied especially to baptism (***Jn 3:5***), in itself represents the significant turning point in a person's life. This is the single point of the analogy: that which happens as a result of the water-and-Spirit moment is like a new birth. To speculate on some prebaptismal begetting or conception or embryonic life is to go beyond the metaphor and even to obscure its main point.

A second problem with this approach is that it singles out just one metaphor and, by expanding its application, places it in conflict with other metaphors of regeneration. We must remember that *new birth* is only one of several figures that represent the Spirit-wrought change in our inner being, including new creation, circumcision, and resurrection from the dead. None of these lends itself to being expanded into a multiple-step process. This is especially true of the resurrection metaphor. Up until the moment of resurrection there is nothing but death: a spiritually dead self (***Eph 2:1,5***), and the redemptive death of that dead self (***Rom 6:1-6***). There is no "pre-life life." Speculation about a faith-induced "life before birth" is simply not in harmony with the parallel metaphors for regeneration.[4]

New birth is only one of several figures that represent the Spirit-wrought change in our inner being.

[4] ***First Peter 1:23*** does not speak of an act of begetting that is distinct from the new birth in ***John 3:3-5***. The same root word is used in both passages: *gennao* (John) and *anagennao* (Peter). The reference to the seed of the word in ***1Pet 1:23*** does not make this speak of a separate act equivalent to begetting. The word

The most serious problem with this view of the time of regeneration is that it separates this making-alive work of the Spirit from the point where the Bible says it happens, namely, Christian baptism. This leads to our next section.

Our View: Regeneration Happens at the Time of Baptism

It should be indisputable that faith and repentance, as the sinner's own personal moral change, are preconditions for the Holy Spirit's work of regeneration. Whether this regeneration happens in immediate conjunction with faith and repentance, however, is open to serious dispute. Indeed, my thesis here is that the NT clearly teaches that the Holy Spirit works regeneration in the moment of Christian baptism,[5] at some point *after* faith and repentance have begun. This conclusion follows from the following three related facts: 1) The Holy Spirit is the author or agent of the work of regeneration. 2) The regenerating act occurs in baptism. 3) The Holy Spirit is given to the convert in baptism. The first of these three assertions has been established above. Here we will seek to show the basic biblical evidence for the second and third statements.

Regeneration Occurs in Baptism

To say that regeneration occurs in Christian baptism is not to say anything new. Indeed, this was the consensus belief of Christendom for its first fifteen hundred years (see **Cottrell, "Consensus"**). This begins with Justin Martyr in the mid-second century. Describing the current baptismal practice Justin said that new converts "are brought by us where there is water, and are regenerated. . . . For . . . they then receive the washing with water." Justin then quotes ***John 3:5*** (**"Apology," 61**). In the fourth century Gregory of Nyssa said, "Baptism, then, is a purification from

> **That regeneration occurs in Christian baptism was the consensus belief for fifteen hundred years.**

used in ***Jas 1:18***, *apokueo*, means specifically "to be born." James thus says we are *born* through the Word.

[5] Unless specified otherwise I am using "baptism" and "Christian baptism" in the sense of baptism in water.

sins, a remission of trespasses, a cause of renovation and regeneration." The baptismal water "renews the man to spiritual regeneration" (**"Baptism," 518, 520**). This view continued without serious exception up through and including Martin Luther, who declared that it is appropriate to speak of baptism as the time when "a person is thus born again and made new" (**"Baptism," 3; p. 30**). This "new birth . . . is wrought in Baptism" (***Galatians*, 341**).

The man who almost single-handedly derailed this line of thinking and started Protestantism on a new and radically different course was Huldreich Zwingli (see **Cottrell, "Tradition"**). In 1525 he confidently asserted, "In the matter of baptism, all the doctors have been in error from the time of the apostles. . . . For all the doctors have ascribed to the water a power which it does not have and the holy apostles did not teach" (**130**).

Zwingli started Protestantism on a new and radically different course.

The fact is that nearly everyone recognizes that there is *some* relation between baptism and regeneration, because of texts such as ***John 3:5***; ***Romans 6:1-6***; ***Colossians 2:12***; and ***Titus 3:5***. As Miley remarks, "It is true that the Scriptures verbally place baptism close to regeneration" (**II:334**). For many, however, this relation is only *symbolical*. That is, the act of baptism physically symbolizes or portrays the work that the Holy Spirit has done or will do upon the spirit of the baptized person, but has no necessary temporal connection to it. Commenting on ***Romans 6:4*** Moo says that "many evangelical scholars . . . view baptism as a symbolic picture of the transfer from the old life to the new. Immersion represents death to the old life, submersion the 'burial' . . . of that old life, and emersion the rising to new life. In this way baptism pictures what has taken place in the believer's life through conversion" (**361**). William Stevens is an example. He says, "The act of baptism is symbolical only" (**334**). Stott says that water-baptism "dramatizes Spirit-baptism" (***Baptism*, 35**).

In my judgment we must reject this symbolical view because it teaches something that is never once asserted or implied in any biblical passage about baptism, namely, that it is merely *picturing* or *representing* or *symbolizing* the divine action associated with the baptismal event. In every instance such an interpretation does violence to the straightforward language of the text, and it does so not on any exegetical grounds but solely in the interest of a preconceived dogma.

At the other end of the spectrum, there are some that see a *causal* relation between baptism and regeneration. That is, they see baptism as somehow endowed by God with an inherent power to cause the new birth to occur, or to convey new life to the one being baptized. As Erickson describes it, "This is the doctrine of baptismal regeneration: baptism effects a transformation, bringing a person from spiritual death to life." He finds the most extreme form of this view in traditional Catholicism, but says it occurs in classic Lutheranism, too (**1099-1100**). Those who reject this view are absolutely correct. As Miley says, "No man can rationally think it possible that the outward application of water to the body should effect the interior renovation of the soul" (**II:334**).

At the same time, those who attribute such "baptismal regeneration" to the Restoration Movement as such are *absolutely incorrect.* Stevens, for example, lumps "the Disciples of Christ and the Church of Christ" with Catholics, Anglicans, and Lutherans as those "holding the regenerative view of baptism" (**332**). For another example, J.O. Buswell, Jr., makes the following outrageous statement: "It is worthy of note that the most conspicuous religious group in America today vigorously teaching baptismal regeneration in the sense of the *ex opere operato* efficacy of baptism itself, is the so-called 'Christian Church' (sometimes called 'Campbellite')" (**II:238**). Now, I do not claim to have read everything ever written, or heard everything ever spoken, by members of "the so-called 'Christian Church,'" nor do I claim to speak for everyone in it. But I can vehemently testify that *I* do not hold to such a view, nor have I *ever* seen this view so affirmed in our brotherhood of churches.

The view of the relation between regeneration and baptism that I am presenting here falls between the two extremes above, namely, that the Spirit's work of regeneration occurs *at the time of* Christian baptism; it occurs *during* Christian baptism; it *accompanies* Christian baptism; baptism is the *occasion* for it. To say that baptism is the occasion for the new birth is saying much more than saying it merely symbolizes it; but it is absolutely different from saying that baptism in some sense *causes* regeneration, which is what most people are thinking of when they use or hear the phrase "baptismal regeneration." The symbolists are free to disagree with and argue against baptism as the occasion for regeneration, but they should do so without making false accusations.

What is the NT evidence that regeneration takes place in Christian baptism? We may cite four texts: ***John 3:5***; ***Romans 6:1-6***; ***Colossians 2:12***; and ***Titus 3:5***.[6] That ***John 3:5*** refers to regeneration is beyond dispute; the new birth of which Jesus speaks is probably the most widely accepted image of this event. The issue is whether "born of water" refers to baptism. Those who separate baptism and regeneration usually take "water" to mean something entirely different, such as the amniotic fluid of physical birth or the Holy Spirit Himself (since He is elsewhere figuratively spoken of as water, e.g., ***Jn 4:10-14***; ***7:37-39***). The former view does not fit the context, though, since physical birth is spoken of in **verse 6** as being *"born of the flesh,"* not of water; and it is spoken of in a way that *contrasts* it with *"born of the Spirit,"* whereas **verse 5** links the two together as requirements for entering the kingdom. The latter explanation—equating the "water" with the Spirit—makes the phrase *"born of water and the Spirit"* needlessly and confusingly redundant.

What is the NT evidence that regeneration takes place in Christian baptism?

The weakness of taking "born of water" as a reference to Christian baptism, says Morris, is that Nicodemus would not have known what Jesus was talking about; he "could not possibly have perceived an allusion to an as yet non-existent sacrament. It is difficult to think that Jesus would have spoken in such a way that His meaning could not possibly be grasped" (***John*, 218-219**). This objection is invalid for two reasons. First, Nicodemus would certainly have been familiar with John the Baptist's ministry and baptizing work, and it is no stretch to assume that he would have made a connection between water and some kind of baptism. Second, though the baptism to which Jesus was referring was still in the future, this was not the only time He made an unexplained allusion to some future reality. He spoke thus of His resurrection: *"Destroy this temple, and in three days I will raise it up"* (***Jn 2:19***). His statements about the living water (***Jn 4:10-14***; ***7:37-39***) referred to the Pentecostal outpouring and subsequent personal indwelling of the Spirit. Even the rest of Jesus' instruction in ***John 3:5*** itself refers to future realities. Nicodemus would not

[6] One may consult my book *Baptism: A Biblical View* for a detailed discussion of each of these texts.

have known that the "kingdom of God" would be the church. And even regeneration itself—"born of the Spirit"—was a future Pentecostal gift for the church, something that would have been even more difficult for Nicodemus to understand than "born of water"!

We conclude that anyone whose mind is not closed to the "occasional" view of baptism and regeneration (i.e., baptism is the occasion for regeneration) will see baptism as the most reasonable referent for "born of water" in ***John 3:5***.

Another passage describing baptism as the time of regeneration is ***Titus 3:5***, which says that God saved us *"by the washing of regeneration and renewing by the Holy Spirit."* Again, there is no question that Paul is speaking of the saving act of regeneration. But as with "water" in ***John 3:5***, the issue is whether "washing" refers to baptism. Dunn notes that "most commentators unhesitatingly accept that the primary reference is to baptism," but he disagrees: "I believe that we must see here a spiritual washing which is effected by the Spirit" (***Baptism*, 168**). Erickson also disagrees: "If this is an allusion to baptism, it is vague. It seems rather that 'the washing of rebirth' refers to a cleansing and forgiveness of sins" (**1108**).

To anyone steeped in the Zwinglian mind-set, as most Protestants are, the temptation to completely spiritualize the "washing" in ***Titus 3:5*** is often irresistible. But to the early Christians who were steeped in the knowledge of the OT ritual cleansing ceremonies, to understand such "washing" as a literal water ceremony was natural. The word for "washing" is *loutron*, used only here and in ***Ephesians 5:26***; in the latter verse it specifically refers to "the washing *of water*" (see **Cottrell, *Baptism*, 122-125**). The verb form of *loutron*, which is *louo*, is used only five times in the NT. Four are in nonreligious contexts, but ***Hebrews 10:22*** refers to Christians' having *"our bodies washed **with pure water**."* *Apolouo* is used only twice: ***1 Corinthians 6:11*** and ***Acts 22:16***. The latter is clearly a baptismal reference; Ananias exhorts Saul, "Get up and *be baptized*, and *wash away* your sins." Clearly, when the early Christians thought of "washing" in a religious sense, they thought of water—the water of baptism. Oepke correctly says, "All the relevant passages show that, so far as theological usage is concerned, *louein* and *loutron* are baptismal terms" (**303**).

We should also note that the aorist tense of "he saved" points to a specific past event or moment, which would be consistent with an act such as baptism.

It is obvious, though, that when Paul speaks of *"the washing of regeneration and renewing by the Holy Spirit,"* he is *not* saying that the baptismal waters themselves are the cause of the regeneration and renewing; that role is plainly assigned to the Holy Spirit. But we cannot blithely dismiss the intended connection between the baptismal washing and the Spirit's regeneration. Dunn at least makes this concession regarding ***Titus 3:5***: "Of water-baptism as such there is here no mention, though it may be implicit in the thought that water-baptism, which depicts this washing, was also the occasion when it took place" (***Baptism,* 168**). I believe this is explicit rather than implicit.

The other two passages that relate regeneration to baptism are ***Romans 6:1-6*** and ***Colossians 2:12***, where baptism is specifically named as being intimately related to the convert's personal experience of spiritual death and resurrection. ***Romans 6:3-4*** says,

> *Or do you not know that all of us who have been baptized into Christ Jesus have been baptized into His death? Therefore we have been buried with Him through baptism into death, so that as Christ was raised from the dead through the glory of the Father, so we too might walk in newness of life.*

Colossians 2:12 says, *"Having been buried with Him in baptism, in which you were also raised up with Him through faith in the working of God, who raised Him from the dead."*

In the Romans text Paul says we have been *"baptized into Christ Jesus,"* which specifically involves *"being baptized into His death."* This union with Christ in *His* death results in *our own* spiritual death: *"We have been buried with Him* ***through baptism into death****,"* i.e., through the act of baptism we personally experienced death to sin (see ***6:6***). It is implied but not specifically stated here that in the same act we received *"newness of life"* (***6:4***) and became *"alive to God in Christ Jesus"* (***6:11***) and *"alive from the dead"* (***6:13***). The Colossians text makes this more specific. Being *"buried with Him in baptism"* summarizes the point about union with Christ in His death in ***Romans 6:1-6***, and *"in which you were also raised up with Him"* makes explicit that the spiritual resurrection with Christ occurs in baptism.

Through the act of baptism we personally experienced death to sin.

That the main point here is spiritual resurrection, and not just the physical action of raising the immersed person out of the water, is shown by the explanation in the next verse: *"When you were dead in your transgressions and the uncircumcision of your flesh, He made you alive together with Him, having forgiven us all our transgressions"* (***Col 2:13***). That both the burial with Christ and the resurrection with Christ happen in baptism is specifically stated: *"buried with Him **in baptism, in which** you were also raised up with Him."* The words "in which" (*en ho* in the Greek) are not translated in the NIV, obscuring the connection of the spiritual resurrection with baptism. Some interpret the *en ho* as referring to Jesus Himself and translate it "in whom" (as in ***2:11a***), but the proximity with the noun "baptism" makes it grammatically preferable to connect it thereto. Also, the word for "raised up" has the prefix *sun-* ("with"), which itself establishes the link with Jesus.

We conclude that both the Romans and Colossians texts present Christian baptism as the time or occasion when the sinner is regenerated or given new life in Christ.

Some have tried to escape this conclusion by arguing that neither ***Romans 6:3-4*** nor ***Colossians 2:12*** refers to *water* baptism, but that each refers to *spiritual* baptism only. This has been the "standard operating procedure" for symbolists ever since the time of Zwingli. The apostle Paul, says Unger, "is speaking of Spirit baptism . . . in ***Romans 6:3,4***; ***Colossians 2:12***; and ***Galatians 3:27***" (***Baptism,*** **33**). Walvoord asserts that "there are eleven specific references to spiritual baptism in the New Testament," including ***Romans 6:1-4*** and ***Colossians 2:12*** (**139**). What he means by "specific" is somewhat of a mystery, since there is no reference to the Spirit in these two texts. Pache acknowledges this but is not deterred: "Let us again note that these two passages, ***Colossians 2:12*** and ***Romans 6:4***, do not contain the complete expression, 'the baptism of the Spirit,' but only the words 'with Him in baptism' and 'baptism into death.' In both cases, however, the result comprises death and spiritual resurrection with Christ. . . . Baptism by water could not have such an effect. These verses are therefore primarily concerned with the baptism of the Spirit" (**75; see 72-75**).

My immediate response to this idea is to point to ***Ephesians 4:5***, where Paul declares that there is just *"one baptism."* To identify the baptism of which Paul speaks in Romans and Colossians as *Spirit bap-*

tism only is to posit *two* baptisms, since we must acknowledge that water baptism was a normal event in the experience of the early Christians, as attested by the book of Acts. In spite of this, a common symbolist explanation of **Ephesians 4:5** is that the "one baptism" is actually *Spirit* baptism. In Unger's words, "The apostle, in speaking of the 'one baptism' in **Ephesians 4:5**, is speaking of Spirit baptism" (***Baptism*, 33**). Likewise speaking of **Ephesians 4:5**, Walvoord says, "It is patent that this passage could not refer to water baptism, as the sacrament of baptism is observed in various forms and with different interpretations by Christians, and by some few is not observed at all. Instead of the symbol, the reality is in view here, the baptism of the Holy Spirit" (**140**).

Ephesians 4:5 declares that there is just "one baptism."

At the risk of causing embarrassment, we must point out that Walvoord's reasoning assumes that there existed in the apostolic era the same variety and confusion concerning water baptism that exists today. This is a ludicrous assumption. It is also ludicrous to think that the Christians of Paul's day could have read the reference to "one baptism" in **Ephesians 4:5** and immediately understood it to mean spiritual baptism as something distinct from water baptism. In view of the universal conversion experience of water baptism, this is the baptism that would have first come to their minds upon seeing the words "one baptism." Only Zwinglian presuppositions would lead one to think otherwise (see **Cottrell, Tradition, 47**). Stott lays down the principle that should govern our reading of the texts discussed here: "Baptism means water baptism unless in the context it is stated to the contrary" (***Romans*, 173**).

In view of **Ephesians 4:5** we must acknowledge that a sinner is baptized once, period. As we shall see in the next chapter, this one event has an external side, which is immersion in water; it also has an internal side, which is the saving work of God. We may call the latter "Spirit baptism" or "spiritual baptism," but it is not separated in time from the former. Thus unless we want to deny this cardinal truth of Scripture—that there is but one baptism—we must understand the NT passages about baptism and salvation (including regeneration) as referring to our baptism in water.

Biblical teaching thus leads us to speak of Christian baptism as the *occasion* when the Holy Spirit performs His saving work of regeneration. Commenting on ***Titus 3:5***, Lewis Foster says, "This is regeneration. It is not water regeneration, for the power is not in the water but in the presence of God. The occasion is baptism, but it is the Spirit who renews the spirit of man defaced and spotted by sin" (**"Conversion," 9**). Speaking of the supernatural birth bestowed by the Spirit (***Jn 3:5***), Gresham says, "The occasion of this birth is in the loving, obedient submission of the believing person in Christian baptism" (**I:4**).

"It is not water regeneration, for the power is not in the water but in the presence of God."

The Holy Spirit Is Given in Baptism

To establish the thesis that the Holy Spirit works regeneration in Christian baptism we have shown first that the Spirit is the agent of regeneration, and second that regeneration itself happens in baptism. To close the circle completely we will now show that the Holy Spirit is given in Christian baptism. Again, the point will be that baptism is the *occasion* for the reception and working of the Spirit, not the cause thereof. Also, the divine work that takes place in baptism happens not automatically but only on the preconditions of faith and repentance. In baptism we are "raised up with Him through faith" (***Col 2:12***). Repentance must accompany the baptism wherein God bestows the gift of the Spirit (***Acts 2:38***). Christians receive the Spirit *"by hearing with faith"* (***Gal 3:3***); we *"receive the promise of the Spirit through faith"* (***Gal 3:14***). *Through* faith, but *in* baptism.

Two of the texts discussed in the previous section link the Spirit with baptism: ***John 3:5*** and ***Titus 3:5***. If these passages do indeed refer to baptism, as I believe they do, then they show that baptism, the Spirit, and regeneration are inseparably linked together. The grammatical construction of Jesus' phrase in ***John 3:5*** establishes this: one must be born *ex hudatos kai pneumatos*—"from water and Spirit"—to enter the kingdom of God. "Water" and "Spirit" are objects of the single preposition *ek* ("from, of, out of"). The nonrepetition of the preposition before "Spirit" brings the two objects into the closest possible relationship, marking them as two aspects of a single event. Murray J. Harris comments thus (**1178**):

> . . . Sometimes, therefore, the non-use of a second or third [preposition] in NT Gk. may be theologically significant, indicating that the writer regarded the terms that he placed in one regimen as belonging naturally together or as a unit in concept or reality. *Ex hydatos kai pneumatos* (***Jn. 3:5***) shows that for the writer (or speaker) "water" and "Spirit" together form a single means of that regeneration which is a prerequisite for entrance into the kingdom of God. . . . No contrast is intended between an external element of "water" and an inward renewal achieved by the Spirit. Conceptually the two are one. . . .

The whole expression, says Beasley-Murray, defines the manner in which a person is "born again" (**228**). The act of baptism is thus the moment when the Spirit gives the new birth.

Titus 3:5 establishes the same point: baptism ("washing"), regeneration, and the Spirit are inseparably linked. Here Paul affirms that God *"saved us through [the] washing"* (*esosen hemas dia loutrou*). According to Harris, the preposition *dia* can indicate means or instrument, or it can refer to attendant or accompanying circumstances (**1182-1183**). The latter meaning is consistent with the idea of baptism as the *occasion* for regeneration. The word "washing" is then followed by *"of regeneration and renewing by the Holy Spirit"* (*palingenesias kai anakainoseos pneumatos hagiou*). All three of the nouns are in the genitive case, with no prepositions. "Regeneration and renewing" express the *nature* of the spiritual washing that accompanies the baptismal washing, i.e., baptism is the regeneration event. The reference to the Spirit is also in the genitive case, with no preposition. Literally this may be translated "of the Holy Spirit," i.e., the regeneration and renewing are "of the Holy Spirit." Some translations (e.g., NASB, NIV, CSB) render this "by the Holy Spirit," which is no doubt the intended meaning. In other words, the regeneration or renewing that occur during the washing of baptism are caused by the power of the Spirit.

Titus 3:6 confirms this relation between the Holy Spirit and baptism by describing the Spirit as the one *"whom He* ["God our Savior," ***3:4***] *poured out upon us richly through Jesus Christ our Savior."* The word "poured out" (*ekcheo*) is the same word used in ***Acts 2:17,18,33*** for the outpouring of the Spirit on the day of Pentecost. On that day the poured-out Spirit was offered to all who would repent and be baptized in the name of Jesus Christ for the remission of their sins (***Acts 2:38***). The reference to the outpouring of the Spirit in ***Titus 3:6*** refers then either to the original Pentecost event in general, or to the baptismal offer in ***Acts 2:38***. The reference to "washing" in ***Titus 3:5*** suggests the latter. This gives us the picture of Christian baptism as an individual, personalized Pentecost for every penitent believer who submits to this gracious washing.

This leads us to a consideration of ***Acts 2:38*** itself. According to this text, from the very beginning of the new-covenant era the reception of the Holy Spirit has been linked with baptism. The first thing that happened on Pentecost was the outpouring of the Spirit as such (***Acts 2:1-2***). From that moment He was present and available to all who would receive Him. The miraculous signs, including tongues, were the evidence that this was so (***Acts 2:3-13***). When Peter explained this in his Pentecost sermon (***Acts 2:14-36***), his convicted hearers asked for instructions on how to be right with God (***Acts 2:37***). *"Peter said to them, 'Repent, and each of you be baptized in the name of Jesus Christ for the forgiveness of your sins; and you will receive the gift of the Holy Spirit. For the promise is for you and your children and for all who are far off, as many as the Lord our God will call to Himself"* (***Acts 2:38-39***).

From Pentecost on He was present and available to all who would receive Him.

The *main point* of Peter's answer is to explain how individual sinners may receive this promised gift of the Holy Spirit, made available as life-giving water to those dead in their trespasses and sins. His instructions are clear: *"You will receive the gift of the Holy Spirit"* if you repent and are baptized in the name of Jesus Christ for the forgiveness of your sins. That baptism is a condition and the occasion for receiving the Holy Spirit could not be made any plainer. As Bruner explains, "The baptism in the name of Jesus Christ, according to Luke's account, includes both the forgiveness of sins *and* the reception of the gift of the Holy Spirit (***2:38b***)—together" (***Theology*, 167**).

Dunn says, "Luke probably intends ***Acts 2.38*** to establish the pattern and norm for Christian conversion-initiation in his presentation of Christianity's beginnings" (***Baptism*, 90**). As Bruner says, this text "teaches us that since the occurrence of Pentecost Christian baptism becomes the locus of the Spirit's reception in response to the Spirit's pressure in preaching. Henceforth, baptism is Pentecost" (***Theology*, 168**). I agree completely. (See the discussion of ***Tts 3:5-6*** above.)

I agree with Dunn that in ***Acts 2:38*** Peter is not intending to say that baptism *conveys* or *causes* the gift of the Spirit. Dunn says, "As water-baptism does not convey forgiveness, so it does not convey the Spirit. There is absolutely no ground for saying that the Holy Spirit is given by or through water-baptism—especially in Luke" (***Baptism*, 99**). He rightly stresses that ***Acts 2:38*** does not make baptism "the vehicle of the Spirit," as if God bestows the Spirit directly upon whoever gets wet in the water. Rather, "God gives the Spirit directly to faith" as it is expressed in baptism. "Therefore, water-baptism can properly be described as the vehicle of faith; but *not* as the vehicle of the Spirit." Still, "we cannot divorce the Spirit from faith, nor (normally) water-baptism from faith. . . . Faith reaches out to God in and through water-baptism; God reaches out to men and meets that faith in and through his Spirit" (**ibid., 100-101**). This shows how the link between baptism and the gift of the Spirit may be affirmed without resorting to the false view of baptismal regeneration.

"Water-baptism can properly be described as the vehicle of faith; but not as the vehicle of the Spirit."

Two other texts relating baptism and the reception of the Spirit may be noted briefly. One is ***Acts 19:1-5***, where Paul inquires of "some disciples" from Ephesus, *"Did you receive the Holy Spirit when you believed?"* When Paul heard that they had not, he immediately baptized them. This will be discussed further below, but for our present purposes it is sufficient to note that Paul regarded being *"baptized in the name of the Lord Jesus"* as a condition for receiving the Holy Spirit. The other text is ***1 Corinthians 12:13***, where Paul says, *"For by one Spirit we were all baptized into one body."* This, too, will be discussed later. For now we may note that if this reference to baptism in any way relates to water baptism, it shows a clear connection between it and the work of the Holy Spirit.

In conclusion I believe that Bruner is absolutely right when he says, "In Baptism we were given the Holy Spirit. . . . For the Holy Spirit was placed within us at our Baptism" (**"Water," 42**). Where Jesus "received the Spirit is where we receive the Spirit: in Baptism, in water" (**ibid., 44**). Though Dunn rightly distinguishes between baptism as the cause and baptism as the occasion for the Spirit's work of regeneration, he also rightly affirms the latter. Regarding ***Colossians 2:11-13*** he says, "It would be quite wrong to conclude that for Paul baptism was *only* symbolical." He notes that in ***2:12*** Paul

> . . . indicates that baptism was also the occasion of the spiritual transformation depicted by burial (and circumcision), and to some extent the means of burial with Christ. The burial took place in the rite of water-baptism, and baptism was the occasion on which the individual was circumcised with the invisible circumcision of the Spirit. This does not mean that baptism effected that circumcision and that burial. It means simply that the baptisand surrendered himself to the cutting edge of the Spirit's knife by submitting himself to baptism. (***Baptism*, 157**)

Regarding ***Hebrews 10:22*** Dunn says,

> The close complementary nature of the two cleansings (of heart and body) remind us that we cannot separate Christian baptism from conversion. It is related to the cleansing of the heart as the body is related to the heart. It is the outward embodiment of the spiritual transformation which is taking place inside a man. It would simply not occur to the writer, or to early Christians generally, that the two could be separate. The popular idea that conversion precedes baptism, and that baptism is a confession of a commitment made some time previously is not to be found in the NT. **(ibid., 213-214)**

Texts in Acts That Seem to Disagree

One problem with taking the position that the Holy Spirit is received and performs His work of regeneration *in baptism* is that there are two incidents in the book of Acts where it appears that the Spirit is given *before* baptism, and two where it appears He is given *after* baptism. The former are the initial Pentecost outpouring (***Acts 2:1-13***) and the conversion of Cornelius (***Acts 10:44-48***); the latter are the conversions in Samaria (***Acts 8:4-24***) and the conversion of the twelve Ephesian disciples (***Acts 19:1-6***). In view of these incidents, how can we affirm that baptism is *the* time of regeneration?

The beginning point for this discussion is to remember one of the most fundamental truths about the work of the Holy Spirit, and that is the distinction between His *equipping* work and His *saving* work. We have seen that throughout the OT era the Spirit equipped chosen individuals with various abilities and gifts, some of them miraculous in nature. This activity of the Spirit continues into the new-covenant age. We have also seen that the new-covenant era, beginning with Pentecost, brought a new kind of activity by the Holy Spirit; this is His personal indwelling for the purposes of regeneration and sanctification. Thus in the book of Acts we must distinguish those incidents where the Spirit comes upon individuals to equip them with special powers and abilities, from those where He is received by individuals for salvation.

A further distinction must be noted within the former category. Sometimes the powers and abilities with which the Spirit endows chosen individuals are miraculous; sometimes they are not. In the latter category are gifts of service and leadership, which appear to have been present within the men chosen for special tasks of service in ***Acts 6:1-6*** (see ***6:3,5,10***). In the former category are tongue-speaking, prophetic inspiration, and gifts of healing (see ***Acts 8:7***); this category is especially significant in the book of Acts.

But a still further distinction must be made *within* the category of miraculous empowerments. Sometimes, as we will see, the Spirit was bestowed for the purpose of miraculous empowerment via *human instrumentality*, specifically, the laying on of apostles' hands. But at other times—on two occasions to be precise—the Spirit came *directly* upon some individuals for the purpose of miraculous empowerment. These latter two occasions are Pentecost and Cornelius, and they stand out from all the rest because of their unique significance in the establishment of the church. One thing that sets these two incidents apart from the others is the *direct* outpouring of the Spirit.

In thinking about the coming of the Spirit for miraculous empowerment, we should remember the distinct purpose of miracles as such. Miracles are mainly intended to function either as a supernatural source of divine knowledge, as in the gift of prophetic inspiration, or as the supernatural evidence of the truth of such revealed and/or inspired messages. Especially in the latter sense miracles function as *signs from God*.[7]

This brings us back to the question of baptism as the time of regeneration, and the seeming inconsistency between this idea and

[7] Strictly speaking, the term "miracle" is usually limited to this second category (see ch. 11 below). I am using it here in a more inclusive sense for the sake of convenience.

the four incidents in ***Acts 2, 8, 10, and 19***. What I am contending here is that the only way to clear up this apparent problem is to approach the study of Acts in view of the above distinctions. Specifically, we must be aware of three distinct ways of or purposes for "receiving the Holy Spirit" in the book of Acts. First, the gift of the *indwelling* Spirit is received by all believers, for salvation, in baptism. Second, gifts of miraculous empowerment are received from the Holy Spirit by some Christians, *indirectly*, through the laying on of apostles' hands. Third, gifts of miraculous empowerment are received from the Holy Spirit by a few individuals *directly* as a special kind of sign. Unless we approach Acts with these three different possibilities in mind, confusion about the Holy Spirit will continue.

The first thing to notice is that the normal pattern for receiving the Holy Spirit in conversion is established in the very beginning with Peter's instruction to the seekers in ***Acts 2:38***: repent and be baptized, and you will receive the gift of the indwelling Holy Spirit—to fulfill the saving purpose for which He was prophesied, promised, and poured out. ***Acts 2:41*** says about 3,000 received Peter's message and were baptized. Nothing is said about their receiving the indwelling of the Spirit because it was not necessary. We know that they did receive Him because *that was the promise* (***2:38-39***). In ***Acts 5:32*** Peter refers to the Holy Spirit, *"whom God has given to those who obey Him."* The only thing to which this can possibly refer is obedience to the gospel instructions such as are stated in ***Acts 2:38***, including baptism.[8] We may rightly assume that elsewhere in Acts, when anyone was baptized, he received the gift of the indwelling Holy Spirit. It is not necessary for this to be specifically mentioned. See ***Acts 8:38; 9:18; 16:15,33; 18:8***.

But what about ***Acts 8*** and ***Acts 19***? Is it not specifically said that in these cases the Spirit was given at some point *after* baptism? Yes—but which of the three kinds of "receiving the Spirit" is intended? In ***Acts 8:12-13*** we are told that the Samaritan converts were baptized, including Simon the magician. But in ***8:14-17*** Luke reports that it was necessary for the apostles to come to Samaria and pray for these converts *"that they might receive the Holy Spirit. For He had not yet fallen upon*

[8] ***Acts 6:7*** speaks of many priests who "were becoming obedient to the faith." Twice Paul refers to the concept of "obeying the gospel"—***Rom 10:16; 2Th 1:8***. Such obedience is different from the "works of law" (***Rom 3:20,28***). The former is obedience necessary to become a Christian; the latter is the Christian's ongoing obedience to the will of God.

any of them; they had simply been baptized in the name of the Lord Jesus. Then they began laying their hands on them, and they were receiving the Holy Spirit."

How can we explain this? Hoekema says this means "that the Samaritans were not true believers when Philip baptized them" (**36**). Dunn also defends this view (***Baptism*, 56-58**), but is adequately refuted by Keener (**56-59**) and Pettegrew (**122-124**). Others say the Samaritans were converted when baptized, but God *withheld* the Spirit from them until the apostles came for the specific purpose of giving divine confirmation to God's intention to offer the gospel of salvation to this group despised by the Jews. Bruner says that this was a "temporary suspension of the normal," the normal being "the union of baptism and the Spirit" (***Theology*, 178**). Stott presents a similar view, saying that "God deliberately withheld the gift of his Spirit from the Samaritan believers" until two leading apostles came and "confirmed the genuineness of the Samaritans' conversion" (***Baptism*, 33**). This was "clearly abnormal," however; and it is not likely that "the abnormality in the Samaritan reception of the Spirit could be taken as a precedent for today" (**ibid., 33-34**). See Pettegrew for a similar explanation (**125**).

This latter view has some merit, especially in its attempt to do justice to the statement in ***Acts 8:16*** that the Spirit *"had not yet fallen upon any of them."* In my judgment, however, this very point is the weakness of this view. Specifically, the view does not adequately distinguish between the reception of the indwelling Spirit for salvation, and the Spirit's "falling upon" someone for the purpose of bestowing miraculous gifts for revelational and evidential purposes. If the latter is all that is needed (i.e., miraculous evidence), there would be no need to withhold the indwelling of the Spirit at baptism. Thus, even on this view, we can assume that the gift of the indwelling Spirit *was* given in baptism, according to the original Pentecostal promise. What had not yet fallen upon any of the Samaritan Christians was the *miraculous empowerment* for evidential purposes.

I believe this is the best understanding of *"He had not yet fallen upon any of them."* I would explain the *need* for such miraculous gifts in a way different from Bruner's and Stott's rationale, though. From the beginning of the church the apostles were the only group permanently endowed with inspiration and miracle-working power from the Spirit, but they seemed content to remain in Jerusalem. This was sufficient as long as the church itself remained close to Jerusalem. But when the church began to expand beyond there, into Judea and Samaria (**Acts 1:8**), the need arose to select other leaders who would likewise possess miraculous empowerment in order to function as authenticated spokesmen for God in this initial stage of the new era. This was begun in **Acts 6:1-6**, when seven men were chosen to assist the apostles in Jerusalem. The apostles laid their hands on all seven (**Acts 6:6**). Two of them immediately began to be powerful preachers of the gospel, with an accompanying miracle-working power. One was Stephen: *"And Stephen, full of grace and power, was performing great wonders and signs among the people"* (**Acts 6:8**). This is the first reference to anyone other than the apostles working miracles in the early church. Where did Stephen get this power? The apostles had laid their hands on him (see **Acts 8:17-18**).

Philip was another of this group of seven, and he is the one who traveled to Samaria *"and began proclaiming Christ to them"* (**Acts 8:5**). He too was performing *"signs and great miracles"* (**8:13**; see **v. 6**). Where did he get this power? The apostles had laid their hands on him, too. But Philip would not stay in Samaria for very long (see **8:26,40**). Who would continue to evangelize the Samaritans and lead the church there? Who would be God's authenticated spokesmen in Samaria? Herein lies the need for at least some of the new Christians in Samaria to receive miraculous gifts. Since Philip did not pass these along to anyone, but apostles arriving from Jerusalem did, we infer that *only* the apostles had the God-given ability and authority to pass along miraculous empowerments; and they did so through the laying on of their hands. The issue was not whether the Samaritans had received the indwelling at their baptism; it can be assumed that they had. Rather, the Spirit *"had not yet fallen upon any of them"* as He had upon Stephen and Philip, to equip them for continuing foundational ministry in the building of the church.

How do we know that the laying on of apostles' hands conveyed *miraculous* powers? **Acts 8:17** says only that *"they began laying their hands on them, and they were receiving the Holy Spirit."* There is no mention of tongues, for example. But we know that something like this must have happened because of Simon's reaction to this receiving of the Spirit: *"Now when Simon saw that the Spirit was bestowed* *through the laying on of the apostles' hands, he offered them money"* to transfer their power to him (***8:18***). That he *saw* this indicates there were observable manifestations accompanying the reception of the Spirit (something not associated with receiving the Spirit's indwelling), and these manifestations were astonishing enough to tempt this former magician to jeopardize his salvation.

We should note that nothing is said in the text about a need for one-time miraculous signs to confirm the validity of evangelizing the Samaritans. This may be the point, but I think it is more likely that there was a need for continuing prophetic and miraculous powers to facilitate the ongoing task of the church in the absence of apostles. The laying on of apostles' hands, bestowing miraculous powers, met this need.

The incident in ***Acts 19:1-6*** can be explained in basically the same way. Paul encounters about twelve "disciples" in Ephesus. *"He said to them, 'Did you receive the Holy Spirit when you believed?' And they said to him, 'No, we have not even heard whether there is a Holy Spirit.'"* Paul knew immediately that their understanding of the gospel was deficient, and that this deficiency included ignorance of the relation between baptism and the receiving of the Spirit. After their reply to him, the first question he asked them was, *"Into what then were you baptized?"* He knew that if they had been taught the Pentecost gospel, they would know that anyone baptized in the name of Jesus Christ was supposed to receive the gift of the Holy Spirit. They replied, *"Into John's baptism."* This explained everything! They were disciples of John the Baptist, and had not yet heard the Christian gospel, which Paul immediately preached to them. *"When they heard this, they were baptized in the name of the Lord Jesus."*

In my judgment, in keeping with God's promise in ***Acts 2:38-39*** (see ***Acts 5:32***), at this point they received the *indwelling* of the Spirit, though this is not mentioned. But we will remember that this was *never* mentioned in reference to any baptism after Pentecost, though we can be assured that it happened. Then after these men were baptized, the apostle Paul *"laid his hands upon them"* and *"the Holy Spirit came upon them, and they began speaking with tongues and prophesying."*

I agree with Hoekema (**41**) and others that these disciples were not yet Christians when Paul first met them (see also **Stott, *Baptism*, 34**; **Dunn, *Baptism*, 84-85**). As Pettegrew says, they were still "Old Testament saints" (**148**). Thus Paul preached the gospel to them, and they were saved in the normal way, receiving the gift of the Holy Spirit in baptism. Why did he then lay his hands on them? Because as an apostle he had the ability and authority to pass along miraculous gifts to others through the laying on of his hands (see ***Acts 8:17-18***). Hoekema says that this served as evidence that John's baptism was not sufficient but that Christian baptism truly did involve receiving the Spirit (**42-43**). Again there is nothing in the text to indicate that this was so. I prefer here the explanation given above for the Samaritan situation, i.e., Paul was simply giving these Christian servants continuing miraculous abilities to enable them to become authenticated leaders in the spreading of the church.

We conclude, then, that there is nothing in ***Acts 8*** or ***Acts 19*** that is different from the pattern established in ***Acts 2:38*** about the reception of the indwelling of the Spirit in baptism. The postbaptismal reception of the Spirit in these chapters was for the purpose of miraculous empowerment, not the Spirit's saving presence.

What shall we say, then, about the two incidents in Acts where the Holy Spirit is received *before* baptism, namely, Pentecost and Cornelius? Do these events mean that there is no normal pattern for receiving the regenerating presence of the Spirit, as is so often alleged? By no means. The fact is that there is nothing in the text about either incident that actually says that the persons in question received the indwelling gift prior to their baptism. This is just an inference that is based on certain conclusions concerning the phenomenon of baptism in the Holy Spirit (to be discussed in the next chapter). The only thing we truly know about the apostles' and Cornelius's prebaptismal experience of the Holy Spirit is that they received miraculous empowerment, and they received it in a unique way.

There is nothing in the text to say that they received the indwelling gift prior to their baptism.

In ***Acts 2***, at least the twelve apostles (***2:7***), and perhaps the entire 120 followers of Jesus (***Acts 1:15***) spoke in tongues. *"They were **all** filled with the Holy Spirit and began to speak in tongues"* (***2:4***). Whoever was included in this "all," were they later among the approximately 3,000 who were baptized (***2:41***)? We are not told one way or the other. Some assume that the apostles would not have needed to be baptized, even to receive the gift of the Spirit, in view of ***John 20:22***. That is, they were completely saved even before Pentecost. Many others assume that the filling with the Spirit in ***Acts 2:4*** was the promised baptism of the Spirit, and that this in itself involved the regenerating indwelling of the Spirit. Thus whatever salvation was still needed when Pentecost began, either by the apostles only or by the whole group of 120, it was completely bestowed along with the gift of tongues. Under either scenario, those who spoke in tongues would not have needed to be baptized in order to receive the gift of the Holy Spirit. Whether they *were* baptized or not would be irrelevant for their salvation.

The fact is that none of the above issues needs to be resolved in order to come to the proper conclusion concerning baptism as the time of regeneration, since whatever was happening in ***Acts 2:1-13*** was a unique event in the entire history of the church and was thus completely outside of the normal and intended procedure for receiving the new-age gift of the indwelling Spirit. The miraculous tongue-speaking as such was not the new and unique element of Pentecost (see ***Num 11:16-30***), nor was the presence of the Spirit as a source of miraculous powers. What was new was the outpouring of the Holy Spirit for salvation purposes, as had been prophesied and promised for hundreds of years. This was a one-of-a-kind, never-to-be-repeated event, unique in the entire history of redemption.

The tongue-speaking (by the twelve or the 120) was a one-time miraculous endowment for the specific purpose of providing miraculous confirmation of the revealed truth (preached by Peter in ***2:14-36***) that the Holy Spirit is indeed now available as an indwelling, saving presence. The tongue-speaking was a miracle designed to astonish and amaze the audience—which it did (***Acts 2:6-12***), thus preparing them to accept the truth of Peter's sermon. There is absolutely no reason to think that the Spirit-bestowed ability to speak in tongues was accompanied by the gift of the Spirit's indwelling presence. The point was miraculous empowerment, not personal salvation. Thus the events of ***Acts 2:1-13*** cannot be used to cancel out the normative force of ***Acts 2:38***.

This exact form of reasoning applies to the experience of Cornelius and his household as reported in ***Acts 10:44-48***. Though Pentecost was unique and unrepeatable as the initial and general outpouring of the Spirit for saving purposes, the Cornelius event was a limited version of this as it applied specifically to the Gentile world. It is well known that the Jewish prejudice against the Gentiles was almost absolute, affecting the early church (all Jewish) and even the apostles (all Jewish). Not even the Samaritan breakthrough changed this. Thus drastic steps were required to eradicate this prejudice and convince the Jewish church to embrace the Gentiles. ***Acts 10*** is the story of how God accomplished this by bringing the apostle Peter and Cornelius together, through a series of visions and special revelations.

Peter and six other Jewish Christians (***Acts 11:12***) ultimately were led to the house of Cornelius; and when Peter heard about all that had already happened, he was even then convinced that God wanted the Gentiles included in the church (***Acts 10:34-35***). So he gladly preached the gospel to this group of Gentiles (***10:36-43***). While he was still speaking, *"the Holy Spirit fell upon all those who were listening to the message,"* and they were *"speaking with tongues and exalting God"* (***10:44,46***).

What was the result of this miraculous display? *"All the circumcised believers who came with Peter were amazed, because the gift of the Holy Spirit had been poured out on the Gentiles also"* (***10:45***). This was the whole point of this elaborately orchestrated event. Cornelius and his household were given the miraculous ability to speak in tongues in order to *prove* something, just as on the day of Pentecost. And when the witnesses saw this, they were *amazed*, just as on the day of Pentecost. *What* was being proved was different, namely, that God wanted the Gentiles to hear the gospel and be saved, but the formal purpose and result of the tongue-speaking was exactly the same as on Pentecost.

This exact similarity with Pentecost was what clinched the deal for Peter and the other Jewish Christians. When Peter observed the miracle, he said, *"Surely no one can refuse the water for these to be baptized* ***who have received the Holy Spirit just as we did****, can he?"* (***10:47***). *"Just as we did"* refers solely to the original Pentecost event, and not to *any* intervening conversion experience. This is confirmed by Peter's report of this incident to the Jerusalem brethren: *"And as I began to speak, the Holy Spirit fell upon them just as He did upon us* ***at the beginning****"* (***11:15***).

As Bruner observes, this "unique similarity of the Spirit's coming to His coming at Pentecost" provided a certainty that the Gentiles were to be received into the church just as the Jews were (***Theology*, 191**). The miraculous tongues were so "unexpected, unrequired, and unusual—resembled only by Pentecost" that they succeeded in "convincing even the most hard-necked that God wanted the Gentiles as well as the Jews among his people" (**ibid., 191-192**). This "unique similarity" with Pentecost was not the tongue-speaking itself (see ***Acts 8:18*; *19:6***), nor a miraculous display as such (see ***Acts 5:12*; *6:8*; *8:13***). No, the unique thing with Cornelius, the thing that put his experience in a category with Pentecost alone, was that the Spirit fell upon him and his household in the *same way* as on Pentecost: "just as" (*hos*, ***10:47***; *hosper*, ***11:15***). In other words, the Holy Spirit, by His own initiative and without any human intermediary, simply fell *directly* upon the Cornelius group just as He did upon the Pentecost group in the beginning. Not even the laying on of apostles' hands was involved.

Were Cornelius and his household *saved* when the Spirit fell upon them and they began to speak in tongues? Did they at that time receive also the indwelling presence of the Spirit? Many assume this was the case (e.g., **Dunn, *Baptism*, 80**; **Stott, *Baptism*, 37**), and many who so assume use this incident to prove that baptism cannot be the normative time for receiving the regenerating presence of the Spirit. Others deny that the miraculous tongue-speaking was accompanied by the gift of the Spirit's indwelling. "This was an external reception" (**Jacoby, 149**).

The bottom line here is the same as with Pentecost: whether Cornelius and his household were born again when the Spirit fell upon them before their baptism is irrelevant to a determination of the proper view of the time of regeneration. This is true because Cornelius's experience was clearly a unique and exceptional event. It had to be, in order to have the evidential value that was its purpose. What happened there was in no way a normal conversion experience. As Bruner says, we may safely conclude that this "was not the normal initiating experience of the church and that its only correspondence was Pentecost" (***Theology*, 195**).

What happened there was in no way a normal conversion experience.

In my judgment Cornelius and his household were *not* saved when the Spirit fell upon them and enabled them to speak in tongues. Peter knew that the normal occasion for receiving the saving presence of the Spirit was Christian baptism. That is why his *very first reaction* to the tongue-speaking was: "Let's get these people baptized!" (see ***Acts 10:47-48***). We see that he decisively concluded on the basis of the tongues that God wanted the Gentiles to be saved; thus he hastened to see that this was accomplished.

Our conclusion is that these four "contrary" episodes of receiving the Spirit (***Acts 2, 8, 10, 19***) are not salvation experiences at all, but are cases where the Spirit is received for purposes of miraculous empowerment. And even if the Pentecost and Cornelius events did involve the gift of salvation, they cannot be used to negate baptism as the God-appointed time for regeneration because of their unique and deliberately exceptional nature.

Word-only Regeneration and Baptism

In this chapter I have argued that regeneration is a renewing, life-giving act worked directly upon the sinner's heart by the Holy Spirit in Christian baptism. In doing so I have consciously rejected a common Restoration idea that the Holy Spirit never works directly on the heart, but works only indirectly through the influences of the Word. I have also suggested that one reason why many hold to the latter view and cannot accept the former is that they fail to distinguish properly between two different questions. The first question, discussed in the previous chapter, is, how does the Spirit work prior to the moment of conversion, seeking to elicit faith and repentance in the heart of the unbeliever? The answer is, He works primarily indirectly, through the Word. The second question, discussed in this chapter, is different: how does the Spirit work to accomplish regeneration itself? In other words, once faith and repentance are present in the sinner, what more needs to be done by the Spirit in order to bring about regeneration?

The usual answer to the latter question, by most who take the Word-only approach to the Spirit's work, is: *nothing!* Once the Spirit has produced faith and repentance through the Word, the faith and the repentance themselves are sufficient to produce regeneration. The idea is that once faith and repentance are present, regeneration—rebirth to new life—inevitably occurs. For all practical purposes, faith and repentance as inner moral changes are themselves the new birth. Once the Spirit-inspired Word brings forth faith and repentance, regeneration thus immediately follows without any other act by the Spirit. The unbroken line of cause-and-effect is this:

HOLY SPIRIT ➜ WORD OF GOD ➜
FAITH/REPENTANCE ➜ REGENERATION

Thus the Spirit's role in regeneration is actually two steps removed from the actual change called regeneration. That is, the Spirit produces the Word; the Word produces faith and repentance; faith and repentance produce (or *are*) regeneration. In such a view, the Holy Spirit does not regenerate us at all; we actually regenerate ourselves.

What I have said in this chapter is that regeneration is something done upon the heart by the Holy Spirit Himself, *in addition to* His influence upon the mind and heart by the Word, and only after the latter has produced faith and repentance. The Spirit Himself works regeneration upon our hearts *after* we have come to a conscious decision to believe and repent, as motivated by the Word. Thus there are two separate interventions by the Spirit:

SPIRIT ➜ WORD ➜ FAITH/REPENTANCE
[then]
SPIRIT ➜ REGENERATION

The former work is indirect or mediated; the latter is direct and unmediated: "naked Spirit on naked spirit."

An illustration is the way a heart surgeon works to cure a defective heart: A man is feeling very bad and goes to his doctor, who suspects a heart problem and refers the man to a specialist. After a thorough examination the specialist says, "Here's your situation: you have four blocked arteries. But I can correct the problem. When do you want to schedule your surgery?" The patient resists and doubts the diagnosis; he gives excuses and refuses to commit. The specialist persists, explaining the problem in more detail and referring to MRI images for emphasis. He explains the bleak prognosis without treatment. The patient finally yields and consents to the surgery. On the appointed day the operation is actually performed, and the man's healing begins.

Here the surgeon actually does two separate things: 1) through evidence and persuasion, he leads the sick man to believe and commit; 2) in a subsequent and separate act, he performs the actual operation itself. Thus does the Holy Spirit work in two different ways, in two stages, to accomplish regeneration in the spiritually dead sinner.

The reason I am going into so much detail about this issue at this particular point is this: I believe that the Word-only approach to regeneration is inconsistent with the biblical view of baptism as the time when regeneration occurs. Even more seriously, I believe that if the Word-only view is followed consistently, it will ultimately undermine belief in the biblical view of baptism as such.

The Word-only view will ultimately undermine belief in the biblical view of baptism as such.

My reasoning is this. If regeneration is accomplished by the moral influences of the Word alone, then there must be an unbroken sequence begun as soon as the Word engenders faith and repentance. If regeneration itself is accomplished only through "influences mediated by truth," then it *must* take place when the truth is grasped and believed. This process cannot be interrupted by whatever interval of time occurs between the faith-commitment and one's baptism. This approach thus means that regeneration must always occur prior to baptism, and can have no necessary direct connection with baptism whatsoever. After all, what more can be done at baptism that has not already been done prior to baptism, if the Word alone is the mediating instrument of the Spirit's power? But the Bible clearly says that regeneration is connected with baptism, indeed, that it occurs *during* baptism. This shows that it *must* be something more than what the Word itself can effect.

How does the Word-only view ultimately undermine the biblical view of baptism, though? I will use church of Christ author K.C. Moser's book, *The Way of Salvation*, as an example. In general I like this book very much, especially as an explanation of grace; but his view of baptism and regeneration is very weak. In his attempt to explain ***Romans 6:3-4***, Moser argues that "in repentance one dies to sin and is raised to righteousness" (**89**). This occurs at the time of repentance itself, prior to baptism. So how is baptism related to this spiritual death and resurrection (one way of describing regeneration) that occur at repentance? Moser says "it is the work of baptism to represent this change of mind toward sin and righteousness. Baptism cannot effect this change, but it can and does represent it or symbolize it" (**89**). Thus in ***Romans 6:3-4*** Paul is telling Christians "that at the time of their conversion [repentance] they died unto sin, and that their baptism represented this death to sin as well as their resurrection to righteousness" (**89**).

What this means, says Moser, is that although the spiritual death and resurrection actually occur at repentance, "these changes are represented by Paul as taking place in baptism." Surely in ***Romans 6:3-4*** "Paul cannot mean that baptism effects repentance; that one dies to sin and is raised to righteousness in the act of baptism.[9] This would be to ascribe to baptism a miraculous power. . . . Paul certainly means that baptism signifies repentance—the burial standing for death to sin, the emersion representing a resurrection to righteousness" (**90**). "Under Christ, then, baptism is connected with repentance as a symbol of it" (**90**). In other words, "baptism is related to repentance by way of picturing it. In repentance one dies to sin. This death is symbolized in baptism" (**92**).

It should be clear that Moser has just espoused the typical Zwinglian explanation of baptism: salvation event first; baptism later as an outward symbol of it. How then does he maintain the saving necessity of baptism? By making it a requirement for receiving the other half of the double cure, the remission of sins. "We conclude, therefore, that baptism, meaning faith and repentance, must be a condition of the remission of sins." How do we know? Because "just so do the Scriptures plainly represent it." He then quotes ***Acts 2:38*** and declares that "repentance and baptism here precede the promise of the remission of sins" (**103**).

The problem here should be obvious. ***Romans 6:3-4*** *just as plainly* represents baptism as the time of spiritual death and resurrection, which Moser actually acknowledges; but Moser concludes that Paul simply cannot mean this literally and thus assigns to it a symbolic meaning. This leaves him with no defense whatsoever if some

[9] It is obvious that Moser does not adequately distinguish between baptism as the *cause* of regeneration (which would be baptismal regeneration, which he rightly rejects), and baptism as the *occasion* for it.

Zwinglian or baptismal symbolist insists on applying the same reasoning to ***Acts 2:38***, or to any other text about baptism—which they uniformly do. Thus the biblical foundation for baptism as the occasion for salvation is for all practical purposes dismantled.

In my judgment, this is the consistent end for anyone who takes a Word-only approach to regeneration. The passages of Scripture which actually relate regeneration directly to baptism must be symbolized, thus opening the door for doing the same for all other baptismal texts. We can avoid this by accepting the fact that regeneration is indeed a separate, direct act of the Spirit Himself, performed in the moment of baptism.

The next chapter continues to deal with the subject of the work of the Holy Spirit in conversion, as it focuses on the issue of baptism in the Holy Spirit.

CHAPTER EIGHT

BAPTISM IN THE HOLY SPIRIT

The last subject to be discussed in relation to the Spirit's work in conversion is the baptism in the Holy Spirit, or Holy Spirit baptism. There is much controversy over the proper meaning of this concept and over how this term or expression should be used. The main point of disagreement is whether it refers to a conversion experience and thus applies to all believers, or whether it is a nonconversion experience and applies to some but not necessarily all believers. A second issue is whether it involves miraculous experiences, especially tongue-speaking. Those who say it is a conversion experience are more likely to say it is not necessarily related to the miraculous; those who say it is a nonconversion experience often say it involves miraculous manifestations. A third issue is how Spirit baptism is related to water baptism.

HOLY SPIRIT BAPTISM AS A NONCONVERSION EXPERIENCE

We may distinguish three versions of baptism in the Holy Spirit as a nonconversion experience. Two of them see Spirit baptism as a "second work of grace" that follows one's initial conversion; one sees it as an event of salvation history that happened only twice in the beginning years of the church and will never happen again.

The Holiness Movement

The American Holiness movement was built upon the teaching of John Wesley (1703-1791), especially his doctrine of entire sanctification. Wesley taught that full salvation comes in two stages. First, the sinner's guilt and condemnation are removed through the gift of justification. Then in a later crisis experience often called "entire sanctification," the Holy Spirit comes upon the Christian in order to deliver him from the power of sin. This "second work of grace" is actually a new birth and is called many different things, including Christian perfection and perfect love. Interestingly, Wesley himself never called it baptism in the Holy Spirit (**Wynkoop, 355**).

"Originating in the United States in the 1840s and '50s," the Holiness movement "was an endeavor to preserve and propagate John Wesley's teaching on entire sanctification and Christian perfection" (**Pierard, 516**). This "second blessing" or "subsequent experience" was "the theological center of the holiness movement," says Bruner (***Theology*, 42**). Holiness groups have freely referred to this experience as Holy Spirit baptism. As Carter says, "The National Holiness Association has from its inception . . . in 1867 . . . emphasized the 'Baptism in the Holy Spirit' as the means of the believer's crisis experience in sanctification" (**182**). An example is R.A. Torrey, who declared that "the baptism with the Holy Spirit is an operation of the Holy Spirit distinct from and additional to His regenerating work." In fact, "a man may be regenerated by the Holy Spirit and still not be baptized with the Holy Spirit" (**174, 176**). The main purpose of Spirit baptism is to equip Christians for testimony and service (**179**), though this does not necessarily result in the gift of tongues or some ecstatic feeling (**243**).

As a rule Holiness groups do not accept tongues and miraculous gifts as a part of baptism in the Holy Spirit. Carter is quite adamant about this, pointing out that the National Holiness Association, now the Christian Holiness Association, has never recognized tongues as in any way related to the second work of grace. This aspect of Pentecostalism, he says, is not derived from Methodism or from the Holiness movement (**182-183**).

Pentecostals and Charismatics

Nevertheless, says Bruner, "eighteenth-century Methodism is the mother of the nineteenth-century holiness movement which, in turn, bore twentieth-century Pentecostalism" (***Theology*, 37**). The specific element in Wesley's theology that laid the foundation for Pentecostalism's view of Holy Spirit baptism is the "second blessing" doctrine. What distinguishes Pentecostalism and the Charismatic movement from their predecessors is their view that the baptism in the Holy Spirit is usually accompanied by a display of miraculous powers, especially tongues.

Their view is that Holy Spirit baptism is usually accompanied by miraculous powers, especially tongues.

The Pentecostal movement itself began in the first decade of the twentieth century, being traced "to an outbreak of tongue-speaking in Topeka, Kansas, . . . under the leadership of Charles Fox Parham, a former Methodist preacher, . . . after a student in his Bethel Bible School, Agnes Ozman, experienced glossolalia in January, 1901" (**Synan, 835-836**). What "launched Pentecostalism as a worldwide movement," though, was a long revival (1906–1909) in an abandoned church in downtown Los Angeles "led by William J. Seymour, a black Holiness preacher from Houston, Texas, and a student of Parham" (**ibid, 836**). This is called the "Azusa Street revival."

Pentecostalism generally exists as organized denominations such as the Church of God in Christ, the Church of God (Cleveland, TN), the Pentecostal Holiness Church, and the Assemblies of God.

In the early 1950s, especially through the efforts of the Full Gospel Business Men's Fellowship International (begun in 1953), the doctrine and practices of Pentecostalism began to spread outside denominational boundaries and infiltrate all Christian groups, Protestant and Catholic. This began the Neo-Pentecostal or Charismatic movement. Some use 1960 as its formal starting point. The difference between this movement and its predecessor was the fact that Pentecostal doctrine and practice were now accepted by particular individuals and congregations within most mainline churches.

Pentecostals consistently see baptism in the Holy Spirit as a miraculous, postconversion experience. Grudem describes their approach

Pentecostals consistently see baptism in the Holy Spirit as a miraculous, postconversion experience.

thus: "Baptism in the Holy Spirit is an empowering experience subsequent to conversion and should be sought by Christians today"; and "when baptism in the Holy Spirit occurs, people will speak in tongues as a 'sign' that they have received this experience" (**"Preface," 11**). Grudem is basically echoing Bruner's summary of the essence of Pentecostalism's view of Holy Spirit baptism (***Theology*, 61**), which he says is their central doctrine (**ibid., 56-57**).[1]

Neo-Pentecostals, or charismatics, do not all agree on baptism in the Spirit. According to Grudem, "among charismatics there are differing viewpoints on whether baptism in the Holy Spirit is subsequent to conversion and whether speaking in tongues is a sign of baptism in the Spirit" (**"Preface," 11**). Hoekema acknowledges this disagreement, but observes that even those who deny that tongues are a necessary sign of baptism in the Spirit still regard them as "a highly desirable evidence that one has received the 'baptism in the Spirit'" (**30-32**). Keener describes this approach as "the belief that it is normal, but not mandatory, for tongues to accompany baptism in the Spirit" (**63**).

The Two-Episode View

A third nonconversion approach to the baptism in the Holy Spirit has arisen completely outside the Wesleyan tradition and is found mostly (if not exclusively) in the context of the Restoration Movement. It is called the "two-episode view" of Spirit baptism because it says this experience happened on only two occasions, namely, on the day of Pentecost in ***Acts 2***, and when Peter preached the gospel to Cornelius and his household in ***Acts 10***. The idea is that the main purpose for the apostles' baptism in the Spirit in ***Acts 2*** was to empower them to speak in tongues, which served as miraculous confirmation of the new gospel revelation presented on that day. Then in ***Acts 10***, again the main purpose for baptism in the Spirit was to empower

[1] Keener says this applies to "most North American Pentecostals," but that some in places like Chile and Germany do not always link tongue-speaking with Spirit baptism (68).

Cornelius and his household to speak in tongues, providing miraculous proof that God desired the salvation of the Gentiles. These two episodes, and these alone, fulfill all promises concerning the baptism in the Spirit.

According to this view Holy Spirit baptism is neither a conversion experience nor a second work of grace. It necessarily involves miraculous powers, especially speaking in tongues. But since it happened only twice in the early years of the church and will never happen again, it is consistent with a cessationist approach to miraculous spiritual gifts.

J.W. McGarvey's commentary on Acts (1892) has been influential in propagating this view. Concerning Pentecost, McGarvey says, "When the apostles were filled with the Holy Spirit, and began to speak as the Spirit gave them utterance, the promise of a baptism in the Holy Spirit and of power from on high was fulfilled" (**Acts, 22**). Later concerning Cornelius's experience, McGarvey cites Peter's report of it in ***Acts 11:15-16*** where he compared it with Pentecost and says, "In these words he identifies it as a baptism in the Holy Spirit; and these two are the only events that are thus designated in the New Testament" (**ibid., 215**). A recent twenty-first-century commentary on Acts by another Restoration scholar reiterates this view. Commenting on the Pentecost episode in ***Acts 2***, Donald Nash says, "Some claim John the Baptist prophesied that Jesus would baptize all disciples in the Holy Spirit. Not so! . . . This baptism came only on this occasion and in chapter 10 on the household of Cornelius" (**19-20**).

Many other examples could be cited. For example, Spratt says, "It is evident that the fulfillment of the promised baptism of the Holy Spirit included only the apostles and the household of Cornelius" (**"Holy Spirit," 14**). Tribble says, "All converts to Christ receive the Holy Spirit as a gift (***Acts 2:38***), but they do not receive the baptism in the Holy Spirit. Baptism in the Holy Spirit is mentioned only twice in the New Testament"—on Pentecost and in the home of Cornelius (**14**). See also **Boles, 152-153**; and Dave Miller, in a recent article in *Reason & Revelation* (**22**).

A basic assumption of the two-episode view is that Holy Spirit baptism necessarily involves miraculous gifts, especially tongues. Boles says, "In every instance of a Holy Spirit baptism recorded in the New Testament a miracle was wrought in speaking with 'other tongues' and other extraordinary things" (153). "When the baptism of the Holy Spirit takes place, observable signs are present," says James Smith (5). McGarvey says that its main effect is inspiration, and "no one is immersed in the Holy Spirit in whom this inspiration does not take place" ("Immersion," 441). In the book of Acts, says Bales, "Holy Spirit baptism was accompanied by inspiration and by the miraculous" (19). Indeed, if *Acts 2:38-39* includes Holy Spirit baptism, then "all who were baptized into Christ would have spoken in tongues" (17). Bales refers to it as "the miraculous baptism in the Spirit" (20).

Problems with the Nonconversion View

At this point I will briefly explain what I consider to be major problems with the nonconversion view of Holy Spirit baptism. First, I believe it is a serious mistake to link baptism in the Spirit with miraculous gifts, either as a necessary or as a normal accompaniment. This applies in particular to the Pentecostal and Charismatic view, which requires acceptance of modern-day miracles. As a cessationist I believe all miraculous gifts from the Spirit ceased after the first century AD. If this is true, it renders the entire Pentecostal-Charismatic system invalid. This will be discussed in more detail in chapter 11 below.

I believe it is a serious mistake to link baptism in the Spirit with miraculous gifts.

I must also apply this objection to the two-episode theory of Spirit baptism, though I agree with the cessationist stance taken by most who hold this view. Their error, however, is the same as that found in most Pentecostal and Charismatic views, i.e., the idea that Holy Spirit baptism *as such* is inherently connected with miraculous gifts, especially tongues, *even in the first century*. Such a notion is the result of a particular approach to Pentecost, one that assumes that the main point of the outpouring of the Spirit on that day was the miraculous display of tongues. This view is seriously flawed. The outpouring of the Spirit on the day of Pentecost was all about something entirely new in the history of redemption; and miracles as such, including prophesying, *were nothing new*. The Pentecostal outpouring as such

(*Acts 2:1-3*), linked by Peter to Joel's prophecy (*Acts 2:16-21*) and to the Father's promise (*Acts 2:33,38-39*), simply cannot be for the purpose of enabling a few people to speak in tongues. The outpouring is something much bigger than this; it is the fulfillment of a promise of something qualitatively new, a new kind of presence of the Spirit and a new kind of work by the Spirit, indicative of the newness of the new-covenant era. I repeat: *miracles were nothing new*. Compare once again the prophesying in **Numbers 11:25** and the tongue-speaking in *Acts 2*. These are qualitatively identical in their miraculous nature and evidential purpose. McGarvey's comment about *Acts 2* that "such a miracle had never before been witnessed" (*Acts*, 25) is hardly the case.

The Pentecostal outpouring was all about something new, and miracles as such were not new.

The second problem with nonconversion approaches to baptism in the Spirit applies both to the Holiness approach and to the Pentecostal-Charismatic approach. In particular, I believe the whole concept of a two-stage reception of the blessings of salvation, in which Holy Spirit baptism is a second and later work of grace, is wrong. Earlier in this chapter we saw how the gift of the Holy Spirit, including His work of regeneration or new birth, is given in Christian baptism; later in this chapter we will see that this *is* Holy Spirit baptism. Baptism in the Holy Spirit *is* a crisis, a turning point in the life of the individual, but this crisis experience is the *one baptism* (*Eph 4:5*) in water, in which both aspects of the double cure of salvation are received together. A main point of Bruner's book, *A Theology of the Holy Spirit*, is to show that the "second work" concept is contrary to NT teaching; I recommend that this work be consulted for more detail on this subject.

One of the most serious consequences of the two-stage concept is that it completely misses the point of the day of Pentecost in *Acts 2* by treating everything that happened there as a model for an alleged "second blessing" rather than as the inauguration of a new "first blessing." Dunn explains and analyzes this problem very well. He says,

> . . . Pentecostals argue that those who were baptized in the Spirit on the Day of Pentecost were already 'saved' and 'regenerate.' Their reception of the Spirit on that day was not their conversion; it was not the beginning of their Christian life. In

> other words, Pentecost was a second experience subsequent to and distinct from their earlier 'new birth'. As such it gives the pattern for all Christian experience thereafter. As the disciples were baptized in the Spirit at Pentecost, an experience subsequent to their 'regeneration', so may (and should) all Christians be baptized in the Spirit soon after their conversion. (***Baptism*, 38**)

Dunn rightly criticizes this approach. He says, "When we look at Pentecost in the context of Luke–Acts it becomes evident that Pentecostal and Catholic alike have again missed the principal significance of the story. For once again we stand at a watershed in salvation-history, the beginning of the new age and new covenant" (**ibid. 40**). Most specifically to the point he says, "Pentecost is a new beginning—the inauguration of the new age, the age of the Spirit—that which had not been before" (**ibid., 44**). Indeed, Pentecost is a new beginning, both in the general history of redemption and in the lives of every individual who was present in Jerusalem that day.

My third problem with this approach in all its versions is its tendency to interpret everything in ***Acts 2*** (for second-work proponents) and its miraculous elements in particular (for two-episode folks) as the fulfillment of the promise of Holy Spirit baptism. This overlooks the fact that *more than one promise* concerning the Holy Spirit was being fulfilled at Pentecost. John the Baptist's promise of baptism in the Spirit (see ***Acts 1:5***); Jesus' promise of living water (***Jn 4:10-14***; ***7:37-39***); Jesus' promise to send the apostles "another Helper" for purposes of revelation and inspiration (***Jn 14–16***); Jesus' promise to the apostles of "power from on high" (***Lk 24:49***; see ***Acts 1:8***)—why should we assume that these all refer to the same thing? It is wrong to combine them all and equate them all and run them all together in ***Acts 2***. My contention is that ***Acts 1:5*** (see ***Lk 24:49a***) is the same as ***John 4*** and ***John 7*** and is fulfilled in ***Acts 2:1-3*** and ***2:38-39***, while ***John 14–16*** and ***Acts 1:8*** (see ***Lk 24:49b***) refer to the miraculous gifts displayed in ***Acts 2:4-40***, including tongues. With this simple adjustment in our thinking, it is easy to see how baptism in the Holy Spirit is just another way of describing the nonmiraculous gift of the Holy Spirit offered to sinners in Christian baptism for the purpose of regeneration and continued indwelling.

More than one promise concerning the Holy Spirit was being fulfilled at Pentecost.

HOLY SPIRIT BAPTISM AS A CONVERSION EXPERIENCE

The other main approach to baptism in the Spirit is to interpret it as something that happens to every believer at the moment of his conversion from the unsaved to the saved state. Many who take this view equate it with regeneration by the Spirit; others say it happens at the same moment as regeneration. Either way it is related to one's personal salvation, and does not have any connection with miraculous activity such as tongue-speaking. The two versions described below differ mainly regarding the relation of Holy Spirit baptism to water baptism.

A General Protestant View

Many modern-day Protestants agree that baptism in the Holy Spirit is one way of describing what happens at the very beginning of the Christian life for every convert. While rightly recognizing that Pentecost and Cornelius are unique, Leon Morris says that ***1 Corinthians 12:13*** "ascribes to all believers a baptism 'in the Spirit'. . . . The baptism in question obviously refers not to a supreme experience somewhere along the Christian way, but to the very beginning of Christian experience. . . . Believers are never urged to seek the baptism of the Spirit, which is natural enough if they have already received this baptism at the beginning of their Christian life" (***Spirit*, 91-92**). Stott's view is similar; he says in no uncertain terms that "the 'baptism' of the Spirit is identical with the 'gift' of the Spirit, that it is one of the *distinctive* blessings of the new covenant, and, because it is an *initial* blessing, it is also a *universal* blessing for members of the covenant. It is part and parcel of belonging to the new age" (***Baptism*, 43**). "To have been 'baptized' with the Spirit is a vivid figure of speech for to have 'received' the Spirit" (**ibid., 21**).

Some regard this universal, initial baptism in the Spirit as equivalent to regeneration itself. Broomall says, "We believe that when a soul is truly regenerated that soul is baptized into the body of Christ, as taught in ***1 Cor 12:13***. . . . Paul here is speaking about a spiritual baptism. This baptism of the Spirit corresponds to regeneration" (**139**). G. Campbell Morgan says, "The baptism of the Spirit is the primary blessing; it is, in short, the blessing of regeneration" (**169**). Commenting on ***1 Corinthians 12:13*** Hoekema says, "What Paul says here in the plainest of words is that all Christians have been Spirit-baptized. Spirit-baptism is here described as identical with regeneration" (**21**).

Others distinguish Spirit baptism from regeneration but say these two acts are simultaneous. Pache says, "The baptism of the Spirit and regeneration . . . are effected simultaneously" (**72**). How are they different? Regeneration is a change in a person's heart or nature, whereas Holy Spirit baptism is the act whereby God unites us with Christ. He says, "The baptism of the Spirit bears relation, not to the believer's spiritual state, but to his position." It "gives to the believer his position in Jesus Christ" (**ibid., 70**). Unger's view is similar: "Although in this present age of grace regeneration and the baptism with the Spirit are always simultaneous—so that everyone who is regenerated is at the same time baptized by the Spirit into the body of Christ—yet the two operations are distinct" (***Baptism*, 22**). The purpose of Spirit baptism is to unify the believer with Christ and with other Christians: "The baptism of the Spirit . . . brings the believer into organic union with the body and under the imputed merits and power of Christ, the Head. This means the believer is united to Christ and to *all* other believers joined in this manner to Christ" (**ibid., 96-97**). See Walvoord (**139, 149**) for a similar interpretation.

I believe this view is essentially correct in that it sees baptism in the Holy Spirit as an act of God that occurs nonmiraculously for all believers at the moment of salvation or regeneration. My main disagreement with this general Protestant approach is that it usually separates this event from water baptism, whereas I see baptism in water and baptism in the Spirit as two aspects of a single event occurring in a single moment.

Baptism in water and baptism in the Spirit are two aspects of a single event in a single moment.

A Biblical Approach to Baptism in the Holy Spirit

In accord with biblical teaching I will describe Holy Spirit baptism as a nonmiraculous salvation event that happens to all converts in the moment of their baptism in water. This view has been vigorously defended by F.D. Bruner in his book, *A Theology of the Holy Spirit*. His main concern is to refute the Pentecostal view of the Spirit; in so doing he gives a detailed defense of baptism in the Spirit as part of the salvation which God works in Christian baptism. Beginning with **Acts 2:38**, he says that "baptism in the name of Jesus Christ . . . includes both the forgiveness of sins *and* the reception of the Holy Spirit (*2:38b*)—together" (**167**). Thus since Pentecost the gift of the Holy Spirit has been offered, "with forgiveness, in the humble rite of baptism. Baptism becomes the baptism of the Holy Spirit" (**168-169**). "The gift of the Holy Spirit without baptism was as unthinkable to the church as baptism without the gift of the Holy Spirit" (**193**). The apostles knew that "baptism with the Holy Spirit and baptism . . . belonged together in such a way as to form the 'one baptism' of the church. . . . Christian *baptism* and the gift of the *Spirit* come together forming both actually and figuratively the baptism in the Spirit" (**193-194**).

James D.G. Dunn, in his book *Baptism in the Holy Spirit,* presents a similar but more cautious view of Holy Spirit baptism. His study is also an examination of Pentecostalism, and he likewise concludes that Spirit baptism is a conversion event occurring in connection with Christian baptism. He says that **Acts 2:38** was intended by Luke to establish the pattern or norm for conversion-initiation (**90**), though some abnormal events took place from time to time in exceptional circumstances (e.g., the Samaritans, Cornelius). Dunn speaks freely of baptism as the *occasion* for the Spirit's regenerating work (**157, 168-169**), but denies that God gives the Spirit directly to the one being baptized apart from the presence of faith. Rather, the sinner comes to baptism with faith in his heart, and God gives the Spirit directly to his faith. "As the Spirit is the vehicle of saving grace, so baptism is the vehicle of saving faith." In other words, water baptism is "the expression of the faith to which God gives the Spirit" (**227**). Dunn does not combine Spirit baptism and water baptism into a unitary event, as Bruner does, but he sees them as closely related thus: "Spirit-baptism and water-baptism remain distinct and even antithetical, the latter being a preparation for the former and the means by which the believer actually reaches out in faith to receive the former" (**227**).

A growing number of thinkers within the Restoration Movement have come to the same or a similar view. Moses Lard was a kind of pioneer in this regard when in 1864 he published an article called "Baptism in One Spirit into One Body" in his own journal, *Lard's*

Quarterly. Beginning with ***1 Corinthians 12:13*** he concluded that "Baptism in the Spirit does not consist in endowing the mind with miraculous powers, as seems to have been so generally taken for granted" (**275**). "We are all immersed in one Spirit" (**278**), and it happens in Christian baptism:

> . . . At the instant when the body is immersed in water, the instant in which it passes from the world into a kingdom which is not of the world, in that instant the Spirit of that kingdom, which is the Holy Spirit, enters the body. Then it is, if at all, that the immersion of the human Spirit takes place in the Holy Spirit. The inner man is then immersed as well as the outer, that in Spirit, this in water; and both into the one mystic body, which is Christ. (**279**)

The purpose of immersing the soul in the Holy Spirit is to purify it, to cleanse it from the stains of sin (**280**). This is similar to what is usually called regeneration.

Some more recent Restoration representatives of this view of Holy Spirit baptism include Russell Boatman, Jim McGuiggan, Robert L. Gibson, Douglas Jacoby, and William F. Jones. Boatman rejects the more common two-episode theory and concludes, citing ***1 Corinthians 12:13***, that "baptism in the Holy Spirit is one of the facets of our salvation which makes us one body in Christ" (**111**). McGuiggan's conclusion is this: "It seems to me to be much simpler and in line with the NT data to hold that 'baptized in the Holy Spirit' means nothing more than Christ's giving the Spirit to all those who are his and to see the miracles as the divine accompaniment in the first century period" (**276**). Jacoby likewise concludes from ***1 Corinthians 12:13*** "that *all Christians have been baptized with the Spirit*" (**206-207**). Why, then, do not all Christians have miraculous gifts? Jacoby answers, "Where does the Bible say that Spirit baptism confers miraculous powers?" (**209**). Jones, in an e-mail dated 7/16/05, says, "The 'gift' and the 'baptism' of the Holy Spirit are one and the same. . . . 'Christian, You Were BAPTIZED in WATER and SPIRIT' whether you know it or not." Jones here is using the title of Gibson's book, in which he says, "When a convert to Christ is baptized in water, he is also at the same time baptized in

"We were all baptized by one Spirit into one body" (1Cor 12:13a, NIV).

the Holy Spirit" (15). Gibson's book, *Christian, You Were Baptized in Water and Spirit*, is a thorough defense of this view.

ANALYSIS OF BIBLICAL TEXTS

In this section I will survey several relevant biblical texts relating to the subject of baptism in the Holy Spirit. My contention is that all such texts are consistent with and supportive of the conversion (universal, nonmiraculous) approach to Spirit baptism.

The Promise of John the Baptist

The promise that the Messiah would baptize in the Holy Spirit was a major part of John the Baptist's testimony to Jesus. Each Gospel records this promise, no doubt repeated by the Baptist many times in different forms. Luke's record is the most comprehensive: *"John answered and said to them all, 'As for me, I baptize you with water; but One is coming who is mightier than I, and I am not fit to untie the thong of His sandals; He will baptize you with the Holy Spirit and fire'"* (**Lk 3:16**; see **Mt 3:11**; **Mk 1:8**; **Jn 1:33**). Jesus repeats this promise in **Acts 1:5**, and Peter refers to it in **Acts 11:16**.

This way of speaking of Jesus' ministry actually began with God the Father. John the Baptist speaks of Jesus thus: *"I did not recognize Him, but He who sent me to baptize in water said to me, 'He upon whom you see the Spirit descending and remaining upon Him, this is the One who baptizes in the Holy Spirit'"* (**Jn 1:33**). The Baptist here tells us that God was the origin both of his own ministry of baptizing in water (see **Mt 21:25**) and of the description of Jesus as the One who baptizes in the Holy Spirit. John used this language as a way of contrasting his ministry with that of the Messiah, no doubt by God's own design. He declared, *"I baptized you with water; but He will baptize you with the Holy Spirit"* (**Mk 1:8**).

Luke refers to this baptizing ministry of Jesus as *"what the Father had promised"* (**Acts 1:4a**), looking back to **John 1:33** in particular. Shortly before His ascension, Jesus referred to this promise, *"which you heard from me"* (**Acts 1:4b**). This tells us that Jesus Himself had included this promise in His own teaching ministry, though no incident of it is actually recorded in the Gospels. Jesus repeats it here: *"For John baptized with water, but you will be baptized with the Holy Spirit* *not many days from now"* (**Acts 1:5**). In **Acts 11:16** Peter recalls that Jesus had said this, at least in **Acts 1:5** if not on the other occasions implied in **Acts 1:4b**: *"John baptized with water, but you will be baptized with the Holy Spirit."*

Our main question here is whether these texts that speak of Jesus' imminent baptizing ministry can help us decide whether Holy Spirit baptism is a limited nonconversion event, or a conversion blessing received by every believer. The answer is yes; these texts show us that all Christians have been baptized in the Holy Spirit.

These texts show us that all Christians have been baptized in the Holy Spirit.

The first thing that establishes the universal application of Spirit baptism is the language used to describe those to whom John the Baptist spoke this promise. It appears in **Acts 1:4-5** that Jesus is addressing the apostles when He reminds them of this promise, but that circumstance cannot be used to limit its application. The more appropriate question is, to whom did *John the Baptist* address this promise? **Luke 3:16** says, *"John answered and said to **them all**."* Who is included in this "all"? John had been addressing "the crowds" (***Lk 3:7,10***), including tax collectors and soldiers (***Lk 3:12,14***). ***Matthew 3:7*** tells us that He said this to "many of the Pharisees and Sadducees."

To *all* of these people John said, *"I baptize you with water."* The "you" in this statement can hardly be limited to the twelve men who would later become apostles (see **Lard, "Reply," 61**); John was addressing "them all." Now, these are the *same ones* to whom John said, *"He will baptize **you** with the Holy Spirit and fire."* There is absolutely nothing in any of the promissory texts that warrants limiting their application in any way. Does this mean that everyone who was addressed and everyone who heard this promise was later baptized in the Spirit? No, no more so than "I baptize you with water" means that everyone who heard John preach was baptized by John. The references both to John's baptism in water and to Jesus' baptism in the Spirit are statements of fact, but in the sense of *purpose* and *intention*. The actual accomplishment of the purpose is dependent on the hearers' responses. Any limitation in the application of the promise is the result of human refusal to accept it, not the result of divine purpose. John is thus saying, "I am here to baptize you in water, and I am offering to do this for all who will accept it; but there is One coming after me whose purpose will be to baptize you in the Holy Spirit. He offers to do this for anyone who will receive it." As Gibson sums up this point, "both John and Jesus would baptize that class or category that believed and accepted the gospel, John in water and Jesus in the Holy Spirit" (**40**).

The second thing about these texts that establishes their universal application is the reference to *fire* in both ***Matthew 3:11*** and ***Luke 3:16***: *"He will baptize you with the Holy Spirit* ***and fire****."* These two little words—"and fire" (*kai puri*)—are variously interpreted. The main issue is whether the fire baptism is the same as or separate and distinct from the Spirit baptism. Will Jesus give just one baptism, "in Spirit and fire"? Or will He give two baptisms, baptizing some in Spirit and others in fire?

Many say the latter. This was Lard's view. It is "not easy," he said, to divide the "you" to whom John the Baptist spoke into two groups, the good and the bad; "still I believe the circumstances of the case require it." Thus "John's language then means—He shall immerse the good among you in Spirit, but the bad in fire" (**"Baptism," 273**; see **"Reply," 62**). A contemporary example is Keener, who declares that in these texts fire "unquestionably symbolizes judgment." Thus "in this context, baptism in fire can only be a negative promise of baptism in judgment for the wicked, whereas baptism in the Spirit is a positive promise for the righteous" (**27**). The main evidence cited for this view is the immediately following reference to the process of separating the wheat from the chaff, after which *"He will burn up the chaff with unquenchable fire"* (***Lk 3:17***; see ***Mt 3:10,12***). As Robertson says, "***Matthew 3:12*** speaks of the burning of the chaff with 'unquenchable fire' and so makes it clear that the baptism of fire is eternal punishment in hell" (**102**).

Others say that the baptism "in the Holy Spirit and fire" is just one baptism. A.B. Bruce takes the unusual view that it is altogether a baptism of judgment upon the wicked: "The whole baptism of the Messiah, as John conceives it, is a baptism of judgment. . . . I think that the grace of the Christ is not here at all." He takes the word *pneuma* to mean "wind," a "stormy wind of judgment" such as blows away the chaff when the wheat is winnowed (***Lk 3:17***). "Messiah will baptize with wind and fire, sweeping away and consuming the impenitent" (**84**). Bruce has few followers on this point.

The more common unitary view sees Christ's baptism "in the Holy Spirit and fire" as a single saving event. Bruner speaks of "the gift of an inundation or Baptism with a fiery Holy Spirit" (**"Water," 40**). Plummer states his preferred view: "More probably the *puri* ["in fire"] refers to the illuminating, kindling, and *purifying power* of the grace given by the Messiah's baptism. . . . The purifying of the believer rather than the punishment of the unbeliever seems to be intended" (**95**). Chouinard speaks of "the Spirit-fire baptism, received as a blessing by the penitent" (**72**).

Does it matter whether we see this as one baptism or two? Those who hold to the conversion view of Holy Spirit baptism are more comfortable with the two-baptism approach to ***Luke 3:16***, because it implies that the Spirit baptism is universal, or intended for all believers. That is, if the fire baptism embraces all the wicked, then surely the Spirit baptism must apply to all the righteous. This was Lard's argument: "As all the bad were to be immersed in fire, it seems a necessary inference that all the good were to be immersed in Spirit" (**"Baptism," 276**). Boatman says the baptism in the Holy Spirit is set "in the context of a warning concerning the alternative thereto: the baptism of fire. The two baptisms, both of which are the province of Christ to administer, are (together) universal. . . . The two baptisms are plainly said to encompass the entire human race" (**106**). As Keener argues, "But John's prophecy about the outpoured Spirit must at least include conversion, because he explicitly contrasts it with a baptism of judgment for the wicked" (**28**). "To put the question in another form, 'Why must we interpret the "all" of John's prediction (in ***Lk 3:16***) to mean only twelve Jews and a handful of Gentiles, and interpret the same "all" as meaning all the billions of unbelievers who may be cast into hell?'" (**Gibson, 41**).

I agree that a two-baptism approach to the "Spirit and fire" text would give strong support to the view that baptism in the Spirit is a salvation event promised to all believers; and I believe the contextual evidence for it is strong. However, I must reluctantly say that I believe there are problems with this view; or, as Plummer says, it is "very improbable" (**95**). The main problem is the grammatical construction of the phrase "in the Holy Spirit and fire." Here there is only one preposition (*en*, "in") governing the two objects, "thus most naturally indicating one baptism composed of two elements" (**Chouinard,**

71). As Lenski says, "One *en* combines the Spirit and fire: *en Pneumati Hagio kai puri*, and thus regards them as one concept which is also placed over against the one water." The other view "inserts a second 'in' which is not there" (117).

If anyone thinks that such a grammatical "rule" may not be absolute and binding, he should remember that ***John 3:5*** has exactly the same construction, i.e., "unless one is born of [*ek*] water and Spirit, he cannot enter into the Kingdom of God." Many use the single-preposition rule in ***John 3:5*** to show that we cannot separate being born of the Spirit from being born of water (i.e., baptism). If we appeal to the rule in ***John 3:5***, consistency requires us to apply it the same way in ***Matthew 3:11*** and ***Luke 3:16***.

The good thing about this, however, is that the one-baptism view of "the Holy Spirit and fire" is an even stronger argument for the conversion approach to Spirit baptism than is the two-baptism view. If indeed the one baptism applied by the Messiah is a "baptism in the Holy Spirit and fire," the only feasible interpretation of the "fire" is the fire of purification and purging from sin, which is part of the very essence of the Spirit's saving work of regeneration. We cannot assume, as Lenski says, "that 'fire' is always a symbol of judgment and destruction." He refers to "the refiner's fire in ***Mal. 3:2, 3***, fire as an image of purification in ***Zech. 13:9***; ***Isa. 6:6, 7***; ***1 Pet. 1:7***, and the 'spirit of burning' taking away filth in ***Isa. 4:4***" (117). We can also remember the purifying fire that will cleanse the universe of everything sinful and thus "regenerate and renew" it in the eschaton (***2Pet 3:7-13***; see ***Mt 19:28***). In like manner, when the Holy Spirit regenerates the sinner, the "baptism in fire" purifies the soul by putting to death the old man of sin (***Rom 6:1-6***) and making way for new life in the Spirit.

In this view, the only feasible interpretation is the fire of purification and purging from sin.

As we can see, it really does not matter which approach we take to the "baptism in fire" in the Father's promise given through John the Baptist. Both the two-baptism view and the one-baptism view of "the Holy Spirit and fire" strengthen the concept of Spirit baptism as a conversion experience. The very fact that fire is mentioned at all leads to this conclusion.

A third thing about John's promise that points in the same direction is what we may call the lesser-to-greater argument. Without question, the Baptist does his best to emphasize that the Messiah will be so much greater than himself. He *"is mightier than I, and I am not fit to untie the thong of His sandals"* (***Lk 3:16***). That Jesus will baptize in the Spirit, in contrast with John's baptizing in water, is one way of expressing the infinite superiority of Christ over John. Gibson uses this truth to refute the two-episode theory (Pentecost and Cornelius), according to which, he conjectures, only about 40 people would have received Holy Spirit baptism. Why does John give it such prominence, in comparison with his own ministry, if only a few were going to receive it? Gibson says this reduces John's promise to, "I baptize you (thousands) with water; he shall baptize (a few of) you with the Holy Spirit and fire" (**45**). He continues (**45**),

> Our commonly held position would change the scripture to read as follows, *if we made it say what we understand it to say*: "I baptize in water thousands and thousands of you who have come out from Jerusalem, Judea, and all the region round about the Jordan; yet this Jesus who is coming onto the scene and who is much, much greater than I, will baptize about 40 of you with the Holy Spirit and fire." Is that not anticlimactic? Does it really fit? Yet that is "our present position" on the matter.
>
> In contrast, the idea of Jesus continually baptizing converts with the Holy Spirit down through the centuries, seems to fit John's parallelism far better than the idea that Jesus would baptize only a few.

This leads to a final thought, i.e., a consideration of the present participle used in ***John 1:33*** to describe Jesus' baptizing work. Here God identifies Jesus as "the One who baptizes in the Holy Spirit." This surely gives great prominence to Jesus' Messianic role as a *baptizer*. He is the one who baptizes in the Holy Spirit; that's *who He is*! Keener calls Him "Jesus the Spirit Baptizer," as a take-off on "John the Baptizer" (**29**). Stott does the same, saying of ***John 1:33***, "Just as John is called 'the Baptist' or 'the baptizer,' because it was characteristic of his ministry to baptize with water, so Jesus is called 'the Baptist' or 'the baptizer', because it is characteristic of his ministry to baptize with the Holy Spirit" (***Baptism*, 23-**

The Messiah is the one who baptizes in the Holy Spirit; that's who He is!

24). Stott reminds us that the present participle in this verse (translated "who baptizes") "is timeless. It describes not the single event of Pentecost, but the distinctive ministry of Jesus" (ibid., 23). Only the ongoing, universal, salvation approach to Holy Spirit baptism does justice to God's speaking of Jesus in this way.

Only the salvation approach to Holy Spirit baptism does justice to speaking of Jesus in this way.

Holy Spirit Baptism in the Book of Acts

In the Acts of the Apostles, baptism in the Holy Spirit is no longer just a promise; it is now a reality, as explained in the account of the Pentecostal events in **Acts 2**. A key to the correct understanding of **Acts 2** is to properly distinguish between the *two* promises Jesus gives to His apostles in **Acts 1:4-8**. First, He tells them to wait in Jerusalem *"for what the Father had promised."* This promise, He says, *"you heard of from Me; for John baptized with water, but you will be baptized with the Holy Spirit not many days from now"* (**1:4-5**). That is, the time for Jesus' ministry of baptizing in the Holy Spirit and fire was about to begin.

When the apostles asked if this had anything to do with restoring the kingdom to Israel (**1:6**), Jesus told them not to worry about that and just to focus on their immediate task (**1:7**), namely, *"you will receive power when the Holy Spirit has come upon you; and you shall be My witnesses both in Jerusalem, and in all Judea and Samaria, and even to the remotest part of the earth"* (**1:8**).

The usual approach is to equate the promise in **1:5** with the promise in **1:8**, and therefore to equate Holy Spirit baptism with the power that came upon the Apostles in **Acts 2:1-36**. Everything Jesus promised in these two verses is seen as being fulfilled in the miracle of tongues and in Peter's inspired Pentecost sermon. From this it is concluded that Holy Spirit baptism is inseparable from miraculous powers. As Lard put it in 1864, "Heretofore our brethren have very generally held that immersion in the Spirit is identical with miraculous endowment by it" (**"Reply," 60**). Bales says unequivocally, "Holy Spirit baptism was accompanied by inspiration and by the miraculous" (**19**). In a sense this was true in **Acts 2**, but Bales means *always and necessarily* accompanied by the miraculous. This is why ***Acts 2:38-39*** cannot refer to baptism in the Spirit, he says. "If the promise of the Spirit in ***Acts 2:39*** referred to the baptism of the Holy Spirit, all who were baptized into Christ would have spoken in tongues" (17). "If they had all been baptized in the Spirit, on being baptized into Christ, they would all have received miraculous gifts" (**ibid.**). James Smith says, "When the baptism of the Holy Spirit takes place, observable signs are present" (5).

This includes the gift of tongue-speaking, received at least by the apostles (if not by the entire group of 120 disciples).[2] The apostolic speaking in tongues is regarded as the very purpose of Holy Spirit baptism, or at least as the essential sign of it. Some focus more on the gift of divine inspiration, equating or linking Holy Spirit baptism with the ability to speak inspired messages from God, as Peter spoke in his sermon recorded in ***Acts 2:14-36***. This equates the promise of baptism in the Spirit with Jesus' promises to His apostles in ***John 14–16***, a view espoused by Spratt: "I believe that ***Acts 1:4-5*** connects and relates the promise of the baptism of the Holy Spirit to the statements of Jesus Christ as recorded in ***John 14:26, 15:26, 16:7-15***." This, he says, shows that "the promise of the Holy Spirit was exclusively with and directed to His apostles" (**"Holy Spirit,"** 15). In McGarvey's view the main purpose of Holy Spirit baptism was to immerse "the entire intellectual nature of the human spirit" in the Holy Spirit to enable one to speak under divine inspiration. He says that "the direct inspiration of the human soul was an essential part of its immersion in the Holy Spirit. This being the case, no one is immersed in the Holy Spirit in whom this inspiration does not take place." But Christians in general do not have such supernatural power; "therefore, Christians in general, are not immersed in the Holy Spirit" (**"Immersion," 441**).

When the Spirit baptism of ***Acts 1:5*** is thus equated with the "power" from the Holy Spirit in ***Acts 1:8***, everything associated with baptism in the Spirit in ***Acts 2*** has come and gone by the time we reach *2:37*. With the manifestation of the signs (tongues) and with the inspiration of Peter's sermon, the promise of Holy Spirit baptism is fulfilled. Since Joel's prophecy of the coming of the Spirit is representative of all such OT prophecies, and since Joel's prophecy is quot-

[2] We know this is true of the apostles. Since there is some question about whether it applies to the entire group of 120 disciples, from here on I will speak of it as applying only to the apostles.

ed as being fulfilled in the events of ***Acts 2***, then everything the OT prophets predicted about the coming of the Holy Spirit is likewise seen as fulfilled by the time we reach ***2:37***. Thus the promise of the *gift* of the Holy Spirit in ***2:38-39*** is quite anticlimactic. The "main event" has already been played out, exhausting the content of all the promises in the process. The offer of the indwelling Spirit is then brought into the picture without any real connection with the previous context and without any groundwork being laid. It is almost like a postscript, or a "by the way. . . ."

Thus the promise of the gift of the Holy Spirit in 2:38-39 is quite anticlimactic.

I seriously suggest that it is time for another approach to the interpretation of ***Acts 1 and 2***. We may begin by making a distinction between the promise in ***1:5*** and the promise in ***1:8***. The former is about the imminent gift of baptism in the Holy Spirit, ultimately intended for everyone who will accept it; the latter is about empowerment especially for the apostles in their role as Christ's representatives for the building of the church in the new era.

One thing that helps us to discern this distinction is the realization that there were actually *several* promises concerning the Spirit that were fulfilled on the day of Pentecost. These begin with the collective OT prophecies about a new, universal, saving presence of the Holy Spirit, of which Joel's prophecy is an example. Then we have the promise that the Christ would baptize in the Holy Spirit and fire, which is specifically *"what the Father had promised"* (***Jn 1:33; Acts 1:4***). Third, Jesus promised to give the Holy Spirit as *living water* to all those who are spiritually dry and thirsty—a promise that would begin to be kept only after His ascension (***Jn 4:10-14; 7:37-39***). Fourth, Jesus promised that the heavenly Father will "give the Holy Spirit to those who ask Him"—obviously a promise meant for all (***Lk 11:13***). Fifth is Jesus' promise strictly to the apostles to send the Spirit to them after His own departure, to take His place and to guide them into all truth via revelation and inspiration (***John 14–16***). Finally we have Jesus' promise to the apostles just before His ascension, *"And behold, I am sending forth the promise of My Father upon you; but you are to stay in the city until you are clothed with power from on high"* (***Lk 24:49***).

When we examine these many texts, we may discern two main streams of promise and expectation. One is the promise of the Holy

Spirit offered as a gift for salvation purposes to all who will receive Him. The other is the promise especially to the apostles that the Spirit would come upon them to equip them with power to proclaim the Messiah's salvation and to establish His worldwide kingdom. Both of these are important, but it is fair to ask, especially in reference to ***Acts 2*** and the day of Pentecost, which of these two promises is more significant and far-reaching? Which is the more critical and decisive and climactic? Which one is the main point, the "main event"? Which is the end, and which is the means? There should be no doubt about this: the promise of the new universal and saving presence of the Spirit far exceeds and overshadows the importance of the Spirit's empowering presence for the apostles, as essential as the latter is. Surely the former is the main thrust of the OT prophecies. It is also the point of ***Luke 11:13*** and the "living water" promises. It is probably the point of ***Luke 24:49a***. And there is no doubt in my mind that this is what ***Acts 1:4-5*** is referring to.

The promise of the saving presence of the Spirit far exceeds the importance of His empowering presence.

Acts 1:8, on the other hand, refers to something very different. This is Jesus' promise that the Holy Spirit would clothe the apostles with "power from on high" (***Lk 24:49b***), that when the Holy Spirit came upon them they would "receive power." Jesus does not specify the kind of power this would be, but He indicates that its purpose had to do with being *"My witnesses both in Jerusalem, and in all Judea and Samaria, and even to the remotest part of the earth."* Thus we conclude that the Spirit's power would equip them to *proclaim* and *confirm* the message of salvation. This included divine inspiration, and thus is the fulfillment of Jesus' promises to the apostles in ***John 14–16***. It also included miracle-working power, such as the ability to speak in tongues, in order to provide divine confirmation of the truth of the gospel revelation. This is what Jesus meant when He said, *"You will receive power, when the Holy Spirit has come upon you."* This is *not* baptism "in the Holy Spirit and fire."

How are these two promises fulfilled in ***Acts 2***? In ***2:1-2*** we have the "opening bell" of the new era, so to speak. All the promises regarding the Holy Spirit converge upon this moment, and the door is opened for their fulfillment when the Holy Spirit bursts upon the

All the promises converge upon the moment when the Holy Spirit noisily bursts upon the scene.

scene, heralded by a tremendous noise: *"And suddenly there came from heaven a noise like a violent rushing wind, and it filled the whole house where they were sitting"* (**2:2**). This is the initial outpouring of the Spirit, a one-time event that would never be repeated, not even in **Acts 10:44-48**. The floodgates of heaven have opened, and the Holy Spirit is now present. His coming is majestic and unconditional; His presence, like the noise, filled the whole house. In this initial outpouring as such, the Holy Spirit is not given to any individual nor does He "come upon" any individual for any purpose. He is just *there*, with time seemingly suspended in an eternal moment.

The immediate specific result of this general coming of the Spirit is the fulfillment of the promise in **1:8**. *"Tongues as of fire . . . rested on each one of them"* (**2:3**). *"And they were all filled with the Holy Spirit and began to speak with other tongues, as the Spirit was giving them utterance"* (**2:4**).

Here is the apostles' first taste of the promised *"power from on high"* (**Lk 24:49**). Specifically they received miraculous power to speak in unlearned languages. This tongue-speaking gained the immediate attention of those in the vicinity because it was indeed an obvious miracle. As such it served its purpose of causing bewilderment, amazement, astonishment, and perplexity (**2:6-7,12**), thus evidentially and psychologically preparing the audience to attend to and accept the truth of Peter's Pentecost sermon (**2:14-36**). Though it is not specifically stated in **Acts 2**, we can assume that Peter spoke with inspiration of the Spirit as Jesus had promised in **John 14–16**. Indeed, if this does not fulfill that promise, it is difficult to imagine what would. Thus Peter's inspiration was the second taste of the promised "power from on high," fulfilling **1:8**.

I deny, however, that any of this miraculous activity was the fulfillment of the promise in **1:5**, regarding the baptism in the Spirit. McGarvey makes an odd statement about **Acts 2**: "Again, the apostles on the day of Pentecost are expressly declared to have been immersed in the Holy Spirit" (**"Immersion," 430**). I say this is odd because, as a matter of fact, the expression "baptized in the Holy Spirit" in any of

The expression "baptized in the Holy Spirit" is never used in any form in Acts 2.

its forms is never used in ***Acts 2***. ***Verse 4*** says *"they were all **filled** with the Holy Spirit,"* but there is no reason to equate this with "baptized in the Holy Spirit" (though this is usually done).

The main reason why I cannot accept this miraculous activity as baptism in the Spirit is because in all of ***verses 3-36***, there is actually *nothing new* about what the Holy Spirit is doing. Miracles as such were nothing new; certain OT saints worked miracles, and some received gifts of miraculous speaking (***Num 11:25***). Also, miracle-working power was nothing new even for the apostles; Christ had given them this power during His ministry with them (***Mt 10:1,8***; ***Mk 6:13***; ***Lk 9:1***).[3] As far as inspiration is concerned, the gift of inspiration (as in ***John 14–16***) was probably new *for the apostles themselves*, but it was nothing new as such, as the OT attests. Robert Milligan's comment applies here: "I see no evidence whatever that this supernatural power was itself the baptism in the Spirit, or that it was in any way essential to it. Balaam possessed this power in part, and so did Judas; but neither of them was ever *baptized* in the Spirit" (**131**).

The new thing and the main thing about Pentecost was the presence of the Spirit for salvation purposes; "baptism in the Spirit" is a way of describing this reality. The apostles' power to work miracles and speak inspired messages was simply for the purpose of explaining and confirming this greater work of God. The miracles *accompanied* Holy Spirit baptism as *proof* of Peter's sermon explaining it and offering it as a free gift to everyone. As Lard says, baptism in the Spirit was "attended by miraculous endowments. But conferring these endowments was not baptizing in the Spirit" (**"Baptism," 276**). McGuiggan asks, "Why can't we hold that the miracles were given as the credentials of Christ and as visible proof that he does give the Spirit to all who submit to him (***Acts 2:33,38f***)?" (**275**).

We should note that such filling with the Spirit for miraculous endowments did not end with Pentecost. The apostles continued to be given the power to explain the gospel mysteries and to confirm them with miracles (***Acts 2:43***; ***4:31***; ***3:6-9***; ***5:12-16***). The same power

[3] He had given some miracle-working power even to the 70 evangelists in ***Luke 10:9,17***.

was conveyed to others through the laying on of the apostles' hands (e.g., ***Acts 6:6,8***; ***8:6-7,13,17-18***). The promise in ***1:8*** implies this continuation when it refers to the power to witness not just in Jerusalem, but in Judea and Samaria, and even to the ends of the earth.

Up to the end of ***2:36***, *no one*, not even the apostles, has yet been baptized in the Holy Spirit. The Spirit has arrived and is present (***2:1-2***), and He has endowed the apostles with supernatural powers as promised in ***1:8***. But not until we get to ***2:37ff.*** do we see the fulfillment of ***1:5***. The outpoured Spirit has been waiting in the wings, so to speak. But now that the crowd has been thoroughly prepared to accept the offer of the baptism in the Spirit, being brought to conviction and seeking salvation from their sins, Peter tells them what to do: *"Repent, and each of you be baptized in the name of Jesus Christ for the forgiveness of your sins; and you will receive the gift of the Holy Spirit"* (***2:38***). The Spirit is here! He is waiting to enter your heart, to regenerate you and indwell you! *"For the promise is for you and your children and for all who are far off, as many as the Lord our God will call to Himself"* (***2:39***).

The emphatic word in ***2:39*** is "For you!" (*humin*). It is the first word in the sentence, out of the usual order for the purpose of emphasis. In other words, repent and be baptized for the forgiveness of your sins, *"and you will receive the gift of the Holy Spirit"*! You! *You* will receive Him—this same Holy Spirit who is responsible for the tongue-speaking you have just witnessed! "FOR YOU this promise is!" God has been preparing this gift *for you* from ancient times, and it is now here!

While the initial outpouring of the Spirit in ***2:1-2*** was unilateral and unconditional, the actual reception of the Spirit's presence in the individual's life is conditional. One must ask for Him (***Lk 11:13***), calling upon the name of the Lord to bestow what He has promised (***Acts 22:16***). One must believe in Jesus (***Jn 7:37-38***). One must repent and be baptized (***Acts 2:38***). Peter declares that God gives the Holy Spirit to those who obey Him thus (***Acts 5:32***).

The initial outpouring of the Spirit was unilateral and unconditional but the individual's reception of the Spirit's presence is conditional.

What happens when one is baptized in the Holy Spirit, i.e., receives the gift of the Holy Spirit (for these are essentially the same thing)? What is the purpose; what is the result? McGarvey is right to say that it must have some purpose, some intended "vital action" of the Holy Spirit upon the human spirit. "Otherwise, it would be like the immersion of an inanimate block of wood in some inanimate liquid. The promise of immersion in the Spirit would have been a very empty promise, if it meant nothing more than the envelopment of one spirit in another, like the envelopment of a globule of floating gas in the surrounding atmosphere. The Saviour promised more than this" (**"Immersion," 440-441**). McGarvey's error, though, is to think that this "vital action" is endowing the Spirit-baptized person with divine inspiration. The fact is that the *purpose* of Christ's baptizing us in the Spirit is to bring the Holy Spirit into contact with our spiritually dead souls for the purpose of regenerating them and raising them from the dead and endowing them with new spiritual life. The point is not miracles; it is salvation!

The purpose is to bring the Holy Spirit into contact with our spiritually dead souls.

If one says, "How can you be so sure that ***1:5*** is connected with ***2:37ff.*** and not ***2:3ff.***?" I will say, "Follow the language of promise." The Holy Spirit is *"the Holy Spirit of promise"* (***Eph 1:13***); i.e., as the NIV says, He is "the promised Holy Spirit." God has made it possible for us to *"receive the promise of the Spirit through faith"* (***Gal 3:14***). The context for these two texts is salvation, not miraculous power. Then in ***Acts 1 and 2***, Jesus refers to *"what the Father had promised,"* namely, baptism in the Holy Spirit (***1:4-5***). Peter says in ***2:33*** concerning the ascended Christ, *"Therefore having been exalted to the right hand of God, and having received from the Father the promise of the Holy Spirit, He has poured forth this which you both see and hear."* Then He offers the Holy Spirit as a gift to penitent sinners in ***2:38*** with this explanation: *"For the **promise** is for you"* (***2:39***). There is a direct line from ***1:5*** through ***2:33*** to ***2:38-39***.

The experience of Cornelius in ***Acts 10:44-48*** must be understood according to this same pattern. The incident is described thus:

> *While Peter was still speaking these words, the Holy Spirit fell upon all those who were listening to the message. All*

> *the circumcised believers who came with Peter were amazed, because the gift of the Holy Spirit had been poured out on the Gentiles also. For they were hearing them speaking with tongues and exalting God. Then Peter answered, "Surely no one can refuse the water for these to be baptized who have received the Holy Spirit just as we did, can he?" And he ordered them to be baptized in the name of Jesus Christ. Then they asked him to stay on for a few days.*

The expressions used to describe the coming of the Spirit—*"fell upon," "gift of the Holy Spirit," "poured out"*—are not decisive, because none of them seems to be used exclusively for any one form of receiving the Spirit. In my judgment what happens to Cornelius and his household in the beginning (***10:44-45***) is certainly equivalent to what happened to the apostles in ***2:3-13***, i.e., they received "power from on high" to speak in tongues. The purpose was likewise the same as in ***2:3-13***, i.e., to provide miraculous proof for an accompanying revelation from God. In this case the revelation is God's message that the Gentiles are supposed to receive the gospel and be saved just the same as the Jews. The tongue-speaking had the desired effect on the Jewish Christians who came with Peter: they "were amazed." Peter's conclusion is unavoidable: how can we refuse to baptize these people in Jesus' name (***10:47-48***)? I believe they received their salvation, including the baptism in the Holy Spirit, only at this point.

The difficulty with this interpretation is in reconciling it with Peter's report of this incident to the church back in Jerusalem:

> *And as I began to speak, the Holy Spirit fell upon them just as He did upon us at the beginning. And I remembered the word of the Lord, how He used to say, "John baptized with water, but you will be baptized with the Holy Spirit." Therefore if God gave to them the same gift as He gave to us also after believing in the Lord Jesus Christ, who was I that I could stand in God's way?* (***11:15-17***).

One thing that is clarified by Peter's report is what he meant in ***10:47*** when he said that Cornelius and his household had *"received the Holy Spirit just as we did"* (see ***15:8***). That the "we" in this statement refers to "we, the apostles" on the day of Pentecost is indicated when Peter says the Holy Spirit *"fell upon them **just as** He did **upon us at the beginning**"* (***11:15***). Thus the only thing comparable to

Cornelius's experience was the apostles' Pentecost experience. What makes these two events a category to themselves is the way the Holy Spirit fell *directly* upon them, in contrast with coming upon someone through the laying on of apostles' hands or through baptism.

The difficulty, though, is in ***11:16***. Peter says that as soon as he saw that the Spirit had fallen upon Cornelius and his group, he remembered Jesus' words, *"John baptized with water, but you will be baptized with the Holy Spirit."* Most have taken this to mean that Peter is here identifying baptism in the Holy Spirit with the tongue-speaking experience he has just witnessed. I do not agree. I believe his point is this: "As soon as I saw and heard what was happening, I was absolutely convinced that God wants these Gentiles to be saved, i.e., that He wants *them* to receive the baptism in the Spirit also. Thus I immediately said (***10:47***), 'Surely no one can refuse the water for these to be baptized,' can they? After all, they received the miraculous outpouring of the Holy Spirit just as we did on Pentecost (***11:17***). God is surely trying to tell us something, and it is that He wants these and other Gentiles to be saved. So let's get them to the water so they can be baptized in the Holy Spirit! We cannot stand in the way of God and refuse them this gift!"

In other words, Peter's words, *"I remembered the word of the Lord, how He used to say, 'John baptized with water, but you will be baptized with the Holy Spirit,'"* are *forward* looking, not backward looking. These words do not apply to what has just happened, but to what must happen next.

Peter's words are forward looking, not backward looking.

In my judgment, we must abandon all approaches to Acts that inseparably link baptism in the Holy Spirit with miraculous gifts. The assumption that Holy Spirit baptism always or normally involves miracles is the source of all kinds of theological errors. Not the least of these is Pentecostalism and all forms of Neo-Pentecostalism. But also, it leads to a separation between Spirit baptism and water baptism, thus creating *two* baptisms instead of the *one* that Paul affirms in ***Ephesians 4:5***. This separation seems justified when it is assumed on the basis of the presence of tongue-speaking that the apostles (on Pentecost) and Cornelius and his household were baptized in the Holy Spirit *and thus saved* prior to their water baptism. When we understand that baptism in the Spirit is *not* the receiving of miraculous abilities, we have no basis for assuming that the apostles and Cornelius received Spirit baptism (and thus were saved) before they were baptized in water.

1 Corinthians 12:13

Another crucial passage for understanding Holy Spirit baptism is ***1 Corinthians 12:13***, where Paul says, *"For by one Spirit we were all baptized into one body, whether Jews or Greeks, whether slaves or free, and we were all made to drink of one Spirit."* At first glance one might think that this text should resolve many of the controversies surrounding the subject, especially the question of *who* receives baptism in the Spirit. After all, does not Paul say we were *all* so baptized? Yes, but this in itself does not erase all the difficulties. Several issues must be addressed about this verse itself.

The Meaning of the Preposition *en*

The first issue is whether Paul is talking about the same baptism that we have been discussing, i.e., the baptism in the Spirit promised by John the Baptist and then by Jesus in ***Acts 1:5***. Some argue that this baptism in ***1 Corinthians 12:13*** is a totally different baptism, namely, ordinary Christian baptism in water. This conclusion is based mainly on the argument that one of the words in the relevant phrase has a different meaning here, often reflected in a slightly different translation. Instead of *"He will baptize you* ***with*** *the Holy Spirit,"* we have *"**By** one Spirit we were all baptized into one body."* Does this not suggest a different experience or event?

Actually the difference is not as great as some think and as some Bible versions would imply. First, it should be emphasized that Paul is speaking of the Holy Spirit, just as John the Baptist was. This is contrary to Applebury, who argues that *pneuma* here is a spirit in the sense of an *attitude*, i.e., "the spirit of oneness of the believers in Christ who were baptized into His body" (**229**). Such a view can be quickly dismissed, though, in view of the contextual emphasis on the role of the Holy Spirit as unifier of

> **Paul is speaking of the Holy Spirit, just as John the Baptist was.**

the body (see ***12:4-11***). If this is the Holy Spirit, then, why does Paul not *say*, "the *Holy* Spirit"? He does not have to, because the context makes it overwhelmingly certain that his subject is the Holy Spirit. In ***12:1-13*** he refers to the Spirit eleven times, once as "the Spirit of God," once as "the Holy Spirit" (***12:3***), twice as "the Spirit" (***12:7-8***), three times as "the one Spirit" (***12:9,13***), three times as "the same Spirit" (***4,8,9***), and once as "the one and the same Spirit" (***12:11***). In ***verse 13*** he says "*one* Spirit" to reinforce his point about the unity of the body of Christ.

The difference in the word order in ***12:13***, i.e., putting the prepositional phrase "in one Spirit" before the verb instead of after it, should not confuse us. This does not make it a different concept; it is done only for the sake of emphasis.

The main point of controversy about the language is the meaning of the preposition in the phrase *"by one Spirit."* The preposition translated "by" is *en*, the very same preposition used in five of the other six references to baptism "in (*en*) the Holy Spirit" in the gospels and Acts (***Mk 1:8*** has no preposition). Though the preposition (*en*) and its object ("the Holy Spirit," "the one Spirit") are exactly the same in the original language, the dozen Bible versions I sampled here at my desk give an English translation in ***1 Corinthians 12:13*** that is different from the way they render it in the Gospels and Acts. In the five verses in the Gospels and Acts, all the versions say "with (*en*) the Holy Spirit." Then in ***1 Corinthians 12:13***, four of these versions say "in (*en*) one Spirit."[4] This is not a difference in meaning, though. "With" and "in" both refer to the *element* in which one is baptized (cf. "baptized *with* water" and "baptized *in* water"). The other eight versions, however,[5] all use "by (*en*) one Spirit" in ***12:13***. The use of "by" changes the meaning altogether. No longer is the Holy Spirit the element, with or in which one is baptized, with Jesus being the agent or baptizer. To be baptized *by* the Spirit makes the Spirit Himself the agent or baptizer. Thus the use of the different English preposition in ***1 Corinthians 12:13*** implies that *this* baptism *en* the Spirit is different from the baptism *en* the Spirit taught in the Gospels and Acts.

Either translation ("in/with" or "by") is a valid meaning of the preposition *en*, so how do we decide which should be used here?

[4] ASV, NEB, NRSV, ESV.
[5] KJV, NKJV, TEV, RSV, NASB, NIV, NLT, CSB.

Both sides have some valid points. Those who say it should be *"by one Spirit,"* and thus different from what John the Baptist promised, argue from the immediate context, in which the same preposition is used with the Spirit several times in the sense of "by the agency of the Spirit" (***12:3*** [twice], ***12:9*** [twice]; see also ***12:8,11***). James Smith concludes, "This, then, makes it quite likely that the *one Spirit* in ***1 Corinthians 12:13*** is the baptizer, not the one in whom all Christians are baptized" (**8**).

One difficulty with this view is explaining the *sense* in which the Holy Spirit has baptized all Christians into one body. Those who take this view usually agree that the element of this baptism is water and that Paul is referring to ordinary Christian baptism. How, then, is the Holy Spirit the *agent* in a person's being baptized in water? Here is Smith's explanation:

> But in what sense is Great Commission baptism accomplished by the Holy Spirit? Great Commission baptism is performed in the name of the Father, Son and Holy Spirit. The Holy Spirit through accredited messengers commands this baptism. He also reveals in the New Testament the significance of this baptism. The gift of the Holy Spirit imparted at baptism appears to be the indwelling presence of the Spirit. . . . So we are baptized in the name of the Holy Spirit, by an agent of the Holy Spirit in order that we might receive the gift of the same Spirit. This is sufficient to explain *baptized by one Spirit into one body* (**9**).

This explanation says in part that the Holy Spirit is the agent of our Christian baptism by virtue of the fact that the Scripture He inspired leads us to be baptized. Lard in 1864 said that he once held this view, that ***1 Corinthians 12:13*** means "that by the teaching of the one Spirit through the apostles we have all been induced to submit to the one baptism in water," but that he no longer held it (**"Baptism," 282**). McGarvey said he still advocated this interpretation: "By one Spirit, as the divine agent moving us thereto, we were all immersed into one body" (**"Immersion," 435**). This approach is quite common in the Restoration Movement.[6]

The Holy Spirit certainly has a number of connections with Christian baptism, as in the ways cited above. But in my judgment none of these connections—baptism in the name of the Spirit, by the

[6] See the half-dozen examples cited by Robertson, 104-105.

The Holy Spirit has a number of connections with Christian baptism, but none of these warrants calling Him the agent.

command of the Spirit, for the gift of the Spirit—warrants calling the Spirit the *agent* of our baptism. Robertson rightly says that this approach does not do justice to the unity theme of the context. "Paul's argument would be stronger if he spoke of an immediate connection with the Spirit on the part of all Christians, rather than speaking in generalities on the work of the Spirit" (105).

The evidence for the other translation of *en* is quite strong. Its defenders focus on the many other occasions in the NT where "baptized" is followed by this preposition; and they point out that in every other case, baptism *"en"* something indicates the *element* in which one is baptized. As Dunn explains, "In the NT *en* with *Baptizein* never designates the one who performs the baptism; on the contrary, it always indicates the element in which the baptisand is immersed" (***Baptism,*** **128**). This is true not only of the other five references to being "baptized in the Spirit" which use the preposition *en* (***Mt 3:11***; ***Lk 3:16***; ***Jn 1:33***; ***Acts 1:5***; ***11:16***), but also of references to John's baptizing *en* water (***Mt 3:11***; ***Jn 1:26,33***) and *en* the Jordan River (***Mt 3:6***; ***Mk 1:5***). It also includes Paul's own reference to the Israelites' being baptized "*en* the cloud and *en* the sea," in this very letter (***1Cor 10:2***). Also, every time the NT speaks of being baptized *by* someone, the preposition used is *hupo* (***Mt 3:6,13,14***; ***Mk 1:5,9***; ***Lk 3:7***; ***7:30***).

This uniformity of usage of the phrase "baptized *en*" is, I believe, the weightier argument. Thus Paul is saying the same thing John the Baptist, Jesus, and Peter have already said, i.e., that in one Spirit we have all been baptized (by Jesus) into the one body. Stott is correct: "The natural interpretation is that Paul is echoing the words of John the Baptist as first Jesus and then Peter had done (***Acts 1:5***; ***11:16***). It is unnatural to make Jesus Christ the baptizer in six instances, and the Holy Spirit the baptizer in the seventh" (***Baptism,*** **40**). Let us be aware, then, that the translation *"by* one Spirit," which appears in many English versions, is incorrect.

The Meaning of "All"

This in itself does not settle the issue of *who* is thus being baptized in the Holy Spirit. Paul says quite clearly that in one Spirit "we were *all* baptized." But does this "all" really mean *all*, or just *some*? Those who take a two-episode miraculous approach to Holy Spirit baptism have a choice regarding ***1 Corinthians 12:13***. Either they can interpret this "baptism *en* the Spirit" to mean something different from the earlier two-episode version which applied only to the apostles and to Cornelius and his group, as just discussed; or they can find a way to interpret this "all" so that it is consistent with just two episodes of miraculous Spirit baptism. Some have attempted to do the latter by calling attention to the phrase *"whether Jews or Greeks"* in this verse. They say that the Spirit baptism of the apostles on Pentecost was a *representative* baptism that embraces all *Jews*, and the Spirit baptism of Cornelius and his household was a representative baptism that embraces all *Gentiles*. Robertson cites C.C. Crawford as an example of this view.[7]

This approach is extremely weak, however, especially in view of Paul's attempt in this very passage to engender a spirit of unity among all Christians *as individuals*, *"whether Jews or Greeks, whether slaves or free."* In my judgment a much stronger case can be made for the literal meaning of "all" in this verse. First, Paul does not say that all in general or in the abstract have been baptized in one Spirit into one body. He does not make his point rest upon just two episodes remote in time from the date of his writing and very likely experienced by no one who first read this letter. Rather, he makes his comment very personal: "*We*—you and I—were all baptized into one body." The "we" is emphatic, being expressed by the pronoun *hemeis* and not just by the first person plural verb form. Lard adds that "the word '*we*' has here the same extent of signification as the word body, and includes the whole membership of the church of Christ" (**"Baptism," 278**).

A much stronger case can be made for the literal meaning of "all" in 1 Corinthians 12:13.

A second consideration, already intimated, is that Paul's emphasis on unity requires that all Christians be included. In this letter he is battling the rampant divisions in the church at Corinth, caused in part by arguments over the relative merits of the different spiritual

[7] Ibid., 101, citing C.C. Crawford, *The Eternal Spirit: His Word and Works* (Joplin, MO: College Press, 1973), 2:534.

gifts. Paul's point is that it does not matter which spiritual gift an individual has; all the gifts are worthy because they are all bestowed by the same Holy Spirit. Our common relation to the one Spirit makes us one body, and has done so from the very beginning when in that initial moment, being baptized in the one Spirit, we were all baptized into one body. Unless we take this verse to refer to all Christians, it becomes irrelevant to this very point that Paul is making. The oneness of the body is premised on a Spirit baptism shared by *all*. See **Bruner, *Theology*, 292**.

A third reason for taking this Holy Spirit baptism as applying to all Christians is its parallel thought in the latter part of the verse, *"we were all made to drink of one Spirit,"* as explained in the next section.

Drinking of One Spirit

What does Paul mean when he says that we have all been made "to drink of one Spirit"? McGarvey says this must be a completely separate idea, otherwise we would have "useless repetition" (**"Immersion," 439**). Echoing this, Meserve says that equating this with Spirit baptism would be "an unnecessary tautology (vain repetition). Paul by the use of 'and' tells us he is adding another item to the activity of the Holy Spirit, i.e., 'drinking' the Spirit" (**12**). This argument has no merit. The word *kai* ("and") often connects two words or expressions that refer to the same thing (e.g., ***Mt 21:5***; ***Rom 1:5***; ***1Cor 2:10***; ***15:38***). This is called the "explicative" use of *kai*, and is similar to our "i.e." or "namely."

The fact is that both of these descriptions of something that has happened to all Christians refer to the same thing, namely, the reception of the gift of the Holy Spirit in our Christian baptism. The first thing we should ask, upon seeing both of these together in this verse, is, where did Paul get these images, and why does he put them together like this? The answer is that both of these images are from the life and teachings of Jesus. We know them through the Gospels; Paul could have known them through circulating accounts about Jesus but more likely knew them through revelation (***Gal 1:11-17***). The baptism image, of course, began with John the Baptist's promise, and the drinking image comes from Jesus' teaching about the Spirit as living water (***Jn 4:10-14***; ***7:37-39***). Both refer to the same thing, so it is natural for Paul to refer to both of them together.

Understanding this connection with the Gospels sheds light on several issues raised about ***1 Corinthians 12:13*** and baptism in the Holy Spirit. For one thing, that the "drinking of the Holy Spirit" undoubtedly is based on the "living water" teaching of Jesus shows that Paul was thinking about the life of Christ when he wrote this verse, and therefore it would be natural for him to use *en* in the phrase "*en* the Holy Spirit" in the same sense that John the Baptist used it, i.e., to represent the *element* and not the *agent* of Spirit baptism (as in point one above). Also, since there is no question that the Holy Spirit as living water is a salvation gift received by *all* believers, this reinforces the same interpretation of being baptized in the one Spirit. In other words, the parallel with the "drinking" image is a solid argument for the universal understanding of "all" in this verse (as in point two above).

There is no question that the Holy Spirit as living water is a salvation gift received by all believers.

The parallel between being baptized in one Spirit and drinking of one Spirit sheds light on one final issue, namely, exactly what does it mean to be *baptized* in or with the Spirit? What is the significance of the term, which I fully understand to mean "immersion"? Is there some special significance to the notion of being *immersed* in the Spirit? Some think the term represents a kind of quantitative intensity or an experience that is extreme and drastic in nature. As McGarvey explains it, referring to the apostles' speaking in tongues on Pentecost, "As the body, when baptized in water, is sunk beneath its surface and completely overwhelmed, so their spirits were completely under the control of the Holy Spirit, their very words being His and not theirs. The metaphor is justified by the absolute power which the divine Spirit exerted upon their spirits" (***Acts*, 23**). Boles's conclusion is similar: "The baptism of John in water involved as its chief idea an overwhelming, a sudden and complete overpowering of the person submerged by water, and the entering into new conditions and relations, so the baptism of the Holy Spirit was to imply an equally entire subjugation and overmastery of the soul by the Spirit" (**150**). As Giebler says, "When one is immersed, he is at the same time enveloped, overwhelmed, or controlled by the substance into which he is dipped" (**6**). Such exaggerated language is congenial to the two-episode approach (cf. **McGarvey** and **Boles**), as well as to Pentecostalism, as Bruner points out (***Theology*, 60**). It conjures up the idea of being "possessed" by the Spirit.

In my judgment such an interpretation of being "baptized" in the Spirit misses the mark because it attempts to read too much into the figure or metaphor of "immersion." We can of course picture in our minds a person being bodily immersed in a lake or a tank of water. But are we intended to think of the human spirit as being similarly inundated and "overwhelmed" by the Holy Spirit? Such a literal application of the analogy is impossible to visualize, and in fact is not necessary. We can see this is so by considering the companion analogy, *drinking* the Holy Spirit. We know what it means to drink a glass of water and receive it into our stomachs, but there is absolutely no way and no need to think of a *literal* way this could apply to our receiving the gift of the Holy Spirit.

I have concluded that both of these metaphors—baptism in the Spirit and drinking the Spirit—are more or less incidental and have their origin in the historical circumstances in which the teaching was originally given. Why did John the Baptist (under inspiration from God) say that Jesus would *baptize* in the Spirit? Because he himself was *baptizing* in water! It was a convenient and vivid figure to describe the "simple" gift of the Spirit that would begin on Pentecost. Why did Jesus speak of *drinking* the Holy Spirit as living water? Because when He coined this analogy He was at a well where people came to drink water (***Jn 4:4-15***) and later at the Feast of Tabernacles, which involved prominent water ceremonies (***Jn 7:37-39***; see **Morris, *John*, 419-422**). The Holy Spirit had been compared with water before this, but on these occasions it was convenient and appropriate to speak of receiving the Spirit as *drinking* Him, like water. There is nothing inherently significant in either *baptize* or *drink* as a way of depicting the event in which we receive the gift of the Holy Spirit. (Other metaphors that cannot be pressed literally are eating Christ's flesh and drinking His blood [***Jn 6:53-57***], being buried with Christ [***Rom 6:4***], and being crucified with Christ [***Rom 6:6***].)

There is nothing inherently significant in either "baptize" or "drink" as a way of depicting the event.

McGuiggan takes a similar approach, denying that "baptism" in the Spirit must imply being "overwhelmed" by the Spirit. He says, "But the figurative use of 'baptized' need not involve something that 'looks like' a literal baptism. We *eat* and *drink* of Christ without that appropriation of Christ resembling eating or drinking. . . . The reality behind the figure need not resemble the figure" (**276**).

We conclude that ***1 Corinthians 12:13*** reinforces the interpretation of Holy Spirit baptism as another way of describing the salvation experience in which all penitent sinners receive the gift of the regenerating and indwelling Spirit.

THE "ONE BAPTISM" OF EPHESIANS 4:5

"I baptize you with water," said John the Baptist, but the Messiah *"will baptize you with the Holy Spirit and fire"* (***Lk 3:16***). Listening to John preach, one might have concluded that the Messiah's Spirit baptism would simply *replace* John's water baptism. Some ultradispensationalists have actually drawn this conclusion, arguing that once the church was fully established through the work of the apostle Paul, water baptism was set aside so that Spirit baptism alone could continue for the church (**G.R. Lewis, 1120**). An advocate of this view is C.R. Stam, who says that the Great Commission and ***Acts 2:38*** continue the requirement (begun with John the Baptist) of water baptism for the remission of sins. This ended, however, with "the raising up of Paul to proclaim the gospel of the grace of God." In Paul's ministry "water baptism is *never* required for the remission of sins," and Paul never once in his letters commands or exhorts us to be baptized with water. In ***Ephesians 4:5*** he "states emphatically that there is now but 'ONE BAPTISM,'" which is baptism in the Spirit (**228-231**). Most of the Christian world, however, recognizes that in the Great Commission Jesus ordained the practice of water baptism and established it as normative until *"the end of the age"* (***Mt 28:18-20***). That this must refer to water baptism and not Spirit baptism as such is evident from the fact that Jesus commanded His disciples to administer it.

> **Most recognize that Jesus ordained the practice of water baptism and made it normative until "the end of the age."**

Thus we are not surprised to see the clear NT evidence that water baptism continued after Pentecost into the recorded decades of the early church. Water is specifically mentioned in connection with baptism in ***Acts 8:36*** and ***10:47***. Converts are commanded to be baptized, which must refer to water baptism (***Acts 2:38***; ***22:16***). Baptism is pictured as the result of a decision made by sinners, indicating water baptism (***Acts 2:41***; ***19:5***). Evangelists are shown as baptizing converts, which must also refer to water baptism (***Acts 8:38***; ***1Cor 1:14-16***). That Philip baptized the Ethiopian in water (***Acts 8:36,38***) implies that he did the same for the Samaritans (***Acts 8:12-13***). In the final analysis, all these clear references and inferences to water baptism make it more than reasonable to take the other three references to baptism in Acts as water baptism also (***Acts 16:15,33***; ***18:8***).

Thus we are left with this question: since water baptism was normative for the ongoing church, and since Holy Spirit baptism is the saving Messianic gift intended for all Christians, how are these "two baptisms" related? One thing to note immediately is that the church's water baptism (beginning with Pentecost) is *not* equivalent to John's baptism in water. In form they are no doubt the same (i.e., immersion in water), but their meaning and purpose are very different. This can be seen very clearly from ***Acts 19:1-6***, where disciples who had been baptized only with John's baptism were required to be baptized anew *"in the name of the Lord Jesus."* Most significantly, Paul here identifies a key difference between John's baptism and Christian baptism: the latter involves receiving the Holy Spirit!

Paul identifies a key difference between John's baptism and Christian baptism—receiving the Holy Spirit.

Paul's initial question to these disciples was, *"Did you receive the Holy Spirit when you believed?"* "When you believed" must be shorthand or a summary for *all* the acts of obedience already named as conditions for receiving the Spirit, especially repentance and baptism (***Acts 2:38***). This is obviously so, given the fact that when the disciples answered Paul's question, *"No, we have not even heard whether there is a Holy Spirit,"* Paul's follow-up inquiry was not about what they had *believed*, but was about what kind of *baptism* they had received. It is clear that the main reason they had not yet received the Holy Spirit was that they had not been baptized with Christian baptism. When Paul explained this, they immediately were baptized in the name of Jesus, with the implied purpose of receiving the gift of the Holy Spirit.

Two Baptisms

Given the fact that receiving the gift of the Holy Spirit and being baptized in the Holy Spirit are the same thing, what we see in ***Acts 19:1-6*** is a convergence of water baptism and Spirit baptism. However, traditional Protestantism, under the spell of the Zwinglian revolution regarding baptism, has strongly denied such a convergence. Those in this category (e.g., classical Presbyterians, Baptists) usually argue for two baptisms: one in Spirit, the other in water; one a promise, the other a command; one Christ's work, the other man's work; one to bestow salvation, the other to symbolize it. Holy Spirit baptism is thus God's promise that Jesus will baptize sinners in the Spirit for salvation. This is consistently separated from water baptism temporally, with Spirit baptism and thus salvation almost always preceding water baptism (at least in the case of adults). Biblical references to baptism are also separated into two categories, with the assumption that any text that actually ties baptism to salvation must be a reference to Spirit baptism and not water baptism. This is true especially of ***Romans 6:3-4***; ***1 Corinthians 12:13***; ***Galatians 3:27***; and ***Colossians 2:12*** (see **Walvoord, 140, 142; Unger, *Baptism*, 33, 119**). One of my teachers at a Calvinist seminary declared in class one day, "There's not a drop of water in ***Romans 6***!"

The two-stage approach to salvation (wherein Holy Spirit baptism is a "second work of grace"), as well as the two-episode theory of Spirit baptism, likewise discern two distinct baptisms, also with water baptism having nothing to do with Spirit baptism. In the case of the former (two-stage) view, one enters the saved state at the moment of faith, and then is baptized in water as a symbol of that saving event. Then at some still later time, the Christian may receive Holy Spirit baptism for the purpose of either full sanctification (Holiness groups) or miraculous endowments (Pentecostals, Charismatics). In the case of the latter (two-episode) view, the relation between Spirit baptism and water baptism is not an issue since the former has not occurred since ***Acts 10***. Either way, Spirit baptism and water baptism are seen as entirely separate events.

What, then, of ***Ephesians 4:5***, where Paul lists the unifying foundational pillars of the church (***4:4-6***) and declares that there is but "one

Lord, one faith, one baptism"? Many traditional Protestants emphatically insist that this refers to Spirit baptism, not water baptism. Walvoord says, "It is patent that this passage could not refer to water baptism" because so many differences exist today concerning its meaning and practice. Thus, "instead of the symbol, the reality is in view here, the baptism of the Holy Spirit" (**140**). Unger makes this same point over and over: "Paul's clear declaration [is] that there is only *one spiritual* baptism for this age (***Eph 4:5***)" (***Holy Spirit*, 16**). He refers to "Paul's emphatic testimony, 'one [spiritual] baptism' (***Eph 4:5***)" (**ibid., 26**; brackets in the original). Also, "the apostle, in speaking of the 'one baptism' in ***Ephesians 4:5***, is speaking of Spirit baptism" (**ibid., 33**). The idea that ***Ephesians 4:5*** refers to water baptism, he says, "teeters perilously on the precipice of the error of baptismal regeneration" (**ibid., 118**). Martin says of this verse, "The one baptism is undoubtedly the baptism of the Holy Spirit" (**1310**).

On the other hand, many also insist that the one baptism of ***Ephesians 4:5*** is water baptism only. This is especially true for those who espouse the two-episode approach to Spirit baptism, and who thus say that the only form of baptism that exists for the church is water baptism. We have shown, however, that Holy Spirit baptism does continue throughout the church age as a salvation event; thus it cannot be so easily dismissed in ***Ephesians 4:5***.

One Baptism

I.M. Haldemann says of ***Ephesians 4:5***, "If it be Holy Ghost baptism, water baptism is excluded. . . . If it be water baptism, Holy Ghost baptism is no longer operative. Baptism must be either the one or the other, Holy Ghost or water. It cannot be both. Two are no longer permissible" (**4**). Haldemann raises a serious issue: how can we continue to speak of water baptism and Spirit baptism as separate events, if both still exist and there is only *one baptism*? If one of these no longer exists, there is no problem. But if both do in fact exist, in view of ***Ephesians 4:5*** there is no justification for regarding them as two *separate* events rather than as two aspects of one unified event. To say that the "one baptism" of ***Ephesians 4:5*** must be Spirit baptism alone (or water baptism alone) is a fiction born of dogmatism.

Thus I am arguing strongly that the one baptism in ***Ephesians 4:5*** is the one Christian baptism in water, which is also at the same time baptism in the Holy Spirit. The water baptism and the Spirit baptism are not two separate events, but two aspects or sides of one event. While I agree with Dunn that water baptism cannot be *equated* with Spirit baptism (***Baptism*, 4**), I believe he is wrong to refer disparagingly to "Christian water-and-Spirit baptism" as a "curious hybrid unknown to the NT" (**ibid., 100**). ***Ephesians 4:5*** speaks of *"one Lord, one faith, one baptism."* That baptism is one event with two sides is no more "curious" or unacceptable than one *Lord* with two natures (human and divine) and one saving *faith* with two aspects (assent and trust). Thus the one baptism is a single event with two sides: human and divine, physical and spiritual, water and Spirit.

It is a single event with two sides: human and divine, physical and spiritual, water and Spirit.

Water and Spirit are brought together in other places in the NT. We noted earlier in this main section how Paul relates receiving the Spirit with Christian baptism in ***Acts 19:1-6***. ***Acts 2:38*** makes the same connection. ***John 3:5*** speaks of being *born* of these two elements, water and Spirit. Gibson comments, "Nobody argues there are two births because two elements have a part in it. Water and Spirit cooperate in the new birth. Why should it be argued that it would be two baptisms if the same two elements, water and Spirit, cooperate in a convert's baptism? It's one baptism, one birth!" (**15**). Another text that combines the physical and spiritual into the one baptism is ***Hebrews 10:22***, which says that we have had *"our hearts sprinkled clean from an evil conscience and our bodies washed with pure water."*

First Peter 3:21 also reflects the two elements of the one baptism which saves: *"Corresponding to that, baptism now saves you—not the removal of dirt from the flesh, but an appeal to God for a good conscience—through the resurrection of Jesus Christ."* The element of water is implied from the analogy of Noah's flood (***v. 20***) and from the reference to *"removal of dirt from the flesh."* The latter point assumes that the saving baptism is in water, but stresses that it is not the physical action of the water (washing dirt off the body) that saves. What saves is the spiritual side of the event, i.e., the very character of baptism as an appeal to God to keep His promises to those who surrender to Him in this simple act (***Acts 2:38-39***; ***22:16***).

Many students of the Word have accepted this understanding of the "one baptism." Bruner's *Theology of the Holy Spirit* is dedicated to establishing this very point. The "whole teaching of Acts," he says, shows us that "Christian baptism . . . is spiritual baptism. There is only *one* baptism (***Eph. 4:5***)" (***Holy Spirit,*** **170**). The apostles learned from the baptism of Jesus that "the baptism with the Holy Spirit and baptism . . . belonged together in such a way as to form the 'one baptism' of the church," as in ***Ephesians 4:5*** (**ibid., 193-194**). ***John 3:5***, he says, shows us that "spiritually a man is born only once and that 'of water and the Spirit.' That is why baptism[8] is the baptism of the Holy Spirit" (**ibid., 257-258**).

Lard says, "At the instant when the body is immersed in water, . . . the immersion of the human Spirit takes place in the Holy Spirit. The inner man is then immersed as well as the outer, that in Spirit, this in water" (**"Baptism," 279**). Boatman says that in ***Ephesians 4:5*** we have "not water baptism only, nor Holy Spirit baptism only." The water and the Spirit, as in ***John 3:5***, "are two sides, the outward and inward facets, of the *one* baptism" (**109**). "The baptism of the Holy Spirit is the Divine side of the one baptism into the one body" (**ibid., 113**). Referring to ***John 3:5***, Jacoby says,

> We understand that we are born of water and Spirit. We understand that water and spirit are two elements of one birth. We understand that birth of water refers to baptism in water. Isn't it odd that we should not see that birth of the Spirit refers to baptism in the Spirit? Understanding that we are all baptized in the Spirit when we are baptized into Christ is not only the most natural and consistent reading of all the passages on Spirit baptism; it is also the easiest view to defend. (**208**)

Here is a main theme in William Jones's email messages: "The Christian has in reality been baptized in water and Spirit (***Jn 3:5***) which is the ONE baptism of ***Eph. 4:5***. There is an outward (water) side and an inward (Spirit) side to the ONE baptism" (**e-mail, 9/7/05**).

My conclusion is that we must stop dividing the one baptism into two events; it is one event with two distinct aspects. Also, we must stop dividing the biblical texts about baptism into two separate lists, i.e., one with references to water baptism and the other with refer-

[8]When Bruner says "Christian baptism" and just "baptism," he is referring to *water* baptism.

ences to Spirit baptism. There is only one Christian baptism. Whenever baptism is mentioned in the NT in the context of the church, it is *water* baptism; and it is also *Spirit* baptism.

We must stop dividing the one baptism into two events; it is one event with two distinct aspects.

CONCLUSION

In some spheres of Christendom there is a reluctance to deal openly with the subject of baptism in the Holy Spirit. One reason is that the concept has been viewed as inseparably associated with miraculous gifts such as tongue-speaking (**R.E.O. White, 121**). Those with a cessationist approach to such gifts relegate Holy Spirit baptism to the shadows of ancient history and look suspiciously upon anyone who speaks of it as an ongoing blessing for all Christians. Roger Thomas observes, "The phrase 'baptism of the Holy Spirit' has been used so vigorously by Pentecostals and similar religious groups that non-Pentecostals are almost embarrassed to use the words. Worse yet, when we do use the phrase, we assume the Pentecostal definition without ever considering the fact that the New Testament writers may have an entirely different definition in mind" (**"Baptized," 7**). Or as William Jones says, "There has been a neglect of teaching about the baptism of the Holy Spirit because of the fear of being associated with Neo-Pentecostalism and the Charismatic Movement" (**email, 7/16/05**).

This suspicion and fear can exist only where there is a misunderstanding of the true nature of baptism in the Spirit. When we see that being baptized in the Spirit is *not* being overwhelmed with miracle-giving power, but rather is the glorious bestowing of the Holy Spirit so that He may regenerate and indwell us, it should become a topic that we love to contemplate upon and preach about. Stott's observation is appropriate:

> In the light of this biblical testimony it seems to me clear that the "baptism" of the Spirit is the same as the promise or gift of the Spirit and is as much an integral part of the gospel of salvation as is the remission of sins. . . . What a truncated gospel we preach if we proclaim the one without the other! And what a glorious gospel we have to share when we are true to Scripture! (***Baptism*, 25-26**)

CHAPTER NINE

THE WORK OF THE HOLY SPIRIT AFTER CONVERSION: SANCTIFICATION

In this book I am using the word "conversion" to represent the specific moment when a lost person becomes saved, when the sinner is transferred from Satan's "domain of darkness" into the kingdom of Jesus Christ (***Col 1:13***). We have discussed how the Holy Spirit works upon the heart of a sinner prior to this moment, with the purpose of leading him to faith and repentance. We have seen that He accomplishes this mainly through the indirect influence of the Word of God. We have also discussed how the Spirit works upon the sinner's heart in the very moment of conversion, with the purpose of bringing about a literal, metaphysical change therein. We have seen that He accomplishes this during Christian baptism through a direct work upon the heart called (among other things) regeneration, resurrection from the dead, being born again, and baptism in the Holy Spirit.

This event of regeneration is a marvelous supernatural act of the Spirit in which the old self dies and is buried with Jesus, and a new self is brought to life (***Rom 6:1-6***). This does not mean, however, that the Spirit's saving activity is now completed within the life of the individual. Though the sinner has been raised up from spiritual death, he is still weak and must be nursed back to health. Though he has been born again, he is still an infant and must be nurtured to maturity. He is still susceptible to the lusts of the flesh, and is now all the more the target of Satan's temptations and wiles. Candlish puts the problem well:

> Yet his renewal is not complete in any part. The faith of the Christian, though real and sincere, is not perfect at first, but often mingled and interrupted with distrust; his love, though genuine, may not be strong enough to encounter hardships or temptations: in a word, though he has a germ of spiritual life implanted within him, which in principle is higher than anything of which unrenewed men partake, he is still beset with allurements to sin, and possessed with tendencies or habits of yielding to these allurements. He really loves God and hates sin; that is the ruling principle of his soul: but that does not remove all possibility of sin, it does not make the pleasures of sin less attractive to his senses, or the self-denial that God requires less painful to flesh and blood: it does not destroy the power of habit which may have been contracted by former acts of self-indulgence; nor does it obviate the possibility of missing the path of duty through mistake or heedlessness. Such is the state in which the New Testament describes the converts to Christianity as being, with their hearts filled with a new affection, love to God and Christ, yet prone to many sins, sometimes of a gross and shocking nature, and needing to have the most plain moral duties enforced on them. The spirit is willing, but the flesh is weak; nay, the flesh lusteth against the spirit. **(90)**

"The faith of the Christian, though real and sincere, is not perfect at first."

It is certainly true that, because of the Spirit's work of regeneration, we as Christians now have a renewed inner strength to resist such lusts and temptations, and to work toward complete spiritual healing and maturity. God knows, however, that even though we have been regenerated and renewed, we are not able to achieve this healing and maturity through our own strength. This is why the Holy Spirit remains with us and within us, namely, to continue the saving process for which regeneration was merely the beginning. This is usually called *sanctification*, a process in which we must participate through our own decision and effort, but which can actually succeed only insofar as we allow the Spirit's moral power to work within us.

We cannot achieve the desired healing and maturity through our own strength, without the Holy Spirit with us and within us.

The purpose of this chapter is to explain as far as possible the biblical teaching concerning this sanctifying work of the Holy Spirit.

THE INDWELLING OF THE HOLY SPIRIT

To sinners who respond to the gospel call to repent and be baptized, God makes this promise: *"You will receive the gift of the Holy Spirit"* (**Acts 2:38**). Though some have suggested that we may take this to mean that the Holy Spirit is the giver and salvation is the gift (e.g., **John Morrison, Indwelling, 9**), this is true neither to the context nor to NT teaching as a whole. The Spirit Himself is the gift. ***Acts 5:32*** says unequivocally that God has given the Holy Spirit to those who obey Him; ***Romans 5:5*** speaks of *"the Holy Spirit who was given to us."* **Galatians 3:5** says that God *"provides you with the Spirit."* The word translated "provides" is *epichoregeo*, a word in which, says Barclay, the "predominant note is generosity, lavishness, and abundance" (***Promise*, 64**). In other words, God not only *gives* us the Spirit; He *lavishes* the Spirit upon us.

Though the book of Acts does not go into this detail, the rest of the NT makes it clear that, when we receive the gift of the Holy Spirit, He enters into our hearts and bodies, and takes up residence and dwells within us. Thus we speak of the *indwelling* of the Holy Spirit.

THE REALITY OF THE SPIRIT'S INDWELLING

The Bible speaks abundantly and clearly about the fact of the

Spirit's indwelling, first of all as a subject of prophecy. Speaking through Ezekiel God promises the heart-renewing work of regeneration: *"Moreover, I will give you a new heart and put a new spirit within you; and I will remove the heart of stone from your flesh and give you a heart of flesh"* (***Eze 36:26***). Then He says specifically, *"I will put My Spirit within you"* (***Eze 36:27***). Summarizing the main point of several OT prophecies and speaking of Pentecost, Jesus promises, *"If anyone is thirsty, let him come to Me and drink. He who believes in Me, as the Scripture said, 'From his innermost being will flow rivers of living water'"* (***Jn 7:37-38***). John explains, *"But this He spoke of the Spirit, whom those who believed in Him were to receive"* (***Jn 7:39***). "From his innermost being" is literally "out of his belly," which graphically locates the Spirit within the believer's body. This is consistent with Paul's teaching *"that your body is a temple of the Holy Spirit who is in you, whom you have from God"* (***1Cor 6:19***).

Paul uses the language of indwelling several times. In ***Romans 8:9-11*** he says that certain things are true *"if indeed the Spirit of God dwells in you,"* or *"if the Spirit of Him who raised Jesus from the dead dwells in you."* If He does—and of course He does if you are a believer—then *"He who raised Christ Jesus from the dead will also give life to your mortal bodies through His Spirit who dwells in you."* In ***2 Timothy 1:14*** Paul speaks of *"the Holy Spirit who dwells in us."* He also says that *"God has sent forth the Spirit of His Son into [eis] our hearts"* (***Gal 4:6***), and that *"God gave us the Spirit in [en] our hearts"* (***2Cor 1:22***). ***Hebrews 6:4*** speaks of those who *"have been made partakers of the Holy Spirit."* See also ***1 John 3:24***.

The verbs Paul uses in ***Romans 8:9-11*** and ***2 Timothy 1:14*** are *oikeo*, "to dwell," and *enoikeo*, "to dwell in." These are related to the noun *oikos*, which means "house, dwelling place." These verbs imply not a temporary, transient visit, but a permanent settling down. When the Spirit enters into us, He "unpacks His bags," as it were, and becomes a permanent resident. He moves in and makes Himself at home within us. That the body is called His "temple" is an indication of the Spirit's divine nature, since a temple is typically regarded as a dwelling place for deity (***1Kgs 8:10-11***; ***Eph***

This "dwelling" is not a temporary, transient visit, but a permanent settling down.

2:22). "And when the Holy Ghost is thought of as dwelling within us as in a temple, there is the thought that He has not come as it were in passing, but that He has chosen to make His habitation with us" (**Morris, *Spirit*, 74**).

In view of the majesty and awesomeness of God's presence in the tabernacle and temple in OT times (see ***Ex 40:34-38***), it is an absolutely amazing thing to think that our bodies—the body of every individual Christian—are dwelling places for God the Spirit! As Donald Williams says, when Paul said "that we are temples of God and the Spirit dwells in us, he was making the most profound statement imaginable about our access to God and the way we relate to Him" (**189-190**).

It is absolutely amazing to think that our bodies are dwelling places for God.

The Nature of the Spirit's Indwelling

It is easy to picture a human being living in a house, but trying to visualize the Holy Spirit living within our bodies is quite difficult. This is because the concept of the Spirit's indwelling our bodies is of course a metaphor, since our bodies are not literal temples or houses with walls, floors, rooms, or doors. Exactly what does it mean, then, to say that the Holy Spirit dwells within us?

Within the Restoration Movement there has been considerable controversy over how to answer this question. The main issue is whether to take the language of indwelling literally or figuratively. I have just pointed out that there is surely a sense in which the language is metaphorical, insofar as it represents the Holy Spirit as living in our bodies as a person might live in a house. But the present question is something very different from this, namely, whether the Spirit's *presence as such* is literal or figurative. That is, is the Spirit Himself literally present within our bodies, or is He "present" within us only in the sense that His Word or His power or His influence is working within us?

In Restoration circles both views of "the indwelling of the Holy Spirit" have been defended. As Lard explains these views in his 1864 essay on "Spiritual Influence," the first view is "that we are to take the clause literally; and hence to hold that the Holy Spirit actually and literally dwells in Christians." The opposing theory is "that we are to take the clause not literally but figuratively; and hence to hold that the Holy Spirit dwells in Christians not actually and literally but representatively or through the truth" (**236**).

A Figurative Indwelling

The latter view is as Lard indicates, namely, that the Spirit "dwells" within a person only insofar as and in the sense that the truth of Spirit-inspired Scripture has been received and believed with one's mind and accepted into one's heart. To be sure, there is such a thing as having the Word of God abiding within the heart. As David said, *"I have hidden your word in my heart that I might not sin against you"* (***Ps 119:11***, NIV). Paul exhorts us, *"Let the word of Christ richly dwell within you"* (***Col 3:16***). Earlier in this book (pp. 82-85) I have argued that "the anointing" which abides in us (***1Jn 2:20,27***) is the Word of God (***1Jn 2:24***). The question here, however, is whether the indwelling of the Holy Spirit is just another way of describing this heartfelt faith in and commitment to the truth of God's Word.

This is what some were arguing in Lard's day, and Lard is very eager to explain what this view implies: "When it is said that the Holy Spirit dwells in Christians not actually and literally, but merely through the truth or representatively, the implication clearly is, *that the Spirit itself* [*sic*] *does not dwell in them at all*. On the contrary, *the truth only* dwells in them, and this stands for or is in the place of the Spirit. This unquestionably is the meaning of the language" (**Influence, 236**).

This view was defended by G.W. Longan in the 1879 *Symposium on the Holy Spirit*. Longan first notes the literal view, then describes and espouses the "metonymical" view, i.e., the view that says that "the indwelling of the Spirit" is a metonymy, or a figure of speech in which one object is used to represent another to which it is related (like "drinking the *cup*, ***1Cor 11:26***). The latter is "a presence of power, of influence." The Spirit is said to be present in Christians "because his life-giving power is ever active in them" (**62**). Since this power or influence is really the power of gospel truth as believed and appropriated by the soul, we can say that the Spirit's indwelling is in fact "the unfailing presence in the soul of God's holy truth" (**63-64**). Following

Alexander Campbell, Longan ... ay the divine Spirit can impact the ... mediated by truth" (75-7...

Mor... view in a 1971 arti... 's indwelling, he sa... er of the Word of G... entance, then the W... live a Christian lif... literal indwelling is ... ting. . . . I find no re... Holy Spirit can any b... ng me than He can ... is expressed by Ron... od is to have the word of ... when His word dwells in us richly i... Him abiding in us." This answers the question, ... be filled with the Spirit?" (13).

A Literal Indwelling

The other view, which I accept, is that the Holy Spirit does actually, literally, and personally indwell the immersed believer. The main reason why so many have been opposed to this idea, I believe, is their unwarranted fear of any view that implies or involves a direct, immediate influence of God's Spirit upon the human spirit, or in Longan's words, "the notion of an influence by direct, or naked impact" (75). I have already shown, in the discussion of regeneration, that such direct influence is an essential aspect of the Spirit's saving work, and that it is wrong to equate all notions of direct influence with Calvinistic irresistible grace. Thus I can see no reason to interpret the mode of the Spirit's indwelling in a figurative sense. He does, Himself, live within our very hearts and bodies.

This is the view defended by Lard. He argues that there is simply no reason to take the language of indwelling figuratively. The biblical affirmations are not qualified, and there are no contextual or theological reasons why it cannot be taken literally. "I hence decide that

There is simply no reason to take the language of indwelling figuratively.

the clause, *'dwells in you,'* is to be taken in its ordinary literal sense. . . . Therefore that the Holy Spirit actually and literally dwells in Christians is indisputably affirmed in the word of God; and hence cannot be rejected" (**Influence, 236-237**).

In the *Symposium on the Holy Spirit* the same view is argued by Elder T. Munnell. He shows that it is not inherently impossible for God's Spirit to directly impact the human spirit, since this happens in divine inspiration and some miracles (**83ff.**) There is no reason, then, to deny that the Spirit can impart moral powers directly to the soul (**89**). Munnell concludes that the gift of the Holy Spirit promised by Peter on Pentecost must be the Holy Spirit Himself. "When Peter promised them the gift of the Holy Spirit, did he mean nothing but the moral effect of the Word in their minds? This will not do" (**89-90**). Munnell asks again if the indwelling of the Spirit mentioned in ***Romans 8:9-11*** is simply "the moral effect of the Word? No, for it is the same Spirit that is to 'quicken your mortal bodies.'" Surely this cannot be done by anything less than the Spirit Himself (**91**). If everything the NT says the Spirit does for the Christian is "all done by the *Word* alone," then "the language of the New Testament would seem rather misleading" (**93**).

This view has been widely held in recent times. James Bales agrees with Lard and affirms, "Our conclusion is that in some sense and in some way the Holy Spirit dwells in us" (**14**). H. Leo Boles refers to "the gross error . . . that the indwelling of the Holy Spirit is nothing more than the presence of the word of God in the mind or memory of the Christian. . . . The New Testament abundantly teaches that Christians have the Holy Spirit" (**205**). Douglas Jacoby likewise rejects the view that "the Spirit works in us only through his representative, the Word." The "natural reading" of verses such as ***Acts 2:38*** and ***Acts 5:32*** "is not that God has given us his representative but his actual presence" (**220-221**).

We should note that the NT affirms also that both God the Father and God the Son are present in believers: *"Jesus answered and said to him, 'If anyone loves Me, he will keep My word; and My Father will love him, and We will come to him and make Our abode with him'"* (***Jn 14:23***). Christ is in us (***Rom 8:10***; ***Gal 2:20***; ***Eph 3:17***; ***Col 1:27***), and God is in us (***1Jn 4:12,15***). Some say the Father and Son dwell in us only through their representative, the Holy Spirit. Boles says, "Neither God nor Christ dwells personally in us." Christ "dwells in us through His representative. The Holy Spirit represents God and Christ on the earth. When the Holy Spirit dwells in Christians, God and Christ dwell in them" (207). Lard says, "The Spirit dwells literally in us, Christ, by the Spirit" (***Romans*, 258**). It seems rather inconsistent, though, to insist that the same sort of language must apply literally to the Spirit but only representatively to the Father and the Son. In any case, I believe what Edwin Palmer says is correct, that even if the Father and the Son do dwell in us personally, sanctification is still primarily and chiefly the work of the Holy Spirit (91). Our further discussion in this chapter will show this to be the case.

Someone may ask, exactly in what manner does the Holy Spirit dwell within the bodies of Christians? Perhaps the easiest part of the answer is to name the ways the Spirit does *not* live within us. His is not a visible presence, unlike the theophany of God's glory within the OT temple. Nor is His indwelling just the result of divine omnipresence, which is God's universal ontological presence to every point of created space, including the bodies of all human beings (see **Cottrell, *Creator*, 267-273**). Also, the Spirit's indwelling is not like the incarnation of God the Son in the person of Jesus of Nazareth, where the divine and human natures were united into a single person or center of consciousness. Nor should the Spirit's indwelling be associated in any way with the pagan notion of a divine spark that is naturally present within all human beings. Finally, the Spirit's presence within the Christian is qualitatively different from the way a demonic spirit may enter into and become spatially present within a person's body.

In what manner does the Holy Spirit dwell within the bodies of Christians?

Can we then say anything *positive* about how the Spirit indwells? Probably not. As A.B. Jones says, "It is impossible for us to understand just how the Holy Spirit 'dwells' in us. Nor is it a matter of vital importance that we should understand this" (263). Most agree that we cannot explain the mechanics of the indwelling. In fact, as Boles says, we cannot even explain how *our own* spirits dwell in our bodies. Thus we must be willing to accept an element of mystery here, being content to know *that* He dwells in Christians (206), and also *why* He dwells in us—namely, for our sanctification. When we deny the fact of His presence and thus the accompanying purpose of it, we are seriously impoverished in our Christian lives. We will then understand the great feeling with which Lard declares, "O! deliver me from the cold material philosophy which denies that God has placed within me a comforter, a strengthener. I cling to the belief as I do to the shreds that knit my heart together" (**Influence, 241**).

How Do We Know?

A related question is this: how do we *know* that the Holy Spirit dwells within us? Some have suggested that if the Spirit Himself were actually present within us, there would have to be some kind of perceptible signs, some sort of bodily sensations of which we should be conscious. This was Longan's contention: "If the presence of the Spirit in Christians is literal, substantive, personal, . . . is it, as such, a fact of consciousness? Can the soul of the saint turn its gaze in upon itself, and perceive the reality of this presence? Certainly, if there be such a presence, it would appear that there ought to be some mode of cognition, whereby one may become assured of the fact" (**66**). He asks, "But if I admit a direct influence, on what tenable ground can I deny some form of immediate cognition?" (**68**). Guy Woods (**2**) likewise questions whether one could have the actual presence of the Spirit without some "tangible evidence" of it: "Did we know the moment the gift came and were we conscious of the reception? Who will dare say yes? Who can honestly and intelligently confess to a consciousness of its abiding presence?—If one can have it and never know it, of what use is it?" (cited in **Garth Black, 78**).

Two things may be said in reply. First, the very idea that the Spirit's presence would have to be accompanied by perceptible signs or evidence is contrary to the very nature of spiritual being, especially the Divine Spirit. Spiritual essence simply does not interact with material essence in this way, as evidenced by the fact that we have no perceivable sensations of the presence of our own spirits within our bodies. Munnell comments, "It is not the province of consciousness to say whether the Spirit's presence in the soul is

The idea that the Spirit's presence would have to be seen is contrary to the nature of spiritual being.

personal or not" (**100**). Lard rightly says, "Surely a literal indwelling is not doubted on the ground that we have no *sensible* evidence of the Spirit's presence. For neither *a priori* nor from the Bible have we any reason to conclude that such evidence would be afforded us. And gratuitously to assume it, and then make the assumption a ground on which to doubt the indwelling, is most unwarrantable indeed" (**Influence, 239**).

Second, subjective feelings and spiritual experiences of all kinds are inherently ambiguous apart from a trustworthy objective framework within which to interpret them. Sometimes our feelings and bodily sensations have a physiological origin. As Longan somewhat humorously remarks, "Atrabilarious Christians have sometimes derived more spiritual advantage from the administration of a good cholagogue than from the most potent doses of mystic theology, and even preachers may have mistaken the exhilarating effect of a fragrant cup of tea for direct spiritual aid in the delivery of a sermon" (**70**).[1] More seriously, Jesus warns that even such objective experiences as prophesying (which includes tongue-speaking) and performing miracles are no sure sign of God's approval and personal salvation (***Mt 7:21-23***).

If our assurance of the presence of the Spirit within us has no experiential basis, *how do* we know that He is there? The answer is quite simple: God says so. "May we . . . learn to believe that the Spirit is in us, children of God, simply because the Bible tells us so" (**Pache, 102**). It is a matter of *believing God's promise.* God promises to give the Holy Spirit to those who obey Him (***Acts 5:32***), i.e., those who obey the gospel instructions concerning how to be saved (e.g., ***Jn 7:38***; ***Acts 2:38***; ***Rom 10:9-10***). If we believe God keeps His promises, then we have all the assurance we need of the Spirit's presence within us. In fact, this is exactly the same way we know our sins are forgiven. Garth Black says it well:

How do we know? God says so.

> The Christian can know that the Holy Spirit dwells within him as certainly as he knows that his sins have been pardoned. He has no "tangible" evidence that he has received the remission of his sins, nor is he actually conscious of his par-

[1]I admit that I had to consult my unabridged dictionary for these words: "atrabilarious" means gloomy, irritable, bad-tempered; a "cholagogue" is something that promotes the flow of bile.

> don, but he knows from the Bible that if he has obeyed God he has received the promise of remission of sins (***Acts 2:38***). In a like manner the Christian knows that if he obeys God he will receive the gift of the Holy Spirit (***Acts 2:38, 5:32***). The indwelling presence of the Holy Spirit is a matter of faith with the Christian just as is the knowledge of his pardon. It is not a matter of "feelings" any more than the knowledge of our being pardoned is based on feelings. The criterion is God's word in both instances, not feelings. If God says that his Spirit dwells within us, then we believe that He does. (**79**)

The Purpose of the Spirit's Indwelling

God has given the Holy Spirit to those who obey Him (***Acts 5:32***); the Holy Spirit personally dwells within us. This is one of the greatest blessings that God reserved for saints of this new age of the Messiah and His kingdom, the church. Surely a gift bestowed upon God's people with such fanfare in its spectacular debut (***Acts 2:1-13***) must be tremendously significant. Thus we must carefully consider the question, for what *purpose* does God give us His indwelling Spirit? Why does the Spirit live within us?

We have said that the two main things the Spirit does for us are these: He gives us *knowledge*, and He gives us *power*. The former He gives to us primarily if not exclusively through the revealed and inspired Word, the Bible. The purpose of His indwelling, then, is not to fill our intellect with more knowledge. The Spirit gives two kinds of power. First of all, He empowers individuals to serve God's purposes and to meet the needs of His people, sometimes with miraculous gifts and sometimes with nonmiraculous gifts. He was doing this long before Pentecost, and He does not need to indwell people in order to give them this kind of power. Thus this cannot be the purpose of His indwelling.

Why does the Spirit live within us? To give us power to be holy.

What remains, then, is the other kind of power which the Spirit can bestow upon us, namely, the empowerment of the will to obey God's commands and to live a holy life. This is the purpose for which the Spirit dwells within us: to fill us with *moral power*, to strengthen our wills so that we may be able both to desire and to do what is right. The name usually given to this work of the Spirit is *sanctification*. As Swete says, "No one term, indeed, so fully covers the effects upon human nature of the presence in it of the Holy Spirit of God as the word 'sanctification'" (**345**).

The term "sanctification" is part of the word family having to do with holiness. Though some disagree, I believe the root idea in this word family is *separation*. The OT word for "holy" (*qadosh*) most likely comes from a word that means "to cut, to divide, to separate." Thus a holy person or thing is one that is separated or set apart from others.

In the NT the main adjective for "holy" is *hagios*. Variations are the verb *hagiazo*, "to make holy, to set apart or consecrate, to sanctify"; and the noun *hagiasmos*, "holiness, sanctification, consecration." Thus sanctification is basically the same concept as holiness. We should also note that the adjective *hagios* is often used as a noun, i.e., "holy one." When used thus of Christians, it is usually translated "saint."

We may identify three main aspects or steps that are involved in the Spirit's sanctifying work: initial sanctification, progressive sanctification, and final sanctification. Others may used different terminology, e.g., "positional sanctification, experimental or progressive sanctification, and ultimate sanctification" (**Walvoord, 210**). There is general agreement on the meaning of the categories, however, at least among non-Wesleyans.

Initial Sanctification

The first aspect is initial or positional sanctification, also called "definitive sanctification" by Donald Williams (**91**). This is the one-time event in which the unsaved person joins the ranks of the saved, the moment in which he is set apart from the world as such, from his old way of life, and from *"this present evil age"* (***Gal 1:4***). Unlike the inward change of regeneration, it is an external or objective change of status or position in relation to God and in relation to the world. It is the formal transfer of the sinner from the domain of darkness into the kingdom of Christ (***Col 1:13***), from the old sinful and condemned creation into the new creation.

Initial sanctification is the one-time event in which the unsaved person joins the ranks of the saved.

This act of initial sanctification is mentioned in a number of texts, including ***1 Corinthians 6:11***: *"Such were some of you; but you were washed, but you were sanctified, but you were justified in the name of the Lord Jesus Christ and in the Spirit of our God."* That Paul is speaking here of the one-time event of initial sanctification is shown by the aorist tense of the verb, representing completed past action. This is not something that happens as the result of our own efforts; it is accomplished through the power of Jesus' name and the power of the Holy Spirit when we surrender our wills to Him in the baptismal washing (see ***Tts 3:5***).

Other texts most likely referring to initial sanctification[2] include ***Acts 20:32***, which refers to *"all those who are sanctified"*; ***Acts 26:18***, where Jesus speaks of *"those who have been sanctified by faith in Me"*; ***Romans 15:16***, where Paul speaks of Gentiles *"sanctified by the Holy Spirit"*; ***1 Corinthians 1:2***, which refers to the church as *"those who have been sanctified in Christ Jesus"*; and ***Hebrews 10:29***, which refers to the blood of Christ by which one is sanctified. The many NT references to Christians as "holy ones" or "saints" also reflect this initial sanctification, e.g., the *"saints in Jerusalem"* (***Acts 9:13***; ***Rom 15:26***), *"the saints in prisons"* (***Acts 26:10***), *"the needs of the saints"* (***Rom 12:13***), and *"all the churches of the saints"* (***1Cor 14:33***). Such "saints" are not just a select group of special Christians who have reached an especially high level of spiritual maturity through *progressive* sanctification; rather, the term describes the objective status of every Christian from the very moment of conversion, as a result of *initial* sanctification. This is the sense in which the word "sanctification" may be defined as "set apart."

Progressive Sanctification

The second aspect of sanctification is called *progressive* sanctification, because it is the ongoing process in which the Christian becomes more and more separated from sin itself. This aspect of sanctification is not an objective change in status or relationships, but a continuing transformation of our inward character and mental attitudes, as well as our outward behavior and conduct. The possibility

[2]Such a judgment is based on the use of the aorist tense, as in ***1Cor 6:11***, or the perfect tense, which represents action terminated in the past but with an effect existing into the present.

basis for this continuing personal change is the Spirit's work of regeneration, in which our souls underwent that singular experience of being raised from spiritual death and being born again. This Spirit-wrought change within our hearts set us free from slavery to sin and liberated our wills to operate as God intended, i.e., to freely choose to love Him and obey His laws. The result of receiving a new heart and of receiving the indwelling of the Spirit, says ***Ezekiel 36:25-27***, is that we are now able to walk in God's statutes and observe His ordinances. In Paul's words, *"We are His workmanship, created in Christ Jesus"* in that regenerating new-creation event, for one purpose: *"for good works"* (***Eph 2:10***). That is, regeneration restores us to a proper working order for the very purpose of making sanctification possible. "The Spirit's work of sanctification is thus the continuance and development of regeneration" (**Candlish, 94**).

Progressive sanctification is the process in which the Christian becomes more separated from sin.

Many Scripture references speak of this progressive sanctification. This is how we *"grow in the grace and knowledge of our Lord and Savior Jesus Christ,"* says ***2 Peter 3:18***, and *"work out [our] own salvation with fear and trembling,"* says ***Philippians 2:12***. In this aspect of sanctification we become more and more like God in righteousness and holiness of truth (***Eph 4:22-24***). Our pattern and goal are God's own ethical holiness, as we are commanded to imitate His perfect moral character: *"But like the Holy One who called you, be holy yourselves also in all your behavior; because it is written, 'You shall be holy, for I am holy'"* (***1Pet 1:15-16***). As Jesus says, *"Therefore you are to be perfect, as your heavenly Father is perfect"* (***Mt 5:48***). Our goal is to *"share His holiness"* (***Heb 12:10***) or to *"become partakers of the divine nature"* (***2Pet 1:4***) in this moral sense. We are to purify ourselves, even as He is pure (***1Jn 3:3***). We must *"present [our] members as slaves to righteousness, resulting in sanctification"* (***Rom 6:19***; see ***v. 22***). We must *"cleanse ourselves of all defilement of flesh and spirit, perfecting holiness in the fear of God"* (***2Cor 7:1***). *"For this is the will of God, your sanctification. . . . For God has not called us for the purpose of impurity, but in sanctification"* (***1Th 4:3,7***).

The fact that most of the passages just cited are exhortations to Christians (who have already been initially sanctified or set apart) shows that this aspect of sanctification is indeed a process and warrants calling it "progressive." This is also seen in Paul's prayer for God to complete the process in ***1 Thessalonians 5:23***, *"Now may the God of peace sanctify you entirely."* It is reflected too in the present participle form of *hagiazo* in **Hebrews 2:11** and ***10:14***, literally, *"the ones being sanctified"* or *"the ones being made holy."* Process is also reflected in the concept of *growth* in ***2 Peter 3:18***.

Final Sanctification

To what goal does progressive sanctification lead? Surely it can be nothing less than perfect holiness or sinless perfection. Paul says in ***Ephesians 5:26-27*** that Christ is now sanctifying the church that He might present her to Himself *"in all her glory, having no spot or wrinkle or any such thing; but that she would be holy and blameless"* (see ***Col 1:22***). We are to be as perfect and as holy as the Father (***Mt 5:48; 1Pet 1:16***), and as pure as Jesus (***1Jn 3:3***).

When will this become a reality? When will the progressive stage of sanctification be completed, and the goal of final sanctification be attained? Some conclude from the fact that we are *commanded* to be perfect (holy, pure) that we can and must achieve such a state in this lifetime. This is doubtful, however. It is true that "ought implies can," but it does not follow that "can implies will."

When will progressive sanctification be succeeded by final sanctification?

A major factor in reaching a decision on this issue is whether Paul in ***Romans 7:14-25*** is speaking of his past or pre-Christian life, or of his present Christian life. Many argue for the former, especially on the basis of Paul's seriously negative self-descriptions: *"sold into bondage to sin"* (***7:14***), *"nothing good dwells in me"* (***7:18***), *"evil is present in me"* (***7:21***), *"prisoner of the law of sin"* (***7:23***), and *"wretched man"* (***7:24***). Could such things apply to Paul the Christian? We cannot rule this out. Such confessions are no worse than Paul's present-tense declaration that *"I am the worst"* of sinners (***1Tm 1:15***, NIV).

Actually there are many solid reasons for taking Paul's testimony in ***Romans 7:14-25*** as referring to his Christian life (see **Cottrell, *Romans*, I:443-444**). First, the major theme of this section of Romans (***chs. 6–8***) has to do with the Christian life. Second, Paul uses the present tense throughout. Third, Paul's strongly positive statements about the law and about his desire to obey it, plus his sorrowful confession of sin and his hatred of it, are incompatible with a non-Christian's state of mind. Fourth, the spiritual struggle pictured here exists only in a Christian's heart and life. Fifth, the longing for deliverance (***7:24***) suggests the tender heart of a Christian. Sixth, the assurance of triumph (*7:25*) belongs only to a Christian. Last, the order of the sentences in ***verse 25*** is incompatible with a non-Christian's experience; i.e., even after resting his soul on Christ's salvation, Paul once again laments his conflict with sin.

This and Paul's other teaching in ***Romans 6–8*** strongly supports the probability that the process of sanctification will not be completed—that we will not be perfectly holy and pure—until our spirits have been set free from this old, sin-ridden body at death. In ***Hebrews 12:23*** the phrase *"the spirits of the righteous made perfect"* probably refers to Christians who have died and who are presently existing only as spirits and who are still awaiting the resurrection of their new bodies. These are the ones, says Hebrews, who have been "made perfect." An eschatological completion of the sanctification process is also seen in ***1 Thessalonians 3:13***, which says that our Lord is seeking to *"establish [our] hearts without blame in holiness before our God and Father at the coming of our Lord Jesus with all His saints."* This is when He will present the church to Himself *"in all her glory, having no spot or wrinkle"* (***Eph 5:27***).

This final sanctification is not something we will accomplish for ourselves, nor even something in which we may cooperate. Our participation in sanctification is limited to the middle or progressive stage; the initial sanctification is wholly a divine act, as is the final sanctification. However far along we may be in the process of maturing toward the goal of perfection, at the moment of death, God completes the process for us. He not only supernaturally brings our spirits to a state of perfect holiness, but also on the day of resurrection gives us new bodies unstained by sin. The latter is specifically stated to be the work of the Holy Spirit (***Rom 8:11***), and the former probably is as well. Final sanctification is

Final sanctification is not something we accomplish for ourselves, nor even in which we may cooperate.

thus our confident expectation. As Kuyper says, "That which belongs to Jesus enters heaven perfectly holy. The slightest lack would indicate something internally sinful; would annihilate . . . the positive declaration of Scripture, that nothing that defiles shall enter the gates of the city. Hence it is the unalterable rule of sanctification that every redeemed soul entering heaven is perfectly sanctified" (***450***).

The Spirit as Seal and Pledge

In the New Testament two rather vivid images are applied to the Holy Spirit in reference to His indwelling presence within Christians, namely, the Spirit as a *seal* and the Spirit as a *pledge*. Here are the references: *"Now He who establishes us with you in Christ and anointed us is God, who also sealed us and gave us the Spirit in our hearts as a pledge"* (***2Cor 1:21-22***). *"Now He who prepared us for this very purpose is God, who gave to us the Spirit as a pledge"* (***2Cor 5:5***). *"In Him, you also, after listening to the message of truth, the gospel of your salvation—having also believed, you were sealed in Him with the Holy Spirit of promise, who is given as a pledge of our inheritance, with a view to the redemption of God's own possession, to the praise of His glory"* (***Eph 1:13-14***). *"Do not grieve the Holy Spirit of God, by whom you were sealed for the day of redemption"* (***Eph 4:30***).

The Spirit's function as seal and as pledge are related, and together pertain to our final sanctification.

In my judgment, based on these texts, the Spirit's function as a seal and His function as a pledge are related, and together they are related to the subject of our final sanctification.

The three references to the Spirit's role in our sealing are ***2 Corinthians 1:22***; ***Ephesians 1:13***; and ***Ephesians 4:30***. The verb used is *sphragizo*. In ancient times it referred to the act of physically placing one's unique mark or seal upon an object or document in order to tie that object or document legally to the owner of the seal. The seal itself (*sphragis*) was an image carved in relief on a small object, such as a stone that could be mounted in a signet ring; the act of sealing involved the pressing of that image into soft clay or wax attached to the object or document to be "sealed." Modern counterparts include a branding iron, a notary public's official stamping instrument, a copyright, and even a person's signature.

Such an act of sealing could accomplish several purposes. It might serve as an official mark that would "seal up" something that could be closed, such as a tomb (***Mt 27:66***) or a scroll (***Rev 5:1***). The seal did not make an object physically impenetrable, but was a legal barrier to tampering. A seal could also serve as a mark of genuineness to guarantee authenticity or legal validity, similar to a signature on a check or document, or a notary's seal. Also, a seal could function as a simple mark of ownership, as when a rancher brands a calf to proclaim, "This one belongs to me!"

The Holy Spirit is likewise three times described as a pledge (***2Cor 1:22; 5:5; Eph 1:14***). The Greek word is *arrabon,* a commercial term referring to the earnest money or down payment or deposit that serves to guarantee a purchaser's sincere intention of paying the full amount. It is the first installment, to be followed by full payment.

How do these concepts apply to the Holy Spirit? They both have to do with the fact that when God saves us from our sins, He makes us a part of His own family and guarantees that we will one day share in the full inheritance of eternal glory (***Rom 8:14-17; Gal 4:1-7***). That we are *sealed* with the Spirit means that the Holy Spirit within us is a *mark of ownership,* identifying us as a true member of God's redeemed family. The Spirit is thus like a family crest or coat of arms, marking us as children of God. The Spirit's presence is God's testimony, "This one belongs to me!"

The Spirit's presence is God's testimony, "This one belongs to me!"

This of course is a source of great blessings for us in this present life, but the greatest benefit of being a member of God's family is the promise of our future inheritance. The gift of the Holy Spirit is an *arrabon* or pledge in the sense that God's giving Him to us is His guarantee that we will one day receive all the blessings of heaven. The Spirit is the down payment or "earnest money," giving us the assurance of eternal life. Being *"partakers of the Holy Spirit,"* we have tasted *"the powers of the age to come"* (***Heb 6:4-5***). This inheritance includes not just the grand environment of the new heavens and new earth, and not just the glorified resurrection body, but above all else—*final sanctification,* which is the ultimate and most satisfying gift of redemption. The Spirit's sanctifying presence within us now is but a foretaste of that "glory divine"!

This close connection between the Spirit as a seal and as a pledge, and the further connection with our final sanctification, are clear from the contexts of the passages in ***2 Corinthians*** and ***Ephesians*** that use these images. In ***2 Corinthians 1:22***, being sealed and receiving the Spirit as a pledge are combined into a single act, giving us assurance that the many promises of God (***2Cor 1:20***) will be fulfilled. ***Second Corinthians 5:5*** specifically identifies the Spirit as a pledge that we will one day receive a new resurrection body. In ***Ephesians 1:13-14*** the seal and the pledge are again related. The "Holy Spirit of promise" is God's seal upon us, and thus is "a pledge of our inheritance, with a view to the redemption of God's own possession." That is to say, the Spirit marks us as God's possession and therefore as God's heirs. ***Ephesians 4:30*** repeats the idea that the Spirit seals us *"for the day of redemption."*

Romans 8:23 adds a third image to the mix; here the Spirit is described as *"the first fruits,"* guaranteeing *"the redemption of our body"* (see ***Rom 8:11***), which will be the climactic event of our final sanctification.

THE SPIRIT'S ROLE IN SANCTIFICATION

For the rest of this chapter our focus is on progressive sanctification, and the term will be used in that sense unless noted. The essence of such sanctification is the ongoing development of holy character and conduct as taught and commanded by the Word of God. This includes conquering sin and eradicating it from one's life, and positive growth in all moral virtues. It is equivalent to obeying God's will and doing good works (***Eph 2:10***).

This sanctification is the ongoing development of holy character as commanded by the Word of God.

Such holy living is not optional for Christians; it is commanded in many different ways. God's Word exhorts us to *"be holy"* (***1Pet 1:15***), to *"be perfect"* (***Mt 5:48***), to grow in grace (***2Pet 3:18***), and to work out our salvation (***Php 2:12***). Such exhortations are abundant, e.g., *"Do not let sin reign in your mortal body"* (***Rom 6:12***). *"Abstain from every form of evil"* (***1Th 5:22***). *"Submit therefore to God. Resist the devil*

. . . . *Cleanse your hands, you sinners"* (**Jas 4:7-8**). *"Abhor what is evil; cling to what is good"* (**Rom 12:9**). *"Be imitators of God"* (**Eph 5:1**). *"Glorify God in your body"* (**1Cor 6:20**). *"Seek first His kingdom and His righteousness"* (**Mt 6:33**).

The fact that all these exhortations are addressed to us in the form of commandments shows that we not only have an *obligation* to obey them, but that we also have the free-will *ability* to do so. Sanctification is thus our responsibility; it will happen only as a result of our own decision and effort.

But this is not the whole story. Though God lays the responsibility for sanctification upon us, He does not leave us to accomplish it through our sin-weakened ability alone. The whole point of the second part of the double cure of salvation—regeneration and sanctification—is to give us power from outside ourselves to conquer sin and be holy as God is holy. The power for sanctification thus comes from God, in particular God the Holy Spirit. We are saved, says Paul, *"through sanctification by the Spirit"* (**2Th 2:13**). We have been chosen *"according to the foreknowledge of God the Father, by the sanctifying work of the Spirit"* (**1Pet 1:2**). As A.B. Jones says, "The Holy Spirit is an essential factor in separating a man from sin and making him holy in heart and in life" (**292**).

God lays responsibility for sanctification upon us but does not leave us to do it through our ability alone.

How does the Spirit accomplish this? Does He do it by working directly upon the Christian's heart, or by working upon it only indirectly through the influence of the Word? In my judgment, one of the greatest and most prevalent errors concerning the Spirit's work is to think that we must choose one or the other of these two modes: *either* the Spirit works indirectly, *or* He works directly. As I see it, we are being presented here with what is known as a *false choice*.[3] In reality it is not a matter of either/or; it is both/and: the Spirit works upon our hearts *both* directly *and* indirectly.

As we have seen, prior to our conversion the Spirit acted indirectly upon our hearts through the Word of God, in order to lead us to

[3]Advocates of this fallacy include especially Alexander Campbell and those influenced by him on this matter, such as G.W. Longan. For a more recent example see Harold Ford, "Controversy." For an explanation of Campbell's view see C.E. Allen, "Holy Spirit."

faith and repentance. Then in the moment of conversion itself, He acted directly upon our hearts in the work of regeneration. Now, after conversion, in the course of the Christian life, the Spirit still works upon our hearts in *both* ways. He continues to work indirectly through His inspired Word; but He also works directly upon our wills, giving us the moral power to obey God's commands. The latter is the specific purpose of His indwelling presence.

The Spirit Sanctifies through the Word of God

The first way the Spirit operates in the process of sanctification is through the teaching of the Word of God. Whatever influence the Word has upon our hearts and minds is indirectly the work of the Spirit, of course, since its very existence is due to His works of revelation and inspiration. Just as He works through the Word upon the hearts of sinners to lead them to faith and repentance, so also He works through the Word on the hearts of Christians to teach them the will of God and to motivate them to obey it. This is in answer to Jesus' prayer, *"Sanctify them in the truth; Your word is truth"* (***Jn 17:17***).

Sanctification involves our obligation to become holy even as God Himself is holy (***1Pet 1:15-16***). This means that the norm and goal for sanctification are nothing less than the very nature of God. The more we know about the moral nature of God, the more we will know what we, as creatures made in His image, are supposed to be like.

Our obligation is to become holy even as God Himself is holy.

Whence comes this knowledge? It comes primarily from the Spirit-inspired Word of God. The Word teaches us about God's moral character, which we are to imitate. Probably the most precise and complete knowledge of God's moral nature comes from the law He has revealed to us. The commandments of the law, i.e., the law code that constitutes the moral law of God, are basically God's holiness or His perfect moral character put into verbal form. The moral law is thus the mirror or transcript of divine holiness. This is why the moral law is the primary source of our knowledge of His holiness and therefore the most basic norm for our own holiness or sanctification. In order to imitate God's holiness, we must look to His law and obey His law.

To a degree the content of this law is written on every heart (***Rom 2:15***), but our clearest knowledge of it comes through the Spirit-inspired Word. Thus the written Word of God provides us with the knowledge we need as to the kind of life God wants us to live. Indeed, this is one of the very purposes for which God has given us the Bible. As Paul says, Scripture is *"profitable for teaching, for reproof, for correction, for training in righteousness"* (***2Tm 3:16***). As David said, *"Your word is a lamp to my feet and a light to my path"* (***Ps 119:105***). Thus on a practical level the Bible is our norm for sanctification, our "only rule of faith and practice."

At this point it becomes clear that sanctification is not something the Holy Spirit does or can do unilaterally, without our participation and cooperation. The Word of God is absolutely essential for sanctification, but it will do us no good at all if we do not study it and meditate upon its application to our lives. Thus, as Candlish says, "The Word of God must be the constant study of the believer," since "it is a means that the Holy Spirit uses for his sanctification" (**92**). Edwin Palmer adds, "How can we expect to be holy and to do God's will if we neglect the God-given means of grace and rarely read the only Book which shows us what holiness is?" (**98**).

"The Word of God must be the constant study of the believer."

The Indwelling Spirit Gives Us Power to Obey

One thing that the Holy Spirit does *not* do as a result of His indwelling is to give us more *knowledge*, in addition to what we already have in the Bible. He is not present within us for cognitive purposes, i.e., in order to affect our minds or intellects. To be *"led by the Spirit"* does not mean that He speaks somehow on either a conscious or subconscious level, in order to "tell us what to do" or to show us God's will. We must resist the temptation to apply Jesus' private teaching to His apostles in ***John 14–16*** to all Christians, with the expectation that the indwelling Spirit will guide us into all truth (***Jn 16:13***). Candlish, e.g., is guilty of this error, and concludes that such texts say that the Spirit teaches us via "a direct communication to our souls" (**98**). Such inward illumination, he says, "is just the work wherein our sanctification consists" (**103**).

I strongly disagree with this, and seriously suggest that the key word in reference to the indwelling Spirit's sanctifying work is *not knowledge, but power*. This is the second way the Spirit operates in the process of sanctification, i.e., by empowering *our* spirits to overcome sin and to live in obedience to the will of God. In so doing the Spirit works directly upon the Christian's heart in a way that is similar to His work of regeneration. When the Spirit regenerates and renews a sinner, He endows him with new spiritual life and sets in motion the process of spiritual healing and restoration. In sanctification the Spirit continues to undergird and reinforce our recovering souls, like medicine in a sick body restores the body's own ability to fight the disease and recover its health.

The Spirit operates by empowering our spirits.

Such spiritual empowerment is the direct purpose and result of the indwelling presence of the Spirit. Dwelling within our bodies, He is in constant direct contact with our spirits, providing us with an immediate reservoir of strength for our spiritual battles. If one does not accept the reality of this direct operation of the Spirit, the whole purpose of His indwelling becomes problematic. For anyone to defend the Spirit's literal indwelling, and at the same time to affirm that the Spirit works only indirectly, through the Word (as many do), is quite inconsistent, like having a cause without an effect. The fact is that if the Holy Spirit works only through the Word, there is no necessary rationale for His indwelling.

To say that the Spirit supplies us with power implies that we are in a state of weakness, even after we have been regenerated and have received our initial sanctification. This is in fact the case. Even in our saved state, as long as we are in this world and in these as-yet-unredeemed bodies, we will continue to experience the weakening effects of sin. This is why we need the Spirit's power for sanctification: *"The Spirit helps us in our weakness"* (***Rom 8:26***, NIV). This is a general principle, and applies far beyond the infirmities relating to our prayer life.

This truth is explicitly taught in several NT texts. For example, the sanctifying power of the indwelling Spirit is the substance of Paul's prayer for us in ***Ephesians 3:16***, where he prays that God *"would grant you, according to the riches of His glory, to be strengthened with power through His Spirit in the inner man."* That he is speaking of moral power and not equipping or miraculous power is seen from the reference to the "inner man" (the soul) and from the general subject matter of the epistle.

On the negative side, the Spirit empowers us to fight against sin. ***Romans 8:13*** says that we must be *"putting to death the deeds of the body."* These are the sinful deeds that result from the law of sin that continues to reside in our flesh, in our as-yet-unredeemed bodies (***Rom 6:6***; ***7:18, 23-25***). These sins must be put to death, killed, destroyed, overcome, driven from our lives. How can we do this? Paul specifically says that we can accomplish this *"by the Spirit."* The indwelling Spirit is the key to our victory over sin. On our conscious level we are aggressively putting sin to death, but below the level of our consciousness the Spirit's energizing power is making it possible.

Described in positive terms, sanctification means that we must obey God's commands and work out our salvation in fear and trembling (***Php 2:12***). The overwhelming responsibility to be holy as God is holy predictably fills us with awe and trepidation. What a daunting task! But this is why we cannot stop reading this text at ***verse 12*** but must also read ***verse 13***, *"For it is God who is at work in you, both to will and to work for His good pleasure."* God Himself, in the person of the Holy Spirit, is at work in us, to help us both to *want* to do what is right ("to will") and to help us actually to *do* it ("to work").

From passages such as these, says Lard, "it appears that the work of the Spirit within us consists in *strengthening with might the inner man,* and in *helping our infirmities*. Of all the work we can imagine, this is the most important to us. We need not the Spirit's aid to give us new ideas or teach us new lessons. All we need in this way we abundantly have in the word of God." What we need is strength to do what we already know we should do. "How ready we all are to resolve to do right, yet how unequal to the task of performing" (**Influence, 240**). But this is the very reason God gave us His Spirit: *"The Spirit helps us in our weakness"*!

What we need is strength to do what we already know we should do.

As Swete sums it up, the indwelling Spirit is not just "an aggressive force leading the human spirit against the flesh," but "is also a constructive power which builds up a new life within, cooperating with the spirit of man in the work of restoring human life to the image of God" (**344-345**). "The Holy Spirit builds up the ruins of our spiritual nature, restoring the Divine life in man" (**346**).

These thoughts are awesome indeed: that we have the *Holy Spirit* Himself dwelling in us; and that through Him we have *God's own power* enabling us to be holy, even as God is holy! No wonder we approach the task of sanctification with *"fear and trembling"* (***Php 2:12***)! We must emphasize, though, that all this power is useless unless we exercise our own wills and actively *"pursue . . . sanctification"* (***Heb 12:14***). The power is there, but we must claim it and allow it to work within us. We must pray for its application, as Paul did in ***Ephesians 3:16***. *We* must be *"putting to death the deeds of the body"* (***Rom 8:13***). *"Be holy"* (literally, "become holy") in ***1 Peter 1:15*** is an imperative, a command to be obeyed. We must work out our own salvation as it relates to sanctification (***Php 2:12***). We are not puppets being mechanically controlled by the Spirit.

And yet, we must at the same time acknowledge and remember that we can actually do these things only through the power of the Spirit who dwells within us. *"Work out your salvation,"* yes—but *"it is God who is at work in you"* (***Php 2:12-13***). Put sin to death, yes—but *"by the Spirit"* (***Rom 8:13***). As Leon Morris says, "There is not the slightest doubt that the New Testament requires vigorous effort on the part of the believer. But the point is that this effort is to be made in the strength of the divine Spirit, not in the energy of the flesh" (***Spirit*, 78**).

IMAGES OF SANCTIFICATION

The process of sanctification is pictured in a number of different ways in the NT, e.g., fighting a battle, being led by the Spirit, and producing the Spirit's fruit. Some of these images will now be examined.

Spiritual Warfare

"Spiritual warfare" is a justifiable way of describing the Christian life, given the many biblical references to our responsibility to fight against our spiritual enemies. Paul urged Timothy to *"fight the good fight"* (***1Tm 1:18**, strateuo*), and to *"fight the good fight of faith"* (***1Tm 6:12**, agonizomai*). Paul declared near the end of his life, *"I have fought the good fight"* (***2Tm 4:7**, agonizomai*). The verbs used here could refer to contests of various kinds, including battling against one's enemy in warfare. The Christian's enemies are the world, the flesh, and the devil, all of which seek to overcome us with sin. Only the power of the Holy Spirit can help us to prevail against them.

The Christian's enemies are the world, the flesh, and the devil.

The Holy Spirit against the World

From the most general perspective there are two competing worldviews, and two competing spheres within which one must choose to live. These are the old creation vs. the new creation; or the domain of Satan vs. the kingdom of Christ; or *"this present evil world"* (***Gal 1:4***, KJV) vs. the church of Jesus Christ. In ***Romans 8:2*** Paul characterizes these two ways of life as *"the law of sin and death"* and *"the law of the Spirit of life."* These two "laws" are the two competing systems or world orders, the two rival life paradigms. One is dominated by sin and death, the other is controlled by the Spirit of life. These two systems are in conflict. (See **Cottrell, *Romans*, I:457-459**.) In this section of Romans (***8:1-13***) Paul pictures this conflict as a battle between the flesh and the Spirit.

On a cosmic scale we Christians must be aware that we are fighting against organized opposition and whole systems of thought. These anti-Christian forces are depicted in ***Revelation 13*** as two horrible beasts, one arising from the sea and another from the earth. Of the former it is said that his purpose is *"to make war with the saints"* (***13:7***). This beast represents the enemies of Christianity who oppose it with physical power, e.g., the Roman Empire, totalitarian anti-Christian governments, and Islamic terrorism. The beast from the earth represents all those false religions and philosophies that provide a theoretical basis for the anti-Christian powers, e.g., Marxism, Humanism, evolutionism, and the Islamic religion as such. Christians are constantly doing battle with the "world" in various arenas, such as anti-Christian nations, humanistic classrooms, and hedonistic social circles.

Part of our sanctification is to fight successfully against all such forces of this world. This is what it means to *"contend earnestly for the faith which was once for all handed down to the saints"* (***Jude 3***). Over

Over against all others, the Christian must boldly declare, "JESUS IS LORD!"

against those who say "Caesar is Lord!"—"Darwin is Lord!"—"Allah is Lord!"—"Reason is Lord!"—"Sex is Lord!"—"I am Lord"—or even "Nothing is Lord!"—the Christian must boldly declare, "JESUS IS LORD!" Sometimes it is extremely difficult to stay the course against these opposing powers, and we need the internal power of the Holy Spirit to do so. This is the significance of Paul's statement in ***1 Corinthians 12:3***, *"No one can say 'Jesus is Lord,' except by the Holy Spirit."* Here he is not talking about one's initial confession of faith, but his faithful confession made in the face of persecution and even martyrdom (which I believe to be the context of ***vv. 2-3***). We must trust the power of the Spirit to enable us to "stand up for Jesus" in the face of such enemies.

The Holy Spirit against the Flesh

A major theme in the NT is the antagonism between *sarx* ("flesh") and *pneuma* ("spirit"). ***Romans 8:1-13*** is one long contrast between those who live in and according to the flesh, and those who live in and according to the Spirit. ***Galatians 5:16-26*** is another such passage where the Spirit and the flesh are set against one another. The conflict is specifically stated in ***Galatians 5:17***, *"For the flesh sets its desire against the Spirit, and the Spirit against the flesh; for these are in opposition to one another."*

Most agree that *pneuma* in these texts refers to the Holy Spirit; this is my understanding as well. Most agree that *sarx* in these passages does not refer to the body as such, but to a person's entire being, body and spirit, under the power and control of sin. Pache, for example, says that "the flesh is our whole being, our SELF, all that we are by nature when not in Jesus Christ" (**135**). It is our "sinful nature," as the NIV usually translates it in these texts. This "sinful nature" completely dominated us as sinners, was delivered a death blow at conversion, but is still lingering and still working against us as Christians.

This is very important: *I do not accept this interpretation of* sarx, *"the flesh."* In my judgment, the only way to make sense of Paul's teaching in ***Romans 6–8*** is to take "flesh" to mean the *physical body*. I am not espousing a dualistic view of the body as inherently evil. I believe, however, that Paul is teaching us in this section of Romans that sin has corrupted not only our souls but also our bodies, and that the corruption of our bodies is not just physical but is spiritual as well. This means that the sinner's body has become infected with and controlled by sin, and becomes a kind of beachhead or staging point for sins and temptations and lusts of all kinds. (See my discussion of this point in the relevant sections of my *Romans* commentary, especially at passages such as ***6:6***; ***7:5***; ***7:18-25***.)

When the Holy Spirit regenerates a sinner, the body is still unredeemed, under the control of sin.

This is especially important when we consider what happens at conversion. When the Holy Spirit regenerates a sinner, the latter's spirit or soul is renewed and given new life, but *not his flesh*, or *body*. The body is still unredeemed, still under the control of sin, still the source of "the lusts of the flesh." This sets up the conflict, the battle, between our own spirit and our own flesh or body. Paul explains in ***Romans 6:6***, *"Our old self [the spirit] was crucified with Him, in order that our body of sin [the body] might be done away with, so that we would no longer be slaves to sin."* Before conversion we *were* slaves to sin; our sinful bodies dominated our spirits and our sinful spirits were happy to be so dominated. But in regeneration our "old self" or "old man," which I take to refer *only* to the soul or spirit, died with Christ and was raised up and renewed. The intended result of this is that our "body of sin," which is our fleshly body as controlled by sin, is no longer able to dominate our spirit. It has not been "done away with" (a bad translation here), but has been *rendered powerless*. It still fights against our spirits, but we do not have to let it win and "reign" over us (***Rom 6:12***). Instead, Paul exhorts us to bring our bodies under the control of our spirits (***Rom 6:12-13***).

This may work up to a point, but the reality is that our unredeemed bodies often still get the upper hand; and our spirits, though redeemed and renewed, still suffer defeat in our spiritual battles. This, I believe, explains Paul's lament in ***Romans 7:14-25***. His soul is committed to God and to righteousness, but sin is still active and raging in his body (***7:22-23***). This *"different law in the members of my body,"* he says, is *"waging war against the law of my mind and making me a prisoner of the law of sin which is in my members"* (***7:23***). This is real spiritual warfare: the body against the soul. In the agony of battle Paul cries out: *"Wretched man that I am! Who will set me free from the body of this death?"* (***7:24***). *"The body of this death"* is the physical body, still filled with sin, not yet redeemed.

At this point Paul thanks God for Jesus Christ as the source of the rescue for which he pleads in ***7:24***, because he knows that Jesus gives us the two things necessary for winning the war against the flesh: the gift of the Holy Spirit (***8:1-13***) and the hope of a new, redeemed body at the day of resurrection (***8:10,11,23***).

Jesus gives us the gift of the Holy Spirit and the hope of a new, redeemed body.

In other words, in ***Romans 7:14-25*** Paul explains the nature of the spiritual warfare between flesh and *spirit*, but in ***8:1-13*** he celebrates the victory of our spirit over our flesh when we embrace the power of the *Holy* Spirit. The point of ***8:1-13*** is that the Holy Spirit enters the battle on the side of our spirits, gives them power to *put to death the deeds of the body* (***8:13***), and thus leads us to victory in this battle. To quote Swete again, "The Spirit is . . . an aggressive force leading the human spirit against the flesh," and "a defensive power shielding it from attack" (**344-345**).

Doing battle against the as-yet-unredeemed body and its lusts (***Rom 6:12***) is a difficult task, because these *"fleshly lusts . . . wage war against the soul"* (***1Pet 2:11***). We all know how easy it is for bodily appetites to get out of control, even to the point of physical addictions. ***Hebrews 12:4*** chastises us for not fighting hard enough: *"You have not yet resisted to the point of shedding blood in your striving*[4] *against sin."* Paul speaks of his determined regimen: *"I discipline my body and make it my slave, so that, after I have preached to others, I myself will not be disqualified"* (***1Cor 9:27***). Victory will be ours, though, when we call upon and depend upon the power of the indwelling Holy Spirit.

The Holy Spirit against the Devil

When we think of "spiritual warfare," the first thing that usually comes to mind is our battle with the devil and his angels, the demon-

[4]The Greek verb is *antagonizomai*, from which we get the word "antagonist," an adversary or enemy.

ic spirits. ***First Peter 5:8*** warns us against *"your enemy the devil,"* who *"prowls around like a roaring lion looking for someone to devour"* (NIV). *"Resist him,"* Peter exhorts, *"standing firm in the faith"* (***v. 9***). *"Resist the devil and he will flee from you,"* says ***James 4:7***. Resisting the devil is indeed a major aspect of sanctification.

Though Satan, the old dragon, is a defeated enemy (***Rev 12:7-11***), his plan is to attack God's people in whatever ways he can before he is finally and completely banished to hell. *"So the dragon was enraged with the woman and went off to make war with the rest of her children"*—specifically, Christians—*"who keep the commandments of God and hold to the testimony of Jesus"* (***Rev 12:17***). The magnitude of this warfare is seen in Paul's warning in ***Ephesians 6:10-12***,

> *Finally, be strong in the Lord and in the strength of His might. Put on the full armor of God, so that you will be able to stand firm against the schemes of the devil. For our struggle is not against flesh and blood, but against the rulers, against the powers, against the world forces of this darkness, against the spiritual forces of wickedness in the heavenly places.*

Satan usually does not attack us personally, but does so through his minions, i.e., his demons or evil spirits. Their strategy is threefold (see **Cottrell, *Faith*, 174-176**). First, they attack our minds through false teaching, seeking to deceive us with clever lies (***1Tm 4:1***). Second, they attack our wills through temptation, seeking to cause us to sin by manipulating our thoughts and mental states. Third, Satan's forces attack us on the level of our bodies, sometimes gaining entrance into the body itself and taking control of certain aspects of the brain and therefore of our thoughts, words, and behavior. I have no doubt that Satan works in all three of these ways today.

> **Satan's minions attack us (1) through false teaching, (2) through temptation, (3) on the level of our bodies.**

What does this mean for Christians and our spiritual warfare (see **ibid., 176-178**)? Certainly we are constantly bombarded with Satanic lies. Our defense against such attacks is simple: *know, believe, and love the truth*. When Paul tells us to *"put on the full armor of God"* so that we may *"be able to stand firm against the schemes of the devil"* (***Eph 6:11***), the first piece of armor he mentions is *"the belt of truth"* (***v. 14,***

NIV). Then he tells us that the last piece of equipment must be *"the sword of the Spirit, which is the word of God"* (***v. 17***). Thus our primary defense against the devil seems to be the truth of God's Word, by which we are sanctified (***Jn 17:17***) and by which we repel the devil's lies. The role of the Holy Spirit in this aspect of sanctification is clear: through His work of revelation and inspiration, He has given us both this belt and this sword. Thus we see again how a knowledge of the Bible is necessary for sanctification.

The second way we resist the devil is by being strong against his temptations, wherein he attempts to seduce us into sin by exploiting the weaknesses of our flesh and our wills. Most of what is being said in this chapter applies to this point. This is where the main purpose of the Spirit's indwelling presence is fulfilled: He dwells within us to make us strong against temptation and to empower us to put sin to death in our lives (***Rom 8:13***). He gives us the inner strength to walk in paths of righteousness, a strength that is greater than Satan's alluring temptations. In the contest between Satan and the Holy Spirit, the outcome is sure: *"Greater is He who is in you than he who is in the world"* (***1Jn 4:4***). God promises to protect us from whatever flaming arrows of temptation Satan may fling against us: *"No temptation has overtaken you but such as is common to man; and God is faithful, who will not allow you to be tempted beyond what you are able, but with the temptation will provide the way of escape also, so that you will be able to endure it"* (***1Cor 10:13***). God can make this promise because He has given us the gift of the Holy Spirit for this very purpose—to strengthen our wills to resist temptation and to pursue holiness.

In the contest between Satan and the Holy Spirit, the outcome is sure.

The third way we resist the devil is by being vigilant against all attempts by demons to enter into and take control of our bodies. We do this by avoiding sinful and occult activities that give evil spirits an opportunity to enter, and by consciously trusting in the protecting name and blood of Jesus Christ ("the shield of faith," ***Eph 6:16***). When we walk in paths of righteousness and wear the full armor of God, we need not fear being invaded by evil spirits.

A common idea is that demons cannot inhabit the bodies of Christians at all; thus we need not be concerned about this. The main argument is that a demonic spirit and the Holy Spirit cannot be present in a person's body at the same time. Such a view is never taught in Scripture, however; it is an inference based on false assumptions. It assumes that the Holy Spirit and evil spirits are present in a person's body in the same way, as if somehow they would be spatially and/or morally incompatible. This is not true. The Holy Spirit and evil spirits are two completely different kinds of spirits, existing on two vastly different metaphysical levels. The Holy Spirit is divine, infinite, uncreated Spirit; demons are finite, created spirits. They may both indwell the same body because they do not do so in the same sense. Those involved in deliverance ministries are practically unanimous in affirming that Christians may be demonized.

Nonmiraculous deliverance from evil spirits ("casting out demons") is sometimes necessary and always possible today for oppressed Christians who are nonetheless surrendered to the Lordship of Christ. Indeed, at times it may be the only way some Christians will be able to overcome certain addictive sins by which invading demonic powers are holding them captive. *"Release to the captives"* is part of the gospel (***Lk 4:18***). In general the works of Neil Anderson may be used for this purpose, especially the steps he outlines in *The Bondage Breaker*.

In short, Satan and his demons are real, active, powerful, and dangerous; but they are no match for our divine and almighty Redeemer and for His gift of the indwelling Holy Spirit. Through the sanctifying power of the Spirit we can do battle against the world, the flesh, and the devil—and win!

Through the sanctifying power of the Spirit we can do battle and win!

Led by the Spirit

Another key biblical image of the Spirit's sanctifying work is the fact that Christians are *"led by the Spirit."* This language comes from ***Romans 8:14***, *"For all who are being led by the Spirit of God, these are sons of God,"* and from ***Galatians 5:18***, *"But if you are led by the Spirit, you are not under the Law."* Two questions arise here: How does the Spirit "lead" us? and, What does this have to do with His indwelling presence? There are two major approaches to these questions.

One View: The Spirit Enlightens Our Minds

The most common approach to this issue is that the Spirit leads Christians by means of some sort of inward enlightenment of the mind, and that this is a major reason for His indwelling presence. Jacoby summarizes this approach thus: "The popular teaching about being led by the Spirit is that, once the Spirit comes into our hearts, we have an automatic guidance system that enables God to lead us through life and its maze of decisions, like having 'a spiritual gyroscope' in our nosecone" (**66**). Thus many interpret the Spirit's leading cognitively, in terms of *knowledge*. They have been taught to listen for a "still, small voice" giving specific guidance regarding everyday decisions and activities. William Barclay, e.g., says, "If the Christian is led by the Spirit, it means that all his decisions are taken in the guidance of the Spirit. But it is well to remember that a friend cannot give us his advice and his guidance until we seek it, and the guidance of the Spirit is something to which we must open ourselves, and for which we must ask and wait" (***Promise*, 80-81**).

A writer for *Christian Standard* says that we must be open to "the possibility that God might give individual guidance and direction to those who seek Him in matters of personal decision-making and direction," and that He might do this by speaking "personally, in the recesses of a person's heart." The writer identifies this with "the Holy Spirit's leading." He suggests different ways in which "you might feel the Spirit's leading" as He speaks to us in "the still, small voice of God" (**Zustiak, 4, 6**).

In response to this approach I will make three points. First, the biblical texts and language usually associated with the Spirit's "leading" give us absolutely no basis for interpreting this leading as something cognitive, i.e., as something that gives knowledge to the mind or intellect. In ***Romans 8:14*** and ***Galatians 5:18*** the word translated "led" is the verb *ago*, a common word used about 69 times in the NT, most often in the sense of "bringing" something or someone from one place to another. In these other texts, I cannot see that the word ever has the cognitive connotation of leading or guiding by enlightening the mind or "showing the way" to anyone.

The same is true of two other texts using two other words associated with being "led by the Spirit." In ***Galatians 5:16*** Paul exhorts us to *"walk* *by the Spirit."* The Greek verb, *peripateo*, is the common word for "to walk, to walk around." It is often used for a person's general conduct or way of life; the NIV translates it *"live by the Spirit."* There is absolutely nothing in the word or the text connecting this "walking" with inward cognitive guidance from the Spirit. The same is true of ***Galatians 5:25***, where Paul says, *"If we live by the Spirit, let us also walk by the Spirit."* Here, "live" is *zao*, which means "to live one's life, to be alive." The relevant word is *stoicheo*, to *"walk by the Spirit"* (NASB) or *"keep in step with the Spirit"* (NIV). Again there is not one hint in this word or this text of some sort of subjective enlightenment from the Spirit.

My second point about the enlightenment view is the inherent danger of trusting inward feelings and promptings, with the assumption that we can surely distinguish any "leading" by the Spirit from deceptive impressions planted by Satan and his demons. Even our external experiences cannot be trusted, says Jesus (***Mt 7:21-23***), so why should we think we can be so certain about ambiguous and often vague inward impressions or voices? Jacoby is right: "If anything is certain, it is the fact that it is dangerous to follow our feelings. Feelings have little to do with being led by the Spirit" (**65**). In an excellent essay on this subject, Lynn Gardner asks, "When one judges on a subjective basis alone, how can he distinguish between a communication from the Holy Spirit and one from the devil, or even from one's own thought processes?" (***1:11-12***).

My third point is that the Holy Spirit *does* "lead" us by giving us knowledge, but He does this only objectively, through the revealed and inspired Bible. Edwin Palmer notes that every major error concerning the Spirit's guidance "stems from a failure to observe the Biblical principle that the Spirit guides the Christian infallibly only through the Guidebook, the Bible" (**120**). One who walks in the Spirit, says Pettegrew, is one who *"is consistently obeying the promptings of the indwelling Holy Spirit."* But whence come these promptings? "The content of these promptings is essentially biblical truth, of which the Spirit reminds the Christian and encourages him to believe and obey. This means that for a person to be spiritual, he must know well the Word of God. If he does not, the Holy Spirit will not have much content with which to work" (**207**).

This is how we must understand ***Galatians 5:16*** and ***Galatians 5:25***. To "walk" by the Spirit, or to "live" by the Spirit, or to "keep in step with" the Spirit means primarily that we must live our lives according to the teachings of His Word. This is seen especially in the term *stoicheo* (***Gal 5:25***), a word that has to do with lining up items in a row. Conceptually it suggests the state of being in *agreement* with or in *harmony* with something. We should understand ***Galatians 5:25*** thus: "Since we have been given new spiritual life by the Holy Spirit, the least we can do now is to conduct our lives in harmony or conformity with what He has taught us in his inspired Word."

Someone may object, "But how can I know the will of God for my life?" This question arises from a misunderstanding of "the will of God" itself (see **Cottrell, *Ruler*, 299-329**). God does not have a *specific* will for most individuals, unlike David or Jeremiah or Paul. If He has a specific will for someone, there will not be any doubt or equivocation as to what it is; i.e., there will not be vague feelings or impressions. God will speak directly to that person, as to Abraham, or Saul of Tarsus, or Moses. But, as we shall see in chapter 11, this is something that happened only in Bible times, when God was working out His plan of salvation. God's will for us today is basically the *same* for everyone, and it is made known to all through the Bible. This is not a *specific* will about individual decisions, especially in the area of opinions or in the area of applications of the general will as revealed in the Bible. To think that each person has a specific path intended for him by God (even if it is difficult to know this path) is a watered-down form of Calvinism. The Holy Spirit gives us knowledge of this general will for all people through the Bible, not through inward impressions. When we pray for God to help us understand or apply His word, we are actually praying not for knowledge but for wisdom, as we are taught to do in ***James 1:5***. See the discussion of the doctrine of illumination in chapter 2, pp. 64-92.

God does not have a specific will for most individuals, and when He does there will be no ambiguity.

Our View: The Spirit Empowers Our Wills

In what sense, then, can we affirm that we are "led by the Spirit," especially as a result of His indwelling presence? The answer comes from reading the relevant texts in their proper contexts. It is especially important to see that the meaning of ***Romans 8:14a***—*"all who are being led by the Spirit of God"*—is to be found in what goes before it, not in what comes after it. What precedes it is Paul's very personal and very intense teaching about the warfare between flesh and s/Spirit. Paul shows us the possibility, the difficulty, and the necessity of subduing and controlling the flesh; and he shows us that we can do this through the power of the Holy Spirit.

The connecting word *gar* ("for, because") at the beginning of ***verse 14*** suggests that being led by the Spirit is the same as putting sins to death by the Spirit (***v. 13***). When we see this connection we will understand that the Spirit leads us not by subjectively enlightening our minds, but by inwardly empowering our wills. He gives us power to conquer the lusts of the flesh that arise from *"the body of this death"* (***7:24***). His *leading*, then, is an inward prodding of the conscience, an influence upon the heart, an empowerment of the will to do what we already know is right based on the teaching of Scripture. Our problem is not ignorance as such, but moral weakness. The Spirit leads us by taking our hand and giving us the inner strength to walk in the paths of righteousness.

The Spirit leads us not by subjectively enlightening our minds but by inwardly empowering our wills.

The same conflict between flesh and Spirit is the subject in ***Galatians 5:16-26***. Thus ***5:16*** means, "Walk by *the strength of* the Spirit, and you will not carry out the desire of the flesh." ***Verse 18*** means, "If you allow the Spirit to empower you against your enemy the flesh, you are not under law." We can see the same connection between ***verse 24*** and ***verse 25***, *"Now those who belong to Christ Jesus have crucified the flesh with its passions and desires. If we live by the Spirit, let us also walk by the Spirit."* That is to say, we have already died with Christ and been raised up to new life with Him through the regenerating power of the Holy Spirit; let us now live day by day in that same power. As Jacoby says, being led by the Spirit "actually has next to nothing to do with divining God's will. It is not 'reading your feelings'. . . . Rather it is triumphing over the flesh by the Spirit (***Galatians 5:16-26; Romans 8:1-16***)" (**219**).

Gardner makes this point so very well. In each text that speaks of being led by the Spirit, he says, "the context indicates that the meaning is not the Spirit conveying information but rather the Spirit helping to bring about transformation of character and conduct. . . . The leading of the Spirit means sanctification" (**2:11**). Gardner refers positively to these comments by Lard on **Romans 8:14**:

> What kind of leading then is it? I answer, both internal and external. To whatever extent the Holy Spirit by its indwelling strengthens the human spirit, to enable it to control the flesh, to that extent the leading is internal. To whatever extent the motives of the gospel, when brought to bear on the mind in the written word, enlighten and strengthen it, and so enable it to keep the body in subjection, to that extent the leading is external. The leading, then, consists of the whole of the influences of every kind, spent by the Holy Spirit on the human spirit, in enabling it to keep the body under. (***Romans*, 264**)

Gardner's conclusion is appropriate: "Let us determine to follow the leading of the Spirit by instructing our minds through the study of the Scriptures and by submitting our wills to God, whose Spirit will strengthen our inner man so that we can obey the truth" (**2:12**).

The Witness of the Spirit

One thing that causes some to lean toward a cognitive understanding of "led by the Spirit" is the close connection between this idea (**Rom 8:14a**) and the assurance that we are indeed children of God (**Rom 8:14b-16**). Especially significant is **verse 16**: *"The Spirit Himself testifies with our spirit that we are children of God."* This is taken by many to mean that the Spirit speaks inwardly to our hearts.

This verse does in fact say that the Holy Spirit bears witness in relation to our personal spirit (soul, heart). But exactly what does this mean? The verb is *summartureo*, which combines *martureo*, "to testify, to bear witness," with *sun*, "with." Does this mean the Spirit "bears witness *with*" our spirit, or "bears witness *to*" our spirit? Most agree that the former is the literal meaning of the word, but they treat it as if it means the latter. In truth, the crucial question is this: *to whom* is the Spirit's testimony addressed? Most say this verse refers to the inward, experiential, subjective testimony of the Spirit directly to our spirit, a testimony that gives us assurance that we are indeed children of God. It is "a direct operation of the Holy Spirit on our spirit," says

Leon Morris (***Romans*, 317**). This witness of the Spirit is not in some outward manifestation, says Broomall, such as the voice that spoke at Jesus' baptism. "The voice is rather inward" (**148-149**).

I cannot agree with this view of the Spirit's witness, and I will make three points in response to it. First, we need to understand the main point of the entire passage, ***Romans 8:14-17a***:

> *For all who are being led by the Spirit of God, these are sons of God. For you have not received a spirit of slavery leading to fear again, but you have received a spirit of adoption as sons by which we cry out, "Abba! Father!" The Spirit Himself testifies with our spirit that we are children of God, and if children, heirs also, heirs of God and fellow heirs with Christ.*

(See **Cottrell, *Romans*, I:478-485**.) The point can be summed up thus: if we have the Spirit of God, we are His children; and if we are His children, we are His heirs. Precisely what is the Spirit's role in our membership in God's family? The view mentioned above says this passage teaches that the Spirit directly plants knowledge in our minds concerning our status as children of God. I believe the point is very different from this, namely, that the Spirit gives us the power to live the kind of life that is indicative of a child of God, and the power to confidently claim our filial relationship with the Father. In other words, the point is not that the Spirit *makes* us children of God as such, nor that He makes us *aware* that we are children of God through some mystical inner revelation. The idea rather is that the Spirit *marks* us as God's children indirectly through what He enables us to do. By objectively observing His mark upon our lives, we ourselves as well as others can have assurance that we belong to God's family and are heirs of His glory.

If we have the Spirit of God, we are His children, and if we are His children, we are His heirs.

This is the point of ***verse 14***, i.e., the Spirit leads us into battle against the deeds of the body (the works of the flesh) and enables us to conquer them, and this Spirit-led lifestyle becomes a sign of sonship, the mark of belonging to God's family. By allowing the Spirit to lead us to spiritual victory, we bear witness to the fact that we are sons of God. The point of ***verse 15*** is that this gives us a positive attitude, an attitude of assurance about our status before God. Because the

empowerment of the Spirit has enabled us to live the life of a child of God, we can confidently address God as "Abba! Father!"

What, then, of the Spirit's witness in ***verse 16***? This is my second point: we do not *need* an internal witness of the Spirit in order to have assurance of our sonship. Such is not the point of the connection between ***verse 15*** and ***verse 16***. For one thing, ***verse 16*** does not begin with the common particle indicating a causal connection with the previous verse (*gar*, "for, because"). Paul uses *gar* thirteen times with this meaning in ***8:1-26***. Why w… …e omit it here if he wants us to
see a causal relationshi… … Spirit's testimony (***v. 16***) and
our cry of "Abba! F… …nother thing we already have
the *objective* … …r status as children of God
throu… …Bales says, "The only wit-
… …nd in His written Word.
… …voice; not through our
… …" (54).
… …n ***3:21–5:21***, a main
… …e but is the expect-
… …of what it means
t… …See the "much
m… …ng power as it
affe… …nsciousness
(***v. 15***… …bba! Father!"

My … …ot even *say* that the Holy
Spirit be… …are God's children. The word
again is *su*… …or bear witness *along with*." That is,
our own sp… …s that we are children of God (***vv. 14-15***),
and the Holy … …bears witness *along with* our spirits. How does the
latter happen? …he natural understanding of the word is that His testimony is directed toward the same audience as our own, namely, to the Father. When we cry "Abba! Father!" we bear witness to Him that we are His children. Then the Spirit adds His own testimony to ours, likewise bearing witness to the Father that we are His children.

The Holy Spirit bears witness along with our spirits, confirming our testimony to the Father.

We have assurance that someone besides ourselves is confirming our testimony to the Father. The fact that Paul is here *telling* us that the Spirit likewise testifies to the Father that we are His true sons and daughters makes our assurance even more firm. This is similar to the Spirit's intercession between us and the Father in ***Romans 8:26-27***. This is not necessary for the Father's sake, but knowing that it happens gives *us* a sense of calmness and assurance.

All of this is consistent with the main point here, namely, that being "led by the Spirit" means to be empowered to live a life of true sonship.

Bearing the Fruit of the Spirit

A third image depicting the Spirit's work of sanctification is bearing the fruit of the Spirit. When we consider ***Romans 6–8*** and ***Galatians 5:16-26*** together, we can see that spiritual warfare, being led by the Spirit, and bearing the fruit of the Spirit are all just interrelated facets of a larger picture. That is, when we allow the Holy Spirit to lead us through the spiritual power with which He endows us, we can both fight victoriously against sin and develop the positive virtues that are characteristic of God's children. This picture is succinctly given in ***Galatians 5:16-26***. In ***verses 16, 18, and 25*** we are taught to follow the Spirit's leading. ***Verses 19-21*** list major "deeds of the flesh" (*"deeds of the body,"* ***Rom 8:13***) which we must put to death through the Spirit's power. Then ***verses 22-23*** name the principal virtues we must cultivate through the same power, under the image of fruit: *"But the fruit of the Spirit is love, joy, peace, patience, kindness, goodness, faithfulness, gentleness, self-control; against such things there is no law."*

In this book I will not attempt to explain these individual virtues. My main point is that these and all other aspects of holiness are a major reason why we have been given the gift of the Holy Spirit. The presence of the Spirit within us assures us that we *can* bear this fruit. Since we are free-will beings, the Spirit's presence does not guarantee that we *will* bear the fruit; we must still "work out our own salvation" by devoting our own spiritual energy and concentration to the task. But if we are serious about being holy as God is holy, because we have the Spirit within us we know our efforts will not be in vain.

> **The presence of the Spirit within us assures us that we *can* bear the fruit but not that we *will* bear it.**

A question that often arises is whether a person who does not have the *indwelling* of the Holy Spirit can bear the *fruit* of the Spirit. Some folks become confused because they know individuals who have not obeyed ***Acts 2:38***, which connects receiving the Holy Spirit with baptism, and yet who exhibit aspects of the Spirit's fruit. The reason for this confusion is the false assumption that none of these kinds of fruit can be present in a person's life unless he has the indwelling of the Spirit. One cannot draw such a conclusion from ***Galatians 5:22-23***.

There are two reasons why individuals who do not have the Spirit's indwelling presence can still manifest, to a degree at least, the fruit of the Spirit. First, the various virtues listed by Paul—love, joy, peace, and the rest—are in reality the *natural* state for human beings made in God's image. Such *"righteousness and holiness of the truth"* (***Eph 4:24***) are part of the original "image of God" which the Creator gave to the human race in the beginning. This image includes an innate knowledge of God's basic moral laws (***Rom 2:15***). One of the effects of sin is that this image, including these virtues, has been damaged and marred. This does not mean, however, that it is completely destroyed. Every sinner still possesses vestiges of the image, to a degree that depends on how much of himself he has yielded to the power of sin. Thus we can expect these virtues—at least some of them, to some degree—to be present in most people. (From the negative side, this is the same reason why we do not find *all* of the "deeds of the flesh" present in *all* sinners.)

The second reason why individuals who do not have the Spirit's indwelling presence can manifest the fruit of the Spirit is that such folks have been convicted of sin, righteousness, and judgment by the Spirit-inspired Word of God (***Jn 16:8-11***), and they are making an effort to obey the Word and to lead a virtuous life. They are trying to live according to the Bible, under the knowledge and motivation engendered by biblical teaching. Those who have thus come under the influence of the Word (***Heb 4:12-13***) will be able to bear the fruit of the Spirit to some extent. This explains why OT saints, none of whom had the indwelling of the Spirit, were able to exhibit these virtues.

Why, then, does Paul call this list of virtues in ***Galatians 5:22-23*** "the fruit of the Spirit"? We must remember that there are two aspects of the Spirit's sanctifying work: He sanctifies indirectly *through the Word,* and directly through His indwelling presence. When anyone seeks to live according to the moral teaching of the Word of God, the Spirit of God is at work in his life. When that person, through free-will effort, becomes more loving, more patient, or more self-controlled, he is under the influence of the Holy Spirit and is thus producing "the fruit of the Spirit." This does *not* mean that every person who thus bears some of the Spirit's fruit is saved. It does *not* mean that the Spirit is dwelling within him. Though this is a widespread assumption, it is completely false and unwarranted.

We must be careful to avoid a fallacy in logic here. Just because "all A is B," this does not mean that "all B is A." In other words, that "all who have the indwelling of the Spirit will produce His fruit" does not necessarily imply that "all who produce His fruit have the indwelling of the Spirit." Some in the latter group may simply be under conviction through the power of the Word.

So what advantage does the Christian have in his efforts to produce the fruit of the Spirit? The answer should be obvious. The Christian has *not only* the knowledge and power of the Word working in his heart, *but also* the power of the indwelling Holy Spirit Himself, who is able to directly energize our wills and to empower us to produce this fruit far beyond what our unaided efforts could achieve. This does not eliminate struggle in our efforts to become virtuous, but for those who are serious about fruit-bearing it eliminates the fear of defeat. That is why we can affirm that "all who have the indwelling of the Spirit will produce His fruit."

In the final analysis, then, the *presence* of the fruit of the Spirit as listed in ***Galatians 5:22-23*** is not an infallible sign that a person has the indwelling of the Spirit, but the *absence* of this fruit is a likely sign that the Spirit is *not* present.

The presence of the fruit of the Spirit is not an infallible sign of His indwelling, but the absence is a likely sign of His absence.

Praying by the Spirit

Another way the Spirit sanctifies us is that He aids us in our prayer life. Paul says in ***Romans 8:26-27***,

> *In the same way the Spirit also helps our weakness; for we do not know how to pray as we should, but the Spirit*

Himself intercedes for us with groanings too deep for words; and He who searches the hearts knows what the mind of the Spirit is, because He intercedes for the saints according to the will of God.

As finite creatures who have come under the influence of sin, we have many kinds of weakness. In this passage Paul teaches us that the Holy Spirit comes to our aid and gives us inward spiritual power at exactly those points where this weakness puts us in danger of doubt and sin. He shoulders the burdens of our sufferings and fills in the breaches of our defenses against our spiritual enemies. This is His ongoing work of sanctification, and the very reason for His indwelling presence.

One weakness is that we are not even aware of all our weaknesses. Thus, as Paul says, we do not always know exactly what to pray for in the prayer aspect of our quest for holiness. The NASB says that *"we do not know how to pray,"* but this is too ambiguous. Paul is not talking about the manner of prayer, but its content. In our spiritual warfare we may not know exactly what to pray for, or how to word our prayers. Here is one of the ways the Spirit comes to our aid. In our feeble attempts at heartfelt prayer, He intercedes for us, standing between us and the Father. Just as Jesus intercedes for us in heaven at God's right hand (***Rom 8:34***), the Spirit intercedes for us from within our hearts.

One weakness is that we are not even aware of all our weaknesses.

This does not negate Christ's role as a unique intercessor (***1Tm 2:5-6***) because He is the only one who stands between us and the Father's wrath, the only one who secures for us the decree of justification. The Spirit's intercession is in the realm of our sanctification and is specifically related to our prayer life. By His divine power He looks upon the deepest levels of our hearts and gives content to our unspoken and uncertain prayers, then He lays these prayers before the Father's throne. Knowing that this happens alleviates the frustration and despair that might otherwise arise out of our uncertainty concerning God's will and our inability to know what to pray for.

The "groanings too deep for words" involved in this intercession are the Spirit's own groanings, as He extracts the deepest unformed prayers from our hearts and presents them to the Father in a kind of intradivine communication that does not need words. This communication is described as "groanings" because it conveys to the Father not only our thoughts but also the deep feelings associated with them.

If God the Father can directly search our hearts (*v. 27*), why is it necessary for the Spirit to intercede for us? It is not a matter of necessity but of choice. In relation to our redemption the triune God has chosen to divide the various aspects of His redemptive activity among the three persons of the Trinity. Since the Spirit is specifically responsible for our sanctification, and since this weakness in our prayer life is a matter of sanctification, this intercession is part of His distinctive work. It is another reason why we cherish the fact of His indwelling presence.

Receiving God's Love from the Spirit

A final aspect of the Spirit's sanctifying work is that He pours out God's love into our hearts. Paul states in ***Romans 5:4*** that our *"hope does not disappoint, because the love of God has been poured out within our hearts through the Holy Spirit who was given to us."* He is speaking of God's love for us, not our love for God; he says it becomes present within our hearts by being "poured out" within us. This takes place "through the Holy Spirit." Our question naturally is this: *how* is the love of God thus given to us through the Spirit?

We must pay close attention to the wording here. Paul says that the love of God itself is poured out, not our knowledge or consciousness of it. The Spirit does provide us with the *knowledge* of God's love, but this is given through the biblical testimony to that love. The fact that God loves us is objectively revealed in the very events of redemption; and the knowledge of this love is objectively recorded for us in the words of Scripture, which were given through the inspiration of the Spirit. Our subjective knowledge or awareness of this love is thus poured out into our hearts by the Holy Spirit primarily through His inspired Word. This is probably not what Paul is talking about here, though.

The Spirit does provide us with the knowledge of God's love through biblical testimony to that love.

There are three ways in which we may think of God as pouring out His love in our hearts through the Holy Spirit. First, we may think of the gift of the Holy Spirit Himself as being the love that God pours out into our hearts, in objectified form. This same imagery is used in ***Titus 3:6***, which says of the Holy Spirit that He Himself was *"poured out upon us richly through Jesus Christ."* That is, when God pours out the Holy Spirit upon us, He is by that very act pouring out His love upon us. This is why our hope does not disappoint us, because the Holy Spirit as the initial gift of God's love has already been poured out in us and is already present within us as the firstfruits of the fullness of eschatological glory (***Rom 8:23***), and as the earnest or down payment guaranteeing our full and final salvation (***Eph 1:13-14***). This is Paul's primary point, I believe.

Second, the Spirit pours the love of God into our hearts in His role as the agent by which all the other blessings of redemption are applied to us in the initial moment of our salvation. What He bestows upon us is not God's subjective love as such, but the objectification of that love in the form of the many blessings of salvation. After the Spirit Himself is poured out, He in turn lavishly pours out the further gifts of God's love, e.g., the renewing and regeneration of the new birth (***Tts 3:5***; ***Jn 3:5***) and His own ongoing, ever-present sanctifying power (***Rom 8:13***; ***Eph 3:16***).

Third, the Spirit pours the love of God into our hearts by strengthening our inner conviction of the certainty of God's love for us personally. He sharpens our awareness of and faith in God's love as a part of His sanctifying work in our hearts. We must be careful, though, not to separate this from the points already made above, as if some purely subjective experience of God's love were the basis for our hope. However important this inward strengthening of the Spirit may be, our hope is not based on this subjective experience as such. This subjective experience presupposes and supplements several prior *objective* realities: the atoning death of Christ, the Spirit's inspiration of Scripture, our hearing and obeying the gospel, and our reception of the Holy Spirit Himself in our baptism. All of these things together

The Spirit pours the love of God into our hearts by strengthening our certainty of God's personal love.

constitute the outpouring of the love of God into our hearts, and together they assure us that our hope will not make us ashamed.

"BE FILLED WITH THE SPIRIT"

In ***Ephesians 5:18*** the apostle Paul exhorts all Christians thus: *"And do not get drunk with wine, for that is dissipation, but be filled with the Spirit."* What does it mean to "be filled with the Spirit"? It is important that we understand this because this is a command that we must obey. As Stott says, it is "not a tentative suggestion, a mild recommendation, a polite piece of advice. It is a command which comes to us from Christ with all the authority of one of his chosen apostles. . . . The fullness of the Holy Spirit is not optional for the Christian, but obligatory" (*Baptism*, 60).

In the NT a number of people are said to have been filled with the Spirit. This includes individuals such as Jesus (***Lk 4:1***), Elizabeth (***Lk 1:41***), Zacharias (***Lk 1:67***), Peter (***Acts 4:8***), Stephen (***Acts 6:5; 7:55***), Paul (***Acts 9:17; 13:9***), and Barnabas (***Acts 11:24***). Sometimes groups of believers are described as being filled with the Spirit (***Acts 2:4; 4:31; 6:3; 13:52***). Three Greek words are used to represent this filling or fullness. One is the verb *pimplemi*, used in ***Luke 1:15,41,67; Acts 2:4; 4:8,31; 9:17; 13:9***. Another is the verb *pleroo*, used in **Acts 13:52** and **Ephesians 5:18**. The third is *pleres* (the noun form of *pleroo*), used in ***Luke 4:1; Acts 6:3,5; 7:55; 11:24***. Some see differences regarding the way the first word is used compared with the latter two (e.g., **Pettegrew, 197-201**), but I see nothing of significance here.

It is true, however, that we can discern distinct ways in which people are described as being filled with the Spirit in Bible times. Stott (***Baptism*, 48-49**) says there are three categories: (1) Being "filled with the Spirit" as "a normal characteristic of every dedicated Christian," e.g., ***Acts 6:3,5; 11:24; 13:52***. (2) A more or less permanent "endowment for a particular office or ministry," e.g., ***John 1:15-17; Acts 9:17***. (3) A more or less temporary filling "to equip people . . . for an immediate task," such as in ***Luke 1:41,67; Acts 7:55***. Hoekema has a similar threefold distinction (**81-83**). These are valid distinctions, but for our purposes it may be better to discern just two categories: (1) fullness as an equipping for service, whether temporary or lifelong, as bestowed on selected individuals; and (2) fullness as related to the sanctifying presence of the Spirit, available and intended for all Christians. Pettegrew also sees the same two basic categories, and refers to them as special filling and normal filling (**200-201**).

Making Room for the Spirit

Our focus here is on the command in ***Ephesians 5:18***, *"Be filled with the Spirit."* What does this mean? A major issue is, into which of the above two categories does this text belong? Some place it in the category of the Spirit's equipping work, and regard it in terms of an immediate and dramatic "second work of grace," equivalent to the "baptism in the Spirit" defined in the Holiness or Pentecostal sense. This would be an experience subsequent to conversion in which the Spirit is received in His "fullness," often with accompanying or resultant miraculous powers, especially tongues, as in ***Acts 2:4***.

In my judgment this is not the correct understanding of ***Ephesians 5:18***. This verse refers not to any kind of special second work of grace, but to the ongoing sanctifying work of the Spirit. Two main things about the verb, "be filled," support this conclusion. First, the verb is an *imperative,* indicating that it is not an act initiated by the Holy Spirit but is rather something that we ourselves must do. If the filling were a second-work event, equivalent to baptism in the Spirit in a miraculous sense, we could not be commanded to do it, but would simply have to wait for it to happen. The imperative shows, however, that this filling is our responsibility. It involves our submission and our cooperation. We do not wait passively for it; we do not pray for the Spirit to initiate it. We simply *do* it.

The imperative shows that the filling is our responsibility.

Second, the verb is a *present* imperative, which indicates not a one-time episode but a continuing process. Stott explains, "It is well known that, in the Greek language, if the imperative is aorist it refers to a single action, while if it is present the action is continuous." Thus "the present imperative 'be filled with the Spirit' . . . indicates not some dramatic or decisive experience which will settle the issue for good, but a continuous appropriation" (***Baptism*, 61**).

Also, the context supports the view that this command has nothing to do with miraculous empowerment but rather is concerned with ordinary Christian living. The main point in ***Ephesians 4 and 5*** is the contrast between the Ephesians' former immoral pagan life and their new Christian life of holiness. ***Ephesians 5:18*** is a summary of this contrast. Also, "be filled" as a main verb is immediately followed by five present participles which show what kind of conduct is associated with or results from such filling: (1) speaking to one another in psalms, hymns, and spiritual songs; (2) singing and (3) making music with your heart to the Lord; (4) giving thanks always for all things; and (5) submitting to one another in reverence to Christ (***Eph 5:19-21***). It seems clear that the point of this filling is holy living and better moral conduct, not miraculous activity.

The context supports the view that this command is concerned with ordinary Christian living.

With this understanding and expectation, we still must ask, what sort of thing must *we do* in order to "be filled with the Spirit"? Here are two more points about the language that will enlighten us. One, the verb is passive. We are not told to fill something or to fill ourselves, but to *be* filled. Even though it is commanded as something *we* must do, in the final analysis the filling is something the *Spirit* must do. This dual action is captured by the NEB translation, "Let the Holy Spirit fill you." Our part is to submit, to yield, to allow; the Spirit's part is to do the filling.

Two, the phrase usually translated "*with* the Spirit" should probably be translated "*by* the Spirit." The question is, what are we to be filled *with*? The Spirit must fill us, but with what? With Himself? No. We have already been filled *with* the Spirit, when we received the Spirit as a gift at our baptism. The Spirit in all His fullness was given to us at that time; we did not receive just a part of the Spirit with some of the Spirit being withheld for a later time. What Paul is telling us to do here in ***Ephesians 5:18*** is to let the Spirit fill us with something else. The use of the prepositional phrase *en pneumati*, "*by* the Spirit," supports this. In other NT texts, when the concept of being filled *with* something is being expressed, prepositions are seldom used at all. Usually the verb is simply followed by an object in the genitive, dative, or accusative case. Here, then, it would seem to mean, "Let yourselves be filled by the Spirit with His life-giving and sanctifying

power. Let yourselves be filled by the power of the Spirit with all the virtues of the Christian life. Let the Spirit fill you with all things righteous and holy: wisdom (***Lk 2:40***), knowledge (***Col 1:9***), joy (***Acts 13:52; 2Tm 1:4***), joy and peace (***Rom 15:13***), and the fruit of holiness (***Php 1:11***)."

We let the Spirit fill us simply by allowing Him to have more and more control of our lives, by surrendering to Him more and more aspects of our thoughts and activities. When we become Christians, we usually do not become 100% holy as soon as the Spirit enters our lives. Pet sins and pockets of resistance often persist. We have yielded our bodies to the Holy Spirit as a house in which He may dwell, but we have allowed Him access only to certain "rooms" in our house. *"Be filled with the Spirit"* means to unlock those rooms we have been closing off from the Spirit's presence and power, and let Him do a thorough housecleaning. Let Him have control of the way we spend our money, of what we watch on TV or the Internet, of our eating habits, of the way we treat our families. As someone has put it, being filled with the Spirit does not mean that we have more of the Spirit, but that the Spirit has more of us (**Pache, 116**).

Let Him have control of the way we spend our money and every other aspect of life.

We conclude that being filled with the Spirit is really just making more room for the Spirit in our lives, so that He may be able to sanctify us entirely (***1Th 5:23***).

Excluding the Spirit

What happens if we do not allow the Spirit to fill us through and through with His cleansing power and His sanctifying graces? What happens if we continue to exclude the Holy Spirit from various areas of our lives? The Bible gives us several warnings about this: do not grieve the Spirit (***Eph 4:30***); do not quench the Spirit (***1Th 5:19***); and do not insult the Spirit (***Heb 10:29***).

In ***Ephesians 4:30*** Paul says very plainly, *"Do not grieve the Holy Spirit of God, by whom you were sealed for the day of redemption."* We will remember that this is one of the texts that show the Holy Spirit to be a person: He is capable of the emotional state of grief, anguish, sorrow. Since we are commanded *not* to grieve the Spirit, it must be true that we can *do* something that will cause Him to grieve. What would that be?

Since we are commanded not to grieve the Spirit, we must be able to cause Him grief.

We notice first of all that this command is given in the midst of a whole series of commands regarding specific sins and instructions about holy living (cf. ***4:25–5:5***). We will also remember that the Spirit's main purpose for being within us is to help us to be holy. Therefore we can safely infer that *grieving* the Holy Spirit means to spurn His sanctifying presence and power by continuing to sin. He is within us to help us not to sin; when we ignore His presence and refuse to use His power, He grieves. In other words, grieving the Spirit is not a specific sin separate from lying or stealing or using bad language; it is an added dimension that is attached to every sin we commit. As Boles says, "The Holy Spirit is grieved by everything that is contrary to holiness" (**169**). Pache adds, "Every sin consciously committed, whatever its nature, whether great or small, open or hidden, grieves the Spirit" (**106**).

Paul also gives us this command: *"Do not quench the Spirit; do not despise prophetic utterances"* (***1Th 5:19-20***). "Quench" is the Greek verb *sbennumi*, which literally means "to put out a fire" (as it does in its other five NT uses, e.g., ***Mk 9:48***; ***Eph 6:16***). This means that something about the Holy Spirit is like a fire, and that we can do something that will cause that fire to go out. How should we understand this?

We will remember that the Holy Spirit does two main things for us: He gives us knowledge, and He gives us power. Both are involved in sanctification. Through the inspired Word the Spirit tells us what we need to *know* in order to be holy, and through His indwelling power He enables us to live up to this knowledge. One way we can "quench the Spirit" is by *"despising prophetic utterances"* inspired by the Spirit (***v. 20***). Some think this means that we must not prevent Christians who have the gift of prophecy (or any other miraculous gift) from exercising that gift. This is not the point; Paul's instruction has to do not with inspired prophets themselves, but with the prophecies given by them. For those of us living today, such inspired prophecies are the books of the Bible, the inspired writings of prophets and apostles. This Word of God is a lamp to our feet and a light to our path (***Ps 119:105***). In Bible times this "lamp" involved a burning wick. The Bible, like a burning wick, shows us how to *"walk by the Spirit"* (***Gal 5:25***). But when we despise God's Word, and treat it with contempt or neglect, we are simply snuffing out this lamp. We do this when we make no attempt to study and learn God's Word, and to apply it to our lives.

The other way we quench the Spirit's fire is to spurn His sanctifying power, i.e., it is basically the same as grieving the Spirit. We will remember that John the Baptist promised that Jesus would baptize us *"with the Holy Spirit and with fire"* (***Lk 3:16***), and that this "fire" is most likely the purifying effect of the Holy Spirit's presence within us (***Mal 3:1-4***). The Holy Spirit is like a flame-thrower, *"putting to death the deeds of the body"* (***Rom 8:13***) in the purifying process of sanctification. We quench the Spirit's fire when we close ourselves off from this purpose and shield our sins from this consuming flame. We quench the Spirit's cleansing fire when we say to Him, "I'm satisfied with my life the way it is, warts and all. Go work on somebody else." Instead of allowing the Spirit to fill us, we seek to exclude Him from our lives.

We quench the Spirit's fire by spurning His sanctifying power.

The third way to exclude the Spirit is described in ***Hebrews 10:29***: *"How much severer punishment do you think he will deserve who has trampled under foot the Son of God, and has regarded as unclean the blood of the covenant by which he was sanctified, and has insulted the Spirit of grace?"* From the context it seems that this exclusion of the Spirit from one's life is different from grieving and quenching the Spirit, which (in my judgment) a Christian can do without losing his faith and his salvation. However, from the context of ***Hebrews 10:29*** and from the purpose of the book of Hebrews as a whole, we may conclude that "insulting" the Spirit is connected with the sin of apostasy, by which a Christian deliberately repudiates his faith and becomes an unbeliever. In such a situation insulting the Holy Spirit is not a particular sin which is so bad that it causes a Christian to become lost. That is, it is not the cause of such apostasy, but rather the result of it. When one deliberately renounces his trust in Jesus Christ and abandons the Christian faith, this is always a terrible insult to the Holy Spirit, the very one who bestowed the grace of Christ upon us in the first place.

The willful sin of ***Hebrews 10:26*** is most likely this act of apostasy, and the original recipients of the letter to the Hebrews apparently were considering committing it. The writer of Hebrews is trying to convince them not to do it. In this text he warns them of the sure wrath of God which they will suffer if they do. How could God *not* pour out His wrath upon them, if they repudiate their Christian faith? After all, this is equivalent to the three things named in ***10:29***: trampling under foot the Son of God, regarding His blood as unclean, and insulting the Holy Spirit.

The word for "insult" is *enhubrizo*, from *hubris*, meaning a mean-spirited sense of arrogance toward others, a haughty sense of superiority. "Insult" is really too mild a translation in ***Hebrews 10:29***. When one abandons his faith, he despises, reviles, arrogantly ill-treats, and speaks ill of the Holy Spirit. This is not necessarily the same as the blasphemy against the Holy Spirit, but one who commits this sin is bringing himself into a situation where it is possible to take this final step.

Walvoord says that "quenching the Spirit may be simply defined as being unyielded to Him, or saying, 'No'" (197). Actually, all three of these sins—grieving, quenching, insulting—are saying NO! to the Spirit. We Christians still have free will. We must choose, either to say NO! and thus exclude the Spirit, either from part or from all our lives; or we must keep on saying YES! and be filled with the Spirit. The next section shows how to say YES! to the Spirit.

All three of these sins are saying NO! to the Spirit.

THE CHRISTIAN'S EIGHTFOLD PATH OF SANCTIFICATION

The essence of the Buddhist religion begins with its "four noble truths." They are as follows. One, man's basic problem is *suffering*: "to exist is to suffer." Two, the immediate cause of all suffering is *desire* (lust, craving)—for existence, for pleasure, for prosperity. Three, the solution to the problem of suffering thus is to eradicate all desire. Four, desire can be eradicated by following an *eightfold path*, which is as follows: 1) right knowledge (enlightenment), i.e., of the noble truths; 2) right aspirations or intentions; 3) right speech; 4) right conduct or action; 5) right livelihood; 6) right endeavor or effort; 7) right awareness; 8) right meditation or concentration.

Now, when I originally put together the following series of steps for using the Holy Spirit's power, it never occurred to me that I was constructing a *Christian* "eightfold path." That is purely coincidental! Nevertheless I am suggesting that if we want to access the Spirit's power that already resides within us—if we want to allow the Spirit to fill us—we can follow this eightfold path.

Step One: Information

The ideal Christian life is a life of holiness. But what counts as holiness? We cannot begin to be holy until we have this *information,* and the only sure information about it comes from the Bible, God's Word. Thus we must begin by learning from Scripture how God wants us to live. We must allow His Word to be a lamp to our feet and a light to our path (***Ps 119:105***); this is how He guides us in the paths of righteousness (***Ps 23:3***). We must also learn from Scripture what constitutes sin. Contrary to Buddhism, the ideal life is not freedom from desire as such, but freedom from *sin.* We know what counts as sin by studying the Word of God. *"All Scripture is inspired by God and profitable for teaching, for reproof, for correction, for training in righteousness"* (***2Tm 3:16***).

We cannot begin to be holy until we have information from the Bible, God's Word.

We must not only find this information in the Bible; we must also apply it to our own lives. We must honestly compare the state of our own general character and conduct with the ideal given to us in Scripture. This requires not just study of the Bible, but meditation upon its ethical teaching. We must do what David did: *"I will meditate on Your precepts and regard Your ways"* (***Ps 119:15***). *"I shall lift up my hands to Your commandments, which I love; and I will meditate on Your statutes"* (***Ps 119:48***). We must say with David, *"O how I love Your law! It is my meditation all the day"* (***Ps 119:97***).

Step Two: Awareness

The second step of the Christian's eightfold path is *awareness*: we must be aware that we have the Holy Spirit Himself dwelling within us, and that He is in us for the very purpose of giving us the power to be holy. Providing this awareness has been the major point of this chapter.

Step Three: Desire

Buddhism says that desire or craving as such is the root of all suffering; thus we must work to rid ourselves of *all* desire. This is not true. Desire is harmful or wrong only when we are de[illegible]ing something else that is in itself wrong. Our Bi[illegible] [illegible]sually call this "lust" or "evil desire." [illegible] [illegible]*h and the lust of the ey*[illegible] [illegible]*esh"* (**Gal 5:16**). But so[illegible] [illegible]ed heaven (***Php 1:23***[illegible] [illegible]). Most significantly [illegible] [illegible]d *"the desire to do wh*[illegible] [illegible]is evil (***Rom 7:18-21***, [illegible] [illegible]*o live honorably in eve*[illegible] [illegible]*o live godly in Christ Je*[illegible]

This kind of [illegible] [illegible]e sary step to ho[illegible] above all desire [illegible] and to be persona[illegible] rus I remember fr[illegible] puts it this way: "My[illegible] like Jesus! My desire-[illegible]! His Spirit fill me, His love o'erwhelm me; in deed and word—to be like Him."

Step Four: Prayer

The first three steps are in a sense a "warming up" for this one; here is where we begin to personally and directly plug into the Holy Spirit's power for holy living. We must pray specifically for His power to aid us in overcoming specific sins and growing in specific ways. Our model for such a prayer is ***Ephesians 3:16***, where Paul prays for us, that God *"would grant you, according to the riches of His glory, to be strengthened with power through His Spirit in the inner man."*

This prayer, however, is simply the starting point. We must apply it to specific areas of our lives, those areas where we need to put sin to death and grow in holiness. We do not simply pray generically, thus: "I pray for the Holy Spirit to help me to grow as a Christian and to be able to resist temptation." Rather, we pray something like this: "God, please grant me, according to the riches of your glory, to be strengthened with power through your Spirit in my heart *to be able to overcome the anger that comes over me, sometimes for no good cause."* Or, *". . . to be able to fight the feelings of lust that keep popping up in my consciousness."* Such prayers must focus on specific sins, and must involve confessing our sins and laying our heart before God. We should pray that the Spirit would help us not only to get rid of the sin itself, but to overcome the *desire* to commit that sin. We must remember that God is at work in us, *"both to will and to work"* (***Php 2:13***). In other words, God the Spirit will help us not only to *do* the right thing, but to *want* to do the right thing. (See step three above.)

Serious prayer in the pursuit for holiness cannot be just one or two sentences, or just one or two minutes long. Such prayers must be measured more in hours than minutes. They must be strenuous, fervent, and persistent.

Step Five: Surrender

The fifth step is *surrender*. This involves the realization that our own will power is not sufficient to overcome sin and achieve holiness (see ***Rom 7:14-25***). Thus we must confess to God our own personal weakness and helplessness, and our dependence upon the Spirit's power. Then in our hearts we must truly surrender ourselves to that power.

We must confess to God our own personal weakness and helplessness, and our dependence upon the Spirit's power.

It is important to remember this especially in view of the fact that Satan and his demons are working against us, to tempt us and to lead us into sin. We need a power stronger than our own, to combat these enemies. And we have such power: *"Greater is He who is you than he who is in the world"* (***1Jn 4:4***). But we must truly understand that *His* is the power that we are depending on in our spiritual battles.

Step Six: Trust

The sixth step is *trust*. This may be the difficult part. Do we really *believe* everything we have been learning and affirming about the Holy Spirit and His indwelling presence and power? Do we really *believe* that God will answer our prayers for victory over sin, and strengthen us with power through His Spirit in the inner man? In ***Acts***

26:18 Jesus speaks of *"those who have been sanctified by faith in Me."* This applies not only to initial sanctification (as in this verse), but to the ongoing process as well. We must trust God to keep His promises, and one of His greatest promises is that He has given us His Holy Spirit, and that His Spirit will strengthen us with power. Let us remember that the struggle is sometimes hard, and let us resist the temptation to give up.

Step Seven: Action

Even though we have the Spirit's power within us, we cannot sit back like robots and expect the Spirit to just take over our bodies and minds, as if He were "possessing" us, so to speak. We ourselves must *act;* we must work; we must strive; we must fight. We have free will; we must make the *decision* to resist temptation and to do right. This is how we *"work out [our own] salvation with fear and trembling"* (***Php 2:12***). We must take responsibility for our Christian growth, and maintain self-control—but only after we have gone through the first six steps above: information, awareness, desire, prayer, surrender, and trust.

We ourselves must act; we must work; we must strive; we must fight.

Step Eight: Thanksgiving

The last step is to remember to *thank God* for the wonderful gift of the Holy Spirit, and for the power He gives us to conquer the works of the flesh and to produce the fruit of the Spirit. We must give Him the praise and the credit for every victory.

CHAPTER TEN

THE HOLY SPIRIT AND SPIRITUAL GIFTS

We have distinguished between the Holy Spirit's *saving* work and His *equipping* work. The former includes His work of convicting and regenerating sinners, and His work of sanctifying Christians. The latter refers to His bestowing of special ministries and abilities upon specific individuals, enabling them to perform needed services for the people of God. This equipping work was something the Holy Spirit was doing throughout the OT era. We have seen how He gave special abilities to prophets, craftsmen, and administrators.

In NT times the Spirit continues His equipping work, enabling individuals to perform specific tasks necessary for the building of the church as the spiritual house of God (***1Pet 2:5***), just as He empowered craftsmen with physical skills to build the tabernacle in OT times. While not every Israelite received this or other kinds of skills, in the church era it seems that every Christian is so equipped by the Spirit in one way or another. Paul says in ***1 Corinthians 12:7***, *"But to each one is given the manifestation of the Spirit for the common good."* **First Peter 4:10** says, *"As each one* *has received a special gift, employ it in serving one another."* These texts tell us, first, that *each one* has a gift; and second, that each of us is under *obligation to use* whatever gift we have; and, third, that we must use our gifts for the sake of *others*. This should make us eager to understand as much as we can about the NT teaching on spiritual gifts.

THE CONCEPT OF "SPIRITUAL GIFTS"

We should remember first of all that the Holy Spirit *Himself* is God's gift (*dorea*) to Christians in this NT era, beginning with Pentecost. The Pentecostal outpouring as such was God's gift of the Holy Spirit to the church as a whole (***Acts 10:45***; ***11:17***), and the Spirit's indwelling as bestowed in baptism is God's gift of the Holy Spirit to individual believers (***Acts 2:38***).

The Holy Spirit is not only a gift given; He is also the giver of gifts. In addition to His saving gifts of regeneration and sanctification, the Spirit gives us certain abilities or ministries, thus equipping us for service. There is *no connection* between the Spirit as gift and the Spirit as giver, though. OT saints did not receive the gift of the Spirit as an indwelling presence, but the Spirit nonetheless bestowed gifts of service upon some of them. That is, the "gifts of the Spirit" are not the result of and are not related to the fact that the Spirit dwells within us.

The Holy Spirit is not only a gift given; He is also the giver of gifts.

TERMINOLOGY

The complete phrase "spiritual gift" occurs only once in the NT, in ***Romans 1:11***, where Paul says to the Christians in Rome, *"For I long to see you so that I may impart some spiritual gift [charisma pneumatikon] to you."* Some think Paul is here referring to his apostolic ability to bestow miraculous gifts such as prophecy or tongue-speaking, as in ***Acts 19:6*** (e.g., **Lard, *Romans*, 35**). My conclusion, though (**Cottrell, *Romans*, 1:94-95**), is that the gift Paul wanted to bestow upon the Romans was the deeper meaning of the gospel (***Rom 1:15***; ***1Th 2:8-9***; ***1Cor 9:11***). This being the case, the fact is that the full phrase "spiritual gifts" is never used in the NT in the sense in which it is commonly understood today.

The terminology of *gift* or *gifts* is frequently used in the NT in this sense, though. The common verb *didomi* ("to give") is used thus three times, as in ***1 Corinthians 12:7***, *"But to each one is given the manifestation of the Spirit for the common good"* (see ***Rom 12:6***; ***1Cor 12:8***). The related nouns *dorea* (***Eph 4:7***) and *doma* (***Eph 4:8***) also refer to such gifts. The noun most commonly used for this concept is *charisma*, which is related to *charis*, the common word for "grace." The basic meaning of *charis* ("grace") as such is "a gift that pleases or brings joy," and it can be used for gifts other than saving grace. In fact, *charis* itself is used a few times to refer to the equipping gifts of the Spirit. For example, the apostle Peter refers to the whole package of spiritual gifts as *"the manifold grace [charis] of God"* (***1Pet 4:10***; see ***Rom 12:6***; ***Eph 4:7***).[1]

Charisma, though, is the word most commonly used for spiritual gifts in general. Since it is etymologically related to *charis*, our word for "grace," many try to read the concept of grace into *charisma* also. They speak of "spiritual gifts" as "grace-gifts" and think of them as "the result of grace" (e.g., **Griffiths, 13-14**). All the connotations of grace are then read into them, e.g., "the gifts are not only spiritual but also undeserved. They are grace gifts bestowed at conversion" (**ibid., 29**). We should beware of circular reasoning here, however. The main point is that *charisma*, like *charis* itself, basically means "a gift."

In the NT *charisma* is not used exclusively for equipping gifts (see, e.g., ***Rom 5:15-16***; ***6:23***; ***1Cor 7:7***), but it is used most often in this sense: ***Romans 12:6***; ***1 Corinthians 1:7***; ***12:4,9,28,30,31***; ***1 Timothy 4:14***; ***2 Timothy 1:6***; ***1 Peter 4:10***. Its frequent use thus, plus its consistent use in the crucial chapter of ***1 Corinthians 12***, make it the "word of choice" when we are speaking of gifts of the Spirit, as indicated by our anglicized use of it in our word "charismatic." We should note, however, that the NT *charismata* (plural of *charisma*) include both miraculous and non-miraculous gifts.

The word "spiritual," as applied to spiritual gifts, is the adjective *pneumatikos*. This word can be used in two senses. Something is "spiritual" if it is empowered by or derived from the *Holy* Spirit (***1Cor 2:13***; ***15:44,46***), just as a person is "spiritual" if led by the Holy Spirit (***1Cor 2:15***; ***14:37***; ***Gal 6:1***). Thus a "spiritual gift" is a gift bestowed by the Holy Spirit. In its other use, something is called "spiritual" if it is

[1]Paul refers several times to his gift of apostleship as a *charis* from God: ***Rom 1:5***; ***15:15-16***; ***1Cor 3:10***; ***15:10***; ***Gal 1:15***; ***2:9***; ***Eph 3:7-8***.

related to *man's* spirit or to the spiritual world as such (***Rom 15:27***; ***1Cor 9:11***; ***Eph 1:3***; ***6:12***; ***1Pet 2:5***). In this sense a "spiritual gift" is related to the spiritual life of Christians.

The former sense is probably the more dominant one in the two texts where *pneumatikos* is used to refer to spiritual gifts: ***1 Corinthians 12:1*** and ***1 Corinthians 14:1***. In these texts the Greek adjective is used by itself, without the assumed noun *charismata* ("gifts"). Because the subject matter of the context is obviously such gifts, translators often add "gifts" in the Bible versions (e.g., NASB, NIV, ESV). ***First Corinthians 14:12*** is similar, using the plural of the noun *pneuma* instead of the adjective *pneumatikos,* again without the noun *charismata*. Literally it is "of spirits" or "of spirit-things," but is usually translated as "spiritual gifts" (e.g., NASB, NIV, NRSV). The ESV has *"manifestations of the Spirit."* That these terms in these passages are no doubt referring to the Holy Spirit's relation to the "spiritual" gifts is indicated by the seven contextual references to the Holy Spirit as the source of such gifts (***1Cor 12:4,7,8,9,11***).

The Giver of the Gifts

We have become quite comfortable referring to these equipping gifts as "spiritual gifts" or "gifts of the Spirit." It should be noted, though, that God the Father participates in the bestowing of such gifts: ***Romans 12:3***; ***1 Corinthians 12:6,28***; ***1 Peter 4:11***. The same is true of God the Son, Jesus our Lord: ***1 Corinthians 12:5***; ***Ephesians 4:7-11***. Nevertheless we are still warranted in using the term *"spiritual* gifts," since the Spirit's role in bestowing them seems to be predominant. This is seen from the OT data about spiritual gifts as discussed in an earlier chapter, as well as from the use of *pneumatikos* in ***1 Corinthians 12:1*** and ***14:1***, and from the seven references to the Spirit as the source of gifts in ***1 Corinthians 12:4-11***. ***First Corinthians 12:7*** specifically says that each gift is "the manifestation of the Spirit." After naming nine gifts in ***verses 8-10***, Paul says, *"But one and the same Spirit works all these things"* (***v. 11***).

We are warranted in using the term "spiritual gifts," since the Spirit's role seems to be predominant.

We stress again, though, that this equipping work of the Spirit is *not* the result of His indwelling presence. Thus we should not say that "the gifts (plural) flow from the gift (singular) of the Holy Spirit" (contra **Baxter, *Gifts*, 27**), or that a believer thus "receives his spiritual gifts at the moment of conversion" (**ibid., 52**).

THE PURPOSE OF SPIRITUAL GIFTS

The saving work of the Spirit meets the needs of the individual, but His equipping work has a different purpose. The Spirit gives ministries and abilities to individuals, so that those individuals may use these gifts to meet the needs of God's covenant people as a whole. This is the way it was in OT times, and the same is true now in this New Covenant age.

THE INTERDEPENDENCE OF THE MEMBERS OF THE BODY

Peter says we must exercise our gifts in such a way that *"God may be glorified"* (***1Pet 4:11***), which of course is the ultimate goal of everything we do. The more immediate purpose of one's gift, though, is to *"employ it in serving one another"* (***1Pet 4:10***). As Paul states this point in ***1 Corinthians 12:7***, *"But to each one is given the manifestation of the Spirit for the common good,"* or for one another's benefit.

Paul illustrates this point about the purpose of the gifts by comparing the church with the human body. He uses this analogy in each of the three main passages where he discusses the subject: ***Romans 12:4-5***; ***1 Corinthians 12:12-27***; ***Ephesians 4:12,16***. He notes that although the human body is composed of many different parts, each having its own unique purpose, the body is nonetheless a single, unified organism that will function properly only when each part fulfills its own purpose. Also, the well-being of any individual member of the body is dependent upon all the other members carrying out their respective responsibilities.

> **The well-being of any member is dependent upon all others carrying out their responsibilities.**

This is exactly the way the church works, he says. The church is the one body of Jesus Christ, and each Christian is like a member of that body—an eye, an ear, a finger, etc. Each Christian's spiritual gift constitutes his function as a member of the body. Thus by exercising one's spiritual gift, one contributes to the well-being of every other member of the body as well as to the proper functioning of the body as a whole. *"For just as we have many members in one body and all the members do not have the same function, so we, who are many, are one body in Christ, and individually members one of another"* (***Rom 12:4-5***). In ***1 Corinthians 12:12*** Paul says, *"For even as the body is one and yet has many members, and all the members of the body, though they are many, are one body, so also is Christ."* Then in a long discourse on the interdependence of all the members of the body (***1Cor 12:14-26***), Paul stresses this point: we need each other, i.e., we need each others' *spiritual gifts*.

More specifically, our spiritual gifts have been committed to our stewardship (***1Pet 4:10***) so that we may use them to *edify* or build up the church as a whole. This is why the gift of prophecy is better than the gift of tongues (unless the latter are interpreted), because the *"one who prophesies edifies the church"* (***1Cor 14:4***; see ***v. 5***). Paul exhorts the Corinthian church, *"So also you, since you are zealous of spiritual gifts, seek to abound in the edification of the church"* (***1Cor 14:12***). Also, *"Let all things be done for edification"* (***1Cor 14:26b***).

Paul applies the body analogy to the use of the specific gifts named in ***Ephesians 4:11***: apostles, prophets, evangelists, and pastor-teachers. These gifts, he says, are for the purpose of *"the equipping of the saints for the work of service, to the building up of the body of Christ"* (***Eph 4:12***). Through the proper use of these gifts, the church will grow to maturity like a youth that has been well fed and who will ultimately develop a strong, mature body. When "each individual part" of the body exercises its gift, the church will *"grow up in all aspects into Him who is the head, even Christ, from whom the whole body, being fitted and held together by what every joint supplies, according to the proper working of each individual part, causes the growth of the body for the building up of itself in love"* (***Eph 4:15-16***).

"In love," says Paul! The conscientious use of our gifts thus is required by the compulsion of our love for one another (see ***1Pet 4:8-10***). Not to use our gifts, then, is selfish and unloving. "The very nature of the gifts," says Thomas Edgar, "indicates that they are given to enable the recipient to minister to others" (**40**). Schatzmann says, "The intent of individual giftedness for serv-

Not to use our gifts is selfish and unloving.

ice, therefore, cannot lie in individualism but always points to the higher goal of the corporate body in togetherness." He continues, "Charismata, although bestowed upon individuals by the Holy Spirit, are meant for the service unto, and for the upbuilding of, the community as the Spirit directs" (**68**).

The Principle of Need

It is very important to understand that the Holy Spirit bestows the equipping gifts *to meet the needs* of God's people. Specific gifts are given according to specific needs. This principle of need must be grasped in order to have a proper understanding of spiritual gifts. The key idea is that the needs of God's people *will differ* according to changes in time and circumstances. Just because a particular gift is present at one point in the history of redemption does not mean that it must or will be present at all other points. The gifts will vary as the needs vary.

The OT abounds with examples of this principle. The deliverance of God's people from Egypt and the establishment of the old covenant required certain unique and restricted gifts. The role of Moses himself has no real parallel in the subsequent history of God's people, either in the OT or the NT. His specific package of gifts was needed for that time and that time alone. The building of the tabernacle required the bestowing of physical skills for craftsmanship and artisanship that are not necessary and not given in the new-covenant era. God's people no longer have either judges or kings, and therefore have no need for such gifts.

Likewise the era of transition from the old covenant to the new covenant was unique and created many needs that required gifts of a unique and temporary nature. Chief among these needs was leadership that was roughly comparable to that of Moses in some ways (but not others), especially in regard to the overseeing of the establishment of the new covenant and the new-covenant people. This need was fulfilled through the gift of apostleship, a gift that was deliberately and necessarily confined to the foundational era of the church. There was also the need for much new revelation, in order to make known the will of God in various ways with respect to new-covenant faith and practice. This need was fulfilled not only through the gift of apostles but also through the gift of prophets, whose teaching together formed the epistemological foundation for the church (***Eph 2:20***).

The point is that the Spirit bestowed His ministries and abilities, and continues to do so, according to the principle of need. If the church needs it, the Spirit gives it. If the church no longer needs it, the Spirit no longer gives it. (F... discussion of this poi... the next section.)

The Spirit bestows ministries and abilities according to the principle of need.

CATEG...

... ...ut have not yet said ... the NT. In this sectic ... and will ask wheth...

L...

There ... ...nt *1 Peter 4:11* as a li... ...ing gifts and serving ... *...inthians 12:8-10*; *1 Co...* ...e versions often g... ...ious gifts. Here I will giv... ... versions: the NIV, the NASB, and t...

NIV	NASB	NRSV
1. ***Romans 12:3-8***		
a. prophesying	prophecy	prophecy
b. serving	service	ministry
c. teaching	he who teaches	the teacher
d. encouraging	he who exhorts	the exhorter
e. contributing to the needs of others	he who gives	the giver
f. leadership	he who leads	the leader
g. showing mercy	he who shows mercy	the compassionate
2. ***1 Corinthians 12:8-10***		
a. message of wisdom	word of wisdom	utterance of wisdom
b. message of knowledge	word of knowledge	utterance of knowledge
c. faith	faith	faith
d. gifts of healing	gifts of healing	gifts of healing
e. miraculous powers	effecting of miracles	working of miracles
f. prophecy	prophecy	prophecy
g. distinguishing between spirits	distinguishing of spirits	discernment of spirits

h. different kinds of tongues	various kinds of tongues	various kinds of tongues
i. interpretation of tongues	interpretation of tongues	interpretation of tongues
3. ***1 Corinthians 12:28-30***		
a. apostles	apostles	apostles
b. prophets	prophets	prophets
c. teachers	teachers	teachers
d. workers of miracles	miracles	deeds of power
e. gifts of healing	gifts of healing	gifts of healing
f. ability to help others	helps	forms of assistance
g. administration	administrations	forms of leadership
h. kinds of tongues	various kinds of tongues	various kinds of tongues
i. interpretation	interpretation	interpretation
4. ***Ephesians 4:11***		
a. apostles	apostles	apostles
b. prophets	prophets	prophets
c. evangelists	evangelists	evangelists
d. pastors-and-teachers	pastors-and-teachers	pastors-and-teachers

No one of these lists is a formal, complete listing of all the gifts that the Spirit gives to His people. I would not go as far as Keener, who says that Paul's lists are "ad hoc—that is, he is making them up 'on the spot'—and they vary considerably" (**111**). The variations in the lists seem to be at least somewhat explainable. In ***Romans 12*** Paul is dealing with the sanctified life and thus concentrates more heavily on "ordinary" gifts. In ***1 Corinthians 12*** he is dealing with problems in the Corinthian church caused by the misuse of certain miraculous gifts; thus he includes more of these in the listings in that chapter. ***Ephesians 4:11*** focuses on the equipping gifts.

Many will agree that these lists, even when combined, are not necessarily all-inclusive. There may be other gifts not named in the NT that have been or are being bestowed by the Spirit, sometimes in view of new needs that may arise. I agree with Pettegrew: "There probably were other gifts, although the ones that Paul discusses are representative of the types of abilities bestowed on the early Christians" (**163**). Marshall Leggett agrees: "It seems to me that music is a gift the Holy Spirit gives to some Christians which they use to bless the lives of other

There may be other gifts not named in the NT, sometimes in view of new needs that may arise.

Christians. Physical plant management may be a gift needed for the body to be functional in our age" (**Gifts 2:7**). Stott says it may be that each list "is a limited selection from a much larger total" (***Baptism*, 88**). He opines, "Was not Charles Wesley's ability as a hymn-writer as much a *charisma* as his brother John's gift as an evangelist? And what are we to say about gospel singers, Christian poets, and men and women with outstanding spiritual gifts . . . in Christian literature, musical composition, broadcasting and television?" (**ibid., 89**). For our era one might add expertise in computer science or electronics to the list.

DISTINCTIONS WITHIN THE GIFTS

As one reads through the lists of gifts, it seems fairly easy to group some gifts together into one category and others into another category. After doing this, one may look at the lists again and find still other kinds of groupings, without any of them being necessarily comprehensive or lining up neatly with the others. My first inclination is to remember that the Holy Spirit's works can be divided into two main categories: He gives us *knowledge*, and He gives us *power*. When spiritual gifts are considered individually, some involve the gift of knowledge (e.g., prophecy, word of knowledge) and some involve the gift of power (e.g., gifts of healing, effecting of miracles). But some gifts do not fit neatly into either category (e.g., administrations, showing mercy). In another sense, since each gift is an empowerment by the Spirit, *all* gifts are an expression of the Spirit's power.

Another possibility is to think of Peter's summary in ***1 Peter 4:11a*** as implying that there are two categories of gifts: *"Whoever speaks, is to do so as one who is speaking the utterances of God; whoever serves is to do so as one who is serving by the strength which God supplies."* The two categories would be gifts of speaking and gifts of serving. J.I. Packer calls these "gifts of speech and Samaritanship"—as in "the good Samaritan" (**55**); but as he acknowledges, there are also "sign-gifts" such as healing and speaking in tongues (**ibid.**). Hocking thus offers these three categories: speaking gifts, serving gifts, and supernatural gifts (**32**).

Could we simply speak of the *supernatural* gifts, then, as opposed to those that are merely "natural"? This does not really do justice to the concept of the supernatural, though. As Keener observes, "The Christian worldview acknowledges that *everything* in our lives is ultimately 'supernatural,' because even the food on our table is a gift of God's providence" (**107**). This may be going too far, given the distinction between God's *general* providence and His *special* providence (see **Cottrell, *Ruler*, chs. 3–5**). But there is certainly an ambiguity in the word "supernatural" when it is used in reference to spiritual gifts. Since they are indeed gifts from the Holy Spirit, then *every* gift is supernatural with respect to its *origin*, though not all are supernatural in their *effects*. Pettegrew is correct: "We must be careful not to miss the distinction between the bestowal of gifts and the operation of the gifts. Not all gifts produced supernatural, spectacular operations. The gift of helps, for example, was probably not supernatural in its outworking, whereas the gift of miracles was" (**162**). If we remember the distinction between origin on the one hand, and effect or manifestation on the other hand, we could divide the gifts into those that are supernatural in their effect and those that are not.

As gifts from the Holy Spirit, every gift is supernatural in its origin, though not all in effects.

Is this the same as the distinction between *miraculous* and *nonmiraculous* gifts? In the way most people use these terms, yes. But in the strict sense of the word "miracle," some supernatural gifts are not miracles. The supernatural gifts (supernatural in terms of manifestation) can be divided into gifts involving supernatural *knowledge,* and gifts involving supernatural *power*. Strictly speaking, only the latter qualify as miracles or signs. A miracle is a *visible* act, usually performed by an agent, which violates natural law and functions as a *sign* or evidence for the truth of the miracle-worker's claims. Thus if we distinguish between gifts of supernatural knowledge and gifts of supernatural power, only the latter are miracles, in the technical sense.

We recognize, though, that most people do tend to divide spiritual gifts into the two categories of miraculous and nonmiraculous. I use this terminology myself, and will do so in the following pages of this book. But as I use the term "miraculous" in this context, it is a kind of shorthand description for *all* spiritual gifts that are supernatural in their *effect,* including both supernatural knowledge and supernatural power (even though only the latter group qualifies as "miracles" in the strictest sense).[2]

The Main Distinction: Temporary vs. Permanent

We must now discuss what is the most controversial way of categorizing spiritual gifts, namely, the distinction between the *temporary* gifts and the *permanent* gifts. Those who are Pentecostal or Charismatic object to this distinction, believing that all of the gifts in all four lists are intended to be present in the church until Christ's second coming. Others believe that only some of the gifts are intended to continue permanently, with some being intended only for the "start-up" period of the church and thus temporary. Taking the latter view Lewis Foster says, "The gifts of the Spirit can be divided into two types: the temporary gifts and the continuing gifts" (**Gifts,** 3). Those who take the latter view are called "cessationists," since they believe that certain gifts have ceased. This is my view, and I will defend it in the next chapter. In this section I will attempt to explain it.

The justification for speaking of some gifts as temporary and some as permanent is the principle of *need,* as explained above. The Spirit gives His gifts to meet the *needs* of God's people. Since some needs are temporary, so are some gifts. We may remember again the examples from the OT, especially the gifts of physical craftsmanship and artisanship required for the building of the tabernacle. With the possible exception of the time of the building of the original temple, we infer that these gifts have ceased because the unique circumstances that required them have ceased. Their purpose was fulfilled in those circumstances; they are no longer needed.

The same principle applies to the spiritual gifts named in the four NT lists cited above. The Spirit began giving these gifts on the very day the church began (tongues on Pentecost), and continued to bestow them through the earliest decades of the church's existence, as their very mention in Paul's and Peter's letters shows. But it is fair to ask

[2]One can see how difficult it is to keep the categories straight by considering Marshall Leggett's attempt: "Many students of the Bible divide the gifts of the Spirit into two categories. One group is referred to as the supernatural, temporary gifts, sometimes called 'sign gifts.' The others are called the natural, permanent gifts or 'service gifts'" (2:7). We agree at least on "temporary" and "permanent"!

whether there were any circumstances and any needs that were present in those early decades that at some point ceased to exist; and therefore any spiritual gifts, designed to meet those temporary needs, that have also ceased to exist. The answer is surely yes.

The historical situation of the church in its early years was completely unique, and very different from its circumstances after only a few decades and certainly from today. From the day of Pentecost forward, God's people were living under a totally New Covenant, with a new kingdom administration, new worship practices, new evangelistic responsibilities, and new divine realities to be understood, proclaimed, and applied. Yet they lacked an authoritative written revelation, a canon of Scripture comparable to the Old Covenant Scriptures, that explained God's will for His people under these new circumstances. In other words, they did not yet have the written NT, something that did not become completely available until at least the second century and something that we take for granted today.

We do indeed take our possession of the written NT for granted. When we need to know the answers to questions about doctrine and practice, we just get out our Bibles. When we need answers to questions about Jesus and His church, we just consult the NT. It is very difficult for us to identify with the Christians in those early years of the church, and to imagine what it would have been like to live a Christian life and carry on the work of the church without our New Testaments! No wonder Christians in those days needed some spiritual gifts that we do not need today! As Pettegrew notes, "They had the Old Testament Scriptures, of course, but one can imagine how difficult it must have been for their leaders to explain new covenant doctrine and practical Christian living without the New Testament Scriptures" (**158**). Pettegrew gives these examples:

It is very difficult for us to identify with the early Christians who did not have our New Testaments.

> The first generation of Christians would also be perplexed about the basics of the administration of the local church. How was the government supposed to be set up? Who could be a deacon or an elder? The believers could not turn to ***1 Timothy 3*** to find the qualifications for church leaders because that book had not been written yet. They could not

> study the book of Ephesians in discussing dispensational and ecclesiological developments because the apostle Paul had not yet written Ephesians. (**ibid.**)

The main need, of course, was for new revelation. As Walvoord says, "The need for the prophetic gift in the apostolic period is evident. There had been a tremendous doctrinal transition from what was commonly believed by the Jews to what constituted the Christian faith. The New Testament was not written immediately, and there was imperative need for an authoritative source of revelation of the will of God" (**178**).

These new needs created a temporary need for gifts of supernatural knowledge to supply the new revelation, and for gifts of supernatural power to serve as confirming signs or evidence for the new revelation. These are what are usually called "miraculous gifts," even though only the latter produce miracles in a technical sense. These gifts were occasioned by the unique circumstances of the early church, and thus were temporary based on the principle of need.

Some think that Paul's description of apostles and prophets as the epistemological foundation on which the church is built (***Eph 2:20***) implies the temporary nature of their functions. Richard Gaffin explains, "In any construction project . . . the foundation comes at the beginning and does not have to be relaid repeatedly. . . . In terms of this dynamic model for the church, the apostles and prophets belong to the period of the foundation. In other words, by the divine architect's design, the presence of apostles and prophets in the history of the church is temporary" (**43**).

Using the same imagery of constructing a building, some liken the miraculous gifts to the scaffolding which is necessary during the early construction stage. But as Leggett says, "When the building is done the scaffolding comes down because it is no longer necessary." As applied to the church, "In the beginning of the new covenant of grace there were the signs, wonders, miracles, and mighty acts of God used to validate the apostles' message. But when the gospel was fully known, the 'scaffolding' came down. The sign gifts were no longer necessary" (**2:7**). Nor were the revelatory gifts, we should add.

Some liken miraculous gifts to the scaffolding necessary during early construction.

Using the analogy of an individual growing from infancy to maturity, Leon Morris makes the same point. Some gifts, he says, were "for the time of the Church's infancy. They did not last for very long, and in the providence of God evidently they were not expected to last for very long. In those early days there was the outpouring of the Spirit of God to supply every need of the infant community. And some of those needs were not our needs" (***Spirit***, **63-64**).

We conclude that spiritual gifts should be divided into two categories: the temporary and the permanent. The former is the category of the miraculous, the latter of the nonmiraculous.

Miracles without Miraculous Gifts?

Some cessationists—those who believe that miraculous gifts have ceased—believe it is important to distinguish between spiritual gifts that enable someone to work a miracle, and miracles performed directly by God Himself without the intervention of a miracle-worker. In the former case, e.g., a person with the gift of healing may be the channel through which God's healing power works. In the latter case, God may heal directly simply in answer to prayer. To say that the *gift* of healing has ceased does not necessarily mean that God Himself has ceased healing the sick; or to say that *miraculous gifts* have ceased does not mean that *miraculous works of God* have ceased. As Edgar says, we should avoid the tendency "to confuse spiritual gifts with God's miraculous works" (**37**; see **Baxter, *Gifts*, 129**).

To say that miraculous gifts have ceased does not mean that miraculous works of God have ceased.

I agree that it is very important to make this distinction. God does continue to heal many sick people and to perform many wonderful works, especially in answer to prayer. As said earlier, any act of God is certainly a *supernatural* event, and cessationists do not rule out the supernatural. The question is whether we should call such supernatural deeds "miracles," though, since they usually do not function as signs intended to confirm revealed truth. It depends again on how strict we want to be in our terminology. In this case I prefer to call such direct acts of God *special divine providence*. See my book on ***God the Ruler*, chapters 4-5 and pages 261-263**.

EXPLANATION OF THE GIFTS

In this section we shall try to offer a brief explanation of the various spiritual gifts. About some of them we can only speculate, since the NT does not give us details about their use. There will also be some overlapping within subcategories, e.g., healing is a kind of miracle and prophecy would seem to include "word of knowledge." In any case we shall do our best to give the sense of each gift.

TEMPORARY GIFTS

Within the category of temporary gifts we shall distinguish the gift of apostleship, gifts of revealed knowledge, and gifts of miraculous power.

The Office of Apostle

Apostles are named in ***Ephesians 4:11*** and twice in ***1 Corinthians 12:28-30***. The word "apostle" (*apostolos*) comes from a common Greek verb, *apostello*, which means "to send, to send out, to send on a mission." In a generic sense an apostle is anyone sent on a mission, such as the three men (Titus and two others) whom Paul sent to Corinth to facilitate the offering he was collecting for the poor in Jerusalem (***2Cor 8:23***); also Epaphroditus, sent by the church at Philippi to minister to Paul's needs (***Php 2:25***); and Jesus Himself, sent from heaven to be our Savior (***Heb 3:1***).

The word "apostle" is linguistically equivalent to our word "missionary," and is probably used in that sense of "Barnabas and Saul" (***Acts 13:2-4***) in ***Acts 14:4,14***, and of Andronicus and Junias in ***Romans 16:7***. Some think that the spiritual gift of apostleship refers to anyone thus "sent forth to preach the message of the cross" (**Schatzmann, 44**), or "church-planting missionaries" (**Griffiths, 26**). This is possible, but highly unlikely. This function is more likely included in the gift of evangelists.

The word "apostle" is linguistically equivalent to our word "missionary."

It is almost certain that the gift of apostles refers to the *office* of apostle, i.e., to the men chosen by Jesus Christ to be His personal representatives in establishing the church following His ascension. These are "the twelve apostles" (***Mt 10:2***), commonly referred to simply as "the twelve" (with Judas being replaced by Matthias, ***Acts 1:26***), to which was added the apostle Paul (***2Cor 12:11-12***; ***Gal 1:1,17***). When Paul says in ***1 Corinthians 12:28*** that *"God has appointed in the church, first apostles,"* he is saying that this gift is of first importance. It is also the most comprehensive gift, since apostles seem to have been given other gifts as a part of their calling, e.g., prophecy, teaching, administrations (involving their general authoritative leadership), tongues, and miracles (***2Cor 12:12***).

It is also quite clear that the gift of apostles was a temporary gift, intended only for the foundational era of the church universal (***Eph 2:20***). The existence of this gift is limited by the conditions laid down for the choosing of Judas's successor in ***Acts 1:21-26***; i.e., it was necessary for an apostle to have been a direct witness of the earthly ministry of Jesus Christ (or at least to have witnessed the risen Christ, as did Paul, ***Acts 9:1-6***). In any case this inherent limitation upon those who are qualified to be apostles justifies our distinction between temporary and permanent gifts (see **Edgar, 53-63**).

It is quite clear that the gift of apostles was a temporary gift for the foundational era of the church.

Gifts of Revealed Knowledge

Some of the temporary gifts of the Spirit were intended to equip certain individuals to be channels through which revealed and inspired knowledge could be passed along to the early Christians. The need for such an ability, as explained earlier, was occasioned by the lack of an authoritative body of writing (i.e., the NT Scriptures) to guide the church in its formative years. Speaking inspired messages from God was part of the work of an apostle, of course. But as the church grew, and as more and more congregations were planted throughout the Roman empire, there simply were not enough apostles for one to be present in every geographical area much less in every local congregation. This is why gifts of revealed knowledge were given to other selected individuals, probably in each congregation. The knowledge or truth revealed through them was just as authoritative as that which came through the apostles, but the recipients of these gifts were not given the general authority exercised by the apostles.

Prophets. The principal gift of revealed knowledge was prophecy, which is the only gift named in all four of Paul's lists. A prophet literally is someone who speaks on behalf of someone else, a "spokesman." Those who received the gift of prophecy were prophets *of God*, i.e., they spoke on behalf of God.

Some have concluded that the prophesying that results from this gift of the Spirit is just the speaking of God's message, something that is done even today by all who preach and teach the Word of God. Thus they deny that the gift of prophecy is miraculous, much less temporary. Kuyper, for example, says that "by prophecy St. Paul designates animated preaching, wherein the preacher feels himself cheered and inspired by the Holy Spirit" (**187**). John MacArthur calls it "the gift of preaching, of proclaiming the Word of God" (***Romans*, 2:170**). Barry Blackburn says that Pentecost fulfilled Moses' desire (***Num 11:29***) by bestowing the gift of prophecy upon all (***Acts 2:17***), "to enable them to bear faithful witness to their Lord" (**12**).

In my judgment this view simply does not conform to the biblical concept of a prophet, a concept established by its extensive OT use. As Keener rightly observes, "Those who think that prophecy in ***1 Corinthians 12–14*** is merely preaching must treat as irrelevant the Old Testament use of the term (the background Paul shared with his Christian readers), the use in Acts, and the use in the text itself" (**116**). Green agrees that this view "could only be maintained in defiance of the whole weight of New Testament evidence" (**171**). The significance of prophecy was second only to the apostleship itself (***1Cor 12:28***; ***Eph 4:11***), and Paul links prophets with apostles with respect to the foundational function of their teaching authority (***Eph 2:20***; ***3:5***). It was never intended to be given to all Christians, not even in the early church (***1Cor 12:29***).

Thus we must conclude that the gift of prophecy was a *miraculous* spiritual gift in the same category as apostles. What a prophet proclaimed was "inspired speech, words given as from 'without' (by the Spirit) and not consciously formulated by the mind" (**Dunn, *Romans*, 2:727**). An apostle's personal authority was more general and abiding than that of a prophet, but the inspired words of a prophet were just as true and authoritative as the inspired words of an apostle. As Stott says, the biblical prophet is "the mouthpiece of God, the organ of fresh revelation" (***Baptism*, 102**). This is the most generally accepted view, and it should be insisted upon.

Such prophetic revelation could involve prediction of future events (cf. Agabus, ***Acts 11:28***; ***21:10-11***), but more often it was simply the disclosure of God's truth and God's will for the church. Such prophecy was given mostly in local church situations (according to Paul's teaching in ***1 Corinthians 14***), but it could also involve the writing of canonical Scripture (see ***1Pet 1:19-21***; ***Rev 22:18-19***). In my judgment all NT books not written by apostles were written by men who had the gift of prophecy. Thus (NT) prophets and apostles together form the epistemological foundation for the church for all times (***Eph 2:20***; ***3:5***). Though it was bestowed only in the early decades of the church, the importance of this gift is still felt today every time we read from our New Testaments (see **Schatzmann, 21-22**).

The importance of the gift of prophecy is still felt today every time we read from our New Testaments.

Given this revelatory nature of prophecy, if the gift of prophecy existed today, we would have to treat its product as equivalent to Scripture. Thus we would have to abandon the *sola scriptura* principle, i.e., the idea that the Bible alone is our only rule or norm for faith and practice.

Distinguishing of Spirits. In the apostolic era some Christians received the gift of *"the distinguishing of spirits"* (***1Cor 12:10***). This is often taken to be the ability to discern whether or not someone has been invaded by a demon and is in need of deliverance. This may have been a part of it, but it is unlikely in view of the fact that miraculous power is usually not required to discern a demonic presence. The main point of this gift was the ability to discern whether messages alleging to be from God were truly inspired by the *Holy* Spirit, or whether they were false messages from *demonic* spirits (***1Tm 4:1***).

Satan is *"a liar and the father of lies"* (***Jn 8:44***) and is continually seeking to substitute his lies for God's truth. This is why John commanded, *"Beloved, do not believe every spirit, but test the spirits to see whether they are from God, because many false prophets have gone out into the world"* (***1Jn 4:1***). Today we can test truth-claims by comparing them with Scripture, but in the early days of the church there was no NT that could be consulted for this purpose. This is why such a gift was needed. As Walvoord says,

> It was essential to the early church to have divine assistance in detecting the false amidst the true. . . . As the New Testament had not been completed, there was no written Word to appeal to except the Old Testament. With the coming of the completed New Testament, the written Word made this work of the Spirit no longer necessary. (**188**)

In ***1 Corinthians 12:10*** this gift is mentioned immediately after prophecy, reflecting a close connection between the two. This connection is seen in ***1 Corinthians 14:29***, where Paul says concerning the use of the prophetic gift in a church assembly, *"Let two or three prophets speak, and let the others pass judgment."* Some think that even Spirit-inspired prophecy can be distorted by human error, and that is why "maturing prophets had to mentor one another by evaluating one another's prophecies," as in ***1 Corinthians 14:29*** (**Keener, 119**). Such a view must be rejected outright, since it negates the very purpose of prophetic inspiration. The need for the gift of testing prophecies (***1Cor 14:29***), i.e., distinguishing of spirits, arose from the danger of *false* prophets *pretending* to be speaking messages from God. *"Let the others pass judgment"* refers to the other *prophets*, who were probably the main ones to receive the gift of distinguishing of spirits. As Robert Thomas says, "'The others' [***v. 29***] who discerned were none other than the prophets themselves. While one prophet spoke, the rest listened and ruled upon the source and accuracy of his message. From this it is evident that those who possessed the gift of prophecy also possessed the gift of discernment" (**111**).

The need for the gift arose from the danger of false prophets pretending to be from God.

Word of Knowledge (***1Cor 12:8***). We know little about this gift, but it seems to be closely related to the gift of prophecy. Some do not equate it with revealed and infallible knowledge, but with the "ability to speak knowledge publicly, . . . imparting knowledge about God" which was nonetheless "incomplete and sometimes inaccurate" (**Keener, 112-113**). It was simply "the gift of teaching," says Keener (**ibid.**); see **Stott, *Baptism*, 95**. This is not consistent, however, with Paul's further reference to this gift in ***1 Corinthians 13***, where he links it with the obviously miraculous and temporary gifts of tongues and prophecy (***vv. 2,8-9***). All prophets probably had this gift, but some may have had it without having other gifts possessed by prophets, e.g., the ability to predict the future and to distinguish spirits. Their "word of knowledge" was nonetheless authoritative, revealed truth. See **Baxter, *Gifts*, 109-110.**

Word of Wisdom (***1Cor 12:8***). We know even less about this gift. Stott says there is no obvious reason to treat it as miraculous, and that it simply involves "a special measure of wisdom" (***Baptism*, 95**). But since it is grouped with eight other gifts that are clearly miraculous, we are justified in taking this "word of wisdom" to be more than the ordinary wisdom any Christian can receive as an answer to prayer (***Jas 1:5***).

Based on Paul's earlier discussion of wisdom in ***1 Corinthians 1:18–2:16***, Keener says that "the 'utterance of wisdom' . . . may represent the revelation of divine mysteries, based on insight into God's purposes rather than on merely human reasoning" (**112**). This insightful wisdom was focused specifically on the meaning of the death of Jesus, says Schatzmann; thus we can infer that the word of wisdom was "the inspired communication of God's redemptive decrees, especially that of the cross" (**36**).

This is possible, but it raises the question of how this would be different from the word of knowledge. It is more likely that the word of wisdom was the inspired ability to see the *implications* of knowledge revealed through the gift of prophecy or the word of knowledge, i.e., the ability to instruct others on how to apply that Word from God to individual lives and congregations. This is the kind of thing we usually associate with wisdom.

Tongues Plus the Interpretation of Tongues. Speaking in tongues by itself is a gift of miraculous power and functions as a sign, as in ***Acts 2***; but when combined with the gift of interpretation of tongues, the two together function as a source of revealed knowledge. One with the gift of tongues may also have the gift of interpretation of tongues; when used together in a church assembly they are able to edify the hearers in the same way that prophecy does (***1Cor 14:1-5***). As Schatzmann says, "It is the interpretation of tongues which edifies; therefore, at least in terms of effect, it becomes a gift equivalent to prophecy" (**43**). It appears that some who spoke in tongues did not have the gift of interpretation, while others could interpret but not speak in tongues themselves (***1Cor 14:26-28***).

Gifts of Miraculous Power

Another category of temporary gifts includes gifts of *miraculous power*. These are Spirit-bestowed miraculous abilities, i.e., the ability to do things not possible through natural powers as governed by natural laws. Their main purpose was to function as signs or evidence for the authenticity of the inspired messages given through the gifts of revealed knowledge and especially through the ministry of apostles (***2Cor 12:12***). Their connection with these other temporary gifts is a main reason why we say that these gifts of miraculous power are temporary also. Four such gifts are listed in the NT.

Faith. Paul says certain gifts are given to this or that person by the Holy Spirit, and *"to another faith by the same Spirit"* (***1Cor 12:9***). This faith is completely different from the saving faith which is a condition for salvation, which every Christian has as a result of his own free-will decision and not as a gift from the Holy Spirit.

This faith is completely different from the saving faith which is a condition for salvation.

Stott says it is "a special degree of faith . . . for some particular kind of ministry," and is not necessarily related to miracles (***Baptism*, 95**). In my judgment, though, this faith is not just a higher *degree* of our general belief in God's power and providence, but a special *kind* of faith that is directly related to the working of miracles. This is suggested by the way Paul connects it with the miraculous gifts of prophecy, tongues, and knowledge in ***1 Corinthians 13:1-2***. More significant is Paul's description of it as *"all faith, so as to remove mountains"* (***1Cor 13:2***). Keener says, "'Moving mountains' was a Jewish figure of speech for doing what was virtually impossible" (**113**). Jesus used this figure to characterize miracle-working faith in ***Matthew 17:20*** and ***Mark 11:22-24***. The gift of faith "may, therefore, denote a 'mysterious surge of confidence' that God will grant a healing or a miracle" (**Schatzmann, 37**). Thus it probably overlaps or is given in connection with the next two gifts.

Gifts of Healings. To some the Spirit gives "gifts of healings" (***1Cor 12:9,28,30***). This is the ability to apply God's healing power to a sick person, miraculously bringing about the healing of that person. "When in possession of this ability, a person became the specific divine channel for producing a miraculous cure for a physical problem" (**Robert Thomas, 32**). This healing is accomplished by divine power, but the person with the gift is the instrument for applying this power to the sick person. The purpose for such gifts of healings was to provide miraculous signs to confirm the gospel message and the newly revealed prophetic messages from God. Such miraculous healing should be distinguished from God's direct providential healing as an answer to prayer.

> **The purpose was to provide miraculous signs to confirm the gospel message.**

Effecting of Miracles (***1Cor 12:10,28,29***). This gift is basically the same as the previous one in source, manifestation, and purpose, except it enables its recipient to work miracles other than healing. As Keener says, "This gift probably overlaps with 'gifts of healing' and 'faith' elsewhere in the list. But it undoubtedly includes other kinds of miracles as well, such as nature miracles," like calming a storm or controlling rain (**115**). Edgar says it may include the gifts mentioned in ***Matthew 16:17-20*** (**39, 89-90**). It certainly may include miraculous exorcisms, since this gift is not specifically mentioned elsewhere (see ***Mt 7:22***). Deliverance from demons does not always require miraculous power, however.

Kinds of Tongues (***1Cor 12:10,28,30***). Speaking in tongues is the miraculous ability to speak intelligible communications in a language that one has never studied and does not understand. Some speculate that such "tongues" may include ecstatic utterances unrelated to any ordinary human language. Thayer thus describes it as "the gift of men who, rapt in an ecstasy and no longer quite masters of their own reason and consciousness, pour forth their glowing spiritual emotions in strange utterances, rugged, dark, disconnected, quite unfitted to instruct or to influence the minds of others" (**118**).

Most agree on the basis of ***Acts 2*** that at least some tongues must be real human languages; and many argue that all genuine, Spirit-inspired tongues must be real languages, even those discussed by Paul in ***1 Corinthians 12–14***. Keener says, "In contrast to some Pentecostals, I believe that 'tongues' in both ***Acts*** and ***1 Corinthians*** refers to genuine languages unknown to the speaker" (**122**). Walvoord argues for the same position. Beginning with the genuine-language tongues in Acts, he says, "The use of identical terms in reference to speaking with tongues in ***Acts*** and ***1 Corinthians*** leaves no foundation for a distinction" (**183**). The fact that tongues were supposed to function as a sign to unbelievers (***1Cor 14:22***) supports this view, since tongues as sounds intelligible to no one would hardly have this effect.

Some say the content of what was spoken in such tongues was mainly prayer and praise to God (***Acts 2:11***; ***10:46***; ***1Cor 14:14-17***), i.e., "spirit-led prayer" (**Keener, 121**). Since tongues are a form of prophesying (***Acts 2:17-18***; see ***Mt 7:22***; ***Acts 19:6***), and since, when interpreted, tongues could edify the whole church (***1Cor 14:5***), we cannot rule out the possibility that other kinds of messages were communicated through such tongues. In any case the main point of the gift of tongues was not its content but its effectiveness as a sign, i.e., as proof for the truth of NT revelation given otherwise (as in ***Acts 2:11-12***; ***10:44-47***; see ***1Cor 14:22***).

In any case the main point of the gift of tongues was not its content but its effectiveness as a sign.

Permanent Gifts

We consider some spiritual gifts to be permanent because the need which they meet also appears to be permanent and not directly related to the unique circumstances of the first-century church. These permanent gifts fall into three main groups: gifts of leadership, gifts involving preaching and teaching the Word, and general service gifts.

Gifts of Leadership

Some gifts consist of the ability to provide leadership for local congregations of the church through the ages. Three such gifts are named, but there is probably some overlapping among them. All may be taken as applying to the office of elder or overseer (bishop), but there may be some other applications as well.

Leading. In ***Romans 12:8*** Paul names "the one who leads" as a gift bestowed on some members of the body of Christ. The verb translated "leads" literally means "to stand before or in front of." This can mean "to stand before people for the purpose of protecting, aiding, or helping them," or "to stand before people for the purpose of leading, governing, or presiding over them." I take it in the latter sense, i.e., as applying to those who lead the church in the sense of governing it, specifically the elders. This is the sense of the NIV, which says that if one has received this gift of leadership, *"let him govern diligently."* The same word is used of elders in ***1 Thessalonians 5:12***, where Paul refers to those who *"have charge over you in the Lord"*; and in ***1 Timothy***

5:17, which speaks of *"the elders who rule well."* There is no more important permanent gift of the Spirit than this.

Administrations. In ***1 Corinthians 12:28*** Paul names the gift of "administrations." The Greek word is *kubernesis*, and this is the only place it is used in the NT. The related word *kubernetes* is used twice (***Acts 27:11***; ***Rev 18:17***) to refer to the pilot or captain of a ship, which is its basic meaning. Thus when applied to the church, as in ***1 Corinthians 12:28***, "the reference can only be to the specific gifts which qualify a Christian to be a helmsman to his congregation, i.e., a true director of its order and therewith of its life," according to H.W. Beyer (**1036**).

Stott sums up the sense of this gift thus: "*Kubernesis* would seem, then, to be the gift of guiding or governing others, including perhaps organizing ability to take responsibility for some part of the church's programme, or the leadership to take the chair at a meeting and 'steer' the committee's proceedings with wisdom" (***Baptism*, 95**). The primary application would be to the office of elders, who oversee the spiritual direction of an entire congregation; thus the gift would overlap the gift of leading, above. But as Stott indicates, "administrations" could also apply to those who are enabled to organize and guide in other ways, such as leaders of committees or ministry areas, or of certain phases of church life such as education or music or administration as such. Baxter says that Christians who have this gift "can thereby make the local church to be alive with activity. They enjoy organizing, overseeing business matters, helping staff relations, dealing with details and generally making sure the work of the local church runs smoothly" (***Gifts*, 205**).

Pastors and Teachers (***Eph 4:11***). It is generally agreed that the language in Ephesians 4:11 specifies only four gifts: apostles, prophets, evangelists, and "pastors and teachers." In other words, the Lord has equipped some Christians to be "pastor-teachers." A pastor as such (*poimen*) literally is a shepherd, one who takes care of and is responsible for a flock of sheep. In the NT this and related words are used for Jesus Christ (***Jn 10:11***; ***Heb 13:20***; ***1Pet 2:25***; ***Rev 7:17***), but when used in the context of the church, they generally refer to elders (***Acts 20:28-29***; ***1Pet 5:2-3***). This fact, plus the similarity with the two gifts of leadership above, lead us to conclude that the "pastor-teacher" gift is primarily the eldership of the church.

This is supported by the fact that one of the elder's main tasks is that of teaching. One of the listed qualifications is that an elder must be *"able to teach"* (***1Tm 3:2***). ***Titus 1:9*** says that an elder must be *"holding fast the faithful word which is in accordance with the teaching, so that he will be able both to exhort in sound doctrine and to refute those who contradict."* "Exhorting in sound doctrine" is the main way a Christian shepherd feeds his flock, and "refuting those who contradict" is an essential aspect of guarding the flock (***Acts 20:28-31***). Some may be more directly involved in actual teaching than others (***1Tm 5:17***), but all share the responsibility for the teaching ministry of the church. In this sense all pastors (elders) will be teachers, though not all teachers will be pastors.

Some suggest that the pastoral function may also be exercised in more limited ways in the church. Robert Thomas says that the gift of pastor-teacher "can function at other echelons of church life besides the leadership of a whole local body. A Sunday school teacher, for example, may and should exercise shepherdly concern for members of his or her class. Functioning of this gift need not stop at the highest levels of church leadership. It should spread its benefit throughout an entire local body of believers" (**196**).

Gifts of Preaching and Teaching the Word of God

The next category of permanent gifts involves Spirit-given abilities to preach and teach the Word of God. I considered using here the heading "Speaking Gifts" or "Gifts of Speaking" (see ***1Pet 4:11***), since teaching, exhorting, and evangelism all may be done through the spoken word. But the fact is that each (especially teaching) can be done through the *written* word as well. These may thus be called "word gifts" (small "w") since they use both spoken and written words to proclaim and explain the Word.

Teaching. The gift of teaching is mentioned in three of Paul's lists, if we count the "-teacher" aspect of "pastor-teacher" in ***Ephesians 4:11*** (see also ***Rom 12:7*** and ***1Cor 12:28-29***). In ***1 Corinthians 12:28*** Paul seems to say that teaching is the third most important of all the gifts: "first apostles, second prophets, third teachers." Robert Thomas says this shows what a premium Paul "placed upon instruction." Instruction "was always uppermost" in his mind. "He considered an intellectual grasp of the truths of the faith a vital prerequisite to acceptable Christian living and service" (**61**).

Apostles and prophets also teach, but their main teaching is in the form of revealed and inspired material that constitutes the authoritative and infallible Word of God. The gift of teaching, though, presupposes the work of apostles and prophets, since the responsibility of those who have the gift of teaching is to give insightful exposition to the meaning and application of inspired truth, including both OT Scripture and New Covenant revelation. A teacher's authority, then, does not lie in his own words, but in the Word which he is expounding.

A teacher's authority does not lie in his own words, but in the Word which he is expounding.

Such ability is truly a gift of the Spirit. As MacArthur says, a person with the gift of teaching is someone "divinely gifted with special ability to interpret and present God's truth understandably" (***Romans*, 2:172**). As Walvoord notes, many Christians who have a good understanding of the Bible do not have the ability to explain it to others clearly and effectively. The latter is what the gift of teaching supplies (**168-169**).

Exhorting (***Rom 12:8***). There is some ambiguity in this next word-gift. The Greek word is *parakaleo*; the NASB translates it as "exhorts," and the NIV as "encouraging." It is from the same word group as "Paraclete," the word Jesus used of the Holy Spirit Himself and which is usually translated "Helper," "Counselor," or "Comforter" in that context (e.g., ***Jn 14:16,26; 15:26***). Another word in the same group is *paraklesis*, the word used of Barnabas when he is called "Son of Encouragement" (***Acts 4:36***), and also the word translated "comfort" six times in ***2 Corinthians 1:3-7***.

What are we to make of this when considered as a spiritual gift? I take it to be the next step beyond the revealing of the Word of God, and the teaching or explaining of the Word. Whereas teaching is addressed mainly to the intellect, exhorting is directed mainly to the will. It is the ability to motivate one's fellow Christians to action; the ability to move the heart, the conscience, and the will; the ability to encourage and persuade others to act upon the knowledge received through prophecy and teaching; the ability to deliver "a stirring appeal to men to do their duty" (**Lard, *Romans*, 386**).

This gift is a valuable asset to any preaching minister, and is also a gift that can be exercised in the counseling ministry. Schatzmann calls it the gift of "pastoral exhortation," possessed by "one who exercises pastoral care, namely of the afflicted and distressed" (**25**).

Exhorting is a valuable asset to any preaching minister, and to counseling ministry.

Evangelists. The ascended Christ *"gave . . . some as evangelists,"* says Paul in ***Ephesians 4:11***. This particular noun is used in only two other places in the NT: in ***Acts 21:8***, of Philip; and ***2 Timothy 4:5***, of Timothy. The verb form of the word is used 54 times, however, for the work of preaching or proclaiming the gospel. The work of evangelism, then, is preaching the gospel, especially to the unsaved with a view to winning them to Christ. Many may have the gift of teaching but not this gift of evangelism, which requires not only an understanding of the Word but also an ability to relate to people in a loving and appealing manner.

The use of this gift goes beyond simply sharing the gospel with one's neighbor, which is something all of us should do to the best of our ability. On a larger scale it probably includes what we usually think of as missionary work. Hocking says, "The evangelist appears to be a church-planter and would correspond to our word 'missionary' if it is meant by that usage one who would start new churches and establish them" (**14**). As Robert Thomas explains it, "The evangelist's work did not end with conversion. He was responsible for helping a local church get started too, after he had won people to Christ in a given location. . . . In this regard, he functions as what is called in modern times a missionary" (**192**).

Service Gifts

In this last category, which I am calling *service* gifts, we have some gifts of the Spirit which are general in nature and some which are quite specific. These do not have the glamour or the drama of gifts such as prophecy and tongues, and may appear to be what Paul calls the "weaker" members of the body in ***1 Corinthians 14:22***. But we must remember that Paul says that even the weaker members are necessary for the proper functioning of the body as a whole.

Helps. In his list of gifts in ***1 Corinthians 12:28-30*** Paul speaks of the gift of "helps" (*v. 28*), again using a word that appears only this once in the NT, namely, *antilempsis*. It is related to the verb *antilambano*, which means "to help," a word Robert Thomas says has the sense of "to take a burden on oneself in the place of another" (62). The NIV translates the noun in ***1 Corinthians 12:28*** as "those able to help."

We must remember that Paul says even the weaker members are necessary to the body as a whole.

There is no way to know if this gift means anything specific. Most take it in a very general sense as referring to the gift of servanthood, i.e., the spirit of being willing to help out in the church in whatever way help may be needed. Robert Thomas says that it "had the broadest scope of any of the auxiliary gifts," but he does limit it to physical or temporal needs. "It refers to many different kinds of physical help or relief administered wherever a need exists," he says, and he uses ***Acts 6:1-6*** as an example (198).

This may well be the spiritual gift most necessary for anyone who wants to serve as a deacon in the church, though it should not be limited to that office. It is broad enough to include the next three service gifts, all listed by Paul in ***Romans 12***.

Service. In Paul's list of gifts in ***Romans 12:6-8***, the first one he mentions is the gift of service (*v. 7*). He uses the word *diakonia*, which is the term from which we get our word "deacon," as in ***1 Timothy 3:8***. Some take it in the most general sense here, i.e., as equivalent to the spirit of servanthood as such and similar to "helps," above (see also ***1Pet 4:11***). Many others take it in the more narrow sense of "deacon," not necessarily as the formal name of an office but as representing a specific function. A main reason for this is that the word is part of a longer list of specific gifts and therefore seems to be distinguished from them rather than to include them.

If this is the case, what specific function might be in view? The best answer is that it may refer to the ministry of meeting the material needs of the less fortunate in the congregation (***Acts 6:1***), "a ministry of mercy to the poor and infirm" (**Murray, 2:124**), in the sense of church benevolence. In some ways it may be similar to the office of deacon as this is understood by many today, but its more narrow focus is probably the management of the church's ministry to the poor and those otherwise in material need.

Giving. One of the most interesting of all the spiritual gifts is Paul's reference to "he who gives" in ***Romans 12:8***. The Greek word simply means "to share." The NIV translates it as *"contributing to the needs of others,"* and this is no doubt Paul's point. Morris says it refers to "those who had the gift of coming to the assistance of the poor" (***Romans*, 442**). How is this different from the gift discussed in the previous paragraph? The gift of service has to do with the benevolent program of the whole church, while the gift of giving is about those who give their own money and possessions to assist the needy. The essence of the gift includes the ability to earn significant amounts of money (or the simple possession of wealth), plus a "God-given inclination to give" (**Cranfield, 2:625**). But, as Robert Thomas points out, "people with more limited resources can possess that skill, too, as they wisely use what God has put into their hands" (**202**). Paul may be referring to this gift in ***1 Corinthians 13:3***.

Showing Mercy. The final service gift, named in ***Romans 12:8***, is *"the one who shows mercy."* Paul has already named the gift of serving (general church benevolence) and the gift of sharing (private benevolence). But there are many acts of mercy that do not involve the giving of money or material goods, and these are probably what Paul refers to here. These include such things as visiting the sick at home or in hospitals, visiting and helping shut-ins, comforting the dying and the bereaved, visiting and corresponding with prisoners, and sending cards to or telephoning any of these.

Money may be given anonymously but the gift of showing mercy is exercised one-on-one.

Such acts of mercy do not emphasize the giving of money but rather the giving of one's heart in genuine love, caring, and sympathy. The one who has this gift is "divinely endowed with special sensitivity to suffering and sorrow," which includes the ability to notice when others are in misery and distress, and the desire to alleviate such distress (**MacArthur, *Romans*, 2:177**). Money may be given anonymously and without personal involvement, but the gift of showing mercy is exercised through interpersonal, one-on-one, intimate contacts with people in need. Thus such a gift may be manifested in any Christian, rich or poor; and in many ways it is more vital than the giving of material goods.

ARE SPIRITUAL GIFTS *TALENTS* OR *TASKS*?

When we speak of "spiritual gifts" or "gifts of the Spirit," an important question is this: exactly *what* does the Spirit give? Our usual assumption is that, in order to meet the needs of God's people as a whole, the Spirit gives certain *abilities* or *talents* to chosen individuals. Through a supernatural act of enablement, the Spirit equips these individuals with one of the specific abilities discussed in the previous section (or some other ability not named). Then when the question arises, "How can I identify my spiritual gift?" we all engage in anxious introspection, comparing ourselves with these lists and hoping to uncover some latent talent mysteriously bestowed upon us by the Spirit.

Is this the right approach to the concept of spiritual gifts? In a significant article in *Journal of the Evangelical Theological Society* in March 2000, Kenneth Berding says it is not. He challenges the idea that the *charismata* in the NT lists should be defined in terms of ability, and suggests that they should be understood as *ministries* instead. "Spirit-given ministries rather than abilities is what links these passages together," he says, as he argues that "ministries (roles, functions) rather than special ability is the theological entity lying behind" the passages (**39**). Some of the gifts do require "extraordinary enablement," but others do not. "Spirit-given ministries is a concept which accounts for all of these passages; special abilities/enablements is not" (**47**).

Thus we ask: are spiritual gifts *talents* or *tasks*? Are they abilities or ministries? What we will see in this section is that this is not an "either-or" issue; both talents and tasks are involved in spiritual gifts. The Holy Spirit gives both abilities and ministries. But here is a very important point: they are not always given in equal proportions. That is, in bestowing spiritual gifts the Holy Spirit *always* gives a task or ministry, but the kind and degree of ability bestowed will vary from task to task. The bottom line is this: when seeking to identify our own spiritual gifts, we should seek to discover first of all what ministry or task the Spirit is calling us to fulfill, and only sec-

We should seek to discover first of all what ministry or task the Spirit is calling us to fulfill.

ondarily should we be concerned about ability. This is the direction in which Berding is pointing us, and I believe he is right.

The Spirit Gives Abilities

Obviously, all miraculous spiritual gifts included the bestowing of miraculous abilities. All such gifts may be viewed as ministries or tasks, e.g., the office of apostle, the ministry of prophesying or healing, the function of speaking in tongues or distinguishing of spirits. But in order for any individual to perform these functions or tasks, it was necessary for the Holy Spirit to bestow upon him or her a truly supernatural power. Human beings simply do not have innate *natural* abilities to do *supernatural* things. This applies especially to the gifts named in ***1 Corinthians 12:8-10***, after which Paul says, *"But one and the same Spirit works all these things, distributing to each one individually just as He wills"* (***v. 11***). Such an ability is altogether from the Holy Spirit; He does not simply build upon some already-present talent for working miracles or speaking in tongues.

What about the nonmiraculous, permanent gifts, such as teaching, helps, and showing mercy? Most students of spiritual gifts regard every such gift as having some measure of Spirit-empowerment. Stott tentatively says that "we might perhaps define spiritual gifts as 'certain capacities, bestowed by God's grace and power, which fit people for specific and corresponding service'" (***Baptism*, 87**). Edgar's definition is similar: "A spiritual gift is an ability given to an individual supernaturally by God through the Holy Spirit so that the recipient may utilize that ability to minister to the needs of the church" (**36**). Baxter says, "The gifts are not 'natural' abilities, but the supernatural capabilities given by God, the Holy Spirit" (***Gifts*, 40**). According to David Clemens, "By definition a spiritual gift is the ability given by God for a special type of service. It is not a place of service, nor is it a ministry to a particular age group. It is, rather, the ability itself, such as teaching or pastoring" (**314**; cited in **Baxter, *Gifts*, 27**).

At this point it is important to distinguish between *providential* abilities and *Spirit-given* abilities. Providential abilities are those talents and capabilities which are present in all persons totally apart from any connection they may or may not have with the church. These may be innate talents, or they may be capabilities that individuals themselves have nurtured and developed through intense education and practice. These include musical talent, leadership abilities, and speaking skills. Many non-Christians have such providential abilities; thus many Christians already possess such talents from the moment of their conversion.

But is the sheer presence of such an ability, whether natural or developed, the equivalent of a spiritual gift? No. This is extremely important to understand at this point. Marshall Leggett explains, "A 'gift' in the New Testament sense is not a talent. A talent is given indiscriminately by God at birth both to those who will become Christians and those who will not become Christians. Many talented people do not use their talent to build up the body of Christ. But a gift is given only to Christians and given to them by the Holy Spirit" (**2:7**). J.I. Packer concurs: "Natural abilities, however spectacular, are not spiritual gifts as such" (**55**).

Providential gifts are from God, in the general sense of ***James 1:17***: *"Every good thing given and every perfect gift is from above, coming down from the Father of lights."* As Jacoby says, "every good thing" which every great athlete, expert, or superhero has, "God has given him—directly or indirectly." Jacoby then calls attention to ***1 Corinthians 4:7*** (NIV): *"For who makes you different from anyone else? What do you have that you did not receive?"* (**55**). But the point is that there is no necessary relation between these providential gifts and the gifts of the Holy Spirit.

Stott argues that God in His special providence may very early begin to endow chosen individuals with skills that he will later use when God calls him to service as a prophet (***Jer 1:5***) or an apostle (***Gal 1:15-16***), or even as an ordinary Christian working in the church today (***Baptism*, 90-91**). There is more than a little Calvinistic predeterminism involved in Stott's argument (**ibid., 91**). But even if this may happen on occasion, we still are not warranted in assuming that a natural talent just automatically becomes a spiritual gift once someone becomes a Christian. Baxter may go to the other extreme in refuting Stott when he says that "the totality of spiritual ability is from God" as a supernatural gift, but he is certainly right to say, "The 'natural' is not enough" (***Gifts*, 38-39**).

We are not warranted in assuming a natural talent automatically becomes a spiritual gift when one becomes a Christian.

What does happen when a naturally gifted or skilled person becomes a Christian? How does that talent become a "spiritual gift"? The first step is for the Christian to acknowledge that his talent is indeed a providential gift of God (***Jas 1:17***; ***1Cor 4:7***), and the second step is for that person to prayerfully and submissively dedicate that talent to the service of God and God's people. The third step is then to wait for the Spirit to give him or her a *ministry*.

The Spirit Gives Ministries

Ability as such, whether providential or Spirit-given, does not constitute a spiritual gift. Here we can learn from Berding. The crucial element in a spiritual gift—indeed, its main essence—is the ministry or task to which one is called and appointed by the Spirit. Listen again to Marshall Leggett: "Let me attempt to define the gifts of the Holy Spirit. *The gifts of the Holy Spirit are responsibilities given to Christians for them to use to bless the lives of other Christians in the church in order to make the body strong.* They are services or ministries" (2:7). What was given in ***Ephesians 4:11***? Apostles, prophets, evangelists, pastors-teachers—these are *ministries*. In preparing to name the gifts in ***Romans 12:6-8***, Paul says that *"we have many members in one body and all the members do not have the same function"* (***Rom 12:4***). Then when he names the gifts, all except the first one are verbal forms (participles), i.e., actions, functions, tasks. In ***1 Corinthians 12:4-6*** Paul equates gifts with *ministries* and *effects* (or "kinds of working," NIV).

The main essence of a spiritual gift is the ministry or task.

Thus it simply cannot be disputed that what the Holy Spirit gives is a ministry, a function, a role, a responsibility. How does ability fit in? Three ways may be distinguished. (1) When the Spirit bestows a ministry upon someone, He may certainly take into consideration the providential talents already present and may simply appropriate them for His use. (2) Or He may take an already-present, modest skill and heighten or enhance it for more effective service, as He did with the craftsmen in the building of the tabernacle: *"And in the hearts of all who are skillful I have put skill, that you may make all that I have commanded you"* (***Ex 31:6***). Such "natural gifts" are thus "dedicated, consecrated, and enhanced by the Spirit for use in the Lord's service"

(**Donald Williams, 169**). As Lewis Foster says, "The person who uses his abilities for the glory of God finds that his abilities are sharpened and heightened. This is a part of the work of the Spirit" (**Gift, 7**). (3) Finally, the ability to fulfill a Spirit-given task may be altogether a gift of the Spirit, which is certainly true of tasks requiring miraculous powers. We should not rule out this possibility, though, even where the ministry is not of a miraculous nature.

John Stott reflects the dual nature of spiritual gifts (ministry + ability) in this statement: "A spiritual gift or *charisma* is, then, neither a capacity by itself, nor a ministry or office by itself, but rather a capacity which qualifies a person for a ministry. More simply it may be regarded either as a gift and the job in which to exercise it, or a job and the gift with which to do it" (***Baptism*, 87**). Though it is probably unintended, Stott's statement is confusing because in the beginning he says that the spiritual *gift* is neither the capacity nor the ministry by itself, but in the end he distinguishes the gift from the job. So that there is no ambiguity, I will say that in my judgment a spiritual gift is both the gift of the "job" or ministry, and the gift of whatever ability is needed for it. Also in my judgment, the primary aspect of a spiritual gift is the *ministry*.

In my judgment a spiritual gift is both the gift of the ministry, and whatever ability is needed.

This raises the question, *how* does the Holy Spirit bestow a task or ministry upon someone? Several times in the preceding discussion I have referred to the fact that the Spirit *calls* us to fulfill a certain ministry. This is my answer to the present question, i.e., the Spirit bestows a ministry upon any individual by *calling* him or her to that task. When the Spirit issues the call, this is one's *spiritual gift*.

How does the Spirit call someone to ministry? I repudiate from the beginning all mystical or subjective concepts of calling. I believe the Spirit's call is objective, and that it will be either direct or indirect. I am also suggesting that such a call is an essential part of a spiritual gift; that is, a spiritual gift = calling + ministry + ability.

In Bible times, when God spoke directly to individuals such as Moses and Samuel, and when Jesus as God the Son spoke directly to His followers, direct calls were given to chosen individuals. God called Moses through direct speech (***Ex 3:4***), and through Moses He called the overse[illegible] *"See, I have called by name Bezale*[illegible] *appointed with him Oholiab"* [illegible] by Jesus into the role [illegible] abilities these [illegible] em into this [illegible] talent and e[illegible] im (***Acts* *26:***[illegible] irit to the ro[illegible]

But w[illegible] God no longer spe[illegible] individuals into specific roles [illegible] upon them? He does this not [illegible] the church and its appointed leaders [illegible] ders were chosen to assist Moses in his task [illegible] aelite nation, and they were empowered by the Sp[illegible] ity to do so (***v. 17***). But at God's direction it was Moses w[illegible] lled these men to take this task upon themselves (***vv. 16,24***). In ***Acts 6:1-6*** the apostles instructed the Jerusalem church to call seven men to a ministry of benevolence, through which call the Spirit bestowed upon these men the spiritual gifts of helps (***1Cor 12:28***) and service (***Rom 12:7***).

Timothy was called to the ministry of an evangelist by Paul himself (***Acts 16:1-3***; ***2Tm 4:5***), along with elders who laid their hands on him (***1Tm 4:14***). Elders themselves are appointed by the Holy Spirit (***Acts 20:28***), but only indirectly through the call of other church leaders (***Acts 14:23***; ***Tts 1:5***). Sometimes the call comes from the church collectively, in the selection of various ones for various forms of service (***Acts 6:3***; ***15:22***).

When the church today, either collectively or through its leaders, participates in the bestowing of spiritual gifts by calling or appointing someone to service, this must always be done in accordance with the instructions and qualifications laid down in God's Word. Usually included in the qualifications, of course, would be the presence of certain innate abilities or talents or inclinations (see ***1Tm 3:1-13***). But we must remember this: the possession of ability as such is *not* equivalent to possessing a gift from

The possession of ability as such is not equivalent to a gift from the Holy Spirit.

the Holy Spirit. Even a "gifted" person must be *called* to ministry, and then only in accord with any specific limitations or qualifications given in Scripture (e.g., ***1Tm 2:12***).

We should not think that we are being presumptuous or that we are usurping the Spirit's role when we realize that we ourselves are the human instruments through which the Holy Spirit bestows His spiritual gifts upon people. What distinguishes the Pentecostal experience in ***Acts 2*** and Cornelius's experience in ***Acts 10*** is the fact that on these two occasions the Spirit came *directly* upon those so gifted with tongues. According to the NT, in every other way the Holy Spirit comes upon anyone in the NT era, He does so through the instrumentality of human intermediaries. Miraculous spiritual gifts (except for Pentecost and Cornelius) were bestowed through the laying on of apostles' hands.[3] Even the indwelling of the Spirit comes through being baptized by another person. So when we say that the Spirit's gifts today come through a calling by the church and its leaders, we are simply being consistent with this pattern.

IDENTIFYING ONE'S SPIRITUAL GIFT

Thinking of spiritual gifts more in terms of ministry than abilities helps us to deal more comfortably with the question of how to "identify one's spiritual gift." An individual may engage in self-assessment, may discern some talent, and may desire or be zealous to use it in a certain ministry (e.g., ***1Tm 3:1***). He or she may then communicate this desire to the church leaders for consideration. It does not have to be complicated. Donald Williams observes,

> It seems to me that a great deal of our popular teaching on this subject has actually had the effect of bringing people into bondage and making it unnecessarily difficult for them to discover what their spiritual gifts are. . . . But the way to discover what your gift is is not to concentrate on Paul's lists of gifts but to be sensitive to needs within the body and ask yourself how God has positioned you to meet them. Exercising your spiritual gifts is the path to fulfillment as a Christian, but the whole point of them is ministry, service, edification, meeting needs. Yours does not have to be something different from

[3]Exactly *which* miraculous gift the Spirit would bestow with the laying on of apostles' hands was the Spirit's choice, according to ***1Cor 12:11***. This principle does not necessarily apply to nonmiraculous gifts.

> your natural gifts and abilities; it does not have to be one which appears in the lists . . . ; it does not even have to be the same thing at all times. Anything God has given you which you can use to meet a need in the body can be your spiritual gift. You discover it by serving, by caring, living the life of the body. When you find that God consistently blesses your efforts in a certain area you can confidently conclude that there lies one of your gifts.
>
> 
> You do not wait to serve until you somehow mystically discover your gift; you discover it by serving. **(171-172)**

In keeping with what was said above about calling, I believe that the identification of one's spiritual gift may also be initiated by others besides oneself. The church itself, usually through its leaders, may see a task that needs to be filled and may issue a call to a qualified individual to serve in that capacity. Simply by receiving this call from the church or from its eldership, one may "identify" his or her spiritual gift. Church leaders themselves need to recognize their essential role in helping to match individual Christians with their "gifts," i.e., ministries. And every Christian must be open to the Spirit's call to ministry as issued to them through the church collectively or through its leaders.

Identification of one's spiritual gift may be initiated by others.

What, then, shall we teach our classes and congregations about spiritual gifts and how to identify them? When Berding is asked this question, here is how he answers:

> You can begin by teaching that the word *charismata* does not inherently mean Spirit-given ability. . . . You can teach that Paul's list-passages discuss ministries rather than abilities (though God gives general spiritual enablement to every spiritual task). You can teach that the items listed by Paul . . . are in fact ministries (large and small) given by God to members of the Christian community to build that community up in Christ. You can teach your class to get involved in ministry and not wait around until they have figured out what special abilities they do or do not have. You can tell them to dispense with their "spiritual gift tests." You can stop using the word "gift" and talk about ministries instead. And after you have done all these, you might consider cancelling your Spiritual Gifts Class altogether and start another called "Ministering to One Another." **(51)**

CHAPTER ELEVEN

DOES THE HOLY SPIRIT GIVE MIRACULOUS GIFTS TODAY?

Within the boundaries of Christendom today, most believe that the Holy Spirit is presently active in the church, and that He is now working in the lives of individual Christians. Most believe that the Spirit acts upon sinners to regenerate them, and that He acts within Christians to sanctify them. Most believe that the Spirit also gives spiritual gifts to the members of Christ's body. There is a general unity on these issues.

One issue where there is serious disagreement, however, is the question of whether the Holy Spirit gives *miraculous* gifts to Christians today. Many claim that He does, some going so far as to say that you are not a true Christian unless you have spoken in tongues. Others argue that the Holy Spirit is *not* giving miraculous gifts to Christians today, and that He has not done so since approximately the end of the first century, when the last Apostle (John) died.

Publishers Note: *Some views and opinions expressed in this final chapter do not necessarily reflect the views and opinions of the staff and management of College Press Publishing Company, Inc.*

III. Explaining Modern-Day Miracle Claims within Christendom
   A. "Miraculous" Phenomena
   B. Possible Explanations
      1. Natural Explanations
      2. Supernatural Explanations
   C. The Occult Origin of "Christian" Miracles Today
      1. The Reality of Demonic Miracles
      2. The Reality of Demonic Miracles Today
      3. The Reality of Demonic Miracles within Christian Circles
IV. Conclusion

This latter view is sometimes called *cessationism*, since it argues that miraculous gifts have *ceased*, in the language of ***1 Corinthians 13:8***. This is my personal conviction. I believe that the Holy Spirit does *not* give gifts of revelatory knowledge and miraculous power to Christians today. This chapter will make the case for this view.

WHAT IS A MIRACLE?

Some Christians get upset at the suggestion that miracles have ceased, because they do not have a clear understanding of what a miracle actually is. Some think that anything God does is a miracle, or that any phenomenon that causes wonder is a miracle. One writer has claimed that "a miracle is anything that causes us to stop and acknowledge God's intervention in our ordinary human lives." Things that may thus be called miracles include a rosebud, a sunset, a phone call from a loved one, and finding a needed dress on a sales rack. The author concludes, "Miracles are around us every day. Our life and breath are miracles of God's creative thought. . . . Surely, the least we can do is acknowledge His provision and call it by name—a miracle" (**Manes, 13**).

These well-intentioned sentiments are certainly expressions of sincere piety. However, when measured by biblical teaching they must be called not just superficial but confused, misleading, and false. The author takes no account whatever of the way the Bible uses the terms for miracles, and shows no awareness of what is at stake in defining miracles so loosely.

Others may not be so naïve as to call a rosebud a miracle, but they still get upset at the suggestion that miraculous gifts have ceased, because they think this somehow puts limits upon God and upon His power. Some even assume that the cessation of miraculous gifts would mean that God cannot heal the sick today.

The problem with this kind of thinking is the assumption that every act of God—every divine or supernatural act—must be called a *miracle*. Thus if there are no miracles, then God is not acting. This is simply not true to Scripture. What is true is this: all works of God are *supernatural* acts, but not all works of God are *miracles*. To say it another way, all miracles are supernatural events, but not all supernatural events are miracles. Miracles are a quite narrow and specific kind of divine activity.

All works of God are supernatural acts, but not all are miracles.

To give an overview, there are basically four kinds of events. First, some events fall under the heading of "general providence" (see **Cottrell, *Ruler*, ch. 3**). These are things that happen the way they do because of the way God created the world in the first place. They are the result of two relatively independent forces that God chose to bring into existence and which He allows most of the time to operate on their own. These forces are the laws of nature and free-will beings. Events that happen as the result of unaided natural law and human free-will choices are *not* caused by God, except indirectly insofar as He is the one who created this system to begin with. Such events are neither miraculous nor supernatural. Rosebuds, sunsets, phone calls, and department store sales are usually in this category, as far away from true miracles as possible.

The other three kinds of events are all different from the above because all three *are* the result of God's direct divine intervention into the world. They are all acts of God and thus are all supernatural. However, not all of these are miracles. The first such kind of supernatural event (and the second overall kind of event) is what we call acts of "special providence" (**ibid., chs. 4, 5**). These are the occasions when God intervenes in the course of nature and the flow of history, usually in ways that are so subtle that no one will actually observe or recognize them as supernatural. They generally occur within the boundaries of natural law and do not violate natural law, but are nonetheless events that would not have happened without God's special causation. An example is the healing of a sick person in answer to prayer (***Jas 5:16***). This is something that still happens today, but it is not a miracle because from our perspective the healing process usually conforms to natural laws.

The second kind of supernatural event (and third overall kind of event) is what I call "supernatural spiritual events." These are very special works of God that do not involve the physical world and thus are beyond the very sphere of natural laws. These are things God does on the level of the spirit. They may happen in conjunction with physical events (e.g., as the atonement occurs in the crucifixion), but they actually occur in the dimension of the spirit (divine and human).

One kind of supernatural spiritual event is the *saving* works of God. This category includes the main redemptive works associated with Jesus: His incarnation, atonement, and enthronement at God's right hand. It includes the outpouring of the Holy Spirit on Pentecost. It includes works of salvation applied to us as individuals: forgiveness, regeneration, the Spirit's continuing indwelling. Strictly speaking these are not miracles, because they are outside the realm of the physical and thus cannot be observed by our senses. They are definitely supernatural, however.

The other kind of supernatural spiritual event is God's *revelatory* activity, especially the Holy Spirit's work of revelation and inspiration within apostles and prophets. The main purpose of this supernatural activity is to give us revealed explanations concerning the reality and meaning of the saving works of God mentioned in the previous paragraph. For instance, we could never know that Jesus of Nazareth is the incarnate Son of God, or that His death on the cross makes us right with God, unless that were revealed to us by the Holy Spirit, as in Scripture. Such revelatory activity is definitely supernatural, but strictly speaking it is still not miraculous—even though at times we may include such supernatural working in the general category of "miraculous spiritual gifts" (as I myself am doing in this very chapter).

The third and final category of supernatural events (and the fourth overall) is *miracles* (**ibid., ch. 6**). Like the last two categories, miracles are acts of God; but they are unlike the other two in crucial ways. Miracles are unlike supernatural spiritual events because they are visible acts occurring on the level of the physical. Also they are unlike acts of special providence because they are obviously contrary to natural law. For example, instead of a gradual healing brought about in answer to prayer, a miracle is an immediate healing of a lame or blind man. The reason why miracles must be visible events obviously contrary to natural law has to do with their

The reason miracles have the characteristics they do is because of their purpose as proof.

purpose, which is to serve as *proof* or evidence of the truth of the claimed revelatory explanation of God's redemptive works. This will be explained further in the next section.

Another distinction between miracle and the previous categories is that a miracle is performed by a human agent, i.e., by someone empowered by God to work miracles (cf. the Spirit's gift of *"the working of miracles,"* ***1Cor 12:10***, ESV). A miracle happens when a *miracle-worker* deliberately channels the supernatural power of God in a way that produces a visible, physical event that could not have been produced by natural law. This aspect of a miracle also is directly related to the *purpose* of miracles, as seen in the next section.

At this point we should note that many make a distinction between a miracle produced by a human miracle-worker, and a miracle worked directly by God. Some cessationists believe that the *gift* of miracles has ceased, i.e., the Spirit no longer empowers individuals to work miracles; but they affirm that God may occasionally and directly work a miracle, especially in order to heal a serious illness. Baxter makes this distinction, calling the latter "generalized miracles" and allowing for their continuing presence while denying the gift of miracles today (***Gifts*, 141-142**). Geisler accepts the same distinction, asserting that direct miraculous healings "are always possible," but "are seldom necessary" in view of the wonderful ways God can work through special providence (***Signs*, 131-133**).

Personally I prefer to reserve the term "miracle" for a visible act performed by a human agent, an act which violates natural law and functions as a sign or evidence for the truth of the miracle-worker's claims. God's special providential healing may sometimes appear to be quite miraculous in its effect. I still prefer to call this "special providence," however, even if it stretches the borders of providence somewhat.

In any case we can see why we must be very precise in what we call a "miracle." Many marvelous things happen in the world, and many of them are directly caused by God; but this does not mean they are miracles. We do not honor God when we *call* things miracles that are not.

We do not honor God when we call things miracles that are not.

THE CASE AGAINST MIRACULOUS GIFTS TODAY

Arguing that miraculous gifts of the Spirit are valid today, Storms says first of all that "the Bible gives no evidence indicating that they are *not* valid" (**205**). I find this statement to be incredible, in view of the fact that several lines of evidence against the validity of continuing miraculous gifts may be drawn directly from the Bible. This section presents that evidence.

The Purpose of Miracles

The first and perhaps primary reason for denying the existence of miraculous gifts today is the Bible's own teaching about the *purpose* of miracles in the history of redemption. Once we understand that purpose, we can see why the Holy Spirit ceased bestowing miraculous powers after the apostolic age.

The starting point for this understanding is the NT terminology for miracles, which consists of three main words. One is *dunamis,* a common Greek word for "power," often translated simply as "miracle." This word emphasizes the *source* of a miracle, namely, God's divine power. A second word is *teras,* usually translated as "wonder." It emphasizes the immediate *result* of a miracle, i.e., it produces amazement and wonder. The third word is *semeion,* usually translated as "sign." This key word tells us the *purpose* of a miracle, namely, to function as a *sign* (proof, confirmation, evidence) of something.

The word *semeion* is used about 77 times in the NT; more than 50 times it refers to miracles. *Teras* is used sixteen times, always for miracles; in all sixteen cases it is used along with *semeion,* i.e., "signs and wonders." *Dunamis* is used 23 times (out of 119) for miracles; it occurs five times with *semeion.* In four texts all three words are used (***Acts 2:22***; ***2Cor 12:12***; ***2Th 2:9***; ***Heb 2:4***). The word *semeion* is obviously predominant, and we conclude that this predominance shows how important it is to emphasize that the *purpose* of miracles is to give a sign or evidence for something.

The purpose of miracles is to give a sign or evidence for something.

When we say that a miracle functions as a sign or proof for something, the question is, proof of *what*? At the most fundamental level, when a person uses divine power to enact an event that could not have resulted from natural causes, that is proof that this person is acting on behalf of God. Such a miracle authenticates the *person* as being from God. When Moses performed miracles, he was authenticated as a messenger from Yahweh. When he was first commissioned as God's prophet or spokesman, God said to him, *"Thus you shall say to the sons of Israel, 'The Lord . . . has sent me to you'"* (**Ex 3:15**). When Moses replied, *"What if they will not believe me?"* God gave him the power to work miracles, *"that they may believe that the Lord . . . has appeared to you"* (**Ex 4:1-5**). After He led Moses through a demonstration of two such miracles (the serpentine rod and the leprous hand), God said, *"If they will not believe you or heed the witness of the first sign, they may believe the witness of the last sign"* (**Ex 4:8**).

Jesus' miracles likewise served the purpose of authenticating Him as being sent from God: *"Men of Israel, listen to these words: Jesus the Nazarene, a man attested to you by God with miracles and wonders and signs which God performed through Him in your midst, just as you yourselves know"* (**Acts 2:22**; see **Jn 10:24-25**; **14:11**). An example is His healing of the paralytic (**Mk 2:1-12**). He first forgave the man's sins (**v. 5**), an implicit claim to deity (**v. 7**). Then He declared before all, especially the skeptics, *"But so that you may know that the Son of Man has authority on earth to forgive sins"* (**v. 10**)—then He healed the man (**vv. 11-12**). *"So that you may know"* sums up the purpose of all miracles.

Jesus' miracles likewise served the purpose of authenticating Him as being sent from God.

The apostles' ability to work miracles proved that they too were divinely sent. In defending his apostolic authority Paul said, *"The signs of a true apostle were performed among you with all perseverance, by signs and wonders and miracles"* (**2Cor 12:12**). B.B. Warfield says that in the apostolic age, miracles "were distinctively the authentication of the Apostles. They were part of the credentials of the Apostles as the authoritative agents of God in founding the church" (6).

We must take this one step further, however. Miracles confirm not only that a *person* has been sent from God, but also that his *message* is from God. This is indeed the ultimate purpose of a miracle, i.e., the miracle is a sign or evidence that the miracle-worker's message comes

Miracles confirm not only the person but the message as coming from God.

from God and is therefore true and authoritative. This connection between the miracle and the message is crucial. As MacArthur says, "Miracles always are designed to authenticate the human instrument God has chosen to declare a specific revelation to those who witness the miracle" (***Chaos*, 128**). "They were not simply divine exhibitionism; they substantiated and authenticated the prophets' claim that they spoke for God" (**ibid., 138**).

But one may ask, how is this an argument against miraculous gifts today? The answer is that not only are miracles inseparably tied with prophetic revelation, but that miracles and revelation are also inseparably tied together with God's great redemptive events. There is a threefold package of interlocking components: God empowers individuals to work *miracles*, which are signs from God to confirm the *revelation* spoken by the miracle-workers; and the revelation is necessary to promise and to explain the great *redemptive works* of God.

This threefold package explains why miraculous gifts are not given simply at random in the history of redemption, but seem to be clustered around three main eras: the time of Moses and Joshua, when God delivered His people from Egyptian bondage; the time of Elijah and Elisha, representing the prophets whom God sent to explain His continuing intervention in the history of Israel; and the time of Jesus and the apostles, when God's climactic and final works of redemption were accomplished. It has been suggested that each of these three miracle-working eras lasted about 70 years (see **Baxter, *Gifts*, 134-138**).[1]

This view of miracles is usually associated with B.B. Warfield, who emphasized it in his 1918 work against modern miracles. He argued for "the inseparable connection of miracles with revelation, as its mark and credential." He said that miracle-workers "belong to revelation periods, and appear only when God is speaking to His people through accredited messengers, declaring His gracious purposes." The period of Christ and the apostles is the last such period. Thus "when this revelation period closed, the period of miracle-working had

[1]This does not mean that God Himself was not directly intervening in wondrous ways in the history of His people in the interim centuries. The three eras of miracles are the times when certain human beings were endowed with miracle-working power. See Edgar, 37; MacArthur, *Chaos*, 134-136.

passed by also, as a mere matter of course" (**25-26**). "Therefore it is that the miraculous working which is but a sign of God's revealing power, cannot be expected to continue, and in point of fact does not continue, after the revelation of which it is the accompaniment has been completed" (**26-27**).

While Warfield emphasized the connection between miracles and revelation, Reymond credits Geerhardus Vos with pointing out the equally necessary connection between *revelation* and *redemption*. Vos says that "revelation does not stand alone by itself, but is . . . inseparably attached to another activity of God, which we call *Redemption*. . . . Revelation is the interpretation of redemption" (**Vos, 14**; cited in **Reymond, 51**). Reymond sums up this threefold package thus: "Non-repeatable historical events of redemption" are accompanied by "explanatory special revelation," which is accompanied by "authenticating miracles of power" (**55**).

These three elements and their connections can be seen in ***Hebrews 2:3-4***:

> *How will we escape if we neglect so great a salvation? After it was at the first spoken through the Lord, it was confirmed to us by those who heard, God also testifying with them, both by signs and wonders and by various miracles and by gifts of the Holy Spirit according to His own will.*

The primary element consists of *redemptive events*, which are *acts* of God which save His people (in this case, *"so great a salvation,"* referring to the climactic saving work of Jesus). The second element is the *revelation*, i.e., *words* from God to promise and explain the redemptive events (*"at the first spoken"*). The third element consists of *miracles*, which are *signs* from God to confirm the revelation (*"confirmed to us . . . God also testifying"* by signs, wonders, miracles, and gifts of the Spirit).

How does this relate to the question of whether miracles are still occurring today? As long as God is performing new redemptive works, we can expect new revelation to be given, in order to explain these new works. In this case we can then expect more miracles to happen, to authenticate the new revelation. But once God's redemptive works have been accomplished, explained, and confirmed,

The very purpose of miracles argues against their continuation beyond the first century.

we should not expect any further miracles. That is, we would expect miracles today only if new redemptive works are taking place, which is not happening. Thus the very purpose of miracles argues against their continuation beyond the first century.

Storms claims, though, that we need *continuing* authentication of the original, first-century revelation. "If signs, wonders, and the power of the Holy Spirit were essential in bearing witness to the truth of the gospel *then*, why not *now*? In other words, it seems reasonable to assume that the miracles that confirmed the gospel in the first century, wherever it was preached, would serve no less to confirm the gospel in subsequent centuries, even our own" (**200**). This diminishes the primary purpose of a miracle, however, which was to confirm the divine authority of the miracle-worker and his revealed message *once and for all.* Once the message is delivered and divinely authenticated by miracles, it has been authenticated for all time and does not need repeated confirmation. Trench has said, "That the Church *has had* these wonders, —of this it preserves a record and attestation in the Scriptures of truth. The miracles recorded there live for the Church; they are as much present witnesses for Christ to us now as to them who actually saw them with their eyes" (***Miracles*, 32**). This very point is asserted by no less than the apostle John, near the end of his Gospel: *"Therefore many other signs Jesus also performed in the presence of the disciples, which are not written in this book; but these have been written so that you may believe that Jesus is the Christ, the Son of God; and that believing you may have life in His name"* (***Jn* 20:30-31**). To say that we need continuing authentication of the gospel is to deny the very purpose, power, and sufficiency of the written word.

To say that we need continuing authentication of the gospel is to deny the sufficiency of the written word.

The Laying-on of Apostles' Hands

Another reason for denying the presence of miraculous gifts in the church today is the connection between one's receiving miraculous gifts and having an apostle's hands laid on him. This connection is established by the events recorded in the book of Acts.

In the earliest days of the church, though thousands were being baptized and thus were receiving the indwelling presence of the Spirit as promised (**Acts 2:38-41**; **4:4**; **5:14,32**), only the apostles are said to be performing miracles (**Acts 2:43**; **3:6**; **4:33**; **5:12-16**). Only after the apostles laid their hands on the seven servants in **Acts 6:1-6** do we have a record of anyone else—two of the seven—working miracles (Stephen, **6:8**; Philip, **8:6-7,13**).

The necessary connection between miraculous gifts and the laying-on of apostles' hands is clearly seen in Philip's ministry in Samaria in **Acts 8**. Though Philip was working miracles (after the apostles laid hands on him in **Acts 6**), and though many were being converted, none of the converts was given miracle-working power until the apostles Peter and John came down from Jerusalem *"and prayed for them that might receive the Holy Spirit"* (**v. 15**). Though they had surely received the indwelling of the Spirit at their baptism, since that was God's general Pentecost promise (**Acts 2:38-39**; **5:32**), the Spirit had *"not yet fallen upon any of them"* (**v. 16**) in a miracle-giving way. Then the apostles *"began laying their hands on them, and they were receiving the Holy Spirit"* (**v. 17**).

At this point a converted sorcerer named Simon *"saw that the Spirit was bestowed through the laying on of the apostles' hands."* This so impressed him that he tried to purchase this apostolic power with money, and thus experienced a fall from grace (**vv. 18-24**). The result of the laying-on of the apostles' hands could not have been the normal indwelling of the Spirit, since God had already promised this in baptism, and especially since the laying-on of hands resulted immediately in something that Simon *saw*, something that was so spectacular that it led Simon to covet the power to bestow it, at the risk of his salvation (**vv. 18-19**). It must have been a manifestation of miraculous abilities, especially speaking in tongues.

Warfield says of this incident in **Acts 8** that it "is not only a very instructive one in itself, but may even be looked upon as the cardinal instance" of the conferring of miraculous gifts only by the laying-on of apostles' hands. Indeed, "it could not be more emphatically stated that the Holy Ghost was conferred by the laying on of the hands, specifically of the Apostles, and of the Apostles alone. . . . And there can be no question that it was specifically the extraordinary gifts of the Spirit that were" at stake here, and not His indwelling presence. Thus this passage is important to us, "to teach us the source of the gifts of power, in the Apostles, apart from whom they were not conferred." This "connection of the supernatural gifts with the Apostles is so obvious that one wonders that so many students have missed it" (22-23).

This connection is confirmed by the incident recorded in ***Acts 19:6***, when the Apostle Paul laid his hands on the twelve Ephesian disciples, and they began to prophesy and speak in tongues.

These data lead us to conclude that there must have been a necessary connection between such miraculous manifestations and the laying-on of apostles' hands. The only two recorded exceptions to this are Pentecost and Cornelius, on which occasions the Spirit was poured out directly because of the need for a special kind of sign. Peter's words in ***Acts 11:15*** suggest that what happened to Cornelius and his family (***Acts 10:44-48***) had not happened since Pentecost itself. That is, no one else had prophesied or spoken in tongues without the laying-on of apostles' hands.

This leads to the conclusion that the bestowing of miraculous gifts must have ceased around AD 100, when John, the last apostle, died. As Warfield puts it, "My conclusion then is, that the power of working miracles was not extended beyond the disciples upon whom the Apostles conferred it by the imposition of their hands" (23).

The bestowing of miraculous gifts must have ceased when John, the last apostle, died.

The Faulty Theological Framework of Continuationism

Those who believe miraculous gifts continue today—let's call them *continuationists*—have reasons for their view, but I believe that their main arguments are based on faulty theological conclusions, or false interpretations of key biblical concepts. Here I will summarize the problems with their reasoning. Since most of these points have been covered extensively in earlier chapters, they will not be dealt with in detail here.

A False View of Pentecost

First of all, in my judgment most continuationists have totally missed the point of Pentecost. They have concluded that the main purpose of Pentecost was to make miraculous spiritual gifts, especially the gifts of prophecy and tongues, available to all. Keener, for example, asks whether the "gift of Pentecost" is intended for today, and answers in the affirmative: "Acts assumes that the gift made available at Pentecost remains in force," i.e., "the gift is permanent (**2:39**)" (**89-90**). This of course is true, but the problem is that Keener and other continuationists interpret this gift to mean "prophetic empowerment," especially the gift of tongues (**90**). This is the sense in which "Luke presents the empowerment of the church at Pentecost as a normative experience for Christians," says Keener (**85**).

I have shown in chapter five above, "The Holy Spirit and the New Age," that this is simply a false view of what was happening on the day of Pentecost. The point of Pentecost is *not* the miraculous gifts, but the *gift* of the Spirit as a regenerating, indwelling, sanctifying presence. We have considered the significant number of OT prophecies pointing ahead to a new, wonderful, life-giving outpouring of the Spirit,[2] and the numerous promises of the coming Holy Spirit recorded in the Gospels.[3] The point of all these prophecies and promises was that, with respect to the work of the Holy Spirit, something *new*, something *different*, something *special* was going to happen.

The point of Pentecost is not the miraculous gifts but the Spirit's presence.

To think that all of these prophecies and promises were pointing ahead simply to a wider distribution of miraculous gifts is a serious distortion of the history of redemption. On the one hand, it minimizes the truly new and marvelous blessing of Pentecost, namely, the indwelling presence of the Spirit. On the other hand, it magnifies and elevates the miraculous gifts to a status they were never intended to have. The Pentecostal tongues, especially, were the wrapping in which the true gift was packaged; but the continuationists treat them as the gift itself. This is all the more unacceptable in view of the fact that miracles were nothing new. How can the miraculous manifestations of Pentecost be considered the purpose and essence of the new-age outpouring of the Spirit, in view of the fact that God had always given such miracles when needed?

[2]*Isa 32:15; 43:19-20; 44:3-4; Eze 36:25-27; Joel 2:28-32; Zec 12:10.*
[3]*Mt 3:11; Mk 1:8; Lk 3:16; 11:13; Jn 1:33; 4:10-14; 7:37-39.*

Here is the true point of Pentecost, as I hear Peter explaining it in *Acts 2*: "This is the day God is beginning to fulfill His promises to give you the Holy Spirit, and the tongues (which are a kind of prophesying) mentioned by Joel are the proof of it [*2:16-18*]. God is now giving the promised Spirit [*1:4-5; 2:33*] to renew you and dwell within you. You have seen the Spirit's presence miraculously manifested in the apostles, so you know that He is here. Now, if you will repent and be baptized in the name of Jesus Christ for the remission of your sins, this same Holy Spirit will be given to YOU also [*2:38*], for this promise is for YOU [*2:39*]. You can believe this because the miracle of the apostles' tongue-speaking proves it."

The gift of the indwelling of the Spirit was the new and glorious purpose of Pentecost as far as the Holy Spirit is concerned; tongue-speaking as the confirming sign that this was true was simply the wrapping in which the gift was enclosed. This wrapping, having served its purpose, may be reverently discarded.

The indwelling Spirit was the purpose of Pentecost; tongue-speaking was simply the gift-wrapping.

A False View of Baptism in the Holy Spirit

Another faulty theological premise of continuationism is a false interpretation of baptism in the Holy Spirit. This is true especially of those in the Pentecostal and Charismatic movements, who see Holy Spirit baptism as a second work or second blessing of the Spirit (subsequent to conversion itself), and who interpret this second blessing as necessarily involving a bestowing of miraculous gifts, especially tongues. Since baptism in the Holy Spirit is a gift God offers to all Christians and expects all Christians to receive, then those who are receiving it today are being endowed with miraculous gifts.

In chapter eight above, I have discussed the subject of baptism in the Holy Spirit in detail, and have already shown that the above interpretation is false. Baptism in the Spirit is another way of describing the saving event of regeneration, which is an aspect of every sinner's initial conversion and occurs specifically in the moment of water baptism. It is connected with salvation, not with miraculous gifts. In the book of Acts the miraculous gift of tongues was connected with the gift of Spirit baptism at least in ***Acts 2*** and ***Acts 10***, but the tongue-speaking was no more than a miraculous sign that Spirit baptism was now available (***Acts 2***) and that it was intended for Gentiles as well as Jews (***Acts 10***).

When the biblical teaching about Holy Spirit baptism is properly understood, the view that miraculous gifts are intended for today loses one of its main supports.

A False View of Spiritual Gifts

Another faulty aspect of continuationist theology is its false view of spiritual gifts as such, especially of the gift of tongues. One of its main errors is the conviction that no distinction should be made between temporary gifts and permanent gifts. As Storms says, "I believe all the gifts of the Holy Spirit are valid for the contemporary church." Throughout the book of Acts, he says, "whenever the Spirit was poured out on new believers, they experienced the manifestation of his *charismata*. There is nothing to indicate this phenomenon was restricted to them and then." The purpose of each gift is to edify the body of Christ, and it still needs edifying today. And, in ***1 Corinthians 13:8-13***, Paul "dates the cessation of the *charismata* at the perfection of the eternal state, consequent upon Christ's return" (**205-206**).

In chapter ten above, I have discussed the subject of spiritual gifts and have shown the validity of the distinction between temporary and permanent gifts, based on the principle of *need*. It is simply incontrovertible that the early church had certain needs that the post-apostolic church does not have, needs based on the lack of a completed and readily available New Testament. What we are calling "miraculous gifts"—gifts involving special revelation from God and gifts of miraculous signs—were needed until the NT writings became available. These gifts were part of the foundation of the church (***Eph 2:20***). Continuationism

It is incontrovertible that the early church had needs that the postapostolic church does not have.

> completely ignores the meaning and purpose of these gifts in connection with the founding days of Christianity. As well might one claim that because God once caused the walls of Jericho to fall He must continue doing so today, as to claim that because God promised these gifts to the early church He

> must keep on giving them through the church age. When the purpose for which these gifts was given was fulfilled, they were withdrawn. (**Baxter, *Gifts*, 85**)

They were "the swaddling-clothes of the infant churches."[4]

The last point of this main section will be a detailed examination of ***1 Corinthians 13:8-13***, where we shall see that the miraculous charismata *must* end *before* Christ's second coming.

THE QUESTIONABLE ATTENDING CIRCUMSTANCES OF MODERN MIRACLES

In those groups where miraculous gifts are accepted today, especially within Pentecostal denominations and charismatic congregations, the very way these gifts are practiced raises questions about their validity when compared with biblical teaching about the Holy Spirit and about miraculous gifts. Several problematic characteristics of the modern practice of gifts will now be noted.

The Holy Spirit Is Often Elevated above Jesus Christ

First, in charismatic and other such circles, the Holy Spirit is often elevated above Jesus Christ, contrary to the Spirit's stated mission as one who will glorify Christ (***Jn 16:13-15***). Matthews says that this text "means that the Holy Spirit will not draw attention to Himself. This profound statement, expressed so simply, indicates that the entire ministry of the Spirit is away from Himself. All endeavors, whether by the individual Christian or by a church or denomination, to place the Holy Spirit at the center of their attention and instruction is, therefore, under divine censure" (**99-100**).

Are continuationists guilty of putting greater emphasis on the Spirit than on Christ, contrary to the teaching of this text? Edward Fudge, in his booklet *Speaking in Tongues*, draws the following sober conclusion: "Those claiming these gifts today nearly always exalt the Spirit above the Christ, preach their supposed experiences rather than the gospel of the Son of God, and (while in word denying it) actually become much more involved with the Holy Spirit than with the Son

[4]Warfield attributes this phrase to someone named Fuller, but gives no further data (21).

at the Father's right hand. This is a serious charge, but I do not make it lightly. I believe the evidence warrants such strong terms" (**29**).

Experience Is Made the Final Norm

"Someone with an experience is never at the mercy of someone with an argument," according to a bit of pseudo-wisdom. In other words, experience will always trump reason. This is one of the most basic assumptions of those who argue for continuing miraculous gifts, and it is one of the most dangerous. The idea is something like this: "I have personally spoken in tongues, thus I *know* the Holy Spirit is giving miraculous gifts today." As a listener to one of MacArthur's radio programs said in a letter to him, "If you haven't experienced it—you can NOT tell someone who HAS that it doesn't exist" (***Chaos*, 25**). As Edgar says, "It is the argument based on personal experience, namely, 'It happened to me.' For many charismatics it is their only argument" (**16**).

In spite of all protestations to the contrary, the fact is that on a practical if not theoretical level, continuationists elevate experience above the Word of God as the final norm for faith and practice. MacArthur speaks of "the charismatic tendency to test doctrine by experience instead of the reverse" (***Chaos*, 17**). As an example he cites charismatics who argue that "those outside the charismatic movement have no right to evaluate it," including one who says that trying "to interpret the Charismatic manifestations of the Holy Spirit without a Charismatic experience" is "fatuous," i.e., foolish, silly, or inane (**ibid., 19**). MacArthur cites a popular charismatic theologian who claims that any real understanding of the gifts of the Spirit "*presupposes a participation in them.* Without such a participation, whatever is said about the gifts may only result in confusion and error" (**ibid., 20**).

MacArthur remarks, "Make no mistake—the practical effect of charismatic teaching is to set one's experience on a higher plane than a proper understanding of Scripture" (**ibid., 36**). Also, "the major flaw in the charismatic movement is that it calls on experience rather than the Word of God to dictate what is true" (**ibid., 41**).

Edgar finds this presupposition at the heart of Jack Deere's influential book, *Surprised by the Power of the Spirit*. Deere's main argument, Edgar says, "is that personal experience . . . validates the charismatic's position and invalidates any arguments against it." Deere argues that "the only reason anyone is a cessationist is because they have not had this experience." Edgar comments, "While this is an argument from experience as it occurred in the life of one man, it is the same basic argument used by charismatics worldwide: 'It happened to me!'" (**15-16**). "According to this, the sole reason one is a charismatic or a cessationist is whether one has had the experience" (**18**).

An example of this experientialism is given by Gardiner: "A well-known leader of the charismatic movement, addressing a group composed of the varied backgrounds mentioned before, after reading a passage of Scripture closed his Bible and said, 'We are not going to agree on the interpretation of this Scripture, so let me tell you about my experience, then we will have something solid'" (**51**). Another example is a letter received by MacArthur: "You resort to Greek translations and fancy words to explain away what the Holy Spirit is doing in the church today. Let me give you a piece of advice that might just save you from the wrath of almighty God: *put away your Bible* and your *books* and *stop studying*. Ask the Holy Ghost to come upon you and give you the gift of tongues. You have no right to question something you have never experienced" (***Chaos*, 25**). MacArthur cites still another letter from a charismatic: "I do not feel the need for study of the Scriptures, for I know Jesus as He has revealed Himself to me within; and as He dwells in me, there is the Word. I go to scripture, and scripture is vital and necessary—but neither central nor crucial, for I have Him—rather He has me. Scriptures are a secondary source" (**ibid., 99**).

Nothing could be more wrong or dangerous than basing one's beliefs on personal experiences.

The fact is that nothing could be more wrong or more dangerous than basing one's beliefs about God, about the Spirit, about spiritual gifts, and about personal salvation upon one's personal experiences. As Gardiner notes, experiences are often contradictory, and are also "dangerously deceptive" (**52**). Jesus Himself tells us this in ***Matthew 7:21-23***:

> *Not everyone who says to Me, "Lord, Lord," will enter the kingdom of heaven, but he who does the will of My Father who is in heaven will enter. Many will say to Me on that day, "Lord, Lord, did we not prophesy in Your name, and in Your name cast out demons, and in Your name perform many miracles?" And then I*

> *will declare to them, "I never knew you; DEPART FROM ME, YOU WHO PRACTICE LAWLESSNESS."*

Jesus does not deny that some people may have exhilarating experiences of the miraculous, but His frightening dismissal—"I never knew you; DEPART FROM ME"—shows that not all such experiences are from the Holy Spirit, even those done *in Jesus' name*, i.e., within the context of Christendom!

The main reason why experience is neither a valid nor a safe basis for one's beliefs is that it is ambiguous with regard to both its origin and its meaning. With the evil Deceiver prowling around *"like a roaring lion, seeking someone to devour"* (***1Pet 5:8***), we must always be aware of the possibility that he is the one who has caused us to have such experiences, even those of a miraculous nature. (In ***Matthew 7:21-23*** Jesus never denies that these unfortunate ones actually prophesied or performed miracles.) Also, in ***Luke 13:25-28*** Jesus warns us once again that our experiences may deceive us if we rely upon them and upon our interpretations of them.

Jesus warns us that our experiences may deceive us.

We need to understand that elevating experience to the place of the final norm is a rejection of the Bible as our only rule of faith and practice, i.e., it is a denial of the basic principle of *sola scriptura*. Charismatics "leave us with an insufficient Scripture," says Edgar (**258**). MacArthur cites one charismatic who says that Christ is increasingly manifesting Himself in miracle-signs and healings, and who concludes, "'We are not to say, therefore, that the word is sufficient.'" MacArthur replies with great emotion, "*Not to say that Scripture is sufficient*? God *Himself* says His Word is sufficient! (***Ps. 19:7-14***; ***2 Tim. 3:15-17***). Who is [this man] to claim that it is not?" MacArthur notes that most charismatics would not state their views in such stark language, but "the truth is, at the core of their belief system is a denial of Scripture's sufficiency" (***Chaos*, 43**).

This is not to say that experience as such must be excluded from the Christian life. The point is rather to recognize that all experience must be tested by the truth of Scripture. As MacArthur says, "Charismatics err because they tend to build their teachings on experience, rather than understanding that authentic experience happens in *response* to truth" (**ibid., 26**). "Experience . . . is not the test of bibli-

All experience must be tested by the truth of Scripture.

cal truth; rather, biblical truth stands in final judgment on experience" (**ibid., 20**).

False Doctrine Is Sanctioned

But then MacArthur laments, "Still the experiential wave rolls on, and doctrine and theology are being washed out the door" (**ibid., 52**). This will always happen. Once experience becomes normative, sound doctrine becomes less and less important; and doctrinal relativism ensues. The fact is that individuals from all across the theological spectrum, from the most conservative to the most liberal, are experiencing what they think is the baptism in the Holy Spirit. Edgar notes, "The centrality of experience rather than Scripture is obvious also in the fact that the charismatics come from almost every branch of the Christian spectrum, including many whose doctrine is not even evangelical" (**18**). But because (it is believed) the Holy Spirit has blessed such individuals with His empowering presence, this is taken to mean that He accepts or tolerates their doctrine, however false it may be in reality. False doctrine is thus sanctioned by the circumstances of continuationist movements.

This is clearly seen in a book by Kevin and Dorothy Ranaghan, pioneers in Roman Catholic pentecostalism. This movement began, they say, when "some renewal-minded Catholics prayed to the Holy Spirit that they might become better Catholics" (**153**). Does this mean that the Spirit led them to renounce the false teachings of Catholicism? On the contrary:

> It is most important to note that the outpouring of the Holy Spirit in these days has occurred to Catholics *within* the Catholic Church. The pentecostal movement has not separated or excluded Catholics from their Church. Rather it has renewed their love of the Church and has built up a lively faith in the Catholic community. (**55**)

As an example they cite the words of Thomas Noe, who was then a senior at Notre Dame: "The Spirit has deepened every aspect of my religious experience. I have found a new level of meaning in all the sacraments, especially in confession and the eucharist. I have come to a greater realization of the eucharist as sacrifice, and I have returned to frequent confession. . . . I have found a deep devotion to Mary" (**70**).

Is this doctrinal relativism to be deplored or welcomed? Clearly, for continuationists it is very welcome. MacArthur cites this example:

> A close associate of mine attended a charismatic businessmen's meeting in Chicago where a Catholic priest testified that Mary had given him the gift of tongues while he was saying the rosary. Then the charismatic pastor leading the meeting got up and said, "What an amazing testimony! Aren't you glad God isn't bound by our ideas of what's doctrinally acceptable? . . . But how you get filled with the Holy Ghost doesn't matter, as long as you know you've got the baptism!" The audience, numbering in the hundreds, broke into wild, sustained applause. (***Chaos*, 17**)

Pyle reports these words of an Assemblies of God preacher: "I know an Episcopalian priest in this city who is so liberal he neither believes in the virgin birth nor the resurrection. Yet he has recently received the baptism in the Spirit and exhibits a marvelous power in his ministry!" Pyle then comments, "The question arises, since an unbeliever, a Bible-denying modernist, is not a Christian in the Bible sense of the word, what kind of 'marvelous power' does he have in his ministry? Surely not *God's* power!" (**23**).

How can we accept the validity of any movement within which the alleged presence of the Holy Spirit is used to sanction false and contradictory doctrines? The Bible clearly tells us not to endorse or encourage false teaching:

> *Anyone who goes too far and does not abide in the teaching of Christ, does not have God; the one who abides in the teaching, he has both the Father and the Son. If anyone comes to you and does not bring this teaching, do not receive him into your house, and do not give him a greeting; for the one who gives him a greeting participates in his evil deeds.* ***(2Jn 9-11)***

How can we believe that the same Holy Spirit who warns *us* not to sanction and encourage false doctrine is Himself doing this very thing? See also ***2 Corinthians 6:14-18***.

A Counterfeit Unity Is Generated

In his book on the *Charismatic Gift of Tongues*, Baxter devotes a chapter to another very questionable aspect of modern continuationism, namely, "The Result of Tongues Is Counterfeit Unity" (**125-134**).

More generally, we can say that the result of the entire charismatic movement, with its acceptance of a miracle-producing baptism in the Holy Spirit, is a counterfeit unity.

Rightly noting that Jesus desires the unity of His followers (***Jn 17:21-22***), Baxter says, "True unity is a precious thing amongst all true believers" (***Tongues,* 125**). The problem, though, is that not all unity is *true* unity; some is counterfeit in the sense that it is not the *kind* of unity Jesus desires. In ***Ephesians 4:13*** Paul says that the very goal of the equipping gifts named in ***Ephesians 4:11*** is *"the unity of the faith, and of the knowledge of the Son of God,"* which can be attained only by avoiding false doctrine (***v. 14***) and *"speaking the truth in love"* (***v. 15***). The problem is that the experience-based unity of the charismatic movement does not seem to be concerned with unity as it relates to the *content* of faith and knowledge.

In ***1 Corinthians 1:10*** (NKJV) Paul exhorts Christians to doctrinal unity, pleading *"that you all speak the same thing, and that there be no divisions among you, but that you be perfectly joined together in the same mind and in the same judgment."* In continuationist ecumenism, though, the concern is not that *"all speak the same thing,"* but that all *experience* the same thing. As Baxter says, "Again the oneness of the movement is on the ground of experience. If one has experienced 'the baptism with the Holy Spirit,' then he is a fellow traveller. It does not matter what other doctrines he might hold, the experience is the thing" (**ibid., 126**). It is, as MacArthur says, "an external unity that is generally indifferent to any doctrinal concerns" (***Chaos,* 20**).

Liberalism had already spawned an ecumenical movement based on a common acceptance of the "lordship" of Jesus (as subjectively defined), regardless of other beliefs. Most conservatives refused to accept such a watered-down unity—until the charismatic movement came along. Then when individuals from all denominations became "Spirit filled," divisions were overcome. "Speaking with tongues became the experience of Episcopalians, Orthodox, Presbyterians, Baptist, Lutherans—indeed it would seem that no segment of the church escaped the Pentecostal invasion. . . . A new ecumenism had been born" (**Baxter, *Tongues,* 127**).

As Catholic pentecostals, the Ranaghans testify to this new "unity": "One of the richest fruits of this contemporary charismatic movement is the binding together of Christians of many denominations in the Spirit of Jesus. Episcopalians, Lutherans, Presbyterians, Methodists, Baptists, Disciples, Nazarenes, Brethren, as well as denominational Pentecostals have become our very dear brothers and sisters in Christ, united by the baptism in the Holy Spirit" (**225**). This common "baptism in the Holy Spirit" is the key. "How else could men and women of such diverse backgrounds, opinions, and desires live together as one? Yet again and again we have seen that they can and do live in a 'harmony of difference'" (**152**). "Thus, what we have been unable to accomplish by ourselves all these years, has been worked among us by the Holy Spirit" (**56**).

Kurt Koch, a German Lutheran and expert in the occult, has quite a different interpretation of this scenario. He says, "I was told that in America, Jesuits, Lutherans, free church people, modern theologians, High Anglicans, and Mormons meet together in order to speak in tongues. They are convinced that this is true Ecumenicalism in action." But Koch is not convinced. Speaking sarcastically, he says, "This sounds fantastic. And yet I heard of a similar group in London. What a wonderful time we live in today! All schisms, all denominational barriers, age-long divisions have been overcome by the new gift of tongues! Does this really mean that what the Word of God could not accomplish, has been brought about by a psychic epidemic?" (**25**).

MacArthur points out that even this counterfeit unity is not the whole picture. In reality, the continuationist movement has produced its share of strife and division as well. "The legacy of such a position is *not* unity and peace, but confusion and turmoil. Proof of that can be seen in the hundreds of churches, missions boards, schools, and other Christian organizations that have allowed charismatic influence to seep in and go unanswered. They ultimately must either sacrifice their non-charismatic position altogether or suffer the devastating effects of a split" (***Chaos*, 14**). He concludes, "The sad truth is, the legacy of the charismatic movement has been mostly one of chaos and doctrinal confusion" (**ibid., 358**).

The Biblical Rules for Tongue-Speaking Are Ignored

A final questionable circumstance commonly present in assemblies where the "gifts" are practiced is that the biblical rules for speaking in tongues, given by Paul in ***1 Corinthians 14***, are usually ignored.

This is a point made by Kurt Koch in his booklet on *The Strife of Tongues* (**39**). He refers, for example to ***1 Corinthians 14:34***, *"The women are to keep silent in the churches; for they are not permitted to speak."* Koch rightly understands this to mean that "women are not to speak publicly in tongues," but "this is not heeded anywhere in the new tongues movement today." Paul's prohibition also applies to women prophesying in the public assembly.

Koch also reminds us of ***1 Corinthians 14:27***, *"If anyone speaks in a tongue, it should be by two or at the most three, and each in turn, and one must interpret."* Koch comments, "No notice is taken of this either in the new tongues movement. Ten, twenty or even more people speak in tongues at the same prayer meeting." Also, they often speak all at once (men and women together). MacArthur notes, "Some men from our church staff recently visited [John] Wimber's Vineyard in Anaheim. The evening they were there, they witnessed virtual pandemonium. Wimber tried to get everyone speaking in tongues at once" (***Chaos*, 157-158**). I heard an entire charismatic congregation not just speaking in tongues but also singing in tongues at the same time, on a recording included with a book on the subject. The injunction that "one must interpret" is often ignored, also.

Citing ***1 Corinthians 14:1,39***, Koch also points out, "Paul affirms twice that the gift of prophecy is greater than the gift of tongues. The gift of tongues is called the lowest gift by Paul, but today it is given first place by the tongues movement" (**39**).

The Teaching of 1 Corinthians 13:8-13

One of the strongest reasons for denying present-day miraculous gifts is the teaching of ***1 Corinthians 13:8-13***, especially ***verse 10***: *"But when the perfect comes, the partial will be done away."* This verse specifically states that a time will come (in the future from the time Paul wrote these words) when certain miraculous gifts will cease. (Pettegrew is right, I believe, when he says that the gifts mentioned here "likely are representative of the whole list of gifts . . . in ***12:8-10***" [**179**], i.e., the entire list of miraculous gifts.)

One of the strongest reasons for denying present-day miraculous gifts is the teaching of 1 Corinthians 13:8-13.

The purpose of this section is to explain this passage, and to show that "the perfect" in ***verse 10*** (*teleion* in Greek) is *the completed New Testament*. This means that when the New Testament writings were completed, miraculous gifts ceased.

Strife over Tongues

The passage of Scripture we are discussing occurs in the midst of a larger section of the first Corinthian letter (***chs. 12–14***), a section in which Paul deals in detail with the whole subject of spiritual gifts. This entire letter shows that the church in Corinth had a number of internal problems. Paul is using his apostolic authority to address these problems and to exhort the church to straighten itself out. From what he writes in ***chapters 12–14***, it is apparent that one of their problems was controversy over the use of spiritual gifts, especially the gift of tongues.

a. The Message of Chapters 12–14. In the very beginning of the letter Paul tells the Corinthians that he is aware of various divisions and quarrels within their congregation (***1:10-11***). One source of division was their attitude toward and practice of spiritual gifts. From ***chapter 12*** we learn that these Christians had decided that there was a definite hierarchical order in the "varieties of gifts" (***12:4***), i.e., some gifts were regarded as more important and prestigious than others. Those who had such gifts enjoyed a higher status within the group, leading to division (***12:25***). For some reason they had concluded that the gift of tongues was the most important (see ***ch. 14***).

The main point of ***chapter 13*** is to put *all* of the spiritual gifts, especially the gift of tongues, into the proper perspective. All of the gifts are important and are not to be neglected (when properly used—***14:20-40***), but these gifts are not to be regarded as the most important aspect of the Christian life. Within the whole list of gifts prophecy seems most important, more important than tongues (***14:1-19***); but overall there are other aspects of the Christian life that are far more important than any such gifts. These are the things you should be concentrating on, says Paul; these are *"a still more excellent way"* (***12:31***).

In ***chapter 13*** Paul explains that this *"more excellent way"* is *love*. Instead of fighting over these other gifts, such as prophecy, supernatural knowledge, and tongues, you *should* be focusing on loving one another. Love must be the matrix within which all other activities occur. Without love, nothing else matters (***13:1-3***).

To make his point Paul compares love (and later, faith and hope, ***v. 13***) with the three representative gifts of prophecy, knowledge, and tongues. Why does he choose these three gifts? Because he wants to make a point, namely, that love is more important than even the most valuable of the spiritual gifts that he names in ***chapter 12***, the gifts that are related to supernatural knowledge. How does he show that even these gifts are relatively less important than love? By asserting that such gifts will come to an end, while love (and faith and hope) will continue to exist in the church's life.

Love must be the matrix within which all other activities occur.

Paul's challenge is this: Why are you getting so excited about things that are temporary? Why are you fighting among yourselves over things that are ready to pass away? Why are you dividing the church over things that will cease? "Pursue love!" (***14:1***).

b. The Structure of 1 Corinthians 13:8-13. The key section for our purposes is ***13:8-13***. It is very important to understand the outline or structure of this paragraph. It consists basically of *two contrasts*.

The first and main contrast is between things that are *temporary* (***v. 8***) and things that are *permanent* (***v. 13***). To get this point these two verses should be read together while setting **verses 9-12** aside as a parenthesis, thus:

> *Love never fails; but if there are gifts of prophecy, they will be done away; if there are tongues, they will cease; if there is knowledge, it will be done away. . . . But now abide faith, hope, love, these three; but the greatest of these is love.*

Some things, Paul says, will cease—the very things you are fighting and dividing over: prophecy, knowledge, and tongues (***v. 8***). But the really crucial things will continue to exist—faith, hope, and love (***v. 13a***). The most important of all is love (***v. 13b***), since love *never* ends (***v. 8a***).

Paul could have written just this much and still have made his point. But he knew that he had to explain the temporary nature of tongues, etc. a bit further. He knew that in the minds of many Corinthians the gift of tongues was the heart and soul of their faith.

One can imagine their reaction to ***verse 8***: "Oh, no, Paul! You can't mean that! Surely you are mistaken; surely tongues are not just temporary! Don't take away our tongues!"

In order to alleviate such concern, in ***verses 9-12***, even before he completes his main contrast between ***verse 8*** and ***verse 13***, Paul inserts a *parenthesis* with a secondary contrast. Here the contrast is to show *why* gifts like tongues, prophecy, and knowledge are only temporary. The reason they are temporary, he says, is because they are only "partial" or piecemeal; something "perfect" or complete will come to take their place. This four-verse parenthesis should be read as a unit:

> *For we know in part and we prophesy in part; but when the perfect comes, the partial will be done away. When I was a child, I used to speak like a child, think like a child, reason like a child; when I became a man, I did away with childish things. For now we see in a mirror dimly, but then face to face; now I know in part, but then I will know fully just as I also have been fully known.*

Though the Corinthians no doubt did not want to hear this, Paul tells them that the very things they have made the centerpiece of their lives will be "done away" because they are only *partial*. As an analogy, their individual episodes of miraculous tongues and prophesying were like single pieces of a jigsaw puzzle. Something is coming, though, that will be like the entire puzzle with all its pieces put together; then you will see the entire picture. Will that not be much better?

Their individual episodes of tongues were like single pieces of a jigsaw puzzle.

What is this coming thing that will take the place of tongues and other such gifts? Paul calls it the *teleion* in ***verse 10***, translated "the perfect." If we can just know what this *teleion* is, we can know *when* the tongues and other things will cease. This is true because Paul specifically says, "WHEN the *teleion* comes," the partial will cease.[5] The coming of the *teleion* will be the occasion for the end of these gifts.

The Identity of the *Teleion*

The case for the cessationist view of miraculous spiritual gifts rests

[5]"When" is the Greek word *hotan*. When used with a subjunctive verb, as is the case here, it means "when, but not before." Thus the tongues and other things must continue up to the time when the *teleion* comes.

to a large extent on our ability to identify the *teleion* to which Paul refers in ***verse 10***. We will now see how this can be done, based on the word itself and the context in which it appears.

a. Not "Perfect," but "Complete." To determine what the *teleion* is, we must first consider the best English translation of the word in this context. The word is an adjective, and in this passage most Bible versions translate it "the perfect." (The original NIV has "perfection.") This is indeed one main meaning of the word, and it is properly so translated in other texts (e.g., ***Rom 12:2; Jas 1:17***). The verb form of the word (*teleioo*) is often translated "make perfect" (e.g., ***Php 3:12; Heb 7:28***). Another main meaning of the adjective is "mature," and it is sometimes translated thus (e.g., ***1Cor 2:6; Eph 4:13***). Still another main meaning is "complete," though the adjective and the verb are seldom translated thus in the NT. The NIV does translate the verb as "make complete" in several places (e.g., ***Jas 2:22; 1Jn 2:5***), and the TNIV translates *teleion* as "completeness" in ***1 Corinthians 13:10***.

Which of these meanings best fits the context of ***1 Corinthians 13:10***? Despite the fact that most Bible versions use "perfect," the obviously intended meaning in this verse is "complete." Why is this obvious? Because the *teleion* here is clearly contrasted with things that are *partial* (*ek merous,* "in part, of a part, partial")! (See **Unger, *Tongues,* 95**.) Does it not make sense to contrast *partial* things with something that is *complete*? In my judgment this is a "no-brainer." Thus even though when reading most Bible versions we will encounter the word "perfect," in our minds we must think the word "complete."

Despite the fact that most Bible versions use "perfect," the intended meaning is "complete."

Among those who agree is Edgar: "The 'perfect' in this passage is specifically contrasted as the opposite to 'that which is partial.' Therefore, the meaning of 'perfect' must be 'complete.' This not only is a common meaning for *teleion,* it is the only one that makes a sensible contrast with 'partial'" (**244**). Other who agree are **Baxter, *Gifts,* 161**; and **Pettegrew, 181-182**.

b. The Complete Thing. A second consideration is to recognize that *teleion* is a neuter adjective. Adjectives ordinarily modify nouns; but in this case no noun is given, thus it must itself be treated as a noun.

In the Greek language adjectives and other parts of speech have different forms according to *gender*, i.e., they can be masculine, feminine, or neuter. If *teleion* here were in its masculine form (*teleios*), since it stands alone, we would translate it as "the complete one" or "the complete man," referring to a person. But in fact the adjective is neuter in gender, thus must be read as "the complete *thing*."

This is very important, because some have seen the translation "When the perfect comes" and have jumped to the conclusion that this must be a reference to the second coming of Christ. After all, Jesus is the only "perfect one," and He definitely is coming again! The implication regarding miraculous gifts, of course, would be that tongues, etc. will continue until the second coming of Jesus.

When we understand, though, that *teleion* is a *neuter* adjective, we will see that it refers not to a person at all, but to a thing. If it referred to a person such as Jesus, the gender would have been masculine. Thus the best translation is "When the complete *thing* comes." Paul is thus saying that the partial things will cease when the complete thing comes.

c. Not Connected with the Second Coming. Do we have any way of discerning what this complete thing is supposed to be? Yes. For one thing, we know the limitations as to the *time* when it will appear. On the one hand, since Paul uses future tense ("*will* cease . . . *will* be done away"), the *teleion* must still be in the future relative to the time he was writing this letter. This means that the complete thing cannot be *love*, since love was surely already present within the church to some degree. It is important to see this since love has upon occasion been suggested as the identity of the *teleion*. But this cannot be.

On the other hand, we know from something Paul says here that the *teleion* must be something that will come *before* the end of the age, before the second coming of Jesus. This is extremely important, because the most common view as to the identity of the complete thing is that it must have something to do with the second coming and with heaven. For example, Keener says that in this text Paul "explicitly declares that our imperfect gifts will cease" at the Lord's return (**85**). Also, "That Paul assumes all gifts will continue until the return of Christ is clear from his argument in ***1 Corinthians 13***"; they will no longer be needed "when we see Christ face to face (***13:12***)" (**96-97**). Thus, says Keener, "Paul is explicit that these gifts will not cease until Christ's return (***13:8-12***)" (**99**).

We reject this view because it is based on the incorrect idea that *teleion* in ***verse 10*** means "the perfect" and thus must refer to the post-second coming era since that is the only state that will be perfect. We have already seen that *teleion* means "complete," not "perfect." Also, this view is based on a faulty understanding of ***verse 12***, especially the phrase "face to face." This verse will be discussed below.

Most significantly, there is evidence in this very text that the complete thing must come *before* the end times and not in connection with the second coming. How do we know that it must come while the church is still existing in this age? Because of what Paul says in ***verse 13***. Here he declares that the *teleion* will come and the partial gifts will cease while faith, hope, and love still abide or remain among God's people. If *hope* is still present, then the *teleion* must come before Christ's second coming, because once Christ comes, all that we are hoping for will become a *reality*, and hope itself will disappear. As Paul explains in ***Romans 8:24***, we hope only for things we do not yet see, *"for who hopes for what he already sees?"* Some would apply this same reasoning to faith as well, since in one sense *sight* replaces faith (***2Cor 5:7***) as well as hope.

Once Christ comes, all that we are hoping for will become a reality, and hope itself will disappear.

Knofel Staton is emphatic about the significance of this point: "***Verse 13*** gives us a clincher: '*Faith, hope, and love abide.*' These will abide after the *perfect* has come. Thus the *perfect* in ***verse 10*** *cannot refer to the 2nd coming of Christ* because when that happens, our faith will be turned into sight and our hope into reality" (***Gifts*, 52**).

In any case, ***verse 13*** rules out any interpretation of the *teleion* that connects it with the second coming. Thus the partial gifts must cease sometime during the church age.

d. The Completed New Testament. A final consideration in our quest to identify the *teleion* is the fact that it is meant to *replace* some very specific kinds of gifts (***v. 8***). Since the complete thing replaces these partial things, it must be something similar in nature to the latter and must serve the same general purpose as the latter. What is the nature of the gifts named in ***verse 8***? Prophecy, supernatural knowledge, and tongues (when interpreted) are all in the category of *revealed knowl-*

edge. Thus the complete thing must also be in the category of revealed knowledge. Yet it is something *complete*, as contrasted with these partial forms.

Again this goes against identifying the complete thing as *love*, since love is not a revealed-knowledge kind of thing. Also, it rules out another view sometimes suggested, namely, that the *teleion* should be translated "mature" and that the "mature thing" is really the *mature church* (e.g., **Robert Thomas, 79**). Paul does seem to be contrasting childhood with maturity in ***verse 11***, suggesting that the partial things are part of the church's childhood stage while the *teleion* is a mark of its maturity (see **Unger, *Tongues*, 96-97**). But the specific identity of the *teleion* must be something other than the mature church itself, since the latter is not a kind of revealed knowledge.

The only thing that meets all the requirements is the completed New Testament.

The only thing that meets all the requirements pointed out in this section is *the completed New Testament*. The *teleion*, the complete thing, is the completed New Testament. When the completed New Testament has come, piecemeal prophecies, tongues, and knowledge will cease. Pettegrew is right: "Interpreting 'the completed' [*teleion*] as the New Testament is still the most natural and logical explanation of the passage—far better than trying to introduce the Rapture, Second Coming, death, or eternal state into the interpretation" (**182**).

This view is supported by the fact that elsewhere in the Bible God's will and word in the new-covenant era are described with this same adjective, *teleios*; see ***Romans 12:2***; ***James 1:25***; and ***Hebrews 5:14–6:1***. Jacoby notes, by the way, that *teleion* is never used of heaven (***Spirit*, 189**).

Some object to the view that the *teleion* is the completed New Testament on the grounds that no such document existed at the time Paul wrote ***1 Corinthians***, so no one would have known what he was talking about. Keener, for example, says that the idea of a completed canon "could not have occurred either to Paul or to the Corinthians in their own historical context (since at that point no one knew that there would *be* a New Testament canon)." Thus we must accept "the impossibility that Paul could have expected the Corinthian

Christians to think he meant the canon" (**97**). This argument is completely without merit, however. All Christians from the church's beginning would be familiar with the old-covenant canon (what "Scriptures" were the Bereans examining in ***Acts 17:11***?). They would also know that they were under a new covenant. Thus it is quite reasonable to think that they would be *expecting* a completed New Testament to guide them in this new-covenant age, in the same way that God's old-covenant people had the Old Testament to guide them. To call such an idea impossible—especially for an inspired apostle—is quite unfounded. "Moreover, how do we know that Paul is not telling them about the New Testament at this point? How else would the apostle explain that one day there would be a completed prophetic volume that would supplant all of the partial prophecies that had been given?" (**Pettegrew, 182**).

The New Testament was completed near the end of the first century, with the last writing of the Apostle John. All the New Testament books were then in circulation. Thus we must conclude that these partial gifts—such as tongues, prophecy, and knowledge—*have ceased*.

The *Teleion* and 1 Corinthians 13:12

For many people a major problem in accepting the view that the *teleion* is the completed New Testament is what Paul says in ***13:12***: *"For now we see in a mirror dimly, but then face to face; now I know in part, but then I will know fully just as I also have been fully known."* At first glance this seems to be a contrast between our present condition and our future heavenly existence. This is what leads many to conclude that the *teleion* must be the result of the second coming.

In my judgment, however, this is a serious misunderstanding of ***verse 12***. The time reference for the contrast between "now" and "then" is the time Paul was writing this letter. Thus the contrast is still between the church's years of piecemeal revelations ("now") and the time when the full New Testament will be available ("then").

a. "In a Mirror Dimly" versus "Face to Face." The first part of this verse is not a contrast between this present earthly life and our future heavenly state, but a contrast between *two kinds of revelation*: the less clear and the more clear. The less clear revelation is compared with trying to see one's face in a poor-quality mirror: *"For now we see in a mirror dimly."* The more clear revelation is then compared with seeing one's face in a very good mirror: *"but then face to face."* That is, "For now we see in a mirror dimly, with only occasional, scattered, incomplete revelations of God's new-covenant will; but then, when the completed New Testament has come, we will see, as it were, face to face."

The key to understanding this statement is ***Numbers 12:8***. The similarity of the imagery and language of ***1 Corinthians 13:12a*** and the Greek version of ***Numbers 12:8*** is so strong that it is nearly certain that Paul has the latter in mind as he writes the former. In ***Numbers 12*** God is explaining to Aaron and Miriam why Moses as a prophet is in a class by himself compared with other prophets. God says He speaks with other prophets in visions and dreams, but with Moses *"I speak mouth to mouth, even openly, and not in dark sayings."* The phrase "mouth to mouth" here corresponds to "face to face" in ***1 Corinthians 13:12a***, and "not in dark sayings" corresponds to "dimly." In the latter phrasing the same Greek word is used in the Septuagint version of Numbers and in Corinthians, namely, *ainigma* ("riddle"). "In dark sayings" (***Num 12:8***) is literally "in riddles," and so is "dimly" in ***1 Corinthians 13:12a***.

For Moses and Paul the point is the same, i.e., a contrast between less clear and more clear revelation. Paul's image is definitely that of "seeing in a mirror." The KJV says, *"For now we see through a glass, darkly,"* leaving the impression that Paul is talking about trying to look through a dirty window pane. Though "remarkably prevalent among Christians," this view is quite erroneous, says Kittel (179). It is also "incorrect to maintain that one of the characteristics of the mirrors of antiquity was to give indistinct pictures"; Kittel speaks of "the archaeological unsoundness of this view" (**ibid.**).

For Moses and Paul the point is the same: a contrast between less clear and more clear revelation.

In the Rabbinic literature relating to ***Numbers 12:8***, with which Paul would have been familiar, "Moses is indeed extolled as the one who received the supreme and most direct revelation of God when he saw Him in a clear mirror" (**ibid.**). This is the point of reference from which we must interpret ***1 Corinthians 13:12***. Paul is *not* contrasting (1) seeing *only* in an allegedly cloudy mirror, and (2) seeing *in person*. Rather, the distinction is between (1) seeing in a *cloudy* mirror, and (2) seeing in a *clear* mirror, which projects a clear image of one's face.

Thus in ***1 Corinthians 13:12*** "dimly" versus "face to face" represents enigmatic, incomplete revelation versus clear, complete revelation. The former is the piecemeal, temporary prophecies and tongues; the latter is the completed New Testament. This is supported by ***2 Corinthians 3:7-18*** and ***James 1:23-25***, where New Testament revelation is compared with looking in a mirror.

Some may still be hung up on the idea of seeing "face to face," thinking this must be a reference to seeing *Jesus* "face to face" (e.g., **Keener, 97**). Actually Paul does not say we shall see Jesus or anyone else face to face. There is no object for the verb "see," since no specific object is intended. The point is not what or whom we will see, but *how* we will see. It refers to the comparative clarity of the revelation in the completed New Testament. This is not to deny, of course, that we *will* see Jesus "face to face" in heaven; it is simply to say that this is not the point of ***1 Corinthians 13:12***.

The point is not what or whom we will see, but how.

An expanded paraphrase of ***13:12a*** is as follows: "For now, in these early days of the church, while we depend on occasional revelations through prophecy or interpreted tongues, it is like trying to see yourself in a scratched and cloudy mirror. But then, when the completed New Testament has come, it will be like seeing a sharp, clear image of yourself in a bright new mirror."

b. "Know in Part" versus "Know Fully." The second part of ***13:12*** says, *"Now I know in part, but then I will know fully just as I also have been fully known."* This has also been interpreted as a contrast between the knowledge we have in this life and the kind of knowledge that will be possible only after Jesus comes. This understanding would also support an eschatological interpretation of the *teleion*. That is, in this life all our knowledge is partial; only in heaven will we "know fully." Thus the partial gifts such as tongues must last until the second coming, for only then will we "know fully."

We maintain, however, that the knowledge of which Paul is speaking in the latter half of this statement is *not* some kind of special, eschatological knowledge available only in heaven. This view is based on a faulty view of the Greek words in ***verse 12b***. Here there are two similar verbs for "to know": *ginosko* and *epiginosko*. The popular belief is that the latter word represents some special, intensified knowledge, such as one might have in heaven. This is why Bible versions translate it as "know *fully*." The "fully" is based solely on the prefix *epi-* on the front of *epiginosko;* there is no word in the Greek that means "fully."

The idea that there is such a contrast between *ginosko* and *epiginosko* is simply not true. The latter term does not necessarily carry any stronger meaning than the former. There is no warrant for translating it "know *fully*," in the sense of some kind of heavenly, quasi-divine knowledge. An examination of parallel uses of these two words in the New Testament shows that they are used interchangeably (e.g., compare ***Lk 24:16,31*** [*epiginosko*] with ***Lk 24:35*** [*ginosko*]). ***Matthew 7:16,20*** says that we human beings shall know (*epiginosko*) them by their fruits, but in ***Matthew 7:23*** *Jesus* says, "I never knew you" (*ginosko*). If the former were the stronger word, we would have expected it in ***verse 23***. In ***Matthew 11:27*** the Father's knowledge of the Son and the Son's knowledge of the Father are described with *epiginosko*, but in ***John 10:15*** the same knowledge is called *ginosko* (in fact, John never uses *epiginosko*). Both *epiginosko* and *epignosis* (verb and noun) are used extensively of our *present* knowledge of God's truth, e.g., ***2 Corinthians 1:13***; ***Ephesians 1:17***; ***4:13***; ***Colossians 1:9***; ***1 Timothy 2:4***; ***4:3***; ***2 Timothy 2:25***; ***3:7***; ***Titus 1:1***; ***Hebrews 10:26***; ***2 Peter 2:21***. Apart from the passage in question (***1Cor 13:12***), neither verb nor noun is used of any kind of eschatological knowledge.

The lengthy article on "Knowledge" in the *New International Dictionary of New Testament Theology* (**2:390-409**) does not even mention a distinction between these words. The major article on *ginosko* in Kittel's *Theological Dictionary of the New Testament* says they are used "interchangeably," and "with no difference in meaning" in the NT. "That there is no general distinction between the simple and compound forms in early Christian writings is shown by a comparison of ***Mk. 2:8*** with ***8:17***; ***Mk. 5:30*** with ***Lk. 8:46***; ***Mk. 6:33, 54*** with ***Lk. 9:11***; ***Mt. 7:16, 20*** with ***Lk. 6:44***; ***Mt. 11:27*** with ***Lk. 10:22***; ***Lk. 24:31*** with ***24:35***; ***Col. 1:6*** with ***2 Cor. 8:9***. . . . Even in ***1 C. 13:12*** the alternation is purely rhetorical" (**Bultmann, 704**).

In this verse the object of our knowledge is not given; it is not important. The point is the contrast between two kinds or two levels of knowledge. Paul does not say we shall know *God* as fully as He knows us, an idea that approaches blasphemy. Knowledge of God is not really the point. It is enough to conclude that with the more complete knowledge we have from the entire New Testament, we should know *ourselves* with more clarity, or know what we *ought* to be in a clearer way (see ***Jas 1:23-25***). All thoughts of *full* knowledge in the sense of omniscience should be excluded altogether. Omniscience belongs to God alone and is impossible for finite creatures, which we will always be, even in heaven.

Thus ***verse 12*** is not speaking of a kind of end-times knowledge that will be ours only when we are glorified or only when we get to heaven or only when Jesus comes again. This verse is quite consistent with the meaning of *teleion* in ***verse 10*** as the completed New Testament, which is a body of knowledge that is relatively clear and complete when compared with the fragments of knowledge given in the earliest days of the church via gifts of supernatural knowledge.

It stands firm that the best understanding of the *teleion* in ***1 Corinthians 13:10*** is that it refers to the completed New Testament. This confirms the fact that miraculous gifts ceased being passed along after the death of the apostles. The miraculous gifts filled a need in the absence of the written New Testament. Once the New Testament writings were in hand, this need ceased; thus the gifts ceased.

The miraculous gifts filled a need in the absence of the written New Testament.

EXPLAINING MODERN-DAY MIRACLE CLAIMS WITHIN CHRISTENDOM

Earlier in this chapter I have presented biblical teaching to support the view that the Holy Spirit has not been giving miraculous spiritual gifts to Christians since late in the first century AD. But there have been countless reports of miracles such as tongues and healings within Christian groups at different points during Christian history, especially since the early twentieth century. What shall we say about these claims? How can we explain them?

I once raised this question in a discussion with a teaching colleague who shares my cessationist convictions. His answer was, "We don't have to explain them. All we must do is teach and follow what the Bible says." This approach will not satisfy many, however; I know it does not satisfy me. Unless we can offer a plausible explanation for the allegedly miraculous phenomena, the case for cessationism is severely weakened. The point of this section is to offer such a plausible explanation.

Unless we can offer a plausible explanation, the case is severely weakened.

Over the past 100 years, in America at least, the experience of miraculous gifts has arisen in three main stages. First came the rise of the Pentecostal movement, which began in 1901. The second stage was the rise of the charismatic movement, beginning slowly in the early 1950s and exploding upon the American church scene about 1960. These two movements were explained on pages 291-292, at the beginning of the chapter on Holy Spirit baptism.

The third stage in the spread of miraculous practices in American Christendom is called the "signs and wonders" movement, or the "third wave" of the Holy Spirit. It can be traced to the late 1970s when John Wimber began the first Vineyard Christian Fellowship in Anaheim, California, with an emphasis on miraculous healing. This caught the attention of C. Peter Wagner, professor of missions and church growth at Fuller Theological Seminary in Pasadena. Wagner became convinced that miracles, especially divine healing, are a key component in church growth today. He and Wimber sparked renewed interest in miraculous gifts within evangelicalism when they began to teach a course at Fuller Seminary—MC510, "Signs, Wonders, and Church Growth"—complete with healing demonstrations. The course broke all enrollment records but caused considerable controversy (**Wagner, 25-30**).

These three movements are linked together by their common belief that Pentecost began the age during which all Christians are intended to receive the gift of the Holy Spirit as a means of enduing them with miraculous powers, especially tongues. They also agree that all of the spiritual gifts named by Paul in ***1 Corinthians 12***, including the miraculous ones, are meant for the entire church age.

In the following discussion I will first in a general way explain the kinds of phenomena found within these movements; then I will outline possible explanations for them, defending one in particular.

"Miraculous" Phenomena

Regardless of how we explain it, we cannot ignore the abundant testimony claiming that miraculous events are occurring within Pentecostalism, the charismatic movement, and the signs and wonders movement. What sorts of phenomena are being reported? The anecdotal material is seemingly inexhaustible.

The most common phenomenon is speaking in tongues. In these circles this has always been important, usually being regarded as a sure sign that the much-coveted baptism of the Spirit has actually been received. Two kinds of tongues (called *glossalalia* from the Greek word for "tongue," *glossa*) are reported. One is the rapid utterance of nonlanguage, nondecipherable strings of syllables. The other is the rational speaking of unlearned foreign languages, similar to what happened on the Day of Pentecost (**Acts 2:1-11**).

There are abundant examples of the former (I have some on tape), but the latter are more dramatic. Lowe reports that a man named Dave Mangan prayed in tongues at a Pittsburgh gathering. A college student near him, a French major, was able to partially translate the prayer. She could not understand it all, though, and concluded it was an old French dialect. A week later a Frenchman named Paul was present and heard Dave again pray in tongues. The Frenchman said Dave *was* speaking French, but not modern French. He said Dave's pronunciation was flawless—but Dave had no background in the French language (**19**).

Wagner tells of a missionary couple, James and Jaime Thomas, who arrived in Argentina with almost no knowledge of Spanish. Early in their ministry James was struggling to translate some announcements into Spanish, when suddenly he "broke into fluent, Argentine-accented Spanish. From that moment on he has spoken it like a native and written it with correct grammar, spelling, and accent marks" (**102-103**).

A former Bible College classmate of mine had a Pentecostal experience and was later reported to have prayed in the (unlearned) Portuguese language while visiting Christians in Brazil. Pyle reports, "Missionaries from the Orient were persuaded, along with their

Lancaster, Pennsylvania, pastor, to attend a tongues service. One woman poured forth a torrent of words which the interpreter said was Chinese. Later the missionaries told the pastor that it was indeed Chinese" (**13**).

As this last incident shows, many also claim to have the gift of the interpretation of tongues.

There are also many reports of sick persons being healed, and not just by questionable and sometimes discredited television or "show business" healers. As mentioned, Wagner and Wimber gave healing demonstrations in their Fuller Seminary classroom. One of Wagner's healing specialities was leg-lengthening, i.e., causing the shorter leg to grow longer on a person whose legs were of uneven length (**Sarles, 63**). Wimber reports an unusual case from one of his healing seminars: "With several physicians present, a woman's toe, which had been cut off, completely grew back, toenail and all" (**Wagner, 34-35**).

We also have claims that the dead have been raised. In evangelistic crusades in Africa, "the blind see, the dead are raised, the lame walk" (**ibid., 88**). Wagner says, "In recent years, when I have traveled to the Third World, I have asked leaders there if they know of the dead being raised. In Brazil I heard three direct accounts of such incidents. I talked to a Nazarene pastor who himself had been raised from the dead when he was two years old. . . . I have heard of similar stories in the Philippines, Indonesia, and India" (**ibid., 111**).

Gifts of supernatural knowledge and prophecy have also been reported. I know a missionary whose associates became charismatic and claimed to be receiving all sorts of prophetic messages by revelation from the Holy Spirit. These were written down, and I read some of them. A charismatic author reports that in the late 1970s he attended many meetings where "the pastor regularly revealed what someone [in the audience] was struggling with at the time, and he was invariably right" (**Keener, 113**).

Numerous other kinds of miraculous phenomena have been reported. Certain Pentecostal groups have long practiced snake-handling, i.e., holding, caressing, and draping oneself with numerous poisonous snakes such as rattlers and copperheads, without protection. A popular practice in some circles is "slaying in the Spirit," or causing someone to lose consciousness and to collapse through a mere gesture or suggestion. Some groups have experienced uncontrollable fits of laughter, dubbed "holy laughter." A former Vineyard church in Toronto made news by claiming that in their services God was turning ordinary dental fillings into gold. They said God was simply keeping His promise in ***Psalm 81:10***, *"Open your mouth wide and I will fill it"* (**Beverly, 17**). In Argentinean crusades, "on a fairly regular basis, decayed teeth are filled and new teeth grow where there were none before" (**Wagner, 96**).

Possible Explanations

How shall we respond to such reports and such claims? In this section I will simply outline the possible explanations, and I will affirm that no one explanation can apply to all of the phenomena.

No one explanation can apply to all of the phenomena.

Natural Explanations

First, we should note that the possible explanations of such reports can be divided into two kinds: natural and supernatural. Natural explanations are those that do not involve any divine or miraculous intervention. In such cases the phenomena are fully explainable in terms of natural processes.

One possible natural explanation of these miracle-claims is that the experiences in question really happened but are psychological in origin. The phenomena may be unusual, but may simply be the result of little-understood yet natural powers of the mind. For example, we are familiar with the concept of psychosomatic healing, where a physical ailment is the result of some kind of mental trauma. The ailment disappears when the trauma is neutralized. Geisler gives an example: "Noted psychiatrist Dr. Paul Meier revealed that he healed a young woman of blindness by merely instructing her to sleep in another room and, when she would awake, she would be able to see. The cure came, just as the doctor ordered. Her sight was restored by the power of suggestion" (***Signs***, 77).

For another example, some kinds of tongue-speaking could be triggered psychologically. In an effort to learn to speak in tongues, some have been told to begin repeating short phrases or nonsense syllables very fast, until the Holy Spirit takes over and bestows the genuine gift. I witnessed a friend's attempt to receive the gift of tongues. He knelt as family members laid their hands on his head and prayed in tongues, but nothing was happening. He was instructed to begin to babble until the Spirit took over. Still nothing happened. Kurt Koch reports that one person was told to repeat a short prayer, such as "Lord help me," five to eight hundred times. "Then your tongue and consciousness will get used to it and suddenly you will speak in 'tongues.'" Koch comments, "The Holy Spirit does not need repetitive exercises or any training of the subconsciousness" (**24**; see **Pyle, 74-76**; **Baxter, *Tongues*, 76-79**).

Another kind of natural explanation is that the alleged miraculous gifts are phony; they are being faked by unscrupulous ministers or attention-seekers. This certainly applies to some cases, especially in reference to certain big-name healers who have been publicly exposed as frauds (see **Geisler, *Signs*, 63-64**). Pyle tells of two women who kept interrupting a revival preacher with their tongue-speaking. One would stand and speak a message in tongues, and the other would give an interpretation. The minister arranged for a native Greek to memorize a short passage from the Greek NT, and to stand and quote it in a service attended by the two women. Once he had done so, one of the women enthusiastically stood and gave its "interpretation," which, of course, had no resemblance to the Bible text that was quoted. When the minister explained what had just happened, and read the relevant Scripture in English, "the 'tongues-speaking' women slunk away from the meeting and never returned" (**76-77**).

A third kind of natural explanation is that the reports that certain miracles have occurred are simply mistaken. Baxter mentions the many miracle stories that came out of the 1971 revival in Indonesia. It was claimed that walking on water, resurrections from the dead, water turning into wine, clothes never getting dirty, and other such marvels had taken place. "However, when others began to trace down and investigate the happenings, they did not find the happenings so miraculous after all. Without exception, those miraculous happenings investigated turned out either to be natural phenomena or not to have happened at all" (***Gifts*, 143**). One investigator interviewed people supposedly raised from the dead and found that in that culture "being dead" did not necessarily mean the same thing as it does to more scientifically-minded Westerners. For example, "many of the people who claimed to have died could hear people in the room near

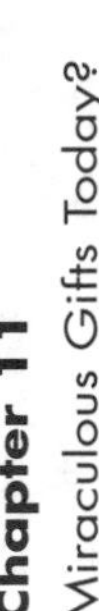

their body. Others admitted they were not 'totally dead'" (**Geisler, *Signs*, 71-72**).

These are just three examples of possible natural explanations. It is likely that many of the allegedly miraculous phenomena can be explained thus. Things may happen through the power of our subconscious minds, and our inability to understand such workings may lead us to mistake them for miracles. Also, there are many naïve and gullible people in the world, and many charlatans who know how to manipulate them and take advantage of them. Finally, some reports are not fraudulent as such but are nonetheless mistaken.

In my judgment, though, it is clear that *not all* of the reported "miraculous" phenomena can be explained by natural means. One cannot conclude from a few obviously fake healings, e.g., that *all* alleged healings are phony.

Supernatural Explanations

If natural explanations cannot account for all allegedly miraculous phenomena, the only other possibility is a *supernatural* explanation. In such a case we would be acknowledging that the event in question is a true miracle. There are two possible supernatural explanations of true miracles. One is that they are from God. The Bible has many reports of miracles performed through the power of God. However, we have already ruled out this explanation for present-day events alleged to be miraculous. We have argued, on biblical grounds, that the Holy Spirit does not give miraculous gifts to Christians today. This does not mean that God is *unable* to work miracles today or unable to give miraculous gifts today. It simply means that He has chosen not to do so.

If someone says, "But I *saw* a genuine miracle," or "I was personally healed by a miracle, and in a church service no less," then I would ask that person to carefully read ***Matthew 7:21-23***, where Jesus says,

Jesus warns that not every miraculous experience comes from God.

Not everyone who says to Me, "Lord, Lord," will enter the kingdom of heaven, but he who does the will of My Father who is in heaven will enter. Many will say to Me on that day, "Lord, Lord, did we not prophesy in Your name, and in Your name cast out

demons, and in Your name perform many miracles?" And then I will declare to them, "I never knew you; depart from Me, you who practice lawlessness."

Here Jesus warns us that not every miraculous experience, including miraculous speaking (such as tongues), even when done in His own name, comes from God.

But if something miraculous is truly happening, and if it is not from God, how do we explain it? There is one other possible supernatural explanation for reports of miraculous events today. If such events are truly miraculous, they must be from Satan and his demonic spirits—even if they are happening in church circles. This will now be explained.

THE OCCULT ORIGIN OF "CHRISTIAN" MIRACLES TODAY

I have reached the conclusion—not easily, I assure you—that all truly miraculous events that occur in Pentecostal, charismatic, and third-wave circles have been and are being caused by demonic spirits working through unsuspecting people. This does not mean that those experiencing such demonic miracles or possessing demonic powers are deliberately allowing themselves to be used by the devil. They are basically victims of demonic deception. Many will think that I am going to a much too radical extreme here, and that this is an overly-harsh judgment; but I see no other possibility.

Miraculous events have been and are being caused by demonic spirits.

The Reality of Demonic Miracles

Though some deny it, the Bible seems adequately clear about the reality of demonic miracles. In the text just quoted (***Mt 7:21-23***) Jesus implicitly affirms the existence of miracles that do not come from God. Pharaoh's magicians, Jannes and Jambres (***2Tm 3:8***), were able to duplicate a limited number of Moses' miracles (***Ex 7:11,22; 8:7,18***). There is no reason to think this was anything less than demonic power at work.

In the New Testament Satanic miracles are linked especially with the end times (***Mt 24:24; Rev 13:13; 16:14; 19:20***). Speaking of a latter-day antichrist figure, Paul says that his *"coming is in accord with the activity of Satan, with all power and signs and false wonders"* (***2Th 2:9***). These are the three main words for miracles. "False wonders" does not mean phony miracles. The phrase is literally "wonders of falsehood," i.e., wonders or miracles performed in connection with falsehood. The old NIV is misleading: "counterfeit miracles, signs and wonders"; but the TNIV improves this to "signs and wonders that serve the lie." If Satan can *cause* illness (***Job 2:7***; ***Lk 13:16***), surely he can *heal* it.

There is no biblical basis for denying the reality of demonic miracles.

Our conclusion is that there is no biblical basis for denying the reality of demonic miracles.

The Reality of Demonic Miracles Today

Until the later 1960s, in America at least, it was easy to deny the reality of demonic miracles in postbiblical and modern times. Unless one spent time on a mission field especially among animistic cultures, there was little overt demonic activity to be seen. In the late 1960s, however, encouraged by the widespread acceptance of relativism and pluralism, occultism and occult practices "came out of the closet," so to speak, and became culturally respectable. For about a decade an explosion of books on occultism appeared, both pro and con.

I confess that until this happened, I had no ready explanation for Pentecostal and charismatic miracles. But the flood of incontrovertible evidence being presented about the reality of occult supernatural practices opened up a new possible explanation. It became very clear that demonic miracles have been and are now occurring in pagan and Satanic circles the world over. Such were simply not openly practiced and openly examined until the late 1960s and following.

I began my career as a seminary professor in 1967, just as this was beginning to happen. Thus from the beginning I felt compelled to prepare and teach courses both on demonism and on occultism. I have learned that all the forms of occultism condemned by the Bible are widespread today. This includes occult or demonic *knowledge* of all sorts: ESP, divination, future-telling, ouija boards, and tongue-speaking in unlearned human languages. Anyone who doubts the reality of supernatural knowledge from demonic sources today should study carefully the life and work of Edgar Cayce. A good beginning place is the chapter on Cayce in Gary North's book, *Unholy Spirits* (**193-225**).

I have also become convinced of the reality of occult or demonic *power* today, involving true miracles. These occur in the context of witchcraft or sorcery, and sometimes involve miraculous healings. Anyone who doubts such possibilities should study the life of the Brazilian healer, Arigo; see especially John Fuller's book, *Arigo: Surgeon of the Rusty Knife*. Also, reports of pagans who "speak in tongues," even unlearned languages, are abundant. Joseph Dillow reports "that in East Africa many persons possessed by demons speak fluently in Swahili or English, although under normal circumstances they do not understand either language" (**172**). Kurt Koch says, "On a mission tour through East Asia and Japan I often heard of Buddhist and Shintoist priests who speak in strange languages and tongues while in trance. . . . Spiritistic mediums all over the world often speak in foreign languages when in trance. The famous medium Mirabelli of Brazil spoke 25 languages in trance which ordinarily were unknown to him" (**32-33**).

The third category of the occult, also prohibited in the Bible, is *spiritism*, or the supposed communication with the spirits of the dead. Both supernatural knowledge and miraculous events take place in this context. The Christian minister Ben Alexander, a former spiritist, testifies to their reality in his book, *Out from Darkness*. He also confirms the fact that the spirits with which spiritists communicate are demons, not the souls of dead people.

The sobering truth is this: the same phenomena that occur in Pentecostal and charismatic circles also occur in pagan and demonic circles. This includes speaking in tongues and miraculous healing. This in itself would not imply that the charismatic phenomena are demonic in origin, of course. But in view of the reasons given earlier in this chapter for denying that the Holy Spirit is giving miraculous powers today, it seems probable that demonic powers are the true source of any truly miraculous or supernatural activity within these Christian circles.

The Reality of Demonic Miracles within Christian Circles

This, of course, is the most difficult aspect of the view I am proposing. How can we possibly think that demonic powers could have a foothold within Christians themselves and within the very sphere of the church? Before dismissing such a possibility out of hand, one should read again Jesus' words in ***Matthew 7:21-23***. Those who were performing the alien miracles were doing so *in Jesus' name*. Thus Jesus must be speaking of individuals who are working miracles within the context of Christendom, but are not doing so by the power of God. There is no other explanation.

Earlier in this chapter I mentioned Pyle's report of missionaries who attended a tongues service in a Lancaster, Pennsylvania, church and heard someone speak in a tongue identified as Chinese. Here is the rest of the story: "Later the missionaries told the pastor that it was indeed Chinese—the most indescribable filth and profanity that could be phrased in the Chinese language!" (13). Without a doubt a demonic spirit was the source of that "tongue."

Many deliverance ministers in recent times have persuaded tongue-speakers to submit to an examination known as "testing tongues." While the subject is calmly speaking in tongues, the tester addresses questions directly to the spirit who is the source of the tongue, who answers in English through the subject's vocal apparatus. I have a tape recording of one such test, in which Ernest Rockstadt, a deliverance ministry pioneer, questions such a spirit. Part of it goes like this:

Rockstadt: "Do you love the blood of Jesus?" Spirit: "NO."

"Do you confess Jesus has come in the flesh?" "NO."

"Is Jesus Christ your Lord?" "NO."

"Is Satan your Lord?" "YES."

"Are you defeated through the cross?" "YES."

"What is your opinion of the blood of the Lord Jesus?" "I HATE IT."

"Is the blood of Jesus holy?" "YES."

"Do you love Him?" "NO."

"Why don't you love Him?" "HE DOESN'T LOVE ME."

"Who have you been praying to?" "THE DEVIL."

"What have you been saying to him?" "I LOVE THE DEVIL."

Many other counselors have had similar experiences; see especially **Ensign and Howe, *Counseling and Demonization*, 294-300**.

For such reasons I find it impossible to deny that demonic powers can work and are working in Christian circles. It is the only consistent explanation of what is going on in the Pentecostal, charismatic, and third-wave movements today.

Many questions and objections may be raised, of course. One is whether it is possible for demonic power to be at work in the life of a God-fearing person. The answer is definitely yes. One may refer again to the life of Edgar Cayce, who began his journey into occultism as a pious, Bible-believing member of a Christian church.

Another question is why would Satan empower works that are good and beneficial to mankind, such as healings? The answer is that this helps him all the more to deceive those who *"did not receive the love of the truth"* (***2Th 2:10***). He is simply using the "checkers" strategy. In the game of checkers a player will often give up one checker because it enables him to catch two. Thus Satan is willing to cause a little good if it will enable him to cause a lot of harm. A possible Satanic goal is a new ecumenical movement based solely upon experience, with a diminished place for sound doctrine, as discussed earlier in this chapter.

Finally, is there any possibility that anyone who affirms that modern tongues and such are demonic is guilty of the unpardonable sin, or blasphemy against the Holy Spirit? Certainly not, if the suggestion is true—which I believe it is. In any case, this is not at all parallel to the kind of sin Jesus calls blasphemy against the Spirit in ***Matthew 12:22-32***. See the discussion of the unpardonable sin in chapter six, pp. 228-236.

CONCLUSION

In view of the above conclusions, how should Christians today respond to the false Pentecostal or charismatic phenomena and experiences within Christendom?

First, *do not seek such gifts!* Doing so makes one vulnerable to becoming demonized.

Remember, these folks are victims, not villains.

Second, pray for those caught up in these entanglements, and try to rescue them. Try to confront them with ***Matthew 7:21-23*** and with other truths set forth here. Always do this in a spirit of love. Remember, these folks are victims, not villains.

Third (this is especially for church leaders), do not allow your congregation to be damaged by such activity. Do not allow a small group of charismatics to exert influence over others and lead them astray. Do not sit by passively while some are practicing these "gifts," even if they are not perceived as a threat to the church as a whole. They are putting themselves in jeopardy.

Fourth (also for leaders), make sure your congregation is educated about these matters before problems arise.

WHAT OTHER AUTHORS

book. In the text itself, all
page number only, except
ore than once, the author
2) If the same author has
d in the title of each of
and the reference in the
ord in the title, and the

College Press, 1985.

...pirit in Regeneration and Sanctification ...to Alexander Campbell," 2 parts. *Restoration Herald* (March 1977) 3-5; and (April 1977) 3-5, 14.

Allen, Leonard, and Richard Hughes. *Rediscovering Our Roots: The Ancestry of Churches of Christ*. Abilene: ACU Press, 1988.

Anderson, Neil. *The Bondage Breaker*. Eugene, OR: Harvest House, 1993.

Applebury, T.R. *Studies in First Corinthians*. Bible Study Textbook series. Joplin, MO: College Press, 1963.

Arndt, William F., and F. Wilbur Gingrich. *A Greek-English Lexicon of the New Testament and Other Early Christian Literature*. 2nd ed., rev. and augmented by F.W. Gingrich and Frederick W. Danker from Walter Bauer's Fifth Edition, 1958. Chicago: University of Chicago Press, 1979.

Baker, Tommy G. "Letter to the Editor." *Christian Standard* (10/4/81) 23.

Bales, James D. *The Holy Spirit and the Christian*. Shreveport, LA: Lambert Book House, 1966.

Barclay, William. *New Testament **Words***. Philadelphia: Westminster Press, 1974.

______________. *The **Promise** of the Spirit*. Philadelphia: Westminster Press, 1960.

Barron, Eugene C. "Blasphemy against the Holy Spirit: Absolute Apostasy," Part One. *The Restoration Herald* (January 1977) 14-15, 18.

Baxter, Ronald E. *The Charismatic Gift of **Tongues***. Grand Rapids: Kregel, 1981.

______________. ***Gifts** of the Spirit*. Grand Rapids: Kregel, 1983.

Beasley-Murray, G.R. *Baptism in the New Testament*. Grand Rapids: Eerdmans, 1962.

Behm, Johannes. "*kainos*" (etc.). In vol. 3, *Theological Dictionary of the New Testament*, Ed. Gerhard Kittel. Trans. Geoffrey W. Bromiley. Grand Rapids: Eerdmans, 1966.

Berding, Kenneth. "Confusing Word and Concept in 'Spiritual Gifts': Have We Forgotten James Barr's Exhortations?" *Journal of the Evangelical Theological Society* (March 2000) 37-51.

Berkhof, Louis. *Systematic Theology*. London: Banner of Truth Trust, 1939.

Bethune-Baker, J.F. *An Introduction to the Early History of Christian Doctrine*. 4th ed. London: Methuen & Co., 1929.

Beverly, James. "Dental Miracle Reports Draw Criticism." *Christianity Today* (5/29/99) 17.

Beyer, Hermann Wolfgang. "*kubernesis*." In vol. 3, *Theological Dictionary of the New Testament*. Ed. Gerhard Kittel. Trans. Geoffrey W. Bromiley. Grand Rapids: Eerdmans, 1965.

Black, Garth. *The Holy Spirit*, rev. ed. The Way of Life series. Abilene, TX: Biblical Research Press, 1973.

Black, Mark C. *Luke*. The College Press NIV Commentary. Joplin, MO: College Press, 1996.

Blackburn, Barry L. "The Holy Spirit in Luke-Acts: A Survey." *Leaven* (Spring 1997) 9-13.

Blaikie, Robert J. *"Secular Christianity" and God Who Acts*. Grand Rapids: Eerdmans, 1970.

Boatman, Russell. *What the Bible Says about the Holy Spirit*. Joplin, MO: College Press, 1989.

Bodey, Richard Allen. "The Spirit and the Word." *Christianity Today* (11/24/61) 16-19.

Boles, H. Leo. *The Holy Spirit: His Personality, Nature, Works*. Nashville: Gospel Advocate, 1956.

Broomall, Wick. *The Holy Spirit: A Scriptural Study of His Person and Work*. Grand Rapids: Baker, 1963.

Bruce, Alexander Balmain. "The Synoptic Gospels." In *The Expositor's Greek Testament*. Ed. W. Robertson Nicoll. New York: George H. Doran Co., n.d..

Bruner, Frederick Dale. *A Theology of the Holy Spirit*. Grand Rapids: Eerdmans, 1970.

_____________. "Of Water and the Spirit." In *The Holy Spirit—Shy Member of the Trinity*. By Frederick Dale Bruner and William Hordern. Minneapolis: Augsburg, 1984.

Büchsel, Friedrich. "*ginomai*" (etc.). In vol. 3, *Theological Dictionary of the New Testament*. Ed. Gerhard Kittel. Trans. Geoffrey W. Bromiley. Grand Rapids: Eerdmans, 1964.

Bultmann, Rudolf. "*ginosko*" (etc.). In vol. 3, *Theological Dictionary of the New Testament*. Ed. Gerhard Kittel. Trans. Geoffrey W. Bromiley. Grand Rapids: Eerdmans, 1964.

Burge, Gary M. "Sin, Unpardonable." *Evangelical Dictionary of Theology*. Ed. Walter A. Elwell. Grand Rapids: Baker, 1984.

Burns, John, ed. *A Symposium on the Holy Spirit*. Joplin, MO: College Press, 1966 reprint of 1879 ed.

Buswell, James Oliver, Jr. *A Systematic Theology of the Christian Religion*. 2 vols. Grand Rapids: Zondervan, 1962, 1963.

Campbell, Alexander. *The Christian System*. Cincinnati: Standard Publishing, n.d. Reprint of 2nd ed., 1839.

Campbell, Alexander, and N.L. Rice. *A Debate . . . on . . . Christian Baptism* [*CRD*]. Lexington, KY: A.T. Skillman and Son, 1844.

Candlish, James S. *The Work of the Holy Spirit*. Edinburgh: T. & T. Clark, n.d.

Carter, Charles Webb. *The Person and Ministry of the Holy Spirit: A Wesleyan Perspective*. Grand Rapids: Baker, 1974.

Chouinard, Larry. *Matthew*. The College Press NIV Commentary. Joplin, MO: College Press, 1997.

Clarke, William Newton. *An Outline of Christian Theology*. 3rd ed. Edinburgh: T. & T. Clark, 1899.

Clemens, David A. *Steps to Maturity*. Vol. 1. Upper Darby, PA: Bible Club Movement, 1975.

Clement of Rome. "Letter of the Romans to the Corinthians, Commonly Known as First Clement." In *The Apostolic Fathers*,

2nd ed. Ed. Michael W. Holmes. Trans. J.B. Lightfoot and J.R. Harmer. Grand Rapids: Baker, 1989.

Cottrell, Jack. ***Baptism**: A Biblical Study*. Joplin, MO: College Press, 1989.

_____________. "Baptism according to the Reformed **Tradition**." In *Baptism and the Remission of Sins*. Ed. David Fletcher. Joplin, MO: College Press, 1990.

_____________. "The Biblical **Consensus**: Historical Backgrounds to Reformed Theology." In *Baptism and the Remission of Sins*. Ed. David Fletcher. Joplin, MO: College Press, 1990.

_____________. *The **Faith** Once for All: Bible Doctrine for Today*. Joplin, MO: College Press, 2002.

_____________. ***Romans***. The College Press NIV Commentary. 2 vols. Joplin, MO: College Press, 1996, 1998.

_____________. *What the Bible Says about God the **Creator***. Joplin, MO: College Press, 1983; reprint, Eugene, OR: Wipf and Stock Publishers.

_____________. *What the Bible Says about God the **Redeemer.*** Joplin, MO: College Press, 1987; reprint, Eugene, OR: Wipf and Stock Publishers.

_____________. *What the Bible Says about God the **Ruler***. Joplin, MO: College Press, 1984; reprint, Eugene, OR; Wipf and Stock Publishers.

Cranfield, C.E.B. *A Critical and Exegetical Commentary on the Epistle to the Romans*. 2 vols. The International Critical Commentary, n.s. Edinburgh: T. & T. Clark, 1990 corrected printing of 1975 edition.

Criminger, Chris. "Don't Lock Holy Spirit in Bible." *Christian Standard* (5/1/94) 23.

Crouch, Owen L. "Two Rabbis and Three Questions." *Christian Standard* (11/24/74) 14-16.

Deere, Jack. *Surprised by the Power of the Spirit*. Grand Rapids: Zondervan, 1993.

DeWelt, Don. *The **Power** of the Holy Spirit*. Joplin, MO; College Press, 1971.

_____________. ***Romans** Realized*. Joplin, MO: College Press, 1959.

Dillow, Joseph. *Speaking in Tongues: Seven Crucial Questions*. Grand Rapids: Zondervan, 1976.

Downer, Arthur. *The Mission and Ministration of the Holy Spirit*. Edinburgh: T. & T. Clark, 1909.

Dunn, James D.G. ***Baptism*** *in the Holy Spirit*. Philadelphia: Westminster, 1970.

_____________. ***Romans***. 2 vols. Word Biblical Commentary. Dallas: Word Books, 1988.

Edgar, Thomas R. *Satisfied by the Promise of the Spirit*. Grand Rapids: Kregel, 1996.

Ensign, Grayson, and Edward Howe. *Counseling and Demonization*. Amarillo: Recovery Publications, 1989.

Erdman, Charles R. *The Spirit of Christ*. New York: George H. Doran, 1926.

Erickson, Millard J. *Christian Theology*. 2nd ed. Grand Rapids: Baker, 1998.

Ford, Harold W. "The Perennial Controversy." *Christian Standard* (5/22/83) 8-9.

Foster, Lewis A. "In Step with the Holy Spirit, Part 3: The Holy Spirit in **Conversion**." *The Lookout* (8/12/79) 7-9.

_____________. "In Step with the Holy Spirit, Part 5: The Miraculous **Gifts** of the Spirit." *The Lookout* (8/26/79) 3-5.

_____________. "In Step with the Holy Spirit, Part 6: The **Gift** of the Spirit Today." *The Lookout* (9/2/79) 5-7, 13.

Fudge, Edward. *Speaking in Tongues*. Athens, AL: C.E.I. Publishing, 1971.

Fuller, John G. *Arigo: Surgeon of the Rusty Knife*. New York: Pocket Books, 1975.

Gaffin, Richard B., Jr. "A Cessationist View." In *Are Miraculous Gifts for Today? Four Views*. Ed. Wayne A. Grudem. Grand Rapids: Zondervan, 1996.

Gardiner, George E. *The Corinthian Catastrophe*. Grand Rapids: Kregel, 1974.

Gardner, Lynn. "Led by the Spirit," 2 parts. *Christian Standard* (10/3/76) 11-12; and (10/10/76) 10-12.

Geisler, Norman L. ***Signs*** *and Wonders*. Wheaton, IL: Tyndale House, 1988.

Geisler, Norman L., ed. ***Inerrancy***. Grand Rapids: Zondervan, 1979.

Geldenhuys, Norval. *Commentary on the Gospel of Luke*. Grand Rapids: Eerdmans, 1951.

Gibson, Robert Leon. *Christian, You Were Baptized in Water* and *Spirit*. Fort Worth: Star Bible Publications, 1987.

Giebler, Brian. "Neither Miracle nor Mystery." *Christian Standard* (3/5/78) 4-6.

Green, Michael. *I Believe in the Holy Spirit.* Grand Rapids: Eerdmans, 1975.

Gregory of Nyssa. "On the Baptism of Christ." Trans. H.A. Wilson. In vol. 5, *Nicene and Post-Nicene Fathers.* Ed. Philip Schaff and Henry Wace. Grand Rapids: Eerdmans reprint, 1979.

Gresham, Charles R. "The Birth of the Spirit." 2 parts. *Christian Standard* (2/22/69) 3-4; and (3/1/69) 5-6.

Griffith Thomas, W.H. *The Holy Spirit of God.* Chicago: Bible Institute Colportage Association, 1913.

Griffiths, Michael. *Grace-Gifts.* Grand Rapids: Eerdmans, 1979.

Gromacki, Robert Glenn. *The Modern Tongues Movement.* Philadelphia: Presbyterian and Reformed, 1967.

Grudem, Wayne A. "**Preface.**" In *Are Miraculous Gifts for Today? Four Views.* Ed. Wayne A. Grudem. Grand Rapids: Zondervan, 1996..

Grudem, Wayne A., ed. *Are Miraculous **Gifts** for Today? Four Views.* Grand Rapids: Zondervan, 1996.

Haarbeck, Herman, H.-G. Link, and Colin Brown. "New." In vol. 2, *The New International Dictionary of New Testament Theology.* Ed. Colin Brown. Grand Rapids: Zondervan, 1976.

Haldeman, I.M. *Holy Ghost or Water?* New York: author, n.d.

Harper, Stanley R. "Holy Spirit." *A Handbook of Christian Theology.* Ed. Marvin Halverson and Arthur Cohen. New York: Meridian Books, 1958.

Harris, Murray J. "Appendix: Prepositions and Theology in the Greek New Testament." In vol. 3, *The New International Dictionary of New Testament Theology.* Ed. Colin Brown. Grand Rapids: Zondervan, 1978.

Heick, Otto W. *A History of Christian Thought.* 2 vols. Philadelphia: Fortress Press, 1966.

Heron, Alasdair I.C. *The Holy Spirit.* Philadelphia: Westminster, 1983.

Hocking, David L. *Spiritual Gifts: Their Necessity and Use in the Local Church.* Long Beach, CA: Sounds of Grace, n.d.

Hodge, Charles. *Systematic Theology.* 3 vols. Grand Rapids: Eerdmans, n.d.

Hoekema, Anthony A. *Holy Spirit Baptism.* Grand Rapids: Eerdmans, 1972

Holmes, Michael W., ed. *The Apostolic Fathers.* 2nd ed. Trans. J.B. Lightfoot and J.R. Harmer. Grand Rapids: Baker, 1989.

Hunley, J.B. *Pentecost and the Holy Spirit.* New York: Revell, 1928.

Hunt, Dave, and James White. *Debating Calvinism*. Sisters, OR: Multnomah Publishers, 2004.

Ignatius of Antioch. "To the Magnesians." In *The Apostolic Fathers.* 2nd ed. Ed. Michael W. Holmes. Trans. J.B. Lightfoot and J.R. Harmer. Grand Rapids: Baker, 1989.

Irenaeus. "Against Heresies." In vol. 1, *The Ante-Nicene Fathers.* Ed. Alexander Roberts and James Donaldson. New York: Charles Scribner's Sons, 1913.

"Is the Holy Spirit a Person?" *Tomorrow's World* (September/October 1970) 31-32.

Jacoby, Douglas. *The Spirit: The Work of the Holy Spirit in the Lives of Disciples*. Rev. ed. Newton Upper Falls, MA: Illumination Publishers, 2005.

Jones, A.B. *The Spiritual Side of Our Plea*. St. Louis: Christian Publishing Co., 1901.

Justin Martyr. "The First Apology of Justin." Trans. Dods & Reith. In vol. 1, *The Ante-Nicene Fathers*. Ed. Alexander Roberts and James Donaldson. Grand Rapids: Eerdmans reprint, 1979.

Keener, Craig S. *Three Crucial Questions about the Holy Spirit*. Grand Rapids: Baker, 1996.

Keil, C.F., and F. Delitzsch. *Biblical Commentary on the Old Testament: The Pentateuch, Vol. 3*. Trans. James Martin. Grand Rapids: Eerdmans, n.d.

Kent, John. "Unitarianism." *The Westminster Dictionary of Christian Theology.* Ed. Alan Richardson and John Bowden. Philadelphia: Westminster, 1983.

Ketcherside, W. Carl. *Heaven Help Us: The Holy Spirit in Your Life.* Cincinnati: Standard Publishing, 1974.

Kik, J. Marcellus. *Matthew Twenty-Four: An Exposition*. Philadelphia: Presbyterian and Reformed, 1948.

Kistemaker, Simon J. *New Testament Commentary: Exposition of the Epistle of James and the Epistles of John*. Grand Rapids: Baker, 1986.

Kittel, Gerhard. "*ainigma.*" In vol. 1, *Theological Dictionary of the New Testament.* Ed. Gerhard Kittel. Trans. Geoffrey W. Bromiley. Grand Rapids: Eerdmans, 1964.

Klein, William W., Craig L. Blomberg, and Robert L. Hubbard. *Introduction to Biblical Interpretation*. Dallas: Word Publishing, 1993.

Koch, Kurt. *The Strife of Tongues*. Grand Rapids: Kregel, 1971.

Kuyper, Abraham. *The Work of the Holy Spirit*. Trans. Henri de Vries. Grand Rapids: Eerdmans, 1966.

Lard, Moses E. "**Baptism** in One Spirit into One Body." *Lard's Quarterly* 1 (March 1864) 271-282. Reprint: Old Paths Book Club, Kansas City, MO, 1949.

______________. *Commentary on Paul's Letter to* ***Romans***. Cincinnati: Standard Publishing, n.d.

______________. "**Reply** to Kappa on Immersion in the Holy Spirit." *Lard's Quarterly* 2 (October 1864) 51-63. Reprint: Old Paths Book Club, Kansas City, MO, 1950.

______________. "Spiritual **Influence** As It Relates to Christians." *Lard's Quarterly* 1 (March 1864) 225-241. Reprint: Old Paths Book Club, Kansas City, MO, 1949.

Laubach, Fritz, et al. "Conversion, Penitence, Repentance, Proselyte." In vol. 1, *The New International Dictionary of New Testament Theology*. Ed. Colin Brown. Grand Rapids: Zondervan, 1975.

Leggett, Marshall J. "A Neglected Emphasis: The Gifts of the Holy Spirit." 2 parts. *Christian Standard* (5/23/99) 6-8; and (5/30/99) 6-8.

Lehman, Chester K. *The Holy Spirit and the Holy Life*. Scottdale, PA: Herald Press, 1959.

Leith, John H., ed. *Creeds of the Churches*. 3rd ed. Atlanta: John Knox Press, 1982.

Lenski, R.C.H. *The Interpretation of St. Matthew's Gospel*. Minneapolis: Augsburg, 1964.

"Let God Be True." Rev. ed. Brooklyn: Watchtower Society, 1952.

Let Your Name Be Sanctified. Brooklyn: Watchtower Society, 1961.

Lewis, Arthur H. "The New Birth under the Old Covenant." *The Evangelical Quarterly* 56 (January/March 1984) 35-44.

Lewis, Gordon R. "Ultradispensationalism." *Evangelical Dictionary of Theology*. Ed. Walter A. Elwell. Grand Rapids: Baker, 1984.

Lindsell, Harold. *The Holy Spirit in the Latter Days*. Nashville: Thomas Nelson, 1983.

Lohse, Eduard. "*pentekoste*." In vol. 6, *Theological Dictionary of the New Testament*. Ed. Gerhard Friedrich. Trans. Geoffrey W. Bromiley. Grand Rapids: Eerdmans, 1968.

Longan, G.W. "The Holy Spirit in Consciousness." In *A Symposium on the Holy Spirit*. Ed. John Burns. Joplin, MO: College Press, 1966 reprint of 1879 ed.

Lowe, William F. *Pentecostalism's Dangers*. Ed. D.A. Waite. Collingswood, NJ: The Bible for Today, 1975.

Luther, Martin. *A Commentary on St. Paul's Epistle to the* ***Galatians.*** Ed. Philip Watson. Westwood, NJ: Revell, n.d.

_____________. "The Holy and Blessed Sacrament of **Baptism**." Trans. Charles Jacobs and E.T. Bachmann. *Luther's Works*, American ed. Vol. 35. *Word and Sacrament.* Vol. 1. Ed. E.T. Bachmann. Philadelphia: Muhlenberg Press, 1960.

MacArthur, John F., Jr. *Charismatic* ***Chaos***. Grand Rapids: Zondervan: 1992.

_____________. ***Romans***. 2 vols. The MacArthur New Testament Commentary. Chicago: Moody, 1991, 1994.

Manes, Josephine. "Are Miracles for Today?" *The Lookout* (11/24/91) 13.

Martin, Alfred. "The Epistle to the Ephesians." In *The Wycliffe Bible Commentary.* Ed. Charles F. Pfeiffer and Everett F. Harrison. Chicago: Moody, 1962.

"Martyrdom of Polycarp." In *The Apostolic Fathers.* 2nd ed. Ed. Michael W. Holmes. Trans. J.B. Lightfoot and J.R. Harmer. Grand Rapids: Baker, 1989.

Matthews, Victor. *Growth in Grace*. Grand Rapids: Zondervan, 1970.

McGarvey, J.W. "**Baptism** in the Holy Spirit." *Lard's Quarterly* 1 (June 1864) 428-442. Reprint: Old Paths Book Club, Kansas City, MO, 1949.

_____________. *New Commentary on* ***Acts*** *of Apostles*. 2 vols. in 1. Cincinnati: Standard Publishing, reprint of 1892 ed.

McQuiggan, Jim. *The Book of 1 Corinthians*. Lubbock, TX: Montex Publishing Co., 1984.

Meserve, Dallas. "A Renewed Look at 1 Corinthians 12:13." *Christian Standard* (12/9/73) 11-12.

Metzger, Bruce M. *The Text of the New Testament.* 2nd ed. New York: Oxford University Press, 1968.

Miley, John. *Systematic Theology.* 3 vols. Peabody, MA: Hendrickson Publishers, 1989 reprint of 1893 ed.

Miller, Dave. "Modern-Day Miracles, Tongue-Speaking, and Holy Spirit Baptism: A Refutation." *Reason & Revelation* (March 2003) 17-23.

Milligan, Robert. *The Great Commission*. Lexington: J.B. Morton & Co., 1873.

Moo, Douglas J. *The Epistle to the Romans*. Grand Rapids: Eerdmans, 1996.

Moody, Dale. *Spirit of the Living God*. Philadelphia: Westminster Press, 1968.

Morgan, G. Campbell. *The Spirit of God*. New York: Revell, 1900.

Morris, Leon. *The Epistle to the **Romans***. Grand Rapids: Eerdmans, 1988.

______________. *The Gospel according to **John***. Grand Rapids: Eerdmans, 1971.

______________. ***Spirit** of the Living God*. London: InterVarsity Press, 1967.

Morrison, John L. "The Holy Spirit's Indwelling." *Christian Standard* (5/30/71) 9-12.

Moser, K.C. *The Way of Salvation*. Delight, AR: Gospel Light, reprint of 1932 ed.

Munnell, Elder T. "The Holy Spirit in Consciousness." In *A Symposium on the Holy Spirit*. Ed. John Burns. Joplin, MO: College Press, 1966 reprint of 1879 ed.

Murray, John. *The Epistle to the Romans*. 2 vols. New International Commentary. Grand Rapids: Eerdmans, 1959, 1965.

Nash, Donald A. *Practical Commentary on Acts*. Grayson, KY: author, n.d.

North, Gary. *Unholy Spirits: Occultism and New Age Humanism*. Fort Worth: Dominion Press, 1986.

Oepke, A. "*louo, apolouo, loutron.*" In vol. 4, *Theological Dictionary of the New Testament*. Ed. Gerhard Kittel. Trans. Geoffrey W. Bromiley. Grand Rapids: Eerdmans, 1967.

"One Man with God." *The Presbyterian Journal* (12/28/66) 9-10.

"Online Etymology Dictionary." www.etymonline.com/index.php?1=g&p=4, accessed 6/29/05.

Pache, Rene. *The Person and Work of the Holy Spirit*. Trans. J.D. Emerson. London: Marshall, Morgan & Scott, 1956.

Packer, J.I. "Experiencing God's Presents." *Christianity Today* (August 2003) 55.

Palmer, Edwin H. *The Person and Ministry of the Holy Spirit: The Traditional Calvinistic Perspective*. Grand Rapids: Baker, 1974.

Pettegrew, Larry D. *The New Covenant Ministry of the Holy Spirit*. 2nd ed. Grand Rapids: Kregel, 2001.

Phillips, Calvin L. "You Must Be Born Again." Oklahoma City, OK: NACC presentation, 7/12/78.

Pierard, Richard V. "Holiness Movement, American." *Evangelical Dictionary of Theology*. Ed. Walter A. Elwell. Grand Rapids: Baker, 1984.

Pink, Arthur. *The Holy Spirit*. Grand Rapids: Baker, 1978.

Plummer, Alfred. *A Critical and Exegetical Commentary on the Gospel according to S. Luke*. 5th ed. The International Critical Commentary. Edinburgh: T. & T. Clark, 1922.

Putman, W.L. (Bill). "Brothers Yet Unborn." *Christian Standard* (8/5/73) 10.

Pyle, Hugh F. *Truth about Tongues*. Denver: Accent Books, 1976.

Ramm, Bernard. *Witness of the Spirit*. Grand Rapids: Eerdmans, 1959.

Ranaghan, Kevin and Dorothy. *Catholic Pentecostals*. Paramus, NJ: Paulist Press, 1969.

Reymond, Robert L. *"What about Continuing Revelations and Miracles in the Presbyterian Church Today?"* Phillipsburg, NJ: Presbyterian and Reformed, 1977.

Richards, Le Grand. *A Marvelous Work and a Wonder*. Rev. ed. Salt Lake City: Deseret Book Co., 1973.

Robertson, Scott. "The Holy Spirit according to I Corinthians 12:13." *The Seminary Review* 23 (December 1977) 95-121.

Root, Orrin. "How To Be **Born Again**." *The Lookout* (2/4/79) 3-4.

____________. "Untying Some **Knots**." *The Lookout* (12/31/78) 11-12.

Russell, Bob. "How God Speaks." *The Lookout* (9/1/02) 14.

Sarles, Ken. "An Appraisal of the Signs and Wonders Movement." *Bibliotheca Sacra* (January/March 1988) 57-82.

Savits, Ronald. "Be Filled with the Spirit." *Christian Standard* (7/10/77) 13-14.

Schatzmann, Siegfreid. *A Pauline Theology of Charismata*. Peabody, MA: Hendrickson, 1987.

Schütz, Eduard, and Ernst Dieter Schmitz. "Knowledge." In vol. 2, *The New International Dictionary of New Testament Theology*. Ed. Colin Brown. Grand Rapids: Zondervan, 1976.

Shaw, Robert W. "Sermon." *The European Evangelist* (September 1977) 1-4.

Smith, Charles R. *Tongues in Biblical Perspective*. Winona Lake, IN: BMH Books, 1973.

Smith, F. Sherwood. "Letter to the editor." *Christian Standard* (6/27/82) 23.

Smith, James E. "Baptize You in the Holy Spirit." http://thecra.org/Smith . . . , accessed 6/27/05.

Smith, Joe Carson. "The New Birth." *Christian Standard* (12/4/77) 9-10.

Spiritual Counterfeits Project form letter. Berkeley, CA: July 26, 1985.

"Spotlight on . . . the Holy Spirit." *Take Our Word for It* 82 (4/17/2000) takeourword.com/Issue082.html, accessed 6/29/05.

Spratt, Walter L. "The **Holy Spirit**: Baptism—Gift." In *The Holy Spirit in Our Lives Today: The Hartford Forum (1966)*. Ed. W. Carl Ketcherside. St. Louis: Mission Messenger, 1966.

____________. "The Unpardonable **Sin**." *The Sentinel* 13 (March 1969) 2, 4.

Sproul, R.C. "The Internal Testimony of the Holy Spirit." In *Inerrancy*. Ed. Norman L. Geisler. Grand Rapids: Zondervan, 1979.

Stam, Cornelius R. *Things That Differ: The Fundamentals of Dispensationalism*. Chicago: Berean Bible Society, 1951.

Staton, Knofel. *Don't Divorce the **Holy Spirit***. Cincinnati: Standard Publishing, 1974.

____________. *Eight Lessons on Spiritual **Gifts** for Christians Today*. Joplin, MO: College Press, 1973.

Stevens, William Wilson. *Doctrines of the Christian Religion*. Nashville: Broadman, 1967.

Storms, C. Samuel. "A Third Wave View." In *Are Miraculous Gifts for Today? Four Views*. Ed. Wayne A. Grudem. Grand Rapids: Zondervan, 1996.

Stott, John R.W. ***Baptism** and Fullness: The Work of the Holy Spirit Today*. 2nd ed. Downers Grove, IL: InterVarsity, 1979.

____________. ***Romans**: God's Good News for the World*. Downers Grove, IL: InterVarsity, 1994.

Sweeney, Z.T. *The Spirit and the Word*. Nashville: Gospel Advocate, n.d.

Swete, Henry Barclay. *The Holy Spirit in the New Testament: A Study of Primitive Christian Teaching*. London: Macmillan, 1921.

Synan, Vinson. "Pentecostalism." *Evangelical Dictionary of Theology*. Ed. Walter A. Elwell. Grand Rapids: Baker, 1984.

Taylor, J.Z. "'The Witness of the Holy Spirit.'" In *A Symposium on the Holy Spirit*. Ed. John Burns. Joplin, MO: College Press, 1966 reprint of 1879 ed.

Thayer, Joseph Henry. *A Greek-English Lexicon of the New Testament.* 4th ed. Edinburgh: T. & T. Clark, 1955 reprint of 1901 ed.

Thomas, J.D. *The Spirit and Spirituality*. Abilene, TX: Biblical Research Press, 1966.

Thomas, Robert L. *Understanding Spiritual Gifts: A Verse-by-Verse Study of 1 Corinthians 12–14*. Rev. ed. Grand Rapids: Kregel, 1999.

Thomas, Roger William. "Baptized in the Spirit." 2 parts. *Christian Standard* (9/30/73) 7-8; and (10/7/73) 7-9.

______________. "A Promise Kept." 2 parts. *Christian Standard* (5/11/75) 15-16; and (5/18/75) 15-16.

Thompson, Marianne Meye. "Committing the Unforgivable Sin." *Christianity Today* (6/14/99) 82.

Torrey, R.A. *The Person and Work of the Holy Spirit*. New York: Revell, 1910.

Trench, Richard Chenevix. *Notes on the **Miracles** of Our Lord*, popular ed. Grand Rapids: Baker, 1956.

______________. ***Synonyms** of the New Testament*. Grand Rapids: Eerdmans, 1958.

Tribble, Noble. "Answers." *The Lookout* (6/28/81) 14.

The Truth That Leads to Eternal Life. Brooklyn: Watchtower Society, 1968.

Unger, Merrill F. *The **Baptism** and Gifts of the Holy Spirit.* Chicago: Moody, 1974.

______________. *New Testament Teaching on **Tongues**.* Grand Rapids: Kregel, 1971.

Van Buren, James G. "When Did I Receive the Holy Spirit?" *The Lookout* (6/7/87) 9.

Van Pelt, Miles V. "*Ruach*." In vol. 3, *New International Dictionary of Old Testament Theology and Exegesis*. Ed. Willem A. VanGemeren. Grand Rapids: Zondervan, 1997.

Vos, Geerhardus. *Biblical Theology: Old and New Testaments*. Grand Rapids: Eerdmans, 1948.

Wagner, C. Peter. *The Third Wave of the Holy Spirit*. Ann Arbor, MI: Servant, 1988.

Walvoord, John F. *The Holy Spirit: A Comprehensive Study of the Person and Work of the Holy Spirit*. Grand Rapids: Zondervan, 1991.

Ware, Bruce A. ***Father**, Son, and Holy Spirit: Relationships, Roles, and Relevance*. Wheaton, IL: Crossway Books, 2005.

______________. "How Shall We Think about the **Trinity**?" In *God* *under Fire*. Ed. Douglas S. Huffman and Eric L. Johnson. Grand Rapids: Zondervan, 2002.

_____________. "Making **Sense** of God's Words." *Moody Magazine* (March/April 2003) 35-38.

Warfield, Benjamin B. *Miracles: Yesterday and Today, True and False*. Grand Rapids: Eerdmans 1965 reprint of 1918 work, *Counterfeit Miracles*.

Wells, David F. *God the Evangelist: How the Holy Spirit Works to Bring Men and Women to Faith*. Grand Rapids: Eerdmans, 1987.

White, James, and Dave Hunt. *Debating Calvinism*. Sisters, OR: Multnomah Publishers, 2004.

White, R.E.O. "Baptism of the Spirit." *Evangelical Dictionary of Theology*. Ed. Walter A. Elwell. Grand Rapids: Baker, 1984.

Wierwille, Victor Paul. *Receiving the Holy Spirit Today*. 4th ed. New Knoxville, OH: The Way International, 1962.

Williams, Donald T. *The Person and Work of the Holy Spirit*. Nashville: Broadman & Holman, 1994.

Williams, J.L. *Victor Paul Wierwille and The Way International*. Chicago: Moody, 1979.

Winter, W.W. "Blasphemy against the Holy Spirit." *The Seminary Review* 3 (Fall 1956) 10-20.

Wood, Leon. *The Holy Spirit in the Old Testament*. Grand Rapids: Zondervan, 1976.

Woods, Guy. "The Gift of the Holy Spirit." *Firm Foundation* (3/22/38).

Wynkoop, Mildred Bangs. *A Theology of Love: The Dynamic of Wesleyanism*. Kansas City, MO: Beacon Hill Press, 1972.

Zustiak, Gary B. "Hearing the Voice of God." *Christian Standard* (10/24/99) 4-6.

Zwingli, Huldreich. "Of Baptism." In *Zwingli and Bullinger*. Library of Christian Classics 24. Ed. & Trans. Geoffrey W. Bromiley. Philadelphia: Westminster, 1953.

Subject Index

I

J

K

L

M

N

O

P

Q

R

Scripture Index

John

Acts

Romans

1 Corinthians

2 Corinthians

Galatians

Ephesians

Philippians

Colossians

1 Thessalonians

2 Thessalonians

1 Timothy

2 Timothy

Titus

Hebrews

James

1 Peter

2 Peter

1 John

2 John

Jude

Revelation

BIBLE PROPHECY
&
THE
END TIMES
A TWELVE-PART
SERMON SERIES
BY
JACK COTTRELL